Mission workers and promoters should welcome Dr. Wang's book with thankful hearts. The study tells how Jesus freed a Chinese scholar's heart to soar above the culture of missionaries who introduced the faith. Will he be a Confucian? A patriotic Chinese? Or simply a Christian? Can he be all of these? The Holy Spirit alone can help him become an example for China over the ages.

In fifty years of promoting foreign missions, especially in China, I was so busy telling the story of missionaries that I did not adequately know the minds and identities of the most important persons – the Chinese believers. I did not even remember the name of Zhang Wen Kai or of his pseudonyms. I am ashamed. I knew the names of American missionaries who ran the China Baptist Publication Society, never stopping to realize that there must have been Chinese Christians doing the daily work and the cutting-edge scholarship and apologetics. I can blame the language barrier, which Dr. Wang helpfully breaks down. I knew "True Light" – the journal, the buildings. Now I can know and applaud the writer, the powerful editor, who embodied the True Light for twenty-five vital years. Thank you, Dr. Wang, for shining that light on my thinking. May he shine on for China today.

Catherine B. Allen, LHD
Author
Former President,
Women's Department, Baptist World Alliance (1995–2000)

Jue Wang's timely study on the life and identity of Zhang Yijing is an essential work for those who wish to understand how modern nationalism, rationalism, and culture have shaped the identity of Chinese Christianity. Further, it probes new avenues by which to understand identity and contextualization of Chinese Christianity and the various challenges this contextualization has overcome to become deeply rooted in China today.

Thomas Alan Harvey, PhD
Academic Dean,
Oxford Centre for Mission Studies,
Oxford, United Kingdom

Within the seams of any historical tapestry that writers weave are the lost stories of forgotten or silenced voices, not least those of non-elite and cultural outsiders. Dr. Wang's meticulous, exhaustive, and culturally attuned analysis of the life and works of Zhang Yijing (张亦镜), an early twentieth century Confucian-trained Chinese Protestant writer and journalist, gives us an insider's perspective on Zhang's strategic trajectories for promoting the integration of Christian and Chinese identities. Dr. Wang helpfully extricates timeless principles from Zhang's three-fold indigenization framework of Confucianism, nationalism, and 'scientism' that can resource contemporary Christians who are seeking relevant and transformative intersections between their personal and social identities.

Ralph Korner, PhD
Platform Coordinator, Kairos
Academic Dean and Associate Professor of Biblical Studies, Taylor Seminary,
Edmonton, Alberta, Canada

Dr. Jue Wang, as a dedicated researcher of the Chinese Christian Community, has written a comprehensive account of Zhang Yijing's search for a Chinese Christian identity. Dr. Wang's understanding of the life and struggles of Zhang Yijing in his desire to bring an identity to the Chinese Christian is unparalleled in the development of China's indigenous church. This is thorough research containing a superb broad overview and great attention to detail. I recommend this book to everyone who has an interest in China, Christianity in China, the impact of Christian outreach throughout China, and the Chinese Christian communities of China. On this subject, there is no book I can recommend more than this volume.

Michael D. Suman, PhD
Missionary with One Mission Society as International Professor
Author, *The Church in China: One Lord Two Systems*

Meticulously researched, this work by Dr. Wang recovers the heritage of Zhang Yijing, a prolific Chinese Christian intellectual of the late Qing and the early Republic. In a tumultuous era when Chinese identity and the fate of the Chinese nation were called into question, Zhang reflected deeply on and engaged actively with the political and intellectual discourse of his day as a Christian. By methodically examining Zhang's revaluation of his own Confucian identity, his sympathetic yet reserved response to the strident nationalism of the 1920s and 1930s, and his resistance to his secular compatriots' unquestioned faith in science even as he embraced the contributions of science to the modern world, Dr. Wang illustrates the dilemmas faced by early twentieth-century Chinese Christians. This work enriches our understanding of the history of Christianity in China, especially as a case study of the fruitful encounter between the gospel and the intellectual and political realities of early twentieth-century China.

Gloria S. Tseng, PhD
Associate Professor of History,
Hope College, Holland, Michigan, USA

Zhang Yijing (1871–1931) and the Search for a Chinese Christian Identity

Jue Wang

© 2021 Jue Wang (王珏)

Published 2021 by Langham Academic (Previously Langham Monographs)
An imprint of Langham Publishing
www.langhampublishing.org

Langham Publishing and its imprints are a ministry of Langham Partnership

Langham Partnership
PO Box 296, Carlisle, Cumbria, CA3 9WZ, UK
www.langham.org

ISBNs:
978-1-83973-218-8 Print
978-1-83973-592-9 ePub
978-1-78368-594-3 PDF

Jue Wang (王珏) has asserted his right under the Copyright, Designs and Patents Act, 1988 to be identified as the Author of this work.

All rights reserved. No part of this publication may be reproduced, stored in a retrieval system or transmitted, in any form or by any means, electronic, mechanical, photocopying, recording or otherwise, without the prior written permission of the publisher or the Copyright Licensing Agency.

Requests to reuse content from Langham Publishing are processed through PLSclear. Please visit www.plsclear.com to complete your request.

Scriptures taken from the Holy Bible, New International Version®, NIV®. Copyright © 1973, 1978, 1984, 2011 by Biblica, Inc.™ Used by permission of Zondervan.

British Library Cataloguing-in-Publication Data
A catalogue record for this book is available from the British Library

ISBN: 978-1-83973-218-8

Cover & Book Design: projectluz.com

Langham Partnership actively supports theological dialogue and an author's right to publish but does not necessarily endorse the views and opinions set forth here or in works referenced within this publication, nor can we guarantee technical and grammatical correctness. Langham Partnership does not accept any responsibility or liability to persons or property as a consequence of the reading, use or interpretation of its published content.

Contents

Acknowledgements xi

Abstract xiv

List of Abbreviations xvii

Chapter 1 1
Introduction and Literature Review
    1.1 Relevance of This Research 1
    1.2 Review of Paradigms of Studying Christianity in China 4
    1.3 Introduction to Identity 15
    1.4 Identity Literature Review 16
        1.4.1 Erikson's Definition of Identity 17
        1.4.2 Ego Identity, Personal Identity, and Social Identity 18
        1.4.3 Marcia's Theory of Identity Statuses Model 21
        1.4.4 Extension of Marcia's Identity Statuses Model 21
        1.4.5 Multiple Identities 23
        1.4.6 The Importance of Spiritual Identity to Ego Identity 25
        1.4.7 The Significance of Commitment to Identity Status 26
        1.4.8 Application of Marcia's Identity Statuses Approach
             to Spiritual Identity 28
        1.4.9 Applicability of Identity Theory to the Eastern Society 29
        1.4.10 Discussion of Christian Identity 30
        1.4.11 Qualitative and Narrative Research Methodologies ... 34
        1.4.12 Disruptive Issues or Crisis in Revealing One's
             Identities 36
        1.4.13 Methodology 36
    1.5 A Brief Introduction to Zhang Yijing 38
    1.6 Current Research on Zhang Yijing 40
    1.7 Conclusion 43

Chapter 2 45
Christianity in China before 1930 and Zhang Yijing's Life
    2.1 A Brief History of Christianity in China before the 1920s 45
    2.2 The Social and Political Context during the 1920s 55
    2.3 Zhang, before Joining *True Light* 63
    2.4 Zhang, after Joining *True Light* 66
        2.4.1 Zhang's Readership 67

  2.4.2 Zhang's Works...67
  2.4.3 Zhang as an Apologist..70
  2.4.4 Zhang's Daily Schedule...92
  2.4.5 Zhang's Views on Some Works of the Church...................93
  2.4.6 Zhang and Missionaries...111
  2.4.7 Zhang's Sensitive Conscience...................................119
  2.4.8 Some Chinese Christians Praised by Zhang.....................121
  2.4.9 Some Other Views of Zhang.....................................122
  2.4.10 Zhang's Last Days...127
 2.5 People's Comments on Zhang..129
 2.6 Conclusion 136

Chapter 3 137
Zhang Yijing's Search for a Christian Confucian Identity
 3.1 Confucianism...137
  3.1.1 Manufacturing the Terms "Confucius" and "Confucianism"..137
  3.1.2 What Is Confucianism?..138
  3.1.3 Is the School of Confucianism a Religion? 139
  3.1.4 Confucianism and Its Three Developmental Epochs 141
  3.1.5 Confucian Values and Confucian Terms and Clichés......145
  3.1.6 Confucianism and the Chinese 146
 3.2 A Confucian or a Christian?..146
  3.2.1 Reasons for the Conflict 147
  3.2.2 An Ignored but Typical Way of Being a Confucian and Being a Christian 148
 3.3 Zhang's Confucian Identity and Christian Identity....................151
  3.3.1 Is Zhang a Confucian?...151
  3.3.2 Becoming a Confucian Christian in the Mid-1890s.........153
  3.3.3 Being a Confucian Christian before 1905....................171
  3.3.4 Being a Confucian Christian after 1905......................183
 3.4 Different Methods of Contextualization 194
  3.4.1 Christians Should Make Sacrifices to Their Ancestors.....195
  3.4.2 Confucianism Should Be China's State Religion 197
 3.5 Conclusion 200

Chapter 4 203
Zhang's Search for a Modern Chinese Christian Identity
 4.1 Nationalism Literature Review...203
  4.1.1 A Brief Review of Research of Nationalism in Modern China 203

  4.1.2 Different Versions of Nationalism in China 206
  4.1.3 Cultural Nationalism and Modern Nationalism 208
 4.2 Nationalism and National Identity..211
  4.2.1 Different Ways of Being Modern Chinese but with
     One Commonality...211
  4.2.2 Competition through Discourses and Narratives.............213
  4.2.3 Competition between National Identity and Other
     Identities 213
  4.2.4 The Way of Studying Zhang's National Identity...............214
 4.3 Being a Modern Chinese or Being a Christian............................214
 4.4 Zhang's National Identity and His Christian Identity 216
  4.4.1 His National Identity in the Cultural Sense 216
  4.4.2 Being a Modern Chinese Christian before 1905...............217
  4.4.3 Being a Modern Chinese Christian before 1920...............220
  4.4.4 Being a Modern Chinese Christian in the 1920s 245
 4.5 Conclusion 274

Chapter 5 279
Zhang's Encounter with Scientism
 5.1 Scientism Literature Review..279
  5.1.1 The Concepts of Scientism 282
  5.1.2 Sources for Scientism in China..283
  5.1.3 The Influence of Scientism in China..................................287
  5.1.4 Being Scientific and Being Chinese 289
 5.2 Zhang's Response to Science and Scientism 291
  5.2.1 Welcoming Science 291
  5.2.2 Being Critical of Scientism...293
  5.2.3 The Difficulty of Answering the Scientistic
     Challenges Outside 297
  5.2.4 Answering Scientism Inside and Discovering Its
     Eastern Root...305
 5.3 Zhang's Dealing with the Early Chapters of Genesis in
   Response to Scientism 312
  5.3.1 Zhang's Pursuit of Being Scientific....................................313
  5.3.2 Science Is Used as a Value in Debate 314
  5.3.3 The Significance of Literal Interpretation to Zhang
     and His Shift..314
  5.3.4 The Elements of Evidence and Reason in His
     Dealing with the Great Flood 321
 5.4 Exploring Zhang's Shift between Biblical Interpretation
   Lines..326

    5.4.1 The Development of Zhang's Nonliteral and
          Nonconcordist Position 326
    5.4.2 Prioritizing between Zhang's Two Interpreting
          Approaches 338
  5.5 Two Christian Leaders' Response to "Scientistism" 344
  5.6 Conclusion 353

Chapter 6 355
Conclusion

Appendix 1 365
The Chronology of Zhang Yijing – My Deceased Father
(先严亦镜年表), By Zhang Qiutao (张秋涛)

Appendix 2 381
The Works of Mr. Zhang Yijing (张亦镜先生的著作)

Appendix 3 385
A Brief History of True Light (1902–1927) (真光小史)

Bibliography 387

List of Tables

Figure 1: A Scale of the Significance of Identities in the Four Christian Versions of Saving China 243

Figure 2: The Scales of the Significance of Identities in the Four Christian Versions of Loving China 272

Figure 3: A Chart of the Development of Zhang's Nonliteral and Nonconcordist Position 338

Figure 4: The Changes of Xu's Identity as a Scientific Chinese and Christian Identities...347

Acknowledgements

I would like to first express my sincere gratitude to my supervisors and mentors. I owe my deepest gratitude to Prof. Rolf Gerhard Tiedemann for his continuous support of my PhD study and related research, as well as for his patience, intense sense of responsibility, and immense knowledge. He guided me throughout my research and writing of this thesis. I could not have imagined having a better supervisor for my PhD study. Prof. Fuk-Tsang Ying's scholarship and integrity are what I admire, and I am heartily thankful to him for pointing me to the primary sources and to Prof. Yee-Cheung Lau. I am really blessed and honoured to have Prof. Yee-Cheung Lau as my supervisor, as he also supervised Prof. Ying in his PhD study. I am indebted to Prof. Lau who has made available his support in a number of ways: his prayers, motivation, laying aside all his other commitments to read my work, and guiding me in life and thesis writing with great patience. I am sincerely grateful to my stage leader, Dr. David Singh. With his excellent scholarship and great patience, he has encouraged me to pursue academic precision and excellence. I am greatly thankful to my tutor, Dr. Tim Keene. He has guided me with his correction, inspiration, and sympathy. Dr. Thomas Harvey's encouragement, guidance, and support from the initial to the final stage of this work enabled me to develop an understanding of the subject. To have Dr. Harvey, Dr. Singh, Prof. Tiedemann, Prof. Ying, Prof. Lau, and Dr. Keene as my supervisors and mentors guiding my doctoral study is indeed a privilege.

Besides my supervisors and mentors, my sincere gratitude also goes to all people of OCMS who have been helping me along the way. Without Dr. Wonsuk Ma and Dr. Julie Ma's encouragement and help, the pursuit of this scholarship could not have started. Dr. Bernard Farr used the imagery of house building to illustrate the process of thesis writing for me. Mr. Brian

Woolnough's encouragement and enthusiasm made me want to speak more. Dr. Damon So helped me to balance faith and scholarship and he spared no effort in finding supervisors for me. I received guidance from the long and interesting chats with Dr. Bill Prevette. Dr. Andy Hartropp was always ready to help and talk. I miss his smile. I am deeply grateful to Dr. Paul Woods. He has encouraged me to have my ideas published, kept my focus in the research from going astray, and spurred me to think from different perspectives. Dr. Ben Knighton taught me many research skills and gave me useful recommendations. I have also been taught, guided, supported, encouraged, loved, and blessed by Dr. Paul Bendor-Samuel, Mr. Ralph Bates, Mr. Andrew Buck, Mr. Terry Garde, Ms. Carole Glendinning, Mrs. Blanche Marslin, Mrs. Rachel McIntyre, Ms. Irim Sarwar, Ms. Nicky Clargo, and others. It is really my good fortune to be able to do research at OCMS.

I would like to thank the team of my thesis examiners, Dr. Damon So and Prof. Chloë Starr, not only for their insightful comments and encouragement, but also for the challenging questions which incentivized me to widen my research to include other perspectives.

The help and encouragement of Prof. Ryan Dunch enabled me to have time to focus on my writing and access to the resources in the library of the University of Alberta. This work would have been full of linguistic faults if Ms. Genevieve Hawkins, a specialist in copyediting and proofreading, Rev. and Mrs. Helmut and Tina Markeli, and Dr. and Mrs. Michael and Nora Suman had not helped me with their speciality free of charge. The Ven. and Mrs. Godfrey and Dot Stone have not only broadened my horizons and deepened my thinking, but also touched my family with their love of Christ. More than always reserving a warm and affordable room for me, Mr. Bill Wilson looks for chances to serve me and China.

I would like to acknowledge that the support from ScholarLeaders International and Dr. Evan Hunter have been extremely critical to this study. The support from the Langham Scholars Programme and Dr. Ian J. Shaw have great significance to my research. I am also grateful to Langham Publishing for transforming the manuscript into a presentable book to the reader.

The leadership and colleagues of Shenzhen University also deserve my gratitude and respect for their encouragement, support, and guidance. Among them, there are Prof. Zhang Xiaohong, Prof. Chen Zhimin, Prof. Tian Jie, Prof. Huang Xuefeng, Prof. Peng Xiaogang, Ms. Tang Hong, Ms. Zeng Xueshan,

Prof. Jiang Daochao, Ms. Chen Zhixing, Prof. Zhang Jiliang, Prof. Ruan Wei, Prof. Wang Hui, Prof. Ji Yinglin, Prof. Liu Yi, Prof. Li Xiaojun, Prof. Hua Weifen, Prof. Hu Yijie, Mrs. Zhang Xinying, Mrs. Zhu Guangwei, Mrs. Li Jing, Mrs. Liu Zhi, Mr. He Yong, and Mr. Li Yi.

The Southern Baptist Convention has my deep respect and gratitude. Their endeavours and sacrifices for China have not only blessed many Chinese like Zhang Yijing nearly one hundred years ago, but also kindly and generously supported me to do my research in its Historical Library and Archives. Dr. Taffey Hall, Mrs. Elyse Rives, and Mr. Arthur Toalston warmly received me so that I had a very enjoyable time there.

I would also like to thank Mr. Ken Osborne for allowing me to use the library of CMS for such an extended period. To my fellow doctoral candidates, I am thankful for their feedback, cooperation, and friendship. I sincerely offer my regards and blessings to all of those who supported me in any respect during the completion of the project.

I want to express my heartfelt gratitude to Rev. and Mrs. Dustin and Niki Stewart and to Rev. and Mrs. Benjamin and Meghan Bowser who have provided my family with spiritual, moral, emotional, educational, and linguistic support in the process. Without their selfless help, I would have had many more difficulties.

The Timothy Group and Mr. Liu Aihua have always been supportive of my study, which I appreciate deeply.

Mr and Mrs. Robert and Carolyn Plunk, Rev. and Mrs. Robert and Judy Carter, and the Trinity Baptist Church have provided us with their best provision, protection, and comfort.

I must express my very profound gratitude to my parents and to my wife, sons, and daughter for providing me with unfailing support and continuous encouragement throughout my years of study and through the process of researching and drafting this work. This accomplishment would not have been possible without them.

Finally, I thank my heavenly Father for putting all those people into my life to nourish, enrich, and bless me.

Abstract

This book aims to understand how Chinese Christians in the early twentieth century attempted to fuse their Christian and Chinese identities by analyzing the life and works of Zhang Yijing (张亦镜).

Chinese Christians' various understandings of their identity are revealed in their different ways of contextualizing the Christian message. This book takes as its subject Zhang Yijing with a conservative Baptist background, who was a very important, but more marginalized, character within the Confucian-trained Chinese Protestant elite. His contributions and importance have not received the recognition and attention they deserve.

By examining the published works of Zhang and contrasting him with several of his contemporaries, this book explores the efforts Zhang has made and the results he has obtained in fusing these two identities. It traces the emergence and development of Zhang Yijng's Christian identity, examines the changing meanings of being a "Chinese" in history, and analyzes how Zhang's Christian identity interact with the different meanings of being a "Chinese." The understanding gained from this research may serve as a reference for the current Christian contextualization or Sinicization movement.

Keywords: identity, Christian, Chinese, Confucianism, nationalism, scientism, contextualization, Sinicization.

内容简介

本书旨在通过分析张亦镜的生活和作品，来了解二十世纪初中国基督徒是如何熔合他们的基督徒身份和中国人身份的.

中国基督徒在各自的处境中对基督信仰有不同表达，这反应出他们对自己的身份有不同的理解。本书以持基督信仰保守立场的张亦镜为研究对象，他是中国新教教会中一个非常重要的领袖人物，但却长期被边缘化，其贡献和重要性没有得到应有的表彰和重视.

本书通过研究张亦镜发表的作品，并将他与其同时代的基督徒进行对比，探讨了张在熔合这两个身份上所付出的努力和所得到的结果。本书追溯了张亦镜的基督徒身份的产生和发展过程，分析了'中国人'这一身份的涵义在历史中的变迁，并分析了张的基督徒身份和'中国人'的不同涵义之间是如何互动的。从中所获得的认识或许可以作为对目前基督教处境化或中国化运动的一种参考.

关键词：身份、基督徒、中国人、儒家、国家主义、唯科学主义、处境化、中国化.

List of Abbreviations

BCC	belief-confirming consultation
BTC	belief-threatening consultation
CACA	China Anti-Cult Association
CBPS	China Baptist Publication Society
CCP	Chinese Communist Party
CIM	China Inland Mission
CPC	Communist Party of China
KMT	Kuomintang of China or Nationalist Party of China
OCMS	Oxford Centre for Mission Studies
YMCA	Young Men's Christian Association
NIV	New International Version

An Explanation of the Different Ways of Writing a Chinese Name

A Chinese name in this text is usually written as "family name – given name(s)" while, for the reference information in the footnote, it is written as "given name(s) – family name." However, in the bibliography, the same name is written as "family name – given name(s)." Thus, "Zhang Yijing" in the text is the same person as "Yijing Zhang" in a footnote reference and "Zhang, Yijing" in the bibliography.

Zhang Yijing (张亦镜, 1871-1931)[1]

---
1. Picture taken from: John Benjamin Powell, *Who Is Who in China* 中国名人录, 5th ed. (Shanghai: The China Weekly Review, 1936), 17.

CHAPTER 1

Introduction and Literature Review

1.1 Relevance of This Research

For the last several decades starting from the 1970s, Christianity in China has regained its momentum of development, along with extreme care, caution, and sacrifice. Though the Chinese people are more open to Christianity, there is still a lot of discrimination, humiliation, and suspicion for Chinese Christians to face. Chinese nationalism, which used to exclude religion from her self-image as a national state, is still developing, but it is continually wary of the possible danger of religion to national solidarity and social stability, especially if used by "foreign hostile forces" for infiltration.[1] Although religion is not necessarily considered the "opiate of the people" anymore, the presence of "scientism" which labelled it superstitious and anachronistic is still easily felt. On 13 November 2000, the "China Anti-Cult Association" (CACA) (*Zhongguo fan xiejiao xiehui*), was established under the administration of the Institute of Science and Technology. Its members are mostly natural scientists, with the exception of two delegates from the State Catholic and Buddhist Association.[2] The underlying presupposition is that natural science decides the legitimacy of religion. The majority of Chinese who reject Christianity claim a faith in science. A typical response of the college students

---

1. Fuk-Tsang Ying 邢福增, "New Wine in Old Wineskins: An Appraisal of Religious Legislation in China and the Regulations on Religious Affairs of 2005," *Religion, State and Society* 34, no. 4 (1 December 2006): 358, 363, https://doi.org/10.1080/09637490600974427.

2. Kristin B. Kupfer, "Christian-Inspired Groups in the People's Republic of China after 1978: Reaction of State and Party Authorities (English)," *Social Compass* 51, no. 2 (2004): 277.

to the Christian message would be "I believe in science, so I don't believe in God." Confucianism, which used to be the core of China's tradition and had condemned Christianity as heterodoxy to its values and social structure, has been revived to some degree with the encouragement of the government,[3] along with other traditional values like Taoism and Buddhism.

In such a milieu, Chinese Christians, in diverse ways, are exploring and presenting their understanding of a Chinese Christian identity. Some feel they have to reveal the prominence of their Chinese identity by resonating with the calling of nationalism. Some consider avoiding an image of being superstitious and outdated is a matter of utmost importance. Some teach religious inquirers the Confucian classics in church, which leaves an impression that Christianity is in a perfect union with Chinese traditional culture, although most of the current religious inquirers, unlike their Chinese ancestors one hundred years ago, have a very limited knowledge of those classics and rarely view themselves as Confucians. Such an effort in seeking Chinese Christian identity also occurs in academic circles. For example, some scholars from academic institutes and universities in China are advocating "Sinicizing Christianity."

In connection with his analysis of the writings of the Christian apologist Zhang Lisheng (Chang Lit-sen, 章力生, 1904–1996), G. Wright Doyle has found the following:

> In the 1920s an "Indigenous Theology" movement began among Chinese scholars. Their aim was "relevance." The leaders of the movement included Zhao Zichen (or T. C. Chao 赵紫宸, 1888–1979), Xie Fuya (谢扶雅, 1892–1991), and Wu Leichuan (吴雷川, 1870–1944). Together they sought to make the Christian gospel acceptable to China through its integration with elements of traditional Chinese culture, especially Confucianism (and, to a lesser extent, Taoism and Buddhism).[4]

---

3. Sébastien Billioud and Joël Thoraval, "Anshen Liming or the Religious Dimension of Confucianism," *China Perspectives* 3, no. 75 (2008): 88–106, https://www.jstor.org/stable/24054196.

4. Wright Doyle, "Lit-Sen Chang (1904–1996) and the Critique of Indigenous Theology," *International Journal for the Study of the Christian Church* 15, no. 4 (2015): 345–46.

Doyle notices that this desire to make Christianity "Chinese" (to some, to "Sinify" or "contextualize" it) remains strong. However, just as Doyle reminds us, Chang Lit-sen also warned of the risk of uncritical indigenization.[5] Maureen W. Yeung's question pinpoints the key: "As for Chinese people who have become Christians, are they first and foremost Christians, and only secondarily Chinese? Or are they first and foremost Chinese, and only secondarily Christian?"[6]

History might provide some insights into the present situation because similar efforts in the search of Chinese Christian identity have been witnessed, especially at the beginning of the twentieth century when Confucianism, modern nationalism, and scientism were the influential ideologies of the milieu. As Chloë Starr points out, "Christian elites who took on the intellectual leadership in the mainstream churches in the 1920s responded robustly to the scientific and nationalist critiques of Christianity of their peers, developing their own visions of what a Chinese Christian church and thought might look like."[7] To them, the central question was identity: "Who are we, as Chinese Christians? To whom is loyalty due? How can an individual identity as a Christian be reconciled with a social identity as a Chinese?"[8]

Therefore, Chinese Christians both in the 1920s and at the present time have had an identity problem. If the contents of those dominant ideologies did not experience fundamental changes, it is proper to conclude that the question of identity faced by Chinese Christians then and now is basically the same problem. Therefore, this study will benefit from the knowledge accumulated by other researchers and narrow its focus down to a study of how Zhang Yijing, an elite Christian from a mainstream Christian press, dealt with this question, and gain a greater understanding of this enduring identity problem in the process.

---

5. Doyle, "Lit-Sen Chang," 346.

6. Maureen W. Yeung, "Boundaries in 'In-Christ Identity' Paul's View on Table Fellowship and Its Implications for Ethnic Identities," in *After Imperialism: Christian Identity in China and the Global Evangelical Movement*, ed. Richard R. Cook and David W. Pao (Cambridge: Lutterworth Press, 2012), 155.

7. Chloë Starr, *Chinese Theology: Text and Context* (New Haven: Yale University Press, 2016), 44.

8. Starr, *Chinese Theology*, 42–43.

1.2 Review of Paradigms of Studying Christianity in China

Hans Kung has subdivided the entire history of Christianity into six major paradigms to reveal a peculiar understanding of the Christian faith. Drawing upon the work of Kung, David Bosch suggests each paradigm also offers a distinctive understanding of Christian mission. The six paradigms are: (1) The apocalyptic paradigm of primitive Christianity, (2) The Hellenistic paradigm of the patristic period, (3) The medieval Roman Catholic paradigm, (4) The Protestant Reformation paradigm, (5) The modern Enlightenment paradigm, and (6) The emerging ecumenical paradigm.[9] Bosch's work reveals how Christians have understood Christian mission. When Christians have carried out their mission, the encounter of Christianity and culture occurred.

H. Richard Niebuhr's *Christ and Culture* has influenced several generations of thinkers so much that the idea of "Christ transforming culture" is easily related to Niebuhr's five categories. These are: Christ against culture and Christ of culture at the two extremes, with the moderating positions of Christ above culture, Christ and culture in paradox and Christ transforming culture in between.[10] Although he is critiqued by Craig Carter who believes Niebuhr's typology has an unarticulated presupposition of Christendom and a negative portrayal of the "Christ against culture" type,[11] his five categories serve as the base for Carter's rehabilitation. Carter defines Christendom as the "concept of Western civilization as having a religious arm (the Church) and a secular arm (civil government), both of which are united in their adherence to Christian faith, which is seen as the so-called soul of Europe or the West" and its essence is the assertion that Western civilization is Christian.[12] His post-Christendom typology consists of three Christendom and three non-Christendom types. The former includes Christ legitimizing culture, Christ humanizing culture, and Christ transforming culture. The latter serves as his attempt to rehabilitate the "Christ against culture" type, including Christ

---

9. David J. Bosch, *Transforming Mission: Paradigm Shifts in Theology of Mission* (Maryknoll: Orbis Books, 1991), 185–86.

10. H. Richard Niebuhr, *Christ and Culture*, exp. 50th anniversary ed. (New York: HarperOne, 2001).

11. Craig A. Carter, *Rethinking Christ and Culture: A Post-Christendom Perspective* (Grand Rapids: Brazos Press, 2006).

12. Carter, *Rethinking Christ and Culture*, 78.

transforming culture, Christ humanizing culture, and Christ separating from culture. The dividing line between Christendom and non-Christendom types lies in the necessity of the church endorsing, requesting, or joining in violent coercion.[13] Gustafson, a pupil of Niebuhr, says that Niebuhr does not intend a taxonomy, but a heuristic ideal-typical method.[14] Carter's purpose is not to provide a how-to manual but to stimulate imaginations so that various groups of people all over the Western world can learn how to follow the leading of the Holy Spirit in their own particular situations.[15] A critical question remains: Why do people relate Christ and culture to each other differently in the first place, resulting in the distinct categories proposed by Niebuhr and Carter?

In the case of China, a clue to the understanding of the encounter of Christianity in China can be found in the meeting of Christendom and Chinese culture. According to Daniel Bays, Christendom substantially shaped the assumptions and perceptions of both the Catholic missions to China in the sixteenth century and the Protestant missionaries of the nineteenth century.[16] The difference between these eras of Western missions in China is in the accompaniment of European imperialism with its gunboats. Thus, the meeting between Christendom and Chinese culture gradually shifted its focal point from meeting *tianxia*, the Chinese divinely ordained system for humankind, to meeting Chinese modern nationalism, worship of science, and Marxism.

Concerning the common ways of studying modern Chinese history, including the encounter of Christianity and China, Paul Cohen lists three approaches: impact-response, tradition-modernity, and imperialism.[17] However, he believes all the three paradigms are faulty because they predefine the West's importance and then go on to demonstrate it.[18] They all display "a Western-centredness that robs China of its autonomy and makes of it, in the end, an

---

13. Carter, 112.
14. Niebuhr, *Christ and Culture*, xxxi.
15. Carter, *Rethinking Christ and Culture*, 202.
16. Daniel H. Bays, "Protestantism in Modern China as 'Foreign Religion' and 'Chinese Religion': Autonomy, Independence, and the Constraints of Foreign Hegemony," in *Confucianism and Spiritual Traditions in Modern China and Beyond*, ed. Fenggang Yang and Joseph B. Tamney (Leiden: Brill, 2012), 232–33.
17. Paul A. Cohen, *Discovering History in China: American Historical Writing on the Recent Chinese Past* (New York: Columbia University Press, 1984).
18. Cohen, *Discovering History in China*, 5.

intellectual possession of the West."¹⁹ Cohen approves of a China-centred approach which looks at China from "a more interior approach" and "begins with Chinese problems set in a Chinese context."²⁰ Following this line, he abandons 1840, China's defeat in the first Opium War against the British, as a general time marker for modern Chinese history and instead extends the time marker back to the 1550s.²¹ In 1552, Saint Francis Xavier, a Spanish priest and missionary, made the Jesuits' first attempt to reach China.

The growing popularity of the China-centred approach to the study of the encounter between Christianity and China is reflected by the fact that, during the last few decades, scholars have been shifting attention from Western missionaries to indigenous Christians. As for the study on Christianity in China from the side of the Chinese, many scholars have made significant contributions. According to Ying's research of Chinese Christians' cultural adaption in the Ming and Qing dynasties, Chinese Christians' attitudes towards the relationship between Christianity and Chinese culture oscillate between two extremes: absolute incompatibility and complete convergence.²²

In his research of Pang Sanjie, R. G. Tiedemann 狄德满 shows how the Chinese response to Christianity was actually a reflection of their attitude towards both Western and local indigenous forces such as ideological systems and traditions.²³

Thomas Harvey's research illustrates how Chinese Christians like Wang Mingdao, John Sung, and Jing Dianying transmitted the Christian message through sermon, story, and song in ways fitting with the Chinese milieu.²⁴ This reflects their understanding of Chinese Christian identity. There are other important works of this kind which are not listed here.

---

19. Cohen, 151.

20. Cohen, 153–54.

21. Cohen, 195.

22. Fuk-Tsang Ying 邢福增, 文化适应与中国基督徒：一八六零至一九一一年 (*Cultural Accommodation and Chinese Christians: 1860–1911*) (香港 Hong Kong: 建道神学院 Alliance Bible Seminary, 1995), 141–43.

23. R. G. Tiedemann, "Anti-Christian Conflict in Local Perspective. The Life and Times of Pang Sanjie: Patriot, Protector, Bandit or Revolutionary?" in *Contextualization of Christianity in China: An Evaluation in Modern Perspective*, ed. Peter Chen-Main Wang (Sankt Augustin, Germany: Monumenta Serica, 2007), 243–75.

24. Thomas Alan Harvey, "Sermon, Story, and Song in the Inculturation of Christianity in China," in *Sinicizing Christianity*, ed. Yangwen Zheng, vol. 49, Studies in Christian Mission Series (Leiden: Brill, 2017).

In short, a series of perspectives are used to understand what attitude, method, or strategy has been adopted by Chinese Christians in their encounter with Christianity. Such efforts can also be understood as a study of contextualization, which Bevans describes as an attempt to understand Christian faith in terms of a particular context made up of cultural, social, religious, political, and economic aspects.[25] In this sense, the study of Christianity in China from a Chinese perspective can also be viewed as a study of contextual theology, for which Bevans proposes six models as lenses for understanding.

Viewed from the perspective of Stephen Bevans,[26] Chinese Christians are doing their own contextual theology because they were or are "expressing their experience in terms of their faith"[27] and reflecting on God's revelation which "is not just a message from God but the manifestation of God's presence in human life and in human society."[28] Bevans says that the texts of the Bible are the result not of heavenly dictation, but of the struggles of women and men of faith to make sense out of that faith in the midst of lives where God's presence was often less than self-evident.[29] In spite of this theological weakness, the models offered by Bevans are helpful to understand the various Chinese approaches to contextual theology. In 2004, he added a "countercultural" model to the translation, anthropological, praxis, synthetic, and transcendental models as presented in 1992.

These models are the results of the interplay of Scripture, tradition, human experience, and other contextual elements. The countercultural model is the most sceptical of context and emphasizes the disjunctions between culture and revelation. This model is reminiscent of the Christ against culture type of Niebuhr and the non-Christendom types of Carter. At the opposite end of the spectrum from the countercultural is the anthropological model which gives its primary attention to each concrete situation in which God already manifests the divine presence and views the human as a source of theology because they are the place of divine revelation. While the countercultural model proceeds from gospel to culture, the anthropological model moves

---

25. Stephen B. Bevans, *Models of Contextual Theology*, rev. and expanded ed. (Maryknoll: Orbis Books, 2004).
26. Bevans, *Models of Contextual Theology*.
27. Bevans, 18.
28. Bevans, 44.
29. Bevans, 44.

from culture to gospel. The other models fall in between. The models are heuristic, inclusive, and complementary, and are not mutually exclusive.[30]

Nonetheless, the question for Niebuhr and Carter is also true of Bevans's models: Why do people relate the gospel to culture differently, even in a similar social, political, historical, cultural context, to the point where their contextualizing methods can be classified as different models?

People may wonder if such models or types are universal or culturally specific. David Lee's work may help us gain insight in this question. Going beyond the scope of Christ and culture, Lee[31] even makes use of the models proposed by Bevans to study the method of contextualization of Islam in China by a Muslim Chinese, Liu Zhi (1662–1730). Thus, the work of David Lee gives support to the feasibility of such models for understanding Christianity in China at least.

As said above, the types and models proposed by Niebuhr, Carter, and Bevans are useful to understanding the practice of Christianity in China because Chinese Christians were or are relating Christ to culture or developing their own contextual theology when negotiating and reconciling their identity as Christians and their identity as Chinese.

Why do people have diverse types and models of the practice of Christianity, as summarized by Niebuhr, Carter, and Bevans? Using the theory of Bevans, we will see that the answer must lie in the personal and communal experiences because only this element can explain the difference between contextual theologians who face similar Scripture, tradition, culture, social location, and social changes.[32] As for the personal and communal experiences, Bevans does say that this element is possible only within the context of culture.[33] However, he does not elaborate on this at all. Though the background information in the examples of each model helps in understanding the models, the connection between the personal and communal experiences and the models is still not truly clear. More investigation should be made in contextual theologians' personal and communal human experience as one of the elements in understanding the models of contextual theology.

---

30. Bevans, 139.

31. David Lee, *Contextualization of Sufi Spirituality in Seventeenth- and Eighteenth-Century China: The Role of Liu Zhi (c. 1662–c. 1730)* (Eugene: Pickwick, 2015).

32. Bevans, *Models of Contextual Theology*, 5–7.

33. Bevans, 6.

At this point, we come back to the discussion of the original purpose of the China-centred approach, which is, as suggested by Cohen, to balance the importance between the West and China. This China-centred approach cannot guarantee an elimination or reduction of ethnocentric distortion. There is an example when Cohen notices an article written by Luo Rongqu, a Beijing University historian, in which Luo wrote, "China and Japan were both Eastern countries with similar historical backgrounds. Moreover, they experienced the same Western capitalist impact. Yet, the attitudes and policies the two countries adopted in responding to the Western impact were vastly different, as were the results. This comparison shows that the changes undergone by different countries in the face of capitalist aggression are shaped by internal factors." Cohen comments, "In the internal context in which Luo Rongqu wrote, however, the use of the impact-response approach, along with the comparison of Japan's successful response to China's unsuccessful one, emphasizing internal factors in each society and deemphasizing the role of imperialism, represented a significant challenge to the standard Maoist historiography of the day."[34]

What exactly is Luo's approach? If it were the impact-response approach, Luo's conclusion about internal factors in China and Japan as the sole cause of the changes would cause a contradiction to Cohen's criticism of the three paradigms listed above because Cohen believes that they are heavily burdened with Western-centric assumptions and lead to an excessive intellectual possession by the West. According to the characteristics of the China-centred approach such as "looking at China from a more interior approach" and "begins with Chinese problems set in a Chinese context," Luo's approach is more likely to be called a China-centred one. It is excessively China-centred to the point where the factors from the West are dismissed.

Nicolas Standaert 钟鸣旦 discusses a paradigm shift to stimulate a discussion about ways of studying Christianity in China.[35] He raises two questions. First, what is ultimately being studied? Second, from what perspective is it being studied?

---

34. Paul A. Cohen, "Cultural China: Some Definitional Issues," *Philosophy East and West* 43, no. 3 (1993): 559, https://doi.org/10.2307/1399582.

35. Nicolas Standaert, "New Trends in the Historiography of Christianity in China," *The Catholic Historical Review* 83, no. 4 (1997): 573–613, http://www.jstor.org/stable/25025062.

Concerning the object of research, Standaert states that one could also go beyond a study of Christianity in China that is strictly limited to either missiology or sinology.[36] The study of Christianity should lead to a better understanding of both Chinese and Western culture and of the interaction between them.

As to the choice between the West-centred/Eurocentric approach and China-centred/Sinocentric approach, he suggests that one should avoid an overly dualistic or essentialist approach to East and West.[37]

Standaert lists four interpretative schemes for the study of Christianity in China: as a type of cultural contact, as a factor in the modernization of China, as a marginal religion, or as a civilizing project. However, he thinks they are all inadequate because the encounter between Christianity and China and its influence is only "a minor thread in the whole tapestry of Chinese history." Because of this, Standaert recommends the paradigm of the "other" and the "self."[38] In his view, the history of Christianity in China can be viewed as a history of defining the "other" and the "self" or "Christianity" and "China." At the same time, he emphasizes that the two entities should be considered as open, dynamic, and mobile and allow for different identifications.

Kwok believes that a remarkably multifaceted relationship exists between Christianity and Chinese culture, consisting of confrontation, interaction, assimilation, and mutual-transformation.[39] He suggests studying the relationship on a micro-level instead of from a totalized, macro, or generalized way.

Ryan Dunch convincingly points out the limitations with the term of "cultural imperialism" when it is adopted to view the history of Christianity in China.[40] He suggests replacing the concepts of "cultural imperialism" and "colonization of consciousness" with "a globalizing cultural modernity" when the missionary movement is in consideration. One advantage of this approach is to provide a foundation for bringing together macro/global and micro/

---

36. Standaert, "New Trends in the Historiography," 581–82.
37. Standaert, 579.
38. Standaert, 611–12.
39. Wai Luen Kwok, "Jia Yuming's Doctrine of Sanctification and the Confucian Nurturing Doctrine of Xin (Heart-Mind)," *Sino-Christian Studies*, no. 17 (2014): 77.
40. Ryan Dunch, "Beyond Cultural Imperialism: Cultural Theory, Christian Missions, and Global Modernity," *History and Theory* 41, no. 3 (2002): 301–25, http://www.jstor.org/stable/3590688.

particular perspectives on the missionary movement as a factor in modern world history.

Concerning the object of study of Christianity in China, I agree with Standaert that it is important to study Chinese and Western cultures and their interaction and that it is important to go beyond a study which is strictly limited to missiology or sinology. In my opinion, it would be better to combine both missiology and sinology together for study. Just as Standaert says, the arrival of Christianity in China is a means to know China better.[41] On the other hand, a good understanding of China would certainly be helpful to missiology, the study of the cross-cultural communication of the Christian faith.

In the study of Christianity in China, Christian message and doctrines cannot be ignored because the encounter of Christianity and China is not merely the meeting of Western and Chinese cultures, although Western missionaries were imbued with Western culture. Moreover, an examination of Western and Chinese Christians' comprehension of Christian message and doctrines is necessary for a better understanding of the different contextualization strategies that they used. Thus, Bevans takes Scripture and tradition as one basic element in making contextual theology. Similarly, Smart shows that there is a motley assortment of Christian thought, experience, and life.[42] A different understanding of God and the Christian message would lead to different strategies in contextualization.

Turning to the choice of approach or perspective, Standaert recommends the paradigm of the "other" and the "self," but as Dunch has shown,[43] "Orientalism," which conflated distinct societies and imputed to them a set of negative attributes contrasting to positive qualities attributed to the "West," is also a way to discourse "self" and "other." Standaert realizes too that both "Orientalism" and "Occidentalism" or "Euro-centred" and "China-centred" approaches are also ways of delineating "self" and "other." They also bear the possible feature of one-sidedness because both types of discourses are subjected to power.[44] However, Standaert does suggest adopting Chen Xiaomei's opinion that "the binary oppositions Orient/Occident and Self/Other can,

---

41. Standaert, "New Trends in the Historiography," 579.

42. Ninian Smart, *In Search of Christianity: Discovering the Diverse Vitality of the Christian Life* (San Francisco: Harper & Row, 1979).

43. Dunch, "Beyond Cultural Imperialism," 303.

44. Standaert, "New Trends in the Historiography," 577.

therefore, best be viewed as in a constant and continuing dialogue."[45] This is a good suggestion, but sometimes it still might go against his original desire of avoiding an overly dualistic or essentialist approach to the East and the West.

Ryan Dunch's recommendation of "globalising cultural modernity" has much to commend it, but Standaert thinks that the interpretative scheme of viewing the encounter of Christianity and China as an encounter of two civilizing projects is inadequate because this encounter and its influence are only "a minor thread in the whole tapestry of Chinese history." It is true that currently the influence of Christians in China is still politically and publicly a minor one. Yet it is also arguable that the current population of Christians is large, and they are changing the Chinese lifestyle in an unobtrusive way, in both the urban and rural areas. The governmental restrictions of Christianity reflect its potential influence. In the future, the encounter of Christianity and China might not be viewed as a minor thread in the whole tapestry of Chinese history. Considering its potential of bringing together macro/global and micro/particular perspectives, "globalizing cultural modernity" is definitely an attractive approach.

Nonetheless, the encounter of Christianity and China is more than an encounter of Western and Chinese cultures. Christianity is not Western and Western culture cannot represent it. Since some missionaries also opposed the idea of Christendom, it would be problematic to call it "the encounter of Christendom and China." The encounter is better described as an encounter between the Chinese and God or Christian faith through the messengers or Western missionaries who were imbued with Western culture.

Therefore, while taking the elements of the Bible and the external context (including culture) into consideration, it would also be wise to include another perspective – the perspective of "identities." There are two reasons. First, the research question is about identity: To what extent did Zhang demonstrate that being a Christian Chinese at that time was possible? As Professor Starr asks: "To whom is loyalty due? How can an individual identity as a Christian be reconciled with a social identity as a Chinese?"[46] Second, this perspective can facilitate the understanding of the individual contextual theologian's personal and communal experience because identity attaches

---

45. Standaert, 577.
46. Starr, *Chinese Theology*, 42.

importance to the process of the personal and communal experiences being organized, synthesized, and integrated with the context. As a psychologist and the founder of identity theory, Erikson points out, "Identity formation is a process 'located' in the core of the individual and yet also in the core of his communal culture, a process which establishes the identity of those two identities."[47] This is a process with a continuous interaction between person and context. As noted above, we should examine the personal and communal experiences that led Christians in early twentieth-century China to relate Christ or the gospel to culture in different ways in the first place so that their choices can be categorized by the typologies proposed by Niebuhr, Carter, and Bevans.

Paul Cohen is also highly interested in "identities" when he suggests utilizing methodologies and techniques from other disciplines in historical analysis. According to him, the central task facing historians is to find ways of exploiting their outsideness that maximize the illumination and minimize the distortion. The way he finds very helpful for scholars of Chinese studies is that "whatever their original ethnic identity, they should be regarded as marginal personalities who belong simultaneously to both the Chinese cultural world and their own heritage" because "moving back and forth between being 'inside' and being 'outside' invests them with the potential to see in new and unusual ways and confers on marginality its special intellectual power."[48]

On 28 September 2004, William S. Campbell presented a lecture at the Oxford Centre for Mission Studies in Oxford. It was entitled, "Identity in Christ according to Paul" and was well received. He is an early adopter of the use of social scientific methodology in biblical interpretation and brings to the fore methodological reflections on identity.[49] J. Brian Tucker of Moody Theological Seminary, a doctoral student of William S. Campbell, uses the lens of identity theory to show how Paul, in his first letter to the Corinthians,

---

47. Erik H. Erikson, *Identity: Youth and Crisis* (New York: W. W. Norton, 1968), 22.

48. Cohen, "Cultural China: Some Definitional," 561–62.

49. J. Brian Tucker, "Diverse Identities in Christ according to Paul: The Enduring Influence of the Work of William S. Campbell," *Journal of Beliefs & Values* 38, no. 2 (2017): 150, https://doi.org/10.1080/13617672.2017.1291255.

is forging a social identity "in Christ" to overcome the competing Roman social identity.[50]

Thus, following their trail, this research aims to trace the development of Zhang Yijing's Christian identity to find out to what extent he reconciled his personal identity as a Christian with his social identity as a Chinese by analyzing his stories, conversations, arguments, and narratives. This study will borrow the fruits of modern psychological research of identity. Its definition originates from Erikson who defines a sense of identity as "a sense of personal sameness and historical continuity."[51] Identity can be analyzed at various levels: ego identity, personal identity, and social identity. More will be given in the next section.

Two of the advantages of using the perspective of identity are personalization and decentralization, which are actually advocated by Dunch[52] and Standaert.[53] In the process of analyzing an individual Christian's identities, researchers and readers are more able to feel and view the surroundings from the perspective of the Christians in question. This creates more sympathy with the Christians' responses.

Furthermore, after the analysis of the Christian's different identities, researchers and readers are more likely to have a bird's-eye view of the Christians being studied and have a self-consciousness of their own identities. This overall view and self-consciousness help the researchers and readers detach themselves more easily from their own nationalistic and ethical identities and feelings. In this way, decentralization can be more likely achieved. Neither the West nor China is at the centre.

In spite of that, there are at least two potential limitations. The perspective of identities is more about research on a micro-level. It cannot promise a description on the macro-level. The second limitation is that, currently, it is hard to evaluate the measure or the strength of faith.

In reality, identities are, of course, combined in one person. In certain contexts or situations, one or the other of these identities will be more prominent

---

50. J. Brian Tucker, *You Belong to Christ: Paul and the Formation of Social Identity in 1 Corinthians 1–4* (Eugene: Pickwick, 2010), 2; J. Brian Tucker, *Remain in Your Calling: Paul and the Continuation of Social Identities in 1 Corinthians* (Eugene: Pickwick, 2011), 48.

51. Erikson, *Identity: Youth and Crisis*, 17.

52. Dunch, "Beyond Cultural Imperialism."

53. Standaert, "New Trends in the Historiography."

than the other identities. Even so, it may serve a useful perspective to present these identities separately for analytical purposes.

In short, this research will try to understand Zhang Yijing's ways of negotiating and reconciling his personal identity as a Christian and his social identity as a Chinese.

1.3 Introduction to Identity

"More so than the later graduates of other Christian colleges, Wenhuiguan[54] graduates seem to have remained committed to a Christian identity." With this sentence, the historian Daniel Bays introduces us once again to the concept of identity as applied to Christian believers and the idea of the differing strengths of Christian identity.[55]

At the beginning of the twentieth century, there were at least four challenges in particular that demanded a response from these graduates and other Chinese Christians – Confucianism, nationalism, Marxism, and scientism. Some people were still very firm Christians while trying to respond to these challenges or being silent. Some people turned to challenge and doubt their belief for its "unscientific" and "unpatriotic" features. Some people requested the church to submit to the demands of nationalism while maintaining a Christian identity. Some gave up their belief completely. Such diverse responses to those ideologies reflect the different ways of being a Christian and being a Chinese, placing a different significance on Christian identity. So, the strength of the Christian identity and the influences of those other ideologies account for the variety of responses. This study will examine the development of Zhang's Christian identity and its interaction with three main ideologies: Confucianism, nationalism, and scientism.

The literature review of identity below might at first seem too detailed for the study of Zhang Yijing. However, there are substantive and strategic considerations. Substantively, to propose the use of identity for an approach, a term still encumbered by alien perceptions, more explanation is needed.

---

54. Wenhuiguan or Tengchow College was established in 1876 by the US Northern Presbyterian, Calvin Mateer.

55. Daniel H. Bays, *A New History of Christianity in China* (Malden: Wiley-Blackwell, 2012), 95.

Strategically, the author, a Chinese-speaking student using poor English to suggest an approach to an English-speaking academic audience, should be more thorough for fear that his marginality could leave the impression of being impotent. The same fear can be observed in Paul Cohen's work on the topic of shaping cultural China, where it motivates him, as a representative of those who are neither ethnically nor culturally Chinese, to blur the boundaries between centre and periphery and between internal and external, so that all are seen as legitimate players in an internal discourse on Chinese history.[56]

Since the theory of identity is developing quickly and widely and is still in the making, this research will take two elements into consideration for its selected literature review: (1) the ideas of widely recognized authorities will be respected; and (2) the research relating to religious identity will be viewed as more relevant. Therefore, the selection of research for analysis will not be totally objective and inclusive.[57]

1.4 Identity Literature Review

In the globalized world today, people are increasingly familiar with the confusion caused by multiple demands being placed upon them simultaneously. McLean and Pasupathi have explained how people who have changed their beliefs have also changed to become different persons.[58] With new values and new beliefs, they also have a new identity. Individuals who have violated their own values and beliefs have violated their identity. In reality, an individual may end up holding different beliefs or values simultaneously, and so may have a number of different identities that intersect or overlap like a Venn diagram, thus creating confusion. From social-psychological and sociological viewpoints, people are said to have "multiple identities."[59] According to

---

56. Cohen, "Cultural China: Some Definitional."

57. In mainland China till now, to the author's knowledge, there is no specific journal for identity study and only a very small number of articles about identity are published in psychology journals. Thus, this study has not been able to include the research of identity done there.

58. Kate C. McLean and Monisha Pasupathi, "Processes of Identity Development: Where I Am and How I Got There," *Identity: An International Journal of Theory and Research* 12, no. 1 (2012): 9, 15.

59. Vassilis Saroglou and Benoît Hanique, "Jewish Identity, Values, and Religion in a Globalized World: A Study of Late Adolescents," *Identity: An International Journal of Theory and Research* 6, no. 3 (2006): 231.

Erikson, these multiple identities lead to "identity confusion."[60] As stated above, Chinese Christians responded in diverse ways to the challenges they faced in the 1920s and some people were more committed to their Christian identity than others. This may have been because people had a different priority order of their multiple identities and different priority orders led to different responses when some identities were being challenged. As Hunsberger et al. have observed,[61] little research has been done on the sociopsychological aspects of this from a religious point of view, and as Schwartz et al. have noted,[62] the ways in which identity develops in non-Western contexts are not well understood. Hence this research also wishes to explore the connections between an individual's "identity confusion" and his Christian identity in China of the 1920s.

1.4.1 Erikson's Definition of Identity

Identity is now an immensely popular word in everyday speech partly because of the influence of psychology on contemporary thinking. Since this study needs to borrow certain perspectives from psychology, it will go in-depth into the psychological writings of Erikson and others to discern how they use these terms.

Most of the theories and approaches to identity can be traced back to Erik H. Erikson who is viewed as the founder and authority of the identity theory, although Erikson received some of his legacy from Freud. Postmodernists like Ann Phoenix and Ali Rattansi try to challenge the necessity of Ericksonian approach.[63] This has not been successful, but instead proves the significance of Erikson.

---

60. Erikson, *Identity: Youth and Crisis*, 166.

61. Bruce Hunsberger, Michael Pratt, and S. Mark Pancer, "Adolescent Identity Formation: Religious Exploration and Commitment," *Identity: An International Journal of Theory and Research* 4, no. 1 (2001): 382.

62. S. J. Schwartz et al., "Identity Development, Personality, and Well-Being in Adolescence and Emerging Adulthood: Theory, Research, and Recent Advances," in *Handbook of Psychology, Vol. 6: Developmental Psychology*, ed. I. B. Weiner et al. (New York: John Wiley and Sons, 2013), 358.

63. Ann Phoenix and Ali Rattansi, "Proliferating Theories: Self and Identity in Post-Eriksonian Context: A Rejoinder to Berzonsky, Kroger, Levine, Phinney, Schachter, and Weigert and Gecas," *Identity* 5, no. 2 (1 April 2005): 205–25, https://doi.org/10.1207/s1532706xid0502_9.

Erikson defines a sense of identity as "a sense of personal sameness and historical continuity."[64] This sense of identity is "based on two simultaneous observations: the perception of the self-sameness and continuity of one's existence in time and space and the perception of the fact that others recognize one's sameness and continuity."[65] Thus, Erikson refers to a sense of identity as a subjective experience of a person's core aspects, the social recognition of these same core aspects, and the interaction of personal and social contextual processes. To achieve this, the ideological structure of the environment (social reality) becomes essential because an ideological simplification of the universe can organize experience and there is a universal psychological need for a system of ideas that provides a convincing world image.[66] Therefore, Erikson sees identity and ideology as complementary.[67] However, ideologies must ask for an uncompromising commitment to some absolute hierarchy of values and some rigid principle of conduct.[68] It is the task of the core aspects (the ego) to attune and integrate these processes. Côté analyses one's sense of identity at different levels: ego identity, personal identity, and social identity.[69]

After Erikson, many researchers began to develop the theory of identity. Seth J. Schwartz tries to bring together different perspectives on self and identity, and identify commonalities between and among them.[70] The writings of Schwartz on this theme give a good summary of the key issues and his works are a good place to start to understand this topic.

1.4.2 Ego Identity, Personal Identity, and Social Identity

According to Erikson, ego identity is defined as the awareness of the fact that there is a self-sameness and continuity to the ego's synthesizing methods, the

---

64. Erikson, *Identity: Youth and Crisis*, 17.
65. Erikson, 50.
66. Erikson, 27, 31.
67. Erikson, 309.
68. Erikson, 191.
69. James E. Côté, "Editor's Note: The Hope and Promise of Identity Theory and Research," *Identity: An International Journal of Theory and Research* 1, no. 1 (2001): 4.
70. Seth J. Schwartz, "The Evolution of Eriksonian and Neo-Eriksonian Identity Theory and Research: A Review and Integration," *Identity: An International Journal of Theory and Research* 1, no. 1 (2001): 7–58; Seth J. Schwartz, "Self and Identity in Early Adolescence: Some Reflections and an Introduction to the Special Issue," *Journal of Early Adolescence* 28, no. 1 (2008): 5–15; Schwartz et al., "Identity Development, Personality."

style of one's individuality, and that this style coincides with the sameness and continuity of one's meaning for others in the immediate community.[71] In short, ego identity represents a coherent picture that one shows both to oneself and to the outside world. Personal identity refers to one's view of oneself in terms of goals, values, and beliefs that one shows to the world.[72] It is studied in content domains like career goals, dating preferences, word choices, and other aspects of self that identify an individual as someone in particular and that help to distinguish the person from other people. Social identities are those aspects of self-definition that derive from groups and corporate group-related behaviour, emotions, or evaluations.[73] Social identity is a sense of inner solidarity with a group's ideals. Aspects of self such as native language, country of origin, and racial background would fall under the heading of group identity.[74]

Levine quoted Erikson to differentiate between ego and personal identity "Ego identity . . . would test, select, and integrate the self-representations derived from the psychosocial crises of childhood."[75] The self-representations are part of the individual's personal identity; ego identity can be understood as "a sense of one's ability to momentarily reflect on the self as an object (i.e. to adopt a marginalised position from which to view one's personal and social identities)." Kunnen and Bosma refer identity to person-context integrations.[76] The contents of these integrations can be seen as components of personal and social identity, and the style or quality of these integrations, as well as a subjective sense of them, can be seen as components of the ego and its identity.

According to the review above, Zhang's ego identity was his awareness of the fact that there is a self-sameness and continuity in his ego's synthesizing methods and his style which tested, selected, and integrated his

---

71. Erikson, *Identity: Youth and Crisis*, 50.

72. Erikson, 1950, cited in Schwartz, "Evolution of Eriksonian and Neo-Eriksonian," 10.

73. H. Tajfel, "Intergroup Behaviour: I. Individualistic Perspectives," in *Introducing Social Psychology: An Analysis of Individual Reaction and Response*, ed. C. Fraser and H. Tajfel (New York: Penguin Books, 1987), 423–46.

74. Schwartz, "Evolution of Eriksonian and Neo-Eriksonian," 10.

75. C. Levine, "Questions Concerning Ego Identity and Its Health: A Commentary on Schwartz's 'The Evolution of Eriksonian and Neo-Eriksonian Identity Theory and Research,'" *Identity: An International Journal of Theory and Research* 1 (2001): 78–79.

76. E. Saskia Kunnen and Harke A. Bosma, "Fischer's Skill Theory Applied to Identity Development: A Response to Kroger," *Identity: An International Journal of Theory and Research* 3, no. 3 (2003): 250.

self-representations including his goals, values, and beliefs which he showed to the world, and other aspects of self-representation which he partly derived from groups and corporate group-related behaviours, emotions, and evaluation. In simple terms, his ego identity was his awareness of the fact that, consistently and continually, in his own way, he tested, selected, and integrated those elements into the self-image he projected to others.

Zhang's social identities, among others, include that of a Chinese, that of a church member, and that of a Baptist church member. His identification with the emotions, behaviours, and values expected of a Chinese was his social identity as a Chinese. His sense of inner solidarity with the ideals and values of the whole Christian church and the Baptist church were his social identities as a church member and as a Baptist church member.

He viewed himself as a Christian (or a follower of Christ) and a preacher-by-writing with beliefs, values, career goals, and word choice which distinguished him from other people. This self-representation as a Christian (or a Christ follower) and a preacher-by-writing are two of his personal identities.

Two questions need to be addressed from the outset. First, are different personal and collective aspects of self actually separate identities? Or, are they separate components of a single identity? Opinions differ. I agree to an integrative view that this is simply a question of terminology – a definitional question rather than a real substantive problem.[77] Therefore, Zhang's different identities could be viewed as the different aspects of him.

Second, how can personal identity relate to social identity? Since identities can be viewed as ways of thinking (or, in some perspectives, ways of talking),[78] the difference between personal identity and social identity can be viewed as the distinction between value references for ways of thinking. Moreover, it is believed that identities are inescapably both personal and social, not only in their content, but also in the processes by which they are formed, maintained, and changed over time.[79] Multiple aspects of identity or multiple identities

---

77. Vivian L. Vignoles, Seth J. Schwartz, and Koen Luyckx, "Introduction: Toward an Integrative View of Identity," in *Handbook of Identity Theory and Research*, ed. Seth J. Schwartz, Koen Luyckx, and Vivian L. Vignoles, vol. 2 (New York: Springer Science + Business Media, 2011), 6.

78. Vignoles, Schwartz, and Luyckx, "Introduction," 4.

79. Vignoles, Schwartz, and Luyckx, 5.

are expected to intersect and interact with each other.[80] Viewed from such perspectives, Zhang's personal identity as a Christian and his social identity as a Chinese were both simultaneously personal and social, and they intersected with each other, functioning as two reference systems (meaning and value) for him. And these two systems interplayed and developed through his personal and relational interaction in his social-historical contexts.

1.4.3 Marcia's Theory of Identity Statuses Model

Marcia is among the first group to elaborate on Erikson's stage-based description of adolescent identity development.[81] He notices two key issues in identity development: (1) exploration of options in the occupational and ideological realms (e.g. choice of career and personal values, respectively), and (2) the person's subsequent commitment to a choice of occupation and set of values to live by and remain faithful to (what Erikson calls "fidelity"). Then he forms and distinguishes four identity statuses by making use of the intersection of these two dimensions of exploration (or crisis) and commitment: identity achievement (commitments achieved after a period of exploration), moratorium (exploration in progress, commitments present but still vague), foreclosure (strong commitments, no exploration period), and identity diffusion (exploration present or absent, no commitments). Marcia also includes political and religious orientations to cover all domains of identity formation, including religious identity.[82]

1.4.4 Extension of Marcia's Identity Statuses Model

Though Marcia's model was important for research on identity development, it was also heavily criticized. Many researchers think Marcia's four statuses model is more descriptive of the reality of one's identity at one moment than reflecting the developmental mode of one's identity.[83] Schwartz et al.

---

80. Maya A. Yampolsky, Catherine E. Amiot, and Roxane de la Sablonnière, "The Multicultural Identity Integration Scale (MULTIIS): Developing a Comprehensive Measure for Configuring One's Multiple Cultural Identities Within the Self," *Cultural Diversity and Ethnic Minority Psychology* 22, no. 2 (2016): 169, https://pubmed.ncbi.nlm.nih.gov/26009944/.

81. J. E. Marcia, "Development and Validation of Ego Identity Status," *Journal of Personality and Social Psychology*, no. 5 (1966): 551–58.

82. Marcia, "Development and Validation of Ego," 551–58.

83. Kunnen and Bosma, "Fischer's Skill Theory Applied"; Lyda Lannegrand-Willems and Harke A. Bosma, "Identity Development-in-Context: The School as an Important Context

question how Marcia's foreclosure and moratorium statuses could fit into Erikson's theories while agreeing that Marcia's identity achievement is similar to Erikson's concept of identity synthesis and diffusion is similar to identity confusion.[84]

In response to these criticisms, theorists are proposing new kinds of approach. Alisat and Pratt suggest understanding the developmental process of one's identity through the study of narrative or life stories in addition to qualitative study,[85] which is also emphasized by Rattansi and Phoenix.[86] Crocetti et al. include reconsideration of commitment,[87] which means dissatisfaction with one's current commitments and a desire to change them. As reviewed by Crocetti and Meeus, the two identity processes have been expanded into more specific forms: exploration in breadth, exploration in depth, reconsideration of commitment, and identification with commitment.[88] Galliher, McLean, and Syed believe that identity processes have been studied quite fruitfully and suggest emphasizing both process and content.[89] Marcia's theory of identity statuses is still widely used by researchers, not only for ego identity, but also for all domains of personal and social identity.

Therefore, Marcia's identity statuses model will be applied to Zhang's Christian identity, the developmental process and content of which will be understood by examining his narrative, stories, arguments, and conversations.

---

for Identity Development," *Identity: An International Journal of Theory and Research* 6, no. 1 (2006): 85–113.

84. Schwartz, "Evolution of Eriksonian and Neo-Eriksonian."

85. Susan Alisat and Michael W. Pratt, "Characteristics of Young Adults' Personal Religious Narratives and Their Relation with the Identity Status Model: A Longitudinal, Mixed Methods Study," *Identity: An International Journal of Theory and Research* 12, no. 1 (2012): 29–52.

86. Ali Rattansi and Ann Phoenix, "Rethinking Youth Identities: Modernist and Postmodernist Frameworks," *Identity* 5, no. 2 (1 April, 2005): 105, https://doi.org/10.1207/s1532706xid0502_2.

87. E. Crocetti, M. Rubini, and W. Meeus, "Capturing the Dynamics of Identity Formation in Various Ethnic Groups: Development and Validation of a Three-Dimensional Model," *Journal of Adolescence* 31, no. 2 (2008): 207–22.

88. Elisabetta Crocetti and Wim Meeus, "The Identity Statuses: Strengths of a Person-Centered Approach," in *The Oxford Handbook of Identity Development*, ed. K. C. McLean and M. Syed (New York: Oxford University Press, 2015), 97–114.

89. R. V. Galliher, K. C. McLean, and M. Syed, "An Integrated Developmental Model for Studying Identity Content in Context," *Developmental Psychology* 53, no. 11 (2017): 2011–22.

1.4.5 Multiple Identities

A person has more than one identity and those identities intersect with each other. Saroglou and Hanique claim that multiple identities are becoming an increasingly important issue in a globalized world.[90]

Those identities may be organized in a structure or hierarchy. By studying women's identities, Graham et al. suggest that one person's identities may be organized: (1) hierarchically, (2) laterally, (3) laterally/hierarchically, or (4) transcendently.[91] Organizing identities transcendently means that personal identity in a structure, including role occupancy and role-related identity, is subordinate to a sense of ego identity and continuity across time and context. Dr. Narváez et al. also suggest that the intersectionality of identities is not always horizontal (or radial), but also vertical (or axial).[92] Okolie concludes that people have multiple identities that often intersect with one another and groups are affected by particular identities that are their core identities, though differently.[93] In contemporary China, when the official line is propagandizing "Loving one's own country is the most thick and lasting emotion in humanity,"[94] it can be viewed as an effort to promote one's national identity as the core identity and consolidating a politically correct way of organizing one's identities.

Apart from having different significance, these identities can be compatible or conflicting.[95] What are the usual means of reconciliation? There are various ways of reconciling apparent inconsistencies in their sense of identity and preserving a subjective sense of self-continuity. For example, people wishing to make a coherent personal narrative may select and reconstruct their past

---

90. Saroglou and Hanique, "Jewish Identity, Values, and Religion," 231.

91. Carolyn W. Graham, Gwendolyn T. Sorell, and Marilyn J. Montgomery, "Role-Related Identity Structure in Adult Women," *Identity: An International Journal of Theory and Research* 4, no. 3 (2004): 255.

92. Rafael F. Narváez et al., "A Qualitative Approach to the Intersection of Sexual, Ethnic, and Gender Identities," *Identity: An International Journal of Theory and Research* 9, no. 1 (2009): 75.

93. Andrew C. Okolie, "Introduction to the Special Issue – Identity: Now You Don't See It; Now You Do," *Identity: An International Journal of Theory and Research* 3, no. 1 (2003): 2, 6–7.

94. "Today, How Are We Patriotic? Hearing What General Secretary Xi Jinping Said, 今天，我们如何爱国？听习近平总书记这样说," *People's Daily Online* 人民网, 8 October 2020, https://baijiahao.baidu.com/s?id=1679940990720387510&wfr=spider&for=pc.

95. Yampolsky, Amiot, and de la Sablonnière, "Multicultural Identity Integration Scale," 180.

experiences;[96] they may also create personalized redefinitions of the meanings of the identity categories they occupy so that group and individual differences can be managed;[97] and they also may deal with their multiple identities by means of categorization, compartmentalization, and integration.[98]

Categorization involves identifying with one cultural group over others by seeing one identity as predominant and excluding other identities from the self. Compartmentalization involves having multiple cultural identities that are kept in their own isolated compartments within the self because the differences between them are seen as conflicting. Integration involves seeing common ground between one's identities while seeing the differences between them as complementary. Moreover, with integration, one may invoke a higher-order, inclusive identity that encompasses the different cultural identities (i.e. a superordinate identity) as a means for reconciling and uniting them. These means could be applied both to personal and to social identities.[99]

Zhang also had multiple identities. This study will focus on how he reconciled his personal identity as a Christian with his social identity as a Chinese and how his way of structuring or organizing them distinguished his way of relating Christ or the gospel to culture from other sources.

Different identities acquire salience in different contexts.[100] Therefore, it is only when they are salient that some of Zhang's other identities will be attended to, namely his identity as a preacher-by-writing and his social identities as a church member and as a Baptist church member. However, for the purpose of this research, some of his other identities, for instance racial identity and gender identity, will not be included.

---

96. Dan P. McAdams, "Narrative Identity," in *Handbook of Identity Theory and Research*, ed. Seth J. Schwartz, Koen Luyckx, and Vivian L. Vignoles, vol. 1 (New York: Springer Science + Business Media, 2011), 111.

97. Alexander Haslam and Naomi Ellemers, "Identity Processes in Organizations," in *Handbook of Identity Theory and Research*, ed. Seth J. Schwartz, Koen Luyckx, and Vivian L. Vignoles, vol. 2 (New York: Springer Science + Business Media, 2011), 737.

98. Catherine E. Amiot et al., "Integration of Social Identities in the Self: Toward a Cognitive-Developmental Model," *Personality and Social Psychology Review* 11, no. 4 (2007): 364–88; Yampolsky, Amiot, and de la Sablonnière, "Multicultural Identity Integration Scale."

99. Yampolsky, Amiot, and de la Sablonnière, 168–69.

100. Rattansi and Phoenix, "Rethinking Youth Identities," 104.

1.4.6 The Importance of Spiritual Identity to Ego Identity

Hunsberger et al. show that research linking an individual sense of ego identity to religion and/or spirituality during adulthood has been rare.[101] Hoare uses her primary sources written by Erik Erikson including both published and unpublished materials to show that Erikson believed that the spiritual belief is very important to a person's ego identity.[102] According to Hoare,[103] Erikson found that spiritual belief is a key identity component among many adults and Erikson held that religion "restores . . . a new sense of wholeness," and wholeness, coherence, and ego vitality are the lifeblood of identity. According to Hunsberger et al.,[104] Erikson's theory of psychosocial development can be interpreted as a model of religious faith development. There is some debate about whether Erikson's final stage exists or not.

Kiesling et al. find spiritual identity very important to the sense of self.[105] Later on, Kiesling and Sorell further find spiritual identity serves a central and integrative function for many of their respondents.[106] Kunnen and Bosma advise that achieving a sense of identity requires an integration of individual and contextual processes which contribute to identity formation.[107] If we connect these findings together, especially when we remember that "Ego identity . . . would test, select, and integrate the self-representations derived from the psychosocial crises of childhood,"[108] we can almost reach a conclusion about the significance of spiritual identity because it carries out the main function of ego identity – integration of individual and contextual processes.

The significance of spiritual identity in the thoughts of Erikson and others is another reason why this research will give more attention to Zhang's spiritual identity or Christian identity among his identities. Zhang chose

---

101. Hunsberger, Pratt, and Pancer, "Adolescent Identity Formation," 365.
102. Carol Hoare, "Identity and Spiritual Development in the Papers of Erik Erikson," *Identity: An International Journal of Theory and Research* 9, no. 3 (2009): 183–200.
103. Erikson, 1954, cited in Hoare, "Identity and Spiritual Development," 188, 192.
104. Hunsberger, Pratt, and Pancer, "Adolescent Identity Formation," 366.
105. Chris Kiesling et al., "Identity and Spirituality: A Psychosocial Exploration of the Sense of Spiritual Self," *Developmental Psychology* 42, no. 6 (2006): 1276.
106. Chris Kiesling and Gwen Sorell, "Joining Erikson and Identity Specialists in the Quest to Characterize Adult Spiritual Identity," *Identity: An International Journal of Theory and Research* 9, no. 3 (2009): 261.
107. Kunnen and Bosma, "Fischer's Skill Theory Applied," 250.
108. Erikson, *Identity: Youth and Crisis*, 210.

his Christian identity in his early twenties. It went through a developmental process, consistently and continually, testing, selecting, and integrating those elements into his self-image to others, up to the point when it functioned as his ego identity. As mentioned above, integration of multiple identities may invoke a superordinate identity as a means of reconciling and uniting them.[109] And Zhang's Christian identity would be the superordinate identity. Therefore, by knowing the developmental process and the content of his Christian identity, we can have a better understanding of his choices and structure of identities.

1.4.7 The Significance of Commitment to Identity Status

Marcia's identity statuses approach is based on the intersection of the two dimensions of exploration (or crisis) and commitment. Luyckx, Schwartz, Goossens, et al. summarize the definitions of exploration and commitment as follows:[110] Exploration is defined as the degree to which people search for different identity alternatives with respect to their goals, values, and convictions (exploration in breadth) and in-depth evaluation of one's current, already existing commitments and choices (exploration in depth). Commitment is defined as the degree to which people have made choices about important identity-relevant issues including ideologies and roles in different domains (commitment making) and identify with and feel certain about their choices or commitments.

Kunnen and Bosma emphasize the importance of commitments to one's identity.[111] According to them, commitments provide a person with a self-definition and with a recognition by others. Commitments are links between persons and contexts and they form the central elements in the process of identity development. Firm commitments in important domains of life are identity choices. For individuals, their commitments are about the things which they care most about or value. These commitments have a social significance and at the same time provide the individual with a definition of

---

109. Yampolsky, Amiot, and de la Sablonnière, "Multicultural Identity Integration Scale," 168–69.

110. Koen Luyckx et al., "Employment, Sense of Coherence, and Identity Formation: Contextual and Psychological Processes on the Pathway to Sense of Adulthood," *Journal of Adolescent Research* 23, no. 5 (2008): 572–73.

111. Kunnen and Bosma, "Fischer's Skill Theory Applied."

oneself.[112] In other words, it is important to know what the subjective meanings of a person's commitments are. The relational nature of identity (the attunement of person-context processes) should be central to any discussion of the process of identity development.[113] Kunnen even believes that a change in commitments can be considered indicative of identity change.[114]

The discussion above has shown the significance of spiritual identity to ego identity and the importance of commitment to identity status. Therefore, Zhang's religious commitment must be very meaningful for his spiritual identity and for his ego identity.

Leak makes use of Erikson and Hoare's theories to test the relationship between identity and faith.[115] He finds that religious commitment is highest for those with an achieved identity status. Hunsberger et al. state that the Eriksonian virtue of fidelity – a commitment to an ideological worldview – is involved in the resolution of the identity versus role-confusion conflict.[116] Religion provides a worldview and an opportunity for fidelity, typically through religious (ideological) institutions such as churches. Markstrom-Adams et al. state that there should be greater fidelity among devoutly religious individuals because they have made serious commitments to key aspects of identity.[117] Religion is one ideology upon which fidelity is anchored. Leak finds that there are a few general trends: (1) identity diffusion has been associated with lower levels of religious commitment (e.g. intrinsic religiousness and church attendance) and faith development, as well as higher levels of immature religiousness (extrinsic religiousness), and (2) identity achievement has been related to higher levels of religious commitment and maturity in faith.[118]

---

112. E. Bourne, cited in Kunnen and Bosma, 250.

113. Kunnen and Bosma, 251–52.

114. E. Saskia Kunnen, "Are Conflicts the Motor in Identity Change?," *Identity: An International Journal of Theory and Research* 6, no. 2 (2006): 170.

115. Gary K. Leak, "An Assessment of the Relationship between Identity Development, Faith Development, and Religious Commitment," *Identity: An International Journal of Theory and Research* 9, no. 3 (2009): 215.

116. Hunsberger, Pratt, and Pancer, "Adolescent Identity Formation."

117. C. Markstrom-Adams, G. Hofstra, and K. Dougher, "The Ego Virtue of Fidelity: A Case for the Study of Religion and Identity Formation in Adolescence," *Journal of Youth and Adolescence* 23 (1994): 455.

118. Leak, "Assessment of the Relationship," 205.

Therefore, to understand the internal struggles of Zhang Yijing from the perspective of identity, religious commitment can provide insight because religious commitment reflects his spiritual identity status while spiritual identity performs a main function of ego identity – to integrate personal and contextual processes.

Since Zhang cannot be interviewed because he died in 1931, attention has to be given to the component of commitment, especially religious commitment through the textual analysis of his writings and narratives, in order to have a general understanding of his spiritual identity status.

1.4.8 Application of Marcia's Identity Statuses Approach to Spiritual Identity

Marcia's identity statuses approach has been widely applied to the study of ego identity as well as other domains of identity, such as ethnic identity and sexual identity. The application of Marcia's identity statuses approach to religious identity has also been explored by some researchers.

Hunsberger et al. apply Marcia's identity statuses theory to religious identity to describe the different stages of one's religious identity.[119] According to them, identity achievement is linked to seeking out both belief-confirming consultation (BCC) and belief-threatening consultation (BTC) in response to religious doubts. A moratorium was modestly related to more religious doubt and lack of religious commitment, and lower religious fundamentalism, and with avoidance of BCC. More foreclosed individuals have indeed made religious commitments, accepting the religious teachings they grew up with. Consultation for the foreclosed tended to involve belief-confirming sources and avoidance of belief-threatening resources. More diffused individuals tended to experience more religious doubts, be religiously uncommitted, disagree with religious teachings, and avoid both BCC and BTC.

Features of achieved spiritual identity are also discussed. Kiesling and Sorell find that in stories of the spiritually achieved, the vision for selfhood was not articulated so much as an expansion of identity choices, but rather as a narrowing devotion whereby the ego becomes single-minded in its faithfulness to a deity.[120] They believe an achieved spiritual identity should not only

---

119. Hunsberger, Pratt, and Pancer, "Adolescent Identity Formation," 365.
120. Kiesling and Sorell, "Joining Erikson and Identity Specialists," 261, 268.

include individuation and separation in the service of freeing the ego, but also include centredness and relatedness. They believe this would be better characterized as the surrender of the ego, receptivity to the transcendent, or a "giving over" of the processes of identity formation to a higher power.

Hence, to reach such a level of spiritual identity, Zhang was required to seek out both BCC and BTC. On reaching this, he should demonstrate the sign of surrendering his will to God. As Poll and Smith note, spiritual identity development is a process of gradually surrendering one's own desires to God.[121] Chapters 3, 4, and 5 will reveal his sources of BCC and BTC and his acts of surrender to God.

1.4.9 Applicability of Identity Theory to the Eastern Society

Most of the research on identity development is conceived as applying to adolescence and emerging adulthood in post-industrial Western contexts where young people are faced with finding their own way into adult roles and responsibilities. Whereas in non-Western cultural contexts like China, where the individual self is expected to submit to the wants, needs, and priorities of the group, how applicable are Erickson and other theorists' concepts of identity?

Schwartz et al. believe that identity development can be guided by an individualist perspective (e.g. "I am") or by a collectivist perspective (e.g. "We are").[122] Stryker argues that across cultural contexts, identity achievement is perceived as making and identifying with commitments.[123] It does not matter if commitments are developed using individualistic and internal standards or based on group norms, they serve the same function, which is, to anchor the person within a set of social roles and responsibilities. Therefore, in both the Eastern and Western societies, the commitments one makes will lay a set of expectations upon one's future choices and behaviour.

On this basis, in this research, I will be applying perspectives from the identity research to Zhang Yijing. And his spiritual identity, in this case, is specifically a Christian identity.

---

121. Justin B. Poll and Timothy B. Smith, "The Spiritual Self: Toward a Conceptualization of Spiritual Identity Development," *Journal of Psychology and Theology* 31, no. 2 (2003): 138.

122. Schwartz et al., "Identity Development, Personality," 339.

123. Sheldon Stryker, 2003, cited in Schwartz et al., "Identity Development, Personality," 355.

1.4.10 Discussion of Christian Identity

In this section, three ideas will be discussed: the working definition of Christian identity, another ongoing spiritual developmental journey after reaching the status of Christian identity achievement, and the rising function of Christian identity as ego identity or primary identity.

"Christ-follower" and "Christian" are viewed as interchangeable terms in this study because "Christ-follower" talks about the actions of Christians as well as about their faith in Jesus as Messiah.[124]

With a humble awareness of the complexity and diversity of Christianity, this research views a Christian identity as a Christ-defined identity or an in-Christ identity.[125] Christians acquire their identity on the basis of who Christ is and what he has done.[126]

Concerning who Christ is: Christ is the Son of God, the same Lord of all, and none other than God of the Old Testament (Matt 26:63–64; Mark 14:61–62; Luke 4:41; John 1:1; 9:35–37).[127] Paul held the same view.[128]

Concerning what Christ has done: Paul summarizes in 1 Corinthians 15:3–4: "For what I received I passed on to you as of first importance: that Christ died for our sins according to the Scriptures, that he was buried, that he was raised on the third day according to the Scriptures." This summary is echoed by many scholars.[129]

Therefore, when people accept Jesus Christ as Lord, they make a commitment to Christ, which establishes their personal relationship with Jesus

---

124. William S. Campbell, *Paul and the Creation of Christian Identity* (London: T&T Clark, 2006), 12.

125. Campbell, *Paul and the Creation*, 148.

126. Yeung, "Boundaries in 'In-Christ Identity,'" 157.

127. Matthew 26:63–64 – "The high priest said to him, 'I charge you under oath by the living God: Tell us if you are the Messiah, the Son of God.' 'You have said so,' Jesus replied." Mark 14:61–62: "Again the high priest asked him, 'Are you the Messiah, the Son of the Blessed One?' 'I am' said Jesus." Luke 4:41 – "Moreover, demons came out of many people, shouting, 'You are the Son of God!' But he rebuked them and would not allow them to speak, because they knew he was the Messiah." John 9:35–37 – "Jesus heard that they had thrown him out, and when he found him, he said, 'Do you believe in the Son of Man?' 'Who is he, sir?' the man asked. 'Tell me so that I may believe in him.' Jesus said, 'You have now seen him; in fact, he is the one speaking with you.'" John 1:1 – "In the beginning was the Word, and the Word was with God, and the Word was God."

128. Yeung, "Boundaries in 'In-Christ Identity,'" 158, 164, and 170; Dietrich Bonhoeffer, 做门徒的代价 (*The Cost of Discipleship*) (北京 Beijing: 新星出版社 New Star Press, 2013), 344–45.

129. Yeung, 158; Campbell, *Paul and the Creation of Christian*, 155.

Christ and God (John 5:24; 1 Cor 15:2).[130] And they immediately gain a new in-Christ identity.[131] Viewed from Jesus Christ who is one side of this relationship, the primary identity-marker of being in Christ is faith in Christ, because God justifies people by their faith in the crucifixion and the resurrection (John 17:3; Rom 3:25–26).[132] The evaluation of faith by Christ and God can be understood as the objective fact of one's faith.

As the other side of this relationship, the individual Christian has his or her subjective sense of Christian identity. According to Erikson, the sense of identity is "based on two simultaneous observations: the perception of the self-sameness and continuity of one's existence in time and space and the perception of the fact that others recognize one's sameness and continuity."[133] As Szucs summarizes,[134] the sameness and continuity in the concept of Christian identity can only be who Christ is and what he has done (Heb 13:8).[135] Therefore, the working definition of a sense of Christian identity is a sense of belonging to God through or in Christ and the perception of the fact that others recognize it including Christ. Zhang's Christian identity is his awareness of the fact that there is a self-sameness and continuity in his belonging to Christ and the perception of the fact that others recognize this.

Since Christian identity is a personal relationship between oneself and Christ and God, the perception of Christ's affirmation should have a paramount significance to one, compared to the perception of other people's recognition. One's sense of one's Christian identity can be understood as the subjective aspect of faith which may sometimes not be completely in

---

130. John 5:24 – "Very truly, I tell you, whoever hears my word and believes him who sent me has eternal life and will not be judged but has crossed over from death to life." 1 Corinthians 15:2 – "By this gospel you are saved, if you hold firmly to the word I preached to you. Otherwise, you have believed in vain."

131. Yeung, "Boundaries in 'In-Christ Identity,'" 154.

132. John 17:3 – "Now this is eternal life: that they know you, the only true God, and Jesus Christ, whom you have sent." Romans 3:25–26 – "God presented Christ as a sacrifice of atonement, through the shedding of his blood – to be received by faith. He did this to demonstrate his righteousness, because in his forbearance he had left the sins committed beforehand unpunished – he did it to demonstrate his righteousness at the present time, so as to be just and the one who justifies those who have faith in Jesus."

133. Erikson, *Identity: Youth and Crisis*, 50.

134. Ferenc Szucs, "Christian Identity and National Identity," in *Studies in Reformed Theology, Vol. 16: Christian Identity*, ed. E. van der Borght (Leiden: Brill, 2008), 83–84.

135. Hebrews 13:8 – "Jesus Christ is the same yesterday and today and forever."

concord with its external judgment. The objective evaluation by Christ and God counts.

This sense of Christian identity can be strong or weak and it is prominently characterized by discipleship – faith and hope in him and love for him.[136] Christians should strive for a stronger commitment to Christ or the maturity of one's Christian identity, but a person's Christian identity cannot be forfeited by a momentary failure to comply with the biblical teaching. In-Christ identity can be attained only through justification by faith apart from works;[137] otherwise, one cannot help wondering if the criminal crucified beside Jesus was in Christ. Just as Paul says in 1 Corinthians 15:2 – "By this gospel you are saved, if you hold firmly to the word I preached to you. Otherwise, you have believed in vain."

This understanding that a Christian identity depends only on one's faith in the gospel means that even disbelief in some parts of the Bible will not necessarily invalidate one's Christian identity. And this perception seems to be shared by some scholars. An example can be found in *Four Views on the Historical Adam* which presents four different kinds of views on the historicity of Adam and Eve:[138] the evolutionary creation view which denies the historical Adam; the archetypal creation view which takes Adam as a representative figure of a group of people; and the old-earth creation view and young-earth creation view which both believe in the existence of a historical Adam. The representative of the evolutionary creation view, Denis O. Lamoureux, denies the existence of a historical Adam, but says:

> I'm a born-again Christian . . . I accepted Jesus Christ as my Lord and Saviour in 1980 . . . It was through reading the gospel of John that the Holy Spirit convinced me of my sins and shameful lifestyle . . . He sent His Son Jesus to die for us on the Cross . . . The Creator of the world loves us so much that He willingly died for us.[139]

---

136. Christiaan Mostert, "Christian Identity as Baptismal Identity," in *Studies in Reformed Theology, Vol. 16: Christian Identity*, ed. E. van der Borght (Leiden: Brill, 2008), 51.

137. Yeung, "Boundaries in 'In-Christ Identity,'" 163, 173.

138. Matthew Barrett and Ardel B. Caneday, eds., *Four Views on the Historical Adam* (Grand Rapids: Zondervan, 2013), 75.

139. Barrett and Caneday, *Four Views*, 75.

Though his view on Adam is critiqued, his own Christian identity is not rejected by the representatives of the other three views because he still holds to the gospel.

Those who have already put their faith in the objective redemptive work of Christ demonstrate different measures of faith (Rom 12:3)[140] and Christians are also described as being either "strong" or "weak." Every believer grows in the knowledge of God at a different pace, being influenced by his or her background, including the ethnic and cultural background. The same Lord Jesus Christ, however, as the gracious Lord, "welcomes" (Rom 15:7)[141] subjective faith. He allows diversity as each believer seeks to please him according to his or her conscience.[142]

When Christians with different measures of faith, after their exploration, have made a commitment to Christ, they have reached the status of Christian identity achievement. However, Marcia's theory does not elaborate on the growth occurring on this status. In fact, another spiritual journey starts from the moment when a person puts his or her faith in Christ.

This process moves at different speeds before one can reach the stage Christ wishes for: to be so fully identified with Christ that one lives in complete union with him.[143] Jesus himself is a model of complete identification with God and he wishes for such a relationship with his followers: with Christ living in the Christian and the Christian living in Christ, that is, two in one.[144] At this stage, a strong sense of belonging to God through or in Christ is accompanied by discipleship – faith and hope in him and love for him.[145]

---

140. Romans 12:3 – "For by the grace given me I say to every one of you: Do not think of yourself more highly than you ought, but rather think of yourself with sober judgment, in accordance with the faith that God has distributed to each of you."

141. Romans 15:7 – "Accept one another, then, just as Christ accepted you, in order to bring praise to God."

142. Yeung, "Boundaries in 'In-Christ Identity,'" 168.

143. John 14:21 – "Whoever has my commands and keeps them is the one who loves me. The one who loves me will be loved by my Father, and I too will love them and show myself to them." John 14:23 – "Jesus replied, "Anyone who loves me will obey my teaching. My Father will love them, and we will come to them and make our home with them.'"

144. John 14:10–11 – "Don't you believe that I am in the Father, and that the Father is in me? The words I say to you I do not speak on my own authority. Rather, it is the Father, living in me, who is doing his work. Believe me when I say that I am in the Father and the Father is in me; or at least believe on the evidence of the works themselves." John 15:4 – "Remain in me, as I also remain in you."

145. Mostert, "Christian Identity as Baptismal," 51.

The Radical Disciple by John Stott [146] and *The Road to Discipleship* by Roy Robertson[147] describe in detail the path of discipleship towards a complete identification with Christ. Paul could be viewed as the model and goal of a Christ-defined identity of other people in Christ at this stage,[148] and his identities were structured hierarchically, with his identity in Christ as his primary identity and others (ethnic, national, and cultural) as sub-identities.[149] The Christian identity wished for by Jesus and demonstrated by Paul can be viewed as the ideal state to which all Christians are striving with their own current state of Christian identity.

As one's Christian identity grows to be one's primary identity, one's other identities are not obliterated but transformed.[150] As noted above, Brian Tucker has demonstrated how Paul counters the Roman social identity of the Corinthian believers.[151] He shows that Paul seeks to transform and reprioritize those Christ-followers' previous identities in their identity hierarchy. The previous identities are not obliterated, but become subservient to the "in Christ" identity.[152]

Therefore, in addition to process and contents, attention will be given to Zhang's commitment, intention, subjective feeling, and other people's comments when his Christian identity is considered in its interaction with his identity as a Chinese.

1.4.11 Qualitative and Narrative Research Methodologies

The research methodologies relevant to these approaches include narrative, qualitative, and narrative-qualitative research.

McAdams is perhaps the most outspoken proponent of a connection between the construction of the life story and a sense of personal meaning.[153] He argues that identity in adulthood is an inner story of the self that integrates

---

146. John Stott, *The Radical Disciple* (Nottingham: Inter-Varsity Press, 2010).
147. Roy Robertson, *The Road to Discipleship* (Singapore: The Navigators, 1992).
148. Campbell, *Paul and the Creation of Christian*, 148, 153.
149. Campbell, 157.
150. Campbell, 89.
151. Tucker, *You Belong to Christ*, 2; Tucker, *Remain in Your Calling*, 48.
152. Tucker, *You Belong to Christ*, 207; Tucker, *Remain in Your Calling*, 47.
153. D. P. McAdams, "What Do We Know When We Know a Person?," *Journal of Personality* 63 (1995): 365.

the reconstructed past, perceived present, and anticipated future to provide a life with unity, purpose, and meaning. Hendry, Mayer, and Kloep also believe that identity is a life story.[154] Kiesling et al. adopt a biographical and narrative approach to contextualize descriptive data.[155] McLean and Pasupathi include short stories, longer biographies, information about chosen pastimes and entertainments and conversation into the types of narration.[156] In addition, Dunlop and Walker argue identity can be constructed within both of the narrative and paradigmatic (i.e. non-narrative) modes of thought.[157]

Some other researchers try to explore a person's identity status, religious identity, or both through religious narratives. Alisat and Pratt try to build a connection between religious narratives and an identity status model.[158] Their research reveals that there exist links between identity status patterns and features of a personal religious identity in life story narratives. They concluded that greater identity maturity was related to more personally meaningful stories and to those reflecting a greater sense of religious development. Kiesling and Sorell use the narratives of spiritually devout adults when they expand the identity status dimensions of exploration and commitment into multiple components of role salience and role flexibility.[159]

In the case of Zhang Yijing, since his publications and other people's memories of him are the only available information about him, this research will use such writings for an exploration of his internal struggles while it tries to recover his heritage. Thus, it will not be possible to depend on any statistical analysis.

---

154. Leo B. Hendry, Peter Mayer, and Marion Kloep, "Belonging or Opposing? A Grounded Theory Approach to Young People's Cultural Identity in a Majority/Minority Societal Context," *Identity: An International Journal of Theory and Research* 7, no. 3 (2007): 183.

155. Chris Kiesling et al., "Identity and Spirituality."

156. McLean and Pasupathi, "Processes of Identity Development," 16.

157. William L. Dunlop and Lawrence J. Walker, "The Life Story: Its Development and Relation to Narration and Personal Identity," *International Journal of Behavioral Development* 37, no. 3 (2013): 243.

158. Alisat and Pratt, "Characteristics of Young Adults' Personal," 47.

159. Kiesling and Sorell, "Joining Erikson and Identity Specialists," 269.

1.4.12 Disruptive Issues or Crisis in Revealing One's Identities

When choosing the writings by Chinese Christians, the author prefers those stories or events which posed challenges or crisis for them, because these disruptive issues and crises can best reveal one's identities.

A conflict includes an external one, such as a conflict with another person, or an internal conflict, such as a distaste for one's career or dissatisfaction with one's own performance. Such a conflict is a trigger for action. Kunnen considers conflict crucial in identity change because a conflict means there is something at odds with the present commitment.[160] McLean and Pasupathi also talk about the importance of a disruptive event because this disruptive event as the issue of uncertainty or crisis could create challenge or threat as potential opportunities for learning about the self of a person.[161] A similar idea can be seen in Nicolas Standaert's saying that Chinese culture shows its features most clearly when it is confronted with something from outside – Buddhism and Christianity.[162]

The beginning of the twentieth century in China was such a period characterized by critical events which captured growing anti-imperialist, anti-Western, and anti-Christian sentiments. The hostility against Christianity created the external conflicts outside of the church. Besides, starting around 1920, the struggle between liberal and fundamental theologies produced internal conflicts within the church.

1.4.13 Methodology

Bays reminds those studying the Christian movement in China that they should remember the very common phrase often heard in the first part of the twentieth century, "one more Christian, one fewer Chinese."[163] This phrase can be viewed as an epitome of the universal context faced by Chinese Christians, which is still a reality in today's mainland China.

"Being Chinese" is a sense of belonging to the group of Chinese. Though it is a social identity or group identity, it concerns one's personal feeling of

---

160. Kunnen, "Are Conflicts the Motor?," 170.
161. McLean and Pasupathi, "Processes of Identity Development," 15.
162. Standaert, "New Trends in the Historiography," 579–80.
163. Bays, "Protestantism in Modern China," 245–46.

belonging and other members' acceptance of this belonging. This personal feeling is usually secured by other members' recognition of this belonging. In essence, seeking "being Chinese" principally is to seek a recognition by the public who are usually represented by Chinese officials and intellectuals more than one's own feeling of belonging. That is to say, recognition from others is more significant than one's own feeling of belonging.

Christian identity is different from Christian social identity and has its own personal and social dimensions. The personal dimension is how an individual understands and accepts Christ and how one perceives Jesus's affirmation of one's belonging, while the social dimension is about one's perception of other people's recognition of this belonging. Christian social identity is the sense of belonging to the group of Christians and the understanding of this group's acceptance. Compared with the social dimension, the personal dimension has paramount importance to an individual and Christian identity is more meaningful than Christian social identity. These dimensions and aspects have mutual influence on each other.

Thus, seeking a Chinese Christian identity is not merely to seek a balance of one's Christian identity and personal feeling of being Chinese, but also a union of one's Christian identity and the admittance of Chinese officials and intellectuals. In many cases, the latter union would critically influence the former one.

Concerning Zhang's search for a Chinese Christian identity, this research intends to find out how he started to choose a Christian identity and how his Christian identity developed by referring to Marcia's identity status and BTC and BCC developed by Hunsberger et al. in a society whose officials and intellectuals were predominantly under the mixed influences of Confucianism, nationalism, or scientism. By examining his responses in some disruptive issues including external and internal conflicts recorded in his and others' writings, this research tries to identify the negotiation and reconciliation between his Christian identity and his sense of "being Chinese"; namely, how his Christian identity was structured in relation to his Confucian identity and national identity and how his Christian identity encountered and interacted with the influence of scientism. It seeks to identify if these identities were structured laterally or hierarchically or otherwise? Following this, there is a discussion about the Chinese official and intellectuals' attitude towards his and other Christians' "being Chinese" and the possible reasons for this. Furthermore, by examining some other Chinese Christians' methods of contextualization and identities, comparison and contrast will be created in the hope that the relationship between contextualization and the "Chinese Christian identity" may be illuminated. As an added benefit, there may be more understanding of the identity development in a non-Western environment.

I probe Zhang's identities through his external and internal conflicts contained in disruptive issues like sacrificing to ancestors,[164] worshipping Confucius, being filial, saving China, the Shaji Massacre, Christian faith charged with being a superstition, the liberal and fundamentalist theological conflict, and interpreting the flood of Genesis. His multiple identities coexisted, but the discussion will be given to the interaction between his Christian identity and his sense of being Chinese under the influence of Confucianism, modern nationalism, and scientism, because these three ideologies strongly influenced the self-image of the Chinese. The discussion will be respectively carried out in three chapters for the sake of analysis and clarity. It does not mean he only had three or four identities or only two aspects of his identity were involved in each conflict. However, when necessary, the discussion will not be limited to two identities.

Examining Zhang in the light of identity theory risks linking the readers to an analytical framework that they might not accept. I justify the approach on the grounds that the benefits of bringing the study of Christianity in China into the debates on identities might outweigh the risks.

The next section will first give a brief introduction to Zhang, which is followed by a review of research already devoted to him.

1.5 A Brief Introduction to Zhang Yijing

Research on Zhang Yijing (or Zhang Wen Kai) has been neglected for a long time although he is an important and famous Chinese Christian.

Zhang Yijing (1871–1931) was a well-known Christian writer. He served as a journalist for the *Chinese Huan Newspaper* (中国郇报) and editor for the *Tan Tian Weekly* (谈天周刊), the *Da Guang Newspaper* or *The Great Light Newspaper* (大光报), and the *True Light* (真光). He was also the sub-editor

---

164. Is sacrificing to the ancestors and worshipping Confucius worshipping or venerating them? Chapter 3 will delineate Zhang's understanding of this.

of the *Xin Xuan* or *Heartstrings* (心弦) with Fan Bihui (or Fan Zimei)[165] (范弼诲/范子美) as the chief editor.

True Light was a publication of the China Baptist Publication Society[166] (CBPS 美华浸会印书局) and Zhang worked on it for more than twenty-five years as writer and editor. His whole writing career focused on the negotiation between Christianity and the cultures and ideologies in China. Before 1919, Zhang's focus was on the relationship between Christianity and the traditional systems in China like Confucianism, Taoism, Mohism, Buddhism, and folk deities. After 1919, he emphasized the relationship between Christianity and modern ideologies in China like nationalism and rationalism from the West. Of course, this division is not absolute. Throughout his career, he advocated the independence of the church. Zhang was a prolific writer and published many works. More than fifty of his works were printed as separate editions.

Around 1921, Zhong Ketuo (钟可托) who later served as the secretary of the National Christian Council of China (中华全国基督教协进会), called Zhang the vanguard of indigenization of Christianity in China. In March 1924, the Publication Committee of the National Christian Council of China carried out a nationwide survey.[167] *True Light* was the most popular.[168]

Concerning the question of who the readers' most cherished authors were, the top four on the list were: Fan Bihui, Zhao Zichen, Chen Jinyong (陈金镛), and Zhang Yijing. Zhang had the fourth ranking. These four were followed by Jian Youwen (简又文), Xu Qian (徐谦), and Liu Tingfang (刘廷芳). Jian Youwen and Xu Qian will be included in chapters 4 and 5 for comparison.

---

165. Fan Zimei or Fan Bihui (范子美/范弼诲, 1866–1939) was a successful candidate in the imperial examinations at the provincial level (or *juren* 举人). Under the influence of Young J. Allen (林乐知), he became a Christian in 1902. After that, he became a Christian writer and the editor of *Youth Progress* (青年进步), a YMCA publication. Some people called him a Confucian Christian.

166. This Society was established in 1899. It was begun jointly by the Southern Baptist Foreign Mission Board and the American Baptist Missionary Union and sought to serve all Baptist Missions in China. In 1937, the Southern Baptist Foreign Mission Board began the process of dissolving the legal partnership, as American Baptists had reduced their participation in the venture.

167. The National Christian Council of China (1924), "The Answers to the Survey among Christians in Preparation for a National Christian Publication (为筹备全国基督教杂志征求同道意见的答案)," *True Light* (真光), 25, no. 10: 75–78.

168. The top four were *True Light* (真光), *Youth Progress* (青年进步), *Life Monthly* (生命月刊) and *Tong Wen Newspaper* (通问报). Next to the top four were *Theology Review* (神学志), *Chinese Christian Advocate* (兴华报), and *The Truth* (真理杂志).

At the Guangzhou Crusade Meeting in 1921, Zhang was invited to be the speaker as a replacement of Cheng Jingyi[169] since Cheng could not make it.

In 1930, the *Chinese Christian Advocate* (兴华报, a publication by the Methodist Publishing House in Shanghai) carried out a poll to look for the ten most famous Chinese Christians. Zhang was the tenth on the list. Around 1930, *China Monthly Review* (密勒评论报), with J. B. Powell as the editor, identified twelve thousand famous Chinese from all walks of society and varying curricula vitae. Zhang was chosen as a representative of the circle of the press.[170]

True Light under his leadership became one of the most influential publications among Chinese churches. Zhang, the apologist, earned his reputation as "an iron man upholding the truth and justice and a sharp writer producing eloquence and persuasiveness" (铁肩担道义, 辣手著文章).[171]

In 1932, CBPS named its new building in Shanghai the "True Light Building" in memory of the part *True Light* had played through the years. In the building was one large room planned for a meeting place for the staff, other Christian bodies, and Baptists from all over China who assembled in Shanghai from time to time. This was to be the "Power Room." It was named in memory of Zhang – the "Wen Kai Memorial Hall."[172]

1.6 Current Research on Zhang Yijing

There has not been much research published on Zhang. Chu briefly mentioned that Zhang, because of his more fundamentalist beliefs than any of

---

169. Cheng Jingyi (诚静怡, 1881–1939) was the Chinese voice at the Edinburgh Conference 1910 and a Chinese Protestant Christian leader who worked for an independent, unified Chinese Christian Church and a non-denominational unity of Christians in China. He received honorary doctorates from Knox College, Toronto, Canada (1916), the College of Wooster, Ohio, US (1923), and St. John's University, Shanghai (1929). He died in Shanghai after his visit to the mission work in Guizhou and other parts of southwest China in 1939.

170. John Benjamin Powell, *Who Is Who in China* 中国名人录, 5th ed. (Shanghai: The China Weekly Review, 1936), 17.

171. Danlin Lu 陆丹林, "Commemorating Mr. Zhang Yijing Who Widely Spread the Way (纪念道满人间的张亦镜先生)," *True Light* 真光 31, no. 9 (1932): 32; Yinwu Sun 孙荫五, "Mourn Mr. Zhang Yijing (悼张亦镜先生)," *The Chinese Christian Intelligencer* 通问报, no. 1496 (1932): 4.

172. Ruth Carver Gardner and Christine Coffee Chambers, *Builder of Dreams: The Life of Robert Edward Chambers* (Nashville, TN: Broadman Press, 1939), 185.

the other Christian writers of the time, lost much of his younger audience.[173] However, Xue's observation presented a different picture which will be discussed in chapter 2.[174]

According to Lam, Zhang was an apologist with a very conservative theological position. He had a deep knowledge of Chinese learning and held a positive attitude towards it even though he insisted on evaluating and improving it by biblical teachings.[175]

In her Master's degree thesis, Zhu Xiulian (朱秀莲) described Zhang's contributions in his negotiation with Confucianism, his response to the Anti-Christian Movement, and his ideas about indigenization.[176]

Candes Wong explored Zhang's role in the Anti-Christian Movement.[177] She rightly pointed out the elements of scientism and nationalism in the Anti-Christian Movement. As Wong noticed, on the one hand, Zhang argued strongly against the anti-Christians in defence of the Christian church; on the other hand, Zhang kept an open and optimistic attitude towards this movement because it could help the church to stay vigilant and strong.

The works of Lam, Zhu, and Wong present a good start and I will deepen their discussions by supplying more details and analyses.

Concerning Chinese Christians' different attitudes towards Chinese religions in Chan Wai Keung's research of Xu Dishan, he classified Zhang Yijing as the "exclusive" type because Zhang Yijing rejects Chinese religions

---

173. Samuel C. Chu 朱昌峻, "Early 20th Century Chinese Christian Writers and the Church Indigenization Movement (二十世纪初期中国基督教作家的教会本土化运动)," in *Bulletin of the Institute of Modern History, Academia Sinica* 中央研究院近代史研究所集刊 *12* (Taipei 台北: Institute of Modern History, Academia Sinica 中央研究院近代史研究所, 1983), 203.

174. Bingyang Xue, "The Letter of My Repentance (我忏悔经过的一封信)," *True Light* 真光 25, no. 9–10 (1926): 95–98.

175. Wing-Hung Lam 林荣洪, *Rising Chinese Church in the Storms* (风潮中奋起的中国教会) (Hong Kong: Tien Dao Publisher 天道书楼, 1980), 119; Wing-Hung Lam 林荣洪, *Fifty Years of Chinese Theology: 1900–1949* (中华神学五十年: 1900–1949) (Hong Kong: China Graduate School of Theology 中国神学研究院, 1998), 228.

176. Xiulian Zhu, "Chinese Apologist's Response in His Era: A Study of Zhang Yijing (中国护教者对时代的回应 - 张亦镜研究)" (Master of Divinity thesis, Alliance Bible Seminary, Hong Kong, 2001).

177. Yuet-Sheung Candes Wong, "The Role of Zhang Wenkai (1871–1931) in the Anti-Christian Movement in the 1920s" (Master's thesis, University of Hong Kong, Hongkong, 1997), http://hdl.handle.net/10722/50446.

as falsity.[178] This categorization of Zhang as an "exclusive" type is misleading because it can leave an impression that Zhang despised Chinese culture and religious systems. The fact is that Zhang had different attitudes towards Chinese culture and religious systems. On the one hand, he was very proud of Chinese culture, for example the lunar calendar, and translated many Chinese classics for English speakers to prove the beauty and truthfulness in Chinese culture.[179] On the other hand, he was also very critical of some aspects of Chinese culture, such as sacrificing to the ancestors and geomancy, which he used to practise. Zhang considered Buddhism to be false, but he valued Taoism. He thought that the truthfulness in some parts of the *Tao Te Ching* (道德经), the Taoist classic attributed to Lao Zi,[180] was on par with the New Testament.[181] He felt Lao Zi had a similar function in preparing people to know Christ though it might be too much to call him "John the Baptist of East Asia." As for the supernatural records in Chinese books, Zhang selectively believed them after his research, especially when they were recorded in classics and history books written in biographical style. Zhang himself was a Confucian. Zhang's attitude towards Confucianism will be examined in chapter 3 where the religiosity of Confucianism will also be discussed.

Fan Daming has published eight papers on Zhang covering Zhang's attitudes towards Buddhism, Confucius, Chinese culture, Taoism, Mo Zi or Mo-tse (墨子, the founder of the Maoist school), and national and educational sovereignty. The research of Fan on this point mainly focuses on introducing Zhang Yijing's ideas through a perspective of cultural communication. As for the cause for the negotiation strategies of Zhang, he looks for reasons in Zhang's education and his social and political surroundings.[182] He calls Zhang

---

178. Wai Keung Chan 陈伟强, "Christianity Meets the Chinese Religions: A Case Study of Xu Dishan 基督教與中國宗教相遇—許地山研究" (PhD Diss., The Chinese University of Hong Kong, Hong Kong, 2002), 4.

179. Zhang had little knowledge of English. He explained the meanings of the classics while his Western co-worker R. E. Chambers put them into English.

180. Lao Zi (老子) was a philosopher in the Spring and Autumn Period 770–476 BC and the founder of Taoism.

181. Yijing Zhang 张亦镜, "Lao Zi (太上老君)," in *A Quarter of a Century of True Light, Selected* 真光丛刊, *Part 4: Religious Evidence and Origins* 关于宗教之考据文字, ed., Yijing Zhang (Shanghai 上海: China Baptist Publication Society 中华浸会书局, 1928), 58.

182. Daming Fan, Ling Li, and Jianming Chen, "True Light: Search for the Relationship between Christianity and Chinese Culture – Taking Zhang Yijing as a Case (真光杂志: 寻索基督教与中国文化的关系 - 以张亦镜为中心的考察)," in *Christian Text Media and Modern*

a "double-faced man (双面人)," a term which sounds like "double-dealer," to indicate Zhang's identity of being a Chinese and being a Christian.[183] Plausibly, Fan thinks Zhang made strained interpretations and ignored the elements of democracy and science in Chinese traditional culture.[184]

Quoting Fan, Li and Zhang's research gives a three-page brief introduction to Zhang as an effective apologist and his Confucian education.[185]

This study is different from past research in two ways. First, it will not only give a more comprehensive description of Zhang's life and contributions to Christianity in China, but also include an analysis of Zhang's contextualization strategies. Second, this analysis is carried out from the perspective of identities in order to reach a deeper understanding of Zhang, the reasons for his contextualization, and the theory of identity itself.

1.7 Conclusion

This chapter has partially and briefly reviewed the research on Christianity in China. The aim of this work has been introduced: Zhang Yijing will be studied to show how he searched for a Chinese Christian identity. In this process, how his contextualization reflected the interaction between his identities in his milieu will be discussed; the perspective of identity will be tested for its aptness as another perspective in understanding Chinese Christians' encounter with Christianity.

The next chapter will introduce Christianity in China and the social and political contexts before 1930. It will also briefly introduce Zhang's life and contributions.

China 基督教文字传媒与中国近代社会 (Shanghai 上海: Shanghai People's Press 上海人民出版社, 2013), 446–49.

183. Daming Fan 范大明, "Exploring Zhang Yijing's Indigenization 审判与选择: 寻索基督教与中国文化的关系——张亦镜本色神学之探," 世界宗教研究 *Studies in World Religions* 3 (2014): 81; Daming Fan 范大明, "New Culture Developed from the Church – Focusing on the Ideas of Zhang Yijing (新文化源于教会论—以张亦镜为中心)," 史林 *Journal of History* 3 (2014): 130.

184. Fan, "Exploring Zhang Yijing's Indigenization," 91.

185. Lanfen Li and Qingjiang Zhang, "Guangzhou's Christian Intellectual Community in the Era of ROC and Their Efforts in Indigenizing Christianity: With Zhong Rongguang and Zhang Yijing as Examples (民国广州基督徒知识分子与基督教中国化的努力 – 以钟荣光、张亦镜为例)," *Open Times* 开放时代, no. 3 (2017), 66–68.

CHAPTER 2

Christianity in China before 1930 and Zhang Yijing's Life

2.1 A Brief History of Christianity in China before the 1920s

The history of Christianity in China can be divided into four separate periods. Missionaries of the Church of the East, popularly known as Nestorians, entered China during the Tang dynasty around AD 635. During the Yuan dynasty founded by Genghis Khan in 1206, Christians (called Erkeun or Arkaim) were mainly found among ruling Mongols and other ethnic minorities. In the sixteenth century, towards the end of the Ming dynasty, the Jesuits brought Christianity into China for the third time. Robert Morrison's arrival in China as the first Protestant missionary in 1807 marked the fourth period of Christianity.[1]

According to Bays, the period of 1800–1950 can be divided into four parts: (1) Protestant beginnings, Catholic Redux, and China's first indigenous Christians, 1800–1860; (2) expansion and institution-building in a declining dynasty, 1860–1902; (3) the "Golden Age" of missions and "the Sino-foreign Protestant establishment," 1902–27; and (4) the multiple crises of Chinese Christianity, 1927–50.[2]

---

1. Jialin Liang 梁家麟, *Blessings on China – Ten Lessons on the Modern Church History of China* 福临中华—中国近代教会史十讲 (香港 Hong Kong: 天道书楼 Tian Dao Press, 1988).
2. Bays, *New History of Christianity*, 41–121.

Before 1842, the missionaries found it extremely difficult to carry out their mission because the Qing government forbade Christianity, and because the gentry and officials believed this foreign religion would subvert their Confucian tradition. The Chinese Rites Controversy is an example: the opposition among some Europeans to the Valignano-Ricci's "accommodation policy" and the papal condemnation of the rites and a rejection of Jesuits policy in 1704 led to the Kangxi Emperor's outrage and finally to the Yongzheng Emperor's labelling of Christianity as an "evil cult" or "heterodox sect" (*xiejiao*), subversive of Chinese culture and values.[3]

Following its defeat in the two Opium Wars (1840–42 and 1856–60), the Qing government was forced to allow the spread of Christianity in China. The item of protecting preachers and Chinese Christians was included in the treaties signed with the United States, the United Kingdom, and France in 1860.[4] This item will be called the Treaty of Protecting Preaching and Believers or simply the Treaty in this study.

During the two wars, some missionaries were involved in translation or treaty negotiation and some gave their approval to the wars. Although Christianity was allowed to spread through religious freedom, the Chinese people became more hostile towards it because this freedom was protected by unequal treaties and because of some missionaries' roles in the Opium Wars. David Aikman notes: "a monstrous albatross for Protestant Christianity in China for more than a century, was the association of Western missionaries with Western traders who came . . . to make money trading opium."[5] Thus, it is

---

3. Bays, 28–31.

4. The treaties did not directly and clearly state that Chinese Protestant believers were protected. According to Zhang's research, this was an over-interpretation of the Eighth Article in the Treaty of Tientsin (or Tianjin) signed with Russia in 1858 and the Sixth Article in the Convention of Peking (or Beijing) signed with France in 1860. Zhang Yijing, "Cleansing the False Accusations against Christianity (诬教雪)," in *A Quarter of a Century of True Light, Selected* 真光丛刊, Part 2: *The Gospel Discussed and Explained* 辩道文, edited by Yijing Zhang, (Shanghai 上海: China Baptist Publication Society 中华浸会书局, 1928), 58. The two Articles can be seen in *The Maritime Custom: Treaties, Conventions, Etc., between China and Foreign States* 1 (1917): 97–98, 888. According to R. G. Tiedemann, the Russian treaty of 1858 referred to the descendants of the Russian captives brought to Beijing during the reign of the Kangxi Emperor. It was their spiritual welfare that the Russians were seeking to protect. The Russian Orthodox Church had not yet developed a mission to the Chinese at this time. The French treaty of 1860 explicitly stipulated the protection of Chinese Catholic believers. However, Protestant missionaries intervened when their Christian believers were persecuted.

5. David Aikman, *Jesus in Beijing: How Christianity Is Transforming China and Changing the Global Balance of Power* (Oxford: Monarch Books, 2006), 51.

no surprise to hear the later Anti-Christian Movement denounce Christianity as the tool of imperialistic economic aggression and cultural aggression. Such accusations still exist in China today. Since some scholars and Christians like Liang and Wang have analyzed the legitimacy of such accusations,[6] this study will not continue in this direction but will do the analysis from the perspective of identity, the responses from Chinese Christians to such accusations in the Anti-Christian Movement during the 1920s.

Bays calls the Taiping Kingdom (1851–64) China's first indigenous Christian movement.[7] It was founded by Hong Xiuquan (洪秀全) who was influenced by Protestant missionaries and later on claimed, on the basis of a revelatory vision, to be the younger brother of Jesus Christ and the Chinese Son of God.

Oppressed by the Western powers and the Taiping Kingdom, the Qing government started a self-strengthening movement between 1861 and 1894 in the hope that China would counter Western countries with the techniques acquired from them. The Qing government hired some missionaries and Chinese graduates from mission schools to assist in this effort and sent some Chinese students to study overseas. During this period, many missionaries arrived in China. The China Inland Mission which gave priority to unreached inland provinces and indigenization was set up in 1865 and its first group of twenty-two missionaries arrived in Shanghai in 1866.[8] Timothy Richard (1845–1919) who was sent to China by the Baptist Missionary Society had an active role in relief operations and the modernization of China. The missionaries established churches, printing presses, schools, and hospitals. They also actively initiated and participated in charity activities. Although the hatred towards Christianity was still intense, more and more Chinese began to welcome Christianity and even became Christians. The number of Catholic Christians was seven hundred thousand to eight hundred thousand 1900.

---

6. Liang, *Blessings on China*; Jue Wang, "Opium Supporters, Missionaries, and Opium (1874–1906) 鸦片贸易支持者、在华新教传教士、与鸦片 (1874–1906)" (Master's thesis, Peking University, Beijing, 2007).

7. Bays, *New History of Christianity*, 53.

8. Jost Oliver Zetzsche, "Protestant Missionaries in Late Nineteenth-Century China," in *Handbook of Christianity in China: Volume Two: 1800–Present*, ed. R. G. Tiedemann (Leiden: Brill, 2010), 177.

The number of Protestants increased from a few hundred in 1860 to about one hundred thousand by 1900.[9]

The number of missionaries in China between 1860 and the early 1900s grew from approximately eighty to more than three thousand.[10] In 1860, eighteen mission societies had representatives in China which increased to thirty-three in 1888 and by 1900 there were sixty-one society representatives.[11] Detailed information about mission societies can be found in *Reference Guide to Christian Missionary Societies in China: From the Sixteenth to the Twentieth Century* by R. G. Tiedemann.[12]

In 1900, the Boxer Unrest occurred in which the Legation Quarter in Beijing was attacked and around 250 Protestant missionaries and their families and 32,000 Chinese converts were killed. The victims suffered some terrrible atrocities.[13] Its causes can be summarized as: the hostility of the gentry and officialdom towards Christianity; rumours and misunderstanding; frequent occurrences of lawsuits involving church, missionaries, and Chinese Christians;[14] conflicts between Christianity and Chinese traditions and culture; xenophobia which increased in reaction to China's defeat by Japan in the war of 1894–95.[15]

Losing almost all wars to Western powers led to the Qing government's self-strengthening effort while losing the war to Japan symbolized the failure of the self-strengthening movement. Then the Boxer Rebellion in 1900 incurred the invasion of the Eight-Power Allied Forces and the Boxer

---

9. Bays, *New History of Christianity*, 77.

10. There were 189 missionaries in 1864; 436 in 1874; 618 in 1881; and 1,296 in 1890. By 1905, there were 3,445 missionaries. Zetzsche, "Protestant Missionaries," 175; R. G. Tiedemann, ed., *Handbook of Christianity in China: Volume Two: 1800–Present* (Leiden: Brill, 2010), 960.

11. Zetzsche, "Protestant Missionaries," 176.

12. R. G. Tiedemann, *Reference Guide to Christian Missionary Societies in China: From the Sixteenth to the Twentieth Century* (Armonk: M. E. Sharpe, 2009).

13. Michael D. Suman, *The Church in China: One Lord Two Systems*, Expanded Edition (India: SAIACS Press, 2007), 151.

14. According to Gary Tiedemann, after 1900, missionaries began to rely less on treaty protection for their Chinese converts. In any case, just like the China Inland Mission operated in a different way from the nineteenth-century mainline missionary societies, after 1900, many new evangelical missionary groups were arriving in China. These new missionary bodies had very little contact, if any, with Western imperialism. By the 1920s, the Protestant missionary enterprise had become far more complex than it was in the nineteenth century. It becomes, therefore, more difficult to make generalizations.

15. Liang, *Blessings on China*; Bays, *New History of Christianity*, 85–86.

indemnity. After a series of failures and frustrations, the Chinese people lost their faith in the Confucian political and cultural system, but their interest in Christianity grew. Although the Qing government started to reform, for example, by abandoning the imperial examination system which had lasted more than one thousand years, it was still too late. The Revolution of 1911 successfully overthrew the Qing government and established the Republic of China in 1912.

Around the early 1900s, the number of missionaries began to double every eight years and over 90 percent of them came from the USA or Britain. Their major Christian ministries included education and medicine. Mission schools offered basic educational opportunities to both boys and girls of meager means and 10 to 12 percent of all Chinese college students were Christians. However, missionary doctors were especially vulnerable to diseases due to their proximity to patients. More missionaries died of diseases than from violence. At the 1907 Protestant centennial celebration, there was not a single Chinese present, which might be evidence that the missionaries had not identified with their Chinese coworkers sufficiently, but in their quest to Christianize China, many missionaries did expand their thinking and lifestyles, embracing both Western and Eastern cultures.[16]

The period between 1910 and 1920 was a golden age for Christianity in terms of preaching opportunities and building up churches in China. Protestant growth between 1900 and 1915 was impressive. Foreign missionaries numbered 5,500 in 1915, well on the way towards their eventual high-water mark of more than 8,000 in the 1920s. As for Chinese Protestants, there were 40,000 converts in 1893;[17] almost 270,000 communicants (330,000 baptized) in 1915; this growth would also continue into the 1920s, reaching about 500,000 before the storms of mass nationalism hit.[18]

During this period, preaching work was freely and actively carried out and there were some famous preachers like the revivalists Jonathan Goforth, Sherwood Eddy, John R. Mott, and Chinese preacher Ding Limei (丁立美 1871–1936) who initiated the Chinese Student Volunteer Movement for the Ministry (中华学生立志传道团). In 1918, seven Chinese, including Shi

---

16. Suman, *The Church in China: One Lord Two Systems*, 152–57.
17. Suman, 152.
18. Bays, *New History of Christianity*, 94.

Meiyu[19] and David Z. T. Yui (余日章, who will be further discussed in a later chapter), started the first Chinese mission – Chinese Home Missionary Society (中华国内布道会). The China Continuation Committee (中华续行委办会) was set up in 1913 and it initiated the Chinese for Christ Movement (中华归主运动) in 1919.[20]

Around this period, Chinese Christians also tried to build up independent churches. In 1873, Pastor Lu and Chen Mengnan (陈梦南 or 陈觉民) formed Guangdong Cantonese Chinese Alliance Church (粤东广肇华人宣道会) with Feng Huoquan (冯活泉) and Zhang Yaoqi (张耀岐).[21] This was the first Chinese independent church in Guangdong Province and the first Chinese independent Baptist church in South China. In 1906, Yu Guozhen (俞国祯) started the China Jesus Independent Church (中国耶稣教自立会);[22] in 1915, Liu Shoushan (刘寿山 1863–1935) set up the Shandong China Self-Reliance Christian Church (山东中华基督教自立会) while Liu Ziru (刘子如 1870–1948) created the Chongqing China Christian Self-Reliance Methodist Church (重庆中华基督教自养美道会); in 1917, the True Jesus Church was established in Peking; Jing Dianying (敬奠瀛) started the Jesus Family in 1921 and Watchman Nee (倪柝声) created the Little Flock (小群教会) in 1922.

During this period, mission schools were gradually extended to higher education. In 1915 there were almost 170,000 students in mission schools (as opposed to 17,000 in 1889). In the mid-1920s the figure reached almost a quarter million.[23] Since so many people wanted to attend, the average tuition fee of mission schools was four to five times higher than that of the government

---

19. Shi Meiyu (石美玉, 1 May 1873–30 December 1954), also known as Mary Stone, was a doctor of medicine who graduated from the University of Michigan. Shi Meiyu was not only well known as a medical professional, but also for her Christian missionary work. Between 1920 and 1937, she was involved in starting multiple hospitals, schools, and churches in China including Elizabeth Skelton Danforth Hospital in Jiujiang, named after Dr. Sanforth's wife, which later became the Jiujiang Women and Children's Hospital.

20. At the World Missionary Conference in Edinburgh in 1910, Protestant Christian leaders decided to set up regional Continuation Committees for greater cooperation among Protestant denominations. China Continuation Committee was formed in 1913 with the help of John R. Mott in Shanghai.

21. Yijing Zhang 张亦镜, "The Age of Moral Education: Evangelizers and Their Motherland (德育春秋: 传福音之人与其国)," *Shanghai Youth* 上海青年 27, no. 4 (1928): 159-60.

22. Bays, *New History of Christianity*, 96.

23. Bays, 94.

schools. When mission schools had more non-believer students and became more formal and more self-sufficient, their existence was more for education than mission purpose. Medical work also expanded quickly. By 1920, there were 347 mission hospitals and 473 clinics. Peking Union Medical College was set up in 1919 and became the best medical college in China. Some publishing houses were also active in offering Christian literature, for instance, the Christian Literature Society for China (广学会), CBPS, the American Presbyterian Mission Press, the China Sunday School Association (中国主日学协会), and the National Committee of the YMCA in China (中华基督教青年会组合).

There were some reasons for this golden age: a period characterized by flexibility, openness, and an active quest for alternative political and social models;[24] Chinese Protestants' participation in overthrowing the imperial political order;[25] Chinese Christians were no longer protégés of Western missionaries, but Chinese citizens with the liberty of faith in the Republic of China;[26] many Christians taking high-level official positions, a basically good relationship between the government and the church; Christians' elevated social and economic status after acquiring Western knowledge in mission schools, and; the popular belief that Western culture was Christian, and that Christianity would lead to China's salvation.[27]

Before the Revolution of 1911, many people, especially the young, believed that China could not achieve salvation unless the Qing government was overthrown. To their disappointment, shortly after the establishment of the Republic, Yuan Shikai[28] seized the presidency of the Republic, then became the first dictator, and finally "emperor" in 1915. Japan pressured Yuan Shikai in 1915 to sign the Twenty-One Demands to make China its client state. Yuan agreed, in order to obtain loans from Japan. After Yuan's death in 1916, his generals fought against each other for the control of the

---

24. Ryan Dunch, *Fuzhou Protestants and the Making of a Modern China, 1857–1927* (New Haven: Yale University Press, 2001), 121, 179.

25. Dunch, *Fuzhou Protestants*, xviii.

26. Bays, *New History of Christianity*, 96.

27. Dunch, *Fuzhou Protestants, 1857–1927*, xviii.

28. Yuan Shikai (袁世凯, 1859–1916) was a Chinese general, politician, and emperor. He was the first formal president of the Republic of China, but he restored the monarchy in China on 20 November 1915 to be the Hongxian Emperor (洪宪皇帝).

Peking government. Sun Yat-sen or Sun Zhongshan[29] combined the warlords in southern China to form a Military Government of Guangdong to oppose the Peking government.

China's intellectuals and youth realized that political revolution could not save China because most of the Chinese were ignorant and apathetic. They concluded that their primary task was to wake up the nation, especially the youth. To achieve this, they first had to liberate the Chinese people from the bonds of the traditional culture and its mindset. Thus, began the New Culture Movement in 1915.[30] The New Culture Movement totally repudiated traditional culture and introduced all kinds of ideas and theories from the West for China's salvation. Some scholars believe that the total rebuttal of the traditional culture greatly benefited Christianity because the Confucian traditions and theories had formerly been a big barrier. Now Christianity was welcomed because the Chinese equated Western culture with the Christian culture and believed that Christianity was a possible way to China's national salvation.

The New Culture Movement may have benefited Christianity to some degree by its total denial of China's traditional culture, but it also bred seeds of anti-Christianity. After the founding of the Republic in 1912, more and more Chinese students returned from overseas. They brought back not only Western scientific and technological knowledge but also atheism, secularism, and scepticism. They had found that Western culture was not the same as Christianity and even more, they had learned that Christianity had been challenged and doubted in the West for a couple of centuries. The New Culture

---

29. Sun Yat-sen (孙中山, 1866–1925) was a Chinese physician, writer, philosopher, calligrapher, and revolutionary, the first president and founding father of the Republic of China. Sun played an instrumental role in the overthrow of the Qing dynasty during the years leading up to the Xinhai Revolution.

30. The New Culture Movement (新文化运动) of the mid 1910s and 1920s, often understood as the Chinese Enlightenment, sprang from the disillusionment with traditional Chinese culture following the failure of the Chinese Republic, founded in 1912, to address China's problems. Scholars had classical education but began to lead a revolt against Confucianism. They called for the creation of a new Chinese culture based on global and Western standards, especially democracy and science. Younger followers took up their call for: vernacular literature, an end to the patriarchal family in favour of individual freedom and women's liberation, a new view of China as a nation among nations rather than a uniquely Confucian culture, the re-examination of Confucian texts and ancient classics using modern textual and critical methods, known as the Doubting Antiquity School, democratic and egalitarian values, and an orientation towards the future rather than the past. For an introduction to its intellectual context in English, see Vera Schwarcz, *The Chinese Enlightenment* (Berkeley: University of California Press, 1986).

Movement was to seek China's national salvation by introducing Western ideas. Its two banners were democracy and science. Darwinism was introduced and was extended and applied to social studies. Science was widely accepted and admired. Many Chinese intellectuals not only accepted the results of scientific research but also adopted the research methods and evaluations of natural science, imposing and applying them to the study of society and life. After the Debate on Science and Metaphysics in 1923,[31] "being scientific" became one of the standards for one's validity. As a result, many Chinese intellectuals rejected all things which were beyond or against rationality and experience, such as myth, fairy tales, and Christian theism. Science ceased to be merely the knowledge and understanding of this world and was given the status of absolute truth; anything against scientific knowledge was judged as false or superstitious. To denote such an undue attitude or faith in science prevalent in China, contemporary scholars, especially Chinese scholars, adopt the term scientism. Though he never used the term scientism, Zhang Yijing also noticed this undue confidence in science and called it "a superstition in science (科学上地迷信)."[32] More will be discussed in chapter 5.

Nationalism flourished also in the New Culture Movement. Though the leaders of the New Culture Movement advocated democracy, freedom, and human rights and sought to reform Chinese servility and weakness of character, they tended to attribute these to a general lack of national and racial consciousness.[33] Many articles written during this period either pointed out Chinese weakness of national character, praised other countries' more excellent national character, or elaborated China's national crisis. Also, many

---

31. The Debate on Science and Metaphysics is also called "The Debate on Science and the Philosophy of Life."

32. Zhang Yijing and Jun Mo Liang, "Criticizing Qi Yuan's 'Christianity and Communism' (批评绮园的基督教与共产主义)," *True Light* 真光 21, no. 8–9 (1922): 70.

33. Ping-yi Peng, "The Influence of Early New Culture Movement on the May Fourth Patriotic Movement," *Journal of Hunan University of Technology Social Science Edition* 14, no. 6 (2009): 28–33.

thinkers and leaders such as Chen Duxiu[34] and Li Dazhao[35] recommended national education as a solution.[36] Consequently, the discussion on reforming the weak Chinese national character in the Movement aroused and incited Chinese nationalism. With this influence, Yu Jiaju,[37] Li Huang,[38] and Zeng Qi,[39] who shared the background of education in France, became the advocates of a radical nationalism in the 1920s. They believed that it was nationalism rather than anarchism, Communism, or Christianity that could save China.[40]

Nationalism flared up in the May Fourth Movement. The May Fourth Movement in 1919 was a patriotic demonstration against imperialism and feudalism. It was prepared by the New Culture Movement and triggered by the unfairness of the treaty signed at the Versailles Peace Conference. There the great powers ignored China's sovereign rights and China's claims by transferring the control of certain economic and territorial concessions in Shandong Province from Germany to Japan, which gave free rein to Japanese ambitions in northern China. This provided a catalyst to the demonstrations against imperialist abuse of a weak China on 4 May 1919. Its slogan "fighting for national sovereignty on the outside and eradicating traitors on the inside" demonstrated the growing national consciousness.

---

34. Chen Duxiu (陈独秀, 1879–1942) was a Chinese revolutionary socialist, educator, philosopher, and author. He was one of the founders of the Chinese Communist Party in 1921. Chen was a leading figure in the May Fourth Movement for Science and Democracy. Politically, he advocated the Trotskyist theory of Marxism. Chen's ancestral home was in Anqing, Anhui, where he established the influential vernacular Chinese periodical *New Youth* or *La Jeunesse* (新青年).

35. Li Dazhao (李大钊, 1888–1927) was a Chinese intellectual who was one of the founders of the Communist Party of China in 1921.

36. Duxiu Chen 陈独秀, "My Patriotism (我之爱国主义)," *La Jeunesse* 新青年 2, no. 2 (1916): 1–6; Dazhao Li 李大钊, "Youth (青春)," *La Jeunesse* 新青年 2, no. 1 (1916): 1–12.

37. Yu Jiaju (余家菊, 1898–1976) was a famous educator and thinker. He was a representative figure for the nationalistic education school and a leader of the Chinese Youth Party (中国青年党).

38. Li Huang (李璜, 1895–1991) was a scholar and advocate for nationalism. In 1913, he studied at Aurora University in Shanghai and joined The Young China Association in 1918. In 1919, he went to study in Paris University and obtained his Master's degree. In 1923, he participated in founding the Chinese Youth Party (中国青年党) to advocate nationalism. Later on, he served as a history professor in Wuchang University, Peking University, and Chengdu University.

39. Zeng Qi (曾琦, 1892–1951) was a founder and leader of the Chinese Youth Party (中国青年党).

40. *The First Selection of the Speeches on Nationalism* 国家主义讲演集第一集. Shanghai: Shanghai Awakening Lion Weekly 上海醒狮周报社, 1926: 1–70.

I have briefly reviewed above the history of Christianity in China before 1920 and found that 1911–20 was both a golden age for the development of Christianity in China and a time for the growth of scientism and nationalism which brought challenges to Christianity in the 1920s. The next section will first introduce a few events which turned against Christianity in China and will then look at the response of some Chinese Christians.

2.2 The Social and Political Context during the 1920s

The nature of the May Fourth Movement was defined as "a combined intellectual and socio-political movement to achieve national independence, the emancipation of the individual, and a just society by the modernization of China."[41] With the humiliation of more than half a century of unequal treaties and Japan's Twenty-One Demands in 1915, the intellectuals desired to modify traditional Chinese thought in light of Western ideologies. Dr. Chow identifies the various foreign philosophies as: liberalism, agnosticism, individualism, socialism, Darwinism, pragmatism, utilitarianism, democracy, beliefs in science, and Marxism.[42]

In the May Fourth Movement, the intellectuals underwent persecutions by the Peking government in return. While that made them lose their faith in the Peking government, the Bolsheviks' success excited the intellectuals to new hope and desire for actions rather than mere theories. From around 1919, many political associations and parties were formed such as the Communist Party. Unavoidably, they debated, competed with, and even attacked each other.

In addition to the rise of radical nationalism and revolutionary movements, militant political activists and foreign agitators mobilized people by using more extremist language and by providing concrete, radical, and even financial support, especially in many urban centres of China. For example, a new vocabulary from Europe, such as "imperialism" and "cultural aggression," was abused. Agents from the Communist International (Comintern) were active in Guangzhou and at the Whampoa Military Academy (黃埔

---

41. Tse-tung Chow, *The May Fourth Movement: Intellectual Revolution in Modern China* (Cambridge, MA: Harvard University Press, 1960), 358–59.

42. Chow, *May Fourth Movement*, 1, 58–59, 218.

军校). In this light, foreigners (or strangers or outsiders) and their Chinese connections became easy scapegoats.

Under such circumstances, religions were attacked.[43] Christianity was targeted because it was believed to be both superstitious and connected with imperial countries. Furthermore, it could not offer a concrete plan for action. The slogan "saving China through personal character" seemed too abstract and too soft. Some leading intellectuals such as Cai Yuanpei,[44] showed their negative attitude towards Christianity by advocating the substitution of religion with aesthetic education;[45] Chen Duxiu called Christianity a cheating idol,[46] and Zhu Zhixin[47] published *What the Heck Is Jesus*? (耶稣是什么东西?) According to Yang Tianhong, since the leaders of the New Culture Movement called themselves the successors of the modern European thinkers, they were necessarily influenced by modern humanism and the criticism of religion.[48]

The worldwide "Fundamentalist-Modernist Controversy" began in China in the summer of 1920. Theological liberalism has caused the disintegration of their former consensus over biblical authority, higher criticism, evolution, and the like.[49]

The first wave of the attack on religion was initiated by the Young China Society in 1921 when the legitimacy of Christianity was challenged in this debate. This Society held a few seminars and published three Religion Problem Issues in its journal of *Young China*. Many Chinese and Western scholars

---

43. Chow, 320–27.

44. Cai Yuanpei (蔡元培, 1868–1940) was a Chinese educator, Esperantist, president of Peking University, and founder of the Academia Sinica. He was known for his critical evaluation of Chinese culture and synthesis of Chinese and Western thinking, including anarchism. At Peking University, he assembled influential figures in the New Culture and May Fourth Movements.

45. Yuanpei Cai, "On Substituting Aesthetic Education for Religion (以美育代宗教说)," *La Jeunesse* 新青年 3, no. 6 (1917): 1–5.

46. Duxiu Chen 陈独秀, "On Destroying Idols (偶像破坏论)," *La Jeunesse* 新青年 5, no. 2 (1918): 89.

47. Zhu Zhixin (朱执信, 1885–1920) was a colleague of Sun Yat-sen in his early organizing of the anti-Manchu revolutionary party, the Tong Meng Hui, and helped Sun develop and spread his revolutionary philosophy. Zhu was a gifted writer and polemicist known among other writers.

48. Tianhong Yang 杨天宏, 基督教与民国知识分子 *Christianity and Intellectuals of Republic of China* (北京 Beijing: 人民出版社人民出版社 People's Publishing House, 2005), 53.

49. Bays, *New History of Christianity*, 106.

were invited to give their opinions on the following questions: (1) Is human being the animal of religion? (2) Is there still value in the survival of the old and new religions? and (3) Does new China need religion? The focus was on the usefulness of religion for China and the evaluation standards came from nationalism, scientism, Marxist historical materialism, liberalism, anarchism, and the theory of evolution.[50] For the three Religion Problem Issues in the *Young China* journal, the first two included articles from both sides, but the third issue only had the anti-religion side. In hindsight, the Anti-Christian Movement was inevitable for the widespread criticism of religions.

The Anti-Christian Movement began in 1922 and lasted throughout the 1920s. The angry accusations against Christianity included it being a superstition, a cultural aggression, a tool for imperialistic invasion, and an enemy of the Chinese people and government. Chinese Christians were mentally tortured by the charges of being the foreigners' slaves, running dogs of imperialists, and traitors to China. In short, the propaganda against Christianity was "One more Christian, one fewer Chinese."[51]

The Anti-Christian Movement (1922–27) was launched as follows. A foreign commission, the Burton Commission, finished its report, *Christian Education in China*, on the thirteen Protestant colleges and universities and recommended the expansion of Christian higher education. This aroused the antipathy of many Chinese students and intellectuals. Then a few weeks later, the China Continuation Committee, in preparation for the National Christian Conference held in Shandong Province in 1922, published a large volume of statistics and analysis of Protestant enterprise in China with its English name, *The Christian Occupation of China* (中华归主). This angered many Chinese people and confirmed their belief that Christianity was a tool for imperialist aggression. Then came the news that Tsinghwa (Qinghua) University was going to host the international meeting of the 13th World Student Christian Federation in April. Then on 9 March 1922, students in Shanghai set up the Anti-Christian Student Federation (非基督教学生同盟) and in its Declaration condemned Christianity for its connection with capitalism and called for support nationwide. On 11 March, the Anti-Religion

---

50. Liang, *Blessings on China*, chapter 8, http://cclw.net/gospel/explore/fulingzhonghua/index.html.

51. Bays, "Protestantism in Modern China," 245–46.

Alliance (非宗教大同盟) was started in Peking and seventy-seven members issued a Manifesto to denounce Christianity for its opposition to science and humanism. The Socialist Youth League (中国社会主义青年团), a branch of the Chinese Communist Party, and the Young China Association gave their help to these activities.[52] Thus, in many cities and many campuses anti-Christian and anti-religion demonstrations and denunciations took place, but most of them were not co-ordinated. When the summer vacation came, the wave died down. However, from time to time, some anti-Christian articles could still be found in *The China Youth* (中国青年), a journal published by the Socialist Youth League. This was the first stage of the Anti-Christian Movement and it was basically non-violent.

Before the fire of the Anti-Christian Movement was rekindled in 1924, the Debate on Science and Metaphysics (1923–24) took place. The Debate included questions such as: Should science dictate the philosophy of life or should the philosophy of life be consistent with science? What was the scientific philosophy of life? What was the relationship between matter and spirit? Communist Chen Duxiu, Deng Zhongxia,[53] and Qu Qiubai[54] as representatives of historical materialism joined the debate and presented historical materialism as the only theory wholly true to science.[55] This debate aroused the Chinese interest in Marxism and further strengthened the status of science in the Chinese mind, but metaphysics was depicted as backward, abstract, superstitious, and unscientific. Christianity as a view on life suffered the same fate.

Around 1924, political and educational changes also happened. In the political arena, Sun Yat-sen and his KMT party wanted to abrogate the unequal treaties and regain tariff autonomy, but they felt frustrated with the

---

52. Yang, 基督教与民国知识分子 *Christianity and Intellectuals*, 113–14; Bays, *New History of Christianity*, 109.

53. Deng Zhongxia (邓中夏, 1894–1933) was an early member of the Communist Party of China and an important Marxist intellectual and labour movement leader.

54. Qu Qiubai (瞿秋白, 1899–1935) was a leader of the Communist Party of China in the late 1920s.

55. Zhonghua He 何中华, "The Debate on Science and Metaphysics and the Direction of Philosophy in China in the 20th Century ('科玄论战'与20世纪中国哲学走向)," *Journal of Literature, History and Philosophy* 文史哲, no. 2 (1998): 12–13; Xiaonan Hong 洪晓楠, "Effects of the Polemics between Science and Metaphysics on the Development of Chinese Cultural Philosophy ('科玄论战'对中国文化哲学的影响)," *Journal of Nanchang University* 南昌大学学报 (人社版) 33, no. 3 (July 2000): 17–18.

responses of Western powers, except for the Soviet Union as it abolished all the unequal treaties signed by the Russian Empire. Then Sun Yat-sen and his Guangdong government began to show an inclination towards the Soviet Union and eventually formed a united front with the Chinese Communist Party (CCP). The name of Lenin and his opposition to the colonial aggression of imperialism were widely circulated.

In the field of education, Chinese began to increasingly believe that education was significant to the development of a country and that education in China should serve the national interest, but mission schools were moving in a different direction. On 14 October 1923, the Young China Association declared at its Suzhou meeting:

> The general scholarly leaders under the influence of foreign cultural aggression and mission school education only knew to praise US, UK and Europe but ignored the questions critical to their own country's survival . . . The general youth under the influence of such scholarly leaders had no idea what kind of country China was and that China's independence was their important mission. They were used to international oppression and have lost the spirit of an independent nation because the devils of the foreign cultural aggression and mission school education had erased their national spirit.[56]

Among the nine guiding principles announced in this declaration, the third principle was that national character education should include the cultivation of the love of motherland and nationality, and that aggressive foreign cultural policy and mission school education should be opposed.[57] Yu Jiaju accused the mission school education of being the biggest danger to China's future.[58] Quoting from *The Christian Education in China*, he pointed out that the final goal of Christian schools, which were protected by extra-territoriality and numberless warships, was to convert the whole country and that Christian schools served the interest of Christianity. Then he listed three

---

56. "The Declaration of The Young China Association at Its Suzhou Conference (少年中国学会苏州大会宣言)," *The Young China* 4, no. 8 (1923): 2.

57. "Declaration of The Young China," 3.

58. Jiaju Yu 余家菊, "The Problems with Christian Education (教会教育问题)," *Young China* 少年中国 4, no. 7 (1923): 1–19.

evils of Christian schools: (1) being aggressive; (2) producing a social class composed of religious personages; and (3) impeding the union of China's education.[59] Then he offered his five solutions: (1) education must be neutral; (2) school must get registered; (3) the teacher's qualifications must be examined; (4) the law of compulsory education must be strictly implemented; and (5) graduates from unregistered schools should not have the same treatment for registered graduates at the same level.[60] Under the second solution, in addition to more detailed rules (no church on campus, no teaching of prayers, no religion course and no seminary in university, no advocating religion, no teacher working as a pastor or religious movement activist, and so on), he clearly stated that the urgent need at that time was to reclaim the educational rights.[61] Yu Jiaju is believed to have been the first to clearly proclaim that educational rights should be reclaimed.[62]

Apart from the political and educational changes above, two other events fuelled the forthcoming fire. One was the news report that the Turkish government had expelled church leaders and closed mission schools. Another was that the Education Bureau in northeast China, controlled by a warlord Zhang Zuolin (张作霖), tried to take back the education rights from colonial Japan. These two events greatly fostered nationalism in other parts of China.

The second stage of the Anti-Christian Movement started in 1924 and called for the Chinese to take back educational rights by controlling the mission schools. Since both the Chinese Nationalist Party (KMT) and the CCP depicted themselves as the guardians of China's sovereign rights, with the Bolshevists' active help, they chose Christianity as their target. They made use of the issues of imperialism and unequal rights to propagandize and mobilize, and the wave of nationalism gradually gained strength, especially among the young. Not only did the students from non-Christian schools shout "down with imperialistic aggression and enslaving education," but the students from the mission schools shouted the same slogans as well. On 22 April 1924, the first student unrest occurred at the Anglican Trinity College of Guangzhou (广州圣三一学校). Then student walkouts and boycotts against classes

---

59. Yu, "Problems with Christian Education," 6–11.
60. Yu, 16–19.
61. Yu, 17.
62. Yang, 基督教与民国知识分子 Christianity and Intellectuals, 204.

and examinations took place in mission schools in many places, such as the Guangzhou Sacred Heart School (广州圣心), Xuzhou Heart Cultivating School (徐州培心), Nanjing Mingde School (南京明德), Changsha Xiang-Ya School (长沙湘雅) and Fuzhou Union School (福州协和), and so on. Between 1925 and 1926, such kinds of disturbance happened more than sixty times in mission schools nationwide.[63]

On 13 August 1924, an association called the Anti-Christian Society (非基督教同盟) came into being. *Juewu* or *Wake Up* newspaper (觉悟) which was affiliated to *Republican Daily* (民国日报), the KMT Party newspaper, published twenty-five *Anti-Christian Special Issues* (非基督教特刊). *The Guide* (向导) which was the Chinese Communist Party newspaper and *The China Youth* (中国青年) of the Socialist Youth League published a large number of articles attacking Christianity. The youth organizations under the two parties' leadership participated in this movement with rallies, petitions, announcements by nationwide telegrams and rhetoric. During 22–27 December 1924, named as an Anti-Christian Week by the Guangzhou Branch of the Anti-Christian Society, masses were mobilized to demonstrate, distribute handbills, give speeches, occupy the podium in the church and drive Christians out.

W. F. Yeung, as quoted by Lide, the Business Manager of *True Light* wrote: "When Borodin was in Canton in 1925, he boasted that the Bolshevists had done more in one year than all the missionaries had done in one hundred years."[64]

Then in 1925, the May 30th Massacre[65] (五卅惨案) took place. This ignited Chinese anger against imperialism, nationwide. People from all walks of society joined strikes to demand the abrogation of extra-territoriality and the taking back of foreign concessions. On 7 July 1925, the National Union of Students (全国学生联合会) declared their take over of the Anti-Christian Movement to disseminate the evils of Christianity. Around Christmas 1925, activists occupied church buildings in many places and preachers were beaten

---

63. Liang, *Blessings on China*.

64. R. W. Lide, "Dr. Rosewell H. Graves" (1934), 6, FMB AR 551-1, MISS. MINUTES, BOX – 229, Mission South China, Articles, 1925–39, 229–34.

65. On 30 May 1925, British policemen shot at workers who were demonstrating in the Shanghai foreign concession against a Japanese factory owner's cruelty to his workers. This became known as the May 30th Massacre and led to more demonstrations nationwide. On 23 June 1925, the British Marines fired at a demonstration near Shamian Island in Guangzhou, which is called the Shaji Massacre.

up. Compared with the many other massacres that were occurring in China at this time, the May 30th Massacre was essentially a minor affair. However, the activists effectively exploited it to trigger a nationwide anger. The missionary enterprise was accused – without distinction – of cultural aggression from the West. These activists proved to be intolerant in these activities. Many foreign missionaries were forced to leave because of the intense anti-foreigner feeling.

Then in 1926, the KMT and the CCP started the Northern Expedition to destroy the warlords and reunite the country. Many leaders of the Northern Expeditionary Army were graduates from Whampoa Military Academy where many students had actively taken part in the Anti-Christian Movement. The places reached by the Northern Expeditionary Army witnessed harassment, disruption, occupations and destruction of church buildings, mission hospitals, and mission schools. Some Christians were killed, like J. E. Williams, the vice-president of Nanking University. The foreign consuls ordered evacuation; the majority of missionaries fled to the coast and many never returned.

In April 1927, Jiang Jieshi[66] established the Nanjing KMT government which repelled the CCP and showed an inclination towards Western powers instead of the Soviet Union. Thus, the banner of anti-imperialism was not as highly raised as before. Since then, the Anti-Christian Movement lost its strong parties' leadership. Furthermore, Chiang was converted to Christianity by his wife. Following this, within the places controlled by the KMT government, there was no more large-scale anti-Christian activity and a basically good relationship was maintained between the government and the church. In spite of this, the anti-Christian momentum remained, and anti-Christian articles and activities still appeared from time to time.

For example, at Christmas in 1929, the atmosphere was still tense during the Anti-Christian Week in Guangdong Province, like a few years before. The Muslims also joined the Anti-Christian Movement. *Arabian Theory Monthly* or *Tianfang Xueli Monthly* (天方学理月刊), a publication by Muslims, had published *A Special Issue of Comparing Islam and Christianity for the Truth*. *Forward Weekly* (前锋周刊), a publication of KMT Branch in Guangzhou, published *A Special Issue of Anti-Christianity* for its 24th issue. In Shanghai,

---

66. Jiang Jieshi (or Chiang Kai-shek, 蒋介石, 1887–1975) was a Chinese political and military leader who served as the leader of the Republic of China between 1928 and 1975.

only the KMT branch in the 7th district held a meeting and decided to carry out an anti-Christian propaganda.[67]

During the period between 1807, when Robert Morrison arrived, and the Boxer Unrest of 1900, Christian identity had not really been accepted by the Chinese, from officialdom and gentry down to the peasantry. At that time, admitting one's Christian identity must have been very difficult, and sometimes even dangerous. One example is Wang Tao (a Christian scholar and journalist, 王韬 1828–1897) who tried hard to hide his relationship with the church.[68] After 1900, and especially after 1911 when the Republic of China was founded, Chinese became more open to Christian identity. It was as close to being accepted by the Chinese as was a Buddhist or Taoist identity. Beyond all expectations, this course was suddenly and completely reversed during the 1920s. As we can see, China in the 1920s was filled with upheavals, in which one of the common threads was anti-Christianity. Correspondingly, the shared feature among Christians was their search for a Chinese Christian identity.

2.3 Zhang, before Joining *True Light*[69]

Zhang Yijing (张亦镜) was the most well-known pen name of Zhang Wen Kai (张文开) whose courtesy name was Jianru (鉴如). His other early pen names included Jianyu (检余), Qiuchan (秋蟾), Zhishui (止水), Donghong (冬烘), Liusheng (流升), Mujun (亩均), Heyin (荷寅), Pingji (萍寄), and

---

67. Yijing Zhang 张亦镜, "The Anti-Christian Movement in the Last Christmas in Guang Dong Province (广州本届圣诞节之非教运动 广东)," *True Light* 真光 29, no. 1 (1930): 87.

68. Fuk-Tsang Ying 邢福增, "知识分子与中国教会 Intellectuals and the Chinese Church," 2002, http://www.godoor.net/text/history/zhjh16.htm.

69. This part is a combination of Yijing Zhang, "The Last Twenty-Five Years after the Birth of True Light and the Twenty-Two Years of My Humble Involvement (真光杂志出世迄今二十五年及余滥竽其中廿二年之经过)," *True Light* 真光, 26, no. 6 (1927): 1–7, and "How I Became a Christian and My Experiences during the Past Thirty Years after Conversion (我信基督教的缘起和信教后迄今三十年的经过)," 1923, Part 10: Conclusion 备数文, 1–12, in Yijing Zhang, ed. *A Quarter of a Century of True Light, Selected* 真光丛刊 (Shanghai 上海：China Baptist Publication Society 中华浸会书局). (In 1928, when Zhang included this article written in 1923, he omitted about one thousand words. Thus, I also refer to the same article published in *Life* in 1923.) "The Chronology of Zhang Yijing" by his son is also referred to. Qiutao Zhang, "The Chronology of Zhang Yijing, My Deceased Father (先严亦镜年表)," *True Light* 真光, 40, no. 12 (1941): 16–22.

Zhenmei (珍枚).⁷⁰ His family had originally lived in Fengshun County (丰顺) of Chaozhou (潮州) in Guangdong Province. His grandfather moved his family to Guangxi Province. Zhang's father was a normal peasant who could make a living, but was far from being wealthy. Zhang was born on 26 March 1871 in Huangbao village (黄宝) of Zhongshan County (钟山) in Guangxi Province and died on 10 December 1931 in the same village. Zhang was the first Christian in his family. From childhood, he received a Confucian education in his hometown and in Shatianxu (沙田圩), another town in He County (贺县). Later he became a Confucian teacher in a village in 1888. In the winter of 1887, he was married to the daughter of the Chen family. In the winter of 1892, three Chinese preachers from a Baptist church in Guangzhou helped Zhang understand what Christianity advocates and he decided to become a Christian. In the spring of 1893, a Baptist pastor named Lu Zizhen (鲁子珍) came and baptized him.

In the summer, Zhang went to Guangzhou and joined a Bible class at a Baptist church for three months. Then he was sent to sell Christian publications in the areas of Guangning (广宁) and Sihui (四会) in Guangdong Province where he suffered a lot of insults. In the autumn, he had to go back to Guangxi Province because his parents worried about him too much. Zhang's father was very displeased with his conversion because it was impossible for Zhang, as a Christian, to seek a position in a government office.

In 1899, Zhang became a journalist for the *Chinese Huan Newspaper* in Hong Kong. This weekly newspaper was founded by Chinese Christians and Mr. Liao Zhuoan (廖卓庵) oversaw it. This was a preparation for his later work in the *True Light*. However, after half a year, he quit the job because he was irritated by the unequal treatment of the Chinese people. For the next five years, he stopped communication with any church.

In 1900, while he was at home, he was involved in a lawsuit. A father and his son who had no relationship with Zhang were falsely accused of being bandits and were going to be executed. Zhang, out of sympathy, went to the county magistrate to voice grievances for them. The county magistrate took

---

70. There are also some other pen names he used to use: Jianru (谏儒), Ganyu (感予), Ganyu (感遇), Ganyu (甘雨), Jianyi (监彝), Yingjian Ruyi (影鉴如义), Fangtang (方塘), Bantang (半塘), Wuming (庑铭), Gujing (古井), and Zhenwei (甽限).

him as their accomplice and beat him up. Zhang kept scolding the official loudly and angrily for the cruel way the official treated the ordinary people.

One of Zhang's friends was the magistrate's subordinate. He recognized Zhang and secretly pleaded with the magistrate's son. Then the magistrate stopped beating him. Later when this friend asked him why he had not told the magistrate that he was a *jiaomin* (a term meant for a church member in the late Qing dynasty with a derogatory sense, 教民) so that he certainly would not have suffered this beating. Zhang answered:

> I have become a believer without a denomination. Furthermore, at present many people are joining the Church so that they could play like overlords. If I had called myself a *jiaomin*, the magistrate would have been more likely to believe that I had been trying to protect bad people by the power of the Church. Maybe he would not have beaten me, but the two innocent people would have been more likely taken as bad people.[71]

Zhang did not want to shame the church. He thanked God for his friend saving him; otherwise, he would have been beaten either crippled or dead. Still, he had no connection with any denomination or church.

After this issue, Zhang won the fame of "scolding the official and saving the innocent from death" among the neighbouring counties. When Zhang passed away, the father and the son saved by Zhang sent their elegiac couplets to mourn over him.

In 1901, Zhang suggested to Liao Zhuoan not to practise writing the eight-part essay (八股) for passing the Imperial Examination (科举考试), but to study practical learning (实学) or Western learning. Zhang predicted that the eight-part essay would be stopped, and practical learning would be chosen for the Imperial Examination. Four years later (1905), it actually happened.

In the winter of 1904, a local merchant bought a lottery ticket in Zhang's name in spite of Zhang's objection because many local people had a superstitious belief in the power of Zhang's name. He won a lot of money and wanted to give a share to Zhang. Zhang refused to accept it because he did not want to be viewed as a "gambler." When a local preacher named Yu Jianpan (余建磐) heard of this, he came to visit Zhang and then Zhang returned to the church.

---

71. Zhang, "How I Became a Christian," 4–5.

Under his influence, his entire family became Christian. Every evening, he would gather his family members and students for a Bible reading.

In the winter of 1905 when he brought one of his students to Guangzhou for a Bible study, he met his former co-worker Mr. Liao Zhuoan in the street accidentally who invited him to join the *True Light*,[72] a publication of the CBPS.

2.4 Zhang, after Joining *True Light*

From joining *True Light* in 1905 to his sick leave in 1931, Zhang devoted his life to serving the Lord by writing. Jiang Jianbang[73] said that Zhang was the worker in the Baptist church who reaped the richest harvest in the first one hundred years after the Baptist church's arrival in China.[74]

Zhang viewed himself as a preacher through the pen.[75] The mission for *True Light* and himself was to lead people to Christ, to build up Christians' spiritual life, and to defend Christianity from attacks.

To lead Chinese people to Christ, Zhang poured his efforts into bridging Christianity and the cultures and ideologies in China. His works did not only cover the relationship between Christianity and the main traditional systems in China like Confucianism, Taoism, Mohism, Buddhism, Muslim, and folk deities but also dealt with modern ideologies in China like nationalism and scientism (which denotes undue confidence in science or Zhang's term "a superstition in science 科学上地迷信"). To build up Christians' spiritual life, Zhang wrote many articles to interpret the Bible and to discuss the indigenization of Christianity in China. To defend Christianity from attacks,

---

72. It was founded by Dr. Robert E. Chambers (湛罗弼, 24 April 1870–20 April 1932) in 1902 in China under appointment of the Southern Baptist Foreign Mission Board. *True Light* was under the leadership of Dr. Chambers and Pastor Jacob Speicher (师雅各 or 师雅古; 1866–1930). Speicher was an appointee of the American Baptist Missionary Union (from 1910 known as the American Baptist Foreign Missionary Society).

73. Jiang Jianbang (姜建邦) was the author of *The History of Hymns* (圣诗史话) and *The Charm of the Chinese Language* (国文趣味) which is still a popular book in China.

74. Jianbang Jiang 姜建邦, "The Works of Mr. Zhang Yijing (张亦镜先生的著作)," *True Light* 真光 40, no. 12 (1941): 15.

75. Yijing Zhang 张亦镜, "Refuting a Plagiarism of Zhang Taiyan's Atheistic Attack on Religion (驳抄太炎无神论之非宗教文)," in *(1928), A Quarter of a Century of True Light, Selected* 真光丛刊, Part 2: *The Gospel Discussed and Explained* 辩道文, ed. Yijing Zhang (Shanghai 上海: China Baptist Publication Society 中华浸会书局, 1920), 224.

Zhang's labours can be seen from three wars of words, which had significant influences.

2.4.1 Zhang's Readership

Zhang's readers were not only in China but also in the US, Europe, and Southeast Asia. He had three target groups of readers.

The first group was atheists who were mainly young people and were deeply influenced by science. Zhang tried to lead them to God by adopting scientific knowledge and the biblical truth. The second group was the people of the old school. They were mainly the old pedants. They stuck with the traditions and took the classics of Confucianism as sacred. Zhang skilfully and widely quoted the traditional learning from those classics to explain Jesus and Christianity. The third group had a low literacy rate and they were idol-worshippers. Zhang used simple and easy words and popular ballads to lead them into the light.[76]

Zhang's writings were not only popular among the Christians who had low literacy, but also among those people with much learning. For example, Dan Tu (丹徒), Yan Jiqing (a Christian poet, 严霁青), and Lü Banjiao (an educator, 吕半教, 1889–?) discussed Christianity and Confucianism with Zhang in poems.

2.4.2 Zhang's Works

Zhang's works were put into five categories in *A Quarter of a Century of True Light, Selected* (真光丛刊): (1) explaining the verses in the Bible for preaching; (2) apologetic writings; (3) writing on general topics; (4) religious textual criticism; and (5) answering questions. In addition to articles and comments, more than fifty of Zhang's works were printed as separate editions. Some of Zhang's writings were reprinted six to seven times. Combining Zhang Yijing and Jiang Jianbang,[77] the readers can have a bird's-eye view of Zhang's works. A list of Zhang's works printed in separate editions can be found in Appendix 2.

---

76. Cheng Hao 郝城, "The Works of Mr. Zhang Yijing (张亦镜先生的著作)," *True Light* 真光 31, no. 9 (1932): 37.

77. Yijing Zhang 张亦镜, "Answering Another Four Questions from Mr. Lu Zhensheng (答吕振声先生之另函四问)," *True Light* 真光 28, no. 12 (1929): 64–68; Jiang, "Works of Mr. Zhang Yijing."

His works on Confucianism and Christianity were:

- *Jesus and Confucius* (耶儒辩, 1910),
- *A Research of Christianity and Confucianism* (耶儒之研究),
- *Break the Obstinacy in Ancestor-Worshipping* (破祭先执, 1925),
- *Study of the Source and History of Ancestor-Worshipping* (祭先源流考, 1916),
- *Study of Tomb-Sweeping at the Qingming Festival* (清明扫墓考, 1916),
- *Cleansing the False Accusations against Christianity* (诬教雪, 1910),
- *Dissecting the Theory for a State Religion* (国教说解剖, 1913),
- *A Hoe for Brambles* (去荆锄, 1913) and
- *Talk with an Old Pedant* (与老学究语, 1918).

Zhang's works on Buddhism were:

- *The Biography of Śākyamuni* (释迦摩尼传, 1925) and
- *Bodhisattva* (观世音, 1918).

With regard to Taoism, Zhang wrote:

- *The Relationship between Taoism and Buddhism* (道释关系, 1916),
- *Tai Shang Lao Jun* or *Lao-tzu* (太上老君, 1918), and
- *Two Cases of the Hatred of Taoism towards Buddhism* (道仇释两大案).

As for Islam, he wrote:

- *A Defence against Mr. Yin Guangyu's Criticism of the Speech on the World's Problems at Guangdong Y.M.C.A.* (读尹光宇君对于广东青年会演讲世界问题之批评摘辩).[78]

Zhang authored gospel booklets:

- *Five Answers to the Basic Truth* (要道五答) – Between August 1930 and 21 January 1931, over one hundred thousand copies of *Five Answers to the Basic Truth* (要道五答) were sold.
- *Challenging Equivocation from the Unbelievers* (诘推诿不信者).

---

78. Yin Guangyu (尹光宇) was a famous Muslim scholar and one of the initiators of the Chinese Islamic Mission (中国伊斯兰布道会).

Zeng Guren (曾骨人), a reader, asked Zhang if there was really an eternal God. One hundred and thirty thousand copies of Zhang's answer were printed by Zheng Deyin (郑德音), a Christian from the Gospel Freedom Church (美瑞丹教会) in Guangzhou, as leaflets for spreading the gospel.[79]

Zhang's apologetical writings were his most significant contribution. According to Jiang Jianbang, Zhang was the only one who had the courage and capability to fight against the Anti-Christian Movement.[80] Such works included:

- *Answering Attacks upon Christianity* (批评非基督教言论汇刊全编, 1927),
- *The Records and Comments on the Ferocious Anti-Christian Movement in 1924* (民十三之剧烈反基督教运动记评),
- *Review of the Anti-Christian Agitation* (最近反基督教纪评),
- *New Collection of Correcting Absurdity* (纠谬新编, after 1922), and
- *Argue against Chen Duxiu and Shen Xuanlu over Christianity* (与陈独秀沈玄庐辩道).

A Christian named Hao Cheng said that Zhang was a purely spiritual person and his works were purely spiritual. Many unbelievers were converted to Christianity after reading his books and many Christians were encouraged by him. Many Christians said that *True Light* was the only spiritual one among the publications of the churches in China.[81]

As mentioned in chapter 1, Lam labelled Zhang's theological position as very conservative.[82] Zhang also identified himself as a conservative because he criticized liberal theology (see ch. 5) and was critical of the Social Gospel movement. Seeing that Hu Shi categorized Christianity as a kind of man-made religion, Zhang advised him to read works by people who took a conservative standpoint.[83] I would consider him as a conservative because he

---

79. Yijing Zhang 张亦镜, "Sending Gospel Leaflets Once a Month (逐家每月派书一次之传道新法)," *True Light* 真光 29, no. 4 (1930): 92–93.

80. Jiang, "Works of Mr. Zhang Yijing," 12–13.

81. Hao, "Works of Mr. Zhang Yijing," 34.

82. Lam, *Rising Chinese Church*, 119; Lam, *Fifty Years of Chinese*, 228.

83. Yijing Zhang 张亦镜, "A Fair Judgment on the Liu Hongru's Threat of Slapping Dr. Hu Shi (对刘鸿儒要打胡适之博士嘴巴的话的一个公正评判)," *True Light* 真光 28, no. 12 (1929): 19–23.

consistently and continually believed in the existence of God the Creator, the sinfulness of people, the blood of Jesus, the virgin birth, the last judgment, and heaven and hell, which differentiated him from the liberal's position which usually considered Jesus only as a human being or at best a perfect human model. Although he insisted on the authority of the Bible, he doubted the reality of the great flood all his life. Furthermore, he took an attitude of engagement towards the secular world rather than isolation, which was also the positive function he praised the Social Gospel movement for. If the word "fundamental" has evolved from "being loyal to the original" to mean "extremely self-righteous," he should not be put into this category.

2.4.3 Zhang as an Apologist

Zhang viewed himself, and as did many Christians, as a preacher through the pen. Many Chinese Christians called him "a star apologist" or "a warrior defender of Christianity." Among his battles by writing, three were particularly significant, so this research calls them his three wars of words.

2.4.3.1 War against the Confucian Association (孔教会)

The first war was against the Confucian Association. The Confucian Association advocated the establishment of Confucianism as China's state religion twice between 1913 and 1917. In this process, it attacked Christianity.

Between 1913 and 1914, the representatives of the Confucian Association Chen Huanzhang[84] and Kang Youwei,[85] who was based in Hong Kong, sought help from then president Yuan Shikai, to establish Confucianism as China's state religion. Yuan intended to restore the monarchy and become the emperor himself by making use of the theories provided by the Confucian Association, so he gave his support to this effort.

In 1913, Zhang wrote *Refuting Chen Huanzhang and Four Other People's Petition for Establishing Confucianism as the State Religion* (驳陈焕章等请定

---

84. Chen Huanzhang (陈焕章, 1880–1933) was a presented scholar (*jinshi* 進士) after passing the imperial examination in the Qing dynasty. He received his PhD from Columbia University in 1911. He was the student of Kang Youwei and was the leading figure in the movement of establishing Confucianism as China's state religion in the 1910s.

85. Kang Youwei (康有为, 1858–1927) was a very important statesman, thinker, educator, and Confucian scholar. He supported constitutional monarchy. He was a leader in the Reform Movement of 1898 (戊戌变法).

孔教为国教呈文) while in 1914, Zhang wrote *Correcting Errors in Dr. Chen Huanzhang's Speech on Confucianism* (读陈焕章博士孔教讲义辩谬). In 1919, these two books were compiled into *Answering Dr. Chen Huanzhang's Error concerning Religion* (驳陈焕章博士说教之谬).

Huang Naishang visited Guangzhou in 1921 at the age of seventy-four.[86] When he found more than thirty kinds of books on Christianity written by Zhang, in amazement he visited Zhang and praised Zhang as the Chinese successor of apostle Paul.[87] Wong said he was not bored at all even after having read *Answering Dr. Chan Huan Chang's Error Concerning Religion* four times.[88] He bought many copies of all Zhang's works and sent them to friends as gifts. Wong loved Zhang so much that, even in sickness two months before death, he had a happy conversation with Zhang in his dream.

Yan Jiqing (严霁青), a Christian poet, wrote a poem in praise of Jesus after reading *Refuting Chen Huanzhang and Other Four People's Petition for Establishing Confucianism as the State Religion* (驳陈焕章等请定孔教为国教呈文), in which he praised Jesus, compared Zhang to Moses, and exhorted the anti-Christians to follow the example of Paul and repent.[89]

In 1917, the Confucian Association sought to ordain Confucianism as China's state religion again by soliciting the political power from Zhang Xun,[90] a warlord, who planned to restore the Qing dynasty. Zhang was entitled "warrior saint (武圣)" while Kang Youwei was called "scholar saint (文圣)" by the Confucian advocates.

The Confucian Association in Hong Kong took *Guo Shi Newspaper* or *National Affairs* (国是报) as their base to advocate establishing Confucianism

---

86. Huang Naishang or Wong Nai Siong (黄乃裳, 1849–1924), as a Chinese revolutionary leader and educator from Fujian Province, served in the Methodist Episcopal Church for many years and participated in the Xinhai Revolution which resulted in the formation of the Republic of China. He also led people from Fujian Province to migrate to other countries including Malaysia, especially Sibu, Sarawak.

87. Yijing Zhang 张亦镜, "Wong Nai-Siong, A Great Christian (重印绂丞先生七十自叙序)," *True Light* 真光 28, no. 7 (1929): 57–59.

88. Yijing Zhang 张亦镜, "Two Papers of Correcting Errors with Dr. Chen Huan-Chang's Speech on Confucianism (驳陈焕章博士说教之谬两种)," *True Light* 真光 30, no. 7 (1931): 1.

89. Jiqing Yan 严霁青, "After Reading Mr. Zhang Yijing's Refuting Chen Huanzhang and Other Four People's Petition for Establishing Confucianism as the State Religion (读亦镜先生驳陈焕章请定孔教为国教论题后)," *True Light* 真光 26, no. 10 (1927): 80.

90. Zhang Xun (张勋16 September 1854–11 September 1923) was a Qing-loyalist general who attempted to restore the abdicated Emperor Puyi in the Manchu Restoration of 1917. He supported Yuan Shikai during his time as president.

as the state religion and to attack Christianity ferociously. Zhang, with his mastery of Confucianism and Chinese culture at the invitation of denominations in Hong Kong, took *Da Guang Newspaper* or *The Great Light Newspaper* (大光报) as his battlefield to fight a war with the pen against *Guo Shi Newspaper*. Within thirty days, *Guo Shi Newspaper* changed its writers three times, but it still could not avoid the fate of being defeated into silence. The three Confucian debaters respectively used the names of Linghua (菱花), Canxia (餐霞), and Chengfu (澄父). The denominations in Hong Kong rejoiced greatly, and put the arguments from both sides into a collection, *Da Guang Po An Ji* or *The Collection of the Great Light Breaking Darkness* (大光破暗集).

2.4.3.2 War against the Anti-Christian Movement in the 1920s

The second war of words was against the anti-Christian publications. Between 1921 and 1922, because of the defamations of Christianity in the *Wuzhou Saving China Daily* (梧州救国日报), Zhang published a book, *New Collection of Correcting Absurdity* (纠谬新编), to refute it.

During the 1920s, almost all the intellectuals and publications in China joined the Anti-Christian Movement to attack Christianity vehemently. Facing the intimidating storm, most Christians chose silence. Zhang was one of the few Christians who responded to the Anti-Christian Movement.

In response to the Anti-Christian Student Federation (非基督教学生同盟) and the Anti-Religion Alliance (非宗教大同盟), he published another two books, namely *A Special Issue of Criticising the Theories of Anti-Christian Movement* and *A Sequel to Criticising the Theories of Anti-Christian Movement* (正续 批评非基督教言论汇刊) which sold over fifty thousand copies. *A Special Issue of Criticising the Theories of Anti-Christian Movement* sold more than twenty thousand copies within the first month of its publication, and it had to be reprinted within the same month, which had never happened before among Christian publications in China. These two special issues were combined into a collected book named *Answering Attacks upon Christianity* (批评非基督教言论汇刊全编).

In 1922, Guohua, a member of the Anti-Christian Student Federation in Shanghai, wrote to Zhang to ask for the book. He said in a sarcastic tone by quoting Zhang's words: "Yeah, you guys have a sincere and academic attitude and you are not 'rude and unreasonable.' I write to you because I want you to send dozens of your books to our members. Don't refuse because we do not have money."[91]

In 1924, the Anti-Christian Movement went into its second stage. The Anti-Christian Society (非基督教同盟) was founded and it published many anti-Christian articles in the *Special Issue on Anti-Christianity* in *Awakening* (觉悟). In December 1924, the Anti-Christian Society called on "all comrades in China" to hold a yearly Anti-Christian Week around Christmas Day, and to hold large demonstrations,[92] which caused a lot of disturbance to the church. For more than six years, the Anti-Christian Week was a routine and an unsettling moment for the church.

Facing this challenge, Zhang wrote *The Records and Comments on the Ferocious Anti-Christian Movement in 1924* (民十三之剧烈反基督教运动记评) and *Review of the Anti-Christian Agitation* (最近反基督教纪评) in addition to his articles and comments. In total, he wrote more than one million words in arguing against the anti-Christians. He was viewed as the most active and capable defender of Christianity.

The members of the Anti-Christian Society paid their most intense attention to the responses in *True Light*.[93]

In 1925, a Christian named Guo Jichuan observed that his Christian friends (he meant Zhang Yijing and a few other Christian writers) hammered the anti-Christians to such a degree that they dared not defame Christianity as carelessly and irrationally as before.[94]

Zhang's courageous war by pen against the Anti-Christian Movement draws a picture of a man who almost single-handedly charged into millions of troops on the side of the enemy like David running towards Goliath or Don Quixote charging at the windmill. *True Light* under his leadership became

---

91. Yijing Zhang 张亦镜, "Response to a Letter from Guo Hua (国华) of the Anti-Christian Federation (非基督教同盟)," *True Light* 真光 21, no. 10–11 (1922): 104–5.

92. Chunfan Li 李春蕃, "Anti-Christian Week (非基督教周)," *Awakening* 觉悟, 9 December 1924, 1.

93. Xue, "Letter of My Repentance (我忏悔经过的一封信)," 98.

94. Jichuan Guo 郭济川, "Are the Records in the First Chapter of Genesis Really Not in Accordance with Science? (创世记第一章的记载果与科学不合吗?)," *True Light* 真光 24, no. 2 (1925): 13.

one of the most influential publications among churches. Zhang became well-known for defending the Way by his pen.[95]

In the view of Xu Baoqian[96] (who will be further discussed in chapter 4),[97] at those critical moments, when the whole church was silent under attacks, the ordinary Christians would definitely have felt frustrated. However, all Chinese Christians were greatly encouraged by Zhang, though his works were not able to silence all the opponents of Christianity. Xu said that Zhang debated with those opponents not because he was argumentative. It was a sense of duty and he had no other choice.

According to Lu Danlin,[98] the significance of Zhang's two wars could be compared to the victory of *Minbao Newspaper* or *People's Newspaper* (民报) over *Xinmin Congbao Newspaper* or *New People's Newspaper* (新民从报) at the end of the Qing dynasty,[99] and the uprising of "Republic-Defence Army (护国军)" for "The Republic of China (共和)"[100] in 1916.[101]

---

95. "Mr. Zhang Yijing – Top-Notch Player in the Ministry of Preaching through Writing from the Baptist Church (浸会文字布道的健将:张亦镜先生)," *The Voice of Evangelization* (宣道声) 3, no. 1 (1940): 19.

96. Xu Baoqian (徐宝谦, 1892–1944) was a prominent figure in the history of Chinese Christianity. He obtained his PhD degree from Columbia University in 1930.

97. Baoqian Xu 徐宝谦, "Write in Memory of Mr. Zhang Yijing (为张亦镜先生纪念号写)," *True Light* 真光 40, no. 12 (1941): 6.

98. Lu Danlin (陆丹林) (1897–1972) was a very famous writer, editor, calligrapher, and thinker. He used to be editor of many publications like *Da Guang Newspaper* or *The Great Light Newspaper* (大光报), *Dao Lu Monthly* or *Road Monthly* (道路月刊), *Yi Jing* (逸经), and *Da Feng* or *Typhoon* (大风). The last two publications were about literature and history, founded by Jian Youen. Lu joined Tong Meng Hui or the Chinese Revolutionary League (同盟会) founded by Sun Yat-sen before 1911. In the 1910s, he submitted a paper to *True Light*, and Zhang invited him to have a meeting at his editorial office. Since then, they got to know each other. Zhang and Lu used to be coworkers in *Da Guang Newspaper* (大光报) and Lu named his son Da Guang. In 1948, he was elected as the director of Writers' Association in Shanghai (上海作协理事).

99. In 1906, *Minbao Newspaper* (民报), the voice of the Tong Meng Hui or Chinese Revolutionary League (同盟会) which was founded by Sun Yat-sen, argued against *Xinmin Congbao Newspaper* (新民从报) which was the voice of the monarchists and was supported by Liang Qichao (梁启超). They debated over three questions: revolution or keeping monarchy, parliamentary democracy or constitutional monarchy, and state ownership or private ownership of the land. After the debate, the proposals of the Tong Meng Hui were widely accepted.

100. In 1925, President Yuan Shikai (袁世凯) announced the restoration of monarchy. On 25 December 1915, Generals Tang Jirao (唐继尧), Cai E (蔡锷), and Li Liejun (李烈钧) initiated a nationwide military resistance. In June 1916, Yuan died.

101. Danlin Lu 陆丹林, "Preface," in (1928), *A Quarter of a Century of True Light, Selected* 真光丛刊, ed. Yijing Zhang (Shanghai 上海: China Baptist Publication Society 中华浸会书局, 1927), 5.

2.4.3.3 *War against Scientism*

The third war of words waged by Zhang was his active participation along with other Christians in the Debate on Science and Metaphysics (1923–24). Very few people in China today still remember Christians' participation in this debate. Baidu, the most popular searching engine in China, provides an explanation for the Debate of Science and Metaphysics by quoting Hong Xiaonan.[102] This typical delineation of the debate has already been presented in chapter 2. Hong's explanation is verified by He.[103] There is no trace of Christians' participation, but actually, Zhang Yijing and some Christians joined this debate with enthusiasm.

In 1923, Wang Zhixin[104] called on his students to respond to Wu Zhihui who exalted science and denounced religion.[105] Zhang Yijing actively responded by soliciting articles on *Criticism of Wu Zhihui's "The Views on Universe and Life of a New Faith"* (批评吴稚晖先生的一个新信仰的宇宙观及人生观). The first issue of *True Light* in 1924 was a special collection of such articles.

Maybe the voice of *True Light*, a church publication, was too obtrusive to be noticed by Chinese intellectuals, or maybe the majority of Chinese intellectuals who had already inclined to believe in science despised its voice. The final result was that the belief in science has become a dominant force and a new element of Chinese culture, while metaphysics including Christianity was depicted as backward, abstract, superstitious, and unscientific. People have even forgotten Christians' participation and contribution in this important debate.

---

102. Hong, "Effects of the Polemics," 17–18.

103. He, "Debate on Science and Metaphysics," 12–13.

104. Wang Zhixin (王治心, 1881–1968) was a very important Christian leader. He became a Christian in 1900. After 1911, he worked as the editor of *Chinese Christian Advocate* (上海兴华报). In 1921, he became a philosophy professor in Nanjing Theological Seminary and the editor of *Nanjing Theological Review* (金陵神学志). In 1926, he became the editor of *Wen She* (文社月刊).

105. Zhixin Wang, *Nanjing Theological Review* 神学志, 1923, 10, no. 1, cited in Cheng Yang 杨程, "A Criticism of Wu Zhuhui's *The Views on Universe and Life of a New Faith* (批评吴稚晖先生的一个新信仰的宇宙观及人生观,附图表)," *True Light* 真光 24, no. 1 (1925): 2.

2.4.3.4 Zhang's Positive and Sympathetic View of the Anti-Christians

Although Zhang argued against the anti-Christians consistently, he also saw their positive side. According to his observation, many officials in the KMT government persecuted Christianity because of their tradition and the former influence of Russia. Although the KMT government did not give much freedom to Christianity, Zhang took it as a good opportunity for Christians to return to Christ. Christians should seek freedom in the heart which was promised by the Lord.[106]

He encouraged the Chinese Christians to take advantage of the Anti-Christian activities to examine themselves. In his view, Christians were focusing too much on the external enterprises like running schools or striving for a career of being an official while ignoring the missions commanded by Christ. He asked,

> Did Christ ask us to run schools which teach the worldly knowledge? Did Christ ask us to become an official and win the worldly glory? Although the titles could bring glory to the Lord and bring the Gospel to the politicians, the fact was many Christians lost their faith after being absorbed into the worldly knowledge and many Christians dared not to admit their Christian identity after becoming officials. If Christianity were left alone for a long time, it would surely die out. Considering this, it is lucky for Christianity to be attacked brutally, which was to turn us to the Lord's narrow way, narrow door, and his cross. The current church was corrupted. Jesus sent us into the world like sheep entering the wolves rather than mixing water and milk together.[107]

At the same time, Zhang had a sympathetic and understanding attitude towards the anti-Christians. He said:

> The only solution was that Christians should follow the example of Stephen who prayed for his persecutors just before he died. There should be no resistance at all, especially in the church. This

---

106. Yijing Zhang 张亦镜, "Christianity under the Government of KMT Party (在既定信教自由于约法既许信仰有完全自由权于党纲的中国国民政府底下的基督教 有按)," *True Light* 真光 29, no. 3 (1930): 51–52.

107. Zhang, "Christianity under the Government," 51–52.

would show that the faith and evangelization of the Christians were directly and purely from God. Then the anti-Christian people might be woken up to the fact that they had taken a wrong aim. Then the two sides might have peace and be reconciled. Then the two sides could believe in Jesus together.[108]

2.4.3.5 Famous People Criticized by Zhang

Since Zhang viewed his and *True Light's* mission as defending Christianity, he had to confront many people, especially those who attacked Christianity. Among them were many well-known officials and intellectuals.

2.4.3.5.1 Famous Confucian advocates

Zhang criticized Kang Youwei, Liang Qichao,[109] Chen Huanzhang, and their followers for their misinterpretations of Confucianism.

Kang Youwei, Liang Qichao, and Chen Huanzhang were very prestigious Confucian scholars. They set up the Confucian Association and sought to establish Confucianism as China's state religion by basing their theories on "The Great Harmony or Da Tong (大同, the ideal society for Confucianism)," "The Well-Off (小康)," and "Three Social Stages (三世说)." Liang's theory had a deep influence on *Chinese Academic History* (中国学术源流) by Wang Zhixin.

The advocates of Confucianism claimed that Confucian ideals like "the world is equally shared by all," "the capable and the virtuous are sought for public service," and "the Great Harmony" had been achieved in the Republic of China. In order to remember that the Republic of China was a product of Confucian teachings, Confucianism should be established as the state religion. While in this process, they belittled Christianity.

Zhang referred to the Chinese classics to prove that their interpretations of Confucian ideas were far-fetched. In *Dissecting the Theory for a State Religion* (1913), *On the Great Harmony* (说大同, 1914), and *The Collection of the Great Light Breaking Darkness* (1916), Zhang gave a detailed explanation of the two

---

108. Yijing Zhang 张亦镜, "Students from Chinese Academy Harrassed Hua Xi University (中文院学生纠众滋扰华大校)," *True Light* 真光 29, no. 1 (1930): 90–91.

109. Liang Qichao (梁启超, 1873–1929) was a very famous thinker, statesman, educator, and Confucian scholar. He was Kang Youwei's student and a leader in the Reform Movement of 1898 (戊戌变法).

ideas of "The Great Harmony" in *The Book of Rites* (礼记) and "Three Social Stages (三世说)" in *Gong Yang's Interpretation of the Spring and Autumn Annals* (春秋公羊传).

Yan Fu,[110] Xia Zengyou (夏曾佑), and Wang Shitong (王式通) were included in Zhang's criticism for their participation in Chen Huanzhang and Liang Qichao's endeavour. Yan Fu criticized people who advocated the Republic of China but slandered Confucianism. Zhang pointed out Yan's misinterpretation of Confucius's words and he emphasized that Confucianism was not a religion.[111]

Wang Rongbao (汪荣宝), as a member of the Parliament (or the Congress), supported the establishment of Confucianism as China's state religion. Zhang criticized him for his being a reader of Kang Youwei and Liang Qichao rather than a reader of the Confucian classics.[112]

2.4.3.5.2 Famous atheist advocate

Zhang Taiyan[113] advocated atheism and attacked Christianity. Zhang opposed him in *Refuting a Plagiarism of Zhang Taiyan's Atheistic Attack on Religion* (驳抄太炎无神论之非宗教文, 1920). In 1930, Zhang criticized Zhang Taiyan again.[114]

---

110. Yan Fu (严复, 1854–1921) was a Chinese scholar and translator, most famous for introducing Western ideas, including Darwin's "natural selection," to China in the late nineteenth century.

111. Yijing Zhang 张亦镜, "After Yan Fu's Speech (书严复民可使由之不可使知之演说词后)," in *(1928), A Quarter of a Century of True Light, Selected* 真光丛刊, Part 3: *General Articles* 通论, ed. Yijing Zhang (Shanghai 上海: China Baptist Publication Society 中华浸会书局, 1913), 89–90.

112. Yijing Zhang 张亦镜, "Denouncing Wang Rongbao (斥汪荣宝)," in *(1928), A Quarter of a Century of True Light, Selected* 真光丛刊, Part 3: *General Articles* 通论, ed. Yijing Zhang (Shanghai 上海: China Baptist Publication Society 中华浸会书局, 1914), 93–95.

113. Zhang Taiyan (章太炎, 1869–1936) was a famous thinker, educator, revolutionary, and Confucian scholar. His students included Qian Xuantong (钱玄同), Shen Qianshi (沈兼士), and Lu Xun (鲁迅).

114. Yijing Zhang 张亦镜, "Answering the Questions from Mr. Zeng Guren (答曾骨人先生来函所设问)," *True Light* 真光 29, no. 1 (1930): 65.

2.4.3.5.3 Famous Buddhism advocates

Zhang Zhongru or Zhang Chunyi[115] and Nie Yuntai[116] had formerly been Christians, but both became more inclined to Buddhism. Zhang Chunyi wrote *Reforming Christianity with Buddhism* (佛化基督教) while Nie wrote *The Questions and Answers about Religion* (宗教答问), *Clarifying the Confusions about Religion* (宗教辩惑说), and *Essays of Exposing Harms* (明害诸篇).

When Zhang Yijing analyzed why Zhang Chunyi advocated reforming Christianity through Buddhism, claiming that Jesus was a disciple of Buddha and an incarnation of Bodhisattva, he listed Zhang Chunyi's three identities: Buddhist, Confucian, and Christian. According to Zhang Yijing, Zhang Chunyi often verified the Christian message by seeking evidence from the teachings of Buddhism when he worked for the Christian Literature Society for China. His analysis was to show that, among his three identities, Zhang Chunyi's commitment to Buddhism was the strongest, while his commitment to Christianity was the weakest. He even doubted if Zhang Chunyi had ever really believed in Jesus as he had proclaimed. Although he did not use the modern term "identity," Zhang Yijing actually interpreted Zhang Chunyi's change from the perspective of identities.[117] In the case of Nie, Zhang felt Nie's former church was too lax to call people Christian and the church did not fulfil the responsibility of feeding the lambs of the Lord. To manifest the fallacies of Buddhism, he offered his *Biography of Sakyamuni* (释迦牟尼传) for their reference.

2.4.3.5.4 Famous anti-Christian people in the 1920s

Zhang confronted almost all the famous Chinese intellectuals with an anti-Christian standing at the beginning of the twentieth century. Wang Jingwei

---

115. Zhang Zhongru or Zhang Chunyi (张仲如/张纯一, 1871–1955) was a *xiucai* (秀才) who passed the imperial examination at the prefectural level. In 1904, he was a Chinese teacher in Wenhua Academy (文华学院) run by the Anglican church in Wuchang (武昌). In 1909, he was an editor of *Datong Newspaper* (大同报) in the Christian Literature Society for China (广学会). In the 1920s, he taught in Yenching University and Nankai University.

116. Nie Yuntai (聂云台, 1880–1953) was a *xiucai* (秀才) who passed the imperial examination at the prefectural level. His mother was the daughter of Zeng Guofan (曾国藩). He later studied in America. In 1920, he became the chair of Shanghai General Chamber of Commerce.

117. Yijing Zhang 张亦镜, "A Discussion over Mr. Zhang Zhongru's Reforming Christianity with Buddhism (讨论张仲如先生之佛化基督教)," *True Light* 真光 23, no. 12 (1924): 78–79.

was not only an anti-Christian activist in the 1920s but he was also already hostile to Christianity in the 1910s in Paris.[118]

In 1913, Wang criticized religion in his foreword to the first issue of *Min De Newspaper* or *People's Morality* (民德报) in Paris. Since Wang called Jesus a fool and a scourge and called Christians hypocrites, Zhang made his criticism of Wang in *Correcting Errors with Wang Jingwei's Words for Destroying Christianity in the First Issue of Min De Newspaper* (纠正汪精卫巴黎民德报发刊词毁教语之谬, 1914).

On 29 March 1922, Wang wrote *Strongly Refuting Three Fallacies of Christianity* (力斥耶教三大谬) after he found three fallacies from a Christian message poster stuck on the wall of a park. Wang could not bear the superstitious words in the posters such as heaven, hell, King of kings and God the Creator.

Wang's article was printed by all newspapers in Guangzhou, which proved to be very effective. On 1 and 2 April, the *Journal of the Republic and the Human Rights* published *Agreeing Comments on Strongly Refuting Three Fallacies of Christianity* in classic Chinese by Wu Yiru (吴义如) who used to be a preacher and an elder in the Presbyterian church for more than ten years. To Wang's delight, Wu turned to attack Christianity now.

On 1 April, in his telegram reply to Li Shizeng[119] (李石曾, the initiator of the Anti-Religion Alliance 非宗教大同盟), Wang said, "Jesus cannot be reconciled with science, especially with evolutionism. After Lamarck and Darwin, Christian religionists had to move to Asia with their afflictions because they had no foothold in Europe. Yet to their shock, there were capable people in the East. Your gentleman's great aspiration is to expurgate

---

118. Wang Jingwei (汪精卫, 1883–1944) received his education in Japan and France. He was a famous high-level official in the KMT government. In 1921, he was in charge of education in Guangdong Province. In 1924, he became minister of the Publicity Ministry. He was the one who drafted Sun Yat-sen's will. Later on, he became the second highest official in the KMT government, just after Chiang Kai-shek, the president. After Japan invaded China in 1937, he went to serve as president in the government established by the Japanese.

119. Li Shizeng (李石曾, 1881–1973) was an educator, promoter of anarchist doctrines, political activist, and member of the Chinese Nationalist Party in early Republican China. Li took a graduate degree in chemistry and biology in Paris. He organized cultural exchanges between France and China, established the first factory in Europe to manufacture and sell bean curd, and created Diligent Work-Frugal Study programmes that brought Chinese students to France for work in factories. Along with Wu Zhihui (吴稚晖), Cai Yuanpei (蔡元培), and Zhang Jingjiang (张静江), he was known as one of the fiercely anti-Communist "Four Elders" of the Chinese Nationalist Party in the 1920s. He founded the Anti-Religion Alliance (非宗教大同盟).

Christianity, which has my limitless admiration. I am sending my paper to you now and expecting your corrections."

On 21 April 1922, Wang Jingwei, as the head of the education department of Sun Yat-sen's Guangdong government, published his article *The Crisis of Nationalistic Education* (国民教育之危机论) in all the newspapers in Guangzhou. In the first half of this article, Wang stated the necessity of nationalistic education, but in the second part, Wang attacked the Christian schools for their religious education. Zhang criticized Wang's ideas in *Refuting Wang Jingwei's The Crisis of National Education* (驳汪精卫国民教育之危机论) in which Zhang warned the Christian educators of the upcoming troubles from Wang.

Zhang said that Christians originally welcomed Wang Jingwei, as a follower of Sun Yat-sen (孙中山), to be the leader of education. Beyond all expectations, Wang had published so many articles gratuitiously denigrating Christianity and the Christian schools in this Anti-Christian Movement that Christians would not keep silent to save Wang's face anymore. Zhang questioned Wang:

> Just as the Anti-Religion Alliance used the words "swear to wipe out 扫除 (Christianity)" in its manifesto, you, ringleader Wang, used "expurgate 廓清 (Christianity)" in your reply to Li Shizeng (李石曾). Since you charged the church and the Christian schools with such a serious charge of national and racial elimination, claimed the result was close at hand and called on the Chinese people to be cautious, would it not be counted as a patriotic action if the masses could be incited to destroy the church and the Christian schools? Are you trying to repeat the Boxer Movement? Obviously, you have been deeply poisoned by the stories about how Mencius rejected Yang and Mo (孟子拒杨墨)[120] and how Han Yu attacked Buddhism and Taoism (韩愈辟佛老).[121]

---

120. Mencius (孟子, 372–289 BC) and Han Yu (韩愈, AD 768–824), in safeguarding Confucianism, violently attacked other schools, Buddhism, and Taoism.

121. Yijing Zhang, "Correcting Fallacies in the Sayings of the Anti-Christian Student Federation – General Remarks (纠正非基督教学生同盟的言论之谬误 - 总论)," *True Light* 真光 21, no. 8–9 (1922): 11.

Zhang exhorted Wang to repent. Zhang also wrote *Talking with Wang Jingwei about the Truth* (与汪精卫论道).

Zeng Yugen (曾郁根), the sales director of *True Light*, asked Zhang if he realized he had put himself in danger because he had harshly criticized an important person in the KMT government in Guangzhou (very probably Zeng meant Wang Jingwei). Zhang replied that he was ready to die for defending the truth of Christianity.[122]

Zhu Zhixin (朱执信) wrote *What the Heck Is Jesus* (耶稣是什么东西) in 1919 which was one of the anti-Christian articles in the Special Issue of Jesus (耶稣号), jointly published by *Tianmin Newspaper* or *Heavenly People* (天民报) and Minfeng Publishing House (民风社) in Guangzhou City. Millions of this Special Issue were sent out. Zhu reviled Jesus as one who was worse than the leader of the Boxers; who was born of Mary after being raped by a Roman officer; who was a hypocritical, selfish, angry, narrow-minded and revengeful idol, and; whose cross was a changed form of a male sex organ. This article was reprinted countless times and spread by the anti-Christian people. A person named Yuan Zhenying (袁震瀛) followed Zhu's example and wrote *What the Heck Is God* which was originally published in the New Year's supplement of *Guangdong Newspaper for the Mass Newspaper* (广东群报).

In his criticism of Zhu Zhixin's *What the Heck Is Jesus*, Zhang, writing under the name of Pingji,[123] concluded that Zhu was more vicious than Dao Zhi (盗跖).[124] After analyzing Zhu's article, Zhang thought Zhu was self-contradictory and had a confused mind. Zhang Yijing and Liang Junmo's (梁君默) criticism of Zhu and Zhang's *Comments on Zhu Zhixin's "What the Heck Is Jesus"* (关于朱执信'耶稣是什么东西'的杂评) were included in *Answering Attacks upon Christianity* (批评非基督教言论汇刊全编).

Zhang noticed that the anti-Christian people in the Qing dynasty viewed all Christians as revolutionaries because Sun Yat-sen, Ou Fengchi (区凤墀), and Zuo Doushan (左斗山) were Christians as well as revolutionaries. In

---

122. Yugen Zeng 曾郁根, "The Baptist Church in Guang Dong and Guang Xi Provinces during the Past Twenty-Five Years (二十五年来两广浸信会概观)," *True Light* 真光 26, no. 6 (1927): 33.

123. Pingji 萍寄, "On the Guangzhou Crusade's Achievements and Responses (论广州大布道的成绩与反响)," *True Light* 真光 20, no. 2 (1921): 2.

124. Dao Zhi (盗跖) was a leader of a group of bandits who was well known for bitterly condemning Confucius face to face. Zhu was worse than Dao Zhi (盗跖) in his disdain for the sage.

the Republic of China, the anti-Christian people like Zhu Zhixin and Wang Jingwei ignored the sacrifices of Christians for the revolution and viewed all Christians as counter-revolutionaries.[125]

Zhang criticized Wu Zhihui.[126]

In addition to *The Views on Universe and Life of a New Faith* (一个新信仰的宇宙观及人生观), Wu also wrote *God Is a Cat Which Does Not Catch Mice* (上帝是一只不扑鼠的猫). As described in Zhang's war against scientism, Zhang devoted a special issue of *True Light* to criticize Wu.

Zhang criticized Cai Yuanpei.

Cai Yuanpei, as the president of Peking University, gave a speech at a meeting of the Anti-Religion Alliance held on the campus of Peking University on 9 April 1922.

Cai called for replacing a religious belief with a philosophical belief because all religions were bound by their old and stale teachings. He had a strong dislike for Christian schools and the YMCA because "they drop all kinds of baits to tempt those underage students into believing Christianity." He insisted that education should involve no religion. At the end of his speech, he shouted the slogan "let's carry on this (Anti-Christian) movement freely with no scruple[s]."

Zhang took fifteen and a half pages to argue against him in *Refuting Cai Yuanpei's Speech at the Conference of the Anti-Religion Alliance* (驳蔡元培在非宗教大同盟的演说词).[127]

Zhang criticized Li Shizeng and Li Dazhao (李大钊).

On 17 March 1922, the Anti-Religion Alliance in Peking sent an express mail with seventy-seven signatures including Li Shizeng and Li Dazhao's to all the main newspapers nationwide to attack Christianity on charges of

---

125. Yijing Zhang 张亦镜, "Answering Four Questions from Mr. Lu Zhensheng (答吕振声先生四疑问)," *True Light* 真光 28, no. 12 (1929): 62.

126. Wu Zhihui (吴稚晖, 1865–1953) was titled as "A Great Scholar of Culture of the Century (世界百年文化学术伟人)" by the United Nations. He was a very famous thinker, statesman, educator, and calligrapher. He joined Tong Meng Hui or the Chinese Revolutionary League (同盟会) in 1905 in France. Wu became an anarchist in France. Along with Li Shizeng (李石曾), Zhang Jingjiang (张静江), and Cai Yuanpei (蔡元培), he was known as one of the strongly anti-Communist "Four Elders" of the Nationalist Party in the 1920s. In 1946, Wu was elected to the National Assembly and he was the teacher of Jiang Jieshi's son, Jiang Jingguo (蒋经国).

127. Yijing Zhang 张亦镜, "Refuting Cai Yuanpei's Speech at the Conference of the Anti-Religion Alliance," *True Light* 真光 21, no. 10–11 (1922): 1–17.

being superstitious and anti-human, blocking the way of science and evolution, causing wars, poisoning China – a land without *Jiao* (教, teaching or religion) – and luring the youth. It swore to wipe out (扫除) Christianity in its Manifesto.

Zhang criticized the seventy-seven members in his *Attached Comments on the Telegram of March 17th from the Members of the Anti-Religion Alliance in Peking and Its Manifesto* (附评北京各学校非宗教同人皷电及宣言) which was included in *Answering Attacks upon Christianity* (批评非基督教言论汇刊全编).[128]

Zhang criticized Chen Duxiu and Shen Xuanlu.[129]

On 15 March 1922, a semi-monthly publication named *Vanguard* (先驱) published *A Special Issue for the Anti-Christian Student Federation* (非基督教学生同盟号) which included Chen Duxiu's *Christianity and the Christian Church*, along with the Anti-Christian Student Federation's Declaration, regulations, and a telegram to the public.

Zhang said if *Christianity and the Christian Church* was really written by Chen Duxiu, then it contradicted the views expressed in Chen Duxiu's *Christianity and the Chinese* (基督教和中国人) which was very supportive of the Chinese Christian faith.

Shen Xuanlu was a top player in the Anti-Christian Student Federation and the Anti-Religion Alliance. On 31 March 1922 when the five famous scholars of Zhou Zuoren,[130] Qian Xuantong (钱玄同), Shen Jianshi (沈兼士), Shen Shiyuan (沈士远), and Ma Yuzao (马裕藻) jointly published their *Declaration on Freedom of Faith* which called the Anti-Christian Movement a violation of the Constitution, Zhang Yijing highly praised the *Declaration* because it was written by non-Christians and it had given a deadly blow to the movements of the Anti-Religion Alliance and the Anti-Christian Student Federation. Without it, the whole Anti-Christian Movement would have lost control and plunged into violence. Whereas, Shen Xuanlu wrote an article of

---

128. Yijing Zhang 张亦镜, "Attached Comments on the Telegram of March 17th from the Members of the Anti-Religion Alliance in Peking and Its Manifesto (附评北京各学校非宗教同人皷电及宣言)," *True Light* 真光 21, no. 8–9 (1922): 23–36.

129. Shen Xuanlu (沈玄庐, 1883–1928) was a 1920s-era Chinese revolutionary and intellectual who belonged to both the Kuomintang and the Communist Party of China.

130. Zhou Zuoren (周作人, 16 January 1885–6 May 1967) was a Chinese writer, primarily known as an essayist and a translator. He was the younger brother of Lu Xun (Zhou Shuren), the second of three brothers.

Questioning Non-Religion-Believers' Resistance to Anti-Christian Movement as a criticism of the five scholars' declaration. Shen Xuanlu and Chen Duxiu and others called the five scholars "flatterers of the power." Zhang Yijing took it as his responsibility to defend the five scholars and criticize Shen and Chen.[131]

Zhang said that *The Young China* (少年中国) also published three Religion Issues which contained Anti-Religion articles. Since they peacefully carried out academic research, they were totally different from the current Anti-Christian Movement which, in a threatening manner, called for "expurgating (廓清)," "wiping out (扫除)," "annihilating (歼灭)," "raiding (讨伐)" and "declaring a war against (宣战)" Christianity in its declarations, manifesto, and telegrams. Such behaviour was unlawful. He defended the five scholars above by questioning, "How could the (five scholars') protest be called an interference with your anti-religion freedom? Why so bullying [sic]?"[132]

In *Argument against Chen Duxiu and Shen Xuanlu over Christianity* (与陈独秀沈玄庐论道), Zhang refuted Chen Duxiu's *Christianity and the Chinese* (基督教和中国人) and Shen Xuanlu's *Doubts about Christianity and the Chinese* (对于基督教和中国人的怀疑).

Zhang argued against Yun Daiying.[133]

Yun opposed Christianity in his *Christianity and Saving China by Character* (基督教与人格救国) and *Why Are We against Christianity* (我们为甚么反对基督教). Zhang wrote four commenting articles on Yun.

Zhang was puzzled by Liao Zhongkai.[134]

At a meeting on the evening of 25th and 26th December during the first Anti-Christian Week organized by the Anti-Christian Society in 1924, Liao Zhongkai, Zhou Fohai (周佛海), Zhou Enlai (周恩来), and Wu

---

131. Yijing Zhang 张亦镜, "Refuting Xuanlu Shen's Challenging Non-Religionists' Defending against the Anti-Christian Movement," *True Light* 真光 21, no. 10–11 (1922): 68–85.

132. Yijing Zhang 张亦镜, "Bullying? (欲欺谁哉)," *True Light* 真光 21, no. 10–11 (1922): 109.

133. Yun Daiying (恽代英, 1895–1931) was an early leader of the Communist Party of China.

134. Liao Zhongkai (廖仲恺, 1877–1925) was a Kuomintang leader and financier. He was the principal architect of the first Kuomintang–Chinese Communist Party (KMT–CCP) United Front in the 1920s. Liao became the civil governor of Guangdong from May 1923 to February 1924, and then again from June to September 1924. When the KMT was reformed in 1924, he was named the head of the Department of Workers, and then Department of Peasants. Later he became Minister of Finance of the southern government. He was assassinated in Guangzhou in August 1925. Liao and He Xiangning had a daughter, Liao Mengxing, and a son, Liao Chengzhi.

Haibin (邹海滨) were invited to deliver speeches against Christianity at Guangdong University.

Liao Zhongkai, the former governor and the president of Guangdong University, accused Christianity of cultural aggression, imperialism, political ambition, and disobedience.

Surprisingly, Zhang noticed that Liao's son was a graduate of Pei Zheng Middle School (培正中学) and both his son and daughter graduated from Lingnan University (岭南大学), the two famous Christian schools. A Christian KMT party member told Zhang that some people also questioned Liao on this. Liao responded to them that he had forbidden his children from becoming Christians though he sent them to Christian schools. When these people further challenged him by saying that he had made his children welcome Western cultural aggression and he could not really forbid his children's acceptance of Christianity in the heart, Liao had no reply.[135]

Zhang criticized Dr. Hu Shi.[136]

In his *History of Chinese Philosophy* (中国哲学史大纲), Dr. Hu categorized Christianity as a kind of man-made religion but interpreted the words of Zeng Zi[137] (曾子, 505–435 BC, a student of Confucius) as evidence for Confucianism as a religion – a religion of filial piety. Zhang thought Hu just took parts of Zeng's words into consideration so that he made a quick judgement. Zhang took Zeng Zi's words only as a life principle. Zhang thought Hu's words would give support to Chen Huanzhang who aimed at establishing Confucianism as China's state religion. As for Christianity, Zhang recommended Hu to read the works by people who took a conservative standpoint. Zhang also pointed out a self-contradiction by Dr. Hu and corrected his statement.

Zhang also mentioned many others for their anti-Christian position including: Jiang Shaoyuan (江绍远), Wang Xinggong, Li Da (李达), Zhou

---

135. Yijing Zhang 张亦镜, "The Anti-Christian Activities during the 'Anti-Christian Week' As I Heard (如是我闻之'非基督教周'的反基督教运动)," *True Light* 真光 24, no. 1 (1925): 93.

136. Zhang, "A Fair Judgment," 19–23.

137. The words are: When Master Zeng was sick, he summoned his pupils and said, "Uncover my feet; uncover my hands. Poetry says: 'Trembling with fear, as if standing over a deep abyss, as if treading on thin ice.' My young students, from now on, I know I shall be free from injury" (启于足, 启于手, 诗云, 战战兢兢, 如临深渊, 如履薄冰, 而今而后, 吾知免夫).

Taixuan, Dai Jitao (戴季陶), He Juefu (何觉甫), Miao Fenglin (缪凤林), Yu Jiaju, and Li Chunfan (李春蕃).

Apart from Chinese, Zhang was also critical of some Westerners. As early as 1906, he called evolutionism a cult.[138] In 1930, he showed his feeling about evolutionism again by saying that the prophecies about Jesus's birth, death, and resurrection, and their achievements were much more amazing than the changes described by people like Thomas Henry Huxley (赫胥黎) in *Evolution and Ethics* (天演论).[139]

2.4.3.5.5 Zhang's defence of social justice

Zhang did not only make criticisms for defending Christianity, but also for safeguarding social justice. This chapter has already discussed how Zhang risked his own life to save a father and a son by confronting a county magistrate in the Qing dynasty. He also criticized President Yuan Shikai, congressman Zhao Weixi,[140] warlord Long Jiguang (龙济光), and Zhao Bingjun.[141]

In 1913, Yuan Shikai, the first president of the Republic of China, commanded people to worship Confucius. Zhang predicted that Yuan's deliberate misinterpretation of Confucianism aimed at restoring the monarchy and becoming an emperor.[142]

In 1914, the Parliament controlled by President Yuan discussed whether the practice of awarding posthumous titles[143] should be resumed. Zhang

---

138. Wen Kai Zhang 张文开, "On 'Our Father in Heaven' (吾侪在天之父论)," *True Light* 真光 5, no. 2 (1906): 2–5.

139. Yijing Zhang 张亦镜, "Continuation of Tasting the Way (道源一勺续)," *True Light* 真光 29, no. 9 (1930): 9.

140. Zhao Weixi (赵惟熙, 1859–1917) was a presented scholar (*jinshi* 進士) after passing the imperial examination in the Qing dynasty. He became the governor of Gansu Province with the support of President Yuan Shikai. In 1914, he became a congressman. He petitioned President Yuan to resume the practice of awarding posthumous titles.

141. Zhao Bingjun (赵秉钧, 1859–1914) was the third premier of the Republic of China from 25 September 1912 to 1 May 1913. Zhao was previously a public security official during the Qing dynasty and became minister of the interior during the republic before becoming premier. He was directly implicated in the assassination of Song Jiaoren, the man most likely to be his successor. Zhao protested his innocence but resigned. Then he was made governor of Zhili. Zhao was mysteriously poisoned in 1914.

142. Yijing Zhang 张亦镜, "After President Yuan Commands to Worship Confucius (书袁总统尊孔命令后)," in *(1928), A Quarter of a Century of True Light, Selected* 真光丛刊, Part 3: *General Articles* 通论, ed. Yijing Zhang (Shanghai 上海: China Baptist Publication Society 中华浸会书局, 1913), 76–88.

143. This is a traditional way in China to show respect to the dead.

thought this motion was ridiculous.[144] He pointed out the future of awarding posthumous titles would be a resumption of the title of emperor. Once again, he foresaw that Yuan aimed at becoming an emperor. Because of this event, he called Zhao Weixi, President Yuan, and the Parliament the "Three Clownish Wonders of the Republic of China (民国三绝)."[145]

Yuan was declared as an emperor on 12 December 1915.

In 1915, Zhang criticized President Yuan Shikai because of his restoration of the monarchy and he criticized the warlord Long Jiguang (龙济光), for Long practised hegemony and claimed to be a king in Guangdong Province. Because of this, Long offered a heavy reward for capturing Zhang.

Zhang condemned Zhao Bingjun[146] because Zhao was believed to plot the murder of Song Jiaoren.[147]

In challenging these famous people, Zhang showed he was a man of principle, bravery, and honesty. He once said:

> Although I do not have the expertise, I have perseverance and courage. So over the past years, when the anti-Christian articles showed up and if they contained unreasonable sayings, I would bombard them with this artillery (which means *True Light*) in spite of the fame and status of the authors.[148]

Apart from words, Zhang safeguarded social justice also by deeds. He quit his job two times, refused to take a sedan chair in Lu Shan Mountain, refused to buy Japanese products in Qingdao, and refused to take the tram car in Shanghai. Such events will be described later in chapter 4.

2.4.3.6 Zhang Was Criticized

As Zhang was an upright and frank man, he was also a target for criticism.

---

144. Yijing Zhang 张亦镜, "Denouncing Fallacies of Awarding Posthumous Title (斥溢法之谬)," in *(1928), A Quarter of a Century of True Light, Selected* 真光丛刊, *Part 3: General Articles* 通论, ed. Yijing Zhang (Shanghai 上海: China Baptist Publication Society 中华浸会书局, 1914), 100.

145. Zhang, "Denouncing Fallacies of Awarding," 96.

146. Zhang, "Denouncing Fallacies of Awarding," 99.

147. Song Jiaoren (宋教仁, 1882–1913) was a Chinese republican revolutionary, political leader, and a founder of the Kuomintang (KMT). He was assassinated in 1913 after leading his Kuomintang party to victory in China's first democratic elections.

148. Jiang, "Works of Mr. Zhang Yijing," 12–13.

Since the sayings of the anti-Christian intellectuals like Li Shizeng and Wang Jingwei were filled with provocative and inflammatory words like "expurgating (廓清)," "wiping out (扫除)," "annihilating (歼灭)," "raiding (讨伐)," and "declaring a war against (宣战)" Christianity, Zhang worried that some people with an explosive temper might join the local gangsters to resort to violence, fearing that the disasters of the Boxer Rebellion and the Eight-Power Allied Forces (八国联军) might reoccur.[149]

After reading about Zhang's worry, Mei Jianfeng (梅剑凤) sent an angry letter to Zhang from a girls' primary school of Chikan (赤坎) in Taishan (台山) of Guangdong Province on 15 May 1922. She said that China had not perished because of the invasion of the Eight-Power Allied Forces, but would certainly perish when people believed in God as the Creator and did not do scientific research. A lot of her words were about how all scientists and politicians in America were not Christians but attacked religion. Her conclusion was that people should boldly destroy religion (Christianity). Zhang was not sure if this letter was from a real person named Mei Jianfeng or from an impostor. After expressing admiration of the letter writer for being a daredevil and also agreeing that mainland China would survive foreign invasions, Zhang turned to reconcile Christian faith with science.[150]

In 1922, Xi Cong (锡聪) published an article on the third volume of *Guangdong Anti-Christian Student Federation Weekly* (广东非基督教学生同盟周刊) after reading Zhang Yijing's *Criticising Wang Jingwei's Strongly Refuting Three Fallacies of Christianity*. Xi said Zhang was like a foolish person cursing loudly in a public square when he said: "We will wait for Wang Jingwei to kill all four hundred thousand of [sic] Christians with military force." Then Xi mocked Zhang as a ten-foot high lampstand which could only shine upon others rather than Zhang himself. Zhang Yijing laughed at Xi for only being able to find such a small fault with the last issue of *True Light*.[151]

---

149. Zhang, "Correcting Fallacies in the Sayings," 11.
150. Yijing Zhang 张亦镜, "What a Ms. Mei Jianfeng (好一个梅剑凤女士)," *True Light* 真光 21, no. 10–11 (1922): 109–10.
151. Yijing Zhang 张亦镜, "A Ten-Foot High Lampstand (丈八灯台)," *True Light* 真光 21, no. 10–11 (1922): 110–11.

In the same volume, Ruan Xiaoxian,[152] a student of Guangdong Type A Technical School (广东省立甲种工业学校), wrote an article, *A Group of Unreasonable and Sordid Jerks of True Light* (不可理喻的真光杂志的一班肮脏东西).[153] In this article, Ruan directed his argument against Zhang. He accused Christians of interfering with their reforming cause and scientific research. Zhang himself was charged with insulting China. Zhang noted that Ruan attacked him by fragmenting his text, changing his words, and quoting out of context.[154]

After reading *A Special Issue of Criticising the Theories of the Anti-Christian Movement* and *A Sequel to Criticising the Theories of the Anti-Christian Movement*, a reader named Zhou Qijian[155] responded in his *The Doomsday of Christianity* (基督教的末日): "A group of incurably foolish believers who have received anti-Christian's blows still refuse to change themselves. On the contrary, they bark like insane dogs in *True Light*." Zhang showed that Zhou's own words should reach the opposite conclusion. Then by quoting history, Zhang tried to prove that Christians were not insane but instead very sober reformers.[156]

As for Zhang's argument against the anti-Christians, some people thought his argument was thorough and incisive. Some others, on the contrary, criticized Zhang for being unlike a preacher because he could only persuade through reasoning, but he could not move people into repentance through love.[157]

In 1924, a letter from Wuchang Buddhist Academy (武昌佛学院) to Zhang criticized him as being narrow-minded, foolish, subjective, and irrespective of the reality in his book *Biography of Sakyamuni*. As an attempt to save Zhang, two books authored by Zhang Chunyi (Zhang Zhongru) and

---

152. Ruan Xiaoxian (1897–1935) was a leader of the Communist Party of China in the 1920s.

153. Chunsheng Chen 陈春生, "Ruan Xiaoxian Who Called Others Sordid Jerks (骂人肮脏东西的阮啸仙)," in *Answering Attacks upon Christianity* 批评非基督教言论汇刊全编, ed. Yijing Zhang (Shanghai 上海: China Baptist Publication Society 中华浸会书局, 1927), 351–52.

154. Yijing Zhang 张亦镜, *Answering Attacks upon Christianity* 批评非基督教言论汇刊全编 (Shanghai 上海: China Baptist Publication Society 中华浸会书局, 1927), 340–42.

155. Zhou Qijian (1893–1928) was a leader of the Communist Party of China in the 1920s.

156. Zhang, *Answering Attacks upon Christianity*, 343–45.

157. Yijing Zhang 张亦镜, "A Critique of the Anti-Christian Movement (非宗教运动的批评)," *Chinese Christian Advocate* 兴华 21, no. 1 (1924): 23–37.

Nie Yuntai were mailed to Zhang. The writer of the letter called Zhang Chunyi and Nie Yuntai "the awakening of two cult believers to their senses" (邪教稍觉悟的人), and he called himself "an old friend of Christ." Zhang wondered if Zhang Chunyi and Nie Yuntai would consider their former Christian faith as a cult, and how orthodox an old friend of heterodoxy could be. He then jokingly added that, given the age of an old friend of Christ, he wondered if it was Buddha himself who wrote to scold him after being angered by his book.

In 1924, Li Chunfan[158] stated that a person proclaimed in *True Light* issue of July 1924 that the Anti-Christian Movement fussed and clamoured loudly in 1924. Yet, after Christians wrote polemics against them, they became as silent as cicadas in winter. Then Li announced with pride: "but now, to their surprise, we begin to publish (*Awakening*) *Weekly*. Cicadas in winter start to chirp and they chirp loudly. Facing our new activists, Christians would desperately write polemics again. However, we do not fear."[159] Li sent each new issue of *Awakening* (觉悟) to Zhang Yijing, and of course, he paid close attention to *True Light*.

From Christmas Day of 1925, *Anti-Christian Semi-Weekly* (反基督教半周刊) became a supplement to *Republican Daily* in Guangzhou. In the *Anti-Christian Semi-Weekly* on 25 January 1926, there was an article "A Letter from a Christian" with the author's name "Huang Zhongtian (黄忠天), a true Christian." Huang attacked Christianity vehemently and he called the undertakings of the church a betrayal of China, like Pei Zheng School, YMCA, and the faculty members and students at Lingnan University. He called the Chinese church the fake Chinese church.

In Huang's accusation list, Zhang Yijing was the second one. He accused Zhang of being a "top-notch player for the Church in China" (拥护中国教会健将) and "the number one running dog of a fake pastor" (某伪牧师头号走狗). He claimed he would list Zhang's wicked deeds in the future. In Huang's analysis, Zhang's leaving *True Light* to run *Da Guang Newspaper* or

---

158. Li Chunfan (or Ke Bainian, 1904–1985) was from Chaozhou (潮州) of Guangdong Province. He was a leading figure in the second stage of the Anti-Christian Movement. In 1924, Li formed the Anti-Christian Society (非基督教同盟) with other people and published many anti-Christian articles in *Juewu* or *Awakening* (觉悟). The yearly "Anti-Christian Week" was his masterpiece.

159. Chunfan Li 李春蕃, "The Cicada in Winter Started to Chirp Unexpectedly (寒蝉居然也鸣起来了)," *Awakening* 觉悟, 26 August 1924, 7.

The Great Light Newspaper in Hong Kong was his other strategy to deal with the Anti-Christian Movement.

Zhang felt happy about this attack[160] because he had a chance to be humbled after being praised so much by Christians.[161] He said:

> Mr. Huang's criticism of me still contains more approval than censure, which would add to rather than free me from the trouble of being famous. I wish that Mr. Huang and other anti-Christian gentlemen would express no approval at all when attacking me in the future, but rather devote all their efforts to publicize my misdeeds and sins. If you lack those details, you must be able to pray to God because you claimed to be a true Christian. I believe my misdeeds and sins cannot be hidden from God who must have a record of them all. If you pray earnestly and sincerely, God must gladly reveal them to you. Then Mr. Huang can publicize them, and the readers will stay away from me as if I were a scorpion or a snake. This way, my trouble (of being famous) can be solved.[162]

2.4.4 Zhang's Daily Schedule

Usually, Zhang had supper at 5 pm, and then he would go to sleep. He would wake up at 1 am. After washing and a simple snack, he would write till 7 am. After his morning quiet time, he would go to have morning tea (breakfast). Around 9 am, he would go back to the CBPS for talking business and to visit. Around 12 am, he would go home for lunch. After lunch, he would read manuscripts, and do editing and letter-writing till 5 pm.[163]

---

160. Yijing Zhang 张亦镜, "Comments on the Most Inferior Anti-Christian Work (按最下乘的反基督教文字)," *True Light* 真光 25, no. 7–8 (1926): 8.

161. Some people called him "Saint of Scholar" (文圣) or "Saint" (圣人).

162. Zhang, "Comments on the Most Inferior," 9.

163. Songshi Xu 徐松石, "In Memory of Mr. Zhang Yijing (忆张亦镜先生)," *True Light* 真光 40, no. 12 (1941): 3.

2.4.5 Zhang's Views on Some Works of the Church

2.4.5.1 *The Church Should Serve the Lord*

In 1929, a writer named Waiting (等候) wrote an article to criticize the church in Guilin of Guangxi Province for not serving Jesus. Zhang thought the situation of Guilin Church was a mirror of all other churches in China.[164] Zhang also humbled himself by saying that this article also exposed his problems and he himself should repent.

What does the service of the Lord entail? Zhang listed a few negative examples: Judas who betrayed Jesus, Peter when he denied the Lord three times, Thomas when he doubted, and the two disciples on their way to Emmaus. He believed that Judas, Peter, Thomas, and the other two disciples in the above situations were not capable of serving the Lord. Zhang thought if one's mind was filled with earthly wisdom and knowledge and had no room for the Holy Spirit, and worse still, if they did not have time for the Holy Spirit and could not recognize the works of the Holy Spirit, they would be like the negative examples given above. Then their works could not be called the service of the Lord, and they had no share in the works of the Lord. In fact, no one could really do the works of the Lord unless they were filled with the Holy Spirit.[165]

Zhang also humbled himself by saying that he himself should repent. He also called for repentance. He said that if they did not repent, the pastors, preachers, and the writers for the church publications would be like the traitor Judah, denying Peter, doubting Thomas, or the two disciples on their way to Emmaus. A church which shamed Jesus by crucifying him again could not serve the Lord, nor was it serving the Lord.

2.4.5.2 *Christian Writers Are Also Preachers*

To Zhang, there were oral and written forms of preaching while the Christian writer was a preacher by pen. Zhang once said that,

> The mission of preacher by pen was the same as the mission of pastors and preachers. How a pastor and a preacher will prepare a sermon, so will a preacher by pen. A pastor or preacher is to make people know Jesus and repent, so does a preacher by pen.

---

164. Yijing Zhang 张亦镜, "Introducing to a Sharp Criticism of the Church (介绍一篇针针见血的鍼砭教会文字)," *True Light* 真光 28, no. 5 (1929): 31–32.

165. Zhang, 31–32.

If a pastor or a preacher did not take this as his mission, his work would be of no effect and he was not qualified to be a pastor or a preacher. This applies to a preacher by pen.[166]

Thus, Zhang viewed a Christian writer as another kind of preacher and that is also how he viewed himself – a preacher.

In Zhang's understanding, preaching embodied *jili liren, jida daren* (A Confucian practice which says if one wants to develop himself, he should develop others too; if one wants to build himself up, he should build up others too. 己立立人, 己达达人 《雍也》). For him, real preaching meant preaching the gospel of Jesus with the power of the Holy Spirit for the purpose that the listeners would be moved to repentance.[167]

A preacher should have a close relationship with Jesus. Preaching was to make people repent and understand how Jesus died for the sin of human beings. In other words, preaching was to draw people to Jesus. If this was not taken as one's purpose, they were not fit to be a preacher, neither in the oral or written form. The effect of preaching depended on daily feeding on the Bible and being filled with the Holy Spirit. No one could preach effectively if they just took the Bible as a reference book and looked for a couple of verses for decoration of their speech or writing, if they did not even have one wholehearted prayer in a whole year, and if being spiritual was only a lip service without real meaning in their life. Therefore, for a preacher, Bible reading, praying, and having a rebirth in the Holy Spirit were more important than breathing, food, and drink. Besides, Zhang wished to see a preacher relying on the Holy Spirit, and with good education, especially in Chinese learning (国学).[168]

Seeing a tendency of becoming more and more academic in preaching, he emphasized the priority of Jesus over academics in preaching. In preaching, the arts, literature, and academics could be quoted only for the purpose of supporting the way of Jesus. If a person focused on the arts, literature, and academics instead of Jesus, he was a subject to them instead of Jesus.[169]

---

166. Jiang, "Works of Mr. Zhang Yijing," 12–13.

167. Yijing Zhang 张亦镜, "My View on Preaching through Writing (我之文字布道观)," *True Light* 真光 27, no. 2–3 (1928): 77.

168. Yijing Zhang 张亦镜, "Attached Comments on a Few Answers to Mr. Yijing (附识: 答亦镜先生几句话)," *True Light* 真光 23, no. 7 (1924): 64.

169. Zhang, "My View on Preaching," 78.

Christianity in China before 1930 and Zhang Yijing's Life

Feeling that some preachers did not balance well between being a preacher and a scholar, Zhang drew a clear dividing line between two kinds of preachers. He said:

> If any Christian organization which an individual worked for did not focus on spreading the Gospel of Jesus' salvation, and if that individual himself also did not value a faith based on the Bible, but only took the position of a detached observer and the attitude of a scholar and made objective or neutral criticism, then this person and I were different in purpose, goals, and interests.[170]

In Zhang's view, scholars would usually promote and boast of having a detached atttitude and a neutral position in order to maintain an objective appearance; however, this can weaken their commitment to Christ. In other words, the significance of their Christian identity is lessened.

Seeing many Christians possessing more enthusiasm for the undertakings of the church than preaching God's word, Zhang reminded that Christians should preach salvation rather than preach religion (传教). With the Social Gospel movement in mind, he said:

> Indeed, if we only talked about some doctrines and filled the pages with the ideas of constructing the heavenly kingdom on earth and reforming society, but if we did not faithfully explain the significance of Christ's coming and the reason why people need Him according to the Bible, we were wasting paper even if we could give a long and persuasive speech in words. We couldn't lead people to know Christ, nor would people run to Christ and kneel before Him to confess and beg for salvation. This was a phenomenon of the blind leading the blind.[171]

Here, Zhang was just trying to draw Christians' attention back to the core of the church – Jesus's salvation. As mentioned above, he was very supportive of the engaging attitude of the Social Gospel movement.

Once again, Zhang touched upon the issue of identity, though he did not use this modern term. According to him, preachers must be committed to

---

170. Zhang, 79.
171. Yijing Zhang 张亦镜, "Preface: Being Sick (卷头语: 记者自去年六月至今,一病八月)," *True Light* 真光 30, no. 2 (1931): 1.

their identity as endowed by God. Preachers should view themselves as directly commissioned by God rather than people employed for a salary. They should ask themselves whether their work has pleased God and how they could serve the Lord with all their learning without winning glory for themselves. If preachers, in both the oral and written forms, only took preaching as a tool for making a living or as a chance to demonstrate their strengths, they could not lead people to Jesus; on the contrary, they might even cause other Christians to stumble in their faith.[172]

On the one hand, Zhang encouraged preachers to be loyal to their calling; on the other hand, he also urged their employers to take a good care of them. He once said when Christian publication agencies were looking for employees, they should look for people who really had the interest in devoting their life to Christian writing and had a sense of responsibility. A person with good learning and good writing skills might not be a good Christian writer. Once devoted people are employed, they should be given freedom, flexibility, and good treatment.[173]

To sum up, in Zhang's mind, a Chinese Christian writer's mission is to lead the readers into repentance and accepting Christ. To achieve this, such a writer must be reborn, committed, responsible, obedient to the Holy Spirit, and well-learned, especially in Chinese learning. Once in employment, they should be trusted and well retained.

2.4.5.3 Zhang's Expectations of True Light

Zhang said that *True Light*'s standard was that every article should truly aim at witnessing to Jesus; namely that, every article should be in accordance with the Bible and God's will.[174]

Zhang gave a further explanation. *True Light* was a tool for preaching Jesus. *True Light* should be viewed as a lectern or a church. Each issue was an evangelization conference. The authors were like pastors and preachers who took turns to give a sermon. Of course, each preacher and pastor should be knowledgeable across many fields. The rich knowledge was like a guest while

---

172. Zhang, "Comments on a Few Answers," 64; Zhang, "My View on Preaching," 78.
173. Xu, "In Memory of Mr. Zhang," 3.
174. Yijing Zhang 张亦镜, "Zhang Yijing's Explanation about Why He Did Not Write during the Last Six Months (张亦镜启事:(一)说明半年来不暇作文与不暇作覆书之由)," *True Light* 真光 27, no. 1 (1928): 1.

Jesus was the master. A presumptuous guest should not be allowed to usurp the host's role (不可喧宾夺主).

Zhang worried about the focus and direction of the articles published in *True Light* since 1928. In this year, he transferred the responsibility of the editor to Liu Weihan (刘维汉) so that he could focus his time and emotional energy on writing. In 1929, Zhang clarified again that *True Light* was to lead people to Christ.[175] The pastors led people to Christ through speaking while the writers of the newspaper of the church led people to Christ through writing. The writers should possess all knowledge and be aware of the lifestyles of all kinds of people, but *True Light* was not a place to speak of such knowledge but a place to introduce Christ through such knowledge.

Zhang openly admitted that *Christians* (基督徒报) and *Revival* (复兴报), *The Light of the Spirit* (灵光报) in Nanjing and *Preaching Magazine* (布道杂志) in Hunan were more focused on evangelizing, spreading the gospel, and leading people to Christ than *True Light*. The *Journal of the Church* (会刊) of the Guilin Independent Christian Church (桂林自立基督教会) was also good. Compared with them, *True Light* was too miscellaneous.[176]

Meanwhile, he also confessed that his work at *True Light* was in fact driven by men instead of by Christ. He said that if a person could be like Christ, he would certainly not be driven by men.[177] Here he was confessing he was not like Christ.

In 1930, it seemed that Zhang had to resume the editor's responsibility. In 1931, Zhang highly recommended Yang Jiangxiong's (杨剑雄) article and viewed Yang's opinions of concentrating on Jesus's salvation and devoting to the Bible in accordance with the mission of *True Light*.[178] Thus, Yang's opinion could be taken as the standard of *True Light*. Zhang wished all the staff of *True Light* and the contributors to remember Yang's opinion in this article so that their writings could be consistent with the Bible and God's will. As a result, the readers could be led to Jesus's salvation.

---

175. Yijing Zhang 张亦镜, "Foreword: The Standing Position of the Staff of True Light (卷头语: 我们办真光的人所站的地位)," *True Light* 真光 28, no. 5 (1929): 1.

176. Yijing Zhang 张亦镜, "True Light Was One of the Best Companies for Mr. Tang Yuanfang (唐元放先生称真光为他最好的伴侣之一函 附)," *True Light* 真光 28, no. 6 (1928): 77.

177. Zhang, "Introducing to a Sharp Criticism," 31.

178. Zhang, "Preface: Being Sick," 1.

2.4.5.4 Chinese Church's Independence and Indigenization

In the 1920s, the word "church" in Chinese often meant all the undertakings established by Christianity like Christian churches, Christian schools, and Christian hospitals. Most of them were founded and managed by Western denominations and very few were independently established and run by Chinese.

The background of the Chinese seeking independence and indigenization was their desperation to avoid the charges from anti-Christian people concerning such things as the churches in China having foreign names, rites, rules and features, raising foreign flags, and members viewing themselves as citizens of foreign countries. This background made some people in the church advocate for an indigenized church or a church with Chinese features.[179]

As early as 1907, Zhang advocated the independence of the church.[180] However, it was not until the 1920s that the majority of Chinese Christians felt the urge to become indigenized and independent from the denominations under the nationalistic charges of Christianity being "the vanguard of imperialism,"[181] "cultural aggression," "foreigners' slaves," and "running dogs."[182]

In Zhang's understanding, such accusations had resulted from a misimpression existing among the Chinese masses which was caused by two factors: the financial dependence of Chinese Christians on the denominations[183] and the connection between the Westerners and imperialism and the unequal treaties.[184]

---

179. T. C. Chao 赵紫宸, "My Opinions on Creating Chinese Christian Churches (我对于创造中国基督教会的几个意见)," *True Light* 真光 26, no. 6 (1927): 2; Yijing Zhang, "My View on the Independence of the Church (我之自立教会观)," *True Light* 真光 27, no. 4 (1928): 19.

180. Wen Kai Zhang 张文开, "Author's Preface: A Special Issue for Ten Denominations to Commemorate Robert Morrison (自序:本期报之专载羊城十大公会纪念马礼逊事也)," *True Light* 真光 6, no. 8 (1907): 7.

181. Chunfan Li 李春蕃, "The Mission and Imperialism (传教与帝国主义)," *Awakening* 觉悟, 19 August 1924, 6.

182. Yijing Zhang 张亦镜, "The Current Trends of Thought in the Church (今日教会思潮之趋势)," *True Light* 真光 26, no. 7-8-9 (1927): 93.

183. Yijing Zhang 张亦镜, "The Solution of Jesus and Paul to the Economic Problem of Preachers (耶苏与保罗之传道的经济问题解决法)," *True Light* 真光 28, no. 8 (1929): 1–2.

184. Yijing Zhang 张亦镜, "Christianity and Imperialism (基督教与帝国主义)," *True Light* 真光 26, no. 4 (1927): 28.

Christianity in China before 1930 and Zhang Yijing's Life

In order to correct the misimpression, the first step in Zhang's understanding was that independence should happen before indigenization and that financial independence was essential. Zhang said,

> Independence in my view is that Chinese should take the financial responsibility completely. It is an inappropriate, unreasonable, and robbing behaviour when Chinese ask the mission organisations for a transfer of their money, properties, and ministries to Chinese.[185]

According to Zhang, when the Chinese church strove for a financial independence, the financial burden on Western denominations could be lessened and Chinese members would have more care for the church because they put in their money. Foreigners should not be in charge and they could only be employees or volunteers. Otherwise, Chinese members would be like agents and the development of the church would be hindered. Even if the church witnessed growth, it was due to Westerners' finance rather than to the true Christian spirit. It was a shame on Chinese members.[186]

For a quick comparison, Zhao Zichen[187] believed that Chinese Christians should control the finance and management independently, but mission organizations should continually provide the finance.[188] If the missions stopped providing funds, there would be only two possible negative results: (1) the church would go bankrupt because the Chinese were perfunctory and had

---

185. Zhang, "Solution of Jesus and Paul," 8.

186. Yijing Zhang 张亦镜, "After a Trip to Suzhou City (去苏州一趟回来)," *True Light* 真光 28, no. 5 (1929): 64.

187. Dr. T. C. Chao (1888–1979) was one of the most influential theologians in China. In 1903, Chao attended the Middle School attached to Soochow University (东吴大学) which was founded by the Methodist Episcopal Church, South (美南监理会). In 1907, he was baptized under the influence of John Mott and David L. Anderson (孙乐文, president of the Soochow University). In 1910, he graduated from Soochow University with a BA degree. He obtained a Master's degree from Vanderbilt University in 1916 and a Bachelor's degree in Divinity in 1917. In 1927, he received his PhD degree from Soochow University. During the 1920s, Chao was a theology professor in Yenching University and the editor of *Truth and Life* (真理与生命) and *Wen She* (文社). According to Tang, Chao's theology is ethical theology. Xiaofeng Tang 唐晓峰, "T. C. Chao's Ethical Theology 赵紫宸伦理的神学," in *Christianity in China: The Wisdom of Contextualization (Vol. 1 and 2) 基督教在中国-处境化的智慧-(上. 下册)*, ed. Shilin Zhao and Qi Duan (Beijing 北京: Religion and Culture Press 宗教文化出版社, 2009), 39.

188. T. C. Chao 赵紫宸, "Discussion over the Indigenization of the Church (本色教会的商榷)," *Youth Progress* 青年进步 76 (1924): 9, 11–12.

no serious ambition; and (2) Chinese Christians would establish their own churches without a bond with the missions.[189]

According to Zhang, the second measure to correct the Chinese misimpression was that the missionaries should give their support to China's fight against imperialism and unequal treaties.[190] If so, there would be no grounds for associating Christianity with imperialism and treaties. And then the only accusation left for the anti-Christian people would be that Jesus's salvation was a superstition. At that point, it would not be absolutely necessary to become independent from the missions.[191]

Concerning indigenization, Zhang opposed two extreme and opposing ideas: to Europeanize the church totally, which was held by some Christians with Western education,[192] or to sinicize the church by adopting all means including the features of Buddhism and Taoism to make the church look Chinese. Zhang did not specify the identity of the advocates of this.[193] In his opinion, the true essence of indigenization was to be in accordance with the Bible since neither China's nor Western characteristics were those of Christianity.[194]

At this point, Zhang's view on the indigenization of the church was different from some other Christian leaders, such as Zhao Zichen. To Zhao, indigenization meant the combination of the truth from both Christianity and Chinese culture and ideologies. The indigenized leadership was the most important part since they were the ones that mastered Chinese culture and ideologies, but mission organizations failed in cultivating Chinese Christian leadership. He believed that everything in Chinese churches should be in accordance with Chinese custom and psychology. There should be no awkward feelings and the theology should be freely nurtured by Chinese thought.[195]

Zhang disagreed with Zhao's views on indigenization. He used the example of Pei Zheng School which was independently founded and run by Chinese

---

189. Chao, "My Opinions on Creating Chinese," 4.
190. Zhang, "Christianity and Imperialism," 28.
191. Zhang, 28.
192. Yijing Zhang 张亦镜, "Discussion with Mr. Wei Qing over the Indigenization of the Church (与唯情先生论本色教会)," *True Light* 真光 25, no. 7–8 (1926): 57.
193. Zhang, 54.
194. Zhang, "Current Trends of Thought," 95.
195. Chao, "Discussion over the Indigenization," 9, 11–12.

to prove that faithfully following the guidance of the Holy Spirit was more important for Chinese leadership than deep learning in Chinese culture and ideologies. Nor did he think the missionaries had such a duty to cultivate Chinese leadership. And the Bible and worship songs should be translated faithfully and the translation should also be seen as Chinese literature.[196]

In Zhang's sight, even though Christian doctrines might seem awkward at present, in the future, its strangeness would become familiar and normal to the Chinese.[197] So long as no biblical teachings were violated, Chinese psychology and customs could be adopted. The uncomfortable feelings Chinese felt with some biblical teachings were just temporary. Zhang's translation of baptism demonstrates his accommodation of Chinese culture. Originally, he created a new Chinese character *bo* (液) for baptism. However, he later gave up his invention and insisted on *fu* (被) because in his research, he had found that the Nestorians had not only existed in China a long time ago, (unknown to most Chinese of the time), but had also tried to indigenize by translating baptism as *fu* (被), which he believed would remind people of the long history of the gospel in China and hopefully make Christianity as welcome as Buddhism.[198]

Zhang differentiated between two concepts:[199] (1) "*bense jiaohui* or indigenized Church (本色教会)" which accepts the local characteristics on the condition that the Bible would not be violated; and (2) "Sinicized Church (中国化教会)," which could include all traditions and habits in China. This would produce "a church with superficial features or *mose jiaohui* (末色教会)."[200] He firmly believed that the elite soldiers of Christ could only approve of Christianizing China rather than sinicizing Christianity.[201]

---

196. Yijing Zhang 张亦镜, "Mr. T. C. Chao's 'Discussion over the Indigenization of the Church' and My Thoughts (赵紫宸先生的 '本色教会的商榷' 和我的感想)," *True Light* 真光 23, no. 11 (1924): 24, 30, 32.

197. Zhang, "Discussion with Mr. Wei Qing," 54–55.

198. Jue Wang, "Neither Xi (洗) Nor Jin (浸), But Fu (被): Zhang Yijing's (张亦镜) Translation of Baptism, Viewed from the Perspective of Identity," *Transformation: An International Journal of Holistic Mission Studies* 34, no. 3 (2016): 214–22, https://doi.org/10.1177/0265378816667276.

199. Yijing Zhang 张亦镜, "Indigenized Church (萍庐笔记: 本色教会)," *True Light* 真光 24, no. 3 (1925): 78.

200. Zhang, "Discussion with Mr. Wei Qing," 56.

201. Zhang, 58.

He insisted that indigenization should be completely based on the Bible rather than people's feelings and the features of a certain country's traditions and customs. Indigenization based on the Bible would lead to "a church with the original feature or *bense jiaohui* or indigenized church." By contrast, indigenization based on people's feelings and a certain country's traditions and customs would produce "a church with superficial features or *mose jiaohui* (末色教会)" which was being advocated by the Chinese. *Mose jiaohui* was thousands of miles far away from *bense jiaohui* which was causing unfavourable feelings.[202]

2.4.5.5 Zhang's View on Christian Education

Zhang was a board member for a Chinese Christian school for over ten years. He agreed that the Christian schools should be guided by the governmental educational bureau. Zhang agreed with Cai Yuanpei that education should include education on patriotism, practical living skills, morality, and aesthetics.[203] In his opinion, a public school should not teach only one religion, but Christian schools should be free to teach only Christianity.[204]

In the 1920s, the Republic of China stipulated in "The Article Five in the Regulations for the Private School (私立学校规章第五条)" that the private schools established by the religious organization should not make the religious subject compulsory, do religious publicity on campus or force students to attend religious rites.

Zhang felt it too harsh.[205] If so, it would be better for Christian schools to stop functioning. He believed that the Christian schools should be granted the freedom of religious education and they should not be labelled as being superstitious or contradictory to patriotism.[206]

Zhang said that the freedom of faith included the parents' right to decide on their children's religious education. The Christian schools should be only

---

202. Zhang, 53–56.

203. Yijing Zhang 张亦镜, "Correcting Errors in Dr. Chen Huanzhang's Speech on Confucianism (读陈焕章博士孔教讲义辩谬)," in *(1928), A Quarter of a Century of True Light, Selected* 真光丛刊, Part 2: The Gospel Discussed and Explained 辩道文, ed. Yijing Zhang (Shanghai 上海: China Baptist Publication Society 中华浸会书局, 1914), 121.

204. Zhang, "Correcting Errors in Dr. Chen," 119.

205. Yijing Zhang 张亦镜, "The Christian School Interfered with by the Government (在政府干涉下之教会学校)," *True Light* 真光 28, no. 5 (1929): 14.

206. Zhang, "Christian School Interfered," 12.

for the children from Christian families. They should not enrol students from non-Christian families. If students from a non-Christian family wanted to study in Christian schools, their parents should agree to Christian education and sign an agreement in writing.[207]

The Article Five in the Regulations for Educational Enterprise Founded by the Religious Organisations of the Education Ministry (教育部宗教团体兴办教育事业办法第五条, 22 April 1929) said that if religious organizations wanted to recruit students for spreading their religion, they should not adopt the names used by the national educational system for their schools at any stage. For example, a church or a mission organization could not include "the primary school" or "the middle school" into the names of their educational undertakings.

Facing the governmental restrictions on Christian schools, Zhang believed that Christian schools should not expect recognition by the national educational system. According to his view, Christian organisations in China could set up small-sized informal and unofficial schools for their own church members without a formal school name. The system and facility within their schools could be the same as formal schools. It could have all subjects in addition to religious education and "The Three People's Principles." All students must come from Christian families. The school size being small, the cost would be cheaper and it would not need financial help from Western denominations.[208]

Such kinds of school did not expect recognition and employment from the government. The students could go to study abroad if their families had the means; otherwise, the students could stay in China to spread the gospel, the Three People's Principles, and Christian education in the form of informal schools. Since the students had no hope in promotion in the social ladder, their attention would not be distracted so that it would be quicker to popularize the gospel, Christian education, and the Three People's Principles. In Zhang's view, this was the best and the most needed way. This was much more important than a formal school name.

---

207. Yijing Zhang 张亦镜, "Comments: The Lutheran Church in Shekou Seeking Advice on Religious Education (溉口信义会关于宗教教育之广征意见函附识)," *True Light* 真光 28, no. 2 (1929): 83.

208. Zhang, "Christian School Interfered," 15.

However, a Christian named Hou Shuxian[209] thought Zhang's way might lead the students into persecution. In Zhang's reply, those who entered an "unofficial Christian school" for Christian education valued the way of life in Christ more than the honour, or the shame, and persecutions from men. They were ready to be like the martyrs in the Roman Empire during the first three centuries and those of the Boxer Rebellion.[210]

Nevertheless, Zhang grieved that the time left for religious education would be only one hour each day or every two days. By contrast, ten years ago, students had "been forced"[211] to spend one-third of school time on religious education.[212]

Hou Shuxian also believed that Western missionaries had no love for Christ and Chinese Christians if they did not help financially with their children's education. Zhang refuted Hou.[213] For Zhang, it was always shameful to the church to rely on Western funds for founding schools, which was a waiver of responsibility if not a loss of sovereignty. Zhang felt ashamed of it.[214] As mentioned in the section above, Zhao Zichen insisted that it was the moral responsibility of the church in the West to fund the churches in China to keep them from disappearing.[215]

Zhang has been advocating that the Chinese should take up the financial responsibility for the Christian schools.[216] He found that when the government endeavoured to take back the educational sovereignty, it actually just asked for a Chinese head. The finance was still the responsibility of Westerners. Zhang challenged that the government should take up the financial responsibility for the Christian schools and the salaries of Westerner and Chinese staff; otherwise, the government should not take back the educational sovereignty.

---

209. Hou Shuxian (侯述先) was an educator and a historian. He was the co-author of *The 50th Anniversary of the Baptist Church in Shandong Province* (山东浸信会50周年纪念集).

210. Yijing Zhang 张亦镜, "Answering Mr. Hou Shuxian (答候述先先生)," *True Light* 真光 28, no. 6 (1929): 64.

211. One accusation against Christian schools was that students were forced to have religious education. Zhang uses this phrase ironically.

212. Zhang, "Answering Mr. Hou Shuxian," 64.

213. Zhang, 65.

214. Zhang, 64; Zhang, "Christian School Interfered," 16.

215. Chao, "My Opinions on Creating Chinese," 4.

216. Zhang, "Christian School Interfered," 16.

In spite of this challenge, Zhang did not really want money from the government because he worried about political interference. In his opinion, after Chinese Christians were given Christian schools by Western missionaries, they should stick to the principle of separation of the church from politics. In other words, they should allow no political interference with the religious education in Christian schools which had their own specific and pure goal (developing Christian faith). In order to achieve this independence, Christian schools should accept no financial help from the government at all. If so, then they could keep Christian schools independent.[217]

Christian schools in China were founded by the church from the very beginning. Usually, it was the Westerners who administered them except for the independent Chinese ones like Pei Zheng School. According to Zhang's observation, they took in the children from non-Christian families without limit and charged a high tuition fee. They finally became exclusive schools while children of poor Christian families were kept out. To Zhang, this was a grave sin on the part of the Christian schools.[218] In his understanding, Christian schools should first serve children from Christian families, even though they were poor. Nevertheless, for the sake of making money, Christian schools kept out poor Christians' children. He believed that Christian schools should not include any student without fulfilling certain criteria.

Zhang criticized the current Christian schools for not checking the speakers' religious background when they invited them to give a speech.[219] He also criticized the Christian universities for being too liberal which led to their secular atmosphere.[220]

According to Zhang, Christian education was such an education that the Christian teachers of every subject should manifest the truth of Christ with the spirit of Christ.[221] Their goal was to develop students' Christian life, and they should strive for such an effect. A Bible teacher should be a role model,

---

217. Yijing Zhang 张亦镜, "Comments on 'My View on Reclaiming the Right to Education' (按: 收回教育权的我见)," *True Light* 真光 23, no. 12 (1924): 8.

218. Zhang, "Christian School Interfered," 18.

219. Zhang, "Answering Mr. Hou Shuxian," 63.

220. Yijing Zhang 张亦镜, "Christian Schools in Belgium (比利时的教会学校)," *True Light* 真光 27, no. 4 (1928): 69.

221. Yijing Zhang 张亦镜, "The Significance of Religious Education (宗教教育的意义)," *True Light* 真光 28, no. 6 (1929): 92.

and be good at cultivating students' interest in Bible study. Otherwise, it was a failure and was not a Christian education. The leaders of Christian education should be cautious in choosing teachers of each subject. The standards for the Bible teacher should not be compromised at all.

There is an anecdote. Once a Chinese teacher in a Christian school[222] claimed that he had had three stages in his spiritual journey: (1) superstition; (2) waking up; and (3) realizing that Christianity was fake. Under his influence, some students followed his example and gradually stopped attending worship.

Zhang renamed the three stages of the Chinese teacher as (1) seeing light by accident; (2) retreating into darkness; and (3) being willing to end in hell.[223] Another member of the staff of the Christian school threatened to resign if the school did not fire the Chinese teacher. Zhang said that this person was following Jesus's example of cleaning the temple.

2.4.5.6 *Zhang's View on Preachers' Finance*

Chinese Protestant pastors and preachers came into being with the help of Western missionaries who founded local Bible schools and often offered free meals to their students. The graduates could become preachers who were often paid by Western mission organisations, at least till the 1920s.

Receiving payment from the mission organisations led to a humiliating nickname "rice Christian" given by non-Christians. Besides this humiliation, Zhang noticed other negative effects.

First, Chinese preachers also took this as a natural way and interpreted it as the application of "the worker deserves his wages"[224] and some people would first bargain with Westerners for a satisfactory salary before agreeing to be a pastor or a preacher.[225]

In Zhang's opinion, when such kind of people became pastors and preachers, their sermons usually were superficial and lacked spiritual nourishment. They spent the majority of the sermon time on science, philosophy, sociology, or the current news without much about Christ. Even if they talked about

---

222. Pei Zheng School.

223. Yijing Zhang 张亦镜, "Three Stages (三个时期)," *True Light* 真光 17, no. 12 (1928): 93–94.

224. Zhang, "Solution of Jesus and Paul," 2–3.

225. Zhang, 4–5.

Christ, they mainly focused on the "ism" and characters of Christ without touching on his cross, the key point between God and man. Even when they occasionally and briefly touched on the cross, their words were unable to move listeners to repentance and to love Jesus because their mind was on money. The listeners could immediately tell that the speakers themselves were not convinced of this. Such kinds of people would finally leave Christian organisations for another business with a better payment unless they lacked suitable skills for any other business.

There were famous pastors and preachers who had a deep love for Christ and were very powerful in preaching, but people scoffed at them when they learned that the famous pastors and preachers were receiving a high salary from Westerners.

Second, many Chinese Christian leaders depended more on money than God.[226] A large number received high salaries from the mission organisations. They believed that becoming independent needed a big sum of money and it was hard to raise money among the Chinese. As a result, they either feared becoming independent or they insisted on the mission organisations' continuing provision of the fund when they talked about indigenization and independence.

Third, few people had roots in the rural area.[227] Fourth, the majority of Chinese Christians were believers in money. They were active only when they could obtain money from the church; otherwise, they would become passive to the Lord's works.[228] Many people with good ministry, character, and education actually were working for the money of Western denominations.[229]

In Zhang's view, economics was a theory of economists of Western capitalism.[230] The doctrines of Christianity were more truthful than all the other theories. So evangelization and preaching should not follow other theories at the cost of the Bible.

---

226. Zhang, 4.
227. Zhang, 5.
228. Yijing Zhang 张亦镜, "The Fourth Part in My Answer to Jiang Shuai Concerning Tough Questions from Anti-Christians and Passive People (答姜树蔼君来函所列反教及消极两种人的辩难(四)," *True Light* 真光 29, no. 5 (1930): 67.
229. Zhang, "Solution of Jesus and Paul," 5.
230. Zhang, 6.

Zhang said that the preachers' economic problems were how the preachers and their wives could have decent meals and clothes and how their children could have a decent education, which actually was a result of Western money.[231]

If a person had genuine sympathy for the people living in darkness, they would take the initiative to raise money for theological training. After this, they would return to their hometown to preach immediately. There should be no problem for "self" of today to be the same "self" of yesterday.

Then Zhang asked questions. Why were decent clothes needed? Why must clothes be better than the time before theological education? Why must the preacher and his wife be addressed with a title instead of being plain folks as before?

Zhang believed that such were worldly concerns. He advocated just being content with things as they were. For example, if a preacher lacked financial capability, he could pass his knowledge on to his children. As a result, his children could help him with preaching, which would serve as further evidence of his devotion. By this, the local people would accept his preaching more easily. This was much better than another situation in which his children sought an official position or money after receiving a worldly education. If a person learned how to be content, an economic problem would not necessarily happen after having received a theological education because he could make a living as before.

So Zhang concluded that the one who had an economic problem after theological education very often was a person who aimed at becoming distinguished rather than spreading the gospel. Such people were not spiritual or religious at all.

According to Zhang's interpretation, when Jesus and Paul talked about workers deserving their wages in Matthew, they both meant that the workers of God should receive their pay from the people they shepherded instead of from the one who sent them.[232] Paul even supported himself by working as a tent-maker. Therefore, Zhang insisted:

> According to the solution of Jesus and Paul, all missionaries should immediately stop their denominations raising any money for China and stop giving salaries to their Chinese staff.

---

231. Zhang, 6–7.
232. Zhang, 1.

According to Jesus' and Paul's principle of "the worker deserves his wages," they should receive support from those who received the message of the Gospel from them. This is a good way to solve the economic problem of the preachers.[233]

Zhang said that this was the way of Jesus and Paul. To obey or not was another question.

Zhang encouraged Chinese Christians to give money to preachers and pastors.[234] It would be perfect if Chinese Christians could support Western missionaries as well; if so, the church could become independent immediately.

Zhang offered a touchstone of true disciples of Christ and whole-hearted servants of God instead of money: they endeavoured to seek independence of the churches, hospitals, and schools, they would willingly receive low payment from Chinese independent organizations though being a co-worker of Westerners, and they could turn down offers from all Western organisations and take the hospitality of the local people as payment for evangelizing trips.[235]

Zhang has anticipated the people's challenge of why he received payment from *True Light*, an organisation of Westerners,[236] so he clarified that his purpose was mainly to solve his own economic problem, rather than accusing a certain kind of church, pastor, or preacher.[237]

Zhang viewed himself as a preacher and believed that it was wrong for him to receive payment from Westerners. He himself had already put his belief into practice by forcing *True Light* to suspend his pay. For the first time, he lived on selling his calligraphy during a half year's suspension, which was around 1925. Then *True Light* was forced to a stop by the political situation, and he quit his job (to be able to criticize the imperialist).[238] After his return to *True Light*, he had been trying to support himself although he was not able to completely achieve it. At the moment of writing on this topic in 1929, he was going to have his pay completely suspended, just as he did previously.

---

233. Zhang, 7.
234. Zhang, 8.
235. Zhang, 4.
236. Zhang, 9.
237. Zhang, 9.
238. This happened after the Shaji Massacre in Guangzhou on 23 June 1925 (沙基惨案).

Zhang did not exclude himself when he encouraged all church workers to live a thrifty life. In 1928, he encouraged all those who were hired by the church to wear clothes made of homespun cloth instead of silk. If they could not be content with a simple life, their high living standard would make them unwilling to be financially independent of the mission organisations. He confessed he sometimes wore silk clothes although he belonged to the homespun cloth class. He determined he would only use homespun cloth after his silk clothes were worn out.[239]

Zhang was not rich, but he had a firm resistance to the temptation of money. As mentioned above, once someone won a lot of money from the lottery bought in his name. When he gave a share to Zhang, Zhang refused it because he took it as a kind of gambling. He refused offers with a better pay and higher social status many times.

Though Zhang was not rich, he was generous. He helped his younger brothers and sisters to receive education. He also paid for some of his nephews and nieces' education. However, after giving a generous donation for the new building of the CBPS in Shanghai,[240] he had no money to pay for his nieces' tuition.[241] As a result, he had to write to Mr. Ou and Mr. Tang, the principals of Pei Dao Girls School (培道女中), to see if his two nieces' tuition fees could be delayed, reduced, or even freed.[242]

After reading Zhang's *The Solution of Jesus and Paul to the Economic Problem of Preachers* (耶苏与保罗之传道的经济问题解决法), Chen Chonggui[243] called Zhang's view on finance "purely biblical," and went to visit

---

239. Yijing Zhang 张亦镜, "Clothes Made of Homespun Cloth (布衣)," *True Light* 真光 27, no. 4 (1928): 94.

240. His donation was equivalent to his one-year salary. Zhang asked for a low salary that was around one fourth or one fifth of the pay given to other Chinese Christians employed by Christian organizations, who obtained a Master's degree or a PhD degree. He asked for suspension of his pay by *True Light* and sold his calligraphy to support himself, and also because *True Light* kept losing money.

241. Jianbang Jiang 姜建邦, "Visiting the Family Members of Zhang Yijing (访问张亦镜先生的家属)," *The Voice of Evangelization* 宣道声 8, no. 4 (1948): 32.

242. Jiang, "Visiting the Family Members," 32.

243. Chen Chonggui (or Marcus Cheng, 陈崇桂, 1884–1964) was a famous Christian leader and theological educator who, among other things, was a delegate to the Jerusalem World Missionary Conference of 1928 and the president of Chongqing Theological Seminary (重庆神学院) which was a co-operative project between Chen and the China Inland Mission from 1943 to 1953. He received his education in Wesleyan College Wuchang (Powen Middle School 武昌博文书院) which was founded by W. T. A. Barber (1858–1945), a missionary of

Zhang in Shanghai twice. Regretfully, he failed to find Zhang, which Zhang took as his own misfortune. Chen admired Zhang for his integrity when he found Zhang had been applying his belief into his own life by refusing salary from *True Light*. He wanted Zhang to contribute more articles to *Evangelism Magazine* (布道杂志), which was being run by Chen.

Zhang answered to Chen that it was his confession. He felt unworthy of being Chen's student. Zhang highly respected *The Light of the Spirit* (灵光报) and *Preaching Magazine* and called them purely biblical. Zhang wished all his words were from God and then people might be moved to loving God and to becoming people of the heavenly kingdom.[244]

2.4.6 Zhang and Missionaries
2.4.6.1 Zhang and His Missionary Co-workers of True Light

During Zhang's service in *True Light*, he worked with Dr. Robert E. Chambers, John Lake (力约翰), and Pastor Jacob Speicher. They finally reached mutual trust after overcoming hindrances caused by different languages and cultures. In 1921, *True Light* was fully entrusted to Zhang, a proposal agreed by all the directors of missions of the Southern Baptist Convention in China.

In 1912, Zhang felt that both his traditional and new learning were not sufficient enough for the mission of writing. He especially felt a need for mastering the Chinese classics and so asked for two months' leave, but actually, he was planning to leave for good. Zhang took this as the most serious lying sin he had committed. Since he did not return as agreed, Dr. Chambers sent many letters to urge him to come back. Finally, Chambers even planned to visit Zhang's hometown in Guangxi Province himself. Zhang was compelled to return.

In 1927, Zhang said during the twenty years he served in *True Light*, Dr. Chambers went back to the US three times. During his first absence, he entrusted *True Light* to Rev. John Lake. Zhang had a good relationship with John Lake. Pastor J. Speicher also served as a substitute during one absence of Dr. Chambers and he had a similar fondness for Zhang.[245]

---

the Wesleyan Methodist Church. Chen later received his college education at Wheaton College (惠顿大学) in the US.

244. Yijing Zhang 张亦镜, "A Letter from Mr. Chen Chonggui (陈崇桂先生来函)," *True Light* 真光 28, no. 11 (1929): 88–89.

245. Zhang, "Last Twenty-Five Years," 3–5.

Among his friends, Zhang's friendship with Dr. Chambers was the longest for they were intimate confidants. Mrs. Catherine Coffee Chambers, the wife of Dr. Chambers, called him the chief Chinese colleague, friend, and companion of Dr. Chambers.[246]

Mrs. Chambers remembered that once in 1911, Zhang arrived with some manuscripts at the Chambers' home two hours later than the appointed time, and Dr. Chambers became angry when he remembered his own duties at the office. Immediately upon Zhang's arrival, he scolded Zhang who remained silent. Then it turned out that the manuscript needed more time than estimated, and Zhang decided to quit. When he walked to the door, Dr. Chambers demonstrated his humility by a quick repentance. He rushed after Zhang, grabbed his hand, and begged his forgiveness. Both of them knelt and prayed together. Dr. Chambers said, "I will never mistrust you again." When Zhang related this story to others, he said that he did not realize Dr. Chambers was so great.[247] Dr. Chambers, in Mrs. Chambers' words, had a quick temper but was quick to repent and apologize. This story revealed Zhang had a similar quick temper, but he was quick to forgive. Zhang was also quick to repent, as seen in the example above.

The mutual trust between them could also be felt on the side of Zhang. In his words, Robert E. Chambers had told people in 1917 that "during the first five years of being a co-worker with Zhang, we were unfamiliar with each other so there was friction. However, during the following five years, we had known each other, and all our problems could be solved by talking them out."[248] Chambers often told people that "although Zhang and I come from different countries, we have become blood brothers." Zhang felt he was not worthy of their love because his learning was limited and his temper was not amiable.

In his letter to Rev. Ray D. D. in 1926, Dr. Chambers expressed his deep appreciation of Zhang for his contribution to *True Light* and the church and for his Christian character.

> *The True Light Magazine*, which the Chinese recognize as the best Chinese Christian Magazine in China is now being edited by Zhang Wen Kai. He decides what goes into the paper.

---

246. Gardner and Chambers, *Builder of Dreams*, 184.
247. Gardner and Chambers, 110.
248. Zhang, "Last Twenty-Five Years," 5.

He has been working with me for nearly twenty years, and I regard him as one of the finest Christians I know anywhere. His pen is a mighty implement for the spread of the Truth. The Chinese have shown in many ways their real interest in the work of the Society.[249]

Mrs. Chambers also highly respected Zhang. In her mind, Zhang was a thorough Christian, and a patriot most honest and unselfish. He and Dr. Chambers were about the same age, and much alike in many ways.[250]

2.4.6.2 *Zhang's Criticisms of the Missionaries*

Zhang's criticisms of the missionaries included their practice of paying the Chinese for doing God's work, some missionaries' connection with imperialists, and a small number of missionaries who had an unsympathetic or arrogant attitude towards the Chinese. He felt sad because many missionaries used foreign powers for shelter.

In this aspect, Zhao Zichen had different criticisms: Western missions' reluctance to accept indigenization, their mistrust of Chinese leaders, discrimination against Chinese Christians, neglect of their Chinese personnel, perfunctory training methods, poor talent-retaining practices,[251] control of the church, and involvement in drawing the Treaty.[252]

2.4.6.2.1 Paying Chinese Christians was unbiblical

The previous section reviewed Zhang's observation of many Chinese Christians' attitude towards money, non-Christians' ridicule and his line of interpretation of "the worker deserves his wages." Such elements led to this criticism.

To Zhang, when the denominations from the rich Western countries sent out their missionaries, they did it in a new way of having capital rather than

---

249. Robert Edwards Chambers, "Rev. T. B. Ray D. D., U. S. A," 25 August, 1926, 1, FMB AR 551–52, BOX 81, Chambers Robert Edwards, Ex Secretary, 1925–26.
250. Gardner and Chambers, *Builder of Dreams*, 171.
251. Chao, "Discussion over the Indigenization," 9–11.
252. Chao, "My Opinions on Creating Chinese," 1–2.

Jesus's old way of having no extra possessions.²⁵³ No missionary was said to live on the support from the local people. This was unbiblical.²⁵⁴

Zhang had no objection to the saying that the high living standard of Western missionaries in Chinese was just a normal one in their own countries. It was not necessary to force them to live like beggars by depending on the people from poor countries.

However, when someone said that it was God's will that the mission organizations pay for Chinese preachers' education and work so that the gospel could be spread in poor and weak China, Zhang had a reserved attitude because Jesus's old way of having no extra belongings in the Bible was replaced with the new way of using money as the vanguard of Christianity. Zhang felt it most unfortunate for Christianity to have money as its vanguard because money only produced a large number of fake and unfaithful Christians like the benefit-seeker in the *Pilgrim's Progress*.²⁵⁵

2.4.6.2.2 Some missionaries were arrogant towards Chinese

Zhang said that some missionaries had for a long time despised the Chinese. So they failed in their mission.²⁵⁶

For example, when Zhang recorded and commented on The Lianzhou (or Lienchow) Massacre (连州教案) of 1905,²⁵⁷ he thought that if Dr. Edward Charles Machle (麻义士; 1859–1936) of the American Presbyterian (North) Mission had made a gentle and polite request like his colleague Miss Eleanor Chestnut (1868–1905; 车思纳) MD, the result would not have been so grave even if the local people might not have met his request. In Zhang's view, Dr. Machle had a proud attitude as being a citizen of a powerful country. In this incident, he treated the Chinese in a way worse than the way of slave owner treating the black slaves. He cursed, kicked, and finally took away

---

253. Zhang might be referring to Matthew 10:9–10 – "Do not get any gold or silver or copper to take with you in your belts – no bag for the journey, or extra shirt, or sandals or a staff, for the worker is worth his keep."

254. Zhang, "Solution of Jesus and Paul," 2–3.

255. Zhang, 4.

256. Yijing Zhang 张亦镜, "Attached Comments on the Conflict between Chinese and Westerners in the Church of Guang Xi Province (闻粤西教会中西冲突感言之附识)," *True Light* 真光 25, no. 4-5-6 (1926): 67.

257. Yijing Zhang 张亦镜, "The Massacre at Lienchow in the Record of the Sunset of Xixia Mountain (巾峰夕霞记之连州教案)," *True Light* 真光 29, no. 4 (1930): 59–67.

the cracker firing tools of the local people who had already accumulated grievances against Christianity and came to seek trouble. To avoid a similar mistake, Zhang suggested[258] that no foreigner should view Chinese as foolish and weak while considering himself as wise and strong, nor should they be quick in physically attacking people.[259]

2.4.6.2.3 Many missionaries sought the protection of foreign powers

Zhang felt sad because most missionaries used foreign powers for their shelter. Whenever there were difficulties, they ran like chicks to hide under the wings of the mother hen. He deplored this because missionaries and Chinese Christians missed the chance of obeying God's teachings like "love your enemy," "be patient," and "pray for your persecutors."[260]

Zhang was of the opinion that missionaries should advocate the abolition of the Treaty of Protecting Preaching and Believers. In his analysis, the inclusion of protecting preaching and believers in the treaties was a violation of Jesus's teaching.[261] The harm caused by this inclusion greatly outweighed its benefits. The Treaty became a big obstacle to the gospel. It gave the anti-Christian people a reason to think that Christians were potential traitors to China because they were protected by foreign governments. If protecting preaching and believers had never been included in the treaties, there would have been no false and unworthy believers who joined the church for power, which in turn produced so many enemies for the church. Consequently, the Boxer Movement would not have happened. Zhang blamed the Treaty for the violence against the church.

However, some Western missionaries opined that abolition of the Treaty depended on the strength of the countries in question. If a country became weak, it could automatically give up the Treaty because it was unable to offer protection, but it might not be proper to ask a powerful country to give up its right. Zhang thought such a view did not reflect a will to defend justice but

---

258. Zhang, "Massacre at Lienchow," 67.

259. By 1905, Dr. Machle had already stayed fifteen years in China and one would assume that he had become familiar with Chinese customs and etiquette. There are at least two different versions of the accounts. Whether the version read by Zhang was more accurate or not, his comments revealed both his sadness and his nationalistic feeling.

260. Yijing Zhang 张亦镜, "Personal Comment: Chance for Practising Obedience (随感录: 行道的机会)," *True Light* 真光 26, no. 4 (1927): 102.

261. Zhang, "Current Trends of Thought," 95–96.

rather a faith in power, so these missionaries were imperialists and unworthy of being preachers.[262] He encouraged missionaries to learn from Paul's sacrificial attitude in 1 Corinthians 9:22.[263]

2.4.6.2.4 Some missionaries were taken advantage of by imperialism

Zhang pointed out that the missionaries were hated by the Chinese because of their imperialistic homelands. Besides, there were also a small number of missionaries who were not good. In addition, some missionaries were taken advantage of by the imperialists.[264]

Zhang was very much pained by the connection between some missionaries and the imperialists. In 1925, after the Shaji Massacre and the May 30th Massacre in Shanghai, Zhang quit his job at *True Light* so that he could freely criticize the violence of the imperialists. He felt it very inappropriate for a small number of missionaries to take sides with the imperialists and make unsympathetic comments on Chinese victims.

Zhang believed that the missionaries should separate themselves from imperialism because the Anti-Christian Movement mistook Christianity for the tool of imperialistic aggression. As a result, Chinese Christians were caught in a difficult situation and they had no way to argue against the anti-Christian people.

2.4.6.3 Zhang's Defence of the Missionaries

Although Zhang was critical of some missionaries or some missions on the issues above, he had a high admiration for the missionaries. Actually, he consistently and continually defended them.

As early as 1910, Zhang already began to proclaim that the missionaries had no intention of violating China's sovereignty and territory.[265] Facing a common accusation concerning the Treaty, he explained that the Treaty should not be counted as a total mistake made by the missionaries and it in

---

262. Zhang, "Current Trends of Thought," 96–97.

263. 1 Corinthians 9:22 – "To the weak I became weak, to win the weak. I have become all things to all people so that by all possible means I might save some" (NIV).

264. Yijing Zhang 张亦镜, "On the Anti-Christian Movement on the Christmas Day of 1928 in Shanghai (书民十七耶稣诞日上海的非基运动)," *True Light* 真光 28, no. 2 (1929): 3–4.

265. Zhang, "Cleansing the False Accusations," 57–58.

fact was beneficial under the persecution of the Qing dynasties.²⁶⁶ He even praised missionaries as genuinely loving their neighbours by using the Treaty to protect the Chinese people from their bad governments.²⁶⁷

In the 1920s, Zhang had to push back another popular attack on the missionaries for their relationship with imperialism. A complicated situation was that some missionaries held a sympathetic feeling for the imperialists and that most of the Chinese people had no idea of the difference between the white missionaries and the same white imperialists. Zhang expounded that, since the missionaries were from the same country as the imperialists, as missionaries, they would warn the Chinese to avoid direct conflict with those imperialists; however, as people who shared the same national identity with the imperialists, some of them would blame the Chinese because they ignored their warnings.²⁶⁸ According to Zhang, it was the imperialists who committed crimes in and against China rather than the missionaries.²⁶⁹ In opposition to the popular accusation that imperialists made use of the missionaries for aggression, Zhang argued that it was not imperialists who took advantage of missionaries, but missionaries who took advantage of imperialists.²⁷⁰ It is remarkable that Zhang interpreted some missionaries' attitudes by differentiating their Christian identity from their national identity.

Zhang reiterated that the majority of the missionaries were against imperialism.²⁷¹ He disagreed with Lu Danlin's saying that "ninety-nine percent of missionaries were hypocrites, lamb on the outside and wolf inside."²⁷² Zhang quoted *Western Denominations' Opinions on the Treaty of Protecting Preaching and Believers* published in *China for Christ* (A Chinese Monthly issued by the National Christian Council of China, Shanghai, 中华归主) as evidence for

---

266. Yijing Zhang 张亦镜, "Commenting on Chen Qiulin's On the Anti-Christian Movement (按: 论反基督教运动)," *True Light* 真光 24, no. 1 (1925): 74.

267. Yijing Zhang 张亦镜, "Commenting on the Second Letter to Refute a Foreign Female Believer (按: 驳一位外国女信徒的又一封信)," *True Light* 真光 24, no. 3 (1925): 52.

268. Yijing Zhang 张亦镜, "Answering Lu Danlin's Letter – Mr. Yijing: We Are Looking Forward to the Combined Issues of No. 4 to 6 in Volume 25 . . . (答复陆丹林通讯: 亦镜先生: 盼望许久的真光杂志廿五卷四至六号合刊...)," *True Light* 真光 25, no. 9–10 (1926): 127.

269. Zhang, "On the Anti-Christian Movement," 3–4.

270. Zhang, "Commenting on Chen Qiulin's," 81–82.

271. Yijing Zhang 张亦镜, "Discussion about the Presence of Westerners in China's Delegation for Jerusalem Conference (1928) 讨论有外国人加入出席耶路撒冷大会中国代表团问题," *True Light* 真光 27, no. 2–3 (1928): 108–9.

272. Zhang, "Answering Lu Danlin's Letter," 126.

missionaries' willingness to separate themselves from imperialism. He had it reprinted in *True Light*.

To prove the missionaries' sincere love for the Chinese, Zhang listed their charities in China. He also quoted a lot of examples to show that Western missionaries had been striving for indigenization and independence of the church in China.[273]

In a church of Guangxi Province, some Chinese Christians drove away their missionaries.[274] Zhang called such Christians "the radical side." He said that it was ridiculous for the radical side to ask for money, though Western mission organizations, in fact, would like to help with finance. He called them cruel and unkind (绝情绝义) to drive away the missionaries and condemned their obstructing the missionaries' luggage transfer[275] as incomprehensible and debased (下劣). Zhang said that, after this issue, not only did Chinese Christians on the mature side criticize the radical side but also non-Christians in Wuzhou who heard about this issue despised them.[276]

Facing the requirement of registration from the government, Western missionaries either stopped their schools or registered with the government. Zhang took this as evidence that the missionaries were not backed up by imperialists' warships.[277]

Zhang analyzed the possible reasons on the Chinese side for the arrogant attitude of some Western missionaries: (1) base Chinese around them; (2) the miserable political and social contexts in China contrasted sharply with their own countries' civilization; and (3) Chinese did not live up to their selfless ideals; for example: most officials and merchants worked for their own benefits instead of for their country. Zhang concluded if Lu Danlin and

---

273. Yijing Zhang, "My Sayings Plagiarized and Twisted in 'The Collection of Researches on Unequal Treaties' (不平等条约研究集引用我的文字的地方)," *True Light* 真光 28, no. 3 (1929): 1–12.

274. Zhang, "Comments on the Conflict," 68.

275. When the church members drove the missionaries away, they kept the porters or coolies away from being hired to carry their luggage. The missionaries had to transfer their luggage themselves by pushing wheelbarrows. At the moment when a missionary tried to push his wheelbarrow onto a boat, they shook the board under his feet, both the missionary and his wheelbarrow fell into the river.

276. Zhang, "Comments on the Conflict," 68.

277. Zhang, "Answering Mr. Hou Shuxian," 61.

he himself had been put into the missionaries' shoes, they would have been criticized for similar reasons.

The Collection of Research on Unfair Treaties written by KMT Branch of Shanghai was published in the *Shanghai Republican Daily* (上海民国日报) on 1 January 1929. It plagiarized and twisted some Christians' sayings, especially Zhang's. It said that Western missionaries would never allow indigenization and the independence of the church. Zhang quoted a lot of examples to prove that Western missionaries had been striving for indigenization and independence of the church.[278]

In view of the fact that the Chinese would not easily trust missionaries even if the missionaries showed sympathy for the Chinese, Zhang believed that the best way was for the missionaries to suffer along with the Chinese under the Chinese government after severing their relationship with imperialists and discarding the Treaty. Then the Chinese would treat the missionaries as their own brethren. There would be no criticism and no obstacle to preaching because it was imperialism behind Christianity that the people were attacking.

In Zhang's understanding, the goal of the Anti-Christian Movement in the 1920s was different from that during the Qing dynasty, when people's hatred was directly aimed at Christianity itself and Christian preachers. Levenson shares Zhang's view when he finds out that, in China during the May Fourth period, one could resent foreign political domination, but this resentment was far from traditional anti-foreignism.[279] Paul Cohen understands this anti-foreignism as an expression of cultural resistance and traces China's tradition of despising imported religion (from Buddhism to Christianity) as heterodoxy.[280] In other words, Zhang sensed the difference between modern nationalism and traditional culturalism that are expounded in the next two chapters.

2.4.7 Zhang's Sensitive Conscience

Zhang's pen stood for his conscience. He would never allow his pen to betray his conscience. He once said, "If a person has to keep his conscience silent,

---

278. Zhang, "My Sayings Plagiarized and Twisted," 1–12.
279. Joseph R. Levenson, "The Day Confucius Died," *The Journal of Asian Studies* 20, no. 2 (1961): 222, https://doi.org/10.2307/2050487.
280. Paul A. Cohen, *China and Christianity: The Missionary Movement and the Growth of Chinese Antiforeignism, 1860–1870* (Cambridge, MA: Harvard University Press, 1963).

why not cut off all fetters and leave for being the only man of integrity under the sky?"[281] Zhang's consciousness of his own faults is the best way to reveal that he lived up to his conscience.

This chapter has pointed out how Zhang confessed that his work at *True Light* was in fact driven by men rather than by Christ in 1929 after reading the article by Waiting. If a person could be like Christ, he would certainly not be driven by men. When Zhang criticized the mission organizations' practice of paying the Chinese, he strove to make a living by selling his calligraphy.[282]

In 1924, after getting acquainted with Aunty Zhang Si,[283] Zhang lamented that he could not obey God wholeheartedly to be Jesus's true disciple as a result of some useless knowledge stored in the heart. He felt ashamed when seeing Aunty Zhang Si. Zhang felt that a person could not become a rock to the church unless they had a faith like Aunty Zhang Si's. It was vain to win in argumentation by talent and intelligence. It would be better to spend more intimate time with God in the inner room.[284]

In 1929, he confessed that, during the past thirty years, he was driven by his desire for knowledge and he would read around one hundred thousand words every day. In contrast, he would not read the Bible unless he needed a quotation to answer a question concerning the Bible. His relationship with God was far less intimate than the first few years after his conversion. As a result, his writing could cheer the readers and provoke their thoughts, but it was unable to convert people into believing in Jesus.[285]

Zhang said he really admired a few editors and journalists who were only driven by the words of the Lord without mentioning their names. They fervently prayed and diligently read the Bible. Their writings could draw people to love God and Christ instead of winning applause. He said he would make

---

281. Jiang, "Works of Mr. Zhang Yijing," 14.

282. Zhang, "Introducing to a Sharp Criticism," 31–32.

283. Aunty Zhang Si (张四婶), a woman preacher, was born in 1867 and her husband's name was Zhang Guangxing (张广星). She became a Christian in July or August of 1912 in Da Dong Men Wai (大东门外) Pentecostal church in Guangzhou after experiencing God's healing of her loss of speaking and sight. Formerly, she was illiterate. In October 1912, she suddenly could read after three days and nights' prayer. In the spring of 1913, she was sent as a preacher to Xin Zao (新造). She performed many miracles. Yijing Zhang 张亦镜, "The Story of Aunty Zhang Si (记张四婶事)," *True Light* 24, no. 2 (1925): 63–68.

284. Yijing Zhang 张亦镜, "Awakening (觉悟)," *True Light* 真光 23, no. 11 (1924): 81.

285. Yijing Zhang 张亦镜, "Bible Reading and Praying (读经祈祷)," *True Light* 真光 28, no. 4 (1929): 98.

a change. Instead of limiting his desire for knowledge, he would extend his desire for the knowledge that the Holy Spirit pointed to. The measurement was how God would accept his prayers in the inner room. Then he would be used by God instead of people.[286]

Zhang told Pastor Liang Xigao (梁细羔) that he had a lot of chances of going astray. Nonetheless, he could quickly become aware of his sins and then he became more able to see the truthfulness of God's words. As a result, he had not been shaken by the Antichrist and nasty theories from the West. He owed this to the prayers of intercession by other people.[287]

2.4.8 Some Chinese Christians Praised by Zhang

Among the Chinese Christians praised by Zhang, there were Huang Naishang (or Wong Nai-siong), Watchman Nee (倪柝声), Aunty Zhang Si, Miss Lin Muchao,[288] and Wang Mingdao (王明道).

Zhang called Wong "a great Christian." Zhang and Watchman Nee were good friends for a long time.[289]

Zhang called Aunty Zhang Si an elite soldier of Christ and an example of faith.[290] He praised her as a true and undeniable testimony to the existence of God and the miracles in the Bible. Zhang's own faith in God and the Bible increased after knowing her.

He called Wang Mingdao "Paul of the present age."[291] He called Miss Lin Muchao "a true servant of God" instead of "a true servant of the church" because he believed the church could not totally stand for God. He wished to see such a servant among Chinese male Christians. Then he found God had prepared Wang already. Zhang praised him for his mastery of the Bible and his noble character.[292] He thought Wang's preaching was fundamental because he based all his words on the Bible and connected every thought to

---

286. Zhang, "Bible Reading and Praying," 98.
287. Yijing Zhang 张亦镜, "Pastor Liang Xigao's Visit (记梁细羔牧师来访)," *True Light* 真光 28, no. 10 (1929): 93.
288. Lin Muchao (林慕超) was a very famous and powerful woman preacher and disciple-trainer.
289. Yijing Zhang 张亦镜, "A Spiritual Feast (灵鼎一脔)," *True Light* 真光 28, no. 12 (1929): 44.
290. Zhang, "Awakening," 81.
291. Zhang, "Spiritual Feast," 45.
292. Zhang, 47–49.

the cross without any addition of his own ideas.[293] Zhang and Wang shared many views.

2.4.9 Some Other Views of Zhang

2.4.9.1 Zhang's Self-Image

Zhang took writing as his mission. He not only considered himself to be a preacher through writing, but also a farmer and an ordinary person.[294]

Someone said that Zhang only made friends with the rich and the powerful. Zhang responded by saying that he seldom joined the social association and made friends because: (1) he looked too plain so that few people noticed him; (2) he was not good at speaking so that people could not hear a satisfactory answer; (3) he viewed himself as a farmer so that he felt uneasy when sitting with the rich and the powerful; and (4) he had so much work that he had to start working from three in the morning. He did not want his schedule to be interrupted, so he had few friends in Canton, Hong Kong, Shantou, and Shanghai where he used to work.[295] When many Christians hailed the news that Jiang Jieshi (蒋介石) was baptized by Pastor Jiang Changchuan (江长川), Zhang expressed his preference of hearing the conversion of the common people over the prominent figures.[296]

There was another reason for the impression of being unsociable. Zhang was poor so he did not like to attend parties.[297] He did not feel comfortable with living in the first class and the second class in the ship because people there spoke foreign languages, wore foreign clothes, and looked rich. He would have felt very nervous around rich people.[298] Nonetheless, he was content to be poor.[299] He was very thrifty and had never hired a servant.[300]

---

293. Yijing Zhang 张亦镜, "Mr. Wang Mingdao Preached in Two Cantonese Churches in Shanghai (记王明道先生在上海两个广东教会演讲)," *True Light* 真光 29, no. 4 (1930): 80–81.

294. Yijing Zhang 张亦镜, "My View on Association (我之于社交)," *True Light* 真光 27, no. 7 (1928): 92.

295. Zhang, 92.

296. Yijing Zhang 张亦镜, "Preface: Merry Christmas and Happy New Year (卷头语: 恭祝圣诞,并贺新禧)," *True Light* 真光 29, no. 12 (1930): 1.

297. Yijing Zhang 张亦镜, "Preface (卷头语)," *True Light* 真光 29, no. 5 (1930): 1.

298. Yijing Zhang 张亦镜, "The Third Part of My Two Months in Qingdao (在青岛两个月之经过 三)," *True Light* 真光 27, no. 12 (1928): 63–66.

299. Yijing Zhang 张亦镜, "Poem with the Rhythm Same with Mr. Lu Banjiao (诗歌: 我所学作之诗:用吕半教先生原韵有序)," *True Light* 真光 30, no. 1 (1931): 78–79.

300. Hao, "Works of Mr. Zhang Yijing," 38; Ji Wang 王玑, "The Anecdote of Mr. Zhang Yijing (张亦镜先生轶事)," *True Light* 真光 40, no. 12 (1941): 15–16.

Zhang had many chances to find a job with higher social status, but he turned all of them down.[301] The warlords Shen Hongying (沈鸿英) and Liu Zhenhuan (刘震寰) invited him to serve them. Shen Meixian (沈梅先), the head of Shantou Tax Bureau (汕头税务局长), also invited him to join his service. Zhang refused them also.[302] In his own words, he was not proud but felt humbled. Moreover, he was too busy with writing to accept any job offers.

2.4.9.2 *Zhang's View of Women*

In the 1920s, Chinese families placed more value on a boy than a girl. Sometimes, newborn baby girls would be abandoned or drowned. Zhang advocated that with more daughters there would be a longer lifespan and more blessings.[303]

Zhang attached his comments on Mr. He's report about Jinde Women's School in Wu Xing County (吴兴进德妇女学校) founded by the Woman's American Baptist Foreign Mission Society (美国浸礼女差会). Zhang celebrated its founding and thought highly of this report. He wished the women in Wu Xing would be blessed by this school. He wanted to have more reports of this school published in *True Light*.[304]

Xiaobai (小白), Zhang's younger sister, was a teacher in Pei Zhen Girls' School of Tong An (同安培真女校). The local preacher invited her to lead worship, which was not a practice in the Baptist church of the time. She wrote to Zhang for his opinion. Zhang responded, "The rule was set by men, not by God. If you could honour the Lord, why not do it?"[305]

Zhang denied the charge that the Bible despises women.[306] He was once asked why Jesus was born as the descendant of Tamar, Rahab, and Bathsheba

---

301. Zhang, "My View on Association," 93.

302. Zhang, 93.

303. Yijing Zhang 张亦镜, "With More Daughters Come Longer Age and More Blessings (多福多寿多女子)," *True Light* 真光 28, no. 10 (1929): 90–91.

304. Zhongxiao He 何仲萧, "Jinde Women's School in Wu Xing and Chinese Women (吴兴进德妇女学校与中华妇女界)," *True Light* 真光 23, no. 2 (1924): 67.

305. Yijing Zhang 张亦镜, "Words from a Female Worship Leader Who Made An Exception (女子破例领礼拜者之言)," *True Light* 真光 28, no. 6 (1929): 85.

306. Yijing Zhang 张亦镜, "The First Part in My Answer to Mr. Jiang Shuai Concerning Tough Questions from Anti-Christians and Passive People (答姜树蔼君来函所列反教及消极两种人的辩难)," *True Light* 真光 29, no. 2 (1930): 76.

who were not pure. Zhang answered that their husbands except for Rahab's were also impure.[307]

2.4.9.3 Zhang's Nationalistic Feelings

It was said that in the Shanghai Bund Park (上海外滩公园) there used to hang a board on which it was written "Chinese and dogs, no entrance."[308] This had lasted for several decades. On 1 June 1928, surprisingly and suddenly all the parks were open to the Chinese, only if they bought a ticket. Most people were happy about this change.[309]

Zhang differed from the others in his response; he took this as a cause for shame. He wondered why the Chinese could not build a few similar parks or even better parks in Chinese territory. If they did so, the Chinese master did not have to receive this condescending grace from the bad guests who viewed Chinese as dogs. Moreover, if it was called a public park, it should not be closed to the public.

He also regretted the loss of China's glory in the past.[310] Zhang sighed: "God's noble Chinese descendants of the ancient country with a few thousand years' civilization do not strive to be strong and restore its former glory when Hun people (匈奴) viewed China as heaven. In contrast, currently, they view themselves as a half-civilized race. They take pride in studying in the countries which view Chinese as dogs and in wearing the ugly degree gowns. They are shameless and they insult China."[311]

2.4.9.4 Zhang's View of Chinese Sages in the Ancient Times

Once Zhang preached in a church on the topic "Avoid Perishing but Having Eternal Life." After affirming that all those who did not believe in Jesus would definitely perish, Zhang added that "although the ancient Chinese sages had

---

307. Yijing Zhang 张亦镜, "Answering Five Questions from Mr. Huang Zhenyan (答黄振雁先生五疑问)," *True Light* 真光 28, no. 11 (1929): 75.

308. Although other parks in the International Settlement and foreign concessions did not have such a sign, Chinese dressed in Chinese attire were denied entry.

309. This event was recorded by Zhang in *True Light* 27, no. 6 (1928): 96. This issue of *True Light* was printed in June 1928. By that time, both Zhang and the CBPS were in Shanghai.

310. Yijing Zhang 张亦镜, "Shanghai Park – No Entrance for Chinese and Dogs (华人与犬不许入之上海公园)," *True Light* 真光 27, no. 6 (1928): 96.

311. The author wants to avoid evaluating how objective Zhang's complaints were. However, his comments demonstrated his nationalistic feeling.

no chance of knowing and believing in Jesus, if they were found to have fear and respect for God, God would certainly have helped them from perishing. For example, Zhao Bian (赵抃; 1008–1084), a Confucian scholar of the Northern Song dynasty (960–1126), would burn incense before the Heavenly King (帝) and reported his deeds. If there was anything he dared not to report to the Heavenly King (帝), he dared not to do such things. Such a behaviour was similar to Christians who would not do anything displeasing God."[312]

Chapter 3 will explain how Zhang concluded that Jesus was the heavenly mandate or *ming* (命) and heaven or *tian* (天) pursued by all Confucians and that Confucius was like John the Baptist paving the way for Jesus. In Zhang's example, Zhao would not do anything he was ashamed of. If Zhao really believed in the existence of the heavenly king, he was actually worshipping God, though he did not know his name. If the heavenly king was similar in conscience, Zhao's sincerity and submission to his conscience would make him like the Jewish people born before Jesus. Zhang's way of bridging between Christianity and Confucianism will be discussed in the next chapter.

2.4.9.5 *Zhang's View about Chinese Christians' Citizenship*

Zhang said that, at the moment of reformation, Christianity was the most needed and the most applicable. The darkness of Chinese society could only be wiped away by Christianity, the guide for social reformation. Cultivating a true Christian was not different from moulding a good citizen for the country. He encouraged Christians to share the gospel.[313]

2.4.9.6 *Zhang's View on Modern Chinese and the New Culture Movement*

In China, it was widely believed that it was Hu Shi who advocated the adoption of modern Chinese by replacing the classical Chinese. The fact is that Zhang had called for the adoption of modern Chinese before Hu Shi did.[314]

---

312. Yijing Zhang 张亦镜, "Avoid Perishing but Having Eternal Life (免沉沦得永生)," *True Light* 真光 28, no. 7 (1929): 23.

313. Yijing Zhang 张亦镜, "At the Twenty-First Anniversary of Tong An Church (书同安教会成立廿一周纪念)," *True Light* 真光 17, no. 12 (1928): 52–53.

314. Danlin Lu 陆丹林, "Recollection of Zhang Yijing (追怀张亦镜)," *Spring and Autumn* (春秋) 5, no. 3 (1948): 35; Lu, "Preface," 3.

Zhang advocated the adoption of modern Chinese even before the New Culture Movement.[315]

As early as 1911, Zhang suggested replacing classical Chinese with modern Chinese or *baihua* because only a very small percentage of the Chinese could read articles in classical Chinese.[316] He pointed out that modern Chinese or colloquial Chinese appeared in the Song dynasty (960–1279).[317] The church in modern China was the first to advocate it and the church in modern China had been using it along with classical Chinese for a hundred years. Zhang himself wrote *Challenging Equivocation from the Unbelievers* (诘推诿不信者) in modern Chinese,[318] seven or eight years before the vernacular movement advocated by Hu Shi, Chen Duxiu, Qian Xuantong, and Lu Xun around 1919.[319]

According to Zhang, colloquial language became significant in the West when John Wycliffe translated the Bible from Latin into colloquial English, which facilitated civilization in the West and led to Martin Luther's reform. In fact, modern Chinese or colloquial Chinese appeared one to two hundred years before the West. However, the persons (he was talking about Hu Shi) who advocated colloquial Chinese did not realize its significance until they went to study in the West.

Zhang said, "That is why I said that the doctrines advocated by the current of new thoughts tide are stolen from the oldest Church, and that the Church itself is the new thoughts tide." Zhang questioned that "since the New Culture Movement could not be independent of religion (He meant Christianity) and since the adoption of modern Chinese had been advocated by the church

---

315. Baoqian Xu 徐宝谦, "For Special Issue of Commemorating Zhang Yijing (为张亦镜先生纪念号写)," *True Light* 真光 40, no. 12 (1941): 6.

316. Yijing Zhang, "The Function of Baihua or Modern Chinese (通俗白话之功用)," in *(1928) A Quarter of A Century of True Light, Selected* 真光丛刊, *Part 3: General Articles* 通论, ed. Yijing Zhang (Shanghai 上海: China Baptist Publication Society 中华浸会书局, 1911), 9–13.

317. Yijing Zhang 张亦镜, "The Church and the New Thoughts Tide (教会与新思潮)," in *China Christian Yearbook (*中华基督教年鉴*)*, vol. 6 (Shanghai 上海: China Continuation Committee (中华续行委办会), 1921), 138–39; Yijing Zhang 张亦镜, "After Reading Mr. Lu Banjiao's Criticism of Modern Chinese (读了吕牛教先生白话文的评判以后)," *True Light* 真光 29, no. 6 (1930): 74.

318. Yijing Zhang, "Challenging Equivocation from the Unbelievers (诘推诿不信者)," *True Light* 真光 10, no. 6 (1911): 29–32.

319. There are other Chinese in modern history who used colloquial Chinese before 1919, for instance, Hong Rengan (洪仁玕, 1822–64) and Huang Zunxian (黄遵宪, 1848–1905).

for a few hundreds of years, how could some advocates of the New Culture Movement and modern Chinese despise the church?"³²⁰

Zhang agreed with Lü Banjiao's saying that the New Culture Movement harmed the beautiful morality passed down by the sages.³²¹

2.4.10 Zhang's Last Days

Zhang had a disease in his leg. In 1931, he moved from Shanghai to Guangzhou where doctors said his legs below the knees must be cut off, but he refused amputation. Zhang said if God wanted to stop him from doing God's work, he would wait for death, bearing the pain.³²²

At that time, he gave 1000 yuan as a donation for the new seven-storey building of the China Baptist Publication Society. This sum accounted for his one year's salary. Now he could not sell his calligraphy anymore, so he had to receive a salary from the CBPS again. On his sickbed, Zhang had new ideas to express, but he could not write them out.³²³ He proofread all his writings in the past and mailed them back to the CBPS for publication. Regretfully, there is no trace of it anymore.

Zhang returned to his hometown in Guangxi Province. His mother was over eighty years old and was very happy to see him and massaged his feet and hands every day. Zhang said:

> Parents' love for their children would not change whatever their children's age. Therefore, I am sure of God's love for His children.³²⁴

On 9 December 1931, Zhang joyfully told his family members that Jesus had taken away his illnesses and these illnesses would not be his problems anymore. On the morning of 10 December, he asked his family to sing a song

---

320. Zhang, "Church and the New Thoughts Tide," 138.

321. Banjiao Lü 吕半教, "With the Trend or Against the Trend (随潮流与不随潮流说)," *True Light* 真光 29, no. 1 (1930): 71–72.

322. Yijing Zhang 张亦镜, "Zhang's Letter about Recent Situation of Illness (张亦镜覆古尚勤告知最近病状函)," *True Light* 真光 30, no. 8 (1931): 1.

323. Yijing Zhang 张亦镜, "Zhang Yijing's Notice (亦镜启事:余自三月十一日返至广州后,廿一日进两广浸会医院疗治)," *True Light* 真光 30, no. 5 (1931): 1.

324. Yijing Zhang 张亦镜, "Zhang's First Letter after Returning from Guilin (张亦镜改赴桂林休养报告书第一函)," *True Light* 真光 30, no. 12 (1931): 1.

as a farewell for his return to the heavenly home. His family and Zhang sang *The Place of the Lord's Rest*. Two hours later, he died in peace.

A few months later, on 20 April 1932, Robert E. Chambers also passed away.

Many Chinese Christians felt heartbroken at the news. Many people and churches wrote to commemorate them in the church publications. *True Light* published special issues in their memory in 1932 and 1941 respectively.

Many elegiac couplets were written as a memorial, including the ones from Liu Zhanen[325] and Bao Zheqing.[326] This study chooses two sets of elegiac couplets from *True Light*, among others, to show people's love and condolence for them:[327]

> The two old men, the leading elders in the Church. No more life? Living eternally in heaven! (二老者, 教会之大老也; 不生乎, 天国去永生兮). (From your junior in Christ, Zhao Shizhang 赵仕璋)[328]

> Mr. Chambers, Mr. Zhang, gave their all to their services of the Lord and had no differentiation between the foreigner and the Chinese. You Robert, I Yijing, preached all life to serve people and had no care for death and life (湛先生, 张先生, 鞠躬尽瘁, 为主做工, 何分中外; 你罗弼, 我亦镜, 毕世宣传, 役人服务, 那里死生). (From your junior in Christ, Cui Tongyue 崔通约)[329]

Even in 1949, *The Voice of Evangelization* (宣道声) still praised Zhang as a good housekeeper of the Lord. It said that Zhang not only made a huge

---

325. Liu Zhangen (刘湛恩, 1895–1938) was the chairman of China Christian Baptist Church Alliance (中华基督教全国浸会联合会) and the president of the University of Shanghai (沪江大学). He obtained his PhD from Columbia University.

326. Bao Zheqing (鲍哲庆, 1893–1957) was the general secretary of China Christian Baptist Church Alliance (中华基督教全国浸会联合会) and a teacher of the University of Shanghai (沪江大学) that had been established by the American Baptist Missionary Union and the Southern Baptist Convention.

327. "Elegiac Couplets for Pastor Robert E. Chambers and Mr. Zhang Yijing (湛罗弼牧师、张亦镜先生挽联), *True Light* 真光 31, no. 9 (1932): 72.

328. Zhao Shizhang (赵仕璋) was a pastor in Hong Kong during the 1930s.

329. Cui Tongyue (崔通约, 1864–1937) was a newspaper editor and journalist. He was one of the students of Kang Youwei.

contribution to the writing ministry of the Baptist church but also was extremely significant to Chinese Christianity.³³⁰

2.5 People's Comments on Zhang

Zhang had won the admiration of Westerners and Chinese while he was still alive. Mrs. Chambers recalled:

> He was looked on as one of the outstanding Christian writers and literary critics of China. The Society depended on his opinion in all matters concerning the quality and character of its publications. He had produced more Christian literature than any other Chinese connected with Baptist work in China, and of such high grade that his writings were received with respect everywhere.³³¹

He was "the most gifted and consecrated Chinese ever connected with the China Baptist Publication Society."³³² W. H. Tipton,³³³ Zhang's longtime coworker, confirmed Lide's comment by saying that "after the death of Zhang Wen Kai, it has been most difficult to find a man to measure up to the high standard which had been attained by this unusually gifted editor."³³⁴ In Tipton's memory:

> Chang Wen Kai, whose talent and devotion to the cause perhaps did more than any other man connected with the society to make its influence felt as a witness in Kingdom service. He was the author of a large number of useful books and tracts which

---

330. "Mr. Zhang Yijing – A Good Housekeeper (一个好管家张亦镜先生)," *The Voice of Evangelization* 宣道声 9, no. 1 (1949): 37.
331. Gardner and Chambers, *Builder of Dreams*, 184.
332. Lide, "Dr. Rosewell H. Graves," 6.
333. W. H. Tipton (1875–1950) was an American missionary from the Southern Baptist Convention. He arrived in China in 1904 and was an evangelist and the editor of Sunday School Literature of China Baptist Publication Society. During his more than forty years' ministry, he was located in Wuzhou, Canton, and Shanghai respectively. When the executive secretary was absent, most of the responsibilities of the CBPS were on his shoulders.
334. W. H. Tipton, "Annual Report of China Baptist Publication Society" (1936), 2, FMB AR 551-1, MISS. MINUTES, BOX – 229, Mission South China, Articles, 1930–40, 229–35.

are still being read by multitudes in China today. Thus, it may be said, "He being dead, yet speaketh."³³⁵

Tipton missed the days when Zhang was alive. He said, "Tsao San Ming, our present editor, is succeeding, in a gratifying way, in restoring the paper to the enviable standing it had during the good old days when Zhang Wen Kai was the editor."³³⁶

After his death, many Westerners and thousands of Chinese people shed tears. Dr. and Mrs. Chambers took the loss of Zhang as "almost bewildering." Dr. Chambers led a meeting in memory of Mr. Zhang. Mrs. Chambers observed, "He was filled with emotion as he spoke simply of his love for Mr. Zhang, his faith in him, his sense of loss." A fund of $50,000 Mexican was raised among the Chinese out of their love for Zhang as a permanent memorial to him to be used as an endowment for *True Light*.³³⁷

The Voice of Evangelization called Zhang Yijing the top-notch player in the ministry of preaching through writing from the Baptist church.³³⁸

Yu Boxia (俞伯霞) became a pastor in 1926. Since then, he often used the works written by Zhang Yijing in his preaching and when answering questions. Pastor Yu summarized Zhang's five contributions to Chinese Christianity as: (1) being a light and a great testimony for Christ, (2) safeguarding the truth, (3) providing materials for preaching and ministry, (4) leading people to the Lord, and (5) promoting literature.³³⁹

People often remembered Zhang for his role in apologetics. In the observation of Pastor Yu, facing the storm of the Anti-Christian Movement, all other publications of the church became as mute as a fish, and they did not dare to talk about the gospel anymore.³⁴⁰ The only exception was *True Light*. By Zhang's efforts, the anti-Christian atmosphere became weakened. This view was confirmed by Jiang Jianbang.³⁴¹

---

335. Tipton, "Annual Report of China Baptist," 4.
336. Tipton, 6.
337. Gardner and Chambers, *Builder of Dreams*, 185.
338. "Mr. Zhang Yijing – Top-Notch Player," 15–16.
339. Boxia Yu 俞伯霞, "The Contribution of Mr. Zhang Yijing to Christian Literature (张亦镜先生对于基督教文学的贡献)," *True Light* 真光 31, no. 9 (1932): 44–45.
340. Yu, "Contribution of Mr. Zhang Yijing."
341. Jiang, "Works of Mr. Zhang Yijing," 12–13.

In Lu Danlin's view, Zhang's works deserved the saying that "a brave heart serves justice and a sharp mind produces eloquence (铁肩担道义, 辣手著文章)."342 As to Zhang's fight against the Anti-Christian Movement, Lu said that "the whole process could be seen in *The Collection of the Great Light Breaking Darkness* and *The Whole Collection of Criticising the Theories of Anti-Christian Movement*. In addition, *True Light* was really the Lord's light on the top of the mountain. As a result of its shining, illuminating, and clarifying, evil and corrupted people either became silent or turned their weapon around (照彻云霄, 六合清莹, 一般恶化腐化份子或则匿迹销声或则反戈投降啊)."343

Zhang did not only defend Christianity from attacks, he was enthusiastic about leading people to Christ.344 In fact, Cao Xinming (曹新铭), the successor of Zhang in *True Light*, became a Christian in 1918 under the influence of Zhang Yijing's writings. Since then, Cao became a subscriber of *True Light* until he became the editor. In 1923, he became a preacher and then started to write for *True Light*. In Cao's view, Zhang had a strong faith and noble character. He said that, because of faith, Zhang gave up the Imperial Examination, bore his father's anger, and carried on the burden of *True Light*. He was a very self-sacrificing and very self-disciplined person.345

Zhang's character was highly praised. Xu Songshi346 said: "I extremely admire Zhang's character and scholarship. He was a very humble person. He always inconspicuously sat in a corner in the church. He liked talking with people but did not like preaching. He lived in Christ."347 An anonymous writer also said Zhang seemed to be proud, but actually, he was very amiable.348

---

342. Lu, "Preface," 6.

343. Lu, 6.

344. Hao, "Works of Mr. Zhang Yijing," 34.

345. Xinming Cao 曹新铭, "In Commemoration of Mr. Zhang Yijing the Former Chief Editor (纪念本志前主编张亦镜先生)," *True Light* 真光 40, no. 12 (1941): 1.

346. Xu Songshi (徐松石, 1900–1999) was a well-known educator, theologian, and ethnology expert. He was a co-worker of Zhang Yijing for one year. After Xu turned to education, they shared a close friendship in Shanghai for many years.

347. Xu, "In Memory of Mr. Zhang," 2, 4.

348. "Humour of My Deceased Friend Zhang Yijing (亡友张亦镜的风趣)," *The Weekly of Zhong Zheng Church* (重正堂周刊) 17 (1940): 2.

Xu Baoqian called Zhang a doughty and upright man (血性男子). Zhang had the boldness to resist then President Yuan Shikai. He was farsighted and had insight. His writing was inspiring, and his character was admirable.[349]

Hou Shuxian gave a more detailed description of Zhang's integrity and his influence although he had been criticized by Zhang for his opinion of Christian education.[350] He said that Zhang Yijing's character should be taken as a model by all the staff of *True Light*. In current China, he was indeed a person of integrity. His words matched his deeds.

In Hou's description, Zhang would have been welcomed into the KMT Party. However, he refused to join it because some party members were against Christianity and he wanted to fight against those anti-Christian people to safeguard Christ and the Bible.

Hou recalled that Zhang started as a Confucian and refused to become an official, so he chose to live a poor life. For his thirty years of serving in *True Light*, it was often reported how he was invited to become an official in the government. However, he viewed the work of preaching through writing as his second life. If possible, he would never give up serving the heavenly kingdom to serve the human kingdom for money, fame, glory, and comfort.

Hou said that Zhang could have gone abroad as did many other people in the Baptist church. He refused to go abroad because of his understanding of the Bible, the needs of the church in China, and his integrity. He did not want to become corrupted or be controlled.

In Hou's view, there were many Christians who had more knowledge, power in eloquence, and accuracy in hitting the point than Zhang Yijing. However, they left their original positions when they were offered a better chance in business, government office or other places out of the church. Although they could serve the Lord from the new place, they had forsaken the original earnestness with which they devoted themselves to the Lord. The words of Zhang had the power to touch people's hearts. This power came from the consistency between his words and deeds.

---

349. Xu, "Special Issue of Commemorating Zhang," 6.

350. Shuxian Hou 候述先, "Reflections on Zhang Yijing's Return to Guang Dong Province (对于张亦镜先生返粤的感想)," *True Light* 真光 30, no. 5 (1931): 67–68.

When Zeng Yugen[351] heard that Zhang was selling his calligraphy to support himself and *True Light*, he suggested that Zhang should focus on writing and avoid this distraction. He said that it was normal for evangelizing organizations to lose money, such as the churches of Xing Hua (兴华), Dong Shan (东山), and Dong Shi (东石). *True Light* was more important than them. Many readers in northern China and neighbouring provinces became aware of the Baptist church through this publication and the majority of the readers were expecting to read Zhang's articles.[352]

Fan Bihui believed that the majority of the articles in *True Light* would endure through the ages. He praised Zhang for his diligence in safeguarding the Way and dispelling the mist. Therefore, people nationwide collected *A Quarter of a Century of True Light, Selected* into their treasure-houses.[353]

Zhang was also known as a filial person. There was a story. After school, he would help his mother with the household routines. People at that time were poor and only ate meat at festivals. One time he noticed there was no meat in his mother's bowl while she was eating in the kitchen. He asked why his father, the workers (usually seasonal), and he had meat while they were eating in the living room. She replied that his father and the workers worked hard for a long day in the field, so they should have some alcohol and meat for relaxation and enjoyment. Afterwards, when there was meat in the meal, but it was not a festival, he knew his mother must not have kept a share for herself. Then he would quietly take his share to his mother.[354]

People noticed that Zhang's contribution to Christianity in China was not limited to apologetics; he also made a great contribution to Chinese literature.[355]

Xu Songshi listed three shortcomings with Chinese literature. First, Chinese literature was filled with passive and pessimistic mood and thoughts after the rise of Taoism and Buddhism. Second, Chinese literature was imbued

---

351. Zeng Yugen (曾郁根) was a historian of the Christian church in China.

352. Yijing Zhang 张亦镜, "Discussing over Zhang's Self-Support by Selling Calligraphy (讨论卖字自给问题)," *True Light* 真光 27, no. 2–3 (1928): 114–16.

353. Bihui Fan 范皕诲, "A Preface to the Bound Edition of True Light Volume Twenty-Seven 真光杂志合订本序," *Youth Progress* 青年进步, no. 120 (1929): 93–94.

354. Wang, "Anecdote of Mr. Zhang Yijing," 15–16.

355. Yu, "Contribution of Mr. Zhang Yijing," 46–47.

with the ideas of gods and spirits. Third, Chinese literature lacked spiritual inspiration and comfort.[356]

Wang Zhixin thought Christian writers should: (1) nurture Christianity, a seed from the West, with Chinese culture to be a local produce; (2) encourage all Christians to build up the church with a united heart; and (3) lead believers (and all people) to Christ.[357]

Pastor Yu thought Zhang had spared no effort to overcome the shortcomings listed by Xu Songshi during his thirty years' writing ministry and he had met all the requirements put forward by Wang Zhixin. Pastor Yu commented: Zhang Yijing tried his best to make up for those shortcomings by interpreting Christianity with the features of China's literature while at the same time introducing Christianity into China's literature, which can be seen from his poems.[358]

In 1948, Lu Danlin repeated his comments in his preface for *A Quarter of a Century of True Light, Selected*. Zhang's writing style was penetrating, touching the exact point, fluent, easy to understand like the poems of Bai Xiangshan (白香山),[359] rich in materials, and all-inclusive as Wu Zhihui whose works contained knowledge of a long history and a wide range of subjects.[360]

In the comments of Lu Danlin, Zhang was a faithful Chinese Christian until death with both the old and new learning. His external appearance would make people believe that he was an outdated old pedant. Unexpectedly, his thoughts were the forerunners for society. He had a clear mind, noble faith, a loving heart for people, a striving spirit, the courage of resisting insults from foreigners, freedom from the binding of the old learning, and a revolutionary spirit to fight against the evil force. His learning was erudite and profound. He knew the three religions, all the sages and famous philosophers, and all

---

356. Songshi Xu 徐松石, "Break into the City of Literature (攻入文学之城)," *True Light* 真光 31, no. 7 (1932): 5–6.

357. Zhixin Wang 王治心, "Writing and Christianity (文字事业与基督教)," in (1928), *A Quarter of A Century of True Light, Selected* 真光丛刊, Part 3: *General Articles* 通论, ed. Yijing Zhang (Shanghai 上海: China Baptist Publication Society 中华浸会书局, 1924), 23–24.

358. Yu, "Contribution of Mr. Zhang Yijing," 46–47.

359. Bai Xiangshan (or Bai Juyi 白居易, 772–846) was one of the three greatest poets in the Tang dynasty 618–907. The other two greatest poets were Li Bai (李白) and Du Fu (杜甫).

360. Lu, "Recollection of Zhang Yijing," 34; Lu, "Preface," 2.

the schools of philosophy in China. He knew science, philosophy, painting, calligraphy, seal cutting, Bolshevism, and anarchism.[361]

There is a story. A couplet (对联) of a church was quoted by Zhao Liutang (赵柳塘) in his *The Second Lesson on Galatians* (加拉太书第二讲) in the second volume of *Spirit Cultivating and Preaching* (培灵讲道 第二集). When Zhang read it, Zhang recalled it was he who wrote it twenty years ago for the Christian Alliance Church (宣道会礼拜堂) in Wuzhou (梧州).[362]

In his poem, Zhang exhorted Lü Banjiao (吕半教, an educator and a Confucian) to follow Jesus.[363] Yan Jiqing (a Christian poet, 严霁青) wrote a poem to praise Zhang as both a true Confucian and a true Christian.[364] Xu Baoqian thought Zhang's knowledge of Confucianism reached a specialist level.[365] According to Jiang Jianbang, Zhang did not spend many years at school and his knowledge was mainly obtained through self-education.[366]

Zhang's diligence was very impressive. In the words of Dr. Timothy Tingfang Liu,[367] Zhang had been labouring for China and for Christianity, working for sixteen hours each day during his thirty years' service. His labour and distinctive merits put him on the list for rewards by emperors.[368]

Under Zhang's leadership, *True Light* received a lot of praise too. At the Baptist Conference for Jiangsu Province, Shanghai City, and Wuxi City, after Liang Shichen (梁拭尘), the marketing manager of *True Light*, introduced this publication, he found many people already knew it as a periodical for "defending and preaching the Way."[369]

---

361. Lu, "Recollection of Zhang Yijing," 34; Lu, "Preface," 1–2; Lu, "Commemorating Mr. Zhang Yijing," 30.
362. Yijing Zhang 张亦镜, "Foreword: Couplet (卷头语)," *True Light* 真光 29, no. 4 (1930): 1.
363. Zhang, "Poem with the Rhythm," 78–79.
364. Jiqing Yan 严霁青, "A Poem about a True Confucian (真儒辨)," *True Light* 真光 27, no. 1 (1928): 72.
365. Xu, "Special Issue of Commemorating," 6.
366. Jiang, "Visiting the Family Members," 32.
367. Dr. Timothy Tingfang Liu (刘廷芳, 1891–1947) was a poet and an important leader in the Chinese church during the 1920s and 1940s. He received his education from St. John's University. He obtained his PhD in psychology from Columbia University and a PhD in theology from Yale University. He was also a founder of the Chinese Psychological Society.
368. Weihan Liu 刘维汉, "About the Editing Office (关于编辑室_编辑者言_终日埋头案前)," *True Light* 真光 27, no. 7 (1928): 95.
369. Zhang, "Trip to Suzhou City," 66.

Zhang listed some other readers' responses as an encouragement. Here are some examples.[370]

Tang Yuanfang (唐元放), a Christian from Shashi of Hubei Province, called *True Light*, *Christians* (基督徒报), and *Revival* (复兴报) three necessities among which *True Light* was the most famous one.

Zhang Tengjiao (张腾蛟), a Christian reader, said *True Light* was true of light.

Li Muzong (李慕宗), a subscriber for three years, said *True Light* was the only sharp weapon for the preachers.

Hua Jianyi (华健益), a member of the Anglican Church in Kunshan of Jiangsu (江苏昆山支塘徐市镇圣公会), on 17 January 1929, said that this publication deserved the title of being a light of true light (真光之光).

Fu Daneng (傅达能) said that *True Light* had rich materials and fresh diction (文辞新颖题材丰富).

Huang Youzhuo (黄幼灼) from Southeast Asia (南洋) said that he could not stop reading *True Light*.

Liu Gangyi (刘刚毅) said on 4 March 1929 that he was helped a lot by *True Light*.

Wang Bizu (王弼祖), a preacher from Feng Shi City (峰市), said that *True Light* was a must for the church.

Zhou Fengqi (周凤岐) said on 18 March 1929 that it was really a star in the circle of periodicals.

2.6 Conclusion

Although this chapter is long, it gives only a very brief description of Zhang Yijing's life and contributions. The following chapters will examine the birth and development of his Christian identity, to facilitate a better understanding of his attitudes and ideas. The ensuing chapters will also examine how he was a Chinese according to the terms of the time, how he balanced his Christian identity and "being Chinese," and how the public thought of him as a Chinese.

---

370. Zhang, "True Light Was One," 75–76; Yijing Zhang 张亦镜, "Readers' Responses," *True Light* 真光 28, no. 4 (1929): 79–80.

CHAPTER 3

Zhang Yijing's Search for a Christian Confucian Identity

3.1 Confucianism[1]

Confucianism was a dominant ideology in Chinese society for a long period and the Chinese officials and intellectuals used to identify themselves as "Confucians." Matteo Ricci (1552–1610), the pioneer Italian Jesuit missionary to China, first dressed like a Buddhist monk to identify with the Chinese, but later he gave it up and turned to dress as a Confucian so that he could identify with the mainstream Chinese.

3.1.1 Manufacturing the Terms "Confucius" and "Confucianism"

According to Rule[2] and Jensen,[3] the terms "Confucius" and "Confucianism" were manufactured by Jesuits in the seventeenth century when they tried to

---

1. In this chapter, the Confucian terms in Chinese are translated and explained according to the traditional understanding in China with reference to the translations and explanations by James Legge and Wing-Tsit Chan (陈荣捷, 1901–1994). The works of Chan mostly referred to in this chapter include *The Chinese Classics*, *Basic Chinese Philosophical Concepts*, *Neo-Confucian Terms Explained* (北溪字义) and *Reflections on Things at Hand: The Neo-Confucian Anthology* (近思录).

2. Paul A. Rule, *K'ung-Tzu or Confucius? The Jesuit Interpretation of Confucianism* (London: Allen & Unwin, 1986).

3. Lionel Jensen, *Manufacturing Confucianism: Chinese Traditions and Universal Civilization* (Durham, NC: Duke University Press, 1997).

introduce to Europe the ethical and philosophical knowledge developed from the teachings of Confucius and his disciples. Their aim was to differentiate the social philosophy of Confucianism from that of Buddhism and Taoism, which were labelled as heathen cults, and to reject Neo-Confucians in favour of returning to its source – the original Confucianism. To this end, they simplified, assimilated, and Latinized the ancient and complex system of religion, ethics, and social philosophy into a Christian context. As a result, researchers have questioned to what extent Confucians accepted Matteo Ricci and his colleagues' handling and assessment of their traditions and to what degree Western assumptions about "Confucius," "*kongfuzi*," and "Confucianism" coincide with Chinese understanding of "*kongzi*" and "*rujia*" (儒家), "*ruxue*" (儒学) or "*rujiao*" (儒教).

This chapter's focus is not etymology, nor assimilation and accommodation in the cross-cultural understanding of *rujia* but how *rujia* influenced Chinese Christians in China around the 1920s. In other words, this chapter will partially reflect on how the Chinese during this period understood "*kongzi*" and "*rujia*." As for the usage of terms, since many Chinese scholars like Wing-Tsit Chan and Tu Weiming have habitually used "Confucius" and "Confucianism" for "*kongzi*" and "*rujia*" when they communicate their ideas in English, this chapter will continue with this usage.

3.1.2 What Is Confucianism?

Historically, the school of Confucianism had different branches and different epochs, but all of them share the same features: (1) Confucius viewed as the founder and leader, (2) their common scriptures composed of the Five Classics and the Four Books,[4] among others, (3) their objectives of "Sageliness Within and Kingliness Without" (内圣外王), (4) the path of achieving these objectives being the "three guidelines" and "eight clauses," and (5) their moral standards of kindness, righteousness, loyalty, and filial piety. The objective of "becoming a sage inside and having kingly benevolent governance outside" was borrowed from *Zhuang Zi* (庄子) of Taoism, and its meaning is further explained in *The Great Learning*:

---

[4] The Five Classics are *The Book of Odes* (诗经), *The Book of History* (尚书), *The Book of Changes* (周易), *The Book of Rites* (礼记), and *The Spring and Autumn Annals* (春秋). The Four Books are *The Analects* (论语), *The Book of Mencius* (孟子), *The Great Learning* (大学), and *The Doctrine of the Mean* (中庸).

The ancients who wished to illustrate illustrious virtue throughout the kingdom, first ordered well their own States. Wishing to order well their States, they first regulated their families. Wishing to regulate their families, they first cultivated their persons. Wishing to cultivate their persons, they first rectified their hearts. Wishing to rectify their hearts, they first sought to be sincere in their thoughts. Wishing to be sincere in their thoughts, they first extended to the utmost their knowledge. Such extension of knowledge lay in the investigation of things. (古之欲明明德于天下者, 先治其国, 欲治其国者, 先齐其家, 欲齐其家者, 先修其身, 欲修其身者, 先正其心, 欲正其心者, 先诚其意, 欲诚其意者, 先致其知, 致知在格物).[5]

The "three guidelines" and "eight clauses," the path through which these objectives are achieved are also from *The Great Learning*. The three guidelines are "to illustrate illustrious virtue; to renovate the people; and to rest in the highest excellence" (大学之道在于明明德, 在亲民, 在止于至善).[6] The "eight clauses" are "investigation of things, extension of knowledge, sincerity in the thoughts, rectification of the heart, cultivation of the self, regulation of the family, national order, and world peace or oneness of the world" (格物、致知、诚意、正心、修身、齐家、治国、平天下).

3.1.3 Is the School of Confucianism a Religion?

This question began to be raised following the encounter between imperial China and Europe from the sixteenth century. One example is the Rites Controversy. The religious status of the school of Confucianism is still a controversial issue. Many scholars insist that this school belongs to humanism and non-religiosity by claiming that it aims at solving human problems through human efforts. The questions put forward by Confucianism always circle around "self-discipline" (*xiuji* 修己) and "administering people and the

---

5. James Legge, *The Chinese Classics: With a Translation, Critical and Exegetical Notes, Prolegomena, and Copious Indexes*, 3rd ed., vol. 1 (Hong Kong: Hong Kong University Press, 1982), 357–58.

6. Legge, *Chinese Classics*, 1, 356.

world" (*zhiren* 治人). Tang Yijie (汤一介) denies its religiosity.[7] However, traces of original religion are still found in it. Some scholars like Li Shen 李申[8] insist on the religiosity of Confucianism. He argues that only after the May Fourth Movement did Chinese intellectuals begin to claim that Confucianism is an ethical and educational doctrine but not a religion.[9] Even Tu Weiming, the famous contemporary Chinese Confucian thinker, is increasingly drawn to the religiosity of Confucianism, although in a very cautious and discreet way.[10] Chen says that this debate was complicated by ideological rivalries and linguistic confusion.[11] Therefore, the participants in the debate should be sensitive to their ideological position and their definitions of religion. The work of Billioud and Thoraval[12] traces the process of appropriation of Confucianism into a religion by examining the meanings of the ancient Chinese word *jiao* (teaching) and *zongjiao* (religion) which is a Western category imported from Japan.

While the religiosity of Confucianism is still under discussion, Zhang Yijing's view on this question is also worthy of attention. Zhang thought the ancient sages of China like the Emperor Yao (尧, before the Emperor Shun, 2377–2259 BC) and the Emperor Shun (舜, Yao's successor, around 2277–2178 BC) had a knowledge of God as deep as that of the ancestors of the Jews.[13] The ways of the Emperor Yao and the Emperor Shun were advocated

---

7. Yijie Tang 汤一介, "Confucianism's Features and Basic Spirit 儒学的特质和基本精神," in *China Confucianism Culture Overview* (中国儒学文化大观), ed. Yaonan Zhang, Ming Fang, and Yijie Tang (Beijing: Peking University Press, 2001), 5.

8. Shen Li, *History of the Confucian Religion* 中国儒教史 (Shanghai: Shanghai People's Press 上海人民出版社, 1999).

9. Shen Li 李申, "The Author's Preface to History of the Religion of Confucianism in China 中国儒教史自序," *History of Chinese Philosophy* 中国哲学史 4 (1997): 6.

10. Frederick W. Mote 牟复礼, "The Preface of The Way, Learning and Politics – On Confucian Intellectuals (道、学、政 – 论儒家知识分子)," in *A Collection of Tu Weiming's Works* (杜维明文集第三册), ed. Qi Yong Guo and Wen Long Zheng, vol. 3 (Wuhan 武汉: Wuhan Publisher 武汉出版社, 1988), 496.

11. Yong Chen, *Confucianism as Religion: Controversies and Consequences* (Leiden: Brill, 2013).

12. Billioud and Thoraval, "Anshen Liming or the Religious."

13. Yijing Zhang 张亦镜, "Answering Eleven Questions from Shi Jingcheng's Friends Concerning Christianity (答石精诚示友人对于基督教的十一条疑问)," in *(1928), A Quarter of a Century of True Light, Selected* 真光丛刊, *Part 5: Answers to Inquiries* 答问, ed. Yijing Zhang, vol. 21 (Shanghai 上海: China Baptist Publication Society 中华浸会书局, 1922), 32.

by Confucius and Confucians.[14] Despite this, Confucius was not a religionist, but an educator, statesman, and ethicist.[15]

3.1.4 Confucianism and Its Three Developmental Epochs

According to Mu[16] and Tu,[17] Confucianism can be divided into three epochs. The first epoch is the period of the Pre-Qin dynasty (before 221 BC) and the Former and Later Han dynasties (202 BC–AD 220), which is called the period of the original or classical Confucianism (原始或古典儒家). The second epoch is around the period of the Song, Yuan, Ming, and Qing dynasties (AD 960–1912) and is usually referred to as the period of Neo-Confucianism or *Song-Ming lixue* (宋明理学). The third epoch, called New-Confucianism (新儒家), started around the time of the May Fourth Movement (1919).

3.1.4.1 Original or Classical Confucianism

The original Confucianism of the first epoch was the root of Neo-Confucianism and New-Confucianism. Confucius or Kong Zi (551–479 BC) is viewed as the founder of the school of Confucianism. Modern scholars, especially more recently, have been questioning the role of Kong Zi as the founder of what is known as "Confucianism" in the West as the term *ru* (儒) referred to scholars in general, i.e. not specifically to the followers of Kong Zi in pre-Qin times. Moreover, it was only after the founding of the Han dynasty that Sima Qian labelled the Five Classics as "Confucian." As this paragraph is intended to serve only as a brief introduction, this debate will not be expounded further. The first epoch had Confucius, Mencius (372–289 BC), Xun Zi (313–238 BC), and Dong Zhongshu (179–104 BC) as its representative figures.

According to *The Records of Art and Literature in the History of the Former Han Dynasty* or *hanshu yiwenzhi* (汉书艺文志), the school of Confucianism

---

14. Zhang, "Cleansing the False Accusations," 62.

15. Yijing Zhang 张亦镜, "Answering an Old Scholar Instead of a Friend (代友人答复一老学究)," in *(1928), A Quarter of a Century of True Light, Selected* 真光丛刊, Part 2: *The Gospel Discussed and Explained* 辩道文, ed. Yijing Zhang (Shanghai 上海: China Baptist Publication Society 中华浸会书局, 1918), 197.

16. Zongsan Mu, "The Reason for Reviving Goose Lake Academy and the Rules (重振鹅湖书院缘起暨章则)," in *The Complete Works of Mr. Mou Zongsan* 牟宗三先生全集, 1st ed., vol. 26 (Taibei 台北: Linking Publishing 联经出版社, 2003), 13–20.

17. Weiming Tu, "The Prospect for the Development of Confucianism at Its Third Stage (儒学第三期发展的前景问题)," in *Comments on New-Confucianism (评新儒家)*, ed. Yijun Luo (Shanghai: Shanghai People's Publisher (上海人民出版社), 1989).

that arose from the *situ* officers (司徒, premier level) who helped the monarchs, acted according to the balance between *yin* (negative force 阴) and *yang* (positive force 阳), and offered enlightenment and education. Their style and manner of writing were in accordance with the six classics including a focus on kind-heartedness and justice. They followed the examples of the Emperor Yao and the Emperor Shun, imitated the models of King Wen (文 1152–1056 BC) and King Wu (武 ?–1043 BC), respected Confucius (551–479 BC), and received teachings from him, so as to show the importance of their theory. The Confucians viewed kind-heartedness and justice as the highest achievement.[18]

3.1.4.2 Neo-Confucianism

Neo-Confucianism was the form of Confucianism during the Song and Ming dynasties (宋明儒学) with the Cheng brothers (Cheng Yi 程颐 1033–1107 and Cheng Hao 程颢 1032–85), Zhu Xi (朱熹, 1130–1200), Lu Xiangshan (陆象山, 1139–93), Wang Yangming (王阳明, 1472–1529), Huang Zongxi (黄宗羲, 1610–95), and Wang Fuzhi (王夫之, 1619–92) as leading figures.[19]

How did Neo-Confucianism come into being? According to Fung Yu-Lan, Neo-Confucianism was the result of the combination of Confucianism with Buddhism and Taoism which rose in response to the challenges of Buddhism.[20]

What is the relationship between original Confucianism and Neo-Confucianism? Neo-Confucianism is the inheritor of original Confucianism, Taoism, and Buddhism.[21] According to Xu Fuguan 徐复观, Neo-Confucianism inherited original Confucianism and made improvements on its teaching of "Learning for One's Self/Learning for Oneself" (为己之学) which means that the goal of study is to discover oneself, improve oneself, and reach

---

18. 儒家者, 流盖出于司徒之官, 助人君顺阴、阳明教化者也. 游文于六经之中, 留意于仁义之际, 祖述尧舜, 宪章文武, 宗师仲尼, 以重其言, 于道最为高. 《汉书. 艺文志》 (*The Records of Art and Literature in the History of the Former Han Dynasty* or *hanshu yiwenzhi*. https://www.gushiwen.org/gushiwen_48b00b5a15.aspx).

19. Luo, *Comments on New-Confucianism*, 1.

20. Yu-Lan Fung and Derk Bodde, "The Rise of Neo-Confucianism and Its Borrowings from Buddhism and Taoism," *Harvard Journal of Asiatic Studies* 7, no. 2 (1942): 113.

21. Dongmei Fang 方东美, *Philosophies of the Original Confucianism and Taoism* (原始儒家道家哲学) (Taibei 台北: Taibei Dawn Culture Company (台北黎明文化公司), 1983), 41–44.

self-fulfilment by way of introspection.²² Neo-Confucianism differentiated between innate knowledge (or moral knowledge 德性之知) and acquired knowledge (见闻之知). By studying the phenomena of nature, one might have acquired knowledge. Through personal experience, one would internalize this acquired knowledge and then reconcile it with its corresponding innate knowledge. Finally, innate knowledge would be substantiated and expressed leading to the stage of self-fulfilment (自得). Thus, the neo-Confucians described a state in which a person could feel that "humankind reached harmony with all beings" (与万物同流) and "humankind and Heaven are in union" (天人合一). Xu's point of view was complemented by Li Shen.

According to Li, another important difference lies in the way of dealing with the relationship between heaven and humanity. The Confucians of the Han dynasty believed in a corresponding relationship between heaven and humanity and listened to the dictates of the heavenly will, while the Confucians of the Song and Ming dynasties focused on the mind, nature, and ontology. In other words, religiosity was demonstrated in the Confucians of the Han dynasty while the Confucians of the Song and Ming dynasties made explicit the ethical and educational doctrines.²³

3.1.4.3 New-Confucianism

At the beginning of the twentieth century, Confucianism suffered a series of setbacks. In 1905, the imperial civil service's examination system which was based on Confucianism and/or Neo-Confucianism was abolished. In 1913 and 1917, the Confucians tried to establish Confucianism as the state religion, but their efforts failed partly as a result of the opposition of Zhang Yijing. Following this, the New Culture Movement (1915–1923) and the May Fourth Movement (1919) propagated the popular slogan "Down with Confucianism" on the heels of which a famous Confucian, Carsun Chang,²⁴ suffered a heavy loss in the Debate on Science and Metaphysics (1923–24). Facing the

---

22. Fuguan Xu 徐复观, "The Similarities and Differences between Cheng Brothers and Zhu Xi (程朱异同)," *The Continuation on the History of Chinese Thoughts* 中国思想史论集续篇 (Shanghai 上海: Shanghai Bookstore Publishing House 上海书店出版社, 2004), 396–97.

23. Li, *History of the Confucian Religion*, 454.

24. Carsun Chang (张君劢, 1887–1969) was a politician, philosopher, and a Confucian scholar.

challenges of modernism, the tendency and attempt to revive Confucianism is called New-Confucianism or Contemporary New Confucianism. Liang Shuming,[25] Carsun Chang, Xiong Shili (熊十力, 1885–1968), Liu Shuxian (刘述先, 1934–2016), Tu Weiming (杜维明, born in 1940) and others are its representatives.

According to Luo, New-Confucians shared common roots with original Confucianism. They take pride in the knowledge and practices accumulated in the area of "self-discipline" of original Confucianism while at the same time they are working to make the area of "administering people and the world" more appropriate for a world of democracy and science.[26]

This epoch could be further divided into three phases: the resistance to foreign influence, the temptation to produce an ecclesiastic Confucianism (*kongjiao*), and a withdrawal into philosophy.[27]

3.1.4.4 Confucianism in a General Sense

Generally speaking, the Confucians of every epoch not only respected and followed the teachings of Confucius but also studied ideas, either foreign or native, to enrich Confucianism to meet the demands of their times. Nonetheless, in the nineteenth century only a few Confucian scholars took an interest in foreign learning while most scholars still rejected Western learning.

Zhang lived through the transition from Neo-Confucianism to New-Confucianism. His lifestyle showed the signs of the influences of Confucianism: he had the introspection and self-discipline of original Confucianism, as seen in his couplets (listed below), and his self-disciplined lifestyle. He was fond of studying nature and seeking evidence, as advocated by Neo-Confucianism. He also paid attention to science and democracy, to which New Confucianism tried to adapt. Before he became a strong Christian, he also experienced a short period of resistance to Westerners. After his Christian identity had grown strong, he countered the effort of producing an ecclesiastic Confucianism.

---

25. Liang Shuming (梁漱溟, 1893–1988) was a philosopher, teacher, and leader in the Rural Reconstruction Movement in the late Qing dynasty and early Republican eras of Chinese history.

26. Luo, *Comments on New-Confucianism*, 3.

27. Billioud and Thoraval, "Anshen Liming or the Religious," 93–95.

Thus, this chapter will examine Confucianism's influence on Zhang from its general sense rather than focusing on categorizing his Confucian thought into different epochs.

3.1.5 Confucian Values and Confucian Terms and Clichés

Just as Fung had observed that the Neo-Confucians' answers to the questions of their time could be found within the Confucian classics themselves,[28] New-Confucians are working off the same premise. Neo-Confucians made use of the traditional terms from these ancient classics to support their arguments. Chan thought that Neo-Confucians used those traditional terms or clichés partly because the ancient Confucian classics were the chief source material available to them, partly because they craved support from ancient sages and worthies, partly because the new metaphysics and epistemology developed by the Neo-Confucians were not sufficient to require new terms, and partly because the nature of the Chinese language makes it easier to express new ideas in traditional terms.[29] Metzger agreed that the traditional terms or clichés, as a verbalized symbol of shared cultural orientation, were used by Neo-Confucians for the context of their ideas and to form the pattern of their thought as a whole. The New-Confucians continue to follow this pattern, and many of the traditional terms or clichés are familiar to Chinese-born intellectuals, who can easily sense their meaning and context.[30]

Although the educational system and civil service examinations based on this Confucian curriculum were ended by 1905, Confucianism's influence did not disappear because its traditional terms or clichés are still being used today. Another reason is that Confucians were and are primarily interested in the knowledge of values.[31] Values, as advocated by these Confucians, can be preserved in attitudes and symbols embodied in "virtues" and "rites," and in mythology, legendary history, religious usages, and poetic imagery.[32] As

---

28. Fung and Bodde, "Rise of Neo-Confucianism and Its Borrowings," 113.

29. Wing-Tsit Chan, "Neo-Confucianism: New Ideas in Old Terminology," *Philosophy East and West* 17, no. 1/4 (1967): 16.

30. Thomas A. Metzger, *Escape from Predicament: Neo-Confucianism and China's Evolving Political Culture* (New York: Columbia University Press, 1977), 13.

31. Wing-Tsit Chan, "Neo-Confucianism and Chinese Scientific Thought," *Philosophy East and West* 6, no. 4 (1957): 331.

32. Helmut Wilhelm, "The Reappraisal of Neo-Confucianism," *China Quarterly* 23 (1965): 123–24.

discussed in the literature review, identity can be understood as a commitment to a choice of occupation and set of values to live by and remain faithful to (what Erikson called "fidelity"). Therefore, people's Confucian identity can be detected by their fidelity to Confucian values.

3.1.6 Confucianism and the Chinese

Confucianism is not equal to Chinese culture, but among China's three main philosophies, Confucianism, Taoism, and Buddhism, Confucianism has been the guiding philosophy for Chinese thought. For more than two thousand years from the Former Han dynasty (202 BC – AD 8) to 1905, Confucianism was not only a scholarly institution, but also the dominant ideology in China, and the entire educational system and civil service examinations were based on Confucianism. It is not only the basis of cultural identification for the Chinese but also an embodiment of the civilization of East Asia. It was formerly the mainstream of Chinese scholarly thought and the philosophy of Chinese intellectuals. It has penetrated every stratum of Chinese culture. It is the key element of Chinese culture and plays a decisive role in daily interaction.[33]

In this sense, being a Chinese used to mean being a Confucian. For this reason, being a Chinese Christian used to mean being a Confucian Christian or a Christian Confucian. The Confucian identity sometimes turned out to be an obstacle for a Chinese to become a Christian. Chinese Christians often found it hard to combine these two identities. This point will be further illustrated below. Paradoxically, it could sometimes enable a person to gain confidence in one's Christian identity, as will be seen in Zhang Yijing's case.

3.2 A Confucian or a Christian?

Before the New Culture Movement (1915–23), the main opposition to Christianity in China was Confucianism. Yang Guangxian (杨光先, 1597–1669) and the Yongzheng Emperor (雍正, 1678–1735) were two examples in the early Qing dynasty. Yang, a Confucian with the help of some Chinese

---

33. Tu, "Prospect for the Development," 119.

Muslim astronomers,[34] was fiercely opposed to Catholic missionaries like Johann Adam Schall von Bell (汤若望, 1592–1666) and wrote a pamphlet called *An Exposure of Heresy* (辟邪论).[35] This confrontation resulted in the death of five Chinese Christian astronomers and the flogging and exile of Catholic missionaries Ferdinand Verbiest (南怀仁), Lodovico Buglio (利类思), and Gabriel de Magalhães (安文思). In 1724, the Yongzheng Emperor prohibited all Catholic activities as an extension of the Chinese Rites Controversy, a conflict between Christianity and Confucian rites.

3.2.1 Reasons for the Conflict

The reasons for the hostility of Confucianism towards Christianity are found in the summary of Chen Duxiu. According to Chen,[36] Christianity was either ignored or viewed as a cult in China because people believed that China's Sacred Teaching[37] or *shengjiao* (圣教) would weed out Christianity. He listed two Chinese Confucian values,[38] one worshipping the sage or *zunsheng* (尊圣) and the other rejecting the foreigner or *rangyi* (攘夷). In ancient times, these mentalities had repelled Buddhism, Taoism, and the schools of Yang Mo (楊墨) which were against Confucianism in the period of Warring States (475–221 BC). The third reason for the hostility of Confucianism towards Christianity was the Chinese obsession with holding an office in the government, which made them look down upon Jesus because of his association with fishermen and the sick rather than high-level officials. In contrast, Confucius and Mencius, in the Four Books, made friends with feudal princes and high-level officials.

The above examples show that from the perspective of values, Confucianism, to some degree, created obstacles for the Chinese to become Christians. According to the theories about religious identity proposed by

---

34. Jing Chen 陈静, "Question about Yang Guangxian's Hui Nationality or Muslim Identity 杨光先回族或回教徒问题质疑," *Study of Hui Nationality* 回族研究, no. 2 (1993): 81.

35. Yang Guangxian launched his anti-Christian attack in the late 1650s, i.e. during the early Qing dynasty. *An Exposure of Heresy* was part of Yang's well-known collection *Budeyi* 《不得已》 (I Cannot Do Otherwise), published in 1665.

36. Duxiu Chen 陈独秀, "Christianity and Chinese (基督教和中國人)," *La Jeunesse* (新青年) 7, no. 3 (1920): 15–16.

37. He meant Confucianism by Sacred Teaching.

38. Chen, "Christianity and Chinese," 16.

Hunsberger et al.,[39] before Confucianism was denounced in the New Culture Movement, the opposition of Confucianism created a milieu in Chinese society which stirred up religious doubts concerning Christian identity. This atmosphere was pervasive for a significant period of time. This may explain why the number of Chinese Protestants was only four hundred thousand around 1920, accounting for one-thousandth of the Chinese population, one hundred years after Robert Morrison's arrival in 1807.

3.2.2 An Ignored but Typical Way of Being a Confucian and Being a Christian

When dealing with the relationship between Christianity and Confucianism, Gregg A. Ten Elshof called for the adoption of a dialogue and the avoidance of the approaches of apologetics (Christianity having the superiority over Confucianism) and pluralism (all religions being democratically legitimate in terms of truth) to enable the Christian believer to learn from other sources of truth.[40] In fact, at the beginning of the twentieth century many Chinese Christians engaged externally or internally in such a dialogue and learned from Confucianism. But for many of them, their approach was in direct opposition to the approach of apologetics; namely, that they either consciously or subconsciously took Christianity as a way to achieve their Confucian ideals.

In 1913, the YMCA in China held the Sixth National Convention in Beijing and some Christians were invited to share their faith with the listeners. In his speech, Lin Changmin[41] said,

> If *tiandao* (the Heavenly Way, 天道) and *rendao* (humanly way, 人道) could be communicated, it would be a high way to *shijie datong* (the oneness of world 世界大同) and the highest civilisation. . . . Actually, *tiandao* (Heavenly Way) is expressed through religion . . . and Christianity is this religion . . . Is there any conflict between Confucianism and Christianity? No. The only difference is that Jesus spread love. We who want to reach

---

39. Hunsberger, Pratt, and Pancer, "Adolescent Identity Formation," 365.

40. Gregg A. Ten Elshof, *Confucius for Christians: What an Ancient Chinese Worldview Can Teach Us about Life in Christ* (Grand Rapids, MI: Eerdmans, 2015).

41. Lin Changmin (林长民, 1876–1925) used to be the vice-president of YMCA in Fujian Province.

zhishan zhijing (the supreme goodness or perfection 至善之境) will find no other way than Christianity . . . but we shall never adopt the attitude of *chuzhu runu* (putting a servant into his master chair while casting the master aside 出主入奴) to reject Confucius; otherwise . . . the country would be in utter disorder.[42]

Lin's ideals as revealed in his speech were the ideals of Confucianism such as reaching *shijie datong* (the oneness of world) and reaching *zhishan zhijing* (the supreme goodness or perfection). He valued Christianity because it helped him to achieve his Confucian ideals. Moreover, his usage of the phrase of *chuzhu runu* (putting a servant into his master chair while casting the master aside) illustrated the relationship between Christianity and Confucianism in his mind.

T. B. Woo (拱平) also gave a speech at this meeting. Quoting from Mencius (372–289 BC), whose status in Confucianism is only next to Confucius, Woo tried to prove that *ren* (kindness, 仁) of Confucianism was the same as the love of Christianity. Then he said: "The heaven in Christianity and Utopia in the Western idealism are just other names for *datong shijie* (oneness of the world 大同世界) . . . Who knows that the so-called heaven and Utopia would not become a fact on earth?"[43]

Woo found counterparts in Christianity for his ideals in Confucianism: love for *ren* (kindness) and heaven for *datong shijie* (oneness of the world). Heaven, utopia, and *datong shijie* were all perceived to be the same thing. Thus, his saying that heaven would be achieved on earth expressed his wish that *datong shijie* would come to fruition rather than a hope for heaven in the sense of transcendence and eternality.

F. S. Brockman was the vice-president of YMCA International at that time. When he spoke to his Chinese listeners, he asked:

> Do not we worship the Emperor Yao and the Emperor Shun? Why do we worship them? Isn't it because they could sacrifice their own interest for the sake of all people's happiness? . . . If we all could give up our own selfishness but be witnesses to the

---

42. Changmin Lin 林长民, "Christianity the Essential Factor in the Welfare of Society and the Nation," *China's Young Men* XVI, no. 1–2 (1913): 32–34.

43. T. B. Woo 拱平, "The Source of Transforming the World into a Paradise," *China's Young Men* XVI, no. 6 (1913): 1138–40.

Way with one heart, China would turn to be a strong nation from a weak one within a few years... When everyone in this country becomes the follower of Christ, then the Republic of China would be the heaven, and it would be a model and leader for all nations. Isn't it wonderful?[44]

Brockman's speech revealed that the majority of his listeners worshipped the sages. "Sacrificing one's own interest" was found to be a value common to both Confucianism and Christianity. The final ideals were "making China strong" which appealed to Chinese national pride and "becoming a model for all nations" which highlighted the Confucian ideal of "illustrating illustrious virtue; renovating the people; and resting in the highest excellence" (大学之道在于明明德, 在亲民, 在止于至善).[45] Once again, being a follower of Christ became the way to achieve the Confucian ideal.

The three speakers' speeches above show that, in their understanding, the majority or at least a section of the Chinese Christians at the Conference had a Confucian identity. More than this, at least for Lin and Woo, the function of being a Christian was to achieve their Confucian ideals. In other words, the purpose of assuming a Christian identity was to facilitate the fulfilment of their Confucian identity. Therefore, their Confucian identity took priority over their Christian identity. Assuming his readers' knowledge of the meaning of the Confucian term *shijie datong*, Fan Bihui also said Jesus's ideals were of the globe and *shijie datong* (the oneness of world).[46]

The next section will take a closer look at Zhang Yijing's Christian identity and Confucian identity. His approach to Christianity and Confucianism will present a contrast to many other Confucian Christians of the time, such as the speakers above.

---

44. F. S. Brockman 巴乐满, "Seeking Not for One's Own Greatness," *China's Young Men* XVI, no. 1–2 (1913): 41–42.

45. Legge, *Chinese Classics*, 1, 356.

46. Bihui Fan 范皕诲, "The Missions of YMCA in China (中华基督教青年会的使命)," *Association Progress* 青年进步, no. 55 (1922): 93.

3.3 Zhang's Confucian Identity and Christian Identity

This section will first examine Zhang's Confucian identity before exploring the development of his Christian identity up to 1906.

3.3.1 Is Zhang a Confucian?

The answer to this question can be found externally in his education, words, and his deeds and subjectively in his self-identification.

Externally, before Zhang chose to become a Christian in 1892, he had received a Confucian education and became a teacher of Confucianism in 1888.

In Zhang's writings, Confucius was a sage par excellence.[47] If anyone belittled Confucius, he would strongly oppose him.[48] In 1914, he said that he had studied the Confucian classics more diligently during the past twenty years than at any time before his conversion in 1892.[49] In the 1920s, Confucianism became a target for criticism. When Wu Zhihui accused Neo-Confucians like Zhu Xi and others of creating terrible moral and political codes for life in this world and making Chinese society a lifeless tragedy,[50] Zhang defended Confucians by saying that it was too sweeping to conclude that all Neo-Confucians were useless.[51] Wu, under the name of Wu Jingheng (吳敬恆), said Confucius, Mencius, Lao Zi, and Mo Zi were products of the chaotic world of the Spring and Autumn and the Warring States, so they must be thrown into the latrine for thirty years.[52] Zhang reminded the church in 1925 that Confucius should never be slandered if Christianity wanted to lead China to Christ.[53]

---

47. Yijing Zhang 張亦鏡, "Jesus and Confucius (耶儒辯)," in (1928), *A Quarter of a Century of True Light, Selected* 真光叢刊, Part 2: *The Gospel Discussed and Explained* 辯道文, ed. Yijing Zhang (Shanghai 上海: China Baptist Publication Society 中華浸會書局, 1910), 31, 34.

48. Zhang, "Cleansing the False Accusations," 62.

49. Zhang, "Correcting Errors in Dr. Chen," 162.

50. Zhihui Wu 吳稚暉, "A New Belief's Conception of the Universe and the Philosophy of Life 一個新信仰的宇宙觀及人生觀 (Continuation to Vol. 1 No. 4 續四卷一號)," *Pacific* 太平洋 (Shanghai 上海) 4, no. 3 (1923): 36.

51. Yijing Zhang 張亦鏡, "A Wonderful Argument against the Saying That Neo-Confucians Were Useless (宋儒不適于用妙辯)," *True Light* 真光 23, no. 10 (1924): 67.

52. Jingheng Wu 吳敬恆, "A Critique of the Thought of Foreign Eight-Leggedism 箴洋八股化之理學," *Advance Together* 共進, no. 44 (1923): 4.

53. Yijing Zhang 張亦鏡, "Answer to the Question about Christianity with Buddhism and with Confucianism (答: 討論耶與佛及耶與孔)," *True Light* 真光 24, no. 3 (1925): 81.

In his personal life, Zhang was very filial. He had a keen sense of family responsibility, so he took care of his siblings and their children both financially and intellectually. He creatively found a way to show respect to his ancestors, which proved his commitment to filial piety and his respect for Confucian tradition. He refused money from a lottery win, which reminds us of the concept that the "*junzi* (the noble man) values justice while *xiaoren* (the petty man) values the material gains" in *The Analects*. He also saved two innocent men from execution at the risk of his own life. If we compare his life to the Confucian eight clauses "investigation of things, extension of knowledge, sincerity in the thoughts, rectification of the heart, cultivation of the self, regulation of the family, national order, and world peace or oneness of the world" (格物、致知、诚意、正心、修身、齐家、治国、平天下), it is not difficult to see his commitment.

Subjectively, even in 1927 when he reviewed his struggle after his conversion, he still identified himself as a Confucian at the moment of his conversion. He recalled:[54]

> The other Confucian scholars laughed at us because they believed that we descended from lofty trees to enter into dark valleys or *xia qiaomu ru yougu*.[55]

The words "The other Confucian scholars" signify the other members of the Confucian group with which Zhang identified himself. His sense of belonging to the school of Confucianism was influenced by his perception of other members' disapproval of his new identity as a Christian. We will examine later how he reconciled these two identities, but here we can see his own sense of his social identity as a Confucian.

Zhang's educational background, his words, his deeds, and his own subjective commitment reveal his Confucian identity. Even if the social changes in the 1920s might have weakened the strength of this identity, his commitment

---

54. Yijing Zhang 张亦镜, "Comments on the Theological Thoughts in the U.S.A. during the Last Twenty-Five Years (按: 二十五年来美国神学思想之趋势)," *True Light* 真光 26, no. 6 (1927): 13.

55. James Legge, *The Works of Mencius*, 3rd ed., with a Concordance Table, and Notes by Dr Arthur Waley, vol. 2, The Chinese Classics: With a Translation, Critical and Exegetical Notes, Prolegomena, and Copious Indexes (Taipei: SMC Publishing INC, 1991), 255. The Chinese characters are 下乔木入幽谷 《孟子. 滕文公上》 Part 1 of the Chapter "Teng Wen Gong in *The Mencius*."

to Confucianism was still revealed by his defence of it in the face of the hostility among intellectuals with Western learning. With such a strong Confucian identity, how did he overcome the usual Confucian mentality of worshipping sages and rejecting the foreigners to assume a Christian identity? How did his Christian identity grow into union with his Confucian identity? What was the structure of these two identities?

3.3.2 Becoming a Confucian Christian in the Mid-1890s

There were a few significant time periods in Zhang's early Christian life: the time before the winter of 1892 when he studied the Bible and learned from other Christians as a religious inquirer and finally decided to become a Christian (he was twenty-one years old at the time),[56] his baptism in the spring of 1893, his secret departure to Guangzhou for theological study in the summer of 1893, his return after this six-month trip, and the next two years until the winter of 1895 when his father died. The following analysis will try to follow these time periods.

3.3.2.1 Before Conversion

Zhang's first contact with Christianity was through the New Testament when he was sixteen, but he quickly put it aside because he could not understand it at all. By then, he was already a skilful writer of the eight-legged essay and rhyming verse, which are the best literary examples of Neo-Confucian influence.[57]

He had a short experience with geomancy. At the age of seventeen, he submitted to his father's request that he study geomancy. Since he married at the age of sixteen and became a Confucian tutor, his father might have intended to find an additional source of income for him. After a year's study, he mastered it and was able to accurately locate the surrounding gods and devils according to the theory of geomancy. In this process, a doubt arose in his mind: Were the locations of those gods and devils designed by a bigger god or invented by humankind? If a bigger god was in control, then his location would be unknowable. If humankind invented this theory, then there

---

56. Traditionally, Chinese would add one more year to one's age. Zhang Yijing and his son Zhang Qiutao calculated his age this way, as seen in Appendix 1.
57. Zhang, "How I Became a Christian," 1.

was neither good fortune to pursue nor bad luck to avoid. After a deliberate testing, he gave it up completely.[58] This issue will be discussed further in the category of his commitment to science in chapter 5. Shortly after, his interest in studying Christianity was aroused by one issue. Zhang recalled:

> After giving it [geomancy] up, all my familiars thought I went too far and none of them could understand me. When a colporteur arrived, I picked up two Christian tracts to read. Although the language was not refined enough, the ideas presented in them were true and faultless. Then I studied the doctrines deeper and then I became a Christian. I often say that the philosophical words of the Chinese Confucians in ancient times (中国儒先哲言, *zhongguo ru xian zhe yan*) could serve as a vanguard for preaching Christianity in China. My case serves as proof.[59]

A significant point revealed here is that Zhang, by the benchmark of his Confucian understanding, evaluated the Christian message in the two tracts as correct. Another significant point is that his Confucian identity helped him gain confidence in his future choice of Christian identity.

In the spring of 1892, he began to read the New Testament seriously. Although he was amazed at Jesus's life and teachings as recorded in the New Testament, he had no idea about the purpose of the book. On the contrary, some adverse reports[60] about the Catholic church and Protestant missionaries served to confirm his prejudice so that he described three Christian visitors to his Christian neighbour as evildoers at their first meeting.[61]

3.3.2.2 Conversion

His rejection of geomancy became one of the two reasons for his eventual acceptance of the three Chinese Christian visitors because they also opposed geomancy. The other reason was his approval of their attitude towards gambling and opium. He recalled the process:

---

58. Yijing Zhang 张亦镜, "Mining Knowledge of Quintessence: On Funeral by Sima Guang (国粹采适: 司马光葬论)," *True Light* 真光 10, no. 3 (1911): 43.

59. Zhang, "Mining Knowledge of Quintessence," 43.

60. Zhang did not specify the unfavourable reports. According to the author's reading of his writings, they should be no more than violating Chinese laws and traditions, bullying neighbours, and rumours like killing children.

61. Zhang, "How I Became a Christian," 2–3.

When the three of them arrived, I happened to see Chen Shousheng and them walking in the street of Tong An Xu (同安墟). I asked Chen who they were. Chen told me their names and said they had come to preach the Way of God (传上帝道, *chuan shangdi dao*) from Guangzhou. When I heard "preach the Way of God," I was very surprised. I took "the Way of God" as the Catholic Church and recalled the words (those adverse reports) of my friend, Mr. Mo, so I took them as evildoers and ignored them. Chen Shousheng once tried to convert one of my cousins with the same family name as mine who was an opium addict. Somehow, he believed in a rumour that a Catholic Church member could receive four taels of silver monthly. He seized this opportunity and went to Chen's home to become a believer with his selfish intention. He came across me and forced me to accompany him. And I did not know Chen Shousheng was a Christian until then. At Chen's home, Mr. Tan Baode questioned my cousin as to whether he had habits of gambling and opium-taking. If so, my cousin should first quit them before joining the Church. My cousin sat against a table and silently rejected his words. When I found that Mr. Tan was capable of speaking such words, I knew he was not an evildoer. Then I began to talk with him, saying "I have read your canon. The doctrines are good, but the believers may not be able to carry them out, which might be laughed at by other people." Tan explained to me in detail and showed me a few tracts. By then I finally understood they were protestant Christians, not Catholic members. I also established that they did not give silver to believers and that they firmly opposed the absurdity of geomancy. Thus, I took them as people with the same views and visited them every day to study Christianity. By this, I saw more clearly than before when I studied it on my own. Then I was determined to become a Christian.[62]

---

62. Zhang, 3–4.

Just as Zhang's Confucian understanding served as a value reference in his judgment of the Christian message in the two tracts, his approval of Christians' rejection of gambling and opium-taking also demonstrated the significance of his Confucian values which preceded his future commitment to Christian values.

Since his Confucian identity served as a standard for his acceptance of the value of Christianity and since it existed before his Christian identity, it is safe to say that his Confucian identity was structured hierarchically higher than his Christian identity and his Confucian identity was his primary or focal identity while his commitment to Christianity had a secondary importance at this moment. He found some shared content between the two identities, but he would soon suffer from the conflicting dimensions between the two identities.

3.3.2.3 *Conflicts after Conversion*

In the next spring, he was baptized after which he had a regular Bible study with other Christians in the neighbourhood.

His conversion immediately put him into conflict with his father. Christian identity jeopardized one's fame and even one's safety in nineteenth-century China. Zhang's Christian neighbour was an example of hesitancy to identify as a Christian out of concern for his status and safety. Even though the two families were closely knit, the neighbour withheld information of his Christian identity until the arrival of the three Christian visitors. Zhang himself is another example of prevailing prejudice against Christianity prior to his conversion. Therefore, it is not surprising that Zhang's conversion led to his father's great displeasure. Fearing that his son was departing from the right path, the father was so anxious to stop him that he frequently threatened him with death. One day after his baptism, when Zhang went for a Bible study, his father searched the neighbourhood for him with an iron rod, but his father knocked at the wrong door. Zhang recalled:

> Luckily, I studied at another Christian's home; otherwise, I would have either died or suffered serious wounds. For this reason [his father's anger], I often prayed to God in tears to

change the hearts of my parents and family and to give me a chance to study the Bible in Guang Dong province.[63]

In the summer of 1893, anticipating his father's refusal, he left a letter and went secretly to Guangzhou for five months of theological training. Because of poor transportation, his father did not receive any letter for half a year. In his great worry and anxiety, he was ready to sue his Christian neighbour for his missing son. Zhang reflected:

> He did not calm down until he saw me. This period was the hardest time for me. . . . After that, he put me under close watch and never gave me another chance of returning to Guang Dong. I had to stay at home farming or tutoring. Since I had brought home a few torn old books about Christianity and science, I studied them in my free time, and they enriched my knowledge of Christianity and science. I also kept exchanging letters with other Christians like Liao Zhuoan and Zhang Yunwen through visiting preachers, and they sent me some copies of *The Review of the Times* (万国公报) and other dated newspapers to me which kept me aware of current affairs and alleviated my loneliness. Only one thing became a gnawing regret in my life: I refused to study for the Imperial Examination in spite of the fact that my relatives continued to push me to take it so that I might bring glory to my parents by my possible success in it; (the Manchu official's cap was so ugly that I hated to see it). I also failed in convincing my parents of Jesus' love and salvation. Consequently, my father was very unhappy for different reasons and could not understand me, which resulted in his illness. In the winter of 1895, three years after my conversion, he coughed blood and died. How sad it is.[64]

When Zhang was twenty-four, his father died. He blamed himself because he could neither satisfy his father passing the Examination nor see him obtain

---

63. Zhang, 3.
64. Zhang, 3–4.

salvation.⁶⁵ He abided by the Confucian rite of mourning the death of his father for the next three years.

3.3.2.4 A View from His Father's Perspective

There were a few factors leading to his father's unhappiness. Immediately after Zhang's baptism, his rage would have been stirred by his own prejudice against Christianity and other people's disapproval. Afterwards, the fear that his son might become an evildoer may have dispersed, but he found a new and serious problem when his son's Christian identity precluded him from taking the Imperial Examination. Another factor was that his son stopped offering sacrifice to the ancestors.⁶⁶

Before the Treaty of 1860 which promised to protect Christian preachers and believers, it was stipulated by the Qing government that Chinese Christians could not work in the government. Before 1870, the article which stipulated severe punishment of Christian preachers and believers was still in the Qing Legal Code (大清律例). After 1871, on paper, Christians were allowed to take the Imperial Examination, but in actuality, the majority of the officials adopted an attitude of containment with the motive of safeguarding Confucianism. Christians had to meet two requirements before taking the examination: (1) kowtowing before the image of Confucius at the ceremony of making sacrifice to him; (2) obtaining recommendation from a *linsheng*⁶⁷ (廩生) who usually would not do so because Christians were unwilling to join the sacrificing ceremony.⁶⁸ In 1684, the Kangxi Emperor (1654–1722) had included several elements in the ceremony of making a sacrifice to Confucius:

---

65. Zhang, 4.

66. Yijing Zhang 张亦镜, "Against Song Shixiang's Saying That Christianity Allows Offering Sacrifices to Ancestors 驳宋史香耶稣教不禁人祭先说," in *(1928), A Quarter of a Century of True Light, Selected* 真光丛刊, Part 2: *The Gospel Discussed and Explained* 辩道文, ed. Yijing Zhang (Shanghai 上海: China Baptist Publication Society 中华浸会书局, 1908), 4.

67. *Linsheng* was a Confucian scholar who lived on government grants.

68. Fei Qiao 乔飞, "From Secretly Prevention to Seriously Protection, Enumeration and Analysis on the Christian Regulations in Late Qing Dynasty 从 '密为防闲' 到 '明为保护' – 晚清基督教法律政策之演变及其法史疏释," 17 October 2016, 3–4, http://www.chinaaid.net/2016/10/blog-post_78.html.

welcoming the spirit of Confucius, seeing him out, kneeling three times, and kowtowing nine times.[69]

His father, a peasant, would have been startled when he first heard that his son's Christian identity forfeited his qualification for the Examination. After a more extensive investigation, he might have felt relieved to a certain extent to hear the more accurate information that his son still had the possibility of taking the Examination if he met the two requirements. However, this relief did not last long. When his son publicly refused not only to take the Examination but also to offer sacrifices to the ancestors, he was completely overwhelmed by rage, sadness, and disappointment. He exhausted all available means to persuade his son, but all his attempts failed.

For a Chinese peasant, wealth and respect were natural desires, but opportunities to realize those desires were few. That was the reason why he sent his son to learn geomancy and have a Confucian education. As was the case with most Chinese parents, he had expected his son to bring glory and hope to the family by passing the Imperial Examination. When his son first gave up geomancy he was disappointed, but Zhang's refusal to take the Examination – the only hope for wealth, respect, and future of the family, was a blow from which he could not recover. From his perspective, his son not only chose the shame of following a foreign religion and the disgrace of stopping sacrifice to the ancestors, but he even tried to convert him.

3.3.2.5 *The Reason for Zhang's Refusal to Take the Exam and Offer Sacrifices*

Why did Zhang refuse to take the Examination? Though the Manchu's oppression of Han, political corruption, and the aesthetic value of official trappings might have lessened Zhang's desire for a government office, they could not be the main cause for his refusal to take the Examination. From the very beginning of his education, he had been taught the importance of the Examination, and those elements were not new. Moreover, he did not obviously have this problem until he came back from the study in Guangzhou. Furthermore, in 1901, he did not oppose Liao Zhuoan's intention of taking the Examination

---

69. Zhongping Liu 刘中平, "On the Sacrifice System of Qing Dynasty 论清代祭典制度," *Journal of Liaoning University (Philosophy and Social Sciences Edition)* 辽宁大学学报(哲学社会科学版) 36, no. 6 (2008): 86.

but merely suggested Western learning because he felt that the eight-legged essay would soon become eclipsed by Western education forms. All of this shows that he did not have a major problem with taking the Examination itself. The main reason for his refusal was that he did not want to kowtow before the image of Confucius at the sacrifice ceremony which hinted at the existence of the spirit of Confucius.

Just as the Rites Controversy surrounded the Roman Catholic missionaries during the seventeenth and eighteenth centuries, the controversy over the religiosity of worshipping Confucius and worshipping ancestors surrounded the Protestants during the nineteenth and twentieth centuries. Zhang's *Argument against Offering Sacrifices to the Ancestors* which was written in 1894 and included in his article of 1908 show that he saw religiosity in these rituals.[70] He recalled in 1908:

> In the early days when I learned the Bible, I dared not to transgress the rite of sacrifice. Later on, I found this practice was not ordered by God and it came into being after the death of the Yellow Emperor. This rite was established by the sages out of their ignorance and it was distorted by the following generations. The sages did not really see with their eyes that the souls of the dead needed to eat and drink. Then I decided to forsake it and join the Church to be a Christian. After joining the Church, some friends often criticized me for giving up offering sacrifice, so I wrote *Argument against Offering Sacrifices to the Ancestors*.[71]

The "early days" of his recollection would be the winter of 1892 when he started to question offering sacrifice to the ancestors and Confucius. And "his joining the Church" would refer to his baptism in the spring of 1893 by which time he had decided to forgo such ceremonies. Since the gap between his baptism and his departure for Guangzhou was too short to manifest his new decisions, he did not feel the full impact of these decisions until the period after he returned from Guangzhou. The turmoil he felt after his trip to Guangzhou signified that he was experiencing external conflicts and internal

---

70. Zhang, "Against Song Shixiang's Saying," 4.
71. Zhang, 4.

struggles in a very serious way.[72] His feelings combined with his father's feelings suggest that he openly refused to participate in such activities, which triggered the serious conflict with his father and his own internal struggle.

Social identities are those aspects of self-definition that derive from groups and corporate group-related behaviour, emotions, or evaluations.[73] Social identity is a sense of inner solidarity with a group's ideals and a perception of others' recognition of one's own commitment. Zhang's social identity as a Confucian expected him to keep in harmony with other Confucians by worshipping Confucius and the ancestors as they did. However, worshipping the spirits of the dead conflicted with his commitment to Christianity which teaches him to worship God alone.

After his return from Guangzhou by the end of 1893, to deal with this problem of conflicting identities or conflicting aspects of identity, Zhang chose to identify with his choice of Christianity over Confucianism by seeing God's command as predominant and simply refusing to worship the spirits of the dead, which Yamolsky, Amiot, and de la Sablonnière would call a means of categorization.[74] Externally, other Confucians saw this as a violation of the Confucian tradition. Subjectively, Zhang seemed to be also aware of his departure from the norm understood by the Confucians of the time, including himself.

However, before long, Zhang found another way for Confucian Christians, including himself, to reconcile the two conflicting dimensions by redefining the meaning of worshipping the ancestors so that the difference between their personal identity as Christians and their group identity as Confucians could be managed.[75]

In *The Origin of Making Sacrifice to the Ancestors* (祭先源流考), Zhang found that although there existed the rite of commemorating people of merit and virtue in ancient times, the rite of worshipping the ancestors did not originate with the Yellow Emperor. It was not even established by the emperors Yao and Shun. It started in the Xia dynasty (around 2070–1600 BC) and was limited to the emperors. Afterwards, it was extended to the common people

---

72. Zhang, "How I Became a Christian," 3.
73. Tajfel, "Intergroup Behaviour," 423–46.
74. Yampolsky, Amiot, and de la Sablonnière, "Multicultural Identity Integration Scale," 168–69.
75. Haslam and Ellemers, "Identity Processes in Organizations," 737.

and many practices and procedures began to be invented.⁷⁶ And the practice of burning incense before the ancestral tablets was an indirect result of the Jewish people burning sacrifice before God.⁷⁷ Concerning many practices such as burning paper by way of sending money to the spirits of the ancestors, Zhang concluded:

> They were not included as the sages established this rite. However, people carried them out without checking by whom they were established. One could say they were sinning against the sages in ancient times.⁷⁸

In the end, Zhang bridged the worship of the ancestor and the worship of God by saying that since remembering the ancestor was a merit, people should also commemorate Adam, the first person created by God and the ancestor of all mankind. He said:

> How to cherish the memory of Adam? The best way was to fear God and believe in Christ . . . Christ came to save the descendants of Adam from their sins. The Word of God has become flesh and Christianity should be accepted by all people regardless of colour and race.⁷⁹

Zhang's redefinition of worshipping the ancestors enabled the Confucian Christians to sense a consistency between their loyalty to the Confucian sages and their commitment to God's command, which spared them from feeling that they were violating their Confucian identity.

Before *The Origin of Making Sacrifice to the Ancestors* (祭先源流考) was published in 1916, it had been reprinted five times as a separate edition by CBPS.⁸⁰ During the period of more than ten years before his whole family's conversion in 1905, he had not dared to destroy his family's ancestral hall because he had been searching for a suitable substitute to commemorate the

---

76. Yijing Zhang, "The Origin of Making Sacrifice to the Ancestors (祭先源流考)," in (1928), *A Quarter of a Century of True Light, Selected* 真光丛刊, Part 4: *Religious Evidence and Origins* 关于宗教之考据文字, ed. Yijing Zhang (Shanghai 上海: China Baptist Publication Society 中华浸会书局, 1916), 9–10.

77. Zhang, "Origin of Making Sacrifice," 24.

78. Zhang, 24.

79. Zhang, 29.

80. Zhang, 30.

ancestors.⁸¹ This means that, by 1895 or even earlier, he had already redefined worshipping the ancestors as he searched for a replacement to express his gratitude to his ancestors. Thus, we know he quickly resumed his subjective sense loyalty to this Confucian norm, a transformed Confucian norm with its "true" meaning.

The conflict as explained above can be explained as a conflict between a Confucian idea and a Christian theology; however, this line of explanation risks leaving aside the subject's emotional attachment and meaning-making. Ideology is emotionally irrelevant if there is no commitment to it. For example, if someone had no commitment to "being Chinese" or "being a Muslim," they should not be emotionally influenced by criticism like "as a Chinese, you should hate the Japanese" or "as a Muslim, you should visit Mecca." If native Chinese gave a long talk about Brexit, the British would feel curious about what it meant to them and how it influenced their emotion. Thus, this study attempts to examine Zhang Yijiang and his search for a Chinese Christian identity by using identity theory, a theory which was described by Kunnen and Bosma as person-context integrations.⁸²

More seriously than the rituals, Zhang's act of disobeying his father brought his filial piety into question. Before analyzing the way he dealt with the problem of being filial, we will review the development of Zhang's Christian identity in the next section.

3.3.2.6 *The Development of Zhang's Christian Identity*

According to Marcia, Zhang was in a state called identity diffusion while exploring Christianity and he did not have this kind of identity conflict over the Chinese rituals that he habitually practised.⁸³ After he chose the commitment to Christianity but while his commitment was still weak, his Christian identity was in a state called moratorium. In Leak's understanding, low levels of religious commitment are already associated with identity diffusion.⁸⁴ In any case, during these two stages, Zhang's Confucian identity was in the dominant position relative to his Christian identity. As a result, the conflicts

---

81. Zhang, 29.
82. Kunnen and Bosma, "Fischer's Skill Theory Applied," 250.
83. Marcia, "Development and Validation of Ego."
84. Leak, "Assessment of the Relationship," 205.

of identities were looming, but they would not have caused major difficulties to him, and he still accepted the rituals. As his Christian identity grew and reached the stage called identity achievement, the conflict became more real and serious, and he experienced more inner struggle over it. Even at the stage of identity achievement, the strength of the identity still varies because religious doubts still exist so that belief-confirming consultation (BCC) and belief-threatening consultation (BTC) are sought.[85] In the case of Zhang, by examining his struggle with his father over the Chinese rituals, the development stages of his Christian identity can be roughly delineated as diffusion, moratorium, and achievement. The changes in his attitudes also reflect the development of the strength of his Christian identity and its relationship with his Confucian identity.

3.3.2.6.1 Diffusion

Before his conversion, Zhang must have learned the general attitude of the Qing officials to Christianity and the prerequisites for Christians to take the Examination. However, he decided to explore Christianity anyway, just as he dared to test the power of gods and devils in geomancy at the risk of his own and his family's well-being. This period between the spring and the winter of 1892 was Zhang's diffusion stage. At this stage, the superiority of his Confucian identity was obvious because he judged the thoughts in the two Christian tracts according to his Confucian principles.[86]

3.3.2.6.2 Moratorium to achievement

There was a period of about six months from the winter of 1892, when he decided to become a Christian, to the summer of 1893 when he set off for Guangzhou. During this period, he attended a regular Bible study with other Chinese Christians and was baptized in the spring. He must have gained some basic knowledge of Christianity during this process, such as "worshipping God alone," which is the first of the Ten Commandments. His commitment to Christianity became stronger as he began to decide to stop offering sacrifices to the ancestors. He sensed the religiosity of the Chinese rituals which was contradictory to the Bible's teaching. However, he did not manifest his decisions, so his father did not really worry about his qualifications

---

85. Hunsberger, Pratt, and Pancer, "Adolescent Identity Formation," 365.
86. Zhang, "Mining Knowledge of Quintessence," 43.

for the Examination and was expecting him to meet the two prerequisites. This suggests that either six months were too short of a time period for him to manifest his new decisions or that his determination to sever himself from those Confucian practices might not yet have become strong enough. Even so, Zhang's new Christian identity was seen in his public baptism, his perseverance under his father's persecution, and his tearful prayers for his parents and family. Therefore, his Christian identity was, at least, in the stage of moratorium. According to Leak, identity achievement is related to higher levels of religious commitment and maturity in faith.[87] Zhang demonstrated a higher level of commitment at that time. In fact, when he prayed for a chance to study the Bible in Guangzhou, he might have been subconsciously seeking BCC after receiving BTC involuntarily from his father, which was linked to identity achievement.[88] Thus, it is reasonable to believe that his Christian identity was progressing from moratorium to early achievement during this period.

3.3.2.6.3 Achievement

At the outset of his six-month trip to Guangzhou, Zhang spent two weeks on the outbound road in the company of Mr. Tan who was one of the three Christian visitors. For the next two months in Guangzhou, he became a full-time student of a Bible class under the guidance of Rev. Rosewell H. Graves (纪好弼, 1833–1912) of the Southern Baptist Convention Mission. After this, he travelled around selling Christian publications for two months, mostly in rural areas before he went back to Guangzhou to continue as a full-time Bible student again for one more month. Finally, Pastor Lu accompanied him during the three weeks of travel to return home.

These six months were roughly divided into three parts with his colporteur experience as the middle one. It is possible to view the huge amount of insults and humiliation he suffered in the middle of his sojourn as a BTC in which his religious doubts would have been aroused and his Christian identity challenged. If so, the first and the last parts of his trip would have offered him BCC, thus facilitating his identity achievement. It is a legitimate assumption that, during this period, his Christian identity was further consolidated.

---

87. Leak, "Assessment of the Relationship," 205.
88. Hunsberger, Pratt, and Pancer, "Adolescent Identity Formation," 365.

Zhang's return from Guangzhou would have relieved his parents' worry and anxiety. Why then did he feel worse upon his return? Naturally, Zhang would have felt sorry because his absence had caused his parents' pain. However, this apologetic feeling could not have been the cause of his most painful emotions because his parents knew of his location and safety through the letter he left for them. Moreover, their anxiety subsided at the sight of him. What happened that prompted him to call this period "the most difficult period" for him?

As has been discussed, his father opposed his being a Christian mainly because it was extremely hard for a Christian to take the Imperial Examination and to get a job in the government. His father anticipated that Zhang would find a way to meet the two requirements, though it would be troublesome. His father did not feel that there was anything wrong with fulfilling these two conditions. In the two years following Zhang's return from Guangzhou, he clearly resisted his relatives' pressure to take the Imperial Examination. This shows that his father had failed to persuade him. Based on the teaching he received in Guangzhou and his later constant and open refusal to take the Examination and offer sacrifices, we may conclude that his determination became stronger either in Guangzhou or shortly after his return. His refusal to take the Exam undoubtedly triggered his father's fiercest reaction, which was his external conflict.

However, the real conflict was not between the father and the son, but between the son's two identities. Zhang's refusal to worship Confucius reveals that meeting God's requirement was more important than the prestige of passing the Imperial Examination – a sign of his Christian identity and Confucian identity being hierarchically organized. This was the last thing that his father wanted to see. What's more, he stopped offering sacrifices to his ancestors, which led other Confucians to accuse him of being a traitor (名教罪人),[89] which was another trigger of his father's rage. If these two actions only caused external pressure, then the act of disobeying his father itself led him to a more serious question internally. He had to ask himself whether or not he was filial.

Filial piety also caused his gnawing regret after his father's death two years later. The complication was that not only is filial piety a core value of

---

89. Zhang, "Origin of Making Sacrifice," 8.

Confucianism, but the Ten Commandments also clearly require honouring one's father and mother. Zhang found he was rebelling against both Confucianism and Christianity.

3.3.2.6.4 Reaching the initial union between the two identities

Filial piety in Confucianism required children to obey parents in every case, even when parents were wrong. Disobedience of one's parents could lead to a death sentence. This is different from the similar biblical command which is conditioned by honouring God. Confucius and the Confucian classics did not teach worshipping Confucius, but filial piety was fundamental. The participants of the ceremony of worshipping Confucius were mostly intellectuals while filial piety was a demand for people of all social strata. In this sense, filial piety was a more prominent element in a Confucian identity than worshipping Confucius. Zhang was very filial, which can be seen in his habit of giving his share of meat to his mother. Although his Christian identity grew after coming back from Guangzhou, he was still a strong Confucian. The commandment of honouring one's father and mother in the Bible more likely served as evidence of the value of filial piety in a Confucian sense rather than vice versa. That means that he still understood filial piety in its Confucian sense and therefore felt unfilial because he disobeyed and vexed his father again and again. Therefore, the situation arose that following the command "worshipping God alone" required by his Christian identity caused him to become unfilial, an act despised by his Confucian identity. That explains why he was enduring his most difficult period.[90] Facing his father's rage and friends' rebukes, he was compelled to contemplate this paradox deeply until he could find peace. Then, for the following two years, before his father died in 1895, he did not feel as conflicted as he had when he first returned from Guangzhou.

During the two years before his father's death, his family and relatives continued to try to persuade him to take the Examination and persisted in criticizing him for not offering sacrifices to the ancestors, an unwelcomed BTC. However, it was also during these two years that he received BCC through reading Christian publications and science books and through his

---

90. Zhang, "How I Became a Christian," 3.

communication with other Christians. Another source of BCC was his communication with God:

> At that time, I only became [sic] a Christian for more than one year. I had a very difficult time at home, so the only things I could do were to read the Bible and pray, wishing that God would imperceptibly but inexorably influence them so that they would know that there was nothing wrong with my new faith and grant me the freedom of faith. Really and always, I felt God heard and accepted my prayers. Then I felt comforted and I had joy.[91]

With his Christian identity gaining strength, he embarked upon solving the conflict between his two identities. Since it would be impossible for him to give up either of these two identities, he had to find union in them – he had to learn to be a Confucian Christian or a Christian Confucian.

The rage of his father, the rebuke from other people, and his own internal struggle forced him to think about the meaning of being filial. Finally, in 1894, he poured his thoughts into *Argument against Offering Sacrifices to the Ancestors* which was included in his article written in 1908.

> How to annul the ceremony of sacrificing? The answer lies in the Heavenly Way or *tiandao*. We know *tiandao* treasures life and soul and spirit, so we should treasure this life and exhort our parents to obtain this life. After they understood this, their hope would be put on God's grace rather than descendants' sacrifices. And they would clearly know that they cannot really enjoy the sacrifices so that they would never allow their descendants to offer sacrifices to their tablets. If the descendants insisted on sacrificing, parents would feel sad over their stupidity and ignorance to a degree that they did not want these unworthy to be their descendants any longer. Thus, after knowing *tiandao*, parents would view the descendants who still offered sacrifice to their tablets as a grave violation of filial piety. Then why should [we] bother offering sacrifice to show filial piety? Even though children failed in helping parents to obtain the Way or it was

---

91. Zhang, "Bible Reading and Praying," 98.

too late to obtain it, they should not play a hypocrite to please the world by offering sacrifices because they know their parents' destination after death who did not need sacrifices. It would hurt parents deeper when they saw their descendants sinning by offering sacrifices. Although parents did not know the Way while living, they certainly would know the truth after death and they definitely did not want their descendants to commit the sin anymore.[92]

In this piece of writing, he did not clearly say "helping parents obtain salvation was the true fulfilment of love for parents," as he said in 1908.[93] However, he did say "parents would view descendants' offering sacrifices to their tablets as an unfilial act" and "it is significant to help parents obtain the Way." He reinterpreted the Confucian value of "being filial" and endowed it with a new Christian perspective. This is why he did not feel conflicted as before even though his father did not compromise at all during these two years.

With regard to his father's death, he partially blamed himself because it was his father's perspective of having an unfilial son that caused him to fall ill in the first place. He did say that his father's death was his gnawing regret. By this, he meant two things: (1) he was not able to bring honour to his parents by passing the Examination – in other words, he could not be filial in the way they expected; and (2) he was not able to help his father to find Jesus's salvation.[94]

Interpreting true filial piety as accomplishing one's parents' salvation signifies that Zhang reached a union between his two identities. His refusal to worship Confucius and offer sacrifices to the ancestors did not necessarily mean a betrayal of his Confucian identity, but being unfilial in the Confucian sense was indeed unacceptable to his Confucian identity. However, the reinterpretation of filial piety, the Confucian term, to conform to the Bible would reassure him that he would in fact be unfilial were he to offer sacrifices in the sight of his dead ancestors and that he was truly being filial in his refusal to worship Confucius and offer sacrifices because this was in fact the first step in pointing his parents to *tiandao* or God. According to Burke, a focal identity

---

92. Zhang, "Against Song Shixiang's Saying," 9.
93. Zhang, 13.
94. Zhang, "How I Became a Christian," 4.

that shares a dimension of meaning with a second identity will change the meanings of the second identity to be consistent with the focal identity (and vice versa).[95] Under this lens, we see that Zhang's Christian identity has risen to be his focal or primary identity because he has transformed his Confucian understanding of being filial to be consistent with his comprehension of the Christian message. In other words, his Confucian identity was experiencing transformation by his Christian identity.

It can be seen that, in the initial stage, Zhang became a Confucian Christian with peace between these two identities. Nonetheless, he differed from many other Confucian Christians as listed above in that his Christian identity was hierarchically structured above his Confucian identity. Zhang's search for a Confucian Christian identity did not progress smoothly, and it unexpectedly suffered a setback and regressed. Before an analysis of this, it is worthwhile to take a look at the theological contents of his Christian identity.

3.3.2.7 A Glimpse of the Theological Contents of His Christian Identity around 1894

Zhang's theological understanding may partially be seen in his letter to Liao Zhuoan written in the autumn of 1894 but included in his article of 1929:

> Principles cannot win over selfishness and Satan's attack was unpredictable; nature will be tested by temptations and the test is changing. The brief and illusory life is like a dream, but pitfalls are everywhere. If *xinde* (信德) is not firm, sin would bring about destruction; if we only read the Bible occasionally, then there will be no intimate feeling when we pray to God.[96]

By *xinde* (信德), Zhang meant faith, as seen in his praise of Moses's *xinde*.[97] In *Argument against Offering Sacrifices to the Ancestors* which was written in 1894, he wrote:

> God is the fairest and there is no partiality with Him. God is omniscient, and nothing would escape his notice. He rewards

---

95. P. J. Burke, "Identity Change," *Social Psychology Quarterly* 69 (2006): 86.
96. Zhang, "Bible Reading and Praying," 98.
97. Yijing Zhang 张亦镜, "On Moses (摩西论)," in *(1928), A Quarter of a Century of True Light, Selected* 真光丛刊, Part 1: *Concerning the Scriptures* 说经文, ed. Yijing Zhang (Shanghai 上海: China Baptist Publication Society 中华浸会书局, 1906), 5.

the obedient with virtues and talents while living and eternal life before Him after death. For the rebellious, God overthrows them because they destroyed kind people and morality and justice. When their evils reached to the full, they would fall into the hell and suffer punishment eternally along with the Devil. This is God's justice and a universal principle.[98]

Such writings show that he believed that the presence of God could be felt if one read the Bible often, and he had this kind of experience. To him, Satan was real and active, but the law by itself could not keep one from sinning because of humankind's selfish nature. Prayer and frequent Bible reading could effectively help one achieve victory over temptations if one behaved in accordance with one's faith. However, if one did sin, there were very serious or even irremediable consequences. Such sayings reveal that Zhang realized he was a sinner who constantly faced temptations. It was not a particular sin but the full number of sins that caused people to end up in hell. Seemingly, this idea was a result of the influence of Confucianism as can be seen in the popular saying "The iniquity of Shang is full. Heaven gives command to destroy it[99] (Heaven will not tolerate anymore)."[100] This can serve as another piece of evidence of his Confucian identity's influence. Due to the lack of his writing in 1894, his views on repentance, grace, the forgiveness of sin, Jesus, and the Holy Spirit are not completely clear. Were he to be judged solely according to the material above, it seems that he believed righteousness was won by being obedient.

3.3.3 Being a Confucian Christian before 1905

There are also a few time markers for this period in Zhang's life. After his father's death in the winter of 1895, Zhang observed the Confucian rite of mourning him for three years. After completing this rite, he went to work as a journalist for a Christian newspaper in Hong Kong for six months after which he quit the job and gave up his membership in a church. He had no

---

98. Zhang, "Against Song Shixiang's Saying," 8–9.

99. James Legge, *The Sacred Books of China: The Texts of Confucianism*, Part 1 (Oxford: The Clarendon Press, 1879), 126.

100. 商罪貫盈; 天命誅之. 《尚書. 泰誓》, the chapter "Declaration 1" in *The Book of History*.

connection with any church until five years later. In the winter of 1904, he devoted his life to serving Jesus. During the one year prior to his joining *True Light* in the winter of 1905, he actively led worship and converted people to Christianity.

3.3.3.1 The Development of His Christian Identity between 1895 and 1905

3.3.3.1.1 Ascension

During his three-year mourning period, Zhang would have lived as usual: farming, tutoring, and regularly meeting with other Christians.

His work for the Christian newspaper in Hong Kong was the start of his career of preaching through writing, which meant that he began to share his Christian faith with others. During this six-month period, he would have joined a church pastored by Westerners and had chances of reading a wide range of Christian literature. Since his employment was intensively connected to Christian ministry, his Christian identity must have had a better chance of gaining strength. He said he "lived a religious life with preaching through writing."[101] Everything would have looked good: a decent job in a cosmopolitan city and a nice church. If there had been no disruption, he might have been able to maintain the close connection between his life and ministry for a longer time. However, he often felt deeply humiliated or *xiuru* (羞辱) when he saw the Chinese being bullied by the foreigners. His nationalistic feelings might have been aggravated by a cultural barrier so that he began to identify Western pastors in his church with all the other foreigner bullies. It is not sure if he received any BTC, but the end result was that he decided to quit both his job and his church membership. The nationalistic feeling which led to his first resignation is further analyzed in his commitment to modern nationalism in chapter 4.

3.3.3.1.2 Regression

When Zhang quit his church membership, he did not abandon his Christian identity. He simply asked his Western pastors to allow him to be a believer without denomination. During the next five years while in his hometown, he neither attended church nor joined any Bible study group. Generally speaking,

---

101. Zhang, "How I Became a Christian," 4.

his Christian identity remained stagnant. As his son Qiutao said, he lived a purposeless life like a ship without a rudder.[102] Since there was no obvious exploration and commitment, his Christian identity regressed from a status of achievement back into diffusion.

He continued to work as a farmer and a Confucian tutor, and his Confucian identity remained strong as can be illustrated in the following descriptions.

A couplet written by Zhang hung in his living room on which was written: "Humility can maintain peace with people and thoughtful considerations of a hundred things can preserve the family, which is good, but the opposite is fearful; Reading brings enlightenment and cultivation brings nourishment, which is enough, so what else do I need?" (和众以一谦, 保家以百思, 善哉, 反是则可惧; 读书能明理, 耕田能养生, 足矣, 此外复何求.)[103] In this couplet, not only are humility, peace, thoughtful considerations, and enlightenment the characters of the honourable man,[104] but reading and cultivation stand for the traditional Confucian lifestyle.[105] Preserving the family is the purpose of regulation of the family, one of the eight clauses. Even the Chinese word for "which is good (善哉)" had its origin in the *Legend of Spring and Autumn Century by Zuo Qiuming* (左氏春秋传) and *The Analects*. All of the ideals, means, terms, and expressions in this couplet were typically Confucian.

Additionally, Zhang recorded how he saved two innocent men who were strangers to him at the risk of his own life and how he was harshly beaten in the process.[106] He thought this event was worthy of recording. Why was recording it so important? Perhaps this issue demonstrated two of the three elements of an honourable man, namely kindness and courage. Confucius said "to see what is right and not to do it is want of courage (见义不为, 无勇

---

102. Zhang, "Chronology of Zhang Yijing," 18.

103. Zhang, 18.

104. Fengyan Wang 汪凤炎 and Hong Zheng 郑红, "Confucius' Thirteen Standards for the Noble and the Petty 孔子界定 '君子人格' 与 '小人人格' 的十三条标准," *Morality and Civilization* 道德与文明, no. 4 (2008): 50–51.

105. Zigang Deng 邓子刚, "The Contemporary Significance of Confucius' Idea of Cultivation and Reading 儒家耕读传家思想的现代意义," *Journal of Hunan First Normal College* 湖南第一师范学报 7, no. 1 (2007): 63.

106. Zhang, "How I Became a Christian," 6–9.

也),"¹⁰⁷ while Mencius said "I will let life go, and choose righteousness."¹⁰⁸ In *The Analects*, the most important feature of an honourable man is kindness or benevolence.¹⁰⁹ In this incident, Zhang succeeded in measuring up to the standards for an honourable man or *junzi*.

Another illustration of Zhang's continued Confucian identity can be seen in his second resignation. Although Confucius, Mencius, and Xun Zi composed the sayings about seeking justice through retaliation,¹¹⁰ the keynote of Confucianism is still kindness. In an outward show of benevolence, while working for the local government, Zhang felt very uneasy after having recorded confessions of seventeen people who were executed within one year. Thus, he resigned from this office. Buoye finds that there was a contradiction between the demands of bureaucratic efficiency and Confucian benevolence in the Qing system for adjudicating capital crimes.¹¹¹ Therefore, Zhang's second resignation was caused by his sense of a conflict against Confucian values.

One final example of Zhang's Confucian identity remaining intact is in his opposition to participating in the lottery. Gambling is presented as an evil deed in *Confucius Sayings Collected from His Family* (孔子家语) and one of five unfilial deeds in Mencius's *lilou zhangju xia* (离娄章句下). His commitment to this concept convinced him of the innocence of the three Chinese Christian visitors because he found they too were opposed to gambling. And this commitment explains why he refused to join the activity of buying lottery tickets and later refused the share of money won from lottery gains bought in his name.

From the descriptions in this section, it is reasonable to conclude that Zhang's Confucian identity had also reached the status of achievement. What's more, his Confucian identity was very vigorous. Nevertheless, this does not mean Zhang's Christian identity disappeared completely. On the contrary, even in a state of diffusion, it was still detectable.

---

107. Government chapter in *The Analects* 《论语. 为政》 in Legge, *Chinese Classics*, 1: 154.

108. Part II of the Chapter "Gao Zi" in *The Mencius* 《孟子. 告子上》, in Legge, *Works of Mencius*, 2: 411.

109. Wang and Zheng, "Confucius' Thirteen Standards," 47.

110. Chapter *Quli* in *The Book of Rites*; the first part of Chapter 14 in *Mencius Annotated and Explicated* 《孟子注疏. 卷十四上》; The eleventh verse in Chapter *Fuguo* 富国 in *Xun Zi* 《荀子》, https://ctext.org/xunzi/fu-guo/ens.

111. Thomas Buoye, "Capital Punishment and Confucian Justice: The Limits of Leniency under Traditional Chinese Law," *Studies in Qing History*, no. 4 (2006): 50.

When he rescued the two innocent people, the magistrate in a rage ordered him beaten. While the beating was taking place, Zhang's friend coincidentally came to visit the magistrate's son and was shocked to recognize Zhang. He told the magistrate's son that Zhang was a *jiaomin* or a member of the church. The beating was stopped once the magistrate received his son's warning. After thanking his friend, Zhang was deeply grateful to God. He thought if God had not worked miraculously, his friend would not have come to visit the magistrate's son at the exact time when he was being beaten. Had he endured the full beating of five hundred strikes with the big stick, he would have been either crippled or killed. He owed his survival to God's amazing power.[112] Therefore, the incident became a story of how God saved an honourable man or *junzi*. Perhaps that is where the worth of recording it lies.

Further evidence that his Christian identity was still detectable lies in the fact that, he himself did not tell the magistrate that he was a Christian for three reasons: (1) he had no church; (2) his Christian identity could save him but would bring more trouble on the two innocent men; and (3) he did not want to give cause to confirm the bad reputation of the church which began when some unscrupulous church members bullied their neighbours by exploiting the influence of the church.[113] His motivation for protecting the reputation of the church also revealed his commitment to Christianity.

Even though he felt grateful for God's intervention in this incident, he was still not fond of the idea of attending church. On the contrary, he devoted his energy to becoming a famous Confucian tutor. This situation lasted until the winter of 1904 when Yu Jianpan, a preacher, came to visit him after hearing about his refusal to accept the money won from the lottery. After this visit, Zhang decided to return to the church and devote his life to God.[114] There were two reasons for his return to the church.

First, he learned a lesson from the issue of the lottery: no good could come from associating with mercenary friends from the outside. He must have felt that the temptation of gambling endangered his Confucian values. Thus, he realized he should leave the mercenary friends outside in order to gain closeness to the spiritual friends inside. He was seeking to protect this

---

112. Zhang, "How I Became a Christian," 8–9.
113. Zhang, "How I Became a Christian," 8–9; Zhang, "Chronology of Zhang Yijing," 18.
114. Zhang, "How I Became a Christian," 12; Zhang, "Chronology of Zhang Yijing," 18.

Confucian value by returning to the church. To put it another way, he resumed his Christian identity to better realize his Confucian identity. At this moment, he was similar to the other Confucian Christians discussed previously: the superiority of Confucian identity to Christian identity. This was also in accordance with what his life had been in the previous five years: an achieved Confucian identity and a diffused Christian identity.

Second, preacher Yu visited him to commend him for his refusal of the temptation of money and also to comfort his hurt nationalistic feelings. The BCC offered by preacher Yu reminded Zhang that the church condoned resisting the temptation for money, valued being patriotic, and that there was a difference between missionaries and the other Westerners.

3.3.3.1.3 Restoration

In 1905, his brothers, sisters, and mother all became Christians, which greatly encouraged Zhang. At that time, he was still a famous Confucian tutor. Every night he would gather his family and his Confucian students to read the Bible and pray. Later on, the majority of those students became Christians. His Christian identity was quickly restored to its previous status of achievement. One particular conflict reveals how quickly Zhang's Christian identity gained strength.

As mentioned above, ancestor worship used to be extremely significant in China's history. It was endowed with filial piety in Chinese culture and Confucianism. If a person was found to be unfilial, he would be viewed not only as a traitor to Chinese culture and Confucianism but also to his parents and ancestors. In fact, he would be viewed as being worse than an animal. The person who did not make sacrifices to his ancestors would lose not only his Confucian identity but also his identity as a human being. When King Wu (武, 1046 BC) once made a military attack on King Zhou (纣), one of the accusations against King Zhou was that he deserted his ancestral temple and stopped sacrificing to his ancestors. In the Qing dynasty, it was standard practice for people to set food and drink before the tablets of their deceased parents and ancestors to let them eat, and they would also burn incense and report to them their needs.[115]

---

115. Liu, "On the Sacrifice System," 89.

Zhang's family had a magnificent ancestral hall[116] with ancestral tablets, and his family had been carefully observing the rite of making sacrifices to their ancestors. For twelve years after his conversion, Zhang dared not destroy it. After his entire family came to believe in Jesus, they all felt that sacrificing to the ancestors was contradictory to their new faith.[117] In spite of this, he did not destroy the hall and the tablets right away, for he had no peace at the thought of destroying these sacred and inviolable things without finding another way to express his filial piety. He must first find some equivalent way to demonstrate his commemoration of his ancestors. Finally, he hung a large-sized central scroll of a painting in the hall with a couplet on the two sides. Then he replaced the tablets with well-decorated calligraphy on which his deceased father's biography and genealogy were written. This was mounted on a wooden screen with a base placed on a long table and protected by a glass cover. The records written in calligraphy showed his gratitude to his ancestors. Many visitors praised the new setting. By this, Zhang retained the essence and significance of filial piety but removed the practice of making a sacrifice to the souls of his ancestors.

Zhang had openly ceased offering sacrifice to the ancestors for ten years. However, he dared not remove the ancestral tablets for a long time because his other family members still worshipped before those tablets and because he had not found a substitute for offering sacrifices. This shows the strength of his Confucian identity. However, he had been struggling with it. This struggle and his final removal of the tablets demonstrated his commitment to his Christian identity. The balance reached between keeping the form of being filial in a Confucian sense and worshipping God alone reflected a balance between his Confucian identity and Christian identity. In other words, his two identities were laterally structured at this time.

However, when this conflict in 1905 and his conflict in 1893 are put side by side, the similarities and differences between them can be highlighted. In 1893, his deep inner struggle was caused by a question: Was he violating filial piety, a value defined by his Confucian identity, when he tried "worshipping

---

116. There is no indication how his father, a normal peasant, could afford such a building. Since his grandfather moved his family to this place and Zhang could change the decorations in it, this ancestral hall was unlikely a place that was shared by the larger Zhang lineage.

117. Zhang, "Origin of Making Sacrifice," 28.

God alone," as required by his Christian identity? For the next two years, even though he remained under the same pressure from his father, his struggle abated owing to his reinterpretation of filial piety in accordance with the Bible. During the ten years until 1905, he had been struggling with another question: How could he maintain the form of being filial when he had publicly stopped making sacrifices to his deceased father and other ancestors? He was not concerned about his actual level of filial piety. His father had passed away and his Christian mother consented to the removal of the tablets. Nevertheless, honour for his dead father would have pricked his conscience if he had continued to understand filial piety strictly in the Confucian tradition. Therefore, Zhang was again a Confucian Christian with a union between his two identities and with his Christian identity being restored to a superior position over his Confucian identity.

3.3.3.2 *The Strengthening of His Christian Identity as Evidenced by His Choice of Confucian Heaven (天) or Father in Heaven*

To reach a union between his two identities, Zhang had to deal with conflicts which he felt were incompatible. Heaven (天) in Confucianism and "Father in heaven" in the Lord's prayer (Matt 6:9) presented two conflicting concepts to him.

The religiosity of the Confucian ceremony of making sacrifices is still controversial, but it was an obvious and well-settled issue in Zhang's mind. According to him, after King Mu of the Zhou dynasty (周穆王, 1054 – 949 BC) made god-worshipping a monopoly of kingship, the distance between God and the Chinese people became difficult to cross. Before Zhang understood Christianity, he had not had any question about the Confucian sacrifice ceremony and those Chinese terms containing heaven (天). Later on, when he was presented with the biblical idea of God, he saw a contradiction between polytheism and monotheism, in the same way that he viewed the religious difference between Confucianism and Christianity and the nature of the persecution of Christianity in the Boxer Rebellion.[118]

> When people began the practice of making sacrifices to humans in the way they had been making sacrifices to Heaven,

---

118. Zhang, "Jesus and Confucius," 32–33; Zhang, "Commenting on Chen Qiulin's," 74.

they actually gave humankind and deities equal status. Thus, the Chinese called the emperors "the Heavenly King (天王)," the prestige of kingship "the Heavenly prestige (天威)," the countenance of kingship "the Heavenly countenance (天颜)," the grace of kingship "the Heavenly grace (天恩)," the imperial edict "the Heavenly word (天语)," the benefactor "the second Heaven (二天)," the local civil servants "Lords of Heaven" (青天大老爷), and so on. This kind of deification of humans demonstrated their disrespect to deities. Though such a wrongful practice did not exist in ancient Israel, a similar case can be found in Acts 12:22 in which people shouted to Herod "This is the voice of a god, not of a man." It seems that the people of Tyre and Sidon did not respect deities as much as the Chinese. However, Jesus revealed to us that God in heaven is our Father in heaven. By this, people are shocked to realize that God is the one and only and that there is no other God. Just as no one wants two biological fathers, no one would want to deify the living, nor would they have the courage to deify the dead. The title of "Father" has wiped away all gods and spirits like *xuantian* supreme god (玄天上帝) and *xietian* supreme god (协天上帝) (gods in Taoism). After hearing how Jesus called God "Father," we begin to know more about the only true God and reject all other claims as absurd.[119]

When looking at the choice between the Chinese concept of heaven and Jesus's Father in heaven, identity plays a decisive role. If Zhang had had a strong Buddhist or Taoist identity, very probably he would have been more apt to favour the former one. If he had had a Muslim identity, he would have been more inclined to agree with the latter. If he had been committed to atheism or if he had believed in scientific evidence, he would have been more disposed to dispense with both. The reality was that his commitment to Christianity had grown stronger than his commitment to Confucianism, which was exemplified by his choice.

That does not mean that he rejected all Confucian thoughts, nor does it mean he stopped seeking evidence for the Christian message from

---

119. Zhang, "On 'Our Father,'" 2–3.

Confucian classics. It merely means that he would tend to tally Confucian doctrines against Christian message, and that he would choose on the side of Christianity whenever conflicts between the two were irreconcilable. Furthermore, he would still accept those Christian messages even if he did not find their reference in Confucian thought such as the Holy Spirit.

3.3.3.3 *The Theological Contents of His Christian Identity at the Beginning of 1906*

In January 1906, a couple of months after joining *True Light*, using the name Jianru, he wrote *On Moses* in which he made a comparison between Moses and Jesus.

> Although there are many similarities between them, there are also differences. Moses saved people's body, but Jesus saved people's spirit. Moses was a saviour for Israelites while Jesus is the Saviour for all peoples. Moses controlled people with God's law while Jesus freed people by God's love. Therefore, I have two meditations: (1) I used to be tortured by unseen slavery which was worse than the torture suffered by Israelites in Egypt. Fortunately, Jesus who is greater than Moses saved me at the sacrifice of his own life. I am free of condemnation but have eternal life. Since Jesus' grace is much greater than Moses, shouldn't our love for Jesus be much sincerer than Israelites' respect for Moses?

His second meditation was to encourage Jewish people to believe in Jesus because he was the prophet prophesied by Moses.

> Life is unpredictable, and it passes quickly. The hell [sic] and heaven are two separate destinations at the end of this life. If we did not choose to be in his flock when he is available, all people, both the Jews and the other races, would end up in the hell [sic] without chance of returning. It will be too late to repent then. I wish all people would view themselves as the Israelites sojourning in Egypt and Jesus as Moses and carry up the cross to follow him bravely. Then our names will be listed in the paradise [sic]. How blessed will that be![120]

---

120. Zhang, "On Moses," 6.

Compared to 1894, this statement reveals Zhang's theological understanding more completely. This is partially due to the lack of his available records written in 1894. There are a few features to note: (1) he made a clear contrast between law and grace; (2) he used to struggle with sin, but he has obtained freedom and forgiveness through his belief in Jesus's sacrifice; (3) people should love Jesus as a response to Jesus's love; and (4) heaven and hell exist and all people without faith in Jesus will end up in hell. His statement in 1894 reflects the idea that righteousness can be won by deeds, but the statement in 1906 demonstrates a dependence on grace.

His understanding of God could be seen in his *On "Our Father in Heaven"* published in February 1906. He referred to God as "our Father in heaven," the Creator, and the true governor. He described him as full of love, respectable, approachable, and knowable.[121]

Zhang did not talk about the Holy Spirit until he listened to the preaching of Pastor Gu, a British missionary stationed in Hunan, in August 1906 when he had a summer retreat in Guling (牯岭) of Jiujiang (九江) with Dr. Chambers. His record described the situations before and after the arrival of the Holy Spirit, but there was no description of the conditions for receiving the Holy Spirit.[122]

Thus, it is safe to assume that up to 1905, Zhang's theological understanding was mainly about God and Jesus rather than the Holy Spirit. There was no concept in Chinese culture parallel to the Holy Spirit, so it took him longer to grasp the idea.

3.3.3.4 Encouragement from the Confucian Classics for His Christian Identity

In the development of Zhang's Christian identity, some important elements were: communicating with God through Bible reading and praying, communicating with other Christians by listening to and sharing with them, living out his belief in daily life, and facing challenges and persecutions. One additional significant element was his study of Confucian classics. When Zhang

---

121. Zhang, "On 'Our Father,'" 5.
122. Jianyu 检余, "The Descent of the Holy Spirit Came on the Day of Pentecost (五旬节圣神降临)," in *(1928), A Quarter of a Century of True Light, Selected* 真光丛刊, Part 1: *Concerning the Scriptures* 说经文, ed. Yijing Zhang (Shanghai 上海: China Baptist Publication Society 中华浸会书局, 1906), 12–18.

recalled how his interest in Christianity had been aroused by reading two Christian tracts, he said, "Therefore, I often say that the words of the ancient Confucian philosophers could serve as a bridge for spreading Christianity in China."[123] However, the role the Confucian classics played in his life changed in accordance with the development of his Christian identity.

Before he assumed a Christian identity, Zhang's Confucian identity helped him to distinguish between right and wrong. Why did he think the thoughts in the two Christian tracts were right? His recommendation of the words of Confucian philosophers as the bridge for the Christian message revealed the success of the two Christian tracts in relating to Confucian classics, which convinced his Confucian identity of the legitimacy of the messages in the two Christian tracts.

In the process of his Christian identity gaining strength, the evidence for the Christian message found in the Confucian classics proved decisive. In 1889, a Chinese author Zhu Baidu (朱百度) published a book *The Inscriptions of the Han Dynasty in Line with the Classics* (汉碑征经) which is a collection of the inscriptions which conform to the Confucian classics. Zhang noticed that Chinese readers became very interested in inscriptions after reading Zhu's book and were then motivated to diligently study the Confucian classics. Inspired by this, Zhang published *Those Bible Stories in Line with the Classics* (汉故证经) in 1913 when he was forty-two years old. According to his introduction, he had wanted to compile this book when he was young in order to arouse the Chinese readers' interest in reading the Bible.[124]

Zhang joined *True Light* at the age of thirty-four in 1905, an age considered not young in that era when people got married early. Therefore, he must have wished to compile this book before that time. His own confidence in the biblical stories must have grown stronger as he found the evidence for them in the classics. This is similar to his experience with the two Christian tracts before his conversion. He found at least twenty-nine parallel stories from the classics, and one will serve as an example below.

---

123. Zhang, "Mining Knowledge of Quintessence," 43.

124. Yijing Zhang 张亦镜, "Those Bible Stories in Line with the Classics (汉故证经)," in *(1928), A Quarter of a Century of True Light, Selected* 真光丛刊, Part 6: Brief Selections Translated 谈薮, ed. Yijing Zhang (Shanghai 上海: China Baptist Publication Society 中华浸会书局, 1913), 67.

Zhang found a historical record from *The History of the Later Han Dynasty* (后汉书) which parallels the story of Moses's crossing the Red Sea. In the record, the Emperor Guangwu (光武帝, 5 BC–AD 57) and his army were hotly pursued by his enemy. They were terrified by a large river because they had no boat. Just for a short while, the river was mysteriously frozen. Almost immediately after they crossed on the ice, the ice melted. The Emperor and his army owed the safe crossing to the blessing of the heaven or god.

Zhang used this story to prove God's existence and work in the story of Moses's crossing the Red Sea. After this comparison was published in *Great Light Daily* (大光日报), it was noticed by Mr. Zeng Yueqiao (曾月樵) who used to be a *juren* (a successful candidate in the Imperial Examination at the provincial level) and a prefectural governor. Zeng quoted this comparison in his speech to prove God's realness and to repudiate atheism before the students of Truth School (真理学校) in Jieyang (揭阳).[125]

3.3.4 Being a Confucian Christian after 1905

As a journalist for and editor of a Christian publication and as a preacher through writing, he would have encountered many instances of receiving BTC and BCC, whether voluntarily or involuntarily. His Christian identity remained generally strong from 1905 until his death, but that does not mean there was no fluctuation. The variations that occurred within the relationship between his Christian identity and his commitment to modern nationalism and science will be discussed respectively. However, the relationship of his Christian identity and Confucian identity remained steady after the five-year retrogression of his Christian identity.

3.3.4.1 A Strong Confucian Identity

Zhang's commitment to Confucianism motivated him to preach the gospel. In 1906, Zhang, using the name Jianru,[126] exhorted Christians to preach the gospel and quoted the Confucian teachings "Consider others in one's own

---

125. Zhang, "Those Bible Stories," 71–72.
126. Jianru 鉴如, "Woe to Those Who Do Not Preach the Gospel (不传福音有祸)," *True Light* 真光 5, no. 2 (1906): 3.

shoes (推己及人)"[127] and "all within the four seas will be his brothers."[128] Then he reasoned that if a person did not share the gospel, he allowed his brother to die, which was disrespect to parents and a sin against God. Then he quoted a story about stopping a shooter from *The Mencius*, saying that people failed to save others because they did not regard them as family members.[129] Since Zhang regarded himself as a preacher through writing,[130] when he made this exhortation, he was convinced of the danger of violating Confucian values if one did not preach the gospel. In 1928, he expressed a similar conviction by saying[131] that preaching embodied *jili liren, jida daren* or the man of perfect virtue, wishing to be established himself, seeks also to establish others; wishing to be enlarged himself, he seeks also to enlarge others.[132]

His commitment to Confucianism is also manifested by his love for the Confucian classics. Between 1906 and 1911, Zhang lived a very austere life. For example, in 1908, he moved to a cheaper dwelling in order to be able to walk to work. He lived on a very tight budget because he wished to save money for buying books. The majority of the books he bought were the classics of both Confucianism and other schools such as: *The Explanatory Notes and Commentaries of the Thirteen Classics* (十三经注释), *The Twenty-Four Histories* (二十四史), *Zhu Xi's Compendium* (紫阳纲目), *The Academic History in Four Dynasties* (四朝学案), etc. However, he was too busy to read them, so reading through the several large boxes of books became one of the motivations for his return to his hometown in 1911 where he studied for half a year.

Zhang's words were saturated with Confucian values. In 1906, Zhang encouraged Christians to be "an honourable man" or "*junzi*" to obey Jesus's

---

127. This is a summary made by Zhu Xi of Confucius' saying "What you do not want done to yourself, do not do to others." Legge, *Chinese Classics*, 1: 301.

128. Legge, 1: 253.

129. This story can be found in Part II of the Chapter *Gao Zi* in *The Mencius* 《孟子. 告子下》. Legge, *Works of Mencius*, 2: 427.

130. Yijing Zhang 张亦镜, "Criticizing the Anti-Christian Student Federation's Declaration (批评非基督教学生同盟宣言)," *True Light* 真光 21, no. 8–9 (1922): 12.

131. Zhang, "My View on Preaching," 77.

132. 己立立人, 己达达人 《论语. 雍也》, the chapter "Yong Ye" in *The Analects*, in Legge, *Chinese Classics*, 1: 194.

command of following the words of the Pharisees (Matt 23:2–3)[133] because "the superior man does not promote a man simply on account of his words, nor does he put aside good words because of the man."[134] "*Junzi*" or "honourable man" is a title endowed by Confucius with all the noble characteristics a Confucian and even an average Chinese could imagine. In 1911, when Zhang recommended a book entitled *On Religion* (a translation of 宗教论) by Luke (a transliteration of 陆克氏, whose full name has not been discovered), he said[135] with respect: "This book is written by Luke, a famous British Confucian (英儒)."[136] In Zhang's view, the term "Confucian" was an honourable name for a good scholar.

Confucianism offered him a sanctuary. In 1927, when Zhang reviewed his conversion, he recalled:

> The other Confucian scholars laughed at us because they believed that we descended from lofty trees to enter into dark valleys or *xia qiaomu ru yougu*.[137] Facing this criticism, we sought the peace of mind by quoting another of Mencius' sayings: "The shining greatness which can transform the world is holiness and the holiness which goes beyond understanding is god."[138] This

---

133. "The teachers of the law and the Pharisees sit in Moses' seat. So you must be careful to do everything they tell you. But do not do what they do, for they do not practice what they preach."

134. 君子不以言举人，不以人废言．《论语. 卫灵公》, the chapter "Wei Linggong" in *The Analects*, in Legge, *Chinese Classics* 1: 300.

135. Yijing Zhang 张亦镜, "On Liang Bichen's Proposal of a Reform Following the Banning of Confucianism (书梁弼臣改革孔教乃可以言维新论后)," *True Light* 真光 10, no. 10 (1911): 4.

136. Although "Confucian" or "*ru*" used to mean "scholar" in general rather than the specific scholars who view themselves as followers of Confucius and Mencius, Zhang used it for the specific scholars at the beginning of the twentieth century. One evidence is that, in his debate with the Confucian Association concerning the establishment of Confucianism as China's state religion, the meaning of "Confucian" had never become ambiguous. If Zhang had realized its ambiguity, he would never have let go of such a powerful weapon in his opposition because, by interpreting Confucianism as scholarship, he could easily foil those Confucians' attempt to establish Confucius's school as China's state religion.

137. 下乔木入幽谷 《孟子. 滕文公上》 Part I of the chapter "Teng Wen Gong" in *The Mencius*, in Legge, *Works of Mencius*, 2: 255.

138. 大而化之之谓圣圣而不可知之谓神 《孟子. 尽心下》 (Part II of the Chapter *jinxin xia* in *The Mencius*). Legge's translation is: "When this great man exercises a transforming influence, he is what is called a sage. When the sage is beyond our knowledge, he is what is called a spirit-man." Legge, *Works of Mencius*, 2: 490. Here, the Chinese characters "圣" and "神" are translated into "sage" and "spirit-man" which point to the sphere of humankind. However, the

saying helped us to believe that Jesus was superior to the saints and he was God and he was a man (神人). Then we realized that saint Confucius had not reached the highest level.[139]

Facing other Confucians' mockery, Zhang found comfort and assurance from Mencius's teaching. The word "god" in Mencius's teaching was interpreted as "God" in the Bible. Mencius's teaching reassured Zhang of his choice. In other words, he found peace when he realized that his commitment to Christianity was in union with his commitment to Confucianism.

3.3.4.2 A Stronger Christian Identity as Evidenced by His Overcoming the Obstacles of Confucian Expectations

The previous section regarding Confucianism has discussed how some Confucian mentalities hindered the Chinese from choosing a Christian identity. Specifically, the two Confucian mentalities listed by Chen Duxiu are: worshipping the sage or *zunsheng* (尊圣) and rejecting the foreigner or *rangyi* (攘夷).[140] In addition to these two, worshipping the ancestors will be included here because it has historically preoccupied the Chinese and it is currently experiencing a revival.

3.3.4.2.1 Concerning ancestors

The significance of the ceremony of worshipping ancestors lies in filial piety, and this is what caused Zhang's long hesitation in removing his ancestral tablets.

After researching the Chinese classics and the Bible, Zhang concluded that it was filial to support parents in their old age and commemorate one's ancestors but that sacrificing to them was not necessary.[141]

Then Zhang furthered his argument by saying that one should also commemorate Adam, the first person created on earth by God and the ancestor

---

two characters can also be translated into "holiness" and "god" which belong to the realm of heaven. Since Zhang was claiming that it was reasonable to believe in Jesus because he was also God and was superior to the sage Confucius, "holiness" and "god" are a better choice for this place. Otherwise, there would be no difference between Jesus and Confucius.

139. Zhang, "Comments on the Theological," 13.
140. Chen, "Christianity and Chinese," 16.
141. Zhang, "Origin of Making Sacrifice," 28.

of all human beings, and the best way was to fear God and believe in Christ.[142] Here Chinese history was connected and grafted onto biblical history. Anyone wanting to be the most filial person should seek to be a beloved son of God through believing in Christ. The deceased ancestors would be very happy to see their descendants obey God, believe in Christ, and become righteous. Zhang wished all his fellow countrymen who clung to the rite of commemorating the ancestors to realize this and appease their ancestors' spirits in this way. Otherwise, they would not only be condemned by God's judgment but also be rebuked by the ancestors after death. Here Zhang might have remembered how a rich man after death became jealous of Lazarus and worried about his own five brothers who were still living, as seen in Luke 16.

Zhang reinterpreted the idea of ancestors and opened a new higher level of Confucianism by linking Chinese culture to the Christian message and viewing it from the perspective of the Bible. When Zhang said that the most filial way to commemorate Adam was to believe in God the Creator and Christ, he was giving a higher status to God and Christ than to one's human ancestors. Logically, identification with God and Christ was more significant than identification with ancestors, and Christian identity was the highest form of filial piety. This reveals that, in Zhang's mind, his Christian identity took precedence over his Confucian identity.

3.3.4.2.2 Concerning Confucius

Zhang expressed his views on Confucius, Mencius, Xun Zi, Lao Zi, and Mo Zi. This section will only focus on how the priority between his identities was displayed by his view on Confucius. Since some scholars may wonder if his view on Confucius might have experienced a change during the 1910s,[143] his articles written between 1910 and 1920 will be analyzed here, especially his two articles: *Jesus and Confucius* (耶儒辩, 1910) and *A Study of Christianity and Confucianism* (耶儒之研究, 1920).

Three views were expressed in *Jesus and Confucius*: (1) the significant difference between Confucianism and Christianity was that Jesus was God while Confucius was a man; (2) the relationship between Jesus and Confucius could

---

142. Zhang, 29.

143. Daming Fan 范大明, "A Dialogue between God and Confucius: Are the Sun and the Moon? Setting Zhang Yijing as the Center 上帝与孔子的对话：日与月乎？," *Journal of Hunan City University* 湖南城市学院院报 34, no. 2 (2013): 32–38.

be compared to that of the sun and the moon; and (3) being a Christian was not a betrayal of Confucianism, and faith in Jesus was not incompatible with respecting Confucius. He especially pointed out that "respecting Confucius" was not worshipping Confucius as God.[144]

Jesus and Confucius also listed five shortcomings of Confucius's knowledge of heaven or *tian* (天) which was obtained through Confucius's diligent self-study of the past learning[145]: (1) not knowing there was only one God, which led to polytheism in China; (2) not knowing the difference between the one true God and gods, which resulted in indiscriminately keeping all of them at a distance; (3) not knowing the difference between worshipping God and worshipping all spirits and ghosts which he had even viewed as people's duty; (4) not knowing that God could not be predicted and therefore seeking the practice of divination (占卜); and (5) not knowing that God's punishment could be inflicted on people's invisible spirit and soul, not only on the fleshly body, from which sprang the one-sided belief that physical gains and losses were, in fact, heavenly rewards and punishments. Since Confucius's faulty knowledge of heaven or *tian* was the inheritance of past learning, he was like a moon whose light was reflected from the sun. However, since the past learning which he received and conveyed was passed down by other people rather than straight from its original source, he was unlike the moon whose light was reflected directly from its source; therefore, even the analogy of the moon was too generous for Confucius (喻之以月, 由未免尊之太过).[146]

The truth of Jesus's teaching and the vacuity of Confucius's words can be witnessed in countries where Christianity was popular and in China.[147] The ineffectiveness of Confucius's teaching could be seen through the bad testimonies of Confucians' moral life in Zhang's *Cleansing the False Accusations against Christianity* (诬教雪).[148]

Next, from *A Study of Christianity and Confucianism*, Zhang illustrated the differences between Jesus and Confucius in the aspects of birth, knowledge, ministry, wisdom, capability, and death and further highlighted four

---

144. Zhang, "Jesus and Confucius," 34.
145. Zhang, 32–33.
146. Zhang, 32.
147. Zhang, 34.
148. Zhang, "Cleansing the False Accusations," 65–66.

differences between Christianity and Confucianism: (1) monotheism versus polytheism; (2) everyone being God's son versus an emperor being God's son; (3) knowing God the Creator versus not knowing God clearly; and (4) no ancestor worship versus ancestor worship.

Four of the five differences between Jesus and Confucius in *A Study of Christianity and Confucianism* could also be found in *Jesus and Confucius*: birth,[149] the source of knowledge,[150] ministry, and capability and power.[151] Death was the only difference not explicitly mentioned. The one similarity between Jesus and Confucius was that they were both skilled at using maxims in their teaching.[152]

A consideration of social and political backgrounds will bring to light Zhang's view on Confucius and Jesus in a clearer way.

Although the educational system and civil service examinations based on Confucian curriculum had ended by 1905, the Qing dynasty was still in existence in 1910 and Confucianism still had strong political power. It must have taken significant courage from Zhang when he wrote *Jesus and Confucius* in 1910. He said: "I do not honour Jesus and humble Confucius with dishonesty. If Jesus was not really God and the Way of God, I should be punished for the crime of censuring the Sacred."[153]

A Study of Christianity and Confucianism was written in 1920, a time when the New Culture Movement and the May Fourth Movement were advocating democracy, science, and China's national sovereignty to rejuvenate China as imagined. Therefore, it must have seemed more superstitious than *Jesus and Confucius* when viewed by the intellectuals with Western learning because it advocated not only the virgin birth, salvation, eternal life, and the miracles of God, but also resurrection. This shows that Zhang did not have any intention of separating Christianity from Confucianism in order to avoid attacks from the intellectuals with Western learning. He did adopt some new modern words like "class" and "labour":

---

149. Zhang, "Jesus and Confucius," 27.
150. Zhang, 32.
151. Zhang, 33–34.
152. Zhang, 34.
153. Zhang, 33.

> Furthermore, it is Christianity, a system for equality, freedom, universal love, sacrifice, and labour, rather than Confucianism, a system for class, that is fitting for the current times and meets the current situation's needs.[154]

He used "Furthermore" to remind his readers of one more practical reason for choosing Christianity. This practical consideration is not the focus of this study. The target of both papers was directed at leading people under the influence of Confucianism to faith in Jesus.

Hence, *A Study of Christianity and Confucianism* was just a more systematic development of the ideas in *Jesus and Confucius*. During the 1910s, Zhang had been holding an attitude that Confucianism and Christianity could be bridged but based on an unequal status. This attitude is an external manifestation of his own internal structure of identities.

Several of his further analogies for the relationship between Jesus and Confucius shed light on this unequal status in his mind: the sun and the moon, the sun and a lamp,[155] and the sun and a hill.[156]

Quoting from Matthew 13:17,[157] Zhang stated that before Jesus, Confucius was one of the "many prophets and righteous men who longed to see what Jesus's disciples saw and heard, but he did not see nor hear it."[158] According to Zhang, Confucius's status was similar to that of Jewish holy men or sages, but his status did not surpass that of John the Baptist.[159] Since John the Baptist was the least in heaven and Jesus's followers were higher than John, Jesus's followers had a higher status than Confucius. This lower status for Confucius was not assigned by Westerners but by Jesus himself, the Son of God. It is

---

154. Yijing Zhang 张亦镜, "A Study of Christianity and Confucianism (耶儒之研究)," in *(1928), A Quarter of a Century of True Light, Selected* 真光丛刊, *Part 4: Religious Evidence and Origins* 关于宗教之考据文字, ed. Yijing Zhang (Shanghai 上海: China Baptist Publication Society 中华浸会书局, 1920), 57.

155. Yijing Zhang 张亦镜, "Refuting Chen Huanzhang and Other Four People's Petition for Establishing Confucianism as the State Religion (驳陈焕章等请定孔教为国教呈文)," in *(1928), A Quarter of a Century of True Light, Selected* 真光丛刊, *Part 2: The Gospel Discussed and Explained* 辩道文, ed. Yijing Zhang (Shanghai 上海: China Baptist Publication Society 中华浸会书局, 1913), 105; Zhang, "Correcting Errors in Dr. Chen," 164.

156. Zhang, "Answering an Old Scholar," 218.

157. Matthew 13:17 – "For truly I tell you, many prophets and righteous people longed to see what you see but did not see it, and to hear what you hear but did not hear it."

158. Zhang, "Jesus and Confucius," 33.

159. Zhang, "Cleansing the False Accusations," 61.

remarkable at this stage to see Zhang using the Bible to gauge the status of Confucius which was the opposite of his approach to dealing with the two Christian tracts eighteen years before.

Only once did Zhang show diminished respect to Confucius by calling him "*konglaoer* (孔老二)" or "the second boy of Confucius' father."[160] In 1913, Dr. Chen Huanzhang, Yan Fu, Xia Zengyou (1863–1924), Liang Qichao, and Wang Shitong (1864–1931) appealed for the establishment of Confucianism as China's state religion. Zhang opposed this motion fiercely. In an article of 38 pages, he argued that they had misinterpreted Confucius and his teachings. He denied that Confucius was the founder of a religion. By adopting this less respectful stance, he could remind people that Confucius was just a man. Moreover, this was the only time that he took this stance. Therefore, this single instance of depreciation cannot be seen to take away from his usual admiration for Confucius.

3.3.4.2.3 Concerning rejecting the foreigners

Christianity is often called a "Western religion" or "foreign religion." From Zhang's observation, people made use of the foreignness in this label to reject it and to pass judgment on it. He himself used to intensely hate the foreigners before his conversion, which will be touched on in the discussion of his commitment to modern nationalism in chapter 4. He overcame this barrier by reinterpreting heaven or *tian* (天).

Tian is a significant concept in Confucianism, so Dr. Chen Huanzhang made use of it in his effort to establish Confucianism as China's state religion.[161] In his speech in Guangzhou on 14 June 1914, he quoted "they (thus) made an exhaustive discrimination of what was right, and effected the complete development of (every) nature, till they arrived (in the *Yi*) at what was appointed

---

160. Zhang, "Refuting Chen Huanzhang," 76.
161. Bodde noticed Chen's propagandistic motivation in his exaggerated claims for Chinese culture. Derk Bodde, "Henry A. Wallace and the Ever-Normal Granary (1946)." In *Essays on Chinese Civilization*, ed. Charles Le Blanc and Dorothy Borei (Princeton: Princeton University Press, 1981), 220, http://www.jstor.org/stable/j.ctt7zvh5f.16; Prof. R. G. Tiedemann points out that during the early years of the twentieth century, the confrontation between Christianity and Confucianism was still quite significant. Foreign missionaries only gradually came to appreciate the ethical values of Confucianism. Chinese Confucianists, on the other hand, still rejected Christianity and were convinced of the superiority of Confucianism. Chen was one example.

for it (by Heaven)"¹⁶² from *The Book of Changes* and "to study the knowledge of the nature and build up the characters of kindness and righteousness to conform to Heaven or *tian*" from *The Analects*.¹⁶³

Tian was also significant to Zhang. He felt encouraged by the greatness of being a follower of *tian* approved in Confucius's praise of the Emperor Yao in *The Analects*: "Great indeed was Yao as a sovereign! How majestic was he! It is only Heaven that is grand, and only Yao corresponded to it. How vast was his virtue! The people could find no name for it."¹⁶⁴ He was comforted by the saying "The king is not a foreigner" (because he has the whole world, 王者无外) from *The Spring and Autumn Annals Commentary by Gongyang Gao* (公羊传).¹⁶⁵ He reasoned that if the grace of a follower of *tian* could go beyond description and if a king is not a foreigner, then Christianity should not be regarded as foreign because Jesus was the King of Kings, the Creator and Governor of the universe, and the Saviour. Thus, his teaching was God's teaching from above and people could not treat it as foreign nor judge it.¹⁶⁶

In 1914, he explicitly stated that Jesus was heaven or *tian*. Since Dr. Chen belittled Christianity in his speech, Zhang felt he had to stand up in its defence. He said that Confucians would spare no effort in understanding the heavenly mandate or *ming* and being in agreement with heaven or *tian*.¹⁶⁷ After referring to some verses in the Bible, he reached the conclusion that Jesus was the heavenly mandate or *ming* and heaven or *tian* was pursued by all Confucians. The relevant verses included Matthew 1:23,¹⁶⁸ John 1:1, 14,

---

162. 穷理尽性以至于命. 《周易. 说卦》 "Treatise of Remarks on the Trigrams" in *The Book of Changes*, in James Legge, *The I Ching*, 2nd ed. (New York: Dover Publications, 1963), 422.

163. 下学上达以合乎天. 《论语. 宪问》, the chapter "Xian Wen" in *The Analects*. Chen made a slight change to the original sentence in Chinese: "My studies lie low, and my penetration rises high. But there is Heaven; – that knows me!" Legge, *Chinese Classics*, 1: 289.

164. 大哉, 尧之为君也, 魏巍乎, 唯天为大, 唯尧则之, 荡荡乎, 民无能名焉. 《论语. 泰伯篇》, the chapter "Tai Bo" in *The Analects*, in Legge, 214.

165. This is a Confucian classic. It covers the history of China between 722 BC and 481 BC.

166. Zhang, "Jesus and Confucius," 27.

167. Zhang, "Correcting Errors in Dr. Chen," 118.

168. Matthew 1:23 – "The virgin will conceive and give birth to a son, and they will call him Immanuel (which means, 'God with us')."

18,[169] and Hebrews 1:1–3.[170] Zhang said he made this discovery after much contemplation on such verses.

Here, "Heavenly Mandate" and "Heaven" found their meaning in Jesus, the Word, the Son, and God in Zhang's mind. The reinterpretation of *tian* as Jesus guaranteed all people with a Confucian identity that being a follower of Jesus was not following a foreign religion but reaching the highest goal of Confucianism, just as the Emperor Yao did. In other words, Zhang found that a Christian identity was the final achievement of a Confucian identity. Where Chinese identity was defined by Confucianism, his reinterpretation made a Christian identity a genuine Chinese identity.

Observing from the theory of Bevans, we can see that the method of interpreting Jesus as heaven or *tian* is a typical example of the translation model because Zhang transposed the meaning of the content of faith into another cultural term to reach a dynamic equivalence between concepts belonging to distinct cultures.[171] The relationship between Jesus and Confucius in Zhang's interpretation also illustrates a key presupposition of this model that the essential message of Christianity is supracultural.[172] Both this model and the countercultural model emphasize that Christian identity is more important than cultural identity.[173] Why did Zhang choose this model?

The emphasis on Christian identity over cultural identity is the external feature of the two models summarized by Bevans in 1992 and 2004. When Zhang made his contextualization at the beginning of the twentieth century,

---

169. John 1:1 – "In the beginning was the Word, and the Word was with God, and the Word was God." John 1:14 – "The Word became flesh and made his dwelling among us. We have seen his glory, the glory of the One and Only Son, who came from the Father, full of grace and truth." John 1:18 – "No one has ever seen God, but the One and Only Son, who is himself God and is in closest relationship with the Father, has made him known."

170. Hebrews 1:1–3 – "In the past God spoke to our ancestors through the prophets at many times and in various ways, but in these last days he has spoken to us by his Son, whom he appointed heir of all things, and through whom also he made the universe. The Son is the radiance of God's glory and the exact representation of his being, sustaining all things by his powerful word."

171. Bevans, *Models of Contextual Theology*, 38–39.

172. The translation model insists that there is "something" that must be "put into" other terms. There is always something from the outside that must be made to fit inside; there is always something "given" that must be "received." Bevans, 39. Practitioners of this model speak of a "gospel core." Another basic metaphor that reveals this presupposition is that of the kernel and the husk: there is the kernel of the gospel, which is surrounded in a disposable, nonessential cultural husk. Bevans, 40.

173. Bevans, *Models of Contextual Theology*, 42.

he was probably not aware of the previous dialogues about contextualization, especially those written in foreign languages, such as Ricci and Legge. His contextualization was a natural and instinctive response, just like that of Muslim Chinese Liu Zhi (1662–1730) whose method of contextualization of Islam in China was studied by Lee,[174] making use of the models proposed by Bevans. In other words, Zhang's choice of the external strategy which contains certain features was just a response or a reflection of the internal reality of his identities. To put it another way, Zhang's internal identities led him to relate Christ or the gospel to culture in a way which is summarized later as the translation model emphasizing Christian identity over cultural identity.

When Zhang pondered these Confucian mentalities that were a part of his Confucian identity in order to bring them into union with his Christian identity, he was contextualizing or indigenizing the Christian message in his mind which was already immersed in Confucianism. It is his internal contextualization or indigenization that demonstrated the superiority of his Christian identity to his Confucian identity. When he shared his ideas about how to contextualize the Christian message in China's Confucian society, he was describing to his listeners the result of his own internal contextualization. Since there are differences in the status of identity, contents of identity, and structure of identities, there are various ways of being a Confucian Christian and hence, the methods of contextualization or indigenization show diversity.

3.4 Different Methods of Contextualization

As shown above, both Zhang's Christian identity and Confucian identity reached a status of achievement and they were hierarchically structured in the 1920s.[175] These features of his internal identities were reflected in his external methods of contextualization. In fact, his refusal to participate in the Imperial Examination around 1895 and the modification of his ancestral hall can be viewed as such examples. This section intends to compare Zhang with other Christians who also held a Confucian identity to show how internal identity influenced the external strategy choices.

---

174. Lee, *Contextualization of Sufi Spirituality*.

175. Zhang, "Answering Eleven Questions," 22–24, 32; Zhang, "Discussion over Mr. Zhang," 77–80; Zhang, "Avoid Perishing," 16–23.

3.4.1 Christians Should Make Sacrifices to Their Ancestors

In 1908, an author named Song Shixiang (宋史香) published *Christianity Allows Offering Sacrifices to Ancestors* (耶穌教不禁人祭先說), and some Christians took this as their basis for making sacrifices. Song was a member of the church founded by the Berlin Missionary Society in Hua County (花县) of Guangdong province.

Song's arguments for making sacrifices to ancestors included: (1) the fourth commandment taught people to be filial, which meant to support them while living and sacrifice to them after death; (2) the first two of the Ten Commandments did not prohibit worshipping the ancestors and thus it was allowed indirectly; (3) people worshipped Jesus's pictures and statues in church, so by extension, it was not prohibited for people to worship their own ancestors' pictures and statues; (4) even though the sacrifices were not eaten by the dead, offering sacrifices could maintain a filial heart; (5) it was against the conscience for people to say that worshipping ancestors would disturb Christians' faith because it would not (However, Song included a saying in this section "parents were human when they were alive and became gods after death."); (6) forbidding sacrificing to parents went against God's teaching on being filial and against Jesus who taught love and kindness or *ren*; (7) the sages set up the rites of sacrifice in accordance with God's truth in order that kind and filial people could honour their parents; consequently, forbidding it was an insult to God and a serious insult to Jesus; (8) the early Chinese preachers were selfish, cruel, and ignorant; and they created this ban to protect their monopoly of the profits or *li* of the church; and (9) the church should grant the freedom of sacrificing to ancestors so that people's hearts could be freed from the conflict it engendered.[176]

Song viewed the issue of filial piety to be the bridge between Christianity and Confucianism and quoted both the Bible and the Confucian sages on the topic, which seemed to reveal that Song had both a Christian identity and Confucian identity. His difference from Zhang lay in his interpretation of filial piety. Zhang used the Bible as the benchmark to interpret the meaning of true filial piety to be helping parents obtain salvation, and he held that the destinations of their spirits were determined by God. Song took advantage of the Bible and some churches' traditions to consolidate and confirm his Confucian

---

176. Zhang, "Against Song Shixiang's Saying," 1–3.

understanding of being filial, and he believed that the spirits of the dead parents would become gods. This interpretation disclosed Song's structure of identities: his Confucian identity took priority over his Christian identity.

As can be observed from the models proposed by Bevans, Song's contextualization belongs to the anthropological model. In Song's view, God manifested his divine presence through the Chinese cultural practice of making sacrifices to their ancestors and any challenge to the established practice was viewed with suspicion because the challenge was not from God himself but from a tendency of one contextual perspective to impose its values on another.[177] In contrast, Zhang's approach was more nuanced. The modification of his ancestral hall was similar to his approach when he translated Jesus into heaven or *tian*, but his refusal to make sacrifices to his ancestors was an example of Bevans' countercultural model because this cultural practice and context were viewed as antithetical to the gospel and therefore required a challenge and purification.[178] From the perspective of Niebuhr, Song was an adherent to the "Christ of culture" model because he sensed no tension between God's requirements and this cultural practice[179] while Zhang belonged to both the "Christ transforming culture" model as seen in his preservation of the ancestral hall, which did not exclude him into isolation from society[180] and the "Christ against culture" model as evidenced by his refusal to make sacrifices which affirmed the sole authority of Christ over Christians and resolutely rejected culture's claim to loyalty.[181] According to Carter, Zhang belonged to both the types of Christ transforming culture (type 4) because he transformed his ancestral hall without violent coercion[182] and Christ separating from culture (type 6) because his refusal to worship Confucius and his ancestors pushed him out of the centre of society.[183]

As analyzed above, when Song and Zhang related Christ or gospel to culture in their practice, their decisions and actions were simply natural responses to their internal contextualization, which were in turn consequences

---

177. Bevans, *Models of Contextual Theology*, 54–55.
178. Bevans, 117.
179. Niebuhr, *Christ and Culture*, 83.
180. Niebuhr, 190.
181. Niebuhr, 45.
182. Carter, *Rethinking Christ and Culture*, 122.
183. Carter, 121.

of the interaction between their internal identities. For the sake of remaining focused on the main topic of this study, the development of Song's identities will not be further delineated. However, the descriptions of Zhang's identities have revealed the interaction between his internal identities and the external strategies he used for contextualization.

3.4.2 Confucianism Should Be China's State Religion

In 1913 and 1917, the Confucian Association started a movement seeking to establish Confucianism as the state religion through the National Assembly. This movement was led by Dr. Chen Huanzhang who based the movement on the theories of Kang Youwei and Kang's student, Liang Qichao.

As introduced in chapter 2, Kang and Liang claimed that "the Great Harmony" was the sages' prophecy of democracy and that it had been achieved in the democratic system of the Republic of China. In recognition that the democracy of the Republic of China was an achievement of Confucian teachings, Confucianism should be canonized as China's state religion.

Zhang refuted their theories as far-fetched and presented his explanations of the Great Harmony by referring to *The Book of Rites* and the Three Social Stages in *Gongyang Zhuan* (公羊传). According to Zhang's interpretation, the Great Harmony was nothing more than the extraordinary peace which was observed during the periods of Emperor Yao and Emperor Shun who both practised monarchism as well as other succeeding dynasties. The current democracy owed its inauguration to Christianity rather than Confucianism. For Christians, the Great Harmony meant freedom of faith and no persecution.[184] The reason for Zhang's firm opposition to Confucianism as the state religion of China was because it meant making Confucian sacrifices and kneeling and kowtowing to Confucius's image at schools, which went against his Christian convictions.

At the time, some Christians adhered to the theories of Kang and Liang. The frequency of the word *datong* in the speeches at the Sixth YMCA Annual Convention in 1913, as shown above, seems to suggest the influence of their theories. Even in 1925 when Wang Zhixin wrote his *China Academic History*,

---

184. Zhang, "After President Yuan Commands," 76–88; Zhang, "Denouncing Wang Rongbao," 93–95.

Liang's thoughts formed the basis for the majority of the book. Therefore, Zhang felt the need to repeat his counter-argument in its preface.[185]

Some Christians supported the establishment of a state religion. To explain their support, they claimed that both Confucianism and Christianity advocated the Great Harmony. Their interpretation was that the Great Harmony or *datong* of Confucianism meant having the same way and same direction (道一风同), which was different from Kang and Liang's version. Their evidence included a quote from *The Book of History*,[186] "If you, the shell, the stalks, the ministers and officers, and the common people, all agree about a course, this is what is called a great concord (or *datong*)"[187]; a quote from Liezi,[188] "A man whose soul and *Qi* are kept in harmony becomes one (or *datong*) with his outer reality, therefore nothing might hurt or control him, and things like passing through metal or stone and walking in fire or deep water are out of question to him";[189] and a proverb and classic of Taoism, "be the same in the essentials or *datong* while differing in minor points." They equated this version of Confucian Great Harmony to a version of God's kingdom on earth in which all races and all polities enjoyed equality and freedom before Jesus.

The evidence put forth by the Christians who supported the establishment of a state religion included some ideas that conflicted with Christianity such as divinations in the Confucian classics and physically merging into all things in the Taoist classics. If they really adhered to these ideas, their commitment to Christianity could be called into question. If they were merely exploiting the use of the term *datong* in those classics, they were attempting to moderate Kang and Liang's views on the Great Harmony in order to bridge and then merge it with their own explanation of God's kingdom. Their purpose was to whitewash their support for the movement of a state religion by reinterpreting both the Great Harmony and God's kingdom. In either case, the nature of their acts demonstrated a low commitment to Christianity.

---

185. Yijing Zhang 张亦镜, "Preface," in *China Academic History* 中国学术源流, ed. Zhixin Wang (Nanjing 南京: Nanking Theological Seminary 金陵神学院, 1925), 1–2.

186. 汝则从，龟从，筮从，卿士从，庶民从，是之谓大同。《尚书.洪范》 The Great Plan in *The Book of History*.

187. Legge, *Sacred Books of China*, Part 1: 146.

188. 以商所闻夫子之言，和者大同于物，物无得伤阂者，游金石，蹈水火，皆可也。《列子.皇帝》, the chapter "The Yellow Emperor" in the *Liezi*.

189. Liezi, *Liezi*, trans. Xiaopeng Liang 梁晓鹏 (Beijing 北京: Zhonghua Book Company 中华书局, 2005), 45.

Because Christian and Confucian identities were varied in their levels of commitment and priority, there were many different ways in which contextualization strategies were adopted and identities were expressed. Examples of this are many and varied. For example, some Chinese Christians maintained firmly that Christians should bow deeply three times before the pictures of their deceased parents;[190] some Chinese Christians insisted that holding a stick at parents' funerals was essential in 1926;[191] some suggested setting a place in the church building as the Most Holy Place with Jesus's picture hung in the middle, with an antithetical couplet hung on each side, a pair of candlesticks, and an incense burner placed on a refectory table, and lit candles and incense during worship.[192] Sometimes, a Buddhist identity was involved in contextualization; as Zhang observed, very few Confucians would not revere Buddhism and Taoism.[193] Some suggested adopting the rite of Buddhism at worship.[194] Some suggested putting a tablet in a shrine for God as in other temples; some suggested carrying the ceremonies of weddings and funerals in the traditional ways, following the example of a pastor in Shanghai who hired the Buddhist monks and Taoists to perform rites at the funeral of his mother.[195]

Each of these examples can be categorized by the models proposed by Niebuhr, Carter, and Bevans. By delineating the connection between Zhang's identities and his contextualization, it is not difficult to understand the differences between Zhang and his contemporary Chinese Christians from the perspective of identities – a useful tool for understanding the personal and communal experiences. Chapter 4 will discuss the role that national identity played in Zhang's contextualization in addition to an analysis of the role his identities played.

---

190. Yingcai Guo 郭英材, "Another Discussion with Mr. Yijing over Three Bowing before the Image of the Deceased Parents at Their Funerals (再与亦镜先生讨论关于追悼会时向先亲像行三鞠躬礼的问题)," *True Light* 真光 23, no. 8 (1924): 27–32.

191. Yijing Zhang 张亦镜, "Concerning Holding Stick at the Funeral of Parents (亲丧执杖问题)," *True Light* 真光 25, no. 9–10 (1926): 67–81.

192. Zhang, "Discussion with Mr. Wei Qing."

193. Zhang, "Answering an Old Scholar," 197.

194. Aiguang Cui 崔爱光, "On Sinicization of the Church (论中国化教会)," *True Light* 真光 23, no. 11 (1924): 16.

195. Zhang, "Discussion with Mr. Wei Qing."

3.5 Conclusion

This chapter has discussed the early development of Zhang's Christian identity which transformed many contents of his Confucian identity. It also described the relationship between his Christian and Confucian identities and traced changes within that relationship. Comparing his methods of contextualization with that of others has shown that the external manifestations of contextualization are in fact reflections of internal identities and the way they are structured.

This process of examination has demonstrated Zhang's search for a Chinese Christian identity. When Chinese identity was defined in terms of culture (specifically Confucianism), this identity was a Confucian Christian identity. Both Zhang's Confucian identity and his Christian identity reached the status of achievement, and they were hierarchically structured, which made him a Christian Confucian who was different from other Confucian Christians of his day.

Gregg A. Ten Elshof proposes the adoption of a dialogue mode and the avoidance of the approaches of apologetics and pluralism.[196] Protestant missionaries did gradually come to appreciate Confucianism. Thus, it is legitimate for Ten Elshof to call for a dialogue mode.

Zhang Yijing did adopt such a mode of dialogue and lived a Christian life mixed with Confucian values. As has been demonstrated above, such a dialogue between Confucianism and Christianity took place in Zhang Yijing both externally and internally. External dialogue, which usually means communication between different people, is a conscious choice, but internal dialogue, which happens between one's different identities, could be partially a conscious choice and partially an unconscious, unavoidable, and natural result of internal conflict. In this sense, a dialogue mode is not something new. It happens and has happened throughout history whenever a person has had more than one identity.

In fact, many Chinese Christians of Zhang's time such as Lin Changmin, T. B. Woo, and Fan Bihui had both Confucian and Christian identities. However, when evaluated using the three approaches listed by Ten Elshof, Zhang demonstrated the use of the approaches of dialogue and apologetics while Ling Changmin and T. B. Woo relied upon the approach of dialogue and another

---

196. Elshof, *Confucius for Christians*.

unnamed approach, which led them to look to Christianity as the route that would help them achieve their Confucian ideals. Therefore, Ten Elshof's three approaches are not an either-or choice or phenomenon. More than one approach could be seen in a single person simultaneously.

As seen in this chapter, there were different methods of being a Confucian Christian or a Christian Confucian, which were determined by identities and the ordering of those identities. Even though Zhang subjectively felt a genuine identification with his Confucian identity, externally, he still was accused by other Confucians of being a traitor to Confucianism. The nature of the conflict lay not in the sincerity of his Confucian identity but in the primary position he gave to his Christian identity. If he could have positioned his Confucian identity in a place of superiority over his Christian identity – for example, being a Christian who could continue to offer sacrifices to the ancestors and worship Confucius, he certainly would have faced much less criticism and resistance.

CHAPTER 4

Zhang's Search for a Modern Chinese Christian Identity

4.1 Nationalism Literature Review

Although the term "nationalism" has a variety of meanings, it is generally used to describe two phenomena: (1) the attitude that the members of a nation have when they care about their national identity, and (2) the actions that the members of a nation take when seeking to achieve (or sustain) self-determination.[1] In modern China, various definitions of nationalism lay different expectations on the Chinese concerning their attitudes and actions. Thus, the native Christians in China needed to negotiate and reconcile their identity as Christians and their identity as modern Chinese.

4.1.1 A Brief Review of Research of Nationalism in Modern China

Kuo demonstrates in his paper "Chinese Bourgeois Nationalism in Hong Kong and Singapore in the 1930s"[2] that Chinese ethnic identity is not associated with all the Chinese from the beginning, especially among those who have settled abroad and are enjoying the benefits of their foreign citizenship.

---

1. Nenad Miscevic, "Nationalism," in *The Stanford Encyclopedia of Philosophy*, ed. Edward N. Zalta (Metaphysics Research Lab, Stanford University, 2018), https://plato.stanford.edu/archives/sum2018/entries/nationalism/.

2. Huei-Ying Kuo, "Chinese Bourgeois Nationalism in Hong Kong and Singapore in the 1930s," *Journal of Contemporary Asia* 36, no. 3 (2006): 402.

Cultural and political mobilizations are not always effective in making one associate with one's "homeland." On the contrary, an ethnic and national identity would appeal to people if the identity would lead to a positive economic return. In other words, nationalism is intertwined with economic development.[3]

Robin McNeal points out that Chinese literati during the twentieth century articulated a coherent Chinese mythology, primarily based on ancient texts but eventually, to some extent, drawing from ethnographic materials and folklore.[4] Gu Jiegang (顾颉刚, 1893–1980) is given as an example. This influential historian founded the *Journal of Ancient History* or *Gushi Bian* (古史辨) and led the famous "Doubters of Antiquity" movement in the Republican era. His body of work stands as the most sophisticated attempt to create a modern history of the Chinese nation that would meet the critical standards of the outside world. Culp finds that, as the dominating language shifted from the classical Chinese or *wenyan* to the modern Chinese or *baihua* in the early twentieth-century China, not only did the knowledge of nationalism and scientism spread but also a new culture was created for a modern China.[5] To put it differently, nationalism involves the invention of tradition[6] and national languages could be semi-artificial constructs.[7]

Culp finds that the reforming intellectuals collaborated with commercial publishers to produce textbooks that contributed to the creation of a national language and the delineation of a modern vernacular literature.[8] Karl shows that after 1895 Chinese urban elites began to discover, in journals and

---

3. Ernest Gellner, *Nations and Nationalism* (Oxford: Basil Blackwell, 1983), 140; Wenfang Tang and Benjamin Darr, "Chinese Nationalism and Its Political and Social Origins," *Journal of Contemporary China* 21, no. 77 (2012): 812; H. A. Innis, "Nationalism," *The American Economic Review* 25, no. 1, Supplement, Papers and Proceedings of the Forty-Seventh Annual Meeting of the American Economic Association (1935): 136–39.

4. Robin McNeal, "Constructing Myth in Modern China," *Journal of Asian Studies* 71, no. 3 (2012): 679–80.

5. Robert Culp, "Teaching Baihua: Textbook Publishing and the Production of Vernacular Language and a New Literary Canon in Early Twentieth-Century China," *Twentieth-Century China* 34, no. 1 (2008): 4–41.

6. Eric. J. Hobsbawm, *Nations and Nationalism since 1780: Programme, Myth, Reality*, 2nd ed. (Cambridge: Cambridge University Press, 1992), 16–17.

7. Hobsbawm, 54.

8. Culp, "Teaching Baihua," 40.

journalism, a new form as well as a new practice, of politics.[9] This newly emergent urban intelligentsia appropriated journalism as a mode of political, intellectual, and social activism and advocacy. Harrison points out that the newspaper news did not simply replace oral reports, but became a part of the existing network of communications.[10] In the same way, the kind of nationalism promoted by the newspapers did not simply replace the existing nationalism of the rural population. Instead, as people learned about provincial, national, and international events through rumour, oral reports, letters, and newspapers, their understanding of the nation came to share the characteristics and concerns of all these different sources. In Anderson's view, an imagined community emerged through communication and media.[11]

In Dunch's review, the case of China might not be applicable to Anderson and others' assumption of a radical disjuncture existing between the forms of community in pre-modern societies and the "imagined community" of the modern nation-state.[12] According to Duara, national/ethnic and cultural identities have existed in China for millennia in a porous and overlapping sense, so all forms of community are in some sense "imagined."[13] Despite this, he agrees with Hobsbawm and Anderson that the world system of nation-states[14] is a distinctive development of modern history.

Fung holds that the modern Chinese cultural conservatism, called the new Humanism by Wang,[15] is very nationalistic.[16] The Critical Review Group (学衡派) is an example. Fung[17] and Wang[18] have illuminated the political

---

9. Rebecca E. Karl, "Journalism, Social Value, and a Philosophy of the Everyday in 1920s China," *East Asia Cultures Critique* 16, no. 3 (2008): 539–40.

10. Henrietta Harrison, "Newspapers and Nationalism in Rural China 1890–1929," *Past and Present* 166, no. 1 (2000): 201, 204.

11. Benedict Anderson, *Imagined Communities: Reflections on the Origin and Spread of Nationalism* (London and New York: Verso, 1991).

12. Dunch, *Fuzhou Protestants*, 116–17.

13. Prasenjit Duara, "Transnationalism and the Predicament of Sovereignty: China, 1900–1945," *The American Historical Review* 102, no. 4 (1997): 1030–51.

14. The system of nation-state is defined as "a political form with distinct territorial boundaries within which the sovereign state, 'representing' the nation-people, has steadily expanded its role and power."

15. Chih-Ming Wang, "Geopolitics of Literature," *Cultural Studies* 26, no.5 (2012): 740–64.

16. Edmund S. K. Fung, "Nationalism and Modernity: The Politics of Cultural Conservatism in Republican China," *Modern Asian Studies* 43, no. 3 (2009): 782, 812.

17. Fung, "Nationalism and Modernity."

18. Wang, "Geopolitics of Literature."

dynamics of modern Chinese conservatism or the new Humanism, which emerged as a counter-movement to May Fourth cultural radicalism and as a critique of Western modernity by placing Chinese classics on the same plane as Western literature. It was marked by a faith in traditional values that could be revitalized and harnessed for the purposes of modernization. For new Humanists, the greatest evil of the New Culture Movement is its radical tendency to denounce Chinese traditions and the unjustified validation of Western scientism and modern literature which overflows with Romantic sentimentality and socialist doctrines.[19] The critique of the new Humanism revealed that it asked not only for loyalty due to China, but also for solidarity between fellow Chinese. Loyalty and solidarity come together as a single undivided sentiment.[20]

4.1.2 Different Versions of Nationalism in China

Lei summarizes the following description of Chinese nationalism as a standard Western narrative: China prides itself on being a historically powerful country with a distinguished civilization.[21] Its decline in the nineteenth and twentieth centuries in the face of Western and Japanese incursions indelibly shamed the Chinese people and triggered their widespread attempts to reform their political system. The key to this endeavour is the quest for a strong state. Over the past century and a half, various reform and revolutionary movements sought to build up the power of the state with the objective of reviving China's past glory. Chinese nationalism is thus state-led, anti-Western, and steeped in an acute sense of national humiliation. In a quest for world eminence, it seeks to restore China's historical grandeur.

The contemporary version of nationalism still keeps seeking the restoration of China's historical glory as its goal, but the key is to "Obey the Party and Follow the Party."[22]

---

19. Wang, "Geopolitics of Literature," 755.
20. Anthony D. Smith, "Nationalism," *Current Sociology* 21, no. 7 (1977): 23.
21. Guang Lei, "Realpolitik Nationalism: International Sources of Chinese Nationalism," *Modern China* 31 (2005): 495.
22. "How Are We Patriotic?"

Lu and Fan describe the evolution of the goal of nationalism in different stages before 1927[23] while Zhao gives a brief introduction to the development of nationalism in China.[24] This linear kind of description easily leaves the impression that one form of nationalism replaced another in a developmental way. In reality, the situation is more like the coexistence of different forms of nationalism competing against each other for the loyalty of the people. Mitter says that in the early twentieth century, those living in the northeast parts of the country, like other Chinese, shared a series of coexisting identities: cultural, national, regional, provincial, generational, ethnic, and gendered.[25] Mitter's research hints that there might be a tug of war between the different types of nationalism. Phillips and James argue against the notion that nation formation involves the necessary dissolution of traditional ties.[26] Rather, they suggest that a layering of subjectivities is likely to persist, causing a series of tensions between traditionalism and modernism.

Among all these nationalisms existing in China during the early twentieth century, Duara lists three versions of Chinese identity which competed against each other for the loyalty of overseas Chinese and two types of transnationalism which responded to nationalism.[27] The three versions of Chinese identity were offered by revolutionaries, the Qing imperial state, and the constitutional reformers.

The image of Chinese identity that the revolutionaries offered the Chinese transnationals was one associated not with high cultural traditions but with newly discovered Enlightenment values of adventurousness, enterprise, and expansionism.[28]

---

23. Zhouxiang Lu and Hong Fan, "From Celestial Empire to Nation State: Sport and the Origins of Chinese Nationalism (1840–1927)," *The International Journal of the History of Sport* 27, no. 3 (2010): 479.

24. Suisheng Zhao, "A State-Led Nationalism: The Patriotic Education Campaign in Post-Tiananmen China," *Communist and Post-Communist Studies* 31, no. 3 (1998): 287–302.

25. Rana Mitter, "Complicity, Repression, and Regionalism: Yan Baohang and Centripetal Nationalism, 1931–1949," *Modern China* 25, no. 1 (1999): 45.

26. Andrew Phillips and Paul James, "National Identity between Tradition and Reflexive Modernisation: The Contradictions of Central Asia," *National Identities* 3, no. 1 (2011): 23.

27. Duara, "Transnationalism and the Predicament," 1041.

28. Duara, 1046.

During this period, both the Qing imperial state and the constitutional reformers employed the older Confucian cultural narrative of community through which they tried to gain possession of people's loyalty.[29]

The constitutional reformers like Kang Youwei could appeal to the monarchism or prestige of the imperial state and graft a modern nationalism onto an older discourse of civilization, which is a vision of gradualist modernity, in which Chinese moral and cultural values were commensurate with an elitist constitutional polity and expanding capitalism. They were thus limited in how far it could reform itself without losing power.[30] Therefore, one must consider three types of nationalism: cultural nationalism, modern nationalism, and a synthesis of the two.

4.1.3 Cultural Nationalism and Modern Nationalism

With regard to cultural nationalism and modern nationalism, Lutz makes a similar differentiation.[31] She differentiates between Chinese culturalism and Chinese nationalism by saying that the culturalism of dynastic China had to be transmuted into nationalism as China accepted the challenge of modernization.

Cultural nationalism in China is the philosophy which perceived China as the centre of the world and constituted the Chinese World Order. This is made clear by the Chinese characters for China, "Middle Kingdom." According to Fairbank, the Chinese World Order had lasted for more than one thousand years in China and was characterized by the existence of an emperor who was considered to have been designated by heaven because of his innate virtue.[32] He was referred to as a "son of Heaven" and had the "Mandate of Heaven" to rule. The emperor was considered to rule the world (*tianxia*, "all under Heaven") as a "child of Heaven," and his subjects enjoyed the benefits of benevolent rule reminiscent of the "Golden Age" of Chinese civilization described in ancient sacred texts. One basic principle of the Chinese World Order was that it attempted to enfold the foreign tribes in its system and stave

---

29. Duara, 1045.
30. Duara, 1047–48.
31. Jessie G. Lutz, "Chinese Nationalism and the Anti-Christian Campaigns of the 1920s," *Modern Asian Studies*, 10, no. 3 (1977): 395.
32. J. K. Fairbank, *The Chinese World Order: Traditional China's Foreign Relations* (Cambridge, MA: Harvard University Press, 1968).

off invasion through tributary missions and other rituals: foreign kings were made to recognize the Chinese emperor as the true son of heaven, and more generally the moral and cultural superiority of China, as is also discussed by Gries.[33] It constituted one of China's primary ways of regarding the world.

Chinese worldviews before the nineteenth century were shaped by the conviction that invaders were to be defeated or absorbed into China, while the foreigners beyond the empire paid tribute to Chinese rulers. Zhao says that culturalism perceived China as the only true civilization, embodying a universal set of values.[34] All those who accepted its teachings and principles, including alien dynasties like the Mongol-Yuan and Manchu-Qing courts, could be incorporated within its cultural bounds. Zhao quoted from Levenson the claim that culturalism permeated traditional Chinese thought because Chinese culture was the focus of people's loyalty.[35]

As for the relationship between culturalism and nationalism, Lu and Fan claim that the history of modern China is one in which nationalism replaces culturalism as the dominant Chinese view of their identity and place in the world.[36] Murata describes how nationalism was developed in China during the collapse of the worldview of the Chinese World Order.[37] Lutz observes that the cultural iconoclasm of the May Fourth Movement was no longer sufficient for nationalists.[38] Scientism and anarchism had proved inadequate intellectual guides. Sporadic and spontaneous student protests had had only a slight impact on militarists or imperialists. As reformers and revolutionaries alike turned to politics and holistic ideologies, Sun Yat-sen spelled out the details of his Three Principles of the People, and translations of Marx and Lenin gained popularity despite censorship. Levenson discusses the pains and ideological changes experienced by generations of Chinese scholars in the face of "changes unprecedented in thousands of years" which can be summarized

---

33. Peter Hays Gries, *China's New Nationalism: Pride, Politics, and Diplomacy* (Berkeley, CA: University of California Press, 2004).

34. Suisheng Zhao, "Chinese Nationalism and Its International Orientations," *Political Science Quarterly* 115, no. 1 (2000): 4.

35. Zhao, 4.

36. Lu and Fan, "From Celestial Empire," 479.

37. Y. Murata, "Nationalism, Historical Aspects of: East Asia," *International Encyclopedia of the Social & Behavioral Sciences*, 2001, 10348–51.

38. Lutz, "Chinese Nationalism," 406.

as an attempt to give up "culturalism" and advocate "nationalism" so as to "snatch a victory as a nation (*guo*)" from the "Chinese defeat of *tianxia*."[39]

However, in addition to Phillips and James,[40] Metzger and Myers recognize that there is an inherent connection between culturalism and nationalism.[41] In their view, Chinese nationalism, which has something to do with its realpolitik and the universal ideal of a world order, has an overarching, a morally pure Chinese political centre and an awareness of being a distinct, superior ethnic group with the same blood, customs, and language.[42] Moreover, nationalistic feeling in modern China has often been mixed with a feeling of proud identification with the glories of China's Confucian civilization. This image, in turn, connotes the utopian ethical vision of world harmony mentioned above, not a narrowly ethnic or civic sense of solidarity. And the nationalistic feeling is mixed with familism and culturalism and is to some degree thereby weakened. Wang also succinctly points out these inherent connections as well as a common feature of modern nationalism.[43] Before the nineteenth century, there was no such word as "nationalism" in Chinese[44] and the national consciousness had been about culture and race. During the interaction with the West after 1840, the element of rights, especially the right of sovereignty, was added and the word "nationalism" was imported. Modern nationalism in China has three basic elements: race, culture, and sovereign rights.

---

39. Joseph R. Levenson, *Confucian China and Its Modern Fate* (Berkeley, CA: University of California Press, 1965), 100.

40. Phillips and James, "National Identity between Tradition," 23–35.

41. Thomas A. Metzger and Ramon H. Myers, "Chinese Nationalism and American Policy," *Orbis*, 1998, 33.

42. However, the ideal image in discourses of the past might just reflect "an imagined community" and does not necessarily match its reality.

43. Er Min Wang 王尔敏, *On the History of Modern Thoughts in China* 中国近代思想史论 (Beijing 北京: Social Sciences Literature Press 社会科学文献出版社, 2003), 177–94.

44. According to Meissner, discourses on cultural and national identity have been part of nation-building in Western Europe since the eighteenth century. Werner Meissner, "China's Search for Cultural and National Identity from the Nineteenth Century to the Present," *China Perspectives*, no. 68 (2006): 2, http://chinaperspectives.revues.org/3103; Prof. R. G. Tiedemann points out that the term "nationalism" did not exist in any language before the nineteenth century.

4.2 Nationalism and National Identity

Hence, nationalism is not only a response against an external agent but also an internal battle between conflicting visions for the nation which projected a variety of expectations on its members.

4.2.1 Different Ways of Being Modern Chinese but with One Commonality

As has already been stated above, the different versions of nationalism were presented by the revolutionaries, the Qing imperial court, and the constitutional reformers before 1911. In the 1920s, competition arose among the revolutionaries including the KMT and the CCP, the Awakening Lion School (醒狮派),[45] also known as the Nationalism School, the cultural radicals, the traditional conservatives, and so on. We may view this as a search for identity, both national and cultural.

Rieffer points out that nationalism, like religion, has the potential to provide individuals with an identity, as well as direction and guidance by providing choices, answers, meaning, and a frame of reference by which they can navigate through an often confusing and complex world.[46] By offering a set of values and a frame of reference, nationalism enables a national identity to all who choose to commit to its values. Nationalism offers its members a sense of identity that can be as important as religion. Henderson and McEwen try to prove that the shared values are very important to building up a national identity because shared values may help to bring meaning to the collective

---

45. On 2 December 1923, a group of Chinese students founded the Chinese Youth Party (中国青年党) in Paris. Initially it was called the China National Youth Corps and it acquired its current name in 1929. Given China's weakened condition in the early 1920s, the Chinese Youth Party primarily advocated the elimination of China's warlords and the establishment of a strong central government. It also promoted a nationalist agenda which focused on the abolition of the special privileges and extraterritoriality which foreign powers had obtained in China during the final years of the Qing dynasty. It was also strongly anti-Communist. The *Awakening Lion* (醒狮) weekly periodical was founded in Shanghai in 1924 as the organ of the China National Youth Corps. This party was also known as the Society of the Awakening Lion (or the Nationalism School 醒狮社). During the Northern Expedition, the party supported the northern warlords because they opposed the Communists within the First United Front. After the anti-Communist purge, they still resisted the KMT because of its one-party state. Zeng Qi (曾琦) and Li Huang (李璜) were among its founders.

46. Barbara-Ann J. Rieffer, "Religion and Nationalism: Understanding the Consequences of a Complex Relationship," *Ethnicities* 3, no. 2 (2003): 217–18.

dimension of national identity and emphasize what defines us as a people.[47] They define the "value" as an "enduring belief that guides actions across specific contexts" and hold that national identity has both an individual and a collective dimension. By the set of shared values offered by nationalism, people understand what the nation is and who belongs to it. Kane believes that national identity, like all forms of collective identity, is a subjectively shared sense of belonging and connection to a particular community, based on symbolic conceptualizations of similarity between oneself and one's group, especially in relation to others.[48] Kulyk also connects nationalism with national identity and understands national identity as a particular kind of collective identity.[49]

The different versions of nationalism in China offered different descriptions of Chinese national identity. In other words, there are various interpretations of what it means to be Chinese. However, as pointed out by Wang in the previous section,[50] one commonality shared by all the different versions of modern nationalism in China was sovereign rights.

The great advances in science and technology were (and still are) believed by the Chinese to be the main cause of the Western powers and Japan's victories over China. In the view of most Chinese, the only way to expunge this humiliation (*xiuru*) was (and still is) to catch up with the West in science and technology. The statesman Zhang Zhidong (1837–1909) proposed a famous slogan "Chinese learning as essence (substance), and Western learning for application (function)" (*zhongxue weiti, xixue weiyong* 中学为体, 西学为用). It meant a selective adoption of the science and technology of the West and the maintenance of Chinese culture (specifically Confucianism) as a guide for individual life, society, and state. In fact, modern nationalism in China led to the rise of scientism and also became the grounds for the Confucian Association's attempt to establish Confucianism as the state religion in the 1910s.

---

47. Ailsa Henderson and Nicola McEwen, "Do Shared Values Underpin National Identity? Examining the Role of Values in National Identity in Canada and the United Kingdom," *National Identities* 7, no. 2 (2005): 175–76.

48. Anne Kane, "Narratives of Nationalism: Constructing Irish National Identity during the Land War, 1879–82," *National Identities* 2, no. 3 (2000): 247.

49. Volodymyr Kulyk, "The Media, History and Identity: Competing Narratives of the Past in the Ukrainian Popular Press," *National Identities* 13, no. 3 (2011): 287–303.

50. Wang, *History of Modern Thoughts*, 177–94.

4.2.2 Competition through Discourses and Narratives

This competition among different versions of nationalism was mainly carried out by presenting different discourses and narratives. Kane discusses how discourse and narrative build up national identity.[51] Henderson and McEwen believe national identity is constituted and reconstituted within political and social discourse.[52] Kulyk also connects nationalism with national identity and proposes that there is a hierarchy of influence of the competing narratives on national identity.[53] Korostelina analyses the impact of education in history on social identity through history textbooks, especially in the area of national identity.[54] She includes China as one of her examples. She concludes that education in history plays a major role in the development and strengthening of social identities. The examples presented in her article show how education in history forms and transforms modes, forms, and concepts of identity and influences the processes of forming a national identity.

Hence, on the one hand, Zhang Yijing perceived the expectations of "being Chinese" through the discourses of other versions of nationalism; while on the other hand, he searched for a way to present the union of his Christian identity and his national identity in the hope that his being Chinese could be universally acknowledged by his compatriots.

4.2.3 Competition between National Identity and Other Identities

Kane says the sense of belonging to a group is problematic and unstable, partially because individuals face multiple identity claims.[55] Kulyk believes national identity can be more or less salient than other collective identities because individuals and subgroups within a nation will contest the identity's content. Identification with a nation or another collectivity manifests one's belief or feeling.[56]

---

51. Kane, "Narratives of Nationalism," 245–64.
52. Henderson and McEwen, "Do Shared Values Underpin?," 176.
53. Kulyk, "Media, History and Identity."
54. Karina Korostelina, "History Education and Social Identity," *Identity: An International Journal of Theory and Research* 8, no. 1 (2008): 43.
55. Kane, "Narratives of Nationalism," 247.
56. Kulyk, "Media, History and Identity," 288.

This study discusses Zhang's four identities from among his multiple identities, and this chapter will focus on his Christian identity and his national identity.

4.2.4 The Way of Studying Zhang's National Identity

In the case of Zhang, his national identity is a significant aspect in understanding his search for a Christian Chinese or a Chinese Christian identity when being Chinese was perceived in the sense of culturalism and modern nationalism. Since Confucianism, the mainstream of Chinese culture, has been discussed in chapter 3, Zhang's national identity in its cultural sense will not be the focus of this chapter, but only discussed briefly. The principal focus of this chapter will be given to the development of the relationship between his Christian identity and his commitment to modern nationalism which will be called his modern national identity in this study. This chapter will study his writings to understand his modern national identity by examining his nationalistic feeling which centred around China's right of sovereignty. In contrast to his usual pride in China's culture, his nationalistic feeling was often revealed by a sense of humiliation or *xiuru*.

4.3 Being a Modern Chinese or Being a Christian

Before the importation of the word "nationalism" into Chinese, the defeats inflicted on China by the West, starting from 1840 had already produced a feeling of humiliation or *xiuru* among the Chinese people. They felt that their rights had been violated. This was, and is, the main theme of all versions of modern nationalism in China. Later this sense of humiliation was deliberately instilled into the minds of young students to arouse nationalistic feelings. This feeling of humiliation became part of China's national identity.[57] As a result of the connection between the Protestant missionaries and the Western imperialists who were the perpetrators of the humiliation, Christianity was often interpreted to mean that the missionaries were the enemy of national interests.

Fitzgerald reveals that the KMT Nationalists and the Communists shared similar views in defining the national interests and extending the state power

---

57. Meissner, "China's Search for Cultural," 4.

over the interests of social groups.⁵⁸ They both depicted themselves as the defenders of China's people, culture, and sovereign rights. Between 1922–25, even the Soviet leaders, in an attempt to exploit the nationalist mood, revised their vision of a proletarian revolution against the bourgeoisie in China to a struggle against imperialism.⁵⁹ The translation of Lenin's *On Imperialism* offered a new lens under which Western nations were found to be guilty of "militant, political, and economic imperialism" while Christianity and Western missions were believed to be guilty of "cultural imperialism."⁶⁰ Meanwhile, Sun Yat-sen, the head of KMT, is seen to turn gradually from liberal politics, representation, and pluralism to revolution, mobilization, and the single party-state.⁶¹ Notwithstanding, Fitzgerald does not mention the Society of the Awakening Lion (also called the Nationalism School), which advocated a radical version of nationalism and nationalistic education and attacked Communism as well as Christianity in its *Awakening Lion* publication.

This school positioned love for one's own country as the apex of morality and human nature.⁶² It was one of the first to put forward "reclaiming the educational rights."⁶³ Chinese Christians who took advantage of their compatriots through the power of foreigners were labelled as national traitors or *guozei* (国贼) while sending the missionaries to China was viewed as a demonstration of power to the Chinese.⁶⁴

---

58. John Fitzgerald, "The Misconceived Revolution: State and Society in China's Nationalist Revolution, 1923–26," *The Journal of Asian Studies* 49, no. 2 (1990): 323–43.

59. Alexander Pantsov, *The Bolsheviks and the Chinese Revolution 1919–1927* (Honolulu: University of Hawai'i Press, 2000), 41, 211.

60. Dunch, *Fuzhou Protestants*, 186–87.

61. Dunch, 191.

62. Qi Zeng 曾琦, "The Four Pieces of Evidence for Nationalism Advocates 国家主义者的四大论据," in *The Collection of the Materials of the Modern Philosophy History in China 中国现代哲学史资料选辑1919–1949* (上), ed. Zhenxia Li 李振霞 and Peiyue Guan 管培月 (Beijing: Philosophy Department of the Party School of the CPC Central Committee 中共中央党校哲学教研室编, 1924), 285.

63. Junsheng Wu 吴俊升, "The Progress of the Nationalistic Education and My Comments 国家主义的教育之进展及其评论," in *The Collection of Papers on Nationalism* 国家主义论文集, ed. Huang Li 李璜 (Shanghai: Shanghai China Publishing House 上海中华书局, 1925), 129.

64. Qi Zeng 曾琦, "The Meaning of 'Eradicating Internal National Traitors and Resisting External Powers' 内除国贼外抗强权释义," in *The Collection of Papers on Nationalism* 国家主义论文集, ed. Huang Li 李璜 (Shanghai: Shanghai China Publishing House 上海中华书局, 1925), 98–99.

Although Chinese communists differed from the Society of the Awakening Lion in the means they proposed for saving China, they shared the same enemies: Christian education, imperialistic capitalism, and warlords.[65] This may explain why nationalism caused conflicts among Christians. Nearly all the versions of nationalism in the 1920s required every social group to submit its interests to their political agenda. Those who did not submit were defined as the enemies of the nation.

So how did Zhang become a Chinese Christian or a Christian Chinese? How did he bring his national identity and Christian identity into a unified whole and how were they positioned in his identity structure? Next, I will examine the writings by Zhang.

4.4 Zhang's National Identity and His Christian Identity

4.4.1 His National Identity in the Cultural Sense

Zhang had a strong emotional attachment to Chinese culture. In addition to his commitment to Confucianism, he demonstrated his pride in other Chinese accomplishments such as the Yin-Yang School[66] whose explanation of the solar and lunar eclipses one thousand years ago was amazingly similar to the modern scientific findings.[67]

While Wu Zhihui claimed the Chinese classics must be thrown into the latrine for thirty years,[68] Zhang verified his commitment to Chinese culture by his love for those threadbare books and his translating them into English with Dr. Chambers.[69] He felt the contents of those books were impressive,

---

65. Chunu Xiao 肖楚女, "A Letter on Nationalistic Education 讨论国家主义教育的一封信," in 中国现代哲学史资料选辑1919–1949 (上), ed. Zhenxia Li 李振霞 and Peiyue Guan 管培月 (Beijing: Philosophy Department of the Party School of the CPC Central Committee 中共中央党校哲学教研室编, 1924), 250.

66. The Yin-Yang School (阴阳家) or the School of Positive and Negative Forces was popular in the Period of the Warring States, 475–221 BC.

67. Yijing Zhang 张亦镜, "Thoughts over a Western Pastor's Plan on Mastering Chinese with His Colleagues (闻某西牧欲联同志精习汉文感言)," in *(1928), A Quarter of a Century of True Light, Selected* 真光丛刊, Part 3: General Articles 通论, ed. Yijing Zhang (Shanghai 上海: China Baptist Publication Society 中华浸会书局, 1916), 34.

68. Wu, "Critique of the Thought," 4.

69. Although Zhang's close friendship with R. E. Chambers might have been negatively influenced by the events of the mid-1920s and Zhang's reaction to them, their trip to Qingdao

admirable, and thought-provoking and was fascinated by the peculiar ancient words, practices, knowledge, and humour.[70]

He said that the lunar calendar was a quintessence of Chinese culture because it demonstrated accurate scientific knowledge four thousand years ago. Zhang proudly pointed out that the West did not have such a scientific lunar calendar.[71]

In Zhang's view, Chinese traditional culture did not only embody philosophy, wisdom, and beauty, but also possessed the scientific potential to endow China with an equal or even transcending status in its relationship with the West. Here we see a mixture of cultural nationalism and modern nationalism in Zhang. The next section will be an analysis of his commitment to modern nationalism.

4.4.2 Being a Modern Chinese Christian before 1905
4.4.2.1 *His National Identity and His Conversion*
Before his conversion in 1892, Zhang strongly opposed Christianity:

> Whenever I read anti-Christian books which blamed China's shamefully ceding territory and paying indemnity on Christianity, I felt so furious that I even wished to eat the flesh of Christian preachers and sleep on a sheet made of their skin. If I had not humbled myself to make a search for the truth, which led to my conversion, I would have become a famous anti-Christian writer.[72]

Zhang's fury was his natural response after feeling humiliated by the West. Because of the misguided information he had been given, his national identity turned him against Christianity. With the hostility towards Christianity stemming from his national identity, it could be expected that it would be extremely difficult for him to commit himself to this new religion. However, his Confucian identity seemed to be a mediator. As seen in chapter 3, Zhang

---

where they spent two months together seemed to be evidence that their friendship weathered the storm.

70. Yijing Zhang 张亦镜, "My Two Months in Qingdao (在青岛两个月之经过)," *True Light* 真光 27, no. 10 (1928): 44, 50.

71. Yijing Zhang 张亦镜, "Abolishing the Lunar Calendar (废除阴历)," *True Light* 真光 28, no. 2 (1929): 95–96; Zhang, "Questions from Mr. Zeng Guren," 60.

72. Zhang, "Cleansing the False Accusations," 59.

once came across two Christian tracts and found that their messages were in accordance with his Confucian identity. This might explain why he humbled himself to research until he found out the reasons for China's humiliations that satisfied him and led him to not blame Christianity. In this case, his Confucian identity facilitated the acceptance of his Christian identity by his national identity.

4.4.2.2 *The Conflict between His National Identity and His Christian Group Identity*

Chapter 3 has recorded how in 1899, Zhang, a village farmer and tutor, became a journalist (or a preacher through writing in his understanding) in Hong Kong and how his nationalistic feeling was offended, and this was exacerbated by his unhappiness with Western pastors in his church. This unhappiness might have been caused by his perception of the pride of Western pastors, but more probably it was caused by differences in culture, language, and personality because such differences also led to the frictions between him and Dr. Chambers in their first five years of co-operation. Zhang himself said, "I even doubted that I would be able to identify with Western missionaries of my own denomination (the Baptist churches)."[73] Qiutao, his son, said, "He then doubted that Chinese believers should associate with Westerners in the church because they were ethnically different."[74] The word "doubted" strengthens the conclusion above.

No matter what caused his unhappiness, it exacerbated his feeling of humiliation. To abate this unbearable anger, he decided to sever his relationship with all Westerners at the cost of his church membership. In other words, Zhang's national identity became so salient that he quit his Christian group identity. Although he still viewed himself as a Christian, he basically stopped his communication with God such as Bible reading and praying. During that five-year period, he only became grateful to God once after he was saved from a beating by the magistrate. Hence, his national identity was the reason for the regression of his Christian identity from its achievement status to its diffusion status. Thus, during the half year in Hong Kong, the strength of

---

73. Zhang, "How I Became a Christian," 4.
74. Zhang, "Chronology of Zhang Yijing," 17.

Zhang's national identity kept increasing to such a degree that Zhang was on the verge of giving up his Christian identity altogether.

4.4.2.3 A Discussion of His National, Christian, and Confucian Identities

Zhang's national identity would usually stay calm and unnoticeable, but the sight of a Chinese person being bullied could cause his nationalistic feeling of anger to flare up to a very high degree. As a consequence, his Christian identity became unsteady especially when he had misinformation.

Nevertheless, he did not choose a Christian identity because of his national identity. In the 1910s, many people became interested in Christianity because they attributed China's weakness to Neo-Confucianism and attributed the prosperity and power of the West to Christianity. Zhang held a different opinion. He said, "At the very beginning, my thoughts were distinct from this saying."[75] By this, he meant that when he decided to become a Christian, his motivation was not to make China strong and he did not attribute China's weakness to Neo-Confucianism. Actually, his selection of a Christian identity was connected with his Confucian identity, as seen in chapter 3. This chapter will investigate his fundamental motivation.

In spite of this, the importance of his national identity was evident in his consideration of the causal links between the innocence of Christianity in China's humiliations and his selection of a Christian identity, and between Westerners' arrogance and his giving up church membership and stopping his communication with God. Therefore, it is safe to say that his national identity took priority over his Christian identity before his return to the church in 1904.

As analyzed in chapter 3, Zhang's return to the church was the result of a few elements: (1) his hurt nationalistic feeling may have calmed down after a five-year separation from Westerners; (2) Christianity edified his Confucian values; (3) his refusal of lottery money as a result of his Confucian identity was praised by Pastor Yu; and (4) Pastor Yu may have clarified the difference between Western missionaries and the other Westerners. This was still based on Zhang's usage of "doubted" in 1923 when he recalled his resignation

---

75. Zhang, "Answering an Old Scholar," 218.

of 1899. This word meant that he later realized he had misunderstood his Western pastors in 1899.

Just as his Confucian identity facilitated his national identity's choice of a Christian identity before 1893, his Confucian identity assisted his return to his Christian identity in 1904.

On the surface, Zhang's national identity and Confucian identity were at peace and their positions in his multiple identity structure were hard to distinguish. However, there are signs to trace. As he said, at the very beginning, he did not think Neo-Confucianism could weaken China. In 1910, he reviewed China's humiliations and China's history of persecuting Christianity and rejecting the foreigners which hinted at the role of Confucianism in the shame suffered by China.[76] In the 1910s, he argued against the Confucian Association's theory that Confucianism could save China. In his argument, he once even denied his subjective sense of belonging to the School of Confucianism by claiming, "Although I am not a Confucian, I admire Confucius from the bottom of my heart."[77] From the beginning of the 1890s to the 1910s, his expectation of saving China by Confucianism went from "having no question" to "denial," while during the same period, the status of his Confucian identity, compared to his Christian identity, also declined from "Confucianism as his benchmark" to "Christianity as his standard." Therefore, the dwindling significance of Zhang's Confucian identity was related to his national identity; in other words, the salience of his Confucian identity changed in proportion to its congruity with his national identity. Since the significance of his Confucian identity depended on its harmony with his national identity, his national identity was superior to his Confucian identity in his multiple identity structure.

4.4.3 Being a Modern Chinese Christian before 1920
4.4.3.1 *The Development of His Christian Identity and the Possible Reasons*

Chapter 3 has reviewed the substance of his Christian identity at the end of 1905. This section will explore the following development of his Christian identity until 1920.

---

76. Zhang, "Cleansing the False Accusations," 56–58.
77. Zhang, "After President Yuan Commands," 87.

The continuity in the substance of his Christian identity during this period could be seen in the following aspects: (1) God is the almighty Creator and loves humanity; (2) Jesus is Christ, the Son of God and his blood could cleanse people's sins; he died and was resurrected; (3) the Holy Spirit could help people; and (4) Jesus commands his followers to spread the gospel.

Compared with the substance of his Christian identity at the beginning of his joining *True Light*, the growth of his Christian identity could also be recognized. The most obvious one should be his understanding of the Holy Spirit. His first use of the term "the Holy Spirit" occurred in June and July of 1906 when he wrote about it after hearing the preaching of two missionaries. His first usage in June was *shengshen* (圣神)[78] rather than *shengling* (圣灵) which he used in July[79] and afterwards. Although *shen* and *ling* are often connected to *shenling* to mean gods, more often *shen* leaves an impression of gods while *ling* leaves an impression of spirit. This probably was caused by a lack of uniformity of translation.

For the next five years, although he would say that the Holy Spirit helped Jesus and helped his followers, he did not specifically explain the details of the Holy Spirit's help. In 1911, he reviewed the power of the Holy Spirit as recorded in Acts 2 and said, "The Holy Spirit is one of the Trinity. The Holy Spirit and Jesus are in one while God and the Holy Spirit are in one also."[80] However, that does not mean he had comprehended it clearly because later he said:

> There must be heaven and hell as two destinations. There must be the Holy Spirit and Satan, two supernatural beings. They are either in the future world or in the other spiritual realm. Our

---

78. Jianyu, "Descent of the Holy Spirit."

79. Jianyu 检余, "Church's Prosperity and China's Hope (教会兴与中国之希望)," in *(1928), A Quarter of a Century of True Light, Selected* 真光丛刊*, Part 1: Concerning the Scriptures* 说经文, ed. Yijing Zhang (Shanghai 上海: China Baptist Publication Society 中华浸会书局, 1906), 18–22.

80. Yijing Zhang 张亦镜, "Go and Preach the Good News to All People (尔曹往普天下传福音与万民)," in *(1928), A Quarter of a Century of True Light, Selected* 真光丛刊*, Part 1: Concerning the Scriptures* 说经文, ed. Yijing Zhang (Shanghai 上海: China Baptist Publication Society 中华浸会书局, 1911), 92.

> fleshly eyes could not see them, but we could believe in their existence by reasoning.[81]

Though he was sure of the existence of the Holy Spirit, it still seemed perplexing to him. He admitted,

> The most unlikely point in Christianity was the Holy Spirit. But the history and the spread of Christianity all depended on it. The Holy Spirit is the spirit of God. It cannot be seen, heard, or touched. The Holy Spirit would not come until Jesus' body was resurrected and returned to his original place [heaven].[82]

As he said in the same text, it could not be seen, heard, and touched. Maybe this was why he felt it so unlikely. Nevertheless, Satan had the same characteristics, but on this point, he did not feel so puzzled. Therefore, the true reason for his puzzlement was due to the lack of a parallel concept in Chinese culture, whereas an analogous idea of the devil exists in Chinese tradition. The lack of analogy also caused his predicament in conveying the idea of Jesus's atonement.[83] His faith in the reality of the Holy Spirit was based on two elements: (1) the history and the vast spread of Christianity which should be impossible without the work of the Holy Spirit; and (2) the Bible which records Jesus's teaching of the Holy Spirit in the Gospel of John and his coming on the Day of Pentecost in Acts. However, according to his saying above, this faith was more of a result of reasoning rather than of personal experience.

His knowledge of the works of the Holy Spirit became more specific, such as the rebirth of one's spirit, making the followers of Jesus to be newly created people, bearing the fruits of the Holy Spirit, strengthening their witness with

---

81. Yijing Zhang 张亦镜, "Correcting Wang Jingwei's Slander on Christianity in His Foreword to the First Issue of Min De Newspaper (纠正汪精卫巴黎民德报发刊词毁教语之谬)," in *(1928), A Quarter of a Century of True Light, Selected* 真光丛刊*, Part 2: The Gospel Discussed and Explained* 辩道文, ed. Yijing Zhang (Shanghai 上海: China Baptist Publication Society 中华浸会书局, 1914), 167.

82. Yijing Zhang 张亦镜, "Resurrection (复生)," in *(1928), A Quarter of a Century of True Light, Selected* 真光丛刊*, Part 1: Concerning the Scriptures* 说经文, ed. Yijing Zhang (Shanghai 上海: China Baptist Publication Society 中华浸会书局, 1914), 129.

83. Zhang, "Atonement (代赎)," in *(1928), A Quarter of a Century of True Light, Selected* 真光丛刊*, Part 6: Brief Selections Translated* 谈薮, ed. Yijing Zhang (Shanghai 上海: China Baptist Publication Society 中华浸会书局, 1913), 68–70; "My View on Jesus' Atonement (附耶稣赎罪问题之我见)," in *(1928), A Quarter of a Century of True Light, Selected* 真光丛刊*, Part 2: The Gospel Discussed and Explained* 辩道文, ed. Yijing Zhang (Shanghai 上海: China Baptist Publication Society 中华浸会书局, 1920), 267–71; Zhang, "How I Became a Christian."

miracles and power.[84] Moreover, he stated his understanding of the nature of the Holy Spirit more clearly. For instance, the Holy Spirit is the spirit of God; the Spirit was with Jesus when he lived in this world; the Holy Spirit would not come until Jesus's body was resurrected and returned to his original place. He took the book of Acts as the Holy Spirit's gospel because it came into being by the Holy Spirit's working within people rather than by human power.[85] He was not articulate on this topic before 1911 and the reason was that he had not obtained such knowledge until then. Very probably he gained more knowledge about it through others' preaching, Bible reading, praying, reference books, talks, and his own contemplation.

By 1918, it seemed that he had more personal experience when he compared the difference between the two states with and without the Holy Spirit. He felt that the believers would still do things they disliked when they depended on themselves and they would find it easier to avoid those things with the help of the Holy Spirit.[86] He observed that since sin was a very personal issue, people's awareness of sin within themselves totally depended on the works of the Holy Spirit or God's inspiration.[87] He also became more familiar with the knowledge of the Holy Spirit and more skilled in using the term. When a Confucian scholar claimed that Jesus was also a sinner, that his execution was a penalty for his own rebellion, and that he did not die for other people, Zhang called it "a blasphemy against the Holy Spirit."[88] Nonetheless, he did not talk about the qualifications for the help of the Holy Spirit until the 1920s.

During the period before 1920, another development in his theological understanding was his attitude towards the salvation of those who had already died. Though in 1906 he had said that people who do not believe in Jesus would go to hell and have no chance to repent as discussed in chapter 3, it seems that his opinion fluctuated in the following years. By 1908, he expressed an idea that a believer's faith might incur God's favour towards their dead unbelieving parents and mitigation of their sin:

---

84. Zhang, "Resurrection," 129.
85. Zhang.
86. Zhang, "Answering an Old Scholar," 190.
87. Zhang, 208.
88. Zhang, 189.

> To love our parents with Jesus' love, we should exhort our parents to believe in the Way so that we all have salvation. If unfortunately, our parents have passed away before we believed in the Way, and if we are devoted to loving Jesus, maybe God, in view of our faith, will mercifully take into consideration an excusable situation that our parents had not had the chance to hear the Way so that He would not declare them guilty in the same way with those who heard but did not believe the Way. This is possible but uncertain. God's leniency might make them an exception, but we are not sure of this. We should be a true disciple of Jesus daily to please God and have a good testimony so that our parents will not be shamed by us.[89]

He said this either because he himself wished it so or because he wanted to keep religious inquirers and new believers interested in Christianity by making it sound less harsh. He should have searched for evidence in the Bible, but obviously he failed in his attempt to secure evidence. Thus, he spoke in an ambiguous way to leave the result open. This mirrors an inner tug of war between seeking the accuracy of interpreting the Bible and having regard for people's feelings.

However, this idea is not found in his later writings. Instead, he explicitly stated that there was no second chance after death. In 1911, when he urged the believers to realize the urgency of evangelization:

> By the testimony of the prophets and the apostles in the Bible, we have also learned that if we did not believe him and rely on him before death, we would definitely cry and grind our teeth after death ... we are afraid that, at the moment of seeing his judgment, it will have been too late to call for help.[90]

If the courtesy in his words "we are afraid" was still an expression used from a sense of propriety, he was unequivocal in presenting his biblical understanding in his letter to an old Confucian scholar in 1918 to clarify his misunderstanding of Christianity and exhort him to put his faith in Jesus as quickly as possible.

---

89. Zhang, "Against Song Shixiang's Saying," 13.
90. Zhang, "Go and Preach," 94.

When old age comes, it is getting urgent for us to get salvation. How can we resist by excuses? It is just "believing in heart and confessing by mouth" (Rom 10:9). How can you say it is too troublesome to do it? Don't you know that the older we get, the less time is left before we leave to meet the Lord? If we did not walk on this way of life (Matt 7:14, John 14:6),[91] the chance of repentance would vanish in no time. After that, people will see the righteous reward and righteous punishment, which could be viewed as a result of free will, and it will be useless to ask for help. The believers will be saved while the unbelievers will be condemned, just as the Gospel says. What can people do?[92]

If a person did not believe while alive, there would be no further chance after death and people could do no more. Compared with his words of ten years earlier, the idea of winning God's preferential mitigation of the sins of the unbelieving dead by their descendants' piousness was absent. Some may wonder if Zhang would repeat his doubtful idea expressed in 1908 to comfort those whose parents had already passed away since the recipients of his words in 1911 and 1918 did not need comfort but a realization of the urgency of time. This speculation is reasonable; however, two elements contradict it. First, all his readers had/would have dead parents and ancestors, they would grasp his public insistence on biblical interpretation. Zhang knew the influence of his biblical insistence on people's feelings, which would stop him from a reversion to create a self-contradiction. Second, his idea of 1908 did not reappear in further writings.

Some may think if the age of the Confucian scholar impressed a sense of urgency in Zhang so that he became direct and pressing by using rhetorical questions. Nonetheless, it is precisely the response under the pressure of urgent feeling that could reflect one's truest thoughts.

An observable feature common in the above quotations may be helpful in understanding the development of the theological contents of his Christian identity; namely, that he was increasingly inclined to accept the descriptions

---

91. Matthew 7:14 – "But small is the gate and narrow the road that leads to life, and only a few find it." John 14:6 – "Jesus answered, 'I am the way and the truth and the life. No one comes to the Father except through me.'"

92. Zhang, "Answering an Old Scholar," 221.

in the Bible according to their literal meanings except for the great flood[93] which will be discussed in chapter 5. The importance he attached to the Bible could be seen in his writings and some sentences are listed below, in chronological order, as examples:

> I would rather be ridiculed as stupid and simple all my life because I sing praises, read the Bible, and pray than be rejected by Christ who makes people holy.[94]

> All goodness has been included in the Bible. By knowing the Bible, a person can learn the main points and understand all goodness. The most important thing is to have the wisdom to obtain salvation through faith in Christ Jesus.[95]

> The Old and New Testaments are the standard of truth. If anything is in accordance with the Old and New Testaments, then it is truthful; otherwise, it is not truthful. The Bible should be the standard of truth against which all traditions and cultures are measured.[96]

> Even in the twentieth century, whenever we read the Bible, we see a living God on the page who talks to us and shows us his glory.[97]

> The whole Bible bears witness to God who is omniscient, almighty, and kind. If anyone is humble and without other motives, he would bow down and confess that Jehovah is the Creator and Jesus is the Saviour.[98]

---

93. Yijing Zhang 张亦镜, "A Brief History of People in Old and New Testaments (旧新约人物传略)," in *(1928), A Quarter of a Century of True Light, Selected* 真光丛刊, Part 1: *Concerning the Scriptures* 说经文, ed. Yijing Zhang (Shanghai 上海: China Baptist Publication Society 中华浸会书局, 1913), 162.

94. Yijing Zhang 张亦镜, "Having a Fellowship with Christ (心交基督)," in *(1928), A Quarter of a Century of True Light, Selected* 真光丛刊, Part 1: *Concerning the Scriptures* 说经文, ed. Yijing Zhang (Shanghai 上海: China Baptist Publication Society 中华浸会书局, 1907), 45.

95. Yijing Zhang 张亦镜, "Salvation through Faith in Christ Jesus (尔自幼识圣经因而有智信基督耶稣得救)," in *(1928), A Quarter of a Century of True Light, Selected* 真光丛刊, Part 1: *Concerning the Scriptures* 说经文, ed. Yijing Zhang (Shanghai 上海: China Baptist Publication Society 中华浸会书局, 1907), 25–26.

96. Zhang, "Against Song Shixiang's Saying," 17.

97. Zhang, "Go and Preach," 91.

98. Zhang, "Correcting Wang Jingwei's Slander," 170.

The truth in the Bible is incontestable. All people are sinners. God sent Jesus to save them. He was born of a virgin. Whoever believes and receives baptism has salvation and whoever rejects has condemnation.[99]

The question is how he developed such a faith in the Bible. When such quotations are put together with his sayings in 1894 and 1906, as presented in chapter 3, a link is revealed between Zhang's faith in the Bible and his pursuit of good deeds, awareness of his own sin, his struggle with it, and his gratitude for Jesus's salvation.

Chapter 3 has reviewed his sayings in 1894 starting with "Principles cannot win over selfishness." His words reveal that in the process of sincerely following the principles required by his Confucian identity, he had met with failures and frustrations. Being enlightened by the two Christian tracts and three preachers, he found the reasons for his failures in Satan and the hope of victory in God. Consequently, he diligently read the Bible so that his nature could be strengthened to defend himself against Satan's attack in the hope that he might become righteous before God by his victories.

However, by the end of 1905, he compared Moses's law and Jesus's salvation and his former slavery and current freedom, which shows his disappointment with his efforts of pursuing good deeds and his joy of finding forgiveness in Jesus.

Afterwards, as a sincere Confucian and a firm Christian, he continued the application of his beliefs, and the flow of his failures and successes in the areas of good deeds and sin confirmed his faith in Jesus's blood and atonement. That was why he frequently talked about sin and Jesus's salvation. In this course, he saw a parallel between Moses's law and the requirements of Confucianism because the moral teachings of Confucianism also asked people to discipline themselves to follow the regulations while Jesus taught people to strive for goodness by following his example and asking for the help of the Holy Spirit.[100] Therefore, he argued:

---

99. Zhang, "Answering an Old Scholar," 176, 182–83.

100. Yijing Zhang 张亦镜, "On Falsehood (说伪)," in *(1928), A Quarter of a Century of True Light, Selected* 真光丛刊, *Part 3: General Articles* 通论, ed. Yijing Zhang (Shanghai 上海: China Baptist Publication Society 中华浸会书局, 1914), 55–56.

> Christianity focused on faith in Jesus. With genuine faith, one would naturally produce good deeds. Confucianism emphasized deeds and there was not much faith in it.[101]

In his reasoning, although the canons of Confucianism contain the term *shangdi* (上帝) which could serve as a reference to Jesus's teachings, Confucius made no difference between god and spirit and warned people to stay away from them altogether. He concluded:

> Therefore, Confucianism offers no faith. Without faith, Confucians are good at speaking of kindness and morality. They use them to decorate their articles, but very few would carry them out in practice.[102]

> Why couldn't Confucians live out their ideals? The only answer was the absence of genuine religious faith. Without genuine faith, individuals cannot obtain God's power to help them overcome their sinful nature, so, they are trapped by their stubborn and polluted flesh.[103]

For example, the Confucians often played with prostitutes.[104] According to his personal experience, both Moses's law and the principles of Confucianism were good, but by pursuing them, he was enslaved because he found himself incapable of following them completely. The fact that he repeatedly tasted Jesus's forgiveness led him to the conclusion that:

> The most important and indispensable thing in this world and life is to love Jesus. Life depends on Jesus. Having no love for Jesus is equal to having no love for life.[105]

How did he solve his problems with sin? He found his salvation by believing the teachings of the Bible.

---

101. Zhang, "Study of Christianity," 56.
102. Zhang, 57.
103. Zhang, 52.
104. Zhang, "Cleansing the False Accusations," 63; Zhang, "Study of Christianity," 52.
105. Yijing Zhang 张亦镜, "Jesus Asked Peter If He Loved Him for Three Times (主三以爱我语彼得)," in *(1928), A Quarter of a Century of True Light, Selected* 真光丛刊, *Part 1: Concerning the Scriptures* 说经文, ed. Yijing Zhang (Shanghai 上海: China Baptist Publication Society 中华浸会书局, 1911), 97.

In the Bible he found not only freedom from his bondage but also a helper to overcome temptations. In spite of his gratitude to Jesus for salvation, he was still serious about pursuing goodness, kindness, and morality, as seen in his comparison of Christianity and Confucianism. His concern with a moral life, as required by both his Christian identity and Confucian identity, motivated him to pray. As he said, when people realized the existence of God, their own sin, and their own inability to cleanse themselves from sin, they found they could never stop praying and then they knew God.[106] This concern motivated him to study the Holy Spirit starting in 1906, thirteen years after his conversion. From others' sermons, his Bible reading, and prayer practices, he gained knowledge and a personal experience with the Holy Spirit so that he felt it would be easier to defeat temptations with the help of the Holy Spirit. His first-hand experiences with the Holy Spirit consolidated his faith in the teachings of the Bible.

Such very personal experiences with sin and forgiveness explained his faith in the Bible and constituted his internal evidence and fundamental motivation for his Christian commitment. His increasing faith in the Bible accounted for the shift in his attitude towards the salvation of the dead.

In addition to the internal elements, there are other external reasons for the growth of his commitment to Christianity. One factor came from his work which he viewed as preaching through writing. Preaching and answering questions forced him into seeking answers. His Christian co-workers, especially missionaries like Dr. Chambers, were another source of encouragement and consultation.

In an overview of this period, reflecting on the stage of development of his Christian identity, one could say that its contents became more complex and its strength increased. If the temptations from Satan could be viewed as a BTC in his interior, then the salvation of Jesus, the Holy Spirit, the Bible, and prayer offered him a BCC inside. While the oppositions, challenges, and questions from people formed BTC in his exterior, the encouragements and consultations of other Christians constituted his BCC outside.

---

106. Zhang, "Correcting Wang Jingwei's Slander," 167.

4.4.3.2 A Modern Chinese Christian's Conflicts

Humiliation or *xiuru*, the emotional characteristic of modern Chinese national identity, was deeply felt by Zhang at least twice in this period.

The first incident was Zhang's protest against discrimination in Lu Shan Mountain in 1906 which he wrote about in 1906 and published a second time in 1927. Zhang went to Lu Shan Mountain Summer Resort (庐山) with Robert E. Chambers. Robert E. Chambers hired sedan chairs. At that time, if a Chinese employed by Westerners wanted to sit in a sedan chair, he had to either have the child of a Westerner sitting on his lap, as the child's protector, or have the clothes of Westerners hung on his sedan chair. Zhang said:

> Robert E. Chambers is very rule-abiding, but he could not bear with putting children into my arms, so he hung his wife's bonnet on my chair. I did not know such rules and so I thought it was too big for her suitcase. When we took a rest at Lotus Cave (莲花洞), I saw a board on which the rules were written. I became very angry because the Chinese were discriminated against so severely in China by Westerners that the Chinese were not viewed as human. Bearing with the insults, I reached the top and swore that I would never again sit [in] the sedan chair. And I am left in inerasable disgust toward the inequality between the Chinese and Westerners.[107]

The day of their return, Zhang walked down the mountain without informing Robert E. Chambers. Zhang felt very apologetic when he learned that Robert E. Chambers had hired a sedan chair for him and searched for him everywhere. On their returning ship, Zhang went up to the deck and wanted to sit on a long bench, but a Westerner drove him away in a very offensive way. Zhang sighed:

> It was already very lamentable for the Chinese to be mistreated overseas, but the Chinese in China suffered the same mistreatment also. Is China still a country and are the Chinese still human?[108]

---

107. Zhang, "Last Twenty-Five Years," 1.
108. Zhang, 1.

Then he regretted this trip. When he shared this experience with Mr. Liao after his return, he said he wanted to quit his position. Mr. Liao stopped him by comforting, criticizing, and explaining. Mr. Liao must have exhorted him to focus his attention on the Lord's ministry. In addition to the role of Liao, there was another reason why he gave up the idea of quitting the job. On the return trip, his boat survived a powerful storm which killed many people. His gratitude to God for his protection made him a willing servant of God so that he stayed on to work as a preacher through writing.

In this first incident, Zhang's feeling of being humiliated made his national identity predominant. Consequently, he walked down the mountain without informing Dr. Chambers, which seemed like an act of revenge on Westerners. When he later realized that Dr. Chambers was the wrong target, he felt very apologetic. Another consequence of his salient national identity would have become evident if it had not been for his Christian identity. If he had resigned his job at *True Light*, it would be similar to his resignation in 1899.

In 1907, Zhang did quit his job in *True Light* as a protest over discrimination against the Chinese. By then, *True Light*'s printing house was at Shamian Island of Guangzhou, an area designated for Consulates that had special laws. There were three rules that angered Zhang and led to his resignation: (1) the Chinese could not enter through the main gate; (2) the Chinese could not walk along the riverside which Westerners' courtyards faced; and (3) in the evening, each Chinese must hold a flashlight in spite of the presence of the bright street lights.[109] Zhang had long harboured a grudge against such rules and so he quit his job with an excuse. He swore he would never enter Shamian Island. His Chinese friends, sent by Robert E. Chambers, came to comfort him every day by saying that he should not allow such bad rules to hinder the Lord's works and promised to make him an exception from those rules. To this, Zhang replied:

> I am not giving up the Lord's work. I just could never do the Lord's work at Shamian where the Chinese are not treated as human. Though an exception might be made for me, I am still treated inhumanly because all other Chinese are still treated inhumanly. I have sworn that I would never enter Shamian until

---

109. The author assumes this as a quick way of locating the Chinese.

the rules have been eradicated and the most minor among the
Chinese receive treatment equal to those prideful races.[110]

There was no room for negotiation. Then Zhang accepted the invitation from Pei Zheng School to work there and his new job would commence in two months. Before he started to work at the school, Robert E. Chambers moved his residence from Shamian to another place and asked Zhang if he would go to work at his new location. Zhang replied, "Without the requirement of entering Shamian, what else could be my excuse?" Then he returned and worked at the new place while Robert E. Chambers would take their writings to Shamian for printing. A Westerner thought Zhang should return to work at Shamian since he was an employee of *True Light*. An old pastor answered him, "I am a Chinese and I don't go to Shamian either." Zhang praised the old pastor by saying:

> His frank words are so right and confident that they would shame those Chinese still working on Shamian Island until they die because they tolerate discrimination in order to earn wages.[111]

In this event, his national identity led to his refusal to enter Shamian and resulted in his rejection of being made a single exception. His friends resorted to his Christian identity in their efforts of persuasion and it motivated him to return to work with Robert E. Chambers. His national identity caused his friction with a Western Christian co-worker, his praise of the Chinese pastor, and his scorn of other Chinese. His Western Christian co-worker might have ignored Zhang's feeling of being humiliated, but this did not mean he discriminated against Zhang. However, Zhang must have felt this Western co-worker could not identify with him.

Compared with the event in 1899, his responses in 1906 and 1907 also demonstrated an interaction between his Christian identity and national identity, but in a different way. In 1899, seeing other Chinese being mistreated and doubting his Western pastors, he gave up both his job in a Christian publication and his church membership, which shows the greater importance of his national identity than his Christian identity, at least in its social or group sense. In 1906 and 1907, when he himself was humiliated and his Western

---

110. Zhang, "Last Twenty-Five Years," 2.
111. Zhang, 2–3.

Christian co-worker could not identify with his feelings, he did not give up his job in a Christian publication and church membership because he wanted to serve God even at the cost of feeling that he was being treated unfairly, which reveals that his Christian identity took priority over his national identity.

4.4.3.3 An Easier Social Environment for Being a Modern Chinese Christian

Dunch has raised an important question: Why did Chinese Protestants enjoy such a high level of acceptance in Chinese society in the early twentieth century, when in the previous decades Christian converts had commonly been despised by elite Chinese, and later in the twentieth century the dominant rhetoric of Chinese nationalism defined Chinese Christians as tools of imperialist aggression?[112]

Dunch's research shows that Chinese Protestants and secular nationalists in the Fuzhou area after 1900 shared their agenda of making China a strong, modern nation-state through the renewal of the Chinese people by education including moral education, citizenship, and social reform, which explains the acceptance of the Chinese Protestants in the early twentieth century.[113]

However, in the end their political vision was frustrated by several elements.[114] These included: (1) political upheaval and the lack of a stable constitutional and electoral political order; (2) America, the model for the Protestants, had never, in reality, lived up to the ideal of the Christian republic; (3) the churches' shortage of resources, in finances or personnel, to effect the wholesale reshaping of Chinese society; (4) by the 1920s, the novelty of Protestant social service initiatives like those of the YMCA had worn off in the Fuzhou area, and other public bodies began to use Protestant methods to compete with the Protestants for public support; and (5) more importantly, a new more radical nationalism discredited the Protestant vision of China's future and called into question the very possibility of Chinese Protestants being true nationalists.

The new more radical nature of nationalism could be seen in almost all the versions of nationalism in the 1920s because they required all social groups

---

112. Dunch, *Fuzhou Protestants*, xviii.
113. Dunch, 194.
114. Dunch, 180.

to submit their interests to the political agenda of the nationalist group, as we have noted above. Based on Dunch's findings, this section restates Dunch's answer to his question from the perspective of identity.

As discussed above, before 1900 Chinese national identity was understood in a cultural sense. At that time, most of the elite Chinese viewed themselves as Confucians and saw Christianity as a threat and subversion of the Confucian values and system which were dominant in China. When they called Christians "traitors of Confucius and ancestors (*qishi miezu*)," they were accusing Christians of betraying their Confucian identity while choosing a Christian identity. Therefore, many Christians, including Zhang Yijing, strove to prove their Confucian identity, as seen in chapter 3.

The period between 1900 and 1920, in Dunch's words, was characterized by flexibility, openness, and an active quest for alternative political and social models. Non-Christian nationalists found Christians had the same political agenda of building China into a strong and modern nation through character-building and social service, and so on. In other words, the national identity of Christians was believed to be going along with that of the non-Christians. Therefore, Christians enjoyed acceptance.

In contrast, the versions of nationalism in the 1920s were much more radical. They required all groups to subject their interests to the political agenda of the nationalist group. To put it another way, national identity was to be given the highest priority, which resulted in the Christians' struggle and being given the label of "traitor" or "tool of imperialist aggression."

Though the period from 1900 to 1920 witnessed less pressure of nationalism in China's society, the national identity of Chinese people was still salient. A wide range of propositions were put forward concerning ways to save China such as saving China through agriculture, industry, increasing military power, reducing troops, education, morality, science, preserving traditional rites, aviation, finance, saving money in banks, donations, martial arts, having the courage to die for one's country, frugality, refusing imports, producing textiles, local autonomy, Christianity, and Confucianism. Not only was every trade connected with saving China, people from all walks of life were its ardent supporters, from monks to prostitutes. Even government notices often started with words like "to love people and to save China." This formed a context for Chinese Christians to present their messages.

4.4.3.4 Four Christian Versions of Saving China

This section will select four ways of presenting the Christian message concerning saving China during this period. That does not mean this selection has exhausted all versions. The purpose is to show the interaction of Chinese national identity and Christian identity through their similarities and differences.

The first version believed that the gospel would save and change individuals who would better the world and naturally lead to a strong China. This opinion appeared as early as the beginning of the twentieth century when Sun Yat-sen, the Christian leader of his party, sought to overthrow the Qing dynasty by revolution.[115] It was still popular after Yuan Shikai grabbed the fruit of Sun's revolution by cajolery and coercion.[116] This group would find China's problem either in the evil nature of humanity[117] or in the corruption of people's hearts.[118] Since the problem could be healed by Jesus, the solution was to believe in Jesus.[119] Thus, they assigned an exceptional value on spreading the gospel and church life. Some of them would attribute the prosperity and power of the US and the UK to Christianity.[120]

The second version was represented by Yu Rizhang or David Z. T. Yui[121] who advocated saving China through Christian education in 1915. By then, China, under President Yuan's rule, was regressing from democracy to monarchism while Yui saw the fate of democracy in China as a question of life and death.[122] To him, three elements were necessary for democracy: citizenship,

---

115. Yeyong Yin 殷耶傭, "Believing the Christ Is the Key to Saving People and Saving China (信主是救人救国之最要点)," *Christian Advocate* 华美教保 2, no. 3 (1905): 31–33.

116. Ge Kui 奎阁, "Christianity Can Save China – Mandarin (基督教救国论-官话)," *The Women's Messenger* 女铎 7, no. 4 (1918): 28–31.

117. Yin, "Believing the Christ," 31.

118. Kui, "Christianity Can Save China," 28.

119. Yin, "Believing the Christ," 33; Kui, "Christianity Can Save China," 30.

120. Yin, "Believing the Christ," 32.

121. David Z. T. Yui (余日章, Yu Rizhang, 1882–1936) was a Chinese Protestant Christian leader who led the Chinese National YMCA in the 1920s and 1930s. David Yui was a leader in what the historian Daniel Bays called the "Sino-Foreign Protestant Establishment," a generation of Chinese Protestant Christians who worked to make Christianity independent of foreign control and relevant to the emerging Chinese nation.

122. David Z. T. Yui 余日章, "Education and Democracy in China (教育与民国之关系)," *The Chinese Students* 中华学生界 1, no. 3 (1915): 2.

leadership, and strength of character[123] which could be achieved through Christian education because its chief purpose was to inculcate in the lives of the students the highest moral principles of life and the strongest inspiration to live up to them.[124] After Yuan died, the power fell into the hands of Duan Qirui (段祺瑞) whose government was viewed as the traitor of China's national interests. Yui reduced his remedy to "Saving China through Good Character" because the national traitors (government leaders) had better education, leadership, and skills but were immoral.[125] He saw three characteristics in Christianity: love, service, and self-sacrifice which could solve the problem. As the general secretary of YMCA, he praised it as an organization for saving China because it aimed at building character through education of morality, intelligence, physique, and teamwork.[126] The speakers at YMCA often connected the Western prosperity with Christianity.[127]

The representative of the third version was Xu Qian[128] who followed Sun Yat-sen and initiated the Association of Saving Nations through Christianity (基督教救国会) in 1918. He opposed the sayings that saving the country was not the responsibility of Christians[129] or that individual salvation would naturally solve China's problem.[130] He attributed China's problems like oppression, exploitation, and poverty to the national traitors and to

---

123. Yui, "Education and Democracy in China," 6–12.

124. Yui, 12–13.

125. David Z. T. Yui 余日章, "Saving China by Character: YMCA – An Organization of Saving China and Molding Character (人格救国论:青年会为救国机关,亦造就人格的机关)," *True Light* 真光 20, no. 2 (1921): 19.

126. Yui, "Saving China by Character," 20.

127. Baoqian Xu 徐宝谦, "How I Became a Supporter of Internationalism (我讲国际主义的经过)," *Truth and Life* 真理与生命 2, no. 16 (1927): 13.

128. Xu Qian (George Xu 徐谦, 1871–1940) was a Chinese politician and scholar. He made important contributions to the judicial system of modern China. He passed the highest level of Imperial Examination in 1903 and obtained *jinshi* title. He became a prominent figure after the foundation of the Republic of China. In 1917, he was the general chairman of the Association of Freedom of Religions (信教自由会) with Cheng Jingyi as the chairman of the Protestant church, Ma Xiangbo as the chairman of the Catholic church. With the lobbying efforts of the Association, the motion of establishing Confucianism as the state religion of China was blocked.

129. Qian Xu 徐谦, "Preface to the Journal of Freedom of Faith (信教自由丛刊序)," *Chinese Christian Advocate* 兴华 15, no. 33 (1918): 11.

130. Qian Xu 徐谦, "Practicing Saving Nations through Christianity (基督教救国主义之实行的概念)," *Chinese Christian Advocate* 兴华 15, no. 47 (1918): 4.

internationally low standards of accountability.[131] According to his sermon at Nanguan Anglican Church (南关圣公会) of Canton, nations sinned by oppressing people. As God loved nations, not wanting to destroy them, Jesus was sent to sacrifice himself for nations. Thus, Jesus's gospel was first and foremost a national salvation rather than a salvation for individuals. Therefore, every true Christian should carry one's own cross, die on it, shed blood, wash off one's sin and save one's country.[132] National salvation included individual salvation. If the aim was to save one's country, heaven was near.[133] When Xu saw that the national traitors were trading national interests for their personal gains, he warned, "Christians, God has released you and Jesus has saved you. Are you willing to be sold out? If so, you would betray God and Jesus, and this sin would never be forgiven."[134]

The fourth version was represented by Zhang Yijing. Misguided by anti-Christian books, he originally blamed China's problems on Christianity and the missionaries.[135] Later, his research convinced him that there was a more complicated picture. Politically, before the trade relationship between China and the West was established in the nineteenth century, there had been no humiliation inflicted on China by the West but there had been a few hundred years of persecution of Christianity in the Ming and Qing dynasties.[136] Among the tragedies related to the West, the most humiliating to him was the Treaty of Protecting Preaching and Believers because Chinese believers had to be protected by the foreigners. When some evil-minded people joined the church to take advantage of such protections, it led to numerous malicious lawsuits involving the church and so Christianity was accused of political interference. In Zhang's view, the opponents of Christianity were reasonable in this sense. But considering the facts that formerly the missionaries and Chinese Christians had been harshly persecuted, and that Christianity was still discriminated against after the Treaty, it would be unfair for China to

---

131. Xu, "Practicing Saving Nations," 5–6.

132. Qian Xu 徐谦, "The Gospel of National Salvation (救国福音)," *Canton Hospital* 博济, no. 2 (1918): 25.

133. Xu, "Gospel of National Salvation," 26.

134. Qian Xu 徐谦, "Are Chinese Willing to Be Sold (国人岂甘被卖为猪仔乎)?," *Chinese Christian Advocate* 兴华 15, no. 35 (1918): 10.

135. Zhang, "Cleansing the False Accusations," 59.

136. Zhang, 57–58.

blame all this on others and shun her own responsibilities. His solutions were: (1) China should learn from the example of Japan to respect Christianity rather than being hostile to it;[137] and (2) all denominations should seek independence from foreign organizations and attach importance to teaching the Chinese language. He based his solutions on two observations. First, Christianity could bring changes to China culturally and spiritually because Chinese superstitions, ugly habits, and sins could only be removed by God's Way and the Holy Spirit; therefore, the more devoutly one believed in Jesus, the better one's character. If one country had many such devout and religious people, people from other countries would respect them and extend their respect to the whole nation.[138] Second, Chinese Christians were eager to make contributions to China's prosperity and safety[139] and they would stop those missionaries who tried to interfere with China's internal affairs by means of their home countries' power.[140] Zhang believed that if his solutions could be adopted, then the hatred of Christianity and the missionaries would cease.[141] Later, he expressed his further wishes that Westerners could learn the beauty of Chinese culture through translated works while China would change her backwardness in science and technology.[142]

For a brief comparison, the first group saw China's problem totally as a result of the sinfulness of people; Yui attributed it solely to Chinese people's weak moral character; Xu interpreted it as a purely political problem; and Zhang's view was more comprehensive, as he understood it from the perspectives of sin, culture, and politics.

Next, a consideration will be given to the identities behind the four ways of presenting the Christian message in China at the beginning of the twentieth century. The first group viewed all problems of China as the result of the sinfulness of humankind which could not be solved by the change of political and social system, as seen in Yuan Shikai and the warlords' annihilation of democracy founded after the Revolution of 1911 led by Sun Yat-sen. This point of view could be universally applied to all people, regardless of

---

137. Zhang, 58–59.
138. Zhang, 60.
139. Zhang, 67.
140. Zhang, 60.
141. Zhang, 60.
142. Zhang, "Western Pastor's Plan."

the nation, race, or time and it tended to view the Chinese including themselves as part of humankind. Chinese problems were the problems of humankind which have already been answered in Jesus's salvation. Thus, they felt a union between their Christian identity and their national identity with their Christian identity as their primary one. And this group's contextualization reflected the prominence of Christian identity and extremely low impact of national identity.

David Z. T. Yui was more sensitive to the contexts, as seen in the shift of his solutions. The question is what the real intention of Yui was when he advocated Christian education and YMCA's character-building project: Did he aim at solving China's problems or did he try to use them to attract people so that they could be converted to Christianity?

As he recalled in his article "Why Do I Believe in Jesus?" in 1930, he did not believe in Jesus because of any theological reason but because of his view of life, lifestyle, influence, and teachings.[143] He did not want to touch on the topic whether Jesus was God or a human being, but he thought Jesus, even as a man, was a great human being.[144] In his understanding, Jesus taught three things by his words and life: (1) People and God could become one in heart and in the body. Humankind and God were same in nature and humankind could become as holy and noble as God;[145] (2) There was life after death, but the current life should be emphasized too. There were many sins in the world and people's efforts could reduce some of the sins;[146] and (3) Everyone had their own noble and eternal value.[147] Jesus believed in heaven, communicated with God, had a strong character with determination, courage, self-sacrifice, and so on. Therefore, when Christians followed him to live for others and carried their cross with determination, then an ideal world would be created.[148]

Yui's words revealed the theological contents of his Christian identity. He believed in the existence of God and life after death, but he mentioned neither his own sin nor the divinity of Jesus. On the contrary, he tended to view

---

143. David Z. T. Yui 余日章, "Why Do I Believe in Jesus (我为什么信仰耶稣)?," *The Shanghai Youth (Shanghai 1902)* 上海青年 (上海 1902) 30, no. 46 (1930): 3.
144. Yui, "Why Do I Believe?," 6.
145. Yui, 3.
146. Yui, 4.
147. Yui, 5.
148. Yui, 6.

Jesus as a human being because he was impressed with the human features of Jesus and because Jesus was an example of how God and humankind could become one. The "theological reason" in Yui's understanding should not be about the virgin birth, sin washed away by Jesus's blood, Jesus's resurrection, and so forth. That may be why he avoided talking about Jesus's divinity. In fact, his words depicted the following picture: by following Jesus's example, people could have good character and obtain God's help by communicating with him to reduce the sins in the world so as to produce an ideal world. Therefore, his focus was to create an ideal world on earth. This understanding could be helpful to comprehend his solutions; namely, that the result he expected from Christian education and YMCA was a democratic and righteous China. Therefore, under his leadership, YMCA became an organization for saving China.

Christ in Yui's understanding was different from the definition of Christian identity in this research. However, in his subjective sense, he might still feel that he was faithful to Christ in his understanding and that there was no conflict between his Christian identity and his national identity. Concerning the priority between his two identities, his quick adjustment of his China-saving plan revealed his deep care for the China cause which served the purpose of following Jesus's model. For this reason, his national identity played a major role in his efforts of relating Christianity to China's context.

Xu said his Christian faith was a product of his wish for saving China.[149] He received the influence of Christianity a couple of years before 1911, but he refused to accept it.[150] In 1912, he resigned his job as the Vice Minister of Law as a protest against President Yuan's move towards dictatorship. Seeing his depression, his brother and friends suggested that he should believe in Jesus. He said he would if President Yuan could die after his prayer. Soon after that, in 1916, Yuan died. To keep his word, he was baptized in an Anglican church in Beijing. He called his idea of saving China "the true doctrine of

---

149. Qian Xu 徐谦, "The Course of My Involvement in the Movement of 'Saving Nations through Christ': Or 'Christianity and A New China' (从事 '基督救国' 运动的经过：一名 '基督教与新中国')," *Typhoon (Hong Kong)* 大风 (香港) 61 (1940): 1850.

150. Fuk-Tsang Ying 邢福增, "Christian Doctrine and National Salvation: The Cases of Xu Qian, Feng Yuxiang and Zhang Zhijiang (基督教救國 [electronic resource] : 徐謙, 馮玉祥, 張之江)" (PhD thesis, Chinese University of Hong Kong, Graduate School, Division of History 香港中文大学研究院历史学部, Hong Kong 香港, 1995), 26.

Christianity."¹⁵¹ Xu first named his idea "Saving Nations through Christianity," but he later changed it into "Saving Nations through Christ" because some pastors protested that the name of Christianity should not be used for his acts of saving China. He made the change to declare that no one had a monopoly on interpreting Christianity and that he had no relationship with any church.

In Xu's theory of "Saving Nations through Christ," Jesus did not die for the sins of individuals but for the sins of nations. Nations sinned by oppressing other nations or by oppressing their own people. True Christians should follow Jesus's example to die for all nations (specifically China). If they did not strive for saving China, they committed a sin which could never be forgiven by God. Xu's way of interpreting Christianity to serve his ambition of saving China supplied a parallel to Hong Xiuquan's reinterpretation of Christianity for his Taiping Rebellion against the Qing dynasty which is sometimes viewed by scholars as Chinese Protestant indigenization on a large scale.¹⁵²

Xu's Christian identity was also different from the definition in this study. He may also have felt a union between his Christian identity and his national identity before 1923, with his national identity playing a prominent role. Compared with Yui, Xu's national identity was far more salient in his contextualization.

Zhang's Christian and national identity and their development have been delineated above. Therefore, it becomes easier to detect the interaction of his identities behind his solutions. He looked for the causes of China's humiliation from different sides. China, the West, and Christianity all shared responsibility for it. Based on his analysis of the causes, he offered solutions aimed at wiping out the humiliations suffered by Christianity and China and winning respect for them.

From another perspective, Zhang's solution revealed one of his ways of reconciling his national identity and his Christian identity. That is, the humiliation which featured in his modern Chinese identity should not be blamed on Christianity which was just indirectly and unintentionally involved in the infringement of China's sovereign rights. It had historical and cultural reasons. And the humiliation could be healed by each side taking due responsibility and by promoting Christianity. This minor flaw was indeed no match for

---

151. Xu, "Course of My Involvement," 1850.
152. Bays, "Protestantism in Modern China," 234–35.

the church's contribution and future potential. Thus, subjectively, he felt no contradiction between his commitments to Christianity and to China.

Both Zhang's Christian identity and his national identity seemed to have equal importance in his solution. However, his other sayings could throw further light on his true intention. In 1907, he encouraged Chinese Christians to be patriotic; otherwise, people with the anti-Christian position would have evidence to defame the missionaries for producing traitors of China.[153] His words in 1918 provide further illumination:

> We should not believe in Jesus because Neo-Confucianism would weaken China and Christianity could make other countries powerful. Even if the opposite was true, we still should believe in Jesus. It doesn't matter if a person was from a weak country or a strong country, he or she is a sinner before God and is waiting for salvation.[154]

Some Christians would hint at a connection between Christianity and the prosperity and power of the West in their evangelizing attempts, which was to suggest a Christian identity by resorting to national identity. Zhang opposed this. In his view, even if Christianity led to China's weakness, people still should choose it. In other words, Christian identity was much more significant than national identity. Moreover, he saw a functional value in patriotism and it could shield Christians from nationalistic accusations. At the same time, he admitted that Christianity could indirectly bring about a positive impact on a country.[155] Thus, his Christian identity played the leading role in his solution of removing China's humiliations.

To sum up, if the four Christian versions of saving China are rated on a scale for measuring the significance of Christian identity and national identity in their interactions, the first and third versions, which were almost exclusively focused on one identity, would go to the two extremes, while the second and fourth versions focused on the major and minor roles alternated by the two identities.

---

153. Zhang, "Author's Preface," 2.
154. Zhang, "Answering an Old Scholar," 218.
155. Zhang, 219.

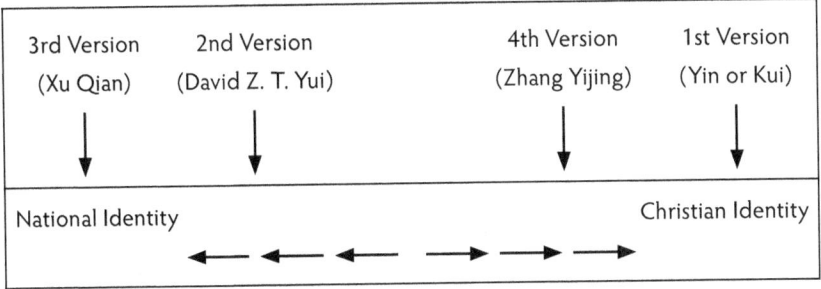

Figure 1: A Scale of the Significance of Identities in the Four Christian Versions of Saving China

4.4.3.5 Identities in His Defence against Confucians' Nationalistic Charge

As seen above, there were many proposals for saving China in this period. Most of them proved harmless to Christianity except Confucianism which charged Christianity and Chinese Christians with jeopardizing the future of China. Xu Fuguan[156] recalled how his teacher Xiong Shili used to say that a country's culture would be destroyed first and the destruction of the nation would follow.[157] This saying motivated Xu to become an expert in Confucianism to save China.[158] In fact, in the 1910s it was not rare for Confucians to compete against Christianity by appealing to Chinese national identity.[159] In one sense, this manoeuvre found its success in Xu.

Zhang's Christian identity in the social sense prompted him to give a defence. He counter-argued by proving that it was Confucianism that betrayed China. As his review showed, the rulers of the Mongols and the Manchus,

---

156. Xu Fuguan or Hsu Fu-Kuan (徐复观, 1902/1903–1982) was a Chinese intellectual and historian who made notable contributions to Confucian studies. He is a leading member of New Confucianism, a philosophical movement initiated by Xu's teacher and friend, Xiong Shili.

157. Xiong Shili (熊十力, 1885–1968) initiated New Confucianism, a philosophical movement. According to Huang, Xiong represented a cultural nationalist Confucian. It was difficult for Christians to develop a dialogue with Xiong. He disputed the idea of a creator in Christianity. Paulos Huang, *Confronting Confucian Understandings of the Christian Doctrine of Salvation: A Systematic Theological Analysis of the Basic Problems in the Confucian-Christian Dialogue*. 3rd ed. (Leiden: Brill, 2009), 131–41.

158. Fuguan Xu 徐复观, "Author's Preface 自序," in *The Continuation on the History of Chinese Thoughts* 中国思想史论集续篇 (Shanghai 上海: Shanghai Bookstore Publishing House 上海书店出版社, 2004), 1.

159. Zhang, "Cleansing the False Accusations," 47.

far from changing China's culture, extolled Confucianism and respected Confucius after their conquest.[160] In his conclusion, Confucians would happily accept a foreigner as the master of the country provided he worshipped Confucius as they did.[161] If Christianity had had any intention of destroying China, it would definitely have tried to win Chinese hearts by supporting the Confucian Association and building up Confucian temples. In addition, he listed the benefits of Christianity for China to become as strong as the Western powers, an act of appealing to national identity also.

Interestingly, Zhang questioned Confucian advocates as to which was more important – protecting the country or protecting Confucianism – which could be restated as, "Which one takes priority, national identity or Confucian identity?" We cannot but be curious as to what he would answer if given a similar question about the priority between Christianity and China. Actually, an answer to such a question has been provided in current China. In most Three-Self churches, there is a watchword "Loving the country and being loyal to the faith." In this watchword, "loving the country" is always placed before "being loyal to the faith." No report has been heard that this watchword has ever been reversed in any of those churches. Zhang's answer could be found from his viewpoint given in the previous section: even if Christianity would weaken China, the Chinese should still choose Jesus.

There was only one occasion when Zhang said: "No love was greater than the love for one's country and no love was sincerer than the love for one's family." The context shows that here he was not making a comparison between the love for Jesus and the love for one's country. He was arguing against Dr. Chen Huanzhang, the leader of the Confucian Association, who belittled Christianity while praising Confucianism. In Zhang's criticism, Dr. Chen was confused about the concept of *zhong* (being true to the originally good nature of the self or being loyal, 忠) and *shu* (the benevolent exercise of the principle of human nature in relation to others or being considerate or forbearing, 恕). Zhang reasoned:

> It would be more illogical if Confucians replaced *ren* (benevolence or kindness, 仁) with *shu*. *Ren* was love. No love was greater than the love for one's country and no love was sincerer

---

160. Zhang, 47–49.
161. Zhang, 67.

than the love for one's family. People would say loving one's country and family, but they would never say *shu* or forbear one's country and one's family.¹⁶²

In this context, Zhang was using "loving one's country" as an example to point out Dr. Chen's misinterpretation of *shu*. He was not ranking different types of love. Furthermore, no other support could be found from all of Zhang's works to support the idea that Zhang valued the love for one's country above the love for Jesus.

In the 1920s, the pressure of modern nationalism increased dramatically. Before an analysis is given of Zhang's national identity in this period, the development of his Christian identity will first be examined in the next section.

4.4.4 Being a Modern Chinese Christian in the 1920s
4.4.4.1 The Continuity and Development of His Christian Identity

The core contents of Zhang's Christian identity during 1905-20 remained basically the same into the 1920s. For example, (1) God is the almighty Creator and loves human beings; (2) Jesus is Christ, who sacrificed himself to atone for people's sin, and he was resurrected. Faith in him as the Saviour could free people from the bondage of sin and his followers were commissioned to spread this good news; (3) the Holy Spirit could help people conquer temptation; (4) there is life after death; and (5) the Bible is the standard for belief and action.¹⁶³

---

162. Zhang, "Correcting Errors in Dr. Chen," 154.
163. Zhang, "Church and the New Thoughts Tide," 137; Zhang, "Answering Eleven Questions," 34-35; Zhang, "How I Became a Christian," 8; Zhang, "Discussion over Mr. Zhang," 79; Yijing Zhang 张亦镜, "Answers to Five Questions (疑问五则)," *True Light* 真光 23, no. 11 (1924): 76-78; Zhang, "Awakening," 81; Zhang, "'Right to Education,'" 8; Yijing Zhang 张亦镜, "The Fourth Comments on Mr. Daiying's 'Christianity and Saving China by Character Formation' and 'Why Are We against Christianity' (读代英君的 '基督教与人格救国' 和 '我们为甚么反对基督教' 慨言 - 四)," *True Light* 真光 23, no. 8 (1924): 51, 57; Yijing Zhang 张亦镜, "A Discussion of Romans 9:14-18 (讨论罗马人书九之十四至十八)," *True Light* 真光 24, no. 3 (1925): 79-80; Yijing Zhang 张亦镜, "Answers to Three Questions Concerning the Bible (疑义三则问答)," *True Light* 真光 24, no. 4 (1925): 81-82; Yijing Zhang 张亦镜, "My View of Jesus' Resurrection (我也来说说耶稣之复活)," *True Light* 真光 24, no. 5 (1925): 37-38; Yijing Zhang 张亦镜, "References about Paul's Teaching of Obeying the Authority (保罗训众宜服秉权者语索隐)," *True Light* 真光 24, no. 3 (1925): 77; Yijing Zhang 张亦镜, "Thoughts after Reading Mr. Langou's 'Argument against Mr. Xu Dingbang's Criticism of Mr.Wu Zhihui' (读浪鸥君 '驳真光杂志徐定邦君批评吴稚晖先生的一个新信仰的宇宙观及人生观' 感言)," *True Light* 真光 24, no. 5 (1925): 22; Zhang, "Discussion with Mr. Wei Qing," 54; Zhang, "Current Trends of Thought," 98-100; Zhang, "At the Twenty-First Anniversary," 52-53;

In this period, the main theme in Zhang's spiritual life was still his desire for a good moral life, the struggle against temptations, and the forgiveness of sins. According to him, one benefit of the Christian faith was the avoidance and resistance to temptations.[164] Lu Danlin recalled that Zhang was firm and serious in resisting temptations.[165]

However, Zhang was not satisfied with himself. He confessed that his heart was not totally subdued before God,[166] that his prayer was hasty and superficial,[167] that he would not read the Bible unless he needed a quotation or the answer to a biblical question, and that his fear of people stopped him from following his conscience.[168] Consequently, he was not as spiritual as others,[169] his relationship with God was far less intimate than in the first few years after his conversion,[170] and his writing was strong in arguing but weak in changing people.[171]

In spite of the fact that he realized he fell short, he knew that he could obtain forgiveness through repenting. In his understanding, everyone had the possibility of behaving like Judas the traitor and that Peter was not too superior to Judas when he denied Jesus three times. The differences between

---

Zhang, "Discussion about the Presence," 111; Yijing Zhang 张亦镜, "My Current View of Jesus (我今日对于耶稣之认识)," *True Light* 真光 27, no. 7 (1928): 45–46; Zhang, "My View on Preaching," 78; Zhang, "Independence of the Church," 21; Zhang, "Age of Moral Education," 16; Zhang, "Spiritual Feast," 47–49, 51; Yijing Zhang 张亦镜, "Answers to the Eight Questions from Miss Lin Huizhen (答林惠贞女士八疑问)," *True Light* 真光 28, no. 6 (1929): 69, 72–73; Zhang, "Avoid Perishing," 21–23; Zhang, "Foreword: Standing Position," 1; Zhang, "Introducing to a Sharp Criticism," 31–32; Zhang, "Solution of Jesus and Paul," 5; Zhang, "Questions from Mr. Zeng Guren"; Yijing Zhang 张亦镜, "The Birth of Jesus and the Births of the Founders of Confucianism, Buddhism and Daoism (耶稣之生与儒释道三教教主之生)," *True Light* 真光 29, no. 12 (1930): 50, 52; Zhang, "My Answer to Mr. Jiang," 77; Zhang, "Preface: Being Sick," 1.

164. Zhang, "Answering Eleven Questions," 35; Zhang, "Awakening," 81; Zhang, "Commenting on Chen Qiulin's," 79.

165. Danlin Lu 陆丹林, "Biography and Comments of Mr. Zhang Yijing (评传:张亦镜先生)," *Beacon* 明灯, no. 275 (1940): 20.

166. Zhang, "Awakening," 81.
167. Zhang, "My View on Preaching," 78.
168. Zhang, "Bible Reading and Praying," 98.
169. Zhang, "Awakening," 80–81.
170. Zhang, "Bible Reading and Praying," 98.
171. Zhang, 98.

these two persons were just motive and repentance.[172] This is why Zhang called other Christians with similar shortcomings to confess and repent.[173]

In the 1920s, Zhang gained more knowledge and personal experience of the Holy Spirit. In 1911, he understood that the Holy Spirit was one member of the Trinity while God, Jesus, and the Holy Spirit were three separate parts in one unit.[174] In 1922, he stated that the Holy Spirit was God and Jesus and the three were one.[175] "The help of the Holy Spirit," his frequent words at the beginning of the 1920s, shifted to "being filled with the Holy Spirit" by the end of the 1920s.[176]

Zhang's focus on "the help of the Holy Spirit" also experienced a change. In his writings of 1920, he was still amazed at the power of the Holy Spirit in its supernatural sense. For example, in 1920, he wrote on how the apostles could perform miracles like Jesus.[177] In 1922, he wrote about the ability of the Holy Spirit to guide people in their decision-making when facing temptations and empower people's minds and emotions in difficulties.[178] In 1924, he discussed the power of the Holy Spirit to change a person's temperament and character.[179] In 1925 he wrote that the Holy Spirit enabled people to know Jesus as the Saviour, to show this to others, and to distinguish between the holy and unholy. Notably, he began to emphasize obedience as a product of the Holy Spirit, as seen in the life of Paul.[180]

---

172. Yijing Zhang 张亦镜, "Answering the Questions from Huang Rongzeng and Liao Yizhi Concerning Why God Did Not Create People Who Would Not Sin (答黄容增寥以智上帝造人何以不使之不会犯罪)," in *(1928), A Quarter of a Century of True Light, Selected* 真光丛刊, *Part 5: Answers to Inquiries* 答问, ed. Yijing Zhang (Shanghai 上海: China Baptist Publication Society 中华浸会书局, 1923), 73–74.

173. Zhang, "Introducing to a Sharp Criticism," 32.

174. Zhang, "Go and Preach," 92.

175. Zhang, "Answering Eleven Questions," 32.

176. Zhang, "My View on Preaching," 78; Zhang, "Introducing to a Sharp Criticism," 32.

177. Zhang, "Study of Christianity," 54.

178. Zhang, "Answering Eleven Questions," 35.

179. Yijing Zhang 张亦镜, "No Self-Examination Will Lead to the Potential for Disaster (人之患在不知自反)," *True Light* 真光 23, no. 2 (1924): 90.

180. Zhang, "Thoughts after Reading Mr. Langou's," 22.

The qualification for the help of the Holy Spirit was true faith.[181] To Zhang, true faith was to have forgiveness in Jesus and it was accompanied by obedience.[182] All true believers could have the Holy Spirit who was the Comforter.[183]

In his mind, "being filled with the Holy Spirit" was similar to having a rebirth in the Holy Spirit. It came about by a time of whole-hearted, long prayers. A Holy Spirit-filled life had a few signs: effective preaching,[184] having no fear of people,[185] and prayers being accepted.[186]

The preconditions for being filled with the Holy Spirit at least included refusing earthly wisdom and knowledge and seeking the Holy Spirit. Then he called for repentance by saying:

> If not repenting, our pastors, preachers, and the journalists for church publications would be like Judah who betrayed Jesus, Peter when he denied the Lord three times, Thomas in doubt, or the two disciples on their way to Emmaus. Our[187] minds were filled with earthly wisdom and knowledge and had no room for the Holy Spirit. Worse still, we did not have time for the Holy Spirit and could not recognize its works. But we would still call our works the service of the Lord. But in fact, who could really do the works of the Lord unless filled with the Holy Spirit? Actually, they had no connection with the works of the Lord. [188]

One important feature of Zhang's knowledge and experience with the Holy Spirit was his own sorrow when he talked about the help of the Holy Spirit and being filled with the Holy Spirit. He lamented that his knowledge and disobedience stopped him from having a relationship with the Holy Spirit

---

181. Zhang, "Answering Eleven Questions," 35.

182. Yijing Zhang 张亦镜, "Christian and Freedom (基督徒与自由)," in *(1928), A Quarter of a Century of True Light, Selected* 真光丛刊, *Part 1: Concerning the Scriptures* 说经文, ed. Yijing Zhang (Shanghai 上海: China Baptist Publication Society 中华浸会书局, 1907), 26–27; Zhang, "Answering Eleven Questions," 28; Zhang, "Questions from Huang Rongzeng," 70.

183. Zhang, "How I Became a Christian," 8.

184. Zhang, "My View on Preaching," 78.

185. Zhang, "Introducing to a Sharp Criticism," 31–32.

186. Zhang, "Bible Reading and Praying," 98.

187. Zhang used "our" and "we" to indicate his identification with them, which is a habit of language use in Chinese.

188. Zhang, "Introducing to a Sharp Criticism," 32.

as intimately as others do.[189] However, he was not against all knowledge, he just prayed for the knowledge the Holy Spirit pointed him to.[190]

There were a few possible reasons for Zhang's development in the knowledge of the Holy Spirit. First, his desire for a good moral life, as required by both his Christian identity and Confucian identity, pushed him into looking for help. Second, the examples of other people, both in the Bible and in real life, spurred him into seeking to live with or being filled with the Holy Spirit. Third, his contact with other Christians enhanced his knowledge of the Holy Spirit. Fourth, the Pentecostal Movement would also have exerted influence on him as suggested in his usage of the expression "being filled with the Holy Spirit." Moreover, some of his readers were from the Assemblies of God. Nevertheless, he rarely spoke of speaking in tongues.

There are a couple of other points noteworthy in the contents of his Christian identity. As in 1913, he still could not believe that the great flood had happened in China.[191] Another point was the change in his attitude towards the first two chapters of Genesis. Before 1920, he still had no problem with their accuracy.[192] While in 1923 he did not trust in their genuineness,[193] he turned around to believe in their authenticity again in 1924.[194] These two points will be discussed in chapter 5.

Summing up this period, on the negative side, Zhang did not read the Bible and pray in the 1920s as frequently and attentively as before, he doubted the truthfulness of records in the Bible (the first two chapters of Genesis between 1920 and 1924 and the great flood throughout his life), and his intimacy with God and the Holy Spirit was unsatisfactory to him.

On the positive side, there were three significant signs of progress. First, he realized Jesus's blood could bring the forgiveness of all sins, including that

---

189. Zhang, "Awakening," 80–81; Zhang, "Bible Reading and Praying," 98.

190. Zhang, "Bible Reading and Praying," 98.

191. Yijing Zhang 张亦镜, "Answering Three Questions from Zhi Xiang Concerning Genesis (答秩亨创世记三疑问)," in *(1928), A Quarter of a Century of True Light, Selected* 真光丛刊, *Part 5: Answers to Inquiries* 答问, ed. Yijing Zhang (Shanghai 上海: China Baptist Publication Society 中华浸会书局, 1923), 66; Zhang, "Questions from Miss Lin," 72.

192. Zhang, "Refuting a Plagiarism," 233–34.

193. Zhang, "Questions from Huang Rongzeng," 70.

194. Yijing Zhang 张亦镜, "Comments on Questioning Mr. Zhang Yijing's Answers to Mr. Huang and Mr. Liao (读亦镜先生答黄廖二君的疑问的质疑有批答)," *True Light* 真光 23, no. 2 (1924): 32.

of Judas the traitor, and he confessed his defects and obtained forgiveness in Jesus. It was predictable that he would dare to confess all his future sins regardless of their severity and believe in Jesus's forgiveness, which would result in a continual increase of his gratitude to Jesus. Second, after 1924, he resumed his faith in the first two chapters of Genesis. Except for this temporary distrust and his disbelief in the extent of the great flood (but he humbly invited criticism of this in 1929),[195] he always took the Bible as his standard point of reference. He learned a lesson from his temporary lapse in faith (which will be discussed in chapter 5). This meant that he was immunized against similar distrust and he tended to completely believe in the inerrancy of the Bible, which would serve as a long-lasting and solid foundation of his faith. Third, before the 1920s, he emphasized obeying the teaching in the Bible; while in the 1920s, he laid stress upon both obeying the teaching of the Bible and following the guidance of the Holy Spirit. This suggested that he began to concentrate on the internal conversation with the Holy Spirit, the supernatural being, which was a field unexplored by him before 1920. By the end of the 1920s, he even denied the ministries of Christians who were not filled with the Holy Spirit. This new experience would certainly add strength, vitality, and excitement to his commitment to Christianity. Therefore, this progress had a very significant impact on his Christian identity.

Moreover, he still took evangelization as the priority of the church. Considering both the negative and positive elements, Zhang's Christian identity, at this stage of achievement, gained new strength. But it is hard to give a precise evaluation of the measure of his faith. Its objective reality should be judged by God. Concerning its subjective side, it is safe to say that the strength of his Christian identity was much greater in the late 1920s than in the time before 1920 and he laid a solid foundation for his future Christian life.

4.4.4.2 A Brief Review of the Context of the 1920s

As said above, a much more radical nationalism rose up and became the dominant voice in the 1920s. This version highlighted the feeling of humiliation the Chinese suffered from the Western powers and endowed the love of China with a paramount moral value for Chinese people.[196]

---

195. Zhang, "Questions from Miss Lin," 72.
196. Zeng, "Four Pieces of Evidence," 285.

The Anti-Christian Movement accused Christianity of being a tool for imperialistic invasion and pressured every Chinese Christian to prove their commitment to China in terms acceptable to the nationalistic requirement of the Movement.[197]

Then, the whole situation was exacerbated by the killings or massacres carried out by Western imperialists: the May 30th Massacre in Shanghai in 1925, the Shaji Massacre in Guangzhou in June 1926, the Massacre in Wan Xian County (万县惨案) in 1926, and the Tang Keng Killing (汤坑惨案) on 12 November 1926. While the whole country was angered, some missionaries publicly sympathized with the imperialists.[198] As a result, Chinese Christians were implicated and put under fire.

It is not easy to reestablish the historical facts and even people living at that time felt confused by the contradictory testimonies. For example, about the Shaji Massacre, Mrs. Chambers said:

> A parade of thousands of students marched with armed soldiers and representatives of all the labour unions. "Perhaps no one will ever know just what happened at that moment when the procession was opposite Shamian. The Chinese truly believed that British soldiers fired on a body of unarmed students. Eye witnesses among the foreigners, not soldiers, declared that the first move was made by a Russian officer mounted higher than the others, who ordered his company to face Shamian and fire." One or two soldiers of the Concession were wounded; one was killed. Of the paraders, reports of the killed varied from one hundred to one thousand.[199]

Therefore, the questions concerning the historical facts cannot be answered in this study and they will be left to the Chinese and Western historians. The

---

197. Ying Lie 列英, "Worthy to Be Answered (值得答复)," *Lingdong Republican Daily News* (岭东民国日报), 1 December 1926.

198. The unsympathetic attitude among a small number of missionaries was noticed by both the Chinese and Westerners. Danlin Lu, "Mr. Yijing: We Are Looking Forward to the Combined Issues of No. 4 to 6 in Volume 25 (通讯:亦镜先生:盼望许久的真光杂志廿五卷四至六号合刊)." *True Light* 真光 25, no. 9–10 (1926): 126; Zhang, "Answering Lu Danlin's Letter," 127; The Committee of Reference and Counsel Foreign Missions Conference of North America, *Present Situation in China and Its Significance for Christian Missions* (New York: Board of Foreign Missions of the Methodist Episcopal Church, 1925), 13.

199. Gardner and Chambers, *Builder of Dreams*, 167.

focus of this research is on Zhang's perception of these events and reactions. Under these situations, Zhang's national identity was more salient than ever. Mrs. Chambers also noticed this:

> The only member of the Publication Society workers who came out in sympathy with the boycott was the Editor of *True Light*, Zhang Wen Kai. He, greatly incensed by the Shamian Incident, resigned because he would not feel free to express his indignation if he remained editor of a publication issued by an American owned organization.... so *True Light* suspended publication for some months. By the time plans were fully made for moving to Shanghai, Mr. Zhang was ready to return to his position as Editor, more loyal and devoted to the ideals of the Society and Christianity than he had ever been before.[200]

4.4.4.3 *The Salience of Zhang's National Identity in the 1920s*

The readers may remember that, after quitting his job for the second time in 1907, Zhang was amazed at the apathy of other Chinese people working on Shamian Island. Almost twenty years later, when many Chinese quit their jobs at Shamian as a protest against the British Consul, he commented:

> Although they took twenty years to wake up, they should be praised for their courage after realising their shame.[201]

As seen above, the feeling of being humiliated or bullied by the West was the typical emotional reaction of the Chinese modern national identity. Zhang felt sorry for other Chinese who could bear with the feeling of humiliation in order to work on Shamian. In his view, their national identity was insignificant to such a degree that it became almost meaningless to them. Thus, he called it "shame."

After the Shaji Massacre, Zhang felt very sympathetic to those victims who were shot by the British army. He was also aggrieved by the British cruelty like shooting the masses with machine guns, for Britain was considered a

---

200. Gardner and Chambers, 171.

201. Yijing Zhang 张亦镜, "The Most Satisfying Protest Reply from the Governor of Guang Dong Province to the British Consul (粤省长为沙面炸弹案一封最快人意之对英领抗议覆函)," *True Light* 真光 23, no. 7 (1924): 93.

Christian nation and it had the largest number of missionaries in China.[202] This massacre offered reasons for people to charge not only against the churches from Britain but also against churches from other countries. Zhang thought he would not be worthy of being a human if he could not strongly condemn the sin of the perpetrators and he would not wash away the shame brought on the church if he could not criticize the sin of the perpetrators in the name of Christianity.[203] At the same time, he thought it best to first quit his job, so he would not bring trouble to his employer, CBPS. It was the third time that his national identity led to his resignation. However, during the short period of his resignation, he urged the striking workers of CBPS to return to work because he did not want to see its business stop.

After moving to Shanghai with CBPS in 1926, Zhang felt conscience-stricken for taking the tram car because the profits made by the tram car business were indirectly used to support the imperialists' army and buy weapons to oppress the Chinese. He felt he would indirectly contribute to the killing of his compatriots if he kept doing so. Therefore, he stopped taking the tram car. Wherever he went, he chose to walk.

In Qingdao, Zhang really wanted a city map. Because he hated the Japanese colonialists, he refused to buy it at a Japanese shop in spite of the fact that he felt the map made by the Chinese was not as good as the one made by the Japanese.[204]

The four issues above illustrate the prominence of Zhang's national identity. The best case which delineates the interaction of Zhang's identities is his response after the Shaji Massacre because several parties were involved in an emotional engagement: the imperialists, the missionaries, the Chinese people, the Chinese Christians, and Zhang. The next section will be devoted to this analysis.

---

202. In 1905, there were 1,304 American missionaries and 1,803 British missionaries. After the First World War, there were more American missionaries. In 1919, there were 3,305 American missionaries and 2,218 British missionaries. Milton T. Stauffer, Tsinforn C. Wong, and M. Gardner Tewksbury, eds., *The Christian Occupation of China: A General Survey of the Numerical Strength and Geographical Distribution of the Christian Forces in China, Made by the Special Committee on Survey and Occupation, China Continuation Committee, 1918–1921* (Shanghai: China Continuation Committee, 1922), 345–46. It seems that Zhang was not aware that the British missionaries had already been outnumbered by the American missionaries.

203. Zhang, "Last Twenty-Five Years," 4.

204. Zhang, "My Two Months," 44, 50.

4.4.4.4 Identities in Zhang's Response after the Shaji Massacre

When Zhang returned to work for *True Light* again, he poured out his anger and criticisms against imperialistic countries, especially Britain, and a small number of missionaries in three articles: *The Anger of the People Who Love Christ* (爱基督者之怒), *The Enemy Who Could Not Be Loved by Christ Lovers and the Way of Removing the Hatred* (爱基督者所不能爱之仇敌与消弭其恨恶此敌仇之方法), and *Seeking to Blame the Chinese* (寻求中国人之罪).

4.4.4.4.1 The Christian countries became the foremost enemies of Christ

Zhang felt angry because it was reported that, when the Chinese governmental leaders sought to reason with the heads of the British side after the Shaji Massacre, the latter flatly refused. Worse still, in his view, they fabricated many charges against the Chinese. In his opinion, it was a whitewash for the imperialists to say that this was a plot of the Russian Communists who sacrificed those victims in the hope that they might have an advantage in any future negotiations.[205]

Since Zhang was in Guangzhou when the Shaji Massacre happened, he offered his analysis to conclude that the patriotic demonstration had neither the means nor the intention to make an attack on Shamian Island, the location of the British Consulate. He enquired what Britain would do if the Chinese had carried out an atrocity in the United Kingdom.[206] Here Zhang's nationalistic feeling was offended because China was treated unfairly, and Chinese sovereignty had been violated. He believed that the theory of the Russian Communists' plot was just an excuse for Britain's refusal to take responsibility for their actions. However, instead of excusing the British, it proved their responsibility for the shootings. In his view, this theory could not justify their killing.[207] Thus, he said that they violated the sixth and ninth commandments.[208] They evaded their responsibility by calling the patriotic demonstration a plot by the Communists, which would offend Chinese

---

205. Yijing Zhang 张亦镜, "Seeking to Blame the Chinese (寻求中国人之罪)," *True Light* 真光 25, no. 4–5-6 (1926): 236.

206. Zhang, "Seeking to Blame," 235.

207. Zhang, 236.

208. The sixth is "You shall not murder," while the ninth is "You shall not give false testimony against your neighbor" (Exod 20:13, 16).

feelings more deeply, just like pouring oil on the flames.[209] More seriously, if all patriotic activities were labelled as the activities of the Communists, it would be no less than promoting Communism because patriotism and Communism would be tightly bound together. Eventually, everyone would take it as the only way of saving China.[210]

At that time, Western powers in China were called Christian countries and Britain claimed Christianity as her state religion. It was Britain that sent the first Protestant missionary to China and had a large number of missionaries there. Naturally, many Chinese Christians esteemed Britain highly. Meanwhile, they were also embarrassed by this country because it was also an imperialistic invader and committed the May 30th Massacre, the Shaji Massacre, and other massacres in China. The ordinary Chinese people did not distinguish between the missionaries and imperialists. They were the same white foreigners in their eyes. Since those countries were called Christian nations, naturally all foreigners such as intellectuals, merchants, politicians, military staff, and diplomats were Christians. Therefore, the ordinary Chinese people saw a confusing phenomenon: Christian countries sent the missionaries to teach the love of Christ and loving one's enemies. Meanwhile, Christian countries invaded China and killed the Chinese, accusing them of being Communists. Thus, Christianity and imperialists were linked together. The massacres offered new evidence for the Anti-Christian movement. Not only did the church sense a sharp increase in anti-Christian feelings on the outside, but it faced splits on the inside.

In fact, the greatest agony for Zhang was the consequences the church in China had to bear. He offered a few examples. In one church, Chinese Christians refused to worship with Western Christians because of this massacre. The preaching of the missionaries was rejected by non-Christians and Christians alike. They challenged the missionaries, saying:

> You preach about loving your neighbour as yourself, so why don't you go back to preach to your own government? You are hypocrites. If you worked as a soldier, you would take the order

---

209. Yijing Zhang 张亦镜, "The Enemy Who Could Not Be Loved by Christ Lovers and the Way of Removing the Hatred (爱基督者所不能爱之仇敌与消弭其恨恶此敌仇之方法)," *True Light* 真光 25, no. 4–5-6 (1926): 233–34.

210. Zhang, "Seeking to Blame," 236.

to shoot the Chinese as your heaven-given duty. Then, would you still sincerely talk about loving people?[211]

There is another example given by Zhang. A church in one county had six hundred to seven hundred members. After the British army bombarded the county, most church members felt heartbroken and left and less than 10 percent stayed.[212] Zhang agonized that Britain and other imperialist countries claimed to be Christian but rebelled against Christ, thus giving a fatal blow to Christianity and creating an obstacle to evangelization. The names of the Lord and God were totally degraded. As a result, it is not surprising to hear Zhang call Britain and other imperialist countries the foremost enemies of Christ.[213]

Zhang's attitude towards the imperialists revealed a mixture of his national identity and his Christian identity. On the one hand, he felt humiliated because China had been bullied by the West yet again so that he posed the question how Britain would feel if the roles had been reversed. On the other hand, the name of Christ and the church suffered serious consequences over which he anguished, such as enmity within and outside the church and the possibility of Bolshevism being taken as the sole way of saving China rather than Christianity. Compared with his sympathy with the dead and wounded and his feeling of being humiliated, his excruciating distress caused by consequences born by Christianity was much more intense. Thus, his Christian identity took a more prominent role in the mixture of identities which motivated his attitude.

4.4.4.4.2 A small number of missionaries were not worthy of their title

The embarrassment of Chinese Christians was also caused by their confusion over the missionaries' own national identity and Christian identity. Zhang had been taking pains to deny the charge that Western missionaries were the vanguards of imperialistic aggression.[214] To many people's surprise, a

---

211. Zhang, "Enemy Who Could Not," 234.
212. Zhang, "Age of Moral Education," 14.
213. Zhang, "Enemy Who Could Not," 233–34.
214. For example, Zhang said that the missionaries were sent either by non-governmental denominations or came on their own and their purpose was no different from the apostles in Rome. This had nothing to do with their countries' governments. They would still come to preach in China even if China had been as strong as Rome and had conquered all Western countries and made them part of the Great China Empire. This could be known from the

small number of the missionaries openly took the side of the imperialists and said that they would also have opened fire, which verified the charge against them. This attitude irritated many Chinese Christians. Zhang gives such an example: A famous Christian was heart-struck to such a degree that he ended his relationship with a missionary whom he respected and loved.[215]

In frustration, Zhang said that those missionaries who supported the imperialist position were not worthy of preaching the gospel. They only deserved to be soldiers of those killer countries because they showed themselves to be the loyal citizens of a powerful country.[216] He actually pointed out a conflict between the missionaries' national identity and their Christian identity. Those who put their national identity before their Christian identity were not worthy of the title of a missionary.

Zhang had a tendency of viewing both Western and Chinese Christians as a group and defending them from anti-Christian attacks, which shows his strong commitment to the group of Christians as a whole or his Christian group identity. It would be painful for him to turn against the missionaries. However, when he perceived that taking the side of the imperialist killer country would jeopardize the name of Christ, evangelization, and Christianity in China, he had to make a sharp criticism of such missionaries. This brought his Christian identity and his Christian group identity to the fore.

4.4.4.4.3 Attacking imperialists can bring a feeling of a union between identities

Another source of pain to Chinese Christians was the conflict between their own national identity and their Christian identity. As stated above, Chinese people naturally connected the humiliation brought by imperialism with Christianity. So Chinese Christians were often called "the foreigners' slaves," "China's traitors," and "running dogs." As for Zhang himself, he was accused of being a "top-notch player for the Church in China" and "the number one running dog of a fake pastor." It was excruciating for Chinese Christians to be

---

Jewish disciples in the second century. Furthermore, the missionaries were not only from powerful countries like Britain, America, and France, but also from small countries like Sweden, Denmark, and Norway. And he asked for a friendly treatment of Western missionaries as guests without defaming them. Zhang, "Commenting on Chen Qiulin's On the Anti-Christian Movement," 80–83.

215. Zhang, "Age of Moral Education," 14.
216. Zhang, "Seeking to Blame," 236.

told that their national identity was in conflict with their Christian identity because the sense of identity is "based on two simultaneous observations: the perception of the self-sameness and continuity of one's existence in time and space and the perception of the fact that others recognize one's sameness and continuity."[217]

Since Zhang had reconciled these two identities in himself, his perception of the self-sameness and continuity in his Chineseness would not be seriously shaken by his perception of others' denial of this on account of his Christian identity. However, not all Chinese Christians have learned that lesson. For this reason, he sensed this agony over the so-called split between identities among Chinese Christians. According to his observation, it was the imperialists who were the enemies both of Christ and of China and caused the split. And recognition of this by the non-Christian Chinese could pave the way for their acceptance of Christ. Accordingly, Chinese Christians would have the chance to show the unity between their Christian identity and their national identity and the missionaries would have the chance to demonstrate their identity as Jesus's servants if they would attack the imperialists and show sympathy with the Chinese victims. Therefore, he called on all Chinese Christians and the missionaries to attack imperialism and expose the sin of killing Chinese more actively than non-Christians did, for the love of Christ and for the future advancement of Christianity in China. Zhang especially emphasized that if any missionaries refused to do this, they were merely loyal citizens of their countries of origin. In order to further the spread of Christianity in China, those who loved Christ must condemn the sin of those imperialistic countries and those who were loyal to those countries.[218]

Of course, Zhang himself would not have been aware of modern terms, like "identity" used in this study. Nevertheless, in all three pieces of writing, he did indeed notice the issue of identity. He actually called on the missionaries to position their Christian identity above their national identity and encouraged Chinese Christians to make their national identity more salient so that their Christian identity might be accepted as a part of being Chinese. However, the union between Chinese national identity and Christian identity

---

217. Erikson, *Identity: Youth and Crisis*, 50.
218. Yijing Zhang 张亦镜, "The Anger of the People Who Love Christ (爱基督者之怒)," *True Light* 真光 25, no. 4–5–6 (1926): 233.

did not mean they were of equal status, as seen in his suggestion to Western missionaries. Nonetheless, this feeling of a union between identities would only belong to each individual Christian and it would never prevent them from being told repeatedly that their identities were in conflict rather than in a union, because the radical version of nationalism asked people to place their commitment and loyalty to their national interest in a superior position: neither lower, nor equal.

To justify his suggestion of hating rather than loving the imperialists, Zhang made a distinction between an individual's personal enemies and a country's public enemy. According to Zhang, when Jesus taught about "loving one's enemy," he meant an individual's personal enemy. By loving a personal enemy, one might move them to repent. As for the countries to be hated, they were the public enemies of a whole country and the foremost enemies of Christ. Personal love would never serve to move the cruel and savage countries into repentance.[219] At one time in 1924, Zhang was inclined to extend the application of Jesus's teaching to the relationship between countries.[220] However, this inclination changed and from then on he limited it to the personal relationship.[221] This narrowing the application of "loving one's enemy" revealed the increase of pressure from nationalism and his despair of the "incorrigible" imperialistic countries, the enemies of China and Christ.

4.4.4.4.4 Exhorting the imperialists to disown their Christian identity voluntarily

Sometimes Zhang's Christian identity and national identity seemed to be entwined and equal. In 1926, he suggested two options to get rid of the bitterness after the Shaji Massacre.[222] First, according to Jesus's teaching on making confession to wronged brothers, the imperialists, the so-called Christians, should immediately denounce the massacre and seek reconciliation. This way,

---

219. Zhang, "Enemy Who Could Not," 233–34.

220. Yijing Zhang 张亦镜, "The Fourth Continuation of Recording and Commenting on the Pen War between Two Official Newspapers of Guomindang Party (录评海外两个国民党机关报关于基督教的笔墨官司 - 续四)," *True Light* 真光 23, no. 2 (1924): 38.

221. Yijing Zhang 张亦镜, "The Anti-Imperialist Articles by Both KMT Party and Christianity and My Opinions (党教相呼应的反帝文章及我的意见)," *True Light* 真光 26, no. 1 (1927): 71; Yijing Zhang 张亦镜, "The Third Part in My Answer to Mr. Jiang Shuai Concerning Tough Questions from Anti-Christian and Passive People (答姜树蔼君来函所列反教及消极两种人的辩难--三)," *True Light* 真光 29, no. 4 (1930): 67–68.

222. Zhang, "Enemy Who Could Not," 233–34.

the abuse of Christ and Chinese Christians could be expunged. Second, the true Western Christians should publicly proclaim that their own countries were in fact enemies of Christianity. The true Christians were just a minority in their countries, and they were given little respect. The intellectuals, politicians, merchants, military staff, and diplomats in their countries were atheists. At the same time, they should revoke the Treaty and declare that the missionaries had been forsaken by their own countries and so they were powerless to offer any protection to Chinese Christians. If these options are followed, the Chinese Christians would be able to speak to their Chinese compatriots with confidence and pride: "The Imperialist murderers are not Christians." Then the defamation that imperialism used Christianity for aggression would be removed. Then Christ and Chinese Christians would not suffer from the shame brought about by the imperialist killers. This would help Chinese people to know there was no connection between Christianity and imperialism and bitterness both inside and outside the church could no longer be justified.

Both options were aimed at clearing away the negative images of Christianity and Chinese Christians in the minds of Chinese people. On the one hand, justice might be done for Chinese people and they might be pleased; on the other hand, the misunderstandings about Christianity and Chinese Christians might be removed. Although the interests of both sides would have been taken care of, Zhang's emphasis was still on the honour of Christ and Chinese Christians. This emphasis could also be sensed in Zhang's final expression of his pessimism about the possibility that the imperialists would repent or deny their Christian identity. He said:

> The imperialists did not have the words "introspection and repentance" in their dictionaries; therefore, they still would celebrate Christmas, Easter, and Pentecost as national holidays. There is no hope to wipe away the shame on Christ and Chinese Christians and the doubly intense bitterness. How miserable it is![223]

With the background of the massacres by the imperialists, the Treaty, and the accusation of the Chinese masses that Christianity was a tool of the

---

223. Zhang, 234.

imperialists to invade China, Chinese Christians heatedly debated the balance between their patriotism and their love of God.

4.4.4.5 Four Christian Versions of Loving China

Essentially, "loving China" in the 1920s was similar to "saving China" because both viewed the imperialist foreigners as the enemy of China. Despite the difference in terms, "loving China" was understood as motivation while "saving China" was the goal. Before the discussion of Christian ways of loving China, the fate of the four Christian versions of saving China before 1920 will be briefly reviewed.

4.4.4.5.1 The fate of the four Christian versions of saving China

All four Christian versions of saving China had a hard time against the backdrop of radical nationalism and Bolshevism. The first version which believed that individual salvation would naturally lead to national salvation still prevailed but was sniffed at by many people. Not only did some Christians oppose this version like Xu Qian[224] and Jian Youwen,[225] but many political leaders and intellectuals scoffed at it as well as most of the other Christian versions mainly because they rejected Christianity as a whole. For example, when Hu Hanmin[226] was asked if Christianity could save China, he replied with disdain, "Christians cannot save themselves, how could they save China?"[227] In

---

224. Qian Xu 徐谦, "The Speech at Guangzhou Bible Study – Part Three (广州研经会讲演)," *New Autonomy* 新自治 1, no. 4 (1921): 7; Qian Xu 徐谦, "The Relationship between the Independence of Chinese Christianity and Saving Nations (中华基督教自立与救国之关联)," *Fellow Christians* 教友, no. 7 (1923): 51; Qian Xu 徐谦, "The Facts about Saving Nations through Christianity (基督教救国事实)," *Chinese Christian Advocate* 兴华 21, no. 1 (1924): 23; Qian Xu 徐谦, "I Bear Witness to Jesus' Truth by Sun Yat-Sen's Faith (我对于孙中山先生的信仰为耶稣所传之真道做证)," *Chinese Christian Advocate* 兴华 22, no. 18 (1925): 6.

225. Youwen Jian 简又文, "What Is Christianity (什么是基督教)?," *Life (Beijing)* 生命 (北京) 2, no. 1 (1921): 7; Youwen Jian 简又文, "An Ethnic Church – Part One (民族的教会 上篇)," *Youth Progress* 青年进步, no. 52 (1922): 38–40; Youwen Jian 简又文, "A National Salvation Seeking Christianity (救国的基督教)," *True Light* 真光 24, no. 11–12 (1925): 25.

226. Hu Hanmin (胡汉民, 1879–1936) was qualified as *juren* at twenty-one years of age. He studied in Japan and firmly held an anti-Christian position. He became a loyal follower of Sun Yat-sen in 1905. Shortly after the Revolution in 1911, he was appointed the governor of Guangdong. In 1924, he acted as vice generalissimo when Sun Yat-sen left Guangzhou for Shaoguan.

227. Hongtu Hu 胡鸿图, "Can Christianity Save China? (基督教可以救国吗?)," *Chinese Christian Advocate* 兴华 17, no. 17 (1920): 30.

view of the opposition within and without the church, naturally this version remained very low profile.

Yui's "Saving China by Improving Character" also received a lot of criticism. The opposition reasons included: (1) The lack of good character was thought to be caused by the foreigners and national traitors; (2) The YMCA could only flatter people in power who lacked good character, not criticize them; (3) Chinese Christians had no qualification to talk about character because they depended on Christian foreigners for salaries and protection and they themselves did not have good character; and (4) There was no real achievement report; so the only way was to overthrow foreign oppression and industrialize China.[228] The criticism did not stop until the alliance of KMT and CCP broke apart in 1927 and it was finally adopted by KMT as its guideline by the late 1920s.[229]

Xu's version that the primary purpose of Christ and Christianity was to save the country persisted till 1924. He established the Association for the Salvation of Nations through Christ in Canton, Shanghai, Changsha, Jilin, Wuchang, Peking, Tianjin, Hangzhou, and many counties.[230] His ideas were preached each week at the headquarters of the Marine base located in Huangpu (Whampoa). His greatest accomplishment was to win the full support of General Feng Yuxiang and his army. In 1925, he went to the Soviet Union as an observer and returned as an active supporter of Communism in 1926. However, he did not finally join the CCP.[231]

There were changes in Xu's version. In 1918, though he said that "Saving Nations through Christianity" was not limited to China, it was applicable to

---

228. Daiying Yun 恽代英, "Christianity and Saving China by Character Formation (基督教与人格救国)," *China Youth (Shanghai 1923)* 中国青年(上海1923) 1, no. 3 (1923): 3–5; Nuliang 女良, "What Is the Achievement of 'Saving China by Character'? ('人格救国' 的成绩如何?)," *Awakening* 觉悟 9, no. 30 (1924): 5; Chunfan Li 李春蕃, "Comments on Christians' Slogan 'Saving the Country by Character' (人格救國！這是基督教教徒所拚命嚷的)," *Awakening* 觉悟, 28 October 1924, 2; Weishuang 味爽, "'Saving China by Character' in the National Day Celebration at Ningbo (宁波国庆大会中的'人格救国')," *Awakening* 觉悟 11, no. 4 (1924): 6.

229. Weibin Lan 蓝渭滨, "Saving China by Character (人格救国)," *Jiangsu Party Affairs Weekly* (江苏党务周刊), no. 5 (1930): 12–13; Zhen Qin 覃振, "Saving China by Character (人格救国)," *Central Committee Weekly (1928)* 中央周刊(1928), no. 191 (1932): 1–2; Zhongzheng Jiang 蒋中正, "Saving China by Character (人格救国)," *Zhejiang Youth (Hangzhou)* 浙江青年(杭州) 3, no. 3 (1937): 1–4.

230. Xu, "Facts about Saving Nations," 25.

231. Danlin Lu 陆丹林, "About Xu Qian (关于徐谦)," *Chat at Tea* 茶话, no. 2 (1946): 102.

all countries in the world,²³² his real intention, as seen in the same text, was to encourage other Christian countries like the US to offer help to China. Later on, the First World War (1914–18) convinced him of the negative side of nationalism because all countries killed and fought out of the love for their own country. Therefore, he denied that his "Saving Nations through Christ" was a version of nationalism but interpreted it as a kind of patriotism or internationalism.²³³ However, the essence of his "Saving Nations through Christ" was still "Saving China through Christ," as seen in the title of his memoirs, "The Course of My Involvement in the Movement of 'Saving Nations through Christ'": or "Christianity and A New China (从事 "基督救国" 运动的经过: 一名 "基督教与新中国")." Furthermore, he has never spared his concern for other countries. Another remarkable change is his inclusion of Communism into his version by 1925.²³⁴

Zhang denied the causal link between Christianity and the humiliations suffered by China, but emphasized the subsidiary contributions of Christianity to a strong China. He offered a comprehensive plan of removing China's humiliations. However, this was far from satisfactory in the view of the advocates of radical nationalism and Communism. Li Chunfan asked Chinese Christians to meet three conditions before claiming their national identity: (1) Christians should insist on overthrowing imperialism by force; (2) Christians should not hold an attitude of non-resistance based on the teaching of loving one's enemy as oneself; and (3) Christianity did not encourage people to passively tolerate their current fate in the light of a heaven that would never come.²³⁵

---

232. Xu, "Practicing Saving Nations," 5.

233. Qian Xu 徐谦 and Xingzhi Su 苏醒之, "A Discussion of Christian Education (基督教育之商榷)," *Christian Educator* 中华基督教育 4, no. 3 (1923): 6; Qian Xu 徐谦, "Save Nations through Christ (基督救国主义)," *The International Journal and Institute Record* 国际公报 2, no. 1 (1923): 20; Qian Xu 徐谦, "Love Nation and Save Nation (爱国与救国)," *Typhoon (Hong Kong)* 大风 (香港), no. 44 (1939): 1398.

234. Xu, "I Bear Witness," 6.

235. Zhang, "Anti-Imperialist Articles," 70.

4.4.4.5.2 Four Christian versions of loving China or being patriotic

The first version of loving one's country could be represented by Lu Boai.[236] Lu thought Christians should not attach importance to or speak highly of it for the following reasons.[237] First, loving one's country was just a stage in the process of development of one's love for mother, family, village, country, and the world. Christians should grow out of this stage quickly to enter the stage of loving all people as God loves the world in John 3. Second, being patriotic in China could be easily manipulated by the warlords who had caused the death of more than a million people.[238] Third, the love of peace, the noblest feature of the Chinese worldview, was more significant than life and property while narrow and revengeful patriotism could not achieve it. Fourth, it would be best for the consciousness of a nation to disappear. If a country encroached on China, the encroachment could be resisted, but the resistance should be carried out with remorse rather than with vengeance. The remorse was for one's own silence before the violence of warlords.[239] Fifth, the weakness of China was the result of moral degradation, thus being moral by having respect and love was the true love of one's country.[240]

Between loving one's own country and loving all people, Lu esteemed the latter as the higher stage, while the former was a lower stage. He urged Christians to exit the lower stage to enter the higher stage because the latter was the way of God. He did not only rank the commitment to Christianity as more valuable than the commitment to one's country, but also saw the commitment to Christianity as a natural and comprehensive solution for the problems of China, compared with the mere commitment to one's country. According to his analysis, the anti-imperialist version of loving China was narrow because it did not pay due attention to the warlords who had killed

---

236. Lu Boai (陆博爱) became a Christian at the beginning of the 1920s after listening to the preaching of two Chinese preachers Zhou Quanxin (周荃馨) and Ou Chitang (区炽堂) at Sanshui Xinan Church (三水西南教会) located in today's Foshan area (佛山). This church located in Xinan came out of the Baptist church and the Assemblies of God. In 1938, Lu became a preacher in the Assemblies of God. In 1982 when the church was reopened, Lu came back to work there. In 1984, he was the head of the local Three-Self Church.

237. Boai Lu 陆博爱, "Talking over Patriotism with Mr. Zhang Yijing (与亦镜先生谈谈爱国)," *True Light* 真光 25, no. 9–10 (1926): 31.

238. Lu, "Talking over Patriotism," 32.

239. Lu, 33.

240. Lu, 34.

more than one million Chinese, a crime graver than that of the imperialists who killed over one hundred in the Shaji Massacre.[241] The root cause of the problem of warlords was a moral degradation, which could only be solved by the reformation of one's heart. Here he meant Christianity as the solution because he believed the Holy Spirit could change everything.[242] Furthermore, the anti-imperialist version of loving China was revengeful, but Christians were supposed to love all people including the enemy. He reminded Christians of Jesus's saying, "My kingdom is not of this world" (John 18:36), and Jesus's respectful attitude to Caesar.[243] Thus, his point of view was that Christians should not advocate patriotism but instead, they should confess the sins of China before God and deepen their relationship with God. The sharp comparison between his very high prominent Christian identity and very low salient national identity might remind the readers of the first Christian version of saving China. Both of them will be viewed as the examples of the Christ against culture type or an anti-cultural model because both viewed the context as a realm under the power of evil and the region of darkness[244] and therefore something to be replaced with a purer Christian one.[245] From his version, Lu felt a union of these two identities with his Christian identity structured as his primary one.

There is another example to show how Lu's identity structure influenced his contextualization. In 1925 when the Anti-Christian Movement reached its peak, Lu said:

> The Holy Spirit, the Comforter, has been given to us. Facing the fierce Anti-Christian Movement, we should only deepen our faith and hold our tongue because the Bible says that every sin and blasphemy will be forgiven, but the blasphemy against the Spirit will not be forgiven.[246]

---

241. Lu, 32–33.
242. Boai Lu 陆博爱, "The Ideal Church (理想的教会)," *True Light* 真光 24, no. 3 (1925): 66–67.
243. Lu, "Talking over Patriotism," 34.
244. Niebuhr, *Christ and Culture*, 48.
245. Bevans, *Models of Contextual Theology*, 119.
246. Lu, "Ideal Church," 67.

He interpreted these verses from Matthew 12 as God's promise that the insults of the Anti-Christian Movement would be taken care of by God in the future. By believing this at that time, he did not have to do anything but develop a close relationship with God. At least before 1927, the strategy of Lu's contextualization was to ignore all external difficulties by solely depending on his commitment to Christianity.

This seems to suggest that one's sense of the self-sameness and continuity in one's own commitment is much more significant than one's perception of others' recognition of this. In Lu's case, his sense of himself as a Chinese was not influenced at all by his perception of others' denial. A possible reason is that his Christian identity was functioning as his ego identity, testing, selecting, and integrating his self-representations. And the contents of his identity as a Chinese, after transformation by his commitment to Christ, were different from the contents of other Chinese.

Xu Baoqian's thought represents the second version.[247] In 1925, on the one hand, Xu was averse to the Chinese being at the beck and call of the foreigners. On the other hand, the version of loving China that was popular at that time was like propaganda from an angry mob to him.[248] Though this version of nationalism had a good motive, it had a tendency towards militarization and there was no guarantee that it would not evolve into imperialism. Since it could not achieve peace, he abandoned it and turned to support internationalism.[249] By 1927, after a series of massacres, he felt this version of nationalism was the only hope to change the fate of China in spite of the fact that this narrow nationalism could not achieve peace because of its two ideals: (1) anyone not from one's clan was considered a traitor; and (2) seeking

---

247. Xu Baoqian (徐宝谦, 1892–1944) was baptized in 1913. After graduating from Beijing School of Taxation (北京税务专门学校) in 1915, he became a secretary of the YMCA in Beijing. In 1921, he went to study in Union Theological Seminary in New York. After returning, he became a teacher, then the dean of the faculty of philosophy in Yanjing University. He also studied in Columbia University and received his PhD in 1930. In 1941, he became the general secretary of YMCA in China. He used to be the editor of *Life Monthly* (生命月刊) and the translator of *Layman's Foreign Missions Inquiry* (宣教事业平议, 1934) and W. E. Hocking's (霍铿) *Meaning of God in Human Experience* (上帝在人类经验中之意义). He died in a car accident in 1944.

248. Baoqian Xu 徐宝谦, "Reminding the Nationalists (敬告今之提倡国家主义者)," *Life (Beijing)* 生命(北京) 5, no. 4 (1925): 1.

249. Baoqian Xu 徐宝谦, "Another Letter to the Nationalists: About Military Power and Mr. Jingzhi (再质国家主义者:论'武力'兼答竞之君)," *Life (Beijing)* 生命(北京) 5, no. 10 (1925): 2.

one's own advantages over others by all means. Therefore, he suggested the radical nationalists include the perspective of internationalism as a remedy.[250]

Xu called the combination of both nationalism and internationalism "the Christian patriotism" or "new nationalism."[251] It had three aspects: (1) the means should serve the goal of peace; (2) being loyal to one's country while respecting other countries' interests; and (3) all the righteous should join together to fight against evil.[252] In his view, the evil was imperialism.[253] Based on Bevans, we can see this kind of contextual theology should be classified as the synthetic model because Xu tried to balance the insights of radical nationalism, internationalism, and the church to develop a plan acceptable to all viewpoints.[254] Yui's version of saving China shares the same feature when he said that humankind and God were the same in nature and humankind could become as holy and noble as God; emphasis should be on both life after death and the current life; there were many sins in the world and people's efforts could reduce sins.[255]

Xu's feeling of humiliation before the foreigners in 1925 was the emotional feature of his national identity, but he did not want to have it eliminated by radical nationalism because of his commitment to internationalism. His international identity enabled him to withstand his feeling of humiliation, which revealed the priority of his international identity.

There was a slight change in his attitude towards radical nationalism. In 1925, he gave it up while he felt it the only hope to change China in 1927. Maybe the success of the Northern Expedition (1926–27) brought him this hope, or maybe the massacres motivated him to push for a faster change, or possibly both were true for him. In all events, his national identity was salient. However, his national identity was still subject to his international identity as seen in his setting boundary lines for nationalism by internationalism. This means that the need to eliminate his feeling of humiliation was conditioned

---

250. Baoqian Xu 徐宝谦, "Is It Necessary to Promote Internationalism in Today's China? (今日中国有无提倡国际主义的必要?)," *Truth and Life* 真理与生命 2, no. 16 (1927): 3.

251. Baoqian Xu 徐宝谦, "The National Obligations of Christians (基督徒对于国家应尽的本分)," *China for Christ* 中华归主, no. 79 (1927): 9.

252. Xu, "National Obligations."

253. Xu, "Is It Necessary?," 2.

254. Bevans, *Models of Contextual Theology*, 89–90.

255. Yui, "Why Do I Believe?," 4.

by his commitment to internationalism. Therefore, his Christian patriotism was the result of the interaction of his international identity and his national identity in which the former took a priority over the latter.

Why did Xu call his version of nationalism the "Christian version" and what did he mean by internationalism? Did he mean cooperation across the nations on earth in the present, the ecumenical church, or the kingdom of God which would come in the future? Xu did ask the Christians to make contributions to China by lifting high the banner of Christ and shining his light quietly in their daily life. However, he did not believe that Jesus Christ experienced the resurrection of the body nor did he believe that Jesus would return to earth.[256] Xu did not believe in the existence of Satan and angels, so the enemy in his "Christian patriotism" was imperialism rather than Satan. Compared with Zhang Yijing and Lu Boai who took the Bible as the sole standard,[257] Xu viewed the Bible only as a history book of the evolution of religious experience of the Israelites and considered some parts of it naive.[258] With the basic understanding of the contents of his Christian identity, it is reasonable to conclude that the internationalism in his version of Christian patriotism was not the kingdom of God which would come in the future. Furthermore, international co-operation in his version was not limited to the Christians around the world as all people who were against imperialism belonged to it. Thus, internationalism in his mind meant co-operation between nations on earth in the present which was the content of his international identity.

The content of Xu's Christian identity was an internationalism.[259] His version reflected a union between his two identities with his international identity taking the lead.

---

256. Baoqian Xu 徐宝谦, "An Advanced View of the Bible (进步的圣经观)," *Truth and Life* 真理与生命 2, no. 5 (1927): 119.

257. Lu, "Ideal Church," 66.

258. Xu, "Advanced View of the Bible," 119.

259. Maybe he experienced changes before or afterwards, or maybe I missed his other writings around 1927. But from those of his writings that I have collected, I feel that the content of his claimed Christian faith around 1927 was an internationalism. Therefore, I marked his Christian identity as an international identity. And I will humbly search for more literature to have this understanding corrected.

The representative of the third version of loving one's country was Jian Youwen.²⁶⁰ Jian believed that Jesus was a patriot. Anyone who denied this did not really know Jesus. Wherever Christianity was, it had to do with patriotism whose expression in China was to save China.²⁶¹

In Jian's theory, Jesus and Christianity existed to save and develop life. Life could be classified as individual life and corporate life.²⁶² Individual life was merged into corporate life and corporate life was more important than individual life.²⁶³ The nation was a corporate body. If a version of Christianity did not save and develop China and did not oppose imperialism and capitalism, this version was not true, the advocates of this version were not true Christians, and Jesus was not with them.²⁶⁴ Jian called his version of patriotism "the theory of Christianity saving China" and the goal of his theory was to strengthen China so that China could enjoy an equal status with other Western powers.²⁶⁵ The contextual theologies of both Jian and Xu Qian had the characteristics of the praxis model because both claimed that true Christians must work against oppressive structures by liberation and transformation, not just gradual development or friendly persuasion.²⁶⁶ They can be viewed as liberation theologians in China.

Jian's version was to call on all Christians to fight against imperialism for a China as strong as the West. Those who challenged this, along with their family, could not enter heaven.²⁶⁷ The sole function of Christianity was to facilitate the achievement of national pride. The high salience of national identity in Jian's version reminds the readers of Xu Qian's version of saving China. The reason for the prominence of national identity in Jian's version can be found in the contents of his Christian identity.

---

260. Jian Youwen (简又文, 1896–1978) was a Chinese historian, public official and Methodist pastor, known in particular for his writings on the Taiping Heavenly Kingdom. He taught at Yenching University, the University of Hong Kong, and Yale University. In 1927, General Feng Yuxiang, the "Christian Warlord," appointed him head of his political department. Afterwards, he held a variety of posts in the government. He founded two important literary magazines: *Yijing* (逸经, in Shanghai) and *Typhoon* (大风, in Hong Kong) in the 1930s.

261. Jian, "National Salvation," 31.

262. Jian, 26–27.

263. Jian, 27–28.

264. Jian, 28–29.

265. Jian, 32.

266. Bevans, *Models of Contextual Theology*, 73.

267. Jian, "National Salvation," 30.

To Jian, all Jesus's teachings were only about ethics, morality, and practical life. He wanted nothing to do with the supernatural and mysterious aspects.[268] There was no life after death. Heaven could only be achieved on earth. After Jesus was stripped to be just a patriot or a liberator of Israel, the only identity left was his national identity. Logically, his followers, such as Jian, should follow his example to make their national identity the most conspicuous. Therefore, in Jian's subjective feeling, there was no contradiction between his Christian identity and his Chinese identity. As a result, his version of loving China came into being.

Zhang Yijing could represent the fourth version. He called on all Christians to criticize imperialistic countries and seek to revoke the Treaty.[269] In his view, Christians had to take the context of rising nationalism into consideration for the sake of the gospel.[270] Therefore, the only acceptable way of expanding Christianity in China[271] was for the Christians to be seen as patriotic.[272] However, he said that this was not out of patriotism but for defending the reputation of Christ and the church[273] and for social justice.[274] If the imperialist countries had not been called Christian countries and not had their missionaries in China, he would have just despised them and left them to the Chinese government rather than being so vociferous personally. Since they were Christians, he had to confront them on their deeds and words even if Zhang had been a British citizen.[275] Under the lens of Bevans, we can find that both Zhang's versions of saving China and loving China can be designated as

---

268. Jian, 29.

269. Yijing Zhang 张亦镜, "Comments on the Christian's Patriotism (按: 基督徒爱国问题)," *True Light* 真光 26, no. 1 (1927): 9–10.

270. Zhang, "Christian's Patriotism," 15.

271. Zhang, 9.

272. In 1907, Zhang under the name of Zhang Wen Kai encouraged Chinese Christians to keep their patriotism; otherwise, the anti-Christians would have evidence to charge the missionaries with producing traitors to China. Zhang, "Author's Preface," 2.
In 1924, commenting on the letters written by Wu Zirui with his blood, Zhang Yijing felt happy that there was such a Christian with sincere love for China. Zhang took Wu as evidence against the accusation that Christians had no national consciousness. So he reprinted Wu's letters in *True Light*. Zhang, "Introducing Mr. Wu Zirui's Blood-Written Petition for Saving China (介绍吴梓瑞先生的救国血书)," *True Light* 真光 23, no. 12 (1924): 28.

273. Yijing Zhang 张亦镜, "Comments on 'Talking over Patriotism with Mr. Zhang Yijing' (与亦镜先生谈谈爱国 -有答)," *True Light* 真光 25, no. 9–10 (1926): 40.

274. Zhang, "'Talking over Patriotism,'" 37–38.

275. Zhang, 40.

the countercultural model because he recognized that the context in China had a strong anti-Christian nature which needs to be challenged and purified[276] and that if the gospel was to be adequately communicated, it had to be done in the language of those to whom it was addressed.[277]

In Zhang's version, the Christians' expression of patriotism, for the most part, was to satisfy the need of contextualizing the gospel rather than for loving one's country, which demonstrated his commitment to Christianity. Though his Christian identity looked very salient in his version, his national identity was also undeniable because in the same text he also wished for the elimination of the humiliation felt by the Chinese.[278]

In fact, there was an increase in the prominence of his national identity in this period. When his three comments, as listed above, were criticized for being too patriotic, he denied it. In his argument, his attitude towards the nationalism that was popular at that time experienced a change. Before the massacres, he used to be critical of it. He did not think this version of loving China could really save China.[279] After the massacres, he dared not criticize nationalism anymore, but he was still far from loving it.[280] In any event, his national identity became more noticeable. Even so, as discussed above, Zhang has reconciled these two identities of his with his Christian identity as the primary one.

If the four Christian versions of loving China are also rated on a scale for the significance of identities, as it has been done with the four Christian versions of saving China above, two kinds of scales are needed. Xu Baoqian's version, the second one, needs a scale with national identity and international identity at the two extremes while the other three need another scale for national identity and Christian identity. The first and third versions would go to the two extremes because of the salience of only one identity. The second and fourth versions would appear at the two places beside the middle point because two identities took turns to play the greater and lesser parts in their interaction.

---

276. Bevans, *Models of Contextual Theology*, 117.
277. Bevans, 119.
278. Zhang, "'Talking over Patriotism,'" 39.
279. Zhang, 35.
280. Zhang, "Christian's Patriotism," 14.

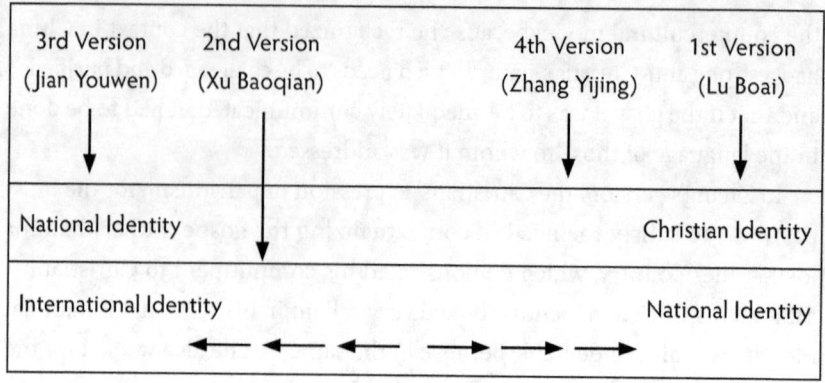

Figure 2: The Scales of the Significance of Identities in the Four Christian Versions of Loving China

4.4.4.6 Identities in His Defence against the Attacks of Modern Nationalism

In 1924, Yun Daiying made use of Chinese nationalistic feeling by charging Chinese Christians of being under the protection of the foreigners.[281] Zhang could not directly deny the charge. He had to restore the social and political context of the past in order to convince the public that seeking foreign protection was partly caused by the brutal treatment of Christians by the Chinese at that time and it was not Chinese Christians' willing choice. Chinese Christians felt ashamed of it and strove for independence because they held their national identity dear to their hearts. However, Zhang considered people who willingly lost their national identity as weak in faith and ones who brought

---

281. Chinese Protestants were not really under the protection of "extraterritoriality." This applied only to foreign missionaries. Chinese Christians were entitled to practise their religion under the treaties. However, when Chinese Christians were involved in lawsuits the missionaries felt obliged to help. For example, a missionary felt it necessary to intercede with the Chinese officials on behalf of the Christians who were being persecuted. *Annual of the Northern Baptist Convention* (American Baptist Publication Society, 1921), 527. The Chinese were left with the impression that Chinese Christians were also under the protection. So, this could be understood as a misapprehension among the Chinese masses about the privileges Chinese Christians were believed to have.

Zhang called extraterritoriality the most shameful and the most painful thing by which strong powers dealt unfairly with a weak country. He looked forward eagerly to its abolition. Yijing Zhang, "The Qualifications for a Preacher (传道人当具何资格)," in *(1928), A Quarter of a Century of True Light, Selected* 真光丛刊, *Part 3: General Articles* 通论, ed. Yijing Zhang (Shanghai 上海: China Baptist Publication Society 中华浸会书局, 1919), 21–22.

shame upon the church.[282] Zhang distinguished between individual Christians in order to defend the church as a whole, which showed his Christian identity in the group sense. In fact, Zhang's Christian identity in the group sense was very obvious in his apologetic writings.

In 1923, Yu Jiaju resorted to Chinese national identity by reviewing Chinese humiliations[283] and depicting Christian education as another violation of China's sovereignty rights.[284] He suggested detailed methods to drive religious education out of all schools.[285]

Zhang guaranteed that the national identity of Christians was strong enough to keep away any harm to China and he suggested replacing humiliation with gratitude because of the contributions Christian education had made to China. He did not try to hide his pride in his Christian identity.[286] Zhang was strongly opposed to applying "reclaiming the right to education by the government" to Christian schools, even those founded by Westerners, because this government was made up of people of all different beliefs.[287] He worried that people with other identities might hate Christianity bitterly and it would interfere with religious education in Christian schools. He said:

> The government could treat us equally or unequally, we did not take their treatment as glory or shame. We should protect the independence of the Church and Christian schools at all costs.[288]

He was concerned with the question whether children from Christian families could still receive Christian education and develop their faith in Jesus. Compared with following Jesus, public recognition was of lesser importance. This demonstrates that Zhang valued his Christian identity in Jesus much more highly than the modern national identity recognized by the government.

---

282. Zhang, "Fourth Comments on Mr. Daiying's," 61; Zhang, "Commenting on Chen Qiulin's," 76.

283. Yu, "Problems with Christian Education," 1.

284. Jiaju Yu 余家菊, "The Independence and Unification of Education in China (中国教育的统一与独立)," *Chung Hua Educational Review* 中华教育界 13, no. 8 (1923): 7; Yu, "Problems with Christian Education," 17.

285. Yu, 16–19.

286. Yijing Zhang 张亦镜, "After Reading Mr. Gu Youchen's Reminder to the Elders Who Donated to Jiaying University (读古有成君'敬告捐款资助嘉应大学诸父老'书后)," *True Light* 真光 23, no. 6 (1924): 59–61.

287. Zhang, "'Right to Education,'" 7–8.

288. Zhang, 8.

Like Lu Boai, Zhang's perception of himself being Chinese was not much influenced by his perception of others' denial of this because his Christian identity, functioning as his ego identity, has transformed his self-representations.

There is another example to show the priority between Zhang's commitments. In the 1920s, many churches used "China or Chinese" before their titles, such as China Christian Baptist Church (中华基督教浸礼会). Zhang deplored this practice except where overseas Chinese adopted such names abroad. Zhang said Guangdong and Guangxi Baptist Church (两广浸信会) had been using "Christian" before its title as Christian Guangdong and Guangxi Baptist Church (基督教两广浸信会) from the very beginning.[289]

To sum up, generally, Zhang's Christian identity took priority over his national identity. That explains why Zhang did not want people to take "making China strong" as the purpose for their conversion. However, this does not mean he was less patriotic than other Chinese, considering the stands he took against the ill-treatment of Chinese, as we saw above.

4.5 Conclusion

This chapter has described four themes for study: nationalism in China, Zhang's Christian identity after 1905, his national identity, and the interaction of these two identities.

Nationalism was another aspect of the context Zhang had to confront. Its development in China can be divided into two stages: culturalism and modern nationalism. The mildness of modern nationalism before 1920 was in sharp contrast to its radicalness in the 1920s.

Development and continuity are evident in Zhang's Christian identity after 1905. The core contents about God and Jesus in his Christian identity basically remained unchanged while the development was visible in his understanding of salvation for the dead, the Holy Spirit, and so on. The reasons for the development and continuity can be summarized as: his fundamental motivational force, and BCC and BTC he received willingly and unwillingly. His fundamental motivation was the combination of the failures in his own pursuit of morality and kindness and the forgiveness he found in Jesus. These two elements became a theme running through his writings. His BCC was

---

289. Yijing Zhang 张亦镜, "The Foreword (卷头语)," *True Light* 真光 29, no. 6 (1930): 1.

comprised of Bible reading, prayer, his preaching through writing, counsels from his Western and Chinese co-workers, the advice of other Christians and his readers, and his own reading. The attacks from the anti-Christians and criticisms from his readers constituted his BTC.

Zhang's national identity was manifested when he demonstrated his pride in Chinese culture, his feeling of humiliation by the West, and his uneasiness with the charge that Chinese Christians had lost their national identity. However, as discussed earlier, he was uneasy not about his own identity as a modern Chinese, but about non-Christian's acceptance of Christ. The examples have been discussed above. It is safe to say that his Chinese identity was not inferior to that of any of his contemporaries.

Nationalism had been posing challenges to Chinese Christians regardless of whether it was defined by culturalism or was understood in modern terms. Zhang's responses to this context or his way of contextualizing the Christian message in these circumstances revealed the interaction of his Christian identity and his national identity.

To answer the challenges of nationalism, on the one hand, he was apologetic in his polemic writings; on the other hand, he was sensitive to nationalistic feelings. He quoted 1 Corinthians 9:19[290] to explain the necessity of adapting to the circumstances.[291] Therefore, facing the charge "one more Christian, one fewer Chinese," he said:

> If Christians could be famous for being patriotic, the Anti-Christians would realize they are wrong. Then the resistance would weaken and even disappear. And then the door to evangelization would be flung open.[292]

Whereas his way of contextualization meant being apologetic and sensitive, after 1906 his Christian identity became more important than his national identity while the reverse was true before 1905. Such a guideline was embodied in his version of saving China and loving China and his other writings.

However, his strong commitment to modern nationalism could not always be satisfactory to its advocates. When nationalism was still mild before 1920,

---

290. 1 Corinthians 9:19 – "Though I am free and belong to no one, I have made myself a slave to everyone, to win as many as possible."
291. Zhang, "Christian's Patriotism," 15.
292. Zhang, 9.

his version of saving China did not receive much criticism. Nevertheless, in the 1920s when radical nationalism became a popular ideology, although he and many other Chinese Christians spared no effort in seeking peace with nationalism, Christianity was still viewed as the enemy of China, as seen in the three conditions put forward by Li Chunfan. In frustration and puzzlement, Zhang sighed:

> In China, the missionaries were formerly suspected of being spies and currently they are viewed as the vanguard of the imperialistic aggression. They are hated even more than before. However kind Chinese Christians have been, however loyal they have been to China, and how many services they have done for the country, they are still being called "slaves of the foreigners" and "running dogs." People will not be content until they wipe out Christians. I really cannot understand it.[293]

The priority of Zhang's Christian identity over his national identity offers an answer to his own bewilderment: Why could Chinese Christians never please other Chinese people saturated with nationalism despite the huge amount of kindness, loyalty, and services they had offered to China? Radical nationalism wants priority of national identity over all other identities because it sets the highest moral standard, such as loyalty to the king in ancient times and love of one's country in modern times, and because it stipulated that human nature was rooted in patriotism.[294] It does not care about how much love one has for one's country, it only cares about its priority. Therefore, the only way left for Zhang and many other Christians to meet the demands of nationalism is to subjugate their Christian identity to their national identity. This was impossible to Zhang and many other Christians who insisted on the priority of Christian identity over national identity. This explains Zhang's bewilderment.

For Christians who made a choice similar to Zhang's, their intentions and loyalty to China were considered suspicious and condemnable. Although subjectively they felt a union between their Christian identity and their transformed national identity, externally non-Christian Chinese still criticized them for not meeting their standards of being Chinese in terms of both

---

293. Yijing Zhang 张亦镜, "The Intellectuals in Japan Respect Christianity (日本知识阶级器重基督教)," *True Light* 真光 27, no. 4 (1928): 95.

294. Zeng, "Four Pieces of Evidence," 285.

priority and content. Later on, many of them turned to seek individual piety. By contrast, many other Christians who were admitted into nation-building found ways to reconcile their Christian identity with the demands of radical nationalism. Wu Yaozong can be taken as an example when he claimed that the similarity between Christianity and Marxism and Leninism reached 99 percent.

The lesson was that success in the search for a modern Chinese Christian identity depends on two elements: the structure and content of one's identities and the radicalness of nationalism. In a context of radical nationalism, anyone who positioned their Christian identity above their national identity with the transformed contents should never expect a public or an official recognition of their success in the search for a modern Chinese Christian identity. However, subjectively one could still live without doubting one's sincere commitment to Christ and China in spite of one's perception of others' denial.

At the beginning of the twentieth century, another element arose which discredited the Protestant vision of China's future: scientism, a new addition to Chinese identity. This is the subject of the next chapter.

CHAPTER 5

Zhang's Encounter with Scientism[1]

5.1 Scientism Literature Review

An important and valuable way to view Chinese history in the last century is to see it as the unfolding of the cultural impact of the West on an entirely different social arrangement, the traditional Chinese system.[2] One important Western influence comes from science. The Chinese were enthusiastic about it to such a degree that they even expected to "Save China through Science."[3]

Jin Guantao and Liu Qingfeng have studied the usage of science in *La Jeunesse* (新青年) between 1915 and 1925, a leading journal in the New Culture Movement. Their statistics show that the word science appeared 1,658 times[4] and that it was mainly used for the following five semantic domains: (1) Marxism-Leninism, (2) technology and applied science, (3) subjects being different from arts and humanities, (4) a system in opposition to superstition, theology, religion, and irrationality, and (5) an equivalent to truth,

---

1. Scientism in this study is a word used by modern scholars to describe a kind of undue trust or faith in the capability of natural science in early twentieth-century China. By reading how the Chinese of the period used phrases containing the word science, readers may have a clearer idea of the meaning of the term.

2. Y. C. Wang, *Chinese Intellectuals and the West, 1872–1949* (North Carolina: University of North Carolina Press, 1966), 497.

3. Zuoyue Wang, "Saving China through Science: The Science Society of China, Scientific Nationalism, and Civil Society in Republican China," *Osiris* 17 (2002): 291–322, https://www.jstor.org/stable/3655275.

4. Guantao Jin 金观涛 and Liu Qingfeng 刘青峰, *A Study of Conceptual History: The Formation of the Key Political Terms in Modern China* 观念史研究：中国现代重要政治术语的形成, 1st ed. (Beijing: Law Press 法律出版社, 2010), 359.

civilization, rationality, and evolution.[5] More noteworthy is that the last two usages for science respectively took up 165 and 113 times. If the 44 times for its usage as a system opposing metaphysics and the 82 times as evidence of materialism are included,[6] then at least nearly one fourth of its usage would directly weaken the position of Christianity and the Bible, quite apart from the usages with indirect negation. Jin and Liu's conclusion is not surprising: "During the New Culture Movement, 'science' was adopted to test 'common sense' and 'religious faith'"[7] and they also note that the scope of meaning of science in today's Chinese is still wider than its usage in the West.[8]

Many scholars from mainland China adopt this term scientism to describe the Chinese thinkers' faith in the power of science in early twentieth-century China.[9] Shen thinks the "persistence of the word 'scientism,' especially among scholars of China" suggests that this is something that cannot be ignored.[10]

According to Shen, when scientism gained currency in the May Fourth Movement, the word itself did not appear in the writings of the Chinese thinkers, but science was indeed presented as a truth-producing system with far-reaching implications. The thinkers most strongly associated with this position, such as Chen Duxiu (1879–1942), Hu Shi (1891–1962), and Ren Hongjun (1886–1961), routinely promoted the scientific method (科学方法), scientific spirit (科学精神), scientific attitude (科学态度), scientific authority (科学权威), and, of course, science itself.[11]

Wu uses the term scientism to describe Hu Shi's idea that "scientific method is almighty (科学方法万能)";[12] Yu uses it for Mao Dun's (1896–1981) com-

---

5. Jin and Qingfeng, *Study of Conceptual History*, 360–61.

6. Jin and Qingfeng, 360–61.

7. Jin and Qingfeng, 585.

8. Jin and Qingfeng, 364.

9. Jianghai Wu 吴江海, "Scientism Thoughts during New Culture Movement: Path, Character and Influence," *Studies in Dialectics of Nature* 自然辩证法研究 24, no. 5 (2008): 88; Zhaoping Yu 俞兆平, "The Centenary Fate of Scientism in China (科学主义在中国的百年命运)," *Cultural Vision* 文化视野, no. 11 (2014): 70; Like Gao 高力克, "'Replacing Religion with Science': Chen Duxiu's Scientism View of Religion," *Journal of Historical Science* 史学月刊, no. 1 (2017): 89; Zhiwen Duan 段治文, "Influence from Modern Scientism on Marxisms Spread and Localization in China," *Journal of Jiaxing University* 嘉兴学院学报 30, no. 4 (2018): 69.

10. Grace Yen Shen, "Scientism in the Twentieth Century," in *Modern Chinese Religion II: 1850–2015* (Leiden, The Netherlands: Interactive Factory, 2016), 91, https://brill.com/view/book/edcoll/9789004304642/B9789004304642_004.xml.

11. Shen, "Scientism in the Twentieth Century," 93.

12. Wu, "Scientism Thoughts," 89.

plaint that application of "scientific method (科学方法)" into novel-writing was required in literature;[13] Gao uses it for Chen Duxiu's advocacy that the world has evolved into an era of "scientific empiricism (科学实证)" and all politics, morality, education, and literature have "scientific and empirical spirit (科学实证的精神)";[14] Duan uses it for Li Dazhao's insistence that "natural science is the only science (自然科学是唯一的科学)" and Chen Duxiu's idea that under the guidance of "scientific thinking (科学思维)," people gradually come to understand the scientific nature (科学性) and advanced nature of historical materialism.[15]

In their debate on the nature of science, Zhang Yijing and his opponents employed similar terms like their contemporaries listed above. In 1922, Qi Yuan, when attacking Christianity, proclaimed, "After natural science (*ziran kexue* 自然科学) has become prosperous, we admit that it has absolute authority (*dudui de quanwei* 绝对的权威)."[16] In his response, Zhang Yijing called Qi Yuan's understanding of science "a superstition in science (科学上地迷信)"[17] and commented, "He superstitiously believes that science is almighty (*ta mixin kexue wanneng* 他迷信科学万能)."[18] Other phrases adopted by Zhang include "overestimate science (*pianzhong kexue* 偏重科学)."[19] As Shen says, scientism in the Chinese context still suggests a fundamental misapprehension of what science really is.[20]

Therefore, this study will follow other scholars' adoption of scientism to denote such an extreme attitude or faith in science which was prevalent in China and was noticed and resisted by Zhang Yijing.[21]

---

13. Yu, "Centenary Fate of Scientism," 74.
14. Gao, "'Replacing Religion,'" 90.
15. Duan, "Influence from Modern Scientism," 71.
16. Zhang and Liang, "Criticizing Qi Yuan's," 65.
17. Zhang, 70.
18. Zhang, 75.
19. Yijing Zhang, "Against a Speech for Atheism (驳无神之演说)," in *(1928), A Quarter of a Century of True Light, Selected* 真光丛刊, *Part 2: The Gospel Discussed and Explained* 辩道义, ed. Yijing Zhang (Shanghai 上海: China Baptist Publication Society 中华浸会书局, 1910), 24.
20. Shen, "Scientism in the Twentieth Century," 92.
21. Professor R. G. Tiedemann says about this research: "'Scientism' was a much-debated issue in 1920s China and is, therefore, relevant to Zhang Yijing's concerns."

5.1.1 The Concepts of Scientism

The adoption of this term scientism denotes that science and scientism are two concepts related but distinct from each other.

D. W. Y. Kwok is among the first group of scholars to trace the Chinese intellectuals' response to Western science and to use scientism for the belief in the omnipotence of science for the solution of human problems. His definition is "that view which places all reality within a natural order and deems all aspects of this order, be they biological, social, physical, or psychological, to be knowable only by the methods of science."[22] Its adjectival form is "scientistic."

Shen refers to global writers and thinkers to describe the features of the Chinese usage of the term. In her description, the most characteristic function of the term "scientism" is "to point to the construction of an image of science that has been positioned as the epistemic and moral reference point for all other human activity."[23]

When Chiu studies how Confucians appropriated the Buddhist ideas in response to the challenge of scientism during that period, he defines it as "a belief that quantitative natural science is the only valuable part of human learning and the only source of truth. Based on this notion, subjects that do not belong to quantitative natural science should imitate the method and language of it, or be seen from a scientific perspective, which leads to a view that only what is measurable in terms of quantitative natural science is considered knowledge."[24]

The manifestations of scientism may be various, but they share similar features: the view of science as the ultimate good that is able to answer moral questions, replace traditional religion, and set the limits of truth, knowledge, and reality; and the view of the scientific method as the only method for all disciplines.[25]

---

22. D. W. Y. Kwok, *Scientism in Chinese Thought 1900–1950* (New Haven, CT: Yale University Press, 1965), 21.

23. Shen, "Scientism in the Twentieth Century," 96–97.

24. King Pong Chiu, *Thomé H. Fang Tang Junyi and Huayan Thought* (Leiden: Brill, 2016), 31, https://doi.org/10.1163/9789004313880.

25. Kwok, *Scientism in Chinese Thought*, 23–24; Mikael Stenmark, *Scientism: Science, Ethics and Religion*, Ashgate Science and Religion Series (Aldershot: Ashgate, 2001), 133–34.

5.1.2 Sources for Scientism in China

Scientism existed in China at the beginning of the twentieth century[26] and is believed to have been imported from the West. Mitter analyses how modernity in a scientific mode prevailed in China and excluded the alternatives.[27]

Although the Jesuits had brought Western science into China in the seventeenth century, scientism did not take root in China until the nineteenth and early twentieth century. In chapter 4 above, we saw that the Chinese attributed the power of the West and Japan mainly to the advances of science and technology, so it was logical that they should look to their own progress in these areas to erase the humiliations or *xiuru* inflicted by them. The more setbacks China experienced in her foreign relationships, the more the Chinese people set their hopes on a China that was strong in science. Thus, modern nationalism in China was closely related to the rise of scientism.

At the beginning of the twentieth century, scientism had a profound influence on Chinese thought.[28] There are basically several sources for scientism in China: Chinese returning students, Western philosophers or educators, and health institutions established by Westerners.[29]

Wang studied the impact of Chinese returning students on China's society.[30] Yang shows that, between the 1870s and the early years of the twentieth century, as many as one hundred thousand Chinese students went to North America, Europe, and Japan to study Western civilization.[31] From 1905 to the 1930s, the largest proportion of Chinese students in the US was in the field of engineering.[32] The foreign-educated Chinese dominated the field of education shortly after their return from abroad.[33] Their impact is most systematically shown in the development of modern education. The new

---

26. D. E. Pollard, "Review of D. W. Y. Kwok 'Scientism in Chinese Thought, 1900–1950,'" *Bulletin of the School of Oriental and African Studies* 30, no. 2 (1967): 29.

27. Rana Mitter, "Modernity, Internationalization, and War in the History of Modern China," *The Historical Journal* 48, no. 2 (2005): 541.

28. Kwok, *Scientism in Chinese Thought*, 17–18.

29. L. G. Tuck 伍连德, "Medical Progress in China Since the Republic," *The Lancet*, 29 May 1920: 1203–4.

30. Wang, *Chinese Intellectuals and the West*.

31. C. K. Yang, "Chinese Intellectuals and the West by Y. C. Wang," *Journal of Asian Studies* 26, no. 1 (1966): 115.

32. Wang, *Chinese Intellectuals and the West*, 510.

33. Wang, 362.

educational system promulgated by the Education Ministry was modelled on the American system.[34]

Ogden indicates the significant influence of Bertrand Russell[35] and John Dewey[36] on the development of science and scientific method in China (the experimental method and empirical verification to social reform).[37] Around 1920–21, Russell visited Peking (Beijing) for a year to lecture on philosophy. Other scholars present in China at the time included John Dewey, Rabindranath Tagore, the Indian Nobel-laureate poet, and Harry Frederick Ward about whom there will be more below.

Bertrand Russell made a commitment to scientism. According to Stenmark, Russell believed that God and sin, central Christian tenets, do not merely fail to be scientifically knowable; there is not even any reason to consider them at all.[38] Christians are thus not rationally justified in believing in them. Being scientific or not becomes a standard for judging whether a (religious) belief is knowable or rationally believable.[39]

Dewey was a disciple of scientism and many leading educational reformers in China were his disciples,[40] such as the literary scholar Hu Shi,[41]

---

34. Wang, 99.

35. Bertrand Arthur William Russell (1872–1970) was a British philosopher, logician, mathematician, historian, writer, social critic, political activist, and Nobel laureate. In the early twentieth century, Russell led the British "revolt against idealism."

36. John Dewey (1859–1952) was an American philosopher, psychologist, and educational reformer. He is one of the primary figures associated with the philosophy of pragmatism.
In 1919, Dewey was invited by Peking University and stayed in China for two years during which he gave nearly 200 lectures to Chinese audiences. Hundreds and sometimes thousands of people attended the lectures. For these audiences, Dewey represented "Mr. Democracy" and "Mr. Science," the two personifications which they thought of as representing modern values; they hailed him as the "Second Confucius."

37. Suzanne P. Ogden, "The Sage in the Inkpot: Bertrand Russell and China's Social Reconstruction in the 1920s," *Modern Asian Studies* 16, no. 4 (1982): 588, 592.

38. Stenmark, *Scientism: Science, Ethics*, 6.

39. Stenmark, 7.

40. Hubert O. Brown, "Tao Xingzhi: Progressive Educator in Republican China," *Biography* 13, no. 1 (1990): 23, 29.

41. Hu Shi (胡适, 1891–1962) was a Chinese philosopher, essayist, and diplomat. Hu is widely recognized today as a key contributor to Chinese liberalism and the use of written vernacular Chinese. At Columbia he was greatly influenced by his professor, John Dewey, and became Dewey's translator and a lifelong advocate of pragmatic evolutionary change, helping Dewey in his 1919–21 lecture series in China. After his PhD study, he returned to lecture in Peking University. Hu soon became one of the leading and most influential intellectuals during the New Culture Movement and later the May Fourth Movement. Hu was the president of Peking University during 1946–48. In 1939, he was nominated for a Nobel Prize in literature.

university presidents Jiang Menglin[42] and Guo Bingwen,[43] textbook author Zhu Jingnong,[44] and the reformer Tao Xingzhi.[45] Many others, such as the author and language reformer Ye Shengtao[46] or the former president of Peking University, Cai Yuanpei, were strongly influenced by the doctrines of Progressivism although they did not study with Dewey. Dewey's theories were spread further by his lectures in China during 1919–21. Dewey and his disciples believed in science as the means of salvation both of education and of society through education.

---

42. Jiang Menglin (蒋梦麟, 1886–1964), also known as Chiang Monlin, was a Chinese educator, writer, and politician. He obtained his PhD from Columbia University under John Dewey's guidance. Between 1919 and 1927, he also served as president of Peking University. He later became president of National Chekiang University.

43. Guo Bingwen (or Kuo Ping-Wen 郭秉文, 1880–1969) was an influential Chinese educator. He graduated with honours from the University of Wooster in 1911 and then undertook graduate studies in education under John Dewey and Paul Monroe at Columbia University, where he received his MA degree in 1912 and his PhD in 1914. In 1921, he became the first chancellor of the Shanghai College of Commerce (上海商科大学), the forerunner of the Shanghai University of Finance and Economics (SUFE) (上海财经大学). Kuo was president of National Nanjing Higher Normal School from 1919 to 1923 and National Southeastern University from 1921 to 1925. Kuo Bingwen was elected three times as vice-chairman of the World Education Congress (世界教育会) and became chairman of its Asian division in 1923.

44. Zhu Jingnong (朱经农, Chu Ching-nong, 1887–1951) was a scholar, educator, and politician. In 1916, he first went to the University of Washington and then shifted to Columbia University. He obtained his Master's degree in education under John Dewey's influence. In 1921, he returned to be a professor in Peking University. Afterwards, he worked at the following positions: editor of the Commercial Press, dean of Chinese Department of University of Shanghai, president of Cheloo University, director of Education Bureau of Shanghai, director of Provincial Education Bureau of Hunan, deputy minister of Education Ministry, and president of Kwang Hua University (光华大学).

45. Tao Xingzhi (陶行知, 1891–1946) was a renowned Chinese educator and reformer in the Republic of China mainland era. He studied at Teachers College, Columbia University, and returned to China to champion progressive education. His career in China as a liberal educator was not derivative of John Dewey, as some have alleged, but creative and adaptive. Returning in 1917, he joined Nanking Higher Normal School and then National Southeastern University (later renamed National Central University and Nanking University). In December 1921, Tao and other educationists founded China Education Improvement Society through which the educationists promoted the forming of the modern education system in China. In August 1923, Tao and Y. C. James Yen organized a National Association of Mass Education Movements (MEM). At the height of its literacy campaign in the 1920s, Yen estimated that the MEM had five million students and more than one hundred thousand volunteer teachers. Tao went on to become the nation's leading promoter of rural teachers' education. In March 1927, he founded the Xiaozhuang Normal College in Nanjing to train teachers and educators for schools in the countryside. It was revived in 2000 as the Nanjing Xiaozhuang University.

46. Ye Shengtao (叶圣陶, 1894–1988) was an influential Chinese author, educator, and publisher. He was a founder of the Association for Literary Studies (文学研究会), the first literature association during the May Fourth Movement in China. He was responsible for a number of posts in the authority.

Yip evaluates the effectiveness of different health agencies' influence on China's mass health and hygiene and shows their role in the spreading of the idea of science in China, especially the efforts of the medical missionaries and the Rockefeller Foundation.[47] The Mass Education Movement led by James Yen[48] was influential too in the 1920s, but, interestingly, the Nationalist government's Ministry of Health, set up in 1928, had little to do with the spreading of science in this period. Through their efforts, a Western-style health system was built up, public health techniques were introduced, and scientific methods began to gain popularity. For example, China's traditional medicine was disdained for its "unscientific" nature by both Western medical workers and Chinese medical staff who were trained either in the West or in the medical institutions established by Westerners.

The Chinese assumption of the unity of moral and natural truth led the Chinese to believe that Western scientific theories were applicable to society and ethics.[49] Hence, the inductive methods and language of the natural sciences were believed to be capable of solving and describing all human and social problems.

To sum up, the essence of scientism features the requirements of empirical evidence and the logic of reason for being scientific and real. Such a scientistic approach could be adopted either consciously or unconsciously.

However, when strictly evaluated against the requirements of scientism, very few people could be called "really scientific." For example, very few would ask for the empirical evidence to prove the safety of their trip by train or car before they board. And very few would refuse to eat the dishes before them till their reason could be perfectly satisfied by finding out all the nutritional elements and their advantages and disadvantages for their bodies. The requirements of scientism are more likely to be applied to others than claimed for oneself, which is a kind of self-righteousness in science.

Then, it is not surprising to know that Chinese "scientists" in the 1920s were not really scientists or even philosophers of science but college dons of

---

47. Ka-Che Yip, "Health and Society In China: Public Health Education for the Community, 1912–1937," *Social Science and Medicine* 16 (1982): 1203.

48. Y. C. James Yen (晏阳初, 1890–1990), known to his many English-speaking friends as "Jimmy," was a Chinese educator and organizer known for his work in mass literacy and rural reconstruction, first in China, then in many other countries.

49. Ogden, "Sage in the Inkpot," 588, 592.

literature and philosophy[50] or intellectuals who were interested in science, and the values and assumptions to which it had given rise, to discredit and eventually replace the traditional body of values.[51]

5.1.3 The Influence of Scientism in China

When the theory of evolution was introduced into China, Chinese scholars immediately saw its practical and moral aspects and extended the theory to the "struggle for existence" and "survival of the fittest" among nations, and so on.[52] One of the two themes of the May Fourth Movement in 1919 was a calling for science. As reviewed in the last chapter, the New Culture Movement was criticized for its iconoclastic denunciation of Chinese traditions and its unjustified validation of Western scientism and modern literature.[53] St. John's University included more science courses after the May Fourth Movement, which could serve as an example of the influence of science.[54]

Yet science did not attain its dominant position in Chinese life until 1923, when the Debate on Science and Metaphysics took place. This debate lasted for one year, after which a large number of Chinese intellectuals accepted the adequacy of science in providing a philosophy of life because of the great accomplishments of Western scientific method.[55] Xiao creatively analyses the relationship between the rhetoric of the pro-science group and that of the pro-metaphysical group and their relationship with the Dao (or the Way) discourse respectively.[56] Then Xiao concludes that the victory of the pro-science group in 1923 was due to its rhetoric being in accordance with Dao discourse, while that of the pro-metaphysical group was not.[57] Since the debate of 1923, trust in the sufficiency of science has become an established element

---

50. Fu-Sheng Mu, "Review of D. W. Y. Kwok 'Scientism in Chinese Thought, 1900–1950,'" *The China Quarterly* 28 (1966): 137.
51. Kwok, *Scientism in Chinese Thought*, 3.
52. Ogden, "Sage in the Inkpot," 590.
53. Wang, "Geopolitics of Literature," 755.
54. Wang, 748.
55. Patricia Uberoi, "Chinese Conversion to Scientism: Scientism in Chinese Thought by D. W. Y. Kwok. Published by the Yale University Press, New Haven (USA), 1965," *China Report* 4, no. 2 (1968): 33–35, https://doi.org/10.1177/000944556800400209.
56. Xiaosui Xiao, "The 1923 Scientific Campaign and Dao-Discourse: A Cross-Cultural Study of the Rhetoric of Science," *Quarterly Journal of Speech* 90, no. 4 (2004): 469–92.
57. Xiao, "1923 Scientistic Campaign," 483–84.

in the thought of most modern Chinese intellectuals, and its most important expression was Marxism.[58]

Virdi believes that Marxism was undoubtedly a scientistic movement.[59] Since the success of the Communist Party in Russia was interpreted as proof of its scientific nature, Marxism (or Marxist ideas) had an increasing appeal among the intelligentsia and the public in China. According to Xiao, Communists appeared at the end of the debate and posed as final judges of the controversy, criticizing pro-science groups for their lack of knowledge of socioeconomic laws and suggesting the socioeconomic formation as the ultimate driving force of the activities of humankind.[60] In Xiao's analysis, they seemed be defending materialism and reason. Afterwards, the Communists became more bent on representing science. The official discourse in contemporary China still presents Marxism as scientific and religion as superstitious.[61]

Not only could the believers and practitioners of scientism be found among leading scholars, educators, and medical staff such as Dewey's disciples, but many political figures supported it. On average, at least one in five Chinese returning students from the US entered the government service between 1917 and 1937.[62] Like most intellectuals of the 1920s, many KMT members were under the influence of scientism, including Ma Junwu,[63] Ren

---

58. Uberoi, "Chinese Conversion to Scientism," 35.
59. Jaipreet Virdi, "Shaping Science and Scientism," *Science as Culture* 20, no. 4 (2011): 543.
60. Xiao, "1923 Scientistic Campaign," 485.
61. Xiaowen Ye, "A Brief Discussion on Theories of Religion and Legal Reconstruction over the Past Twelve Years (略谈十二年来我国的宗教理论和法制建设)," in *Marxism and Religion*, ed. Zhen Chi, Xuezeng Gong, and Daji Lü, vol. 4, Religious Studies in Contemporary China Collection (Leiden: Brill, 2014), 380; Zuoan Wang, "Building a Harmonious Society and New Ideas of Religious Work (构建和谐社会与宗教工作新理念)," in *Marxism and Religion*, ed. Zhen Chi, Xuezeng Gong, and Daji Lü, 390; Xiaoming Zhu, "On the Socialist View of Religion with Chinese Characteristics (论中国特色社会主义宗教观)," in *Marxism and Religion*, ed. Zhen Chi, Xuezeng Gong, and Daji Lü, 354, 366.
62. Wang, *Chinese Intellectuals and the West*, 514.
63. Ma Junwu (马君武, 1881–1940) was a scientist and educator in China and first president of Guangxi University. He studied in Japan and received his engineering degree in metallurgy in Berlin in 1911 and returned to China with his doctorate in 1916. There he resumed leadership positions in various ministries of the government, besides taking up teaching.

Hongjun,⁶⁴ Dai Jitao,⁶⁵ and Wu Zhihui.⁶⁶ Trained in Western science and influenced by Darwinism, Sun Yat-sen also forcefully advocated science, claiming that science had to be the main path if China was to catch up with the West. Lu also says that the understanding of science by the majority of intellectuals, including KMT members, was mainly in terms of spirit and attitude.⁶⁷

Ogden maintains that in the context of the debate over science and democracy, science and scientific method became political issues, but science in China had never been objective and dispassionate.⁶⁸ Just as Wang indicates, the evolutionist theory justified revolutionary measures in the name of national salvation, and reformist literati used science to remove the obstacle of Confucian conservatism in their pursuit of wealth and power.⁶⁹ Such phenomena could be better understood under the lens of scientism.

5.1.4 Being Scientific and Being Chinese

A "crisis of identity" frequently occurs when a new nationalism appears. For many Chinese, the pursuit of science posed a challenge to Chinese "identity,"⁷⁰ for pure science was in conflict with the Chinese tradition of regarding man and nature as an integrated whole and of focusing on ethics and society.⁷¹

---

64. Ren Hongjun (or Jen Hung-Chun, 任鸿隽, 1886–1961) was a Chinese politician, academic, and educator. He was a founding member of the Science Society of China, a major scientific organization in the modern history of China initiated by Chinese students at Cornell University in 1914, and served as its president from 1914 to 1923. He earned a Bachelor's in chemistry from Cornell in 1916 and a Master's from Columbia University in 1917. He was a professor of Chemistry, served as president of universities and in various government agencies and offices. During his lifetime, he helped to promote science in China.

65. Dai Jitao (or Tai Chi-Tao 戴季陶, 1891–1949) studied in Japan between 1905 and 1909. He became Sun's translator and then his confidential secretary, and later served as a high-level official. In 1926, he served as president of the Sun Yat-sen University, and the chief of politics at Whampoa Academy, with Zhou Enlai as his deputy. From 1928 to 1948, he served as head of the Examination Yuan of the Republic of China.

66. Fang-Shang Lu, "The Intellectual Origins of Guomindang Radicalization in the Early 1920s," *Chinese Studies in History* Fall (1992): 8, 31.

67. Lu, "Intellectual Origins of Guomindang," 8, 31.

68. Ogden, "Sage in the Inkpot," 592.

69. Xiuyu Wang, "Review on The People's Peking Man: Popular Science and Human Identity in Twentieth-Century China by Sigrid Schmalzer," *Journal of World History* 21, no. 2 (2010): 356.

70. Ogden, "Sage in the Inkpot," 594.

71. Mu, "Review of D. W. Y. Kwok."

This was the central issue of the "Science versus Metaphysics" debate which had been going on since the nineteenth century.

It is worth mentioning again that Chinese "identity" has different aspects, and traditional Chinese identity was one among others. In the 1920s, different versions of nationalism and the new Marxism were all in competition to prescribe the formula of being "Chinese." As early as 1910, the members of the Science Society[72] sought to save China by science and technology.[73] After the 1923 debate, the different versions of Chinese identity began to share one common aspect: being scientific. In China, both in the Republican period and in the Communist regime that followed it, science was the sign under which the nation and modernity were conceived.[74]

As noted in chapter 4, any version of nationalism would expect certain attitudes and actions from the members of a nation who care about their national identity.[75] In other words, a Chinese who failed to meet the expectation of being scientific and making a scientific contribution to China was considered to be useless. Intellectuals, like Ding Wenjiang,[76] were both followers of modern scientism and inheritors of the traditional legacy;[77] that is to say, they felt they were genuinely Chinese because, in addition to other aspects of their identity, they were scientific so that they were valuable to China. As for those who did not demonstrate a similar commitment to science, they were viewed as useless Chinese or unwanted Chinese.

How should one demonstrate one's commitment to science? The answer lay in their answer to one question: Were they willing to submit every aspect of their life to the requirements of empirical evidence and reason? If their answer was yes and they were willing to denounce any aspect which could not offer empirical evidence or be logical to reason, then they subjectively

---

72. The Science Society of China, the first comprehensive Chinese scientific association, was actually organized in 1914 by a group of Chinese students at Cornell University in the United States.

73. Wang, "Saving China through Science," 292–93.

74. Peter van der Veer, "Religion, Secularism and National Development in India and China," *Third World Quarterly* 33, no. 4 (2012): 730.

75. Miscevic, "Nationalism."

76. Ding Wenjiang (丁文江, 1887–1936) was a Chinese geologist, polymath, writer, politician, administrator, and social activist, active especially in the Republic of China (1912–49). In his own time, his name was transcribed as either V. K. Ting, or Ting Wen-chiang.

77. D. W. Y. Kwok, "Review of Charlotte Furth 'Ting Wenchiang: Science and China's New Culture,'" *China Quarterly* 45 (1971): 186.

felt themselves to be scientific and externally were recognized as scientific. If the answer was no or they were unwilling to denounce those "unscientific" aspects, externally they could certainly be viewed as less Chinese, and even subjectively they themselves felt the same way. This is the consequence of the hegemony of scientism.

The power and hegemony of scientism have remained until the present, as scientism is a main characteristic of Marxism-Leninism.[78] Chinese officials announce: any Chinese superstitious religion believer needs to acquire scientific and cultural knowledge,[79] but it is not realistic to expect religion to die out within a short period.[80]

Since scientism demanded empirical evidence and the logic of reason before it allocated the tag of being scientific and real, it posed a destructive challenge to Christianity, whose preeminent feature is faith. Faith is defined as being sure of what is hoped for and being certain of what is not seen.[81] Within such a context, how did Zhang respond to the claims of scientism? How was he influenced by it? The following sections will be devoted to the examination of his attitude towards science and scientism and the influence of scientism on him.

5.2 Zhang's Response to Science and Scientism
5.2.1 Welcoming Science

Generally, Zhang had a positive attitude towards science, as can be seen from the following aspects.

Under the name of Mujun (亩均) in 1909, Zhang listed two benefits of science. The first was its function in eradicating age-old superstitions. Christians had been accused of rejecting gods. In Zhang's view, this accusation partially contributed to the missionary cases and the Boxer Uprising.[82]

---

78. Chiu, *Thomé H. Fang Tang*, 6.
79. Wang, "Building a Harmonious Society," 390.
80. Zhu, "Socialist View of Religion," 354–55.
81. Hebrews 11:1 – "Now faith is confidence in what we hope for and assurance about what we do not see."
82. Yijing Zhang, "The Relationship between the Advancement of Civilization and the Church (文明进步与教会之关系)," in *(1928), A Quarter of a Century of True Light, Selected* 真光丛刊, *Part 3: General Articles* 通论, ed. Yijing Zhang (Shanghai 上海: China Baptist Publication Society 中华浸会书局, 1909), 37.

Once imported, Western learning quickly labelled idol-related practices as superstitious, which was a help to evangelization.

The second was that science could support Christian faith. Zhang believed that the new discoveries in archaeology confirmed some of the stories in the Bible, like plants and animals being created before humankind and the Israelites crossing the Red Sea.[83] So Zhang concluded that science was a secret key to religion.[84]

Science was the study of God's creation. In 1910, an atheist claimed that no one who knew physics would believe there was a God. Zhang thought that this person must have been poisoned by Darwin's theory of evolution. In his view, though species could change, their origins were from God.[85] Science studied only a small number of physical phenomena among all of God's creations. The fact was that the more advanced the science, the more popular the religion.

Science and Christianity were compatible. In Zhang's explanation, when knowledge and intelligence were still immature, science and religion had conflicted.[86] Later on, each side realized it needed the other. The Christian faith of some scientists was a proof of the compatibility of religion and science. Zhang listed twelve well-known scientists' names, including Darwin, and said that there was only one non-Christian among them. The names of George John Romanes (1848–94) and Alfred Russel Wallace (1823–1913) were on his list.[87]

Science was highly valued by the church. According to Chen Duxiu, new culture included science, religion, morality, arts, literature, and music. Zhang responded that "the Church is the new thoughts tide" and that "all the doctrines advocated by the current new thoughts tide are stolen from the oldest Church."[88] The church had never ignored the importance of science, morality, arts, literature, and music.

Zhang often used modern scientific knowledge to support his argument. As early as 1910, he praised the wonder of creation by attributing to God

---

83. Zhang, "Advancement of Civilization," 38.
84. Zhang, 39.
85. Zhang, "Against a Speech," 23–24.
86. Zhang, "Church and the New Thoughts Tide," 138.
87. Zhang, 138.
88. Zhang, 138.

the fact that the four seasons are caused by the axial tilt.[89] More examples of this kind will follow.

Actually, Zhang's adoption of scientific knowledge was due to his concern to contextualize the Christian messages. Under the name of Zhenmei (珍枚), he said that preachers should be able to bridge the gap between the Bible and their audience's background just as Jesus contextualized his message for people from different backgrounds so as to show their universal relevance.[90] He argued that had Jesus been in China at that time or had science developed in Jesus's time, he would certainly have included modern scientific knowledge and inventions in his parables and teachings. Then those who rejected the Way by a little scientific knowledge would no longer dare to boast about science.

On one occasion Zhang used the sun, sunlight, and the colours of plants as metaphors for the relationship between God, his Son, and his many children. He said that anyone with a knowledge of science would know that the different colours of plants were caused by the same sunlight.[91]

However, despite Zhang's efforts, Christianity was still being depicted by the Anti-Christian Movement as the enemy of science, about which he felt helpless and angry.[92] The reason will be analyzed below.

5.2.2 Being Critical of Scientism

Zhang was positive about science but critical of scientism, that is, he rejected the idea that every aspect of life should be put under the purview of scientism. Although he could not have known the term, he did express a similar idea when he said that he was not against science but against its misuse, which was drawing people away from religion [Christianity].[93]

---

89. Zhang, "Against a Speech," 23.

90. Yijing Zhang 张亦镜, "On Writing for Preaching (论传道文字)," in *(1928), A Quarter of a Century of True Light, Selected* 真光丛刊, Part 3: General Articles 通论, ed. Yijing Zhang (Shanghai 上海: China Baptist Publication Society 中华浸会书局, 1918), 7.

91. Yijing Zhang, "Answering Chen Xiaohan's Three Questions (答陈箫寒三大疑问)," in *(1928), A Quarter of a Century of True Light, Selected* 真光丛刊, Part 5: Answers to Inquiries 答问, ed. Yijing Zhang (Shanghai 上海: China Baptist Publication Society 中华浸会书局, 1913), 3–4.

92. Yijing Zhang 张亦镜, "Preface – A Country with Freedom of Faith (序: 以已有信教自由约法之国家)," *True Light* 真光 21, no. 8–9 (1922): 1–2.

93. Yijing Zhang, "Going to Cinema and Attending to Sermon (看影戏与赴礼拜堂听讲)," *True Light* 真光 28, no. 5 (1929): 55.

Zhang also listed two harms which arose with the arrival of Western civilization. They were products of "a new theory" from the West and Japan and its theorists were usually suspicious and critical of religion.[94] After its arrival, the intellectuals quickly accepted it and became atheists. Then it was taught in schools and disseminated by newspapers. Finally, it became a public opinion and condemned Christianity as a superstition. This was the first harm.

The second harm was to create a new barrier to the gospel. In Zhang's view, the old barrier was that Chinese people, under the influence of Confucianism, were used to seeing people from other countries as *yidi* (夷狄) or foreign barbarians, the gospel as a cult, and Christians as traitors. As a result, Christians used to focus on bridging Christianity and Confucianism in their evangelizing writings. After the arrival of "the new theory," Zhang felt that such writings were becoming outdated:

> Chinese began to reject Christianity by saying that it was against scientific principle or academic principle. They have not realized that human intelligence is not able to exhaust God who has no bounds. So, by pointing to the issues in the Bible people are incapable of doing or knowing, they vainly claim "they are outrageously unreasonable." Though a Chinese person might not totally deny the existence of gods or God, the more knowledge they accumulated, the more opposed they became to the Christian message.[95]

Zhang thought "the new theory" made it more difficult than before for people to accept Jesus.

The two harms illustrated a context for Chinese Christians at the turn of the twentieth century: there existed an old barrier and a new barrier. The old barrier was based on Chinese tradition with Confucianism as the mainstream. The new one in the context was a theory from the West which judged Christianity as a superstition on the grounds that it violated reason. Although Zhang did not use the word scientism, what he described had the distinctive features of scientism: taking the method of natural science and empirical evidence as standards of truth in measuring and judging all experiences. Thus,

---

94. Zhang, "Advancement of Civilization," 37.
95. Zhang, 38.

scientism appeared in China as early as 1909. Since there was no such term as scientism in the Chinese language at that time, Zhang lacked the means to pinpoint the key to the problem. However, as an evangelizing writer, he almost immediately sensed, and responded to, this new challenge.

In the same text, facing the new slogan "when science flourished, religion would perish" – a gap created by scientism between science and Christianity – Zhang proposed another one to bridge the gap: the more progress could be made in science, the more people would welcome religion. He denied the existence of such a gap. Taking the church in the West as evidence, he questioned if the advancement of science had led to the destruction of the church. He continued:

> The Church in the West is growing daily, and the advancement of civilisation did not stop it from practising Jesus' teachings. Plus, the majority of the great scientists were devout religious believers.[96]

Zhang's efforts to oppose scientism were obvious and understandable, but his evidence might not be convincing to everyone. His optimism about the church in the West might not find much resonance among returning Chinese students who had witnessed the challenges and criticisms faced by Christianity in the West.

Evolutionism was, as Zhang saw it, a cult propagated by a few modern philosophers who claimed that God, being invisible, could not exist and that human beings were descended from apes.[97] In response, Zhang pointed out that God was beyond examination and that this now widespread cult could lead only to the loss of self-respect, gross immorality, and damnation.

It was superstitious to believe in the supremacy of science. One slogan in the Anti-Christian Movement was to defeat religion with science.[98] Zhang reminded his readers of the dangers of science as illustrated by the advanced killing machines used in the First World War in Europe.[99] As listed above, he commented that Qi Yuan had a superstitious attitude to science when he

---

96. Zhang, 39.
97. Zhang, "On 'Our Father,'" 5.
98. Yijing Zhang 张亦镜, "The Second Telegram from the Anti-Religion Alliance and My Criticism (非宗教同盟第二次通电 – 也有批)," *True Light* 真光 21, no. 8–9 (1922): 40.
99. Zhang, "Comments on the Telegram," 26.

said that the natural law had absolute authority and every phenomenon was subject to a certain law.[100] This was tantamount to saying that Qi had a strong commitment to scientism when he dealt with Christianity. Interestingly, Zhang showed his disapproval by quoting Dr. Dewey's words that the natural laws concerned the relationships between things and were subject to change like other phenomena. His criticism of Qi could be viewed as a criticism of scientism.[101]

Zhang had never attended mission schools, knew little English, and had few Western contacts with whom he could engage in a discussion in depth. That is to say that his own convictions about the church and Christianity in the West might relate only to the beginning of the twentieth century. Nevertheless, his stance against scientism is clear from the examples above. He also observed that it was only at the start of the twentieth century that the Chinese had rejected Christianity in favour of science, although Western learning had been introduced to China long before 1900.

For the first three decades of the twentieth century, Zhang and other Chinese Christians had to repeatedly face the new conceptualization of state and culture among the intellectuals, in which everything had to be interpreted as scientific. As analyzed above, scientism inclines to extend the methodology and standards of natural science to all disciplines. This means that, in addition to radical nationalism, the demand of scientism became a requirement of being Chinese. As a result, the search for a Chinese Christian identity also meant a search for an identity as a scientific Chinese.

This gives rise to two questions. First, where was the boundary between being scientific and being scientistic? Second, would being scientific win the recognition of being Chinese from the scholars, politicians, and the general public who believed in scientism? On most occasions, the efforts of Christians to be scientific still fell short of the demands of scientism because the evidence and logic offered for belief in the supernatural were never empirical or logical enough according to the terms defined by scientism. Christianity in the 1920s was always depicted by scientism as the enemy of science, which led to feelings of helplessness and anger in Zhang and many other Christians. In his perseverance, Zhang sought inner strength from his faith.

---

100. Zhang and Liang, "Criticizing Qi Yuan's," 70–71.
101. Zhang and Liang, 75.

God protected religion (Christianity) from the attack of scientism. Zhang said:

> Undoubtedly, it is through God's protection that religion [Christianity] has not been destroyed under the ferocious attack from those who had a strong bias toward science. God is "I am who I am," eternal, omnipotent and omniscient, the One and only, and the Supreme with no match, and the Creator. If He wants to promote His beloved religion [Christianity], who, as a negligible and created human being, could obstruct it? The principles studied by science only cover a small part of the physical world created by God. However, after gaining a small amount of knowledge of science, some turn up their noses at all others to such a degree that they not only resist but also arbitrarily deny the existence of God who is the omniscient and omnipotent Lord of all. Is this fair? What makes them overconfident as such?[102]

Even without using the term "scientism," he pointed out that it was not science but an arbitrary overconfidence in the knowledge of science that led to the hostility against God who really exists and is promoting the belief in Christ.

In sum, Zhang defended his faith from the attack of scientism in many ways, such as promoting harmony between science and Christianity, exhibiting the limits of science, critiquing theories such as evolutionism, and pointing out the difference between science and scientism.

5.2.3 The Difficulty of Answering the Scientistic Challenges Outside

The challenges of scientism were severe and hard to answer, so Zhang had to try every possible means to provide a response; however, his responses might not appear impressive to today's readers due to the fact that the discussion of the nature of science in the academic circle at that time was not as comprehensive and sophisticated as today and that Zhang himself had no background of science education at all. Not only might his argument lack

---

102. Zhang, "Against a Speech," 24.

depth and maturity compared to today's understanding, but the effects in his time were also hard to evaluate. Two examples illustrate the level of resistance.

Sun Yat-sen was a Christian while many of his party members were believers in science.[103] Zhang's observation was echoed by Lu, who found that scientism exerted a compelling force on KMT members as well as most intellectuals of the time.[104] Among them, Wang Jingwei was prominent (who is introduced in chapter 2). Zhang argued against him in the 1910s and 1920s.

In Paris in 1913, Wang praised science and criticized religion, especially Christianity. He believed that when scientific knowledge was taken as the touchstone, the difference between truth and falsehood, right and wrong, would be instantly exposed. To his surprise, he found that the superstition of religion still existed in the West.[105] He said the religion in the West (Christianity) was damaging because its founder was a "fool."[106] The followers defended this religion because they were hypocrites. Western clergymen cheated people into superstition with all sorts of sayings about ghosts (魑魅魍魎, demons and monsters). The root reason for all this was that all of them lacked knowledge.[107] Wang also said that morality would improve following scientific progress because new knowledge would bring about a new morality. In addition to the usual scientistic charges against religion, Wang demonstrated another characteristic of scientism, namely that it could answer moral questions and improve morality.

Since Wang claimed Christian beliefs to be false, Jesus to be "stupid," and his disciples to be hypocritical, Zhang was invited by other Christians to refute him.

Zhang admitted that there were stupid and hypocritical people in the church, but according to his observations over twenty years, he found that the largest number of the wise, the sincere, the honest, and the righteous were Western and Chinese Christians.[108]

---

103. Zhang, "Answers to Three Questions," 80.
104. Lu, "Intellectual Origins of Guomindang," 31.
105. Zhang, "Correcting Wang Jingwei's Slander," 171.
106. In China at the beginning of the twentieth century, the Western word "religion" (宗教) was often interchangeable with Christianity.
107. Zhang, "Correcting Wang Jingwei's Slander," 166.
108. Zhang.

To prove the truth of Christian beliefs, Zhang first resorted to faith, an element denied by scientism. He affirmed the existence of the supernatural domain which was invisible to mortal eyes but believable.[109] The entire Bible bore witness to God who was omniscient, almighty, and kind. Anyone who was humble and had the right motives would bow down and confess that Jehovah was the Creator and Jesus was the Saviour.[110]

Then Zhang tried to remind Wang that his assertions were based on a different ontological philosophy rather than on scientific experiment. According to Zhang's analysis, when Wang said that Western clergymen cheated people into superstition with sayings about ghosts, he meant that clergymen talked about God and Satan and worshipped God once every seven days. Zhang argued that what these clergymen said contained inner truth and should never be written off as "ghost stories" unless Wang was sure there was no God. Zhang challenged Wang to prove that God did not exist.[111]

Next, through philosophical analysis and reasoning, Zhang aimed at exposing the flaws in Wang's logic. Wang's atheistic stance was grounded in a theory concerning the "unknowable" held by the anarchist party which had been prominent before the 1920s. Wu Zhihui, a representative of anarchism, exerted an important influence in the victory of Science over Metaphysics in 1923.[112] This theory claimed that "if anyone affirms the existence of a Creator and imagines the state of affairs in the unknowable world by his capacity limited within this knowable world, they are lying. Therefore, the followers of religion are worthless. Similarly, if anyone alleges that there is no existence of a Creator, they are lying. Because people are not able to name the things in the unknowable world, how can people deny the existence of things in the unknowable world?" After describing the main points of this theory, Zhang quoted its further explanations:

> Someone may ask: "When the anti-religion people allege that God does not exist, aren't they denying the existence of a Creator?"

---

109. Zhang, 167.
110. Zhang, 170.
111. Zhang, 169.
112. Shi Hu 胡适, "The Thoughts of Wu Zhihui 吴稚晖先生的思想," in 民国吴稚晖先生敬恒年谱 *The Chronicle of My Teacher Mr. Wu Zhihui*, ed. Kailing Yang (Taipei 台北: Commercial Press 商务印书馆, 1928), 153, 159.

Answer: "They are just denying the existence of God affirmed by the religious believers. When they said, 'not exist,' they were accusing the religious believers' affirmation of 'exist' of being a lie. Their 'not exist' was different from 'denying the existence in the unknowable world.'"

Question: "If it is wrong to deny the existence of things in the unknowable world, wouldn't it be equal to affirming its existence?"

Answer: "No. We can only affirm it is unknowable. Both affirming the existence and denying the existence are lying. Nevertheless, when hearing religious believers falsely affirm the existence, people could immediately refute it by saying 'not exist' because this 'not exist' is incurred by 'exist' and this is just a counterbalance."[113]

Since this theory stipulated that a person was lying when they alleged that God did not exist, Zhang cornered Wang by asking him whether his opposition to talking about God originated in his assertion that God did not exist or from his denial of "the existence of God" as affirmed by the followers of religion. Since the second option was what the theory held as correct, Zhang assumed that Wang must choose the second option. Then Zhang announced that there was no essential difference between "denying the affirmation of its existence" and "alleging that it does not exist." He reasoned:

For example, a person clenched his or her fist and said, "I have a coin in my hand." Both those who did not believe and those who believed did not unfold his or her palm to look at the coin. Those chose to believe because that person's words sounded trustworthy. How could those who chose not to believe claim it was lying for those believers to affirm the existence of the coin? If a person knew there was no coin in the fist, but deliberately said the coin was in the hand, then such a person could be called a liar. On the other hand, if a person believed in the existence of a coin without looking into the hand for an affirmation of "it does not exist," then this person was not lying when he or she

---

113. Zhang, "Correcting Wang Jingwei's Slander," 169–70.

said, "there is a coin." If anyone insisted that this believing person lied and then put aside or cancelled this believing person's saying, what would they do if there was really a coin found in the hand? Since the person who insisted on calling the believing person a liar had not affirmed "the coin does not exist," on what basis did they maintain such an assertion? That's why I hold that it is of the same absurd theory for both "denying or cancelling religion believers' affirmation of its existence" and "alleging that it does not exist."[114]

Zhang's logic was that a person who insisted on the principle of the unknowable should not call the believers "liars" as if they knew. When they insisted that the believers were liars, they share the same presupposition with the unbelievers: both presumed they knew. Both were equally atheistic in Zhang's view. Zhang criticized Wang by the theory of the unknowable, and then he turned to critique this theory.[115] To continue his argument, he said that the Christian affirmation of the existence of God was obtained from God's self-revelation. This was different from imagining the state of affairs in the unknowable world by a capacity limited within this knowable world. Therefore, there was no reason at all to deny it by labelling it a lie.

Since Wang accused Jesus, his disciples, and Western clergymen of lacking scientific knowledge, Zhang tried to prove Wang wrong by seeking evidence from the Bible and empirical observations. He pointed out that the New Testament and the Acts of the Apostles have proved that Jesus was the most knowledgeable person in history and the apostles were sincere in spreading his teaching. Even if all the scientists in history were put together, their total knowledge put together could not equal Jesus's and their total sincerity could not be comparable to that of the apostles.

In addition to the biblical evidence, Zhang also looked for evidence from daily life. For example, he heard that pastors in the West were usually well educated. Often, they had graduated from seminaries after they had finished

---

114. Zhang, 170.
115. This theory sounds like agnosticism, the philosophical view that the existence of God or the supernatural is unknown and unknowable.

their college education. So Zhang questioned how Wang could be so proud of his own scientific knowledge that he regarded them with contempt.[116]

History was another source. As to the moral claim of Wang's scientific faith, Zhang first made a clarification by asking Wang if science was true while religion was false. He assumed Wang's answer would be yes. Then he challenged Wang on history by asking if there had not been any true morality before the progress in science. If Wang insisted on his faith by saying yes, that meant the old morality was not true morality. Only the new morality produced from the progress of science was true morality.[117]

Being immoral was another piece of evidence. Zhang continued:

> If so, Wang's view of morality must be the same as that of the anarchists. They held that there should not be religion, family, and human relationships but sexual freedom. Such behaviours are practised by those who boast of their new knowledge. They accuse the opponents of either having no knowledge or being moral hypocrites. Wang frequently accuses the old morality of religious clergymen of being hypocritical and attributes their foolishness and hypocrisy to their lack of knowledge, which is exactly in accordance with those anarchists.[118]

Then Zhang expressed his dislike for this morality by saying that the true morality that Wang boasted of was the same as the morality of animals. Zhang said that Christians viewed the morality of the anarchists as "unkind" (不善). Since Wang agreed with their morality and since Jesus said "Everyone who does evil hates the light," Wang would obviously oppose religion.[119]

The above dialogue between the two Chinese elites shows that at least for many Chinese, the legitimacy of knowledge needs validation through morality. After building up a connection between the moral views of Wang and the anarchists, Zhang strove to ruin the moral ground of Wang's faith in science by combining both Christian moral standards and the Confucian

---

116. Zhang, "Correcting Wang Jingwei's Slander," 171.
117. Zhang, 171.
118. Zhang, 171–72.
119. Zhang, "Correcting Wang Jingwei's Slander," 172. As noted before, in China at the beginning of the twentieth century, the Western word "religion" (宗教) was often interchangeable with Christianity.

moral term "unkind." What moral appeal did Wang's faith in science have? In Zhang's reply, its legitimacy appeal was to the values embedded in the world of animals. Naturally, in Zhang's view, Wang's faith in science lost its legitimacy in morality.

Zhang did not stop there. He then started to uncover Wang's historical and epistemic roots.[120] He admitted that Wang's motivation was good. However, because he did not know the truth of religion, he formed a prejudicial view after absorbing several fallacies. Zhang's investigation showed that there was a strong atmosphere against religion in France: in 1806, the Institut de France (法兰西学会) listed eighty-five ideals which were believed to be incompatible with the Bible; in September 1905, nearly two hundred thousand people from all over the world attended the meeting in Paris convened by the Global Free Mind Association (万国自由思想会) to denounce superstition and religion; on 9 December 1905, the French Law on the Separation of the Church and the State was passed, categorically denying Christianity, and leaping unprecedentedly into a state with no religion. Zhang guessed that Wang had probably witnessed corruption in the Catholic church in France and the attacks on it initiated by many French scholars. In Zhang's interpretation, France was trying to replace state religion with freedom of faith rather than denying religion. He offered a similar example in China: when the government forbade Confucius-worship on campus, it was rumoured to be aiming at the destruction of Confucianism. As for the attacks from academic circles, such as the eighty-five ideals incompatible with the Bible, Zhang thought their force was becoming exhausted. However, a handful of arrogant and superficial students with no knowledge of the Bible had simply picked a few terms to pose their challenges. Zhang was confident that even if all the scholars joined forces, they would still be unable to pull down religion: let alone the Chinese students in France.

As Zhang saw it, Wang made his observations only on the surface and copied plausible terms without examining their roots and nature. Zhang felt that Wang had wasted his time in France.[121]

It is not known if Wang read Zhang's article. Later he came back to China and became a very high-level official in the KMT government. When the

---

120. Zhang, 172–73.
121. Zhang, 173.

Anti-Christian Movement began in 1922, Wang was living in Guangzhou (Canton) in charge of education in Sun Yat-sen's government. He made another vigorous attack on Christianity. Zhang, who was also in Guangzhou as editor of *True Light*, launched his second polemic against Wang.

Facing Wang's challenge, Zhang laboriously searched for an argument from various sources – faith, the Bible, philosophy, ontology, logic, history, real life, epistemology, and morality. The challenge of scientism in the 1920s became even harder.

Besides using the terms and ideologies from the West for reasoning, Zhang also made use of Chinese materials in history. In 1925, when asked how to prove the existence of the soul and spirit, he admitted they were very hard to prove.[122] He referred to the Chinese traditional belief that people after death became *gui* or "ghosts (鬼)."[123] Since this word and the stories of ghosts were recorded in history books and current newspapers, Zhang took it as evidence for the reality of *gui* or ghosts. In 1914, Parliament[124] discussed the motion of resuming the practice of awarding posthumous titles. Zhang took this to be an expression of their belief in soul and spirit.[125] As for the serpent in Genesis which could speak, Zhang quoted the story of a speaking stone from *Zuo Zhuan*[126] (左传) and said if a stone could speak, much more a snake used by Satan.[127] To verify the authenticity of "the sun stood still, and the moon stopped" in Joshua 10:13, Zhang examined Chinese history to see if there was a record of such a thing.[128] To prove the reality of the virgin birth, Zhang quoted from *The Records of Zhou Dynasty* in *Records of the Historian* (史记. 周本纪) to say that Chinese classics also contained stories of the virgin

---

122. Zhang, "Answers to Three Questions," 80.

123. Zhang, 80.

124. Yuan Shikai was elected provisional president of the Republic of China on 14 February 1912 and began his autocratic rule as the first formal president of the Republic of China. Later, the elected Parliament was also put under his control. After Yuan's death on 6 June 1916, China descended into a period of warlords. For the next decade, the offices of both the president and Parliament in Peking became the tools of militarists and the politicians.

125. Zhang, "Denouncing Fallacies of Awarding," 96.

126. This is a Confucian classic which is a commentary on *The Spring and Autumn Annals*.

127. Yijing Zhang, "Three Questions about Genesis (创世纪三个疑问)," *True Light* 真光 23, no. 12 (1924): 76.

128. Yijing Zhang, "Another Three Questions about the Bible (又三条圣经疑问)," *True Light* 真光 23, no. 2 (1924): 88.

birth.¹²⁹ The approval of such records by Zhu Xi (朱熹, 1130–1200, a significant neo-Confucian scholar leader) provided verification. Zhang said that the drought and rain in the story of Elijah could not be denied by science, as a similar case happened in the story of a filial woman of Dong Hai District (东海孝妇) recorded in both *The History of the Former Han Dynasty* (汉书) and *The Biographies for Chaste Women* (列女传). There are more examples of this kind.¹³⁰

Science was an important source. The British naturalist Alfred Wallace (1823–1913) was often quoted to show that even a founder of the evolution theory believed in the reality of God.¹³¹ The new development in knowledge was adopted to prove God's existence and intelligent design.¹³²

The subsidiary benefits of Christianity were also on his list. For example, Christianity advocated equality, love, and freedom¹³³ and provided a meaning for life.¹³⁴

Nonetheless, Wang and other believers of scientism who asked for empirical evidence were not convinced, although Zhang had been trying to satisfy the requirements of reason. He might have realized that this was an impossible task as long as the terms for being real were set by scientism. In this sense, the conflict was not between Christianity and science but between Christianity and science in the version of scientism.

5.2.4 Answering Scientism Inside and Discovering Its Eastern Root

In 1927, a series of articles were published for the twenty-fifth anniversary of *True Light*. Zhang included a translation of an article *The Theological Thoughts in the U.S.A. during the Last Twenty-five Years* (二十五年来美国神学思

---

129. Zhang, "Questions from Mr. Zeng Guren," 62.
130. Yijing Zhang 张亦镜, "Tasting the Way (道源一勺)," *True Light* 真光 29, no. 8 (1930): 15–16.
131. Zhang, "Refuting a Plagiarism," 249, 262; Yijing Zhang 张亦镜, "The Third Comments on Mr. Daiying's 'Christianity and Saving China by Character Formation' and 'Why Are We against Christianity' (读代英君的'基督教与人格救国'和'我们为什么反对基督教'慨言 – 三)," *True Light* 真光 23, no. 6 (1924): 54.
132. Zhang, "Refuting a Plagiarism," 262–63; Zhang, "Third Comments on Mr. Daiying's," 54.
133. Zhang, "Refuting a Plagiarism," 225.
134. Zhang, "Comments on the Theological," 14.

想之趋势),[135] by Gerald Birney Smith (史美夫, 1868–1929)[136] of the early Chicago School,[137] which had become the centre of the post-Ritschlian school[138] of theological empiricism. According to Dorrien, all the liberal theologies of the nineteenth and early twentieth centuries derived their philosophical bearings from Immanuel Kant's (1724–1804) critiques of "scientific, moral, and aesthetic reason."[139] Liberal theology always appropriated Kantian arguments about the limits of sensual knowledge, the creative role of the mind in producing experience, the transcendental categories of reason, and the boundary between reason and religion.[140] Smith even advocated making theology as scientific as chemistry, or at least as sociology. His scientific ambition for theology was very obvious before his later life.[141] His scientistic position also influenced his theology. Concerning the doctrine of Atonement by Substitution, Smith said:

> To insist dogmatically, as an *à priori* principle, that "without the shedding of blood there is no remission of sin," is both foolish and futile in an age that has abandoned the conception of bloody

---

135. This original text was entitled "Theological Thinking in America" and included in *Religious Thought in The Last Quarter Century* edited by Gerald Birney Smith. "Theological Thinking in America," in *Religious Thought In The Last Quarter Century*, ed. Gerald Birney Smith (Chicago: The University of Chicago Press, 1927), 95–115.

136. Gerald Birney Smith, "The Theological Thoughts in the U.S.A. during the Last Twenty-Five Years (二十五年来美国神学思想之趋势)," *True Light* 真光 26, no. 6 (1927): 1–13.

137. The others included Shailer Mathews, George Burman Foster, Shirley Jackson Case, Edward Scribner Ames, among others.

138. Albrecht Ritschl (1822–89) was a German theologian. Starting in 1852, Ritschl lectured on "Systematic Theology." According to this system, faith was understood to be irreducible to other experiences, beyond the scope of reason. Faith, he said, came not from facts but from value judgments. Jesus's divinity was best understood as expressing "revelational-value" of Christ for the community that trusts him as God. He held Christ's message to be committed to a community. There are two breakpoints between the Ritschlian school and the post-Ritschlian school. The post-Ritschlian school believed that Ritschlian historical scholarship was not sufficiently modern and scientific because of its *a priori* Christian commitments, and that modern Christianity should be wedded to the best philosophy of the modern age – the American pragmatic empiricism rather than Kantian and Hegelian traditions. Gary Dorrien, *The Making of American Liberal Theology: Crisis, Irony, and Postmodernity, 1950–2005* (Louisville, KY: Westminster John Knox Press, 2006), 59.

139. Dorrien, *American Liberal Theology*.

140. Dorrien, 58.

141. Dorrien, 60; Creighton Peden, *Empirical Tradition in American Liberal Religious Thought, 1860–1960* (New York: Peter Lang, 2010), 163–64.

sacrifice and which is loudly demanding the abolition of capital punishment.¹⁴²

For more about the Chicago School and the development of liberal theology, Dorrien and Peden's books could serve as references. Zhang knew that Smith was supportive of liberal theology, but since Smith's article clearly stated the history of the theologies in the US during the past twenty-five years, Zhang published his article.

According to Smith, modernists and fundamentalists existed in every Protestant group.¹⁴³ The fundamentalists insisted on the authority of the Bible and the reality of supernatural phenomena while the modernists objected to the concepts which went against the historical facts. Theological doctrines should be evaluated by personal experience.¹⁴⁴ The fundamentalists wanted the authority of the Bible to be respected so they insisted on its infallibility and the supernatural nature of Christianity, but liberal theology insisted that Christianity should be studied by scientific and historical methods which were critical of the nature of religions and the relationship between theology and religious experience.¹⁴⁵ Liberal theology believed that the Jesus of theology was different from the Jesus of history.¹⁴⁶

For a balance, Zhang also published *The Testimony of Kanamori* (刊南慕利保罗或金森保罗的见证), a speech delivered by the Japanese convert and evangelist Kanamori Tsurin (1857–1945) at a congregation in London on 12 June 1925. In this testimony, Kanamori described how he had been seduced by liberal theology and higher criticism¹⁴⁷ from Germany and had become

---

142. Judson Eber Conant, *The Church, the Schools and Evolution* (Chicago: Bible Institute Colportage Ass'n, 1922), 35.
143. Smith, "Theological Thoughts in the U.S.A.," 5.
144. Smith, 8.
145. Smith, 13.
146. Smith, 9.
147. Higher criticism can be defined as the use of scientific techniques of literary criticism to establish the sources of the books of the Bible (*Collins English Dictionary*, s.v. "higher criticism," accessed April 6, 2016, https://www.collinsdictionary.com/us/dictionary/english/higher-criticism) or the study of the authorship, dates of writing, meaning, and so forth, of the books of the Bible, using the techniques or findings of archaeology, literary criticism, comparative religion, and so on (*Webster's New World College Dictionary*, 4th ed., 1999, s.v. "higher criticism").
  Higher criticism originally referred to the work of German biblical scholars of the Tübingen school. After the path-breaking work on the New Testament by Friedrich Schleiermacher (1768–1834), the next generation – which included scholars such as David Friedrich Strauss

a liberal theologian.¹⁴⁸ He said he had lost his faith in Jesus after becoming a liberal theologian because liberal theology held that the Bible contained not only the word of God, but also the words of men. It included both truth and lies. It comprised errors, superstition, parables, imagination, legends, and stories written by men. It ranked with the Qur'an and the Buddhist sutras. Liberal theology denied the virgin birth, the resurrection, and Jesus as God and Saviour.¹⁴⁹ Zhang thought that "higher criticism" in Kanamori's testimony was the scientific and historical method mentioned by Smith.

Zhang commented on Smith by recalling one phenomenon in China. He noticed that, in China, after reading a few threadbound books and acquiring a little traditional learning, people would criticize the ideas of creation, revelation, prophecy, the virgin birth, miracles, salvation, resurrection, Trinity, the final judgment, heaven, and eternal life in a very similar way to the experts of higher criticism. This showed that these experts had the same mindset as the famous scholars and philosophers of the past three thousand years in China.¹⁵⁰

In 1909, Zhang thought scientism was a new theory imported from Japan and the West, as shown above. By 1927, he realized that the pursuit of reason exemplified in liberal theology already existed among Chinese scholars. He said many Chinese Christians (in his generation) had spent a huge amount of time thinking and debating before they finally gave up their preconceived ideas to accept the teachings of Christ and become his disciples. They were then mocked by other common Confucian scholars who believed that they descended from lofty trees to enter into dark valleys or *xia qiaomu ru*

(1808–74) and Ludwig Feuerbach (1804–72) – in the mid-nineteenth century analysed the historical records of the Middle East from Christian and Old Testament times in search of independent confirmation of events related in the Bible. These latter scholars built on the tradition of Enlightenment and rationalist thinkers such as John Locke, David Hume, Immanuel Kant, Gotthold Lessing, Gottlieb Fichte, G. W. F. Hegel, and the French rationalists. These ideas were imported to England by Samuel Taylor Coleridge and, in particular, by George Eliot's translation of Strauss's *The Life of Jesus* (1846) and Feuerbach's *The Essence of Christianity* (1854).

Higher criticism understands the New Testament texts within a historical context: that is, that they are not adamantine, but writings that express what is handed down. The truth lies in the historical context. In the twenty-first century, "historical criticism" is the more commonly used term for higher criticism. Where historical investigation was unavailable, historical criticism rested on philosophical and theological interpretation. Some scholars, such as Rudolf Bultmann, have used higher criticism of the Bible to "demythologize" it.

148. Kanamori, "The Testimony of Kanamori (刊南慕利保罗的见证)," *True Light* 真光 26, no. 6 (1927): 12.

149. Kanamori, 13.

150. Zhang, "Comments on the Theological," 13.

yougu (下喬木入幽谷).¹⁵¹ Therefore, they sought peace of mind by quoting Mencius:¹⁵² "The shining greatness which can transform the world is holiness and the holiness which goes beyond understanding is god."¹⁵³ This helped them to believe that Jesus was greater than the saints and was God beyond all understanding. They persuaded themselves of their legitimacy because "Saint" Confucius had not reached the highest level. Zhang said:

> If the people who shared the Gospel with us had interpreted Christianity in the same way as the experts of higher criticism, I would have taken Jesus as a Saint in the West who was on the same level with our Saint Confucius and I would have been qualified to be a Christian without having had to drive out my formerly preconceived ideas. Or I could have taken Christianity as one of the religions and I would not have had to be converted to Christianity.¹⁵⁴

Kant (1724–1804) could not have influenced Chinese philosophers and thinkers before 1840. Even at the very beginning of the twentieth century, few Chinese Christians knew the history of the Western ideas and social theories which shaped nineteenth-century thinking in the West. Western countries were still mistakenly called Christian countries and the culture and civilization of the West were still perceived as Christian. Therefore, the scientistic characteristics demonstrated by those scholars with traditional learning, as Zhang noticed, should not have resulted from Western influence.

This could serve as proof for the claims that China already had a rationalistic tradition which had developed independently and separately from the West¹⁵⁵ and that these two rationalistic traditions actually led to similar at-

---

151. Legge, *Works of Mencius*, 2: 255.
152. Zhang, "Comments on the Theological," 13.
153. 大而化之之谓圣, 圣而不可知之谓神 《孟子. 尽心下》 (Part II of the Chapter *jinxin xia* in *The Mencius*).
154. Zhang, "Comments on the Theological," 13.
155. Joseph Needham and Ling Wang explore the intellectual history of Chinese scientific development covering topics such as the *yin-yang* and five-elements theories, astrology and geomancy, among others. *Science & Civilisation in China, Volume II (2): History of Scientific Thought*, 1st ed. (New York: Cambridge University Press, 1956); Wang also notices that Chinese and Western scientific thought are inter-responsive, though they developed separately. Miaoyang Wang, "An Exploration into the Responsiveness between Chinese and the Western Scientific Thoughts (中西科学思想的相应性初探)," *Quarterly Journal of the Shanghai Academy of Social*

titudes, at least towards the Christian message. Zhang felt Christianity would become either unnecessary or degraded if it was bounded by reason or the pursuit of science.

Western terms like "liberal theology," "higher criticism," and "empiricism" may have sounded very new and frightening to Zhang at the outset, but once he learned their meanings, he did not feel impressed at all.

> For the experts of higher criticism, this method might be counted as their new insight. However, from my personal experience, I felt they were turning back the clock. From my current shallow understanding of Christianity, I felt higher criticism was something I had experienced thirty-six years before. On the stage of higher criticism, I could not really understand who Christ was. Now I had known Christ and I felt I had made a step forward. Maybe I was in a superstition, but I had obtained in my spirit a complete knowledge of the truth and a boundless happiness. If I moved back to my former stage, I would feel very dull or even meaningless. My enthusiasm in preaching through writing would also be reduced or even wiped away.[156]

Zhang, as a scholar trained in Chinese traditional learning, also inherited a scientific spirit. In fact, he created a hierarchy between the stage of reason and the stage of going beyond reason. At the stage of reason, Christ was no different from Confucius and people did not have to become Christians. This was a lower stage. Only at the stage of going beyond reason could people really know who Christ was and feel the necessity of converting to Christianity. This was a higher stage, but it was ridiculed as superstition. Since Zhang had experienced both stages and had tasted the benefits of the higher stage, even

---

Sciences 上海社会科学院学术季刊, no. 2 (1992): 71–79; Zarrow suspects that the traditional Chinese conception of a non-anthropomorphic but coherent cosmos clears the way for Chinese acceptance of scientism. Peter Gue Zarrow, *Anarchism and Chinese Political Culture*, Studies of the East Asian Institute (New York: Columbia University Press, 1990), 250; Li thinks China has a long tradition of pragmatic rationalism which paved the way for the popularity of scientism. Li Li, *Scientism in China* 科学主义在中国 (Beijing 北京: People's Publishing House 人民出版社, 2012), 66; When Jian said that the supernatural aspects of Christianity were not for China because the Chinese valued moral principles and pragmatic considerations, he may have meant the rationalistic tradition in China. Jian, "Ethnic Church," 37–39.

156. Zhang, "Comments on the Theological," 14.

if he incurred scorn, he did not want to revert to a life against his current knowledge, a life without passion and meaning.

Here, Zhang revealed how he reconciled his identity as a Christian and his identity as a scientific Chinese. As required by scientism, every aspect of one's life should be inspected by the empirical evidence and reason, but his Christian identity could not meet the requirements in a sufficiently convincing way. These were the conflicting dimensions in his identity. Therefore, he and other Christians, under the magnifier of scientism, were imaged as superstitious, uneducated, and valueless people to China. Externally, Zhang and other Christians' identity as scientific Chinese were denied. Facing others' denial of his self-sameness and continuity in his love of science and his pursuit of being scientific, Zhang maintained his own perception of self being scientific by establishing his Christian faith [going beyond reason] as a higher-order stage to which reason is expected to ascend. By the means which Yampolsky, Amiot, and de la Sablonnière view as integration,[157] Zhang reconciled and united the conflicting aspects. Subjectively, he was sure of his identity as a scientific Chinese, owing to his Confucian understanding as a mediator and his Christian identity as a superordinate. His Christian identity provided him with meaning of life and energy.

In spite of his criticism of liberal theology, Zhang also acknowledged its positive sides. He thought Christ did not want Christians to be isolated from the world. The modernists insisted on uniting with the world, which could be a biblical balance to monk-like Christians. However, as for the fundamental faith which was beyond understanding, Chinese Christians should follow the meaning in the saying of Mencius quoted above by Zhang. Only by this could Chinese Christians be counted as resting in the highest excellence (止于至善).[158]

Concerning the connection between liberal theology, its impact on the Chinese church, and the requirements of scientism, Starr comments:

> The church's strength lay in the proclamation of a variant worldview and in the fortitude demonstrated by its stubborn and unreasonable submission to this alternative ideology – a faith

---

157. Yampolsky, Amiot, and de la Sablonnière, "Multicultural Identity Integration Scale," 168–69.

158. Legge, *Chinese Classics*, 1, 356.

that undermines the proclamation of rational ideology by not acceding to its [atheistic] methodological premise. The "reasonable" faith of liberal Protestants did not offer the opportunity for martyrdom in quite the same way, and their subsequent theologies have yet to deal fully with this period.[159]

Zhang might have liked to read this connection very much because he was ready to die as a martyr and he also critiqued liberal theology for its compromise with scientism.

5.3 Zhang's Dealing with the Early Chapters of Genesis in Response to Scientism

Gerald Rau lays out six different models of treating four major aspects of origins and shows how they make different logical inferences, leading to different interpretations of the same evidence, based on different philosophical presuppositions that are outside the realm of science.[160] Thus, their adherents must take on faith. The six models range from naturalistic evolution (NE) to young-earth creation (YEC) and fit along a continuous spectrum. Each model is described by its distinctive features including basic propositions and underlying philosophical position. Finally, Rau points out that the different understandings of science have resulted in much of the conflict regarding these issues and that the origins debate will continue as long as people hold different worldviews.

Rau compared the six models' different treatments of the first chapters of Genesis.[161] For example, YEC and NE are polar opposites, the former claiming that the Bible overrules scientific evidence, the latter that scientific evidence disproves the Bible.[162] This is helpful in understanding the controversies faced by Zhang and his contemporaries over dealing with the same chapters.

Another finding of Rau is relevant, namely that there is a war going on, not between science and religion but about what science is or whose definition

---

159. Starr, *Chinese Theology*, 184.
160. Gerald Rau, *Mapping the Origins Debate: Six Models of the Beginning of Everything* (Downers Grove, IL: InterVarsity Press, 2012).
161. Rau, *Mapping the Origins Debate*, 206–7.
162. Rau, 51.

counts.[163] Among different definitions of science which rest on different philosophical foundations,[164] one version of science that claims science as the only valid way of knowing and denies other ways of knowing reflects an attitude known as scientism.[165] Rau's finding has confirmed one point of view of this research: the conflict was not between Christianity and science but between Christianity and science in the version of scientism.

In the Chinese context, the dominant standards of being scientific were provided by the version of scientism which labelled everything as unreal or fictional if the requirements of empirical evidence and the logic of reason could not be met. On the opposite side, the Bible requires faith. The nature of the conflicts between the fundamentalists and the people of liberal theology was which parts of the Bible were real or scientific in accordance with the standards defined by scientism. When there was no other definition of science provided as a counter, unsurprisingly, a person might consciously or unconsciously adopt the sole version of being "scientific" to examine the Bible, even with a purpose of protecting Christianity from looking "unscientific," "superstitious," and "valueless" to China.

In this context, Zhang himself was opposed to evolutionism and scientism, but he was unconsciously forced to answer the challenge of scientism in terms of the "scientific" standards it set, whether from the West or the Chinese tradition. This phenomenon of "being unconsciously forced" was mostly revealed in his dealing with the early chapters of Genesis. Before attention is given to his dealing with these early chapters, I will first show that science was more than a tool of evangelization and apology for Zhang, that he did aim to be scientific, and that he sometimes even used it as a standard of value.

5.3.1 Zhang's Pursuit of Being Scientific

Zhang liked to study science. Once he experimentally sprayed water in the sunlight to see if the rainbow was created by the reflection of sunshine. Likewise, he aimed to be accurate and scientific. Readers might still remember how he deliberately violated the principle of geomancy to test its efficacy. In 1924, a Christian named Shenzhi (慎之) criticized the modern doctors of

---

163. Rau, 176, 189.
164. Rau, 180.
165. Rau, 176.

philosophy for attacking Christianity by their shallow knowledge. He thought they should learn from the magi (or wise men) whose knowledge of astronomy enabled them to locate Jesus and worship him. Zhang reminded Shenzhi that the magi's knowledge might not be astronomy although Shenzhi's criticism was valid.[166] This shows that Zhang's enthusiasm for Christianity did not blind him to precision in scholarship.

5.3.2 Science Is Used as a Value in Debate

Huang Mingheng, a preacher in the Shantou Anliu Liyujiang Church, asked Zhang how to convert a Buddhist who believed in the superiority of Buddhist wisdom over Christianity. Zhang's reply questioned what contribution Buddhism made to the advancement of modern science.[167] He was surprised that the *Śūraṅgama Sūtra* (a scripture of Mahāyāna Buddhism, 楞严经) still puzzled over where the fire came from when a mirror under the sun caused a fire. In Zhang's challenge, he adopted the conduciveness to science as a value standard. Of course, the adoption of such a value standard might be only Zhang's technique for a public debate when he sensed the importance of such a standard to the public.

On another occasion, after using the new development in knowledge by telescope and microscope to prove intelligent design by the Creator, Zhang criticized Zhang Taiyan[168] for his ignorance of scientific developments.[169]

However, apart from being scientific, Zhang also showed the signs of being unconsciously influenced by "scientism," which will be discussed below.

5.3.3 The Significance of Literal Interpretation to Zhang and His Shift

The controversy over the early chapters of Genesis is still going on today, just as in China one hundred years ago. Here, the author will quote two questions from a long list so that the readers may understand more clearly the accusations faced by Zhang against the accuracy of Genesis in 1920. The questions

---

166. Shenzhi, "The Example of Magi from the East (可师法的东方博士)," *True Light* 真光 23, no. 2 (1924): 26.

167. Zhang, "Question about Christianity," 80.

168. Zhang Taiyan was a prominent scholar, thinker, revolutionary, and promoter of Yogacara Buddhism.

169. Zhang, "Refuting a Plagiarism," 262–63.

are from Mo He (摩诃) in the Shantou area who had claimed that Christianity was a superstition by repeating Zhang Taiyan's argument.[170] He questioned:

> In the beginning God created the heavens and the earth. Now the earth was formless and empty, darkness was over the surface of the deep, and the Spirit of God was hovering over the waters. Was the water right on the earth's crust? If so, the earth was not created by God; if the crust was created by water, then the light was not created on the first day. Moreover, light comes from the sun. If there was light before the sun, what is the purpose of creating the sun? If the sun was created for sending heat rather than light to facilitate growth, then, when the plants were created on the third day, there was no need of heat anymore. . . . Genesis also says that God created the sun, the moon, and the stars on the fourth day. The land is a part of the earth whose size and weight are very small in the universe. It still took a few days to finish the procedure of creating light, air, plants, animals, and human beings. Nonetheless, billions of stars are in the universe. Why was it more difficult to create a small earth than billions of stars? Therefore, the record of creation causes your religion [Christianity] to go bankrupt.[171]

A typical feature of anti-Christian people's questions was to challenge the truthfulness of the record in its literal sense. One significant characteristic of Zhang's interpretation of the Bible was his consistent inclination to a literal line. Examples of this can be easily found. For instance, when questioned about how literally a snake could speak, Zhang quoted a story of a stone speaking from *Zuo Zhuan* to prove its literal meaning rather than giving an allegorical explanation;[172] when asked about the literal meaning of the soul and spirit, he referred to the Chinese traditional belief about *gui* or "ghosts (鬼)" to prove they really exist;[173] he tried to prove the Israelites crossing the Red Sea according to its literal meaning;[174] he attempted to prove the literal

---

170. Zhang, 225.
171. Zhang, 232.
172. Zhang, "Three Questions about Genesis," 76.
173. Zhang, "Answers to Three Questions," 80.
174. Zhang, "Those Bible Stories," 71–72.

reality of the virgin birth.[175] However, facing the early chapters of Genesis, he demonstrated a shift in his interpretation – namely, from literal to nonliteral[176] and concordist to nonconcordist.[177]

To answer Mo He, Zhang listed two references in his counterargument.[178] The first was Bishop Rev. Francis Lushington Norris of the Anglican Church in Peking.[179] According to Bishop Norris,

> Most of Genesis was oral legend among the Hebrews. The inspiration[180] from God only accounts for a small part of the book. When we read the book, we should carefully differentiate between the oral legend and God's inspiration. Oral legend may contain errors, but God's inspiration must be correct. There are two inspirations from God in the book: God created all things and all creations were good in God's sight. Hence, they are accurate, real, and mysterious. Other sayings are not God's inspiration but oral legend so that they are not liable, for instance, the creation of heaven, earth, the sun, and the moon within six days and the time order and sequence of creation.[181]

The second reference was *Aids to the Understanding of the Bible*[182] which held that the contents of Genesis had already existed before Moses collected and edited them. Then Zhang said:

---

175. Zhang, "Questions from Mr. Zeng Guren," 62.
176. In this research, for the sake of convenience, "nonliteral" and "allegorical" are exchangeable, though "nonliteral" covers a more extensive range than "allegorical."
177. This research refers to Rau for the definitions of the two words. Concordist – A framework for biblical interpretation based on God revealing the order of events of creation in the book of Genesis. Nonconcordist – A framework for biblical interpretation based on Genesis not revealing the order of events of creation, but only God as Creator. Rau, *Mapping the Origins Debate*, 210, 217.
178. Zhang, "Refuting a Plagiarism," 233.
179. Bishop Rev. Francis Lushington Norris (鄂方智, 1864–1945) received education at Winchester College and Trinity College of Cambridge University. He was the first president of Chong De School in Peking (崇德学堂).
180. Inspiration is translated into *qishi* (启示) in Chinese. In the Chinese context, God's inspiration means being real, authentic, and accurate, as seen in the quotation.
181. Zhang, "Refuting a Plagiarism," 233.
182. *Aids to the Understanding of the Bible* (二约释义丛书) was written by various authors. Its first edition was published in Shanghai by the Religious Tract Society in 1882 (Shanghai: Lundun Sheng Shu Hui Yin 伦敦圣书会印 = Religious Tract Society). Its fifth edition was published in 1911. It was edited by Alexander Williamson (韦廉臣) and revised

Since the respected predecessors in the Church had already reached the conclusion that the time order and sequence of creation are unreliable oral legend, it was not the business of outsiders to point the finger. Since this book is just a summary of other books written previously, rather than purely words of God's inspiration through Moses, the precise and appropriate principles of religion [Christianity] are not in this book. The most important sayings, as quoted above, are only "God created all things and all creations were good in God's sight." This point has been universally recognized by the religion [Christianity] advocates equipped with the knowledge of science and this point is the feature of Genesis which is worthy of spreading.[183]

This time, Zhang did not insist on his literal interpretation of the record of creation for two reasons: (1) the experts on the Bible in the church denied the literal reliability of a large part and took a nonconcordist position; and (2) a nonliteral explanation would avoid the charges of being illogical and unscientific. Readers can sense Zhang's surprise and deep disappointment. His former strong faith in the accuracy of the Bible could be shaken and his commitment to the literal interpretation of the Bible could also become unsteady.

He did not argue against or deny those predecessors' opinions, which showed his respect for Christian experts and their interpretations and his lack of confidence in his own expertise. Even so, he still refused to concede victory to the critics in that he excluded them as outsiders. Here Zhang's Christian identity, in the sense of belonging to a particular social group, became prominent. He was protecting his personal faith, or commitment to the faith, by referring to his commitment to the Christian group. In other words, his strong group identity was functioning as a protection of his personal identity.

However, he did not totally give in. He still tried to persist in his literal and concordist line. Following the two references, when he dealt with the criticism of the chronology in the creation of the cosmos, Zhang said that although there was a time order in Genesis, it must all have been created

---

by Donald MacGillivray (季理斐). Zhang probably referred to chapter 4: Special Introductions to the Books of O.T. Supplement (创世纪小引) in the 5th edition, 25–30.

183. Zhang, "Refuting a Plagiarism," 234.

within the same period.[184] He did not say categorically that the time order in the Bible was correct. Zhang's blurring might have been caused by the conflict between his wish for the time order to be correct and the view of the experts that it was not. In other words, he might have hesitated over the choice of concordist or nonconcordist position.

Very soon, he made a choice. One criticism was how plants could appear before the sun. Zhang said that if God could create the sun of light and heat, he could absolutely create light and heat without it. So even before the creation of the sun, light and heat were already created to give light and warmth to the plants. The anti-Christians accused the description in Genesis of being against reason. In order to maintain the consistency and correctness of the creation sequence and its literal meaning, Zhang made a leap of faith by saying that God can produce light and heat without the sun. He chose a literal and concordist position, though he had become aware of another option of nonliteral and nonconcordist. Zhang's persistence demonstrated that his choice of the biblical interpretation was not out of ignorance of another option, it revealed that, in his understanding, this line of interpretation could enable him to feel a stronger sense of belonging to God and Christ. Putting it differently, in his subjective feeling, he could have a stronger Christian identity.

This point will become clearer if his attitude towards the "Fundamentalist-Modernist Controversy" could be recalled. All the parts discarded by the liberal theology for being unscientific and illogical were taken by Zhang as literally true. This point can also be detected from his understanding of the snake speaking and the virgin birth, mentioned above. Concerning the literally unreliable oral legends, he viewed them as a devaluation of Genesis so that "the precise and appropriate principles of religion [Christianity] are not in this book." This point will be further revealed in his separate conversations with Liang Junqing and Guo Jichuan below.

Here it might be worth repeating a point of view in this research: One's sense of one's Christian identity can be understood as the subjective aspect of faith which may sometimes not be completely in concord with its external judgment. It is Jesus's judgment that counts.

---

184. Zhang, 234–35; Zhang did not specify if "the same period" meant the same day. However, he definitely meant "a very short time," for example, "a few days."

After this, he swung from concordist to nonconcordist when dealing with another criticism: How could God create millions and millions of stars within one single day (the fourth day) whereas it took him several days to complete his projects on the earth? Sensing that his literal line would not be accepted as "scientific and logical," he said:

> I would like to give up my theory of "light and heat without the sun" and to adopt the explanation of James Jackson.[185]

As an English-born missionary of the American Church Mission in China, James Jackson (翟雅各, 1851–1918) said that it was not the creation of the sun, moon, and stars that separated day from night. The sun, moon, and stars were already there but they were blocked by thick fog. As the fog dispersed, they could be seen and then day was separated from night. That meant the sun, moon, and stars were not created on the fourth day but had been created before, as the first verse said.[186] This theory was later repeated by Zhang.[187] Then he confessed:

> However, formerly this author did not have knowledge of science; therefore I could only deal with the major principles, but I could not handle the refined explanation of the principles. This is "inappropriate" to the outlook.[188]

Here, he believed that his lack of knowledge of science led to his literal understanding of creation, which was wrong according to Bishop Rev. Francis Lushington Norris. In his words, he realized that the records of six days were observations made by people from the perspective of the earth rather than heaven. If one could have viewed the process from heaven, one could have understood it better because there was no day and night in heaven. Therefore, the sun, moon, and stars had been created before the first day. Zhang repeated this theory and confession later.[189]

---

185. Zhang, "Refuting a Plagiarism," 235–36.
186. Genesis 1:1 – "In the beginning God created the heavens and the earth."
187. Zhang, "Another Three Questions," 87–88; Yijing Zhang, "The Attachment to 'Are the Records in the First Chapter of Genesis Really Not in Accordance with Science?' (附: 创世记第一章的记载果与科学不合吗?)," *True Light* 真光 24, no. 2 (1925): 21–22.
188. Zhang, "Refuting a Plagiarism," 236.
189. Yijing Zhang, "Three Questions about the Bible from Wang Tuoan (圣经疑问三种)," *True Light* 真光 23, no. 2 (1924): 86–87; Zhang, "Another Three Questions," 88.

Zhang's shift between approaches reflected the Chinese context. In the review on China's social and political context around the 1920s, it could be seen that the period 1911–20 was both a golden age for the development of Christianity in China and a time for the growth of scientism and nationalism which brought trials to Christianity in the 1920s. Especially after the Debate on Science and Metaphysics in 1923, most Chinese intellectuals rejected all things which were beyond or against reason and experience, such as myth, fairy tales, and Christian theism. If one item could not prove to be "scientific," it was in danger of being rejected as useless, false or superstitious. One task for this argument written by Zhang was to fight against the accusation of superstition to protect the Christian's positive outlook. Naturally, Zhang tried to come across as rational so that Christianity could avoid this superstitious tag. As said above, one's perception of the fact that others recognize one's self-sameness and continuity is one of the two observations on which one's sense of identity is based. Many Chinese Christians were attracted to the idea of being recognized as a scientific Chinese.

However, one's subjective feeling could not guarantee others' recognition of one's identity as a scientific Chinese. As Rau says, different definitions of science lead to different interpretations of the origins, so this definition has become a central battleground in the origins debate.[190] In the context of China where the science market had been monopolized by scientism, it was not surprising to see that most people living in the cities had consciously or subconsciously accepted reason and empirical evidence as the standards of truth. This was partially true of Zhang because he rated faith at a level higher than reason, a gesture of rejecting this version. Basically, people had accepted the fact that the scientistic version of science set limits of knowledge and reality. This could be viewed as "their being unconsciously forced" to meet the terms set by scientism.

Rau's definition of science may serve as another option, though too late for Zhang and his contemporaries: "The definition of science, like any definition, is a social construct, which changes over time. It is not based on empirical evidence, and therefore cannot be decided using the methods of science."[191]

---

190. Rau, *Mapping the Origins Debate*, 175, 180.
191. Rau, 175.

Thus, Zhang formerly believed in the total accuracy of Genesis, but under the increasing pressure of scientism, his faith in its accuracy was shaken, he admitted his former literal interpretations were errors caused by lack of scientific knowledge, and he accepted explanations against literal interpretation. And he was swinging between literal and concordist, and nonliteral and nonconcordist positions.

5.3.4 The Elements of Evidence and Reason in His Dealing with the Great Flood

When dealing with the early chapters of Genesis, Zhang shifted between interpretation approaches, but this shift lasted only for a short period. However, throughout his life he had a problem with the accuracy of the great flood for lack of evidence.

In 1913, after comparing three sources – Chinese history books, chronologies about the Bible written by Westerners, and the Bible itself – he concluded[192] that Noah's great flood was the flood in the time of the Emperor Yao (2377–2259 BC) and it did not kill all humankind. Otherwise, some errors must have happened to either Chinese historical records or Western chronologies. He concluded that Chinese historical records after the Emperor Yao must be right.

Zhang included[193] two Chinese history books written in the biographical style: *Records of the Historian* (史记) which started from the Yellow Emperor (黄帝, 2717–2599 BC in traditional saying) and *The Time before History as a Mirror* (通鑑外纪) which began with Pao Xi (庖牺, 2852–2738 BC in traditional saying). The chronologies written by Westerners were *The Book of Dates* (四裔编年表),[194] *Chinese and Western Chronology* (中西年表) in *History of Ancient and Modern Nations* (万国通史前编),[195] Chronology of

---

192. Zhang, "Brief History of People," 163.
193. Zhang, 148.
194. According to Prof. R. G. Tiedemann, the author was John Blair (? –1782), a British clergyman. In 1754 he published *The Chronology and History of the World, from the Creation to the Year of Christ 1753*. It was revised and enlarged by J. Willoughby Rosse and then published in Henry George Bohn's (博那, 1796–1884) "Scientific Library" in 1856. Its Chinese version was edited and translated by Young John Allen (林乐知, 1836–1907) and published in 1874. It covered the period between 2349 BC (少昊四十年) and 1862 (同治元年).
195. Its Chinese version was edited and translated by J. L. Rees (李思伦) and published in 1905 by the Christian Literature Society for China in Shanghai.

Emperors (历代帝王年表) in *An Abstract of Chinese General History* (中国纲鉴撮要),[196] *The Old Testament Chronology* (旧约年代表),[197] *The Chronology of Nations* (列国编年纪要),[198] and *Israel Chronology* (以色列人年表) in *A Brief Explanation of the Old Testament*[199] (旧约略释).[200]

After comparing them and referring to 1 Kings 6:1,[201] Zhang concluded that the great flood must have happened around 2500 BC.[202] To Zhang's puzzlement, in China, there was no record of the great flood since Pao Xi (庖牺) who lived around 2900 BC. Therefore, the great flood must have been the flood in the time of the Emperor Yao in which not all Chinese were killed. And naturally, the destruction of all life on earth by the great flood must be an exaggeration.

How could Zhang's conclusion be reconciled with the record in the Bible? Zhang referred to *The Encyclopaedia of the Bible* (圣经典林)[203] which stated that the word "world" in the Bible often meant only a few countries. Therefore, in Zhang's application, the destruction of the earth could also mean a destruction of part of the earth. To give more support to his argument, he used the rainbow as an example. To Zhang, rainbows must have existed before

---

196. It was written by Rev. Philip Wilson Pitcher (毕腓力) and published in 1904. Pitcher was an American missionary who served in Amoy between 1887 and 1916, and his book *In and about Amoy* was published in 1909.

197. It was authored by Joseph Edkins (艾约瑟, 1823–1905), a missionary from London Missionary Society (英国伦敦会). In his book, he started numbering the years from Exodus and did not keep a chronological record of Genesis. In its preface he quoted two Westerners' words: One, whose name in Chinese was Wu Shener (武什耳). According to R. G. Tiedemann, this was Bishop James Ussher, 1581–1656), who said the great flood occurred in 2848 BC, while another, Hei Lisi (黑利斯. According to Prof. Tiedemann, this was William Hales, 1747–1831) said it was 3154 BC.

198. It was written by Zou Tao (鄒弢, 1850–1931), a Chinese scholar, novelist, and supporter of reform. He said it was in 3308 BC. He also said that it was 3102 BC according to Indian history and around 2300 BC according to Jewish history. According to Prof. R. G. Tiedemann, he became a convert to Roman Catholicism in 1900.

199. It was authored by John Shaw Burdon (包尔腾, 1826–1907), a missionary from Church Missionary Society.

200. Zhang, "Brief History of People," 161–63.

201. 1 Kings 6:1 – "In the four hundred and eightieth year after the Israelites came out of Egypt, in the fourth year of Solomon's reign over Israel, in the month of Ziv, the second month, he began to build the temple of the LORD."

202. Zhang, "Brief History of People," 162.

203. The English name is a translation from its Chinese name. It was edited by John Marshall Willoughby Farnham (范约翰, 1829–1917), a missionary from the Presbyterian church in the United States (美北长老会).

the great flood because they are caused by the reflection of sunshine in the water drops in the air. Although the Bible said it was set by God as a sign after the great flood, Zhang could not believe this to be true. Thus, he interpreted it as just a reassurance given by God. It was part of the exaggeration of the destruction of the earth. Zhang extended his conclusion by saying that the Chinese were not the descendants of Noah but the descendants of Cain who had moved towards the east.

As for the possible challenge from other Christians that he was passing judgment on the Bible, Zhang thought this was exactly the essence of interpreting the Bible.[204] He used Rev. Philip Wilson Pitcher (比腓力, 1856–1915) and Joseph Edkins (艾约瑟, 1823–1905) as examples. In his view, these famous pastors also doubted the accuracy of the dates recorded in the Bible. As a result, they either advanced the date of Noah's great flood by one thousand years, as seen in the preface to *The Old Testament Chronology* (旧约年代表序), or acquiesced in saying that the great flood did not kill the Chinese: a note in the Chronology of Emperors (历代帝王年表) said that the tenth year of the Yao Emperor was the time of the great flood and the ninth year of Yao was the time of the tower of Babel. Zhang argued that since so many Christians were happy to take such books as their textbooks for Bible study, there was no call to doubt his conclusion. However, he humbly expected to be corrected. Zhang repeated his view on the great flood later in 1923,[205] 1924,[206] and 1927 when he included his research of the great flood in *A Quarter of a Century of True Light, Selected*. In 1923, he avoided answering the question on whether the rainbow was created after the flood.[207]

What did Zhang mean by saying that his interpretation was the exact essence of Bible interpretation? He said that one should state one's opinions frankly when interpreting the Bible.[208] It would not be truthful to misinterpret the Bible intentionally in order to defend it. Many people made this kind of mistake. Zhang offered three examples. One concerned Abraham and Sarah's laughing on hearing from God that Sarah would give birth to a son in a year,

---

204. Zhang, "Brief History of People," 163.
205. Zhang, "Three Questions from Zhi," 66.
206. Zhang, "Questioning Mr. Zhang Yijing's," 33–34.
207. Zhang, "Three Questions from Zhi," 66.
208. Zhang, "Brief History of People," 175.

while the other two concerned Abraham's age and reproductive capability and Sarah's age and beauty.

Many people claimed that Abraham laughed with happiness while Sarah laughed in disbelief when they heard God's promise of a son. Zhang insisted that both of them laughed in disbelief because Abraham's faith had not reached its peak, as demonstrated in his calling Sarah his sister.[209] In Zhang's view, some people did not want to interpret it in this way lest it damage Abraham's reputation as a father of faith.

For the other two examples, Zhang thought many interpretations were self-contradictory and he offered his own. Abraham's time was not too far away from the time when people could give birth at the age of five hundred, four hundred, three hundred or two hundred. In Abraham and Sarah's time, it was not rare for people of one hundred years old to give birth to children. Therefore, when God told them that Sarah would give birth to a son, they laughed out of disbelief not because they were too old but because they had expected Sarah to remain infertile all her life. This interpretation could satisfy the questions of why Abraham could have six more sons after marrying Keturah at the age of 140 or 150 and why Sarah was abducted at the age of 90. She was like a woman of 20 or 30 in terms of modern life expectancy. Zhang could not believe that a woman as old as 90 should be beautiful enough to be abducted and that Abraham's reproductivity, which was problematic at the age of 100, should become rejuvenated around the age of 140 or 150. Thus, his interpretation moved away from the literal statement in the Bible that Abraham and Sarah were well advanced in years and Sarah was past the age of childbearing.[210]

I will sidestep the argument about the soundness of Zhang's logic by treating his interpretations on his own terms. There are a few notable points in his interpretation. First, Zhang was in search of evidence, as revealed in his comparing the Chinese and the Western chronologies. This is his attempt to be scientific or rational. Second, when his scientific evidence was in conflict with the literal meaning of the Bible, he shifted his literal interpretation of the Bible to a nonliteral way so that the understanding could maintain a

---

209. Zhang, 175–76.

210. Genesis 18:11 – "Abraham and Sarah were already very old, and Sarah was past the age of childbearing; Genesis 23:1 – "Sarah lived to be a hundred and twenty-seven years old."

logical consistency. This could be seen from his conclusions about the flood, the rainbow, and Sarah's age. It was very rare for Zhang to submit his Bible reading to his reason, which mostly took place in his dealing with the early chapters of Genesis. Third, Zhang dared to be truthful. For example, he took Abraham's laughter as an expression of disbelief and he was not afraid of being charged with passing judgment on Abraham. Fourth, Zhang still insisted on his faith in the accuracy of the other records in the Bible, such as those concerning longevity and fertility.

It is interesting and thought-provoking to see Zhang's shift in his interpreting lines as a response to his context monopolized by scientism. If in order to keep consistency, Zhang had extended the nonliteral approach to other parts of the Bible, some contents of his Christian identity around 1920 could have been called into question to some degree, such as: the virgin birth, the resurrection, life after death, and the Bible as the standard for belief and action, etc. If so, some contents of his Christian identity might have had to face a change to some degree, which would definitely have influenced his sense of belonging to God and Christ because the familiar images of them had changed.

Since Zhang believed in the positive relationship between the acceptance of the literal meaning of the Bible and a strong Christian identity, and since his Christian identity had developed to such a degree that his work and life would become dull and meaningless, the hypothesis above did not occur. It seems he used two ways to manage the two inconsistencies in his understanding, namely the two early chapters of Genesis and the great flood.

For the two early chapters, he gradually resumed his literal understanding after one occurrence by the end of 1924. As for the great flood, he seems to put it into an isolated compartment to protect his main stream. This means is called compartmentalization by Yampolsky, Amiot, and de la Sablonnière.[211] However, in 1924, he honestly admitted that he was aware of the priority he had given to his reason on the issue of the great flood,[212] and in 1929 he

---

211. Yampolsky, Amiot, and de la Sablonnière, "Multicultural Identity Integration Scale," 168–69.
212. Zhang, "Questioning Mr. Zhang Yijing's," 34.

humbly invited criticism of this understanding.²¹³ His ways of managing these two inconsistencies will be elaborated in the next section.

5.4 Exploring Zhang's Shift between Biblical Interpretation Lines

Zhang's shift of position is complicated to analyze. In certain parts of the Bible, he chose to meet the requirements of reason and evidence, as required by scientism rooted in both the West and China. As noted in the last section, Zhang's view on the great flood remained unchanged at least between 1913 and 1927. In most parts of the Bible, he followed the line of concordist and literal interpretation. Even among the parts where he had formerly taken a nonliteral and nonconcordist approach, his attitude changed later. Sometimes in a single piece of writing, the two approaches are both in evidence. Especially in 1924, these two approaches alternated among the issues of *True Light*. Therefore, the study on the priority between Zhang's two approaches will be first carried out over his changes.

5.4.1 The Development of Zhang's Nonliteral and Nonconcordist Position

5.4.1.1 Changes

Zhang's nonliteral and nonconcordist position was dynamic rather than static. Before 1913, when this approach was demonstrated in his dealing with the great flood, it was not evidently significant. After 1913, it grew more salient until the end of 1924, a period which was responsive to the development of scientism in China. At the end of 1924, it went into a decline.

In 1913, concerning the truthfulness of the literal meaning of Genesis and creation, Zhang said:

> The book [Genesis] was not all written by Moses. There were some books in ancient times existing previously but related to Exodus. Moses selected and edited them chronologically and placed them before Exodus. The description of creation sounds crazy and unacceptable to the scholars. However, by a detailed

---

213. Zhang, "Questions from Miss Lin," 72.

research of its description, Genesis is a solely accurate history book of ancient times.[214]

From the beginning of the 1920s, he began to express publicly his doubts about Genesis. Zhang said that he did not take the first two chapters of Genesis literally, nor did he base his faith on it.[215] In the second issue of 1924, there was a change in Zhang's attitude towards God's will for Adam and Eve. However, this time he shifted from allegorical and nonconcordist postion to literal and concordist position.

Liang Junqing, a church member of Basel Mission (巴色会) and a student of Tong De Medical University in Shanghai (同德医科大学), criticized Zhang for his superstitious belief in the Old Testament.[216] According to Liang, the Old Testament was only an oral record from a time when there was no written word, so it was not believable. For example, God could not have forbidden Adam and Eve to eat the fruit of the tree because his kindness would not allow him to inflict eternal punishment on all human beings as a result of one mistake. Liang did not believe that doubts about the Old Testament would do any harm to the holiness of Christianity. He said that Zhang's literal understanding had not only led himself to fall into such a superstitious belief in all the records in the Holy Book, but had also resulted in blind interpretations. Thus, Zhang's answers would mislead people into a credulous state. He charged Zhang's literal interpretation with "indulging himself in worshipping (*chongbai* 崇拜) of everything in the Bible."[217] In Liang's view, the right way to understand a particular thing was to take the objective position as a detached observer instead of a subjective position as a receiver.

In his response, Zhang insisted that God was wholly kind and omniscient, that he gave human beings free will, and that he did not create evil.[218] Concerning the Old Testament, Zhang thought that Liang ignored his words at the beginning of his answer to the questions from Mr. Huang and Mr. Liao which said:

---

214. Zhang, "Brief History of People," 148.
215. Zhang, "Questions from Huang Rongzeng," 70; Zhang, "Questioning Mr. Zhang Yijing's," 31–32.
216. Junqing Liang 梁俊青, "Questioning Mr. Zhang Yijing's Answers to Mr. Huang and Mr. Liao (读亦镜先生答黄廖二君的疑问的质疑)," *True Light* 真光 23, no. 2 (1924): 27–28.
217. Zhang, "Questioning Mr. Zhang Yijing's," 28.
218. Zhang, 29.

> These four questions reflect the struggles over the first two chapters in Genesis. Consequently, they questioned God's omniscience and omnipotence. I myself would not take these records as the basis of my faith. Since they have been brought up, I have to discuss them.[219]

After denying that he literally believed in the first two chapters of Genesis, he continued:

> In fact, I had once been as unbelieving as Mr. Liang towards God's command to Adam and Eve. However, after reading the same question from so many people, I made a deep study on it and I found it believable. Currently, I take them as the true facts and there is nothing to be doubted. I have explained my reasons in my answers to the second question from Mr. Huang and Mr. Liao by quoting Mencius.[220]

As he said, he used to take the same allegorical line to understand this command; however, he decided to accept its literal meaning. Just as he quoted *Zuo Zhuan* to prove the literal meaning of a snake speaking, he resumed his faith in the literal meaning of this command by referring to Mencius. Though Zhang changed his attitude towards God's command to Adam and Eve, he still took the other parts in the first two chapters as literally untrue. By saying that Zhang misled people into a credulous state, Liang meant that he misled people into believing in the literal meaning. In fact, developing faith in the literal meaning of the whole Bible was what Zhang wished for. He said:

> Liang took it as my sin to lead people into a believing state, but that is what I have been praying for. I just fear I am not able to achieve it.[221]

As for taking an objective position as an observer, Zhang said that was the position he used to take when dealing with the Bible.[222] Now that he had moved from detached observer position to receiver, it was impossible for him to move back. At the end of his article, he once again explicitly expressed his

---

219. Zhang, 31.
220. Zhang, 31–32.
221. Zhang, 32.
222. Zhang, 33.

conviction that the literal meaning of the great flood went against reason, so that he doubted its truthfulness. He said:

> If the author of Genesis had known that many people and animals around the world survived the Great Flood, he would have written Genesis in a different way. By saying so, I do not mean the Bible had shortcomings. Just as you Mr. Liang has ridiculed, I worship (*chongbai* 崇拜) the Bible. However, sometimes I would refer to my reason (*lixing* 理性) in analysis whenever necessary. If I have to follow the [literal] way as Mr. Liang charges me with, then Mr. Liang seems to respect the Bible more than I do.[223]

We saw earlier that Zhang's readers had noticed Zhang consistently interpreting the Bible in a literal way and accused him of "indulging himself in worshipping of everything in the Bible." However, two places challenged the consistency of Zhang's approach: the early chapters of Genesis and the great flood. He himself was explicitly aware of the reason: going against his reason in lacking evidence.

Zhang used to take the literal position towards the first two chapters before 1913, he changed to the allegorical or nonliteral approach around the early 1920s, and he showed the first sign of resuming the literal position in 1924. In the year 1924, he more frequently made shifts between the two interpreting lines.

5.4.1.2 Alternations

Zhang said he did not take the first two chapters of Genesis literally and did not base his faith on it.[224] Meanwhile, in the same text, he expressed his confidence in the reality of heaven, eternal life, and resurrection.[225]

In the first half of the second issue of 1924, when Zhang criticized the anti-Christian authors for their overconfidence in science, he said:

> [The authors of those books] overestimate (*pianzhong* 偏重) the knowledge of science. As a result, their thoughts are limited by

---

223. Zhang, 34.
224. Zhang, "Questions from Huang Rongzeng," 70.
225. Zhang, 72–73.

the physical world and then blindly denounce the revelation of God who is beyond logic and above reason.[226]

In the second half of the same issue, Zhang tended to demystify the records in the Bible. On one occasion, he was asked about the authenticity of "the sun stood still, and the moon stopped" in Joshua 10:13. Zhang believed that God could do this. Nevertheless, since he found no comparable record in China's history, he interpreted it as "God made Israel so self-sufficient and so successful in avenging itself on its enemies that the result made the people feel that two days must have passed."[227] He did not follow the literal line of interpretation.

5.4.1.3 Increasing Pressure of Scientism in the Context

In 1924, Yun Daiying (introduced in chapter 2) accused Christianity of not wanting to see the popularity of Darwin's evolutionism and of hindering the evolution of humankind. Zhang insisted that God created the world and that no contradiction existed between Christianity and science.[228] For example, Darwin believed that there was a designer behind the universe and Alfred Russel Wallace was a believer in God. He replied: "This charge may be applicable to the Roman Catholic Church or a small number of Christians of the older generation who have stopped learning. The Christian scholars often took Darwin as help and some even referred to him in their interpretation of the Bible."[229] Then Zhang referred to his friend Xie Changho[230] who, in his *Christianity and Science*, called Darwin an honest man and not an enemy of Christianity. So Zhang said there were no grounds to accuse Christianity of hindering the progress of the human race by opposing evolutionism.[231]

---

226. Zhang, "Fourth Continuation of Recording," 36.
227. Zhang, "Another Three Questions," 89.
228. Zhang, "Third Comments on Mr. Daiying's," 56.
229. Zhang, 56.
230. Xie (谢邑候 or 谢洪赉, 1873–1916) was a famous Chinese Christian writer, translator, and professor. His father was a Presbyterian pastor. He studied at the Buffington Institute (博习书院) which became Soochow University (东吴大学) and was founded by the Methodist Episcopal Church, South (美南监理会). Alvin P. Parker (潘慎文), the head of the Institute, thought highly of Xie and invited him to help him with many translations. Xie later worked as an editor of the Commercial Press and Committee member of the YMCA in Shanghai.
231. Zhang, "Third Comments on Mr. Daiying's," 57.

This debate has shown that, in China, the theory of evolution amounted to science and denial of it was an admission of going against reason. It had been changed from a theory to a supreme truth and had been extended from the biological world into human society. Such a public mindset would be the main reason for Zhang's friendly gesture to Darwin and evolutionism. Another possible reason was that Zhang had come round to evolutionism, however briefly. But this seems unlikely, considering that as early as 1906 he had expressed his anger with evolutionism and called it a cult,[232] and in 1922 he had denied Darwin's theory in his polemic against the Anti-Christian Movement,[233] and in 1929 he had again expressed his objections to the idea of a monkey evolving into a human being.[234] If he did accept evolutionism, it must have been very temporary. It is more likely that his provisional compliance was his strategy as an apologist.

Thus, in such a context, what prompted him to try to go against this scientistic trend to resume the literal and concordist position?

5.4.1.4 The Reason for Zhang's Resuming the Literal and Concordist Position

In the eleventh issue of 1924, Zhang realized that the pursuit of reason and scientific knowledge existed in his own mind and lamented that they had hindered him from totally believing in God. In 1924, a Christian named Bao Rixin invited Zhang to refute *Awakening* (觉悟), an anti-Christian newspaper. Bao worried that Christians with weak faith might be confused and misled by *Awakening*.

Zhang delayed his response because the materials used by *Awakening* were those which he had been repeatedly refuting during the past ten years and because he felt Chinese and Western Christians should be aware of the criticisms and value the forthright admonitions of anti-Christians as an aid to self-correction. According to Zhang,[235] Christians with weak faith would be lost anyway in other temptations like money, glory, and lust if not in confusion

---

232. Zhang, "On 'Our Father,'" 5.
233. Zhang, "Comments on the Telegram," 29.
234. Yijing Zhang, "The Question of Old and New (旧新问题)," *True Light* 真光 28, no. 4 (1929): 97.
235. Zhang, "Awakening," 81.

caused by the Anti-Christian Movement. So arguing with anti-Christian friends was less urgent than fighting against other temptations.

In Zhang's view, the majority of Christians in China did not truly believe in the existence of spirit and soul and in the miracles in the Bible. To the anti-Christians' charge that the beliefs of Christians were superstitious, Zhang replied: "We just worry we are not superstitious enough about such things."[236] He deplored the situation that many Christians held back from believing such things because of their superficial rationality and their detached observer's position. They were not committed to being true hosts in the church, believing in their hearts, and communicating intimately with God. Therefore, it would be better to be attacked every day than not to be attacked at all. The attack could help to forge the faith and character of Christians. He was complaining that the majority of Christians did not believe in the Bible as they should for fear of being labelled as superstitious by anti-Christians with scientism as a convenient weapon at hand.

Zhang gave a woman preacher[237] as an example of faith. He described how she experienced God's healing of her loss of speech and sight and how she performed many miracles by faith afterwards. He praised her as a true and undeniable testimony to the existence of God and the miracles in the Bible. Zhang's own faith in God and the Bible increased after meeting her. He said that no one was qualified to be called superstitious unless their faith reached that woman preacher's level. What the church had to fear, he said, was not a lack of rich or intellectual members but a lack of people like that woman preacher whom the anti-Christians regarded as superstitious. He estimated that in the whole body of Chinese Christians, forty at the most had faith so deep and so sincere that they could be labelled superstitious. The rest was dispensable because, regardless of wealth, status, or intellect, the absence of such a faith made them not very different from unbelievers. So they would do well to make use of the attacks of the anti-Christians to fortify their own faith.

Zhang included himself as belonging to the majority. He subjectively felt he was not a true disciple of Christ and could not obey God wholeheartedly. He said:

---

236. Zhang, 81.

237. She was probably Aunty Zhang Si (张四婶) whose story was recorded by Zhang. "The Story of Aunty Zhang Si (记张四婶事)," *True Light* 24, no. 2 (1925): 63–68.

Just as The Analects says, "a troop is valued by its elite soldiers, not by its number." I have only met one elite soldier in my thirty years of being a Christian. Now I regret planting an amount of useless knowledge in my heart which has prevented me from being wholeheartedly obedient to God as a true disciple of Jesus. I feel ashamed of myself on seeing that elite soldier, whose faith is the real rock of the Church and could never be taken away by the anti-Christians. It was vain to win arguments by human talent and intelligence. I would do better to spend more intimate time with God in a private room.[238]

Why did he subjectively feel ashamed and regretful? He realized that he had not been as wholehearted a disciple of Jesus as the woman preacher was. As reviewed in chapter 1, one's perception of Christ's affirmation should have a paramount significance to one's sense of belonging to Christ. Zhang felt that his in-Christ identity was compromised. What was the cause? He owed it to "an amount of useless knowledge" which is "human talent and intelligence." What knowledge did he refer to?

In 1909, he noticed a link between knowledge and rejection of the Christian message. He said "the more knowledge they accumulated, the more opposed they became to the Christian message."[239] In 1910, he said specifically that it was a small amount of knowledge of science that puffed up one's arrogance to resist and deny God's reality.[240] In 1924, he thought that some authors depended on scientific knowledge so that their thoughts were limited by the physical world and then blindly denied the revelation of God who surpasses understanding.[241] In 1927, the link was repeated when he commented on the eastern root of scientism. He said "in China, after reading a few thread-bound books and acquiring a little traditional learning, people would criticize the ideas of creation."[242] In 1929, he repented that he read the Bible only occasionally and his relationship with God was less intimate than the time after his conversion because he spent his time reading many other

---

238. Zhang, "Awakening," 81.
239. Zhang, "Advancement of Civilization," 38.
240. Zhang, "Against a Speech," 24.
241. Zhang, "Fourth Continuation of Recording," 36.
242. Zhang, "Comments on the Theological," 13.

books, driven by his desire for knowledge.[243] However, he was not going to limit his desire for all knowledge; instead, he was going to expand it – for the knowledge the Holy Spirit directed him to.[244]

In addition to seeing his frequent causal link between knowledge and rejecting the correctness of the literal meaning of the Bible, when we connect his words "useless human knowledge" and "the knowledge the Holy Spirit directed him to" with his separating reason and faith into two levels, we may have a clearer understanding of what he meant by this word "knowledge" in this context.

It is safe to conclude that the knowledge he referred to could produce a "scientistic" attitude. He himself realized that he had been unconsciously brought to terms of scientism and subjectively felt that his relationship with God was less intimate and that he was not worthy of being a true disciple of Christ, which was a result of his own realization that he could not wholeheartedly obey God and Christ because his "scientific attitude" questioned the literal accuracy of meaning of some records in the Bible. (For instance, he explicitly confessed that his reason did not allow him to accept the account of the flood literally.)

In other words, his sense of belonging to Christ or his Christian identity was somehow compromised by his awareness of the fact that he rejected the literal meaning of some passages. Thus, whenever, he shifted his interpreting line from literal to nonliteral, he felt an inconsistency. As defined in this study, Christian identity is the awareness of the fact that there is a self-sameness and continuity in one's belonging to Christ and the perception of the fact that others recognize this. Hence, when he shifted away from his literal interpreting line, in his own understanding he was rejecting the literal truthfulness of some passages. Since, in his mind, loyalty to God and Christ meant accepting the Bible literally, logically, his sense of his commitment to God and Christ would be compromised whenever he moved away from his literal approach.

Therefore, he vowed to avoid that kind of knowledge and to embrace the knowledge the Holy Spirit directed him to so that he could believe in the words of the Bible in a way as "superstitious" as that of the woman preacher.

---

243. Zhang, "Bible Reading and Praying," 98.
244. Zhang, 98.

This was a typical demonstration of surrendering his will to God, which Poll and Smith would view as a spiritual identity development.[245] This new development was made on his further spiritual journey after he had achieved his Christian identity. He desired to be fully identified with Christ, a stage Christ wishes for.

Once again, the research should remind us that one's sense of one's Christian identity can be understood as the subjective aspect of faith which may sometimes not be completely in concord with its objective fact which was evaluated by Jesus Christ.

5.4.1.5 Aftermath

Meeting the woman preacher, who was probably Aunty Zhang Si, Zhang experienced a shock and his spirit was somewhat revived. He became conscious of the hindrance to his faith caused by his "scientific knowledge." Here we see an interesting turn: around 1920, he confessed that his former literal position was wrong due to his lack of scientific knowledge; however, by the end of 1924, he mourned over his "scientific knowledge" and decided to believe in a "superstitious" way so that he could be an undeniable witness to the Bible. This might be the reason why a mild decline was apparent in his adoption of a nonliteral and nonconcordist approach in the next three issues of *True Light*.

In the twelfth issue of 1924, Zhang quoted a story of a stone speaking from *Zuo Zhuan* to prove the literal meaning of snake speaking, the example seen above.[246] Nonetheless, he still held there must be some omissions in Genesis. He also said that he seldom referred to Genesis, but his reason now was that it was easy to sound like an ignorant old man from a remote village if one did not then provide a good exposition. Some passages in Genesis still seemed unreasonable and illogical to him, but these might be explained in a rational way if the omitted parts or a good parallel could be provided.

In the first issue of 1925, in response to Chen Qiulin's statement that one should oppose all religions when one realizes the value of science, Zhang explained his view on the possible unscientific records in the Bible.[247] He said that only when there were issues which scientific research proved to be

---

245. Poll and Smith, "Spiritual Self," 138.
246. Zhang, "Three Questions about Genesis," 76.
247. Zhang, "Commenting on Chen Qiulin's," 73.

unreasonable and for which there was no defensible explanation, should people oppose them. The reasonable or unknowable parts should not be opposed. Although Zhang did not totally deny the existence of errors in the Bible, he left a very small space for the possibility. For Zhang himself, the great flood appeared to be the only one.

In the second issue of 1925, a Christian named Guo Jichuan from the Anglican Church in Jingzhou (荆州) made a polite and indirect criticism of Zhang's allegorical and nonconcordist interpreting line.[248] Guo observed that "the anti-Christians attacked Christianity by science. Wu Zhihui was an example. This led to some Christian friends' loss of their faith. They did not believe the first two chapters were by the revelation of God, nor did they believe in the resurrection, Virgin Birth any longer. They wondered if the miracles were exaggerated by Jesus' disciples. This was caused by liberal theology and by the Anti-Christian Movement." Guo said he believed the entire Bible was the revelation of God. (Zhang used to say he did not take the first two chapters as literally real.)

Concerning the difference between the light created on the first day and the two lights created on the fourth day, Guo held that all three lights were the same. Because the earth was surrounded by thick fog at the very beginning, the light was invisible. It took a few million years or a few hundred thousand years for the fog to evaporate, and then the two lights became visible. This was similar to the view adopted by Zhang from James Jackson and Bishop Rev. Francis Lushington Norris of the Anglican Church in Peking in 1920.

Realizing that Guo included him in his criticism, Zhang made no direct comment on Guo. As a silent response, he attached his article written in 1920 in which he did not say that the gap between the first day and the fourth day was a few million or a few hundred thousand years, as Guo hinted.

We could not help asking the question: Why did he not tell Guo Jichuan that he did change his position from literal to nonliteral and insist that his nonliteral position was the correct one?

There are two factors to consider. First, Guo's criticism was that some Christians lost their faith in the first two chapters of Genesis and other miracles under the attack of science. Second, Zhang did give up his former faith in the literal meaning of the first two chapters and confessed that he

---

248. Guo, "Are the Records in the First?," 13.

was wrong because he lacked scientific knowledge. Therefore, Zhang knew Guo's criticism was valid. We may still remember how he lamented that some "useless knowledge" in him, leading to a scientistic attitude, had kept him from becoming a wholehearted witness to God and the Bible. Therefore, with a consciousness of the influence of "human scientific knowledge" on his interpreting position, very likely around the end of 1924 and the beginning of 1925, he was deliberately detaching himself from his nonliteral position and resuming his former faith in the literal meaning of the first two chapters. Consequently, he could not and would not argue that his nonliteral position was the correct one because he was giving it up. He did not argue directly with Guo but attached one article with the literal position, which showed his former position and his current position.

This also suggests that, in Zhang's mind, the literal and concordist interpretation was linked to a stronger Christian identity than a nonliteral and nonconcordist position.

Afterwards, there were no further signs of his criticism of Genesis. To answer Miss Lin in 1929, Zhang said, "All the Bible is the revelation of God. There is no authors' personal opinion. There is no error with the original version. When we feel something wrong with the Bible, usually there are four possible reasons: (1) an error happened at copying; (2) our knowledge is limited; (3) the people at the time could not understand a thing because of the limitation of knowledge, so the Bible had to express it this way; (4) some places focus on making explicit God's will, so other details were missed. Even so, not every seemingly incomprehensible record could be due to one of the four reasons. Everyone who is good at reading the Bible knows the principle."[249]

Concerning the great flood, Zhang still believed that either an error had occurred in Western and Chinese calendars or the great flood in Noah's time did not reach China. Nonetheless, he humbly invited criticism of his understanding of the great flood.[250]

To sum up, after 1924, Zhang became more inclined to literally believe the accuracy of Genesis except for the great flood. As to the issue of the great flood, he still subordinated his interpretation to his nonliteral and nonconcordist approach rather than to literal and concordist line. His adoption of

---

249. Zhang, "Questions from Miss Lin," 69.
250. Zhang, 72.

nonliteral and nonconcordist approach had decreased to some degree, but it never disappeared.

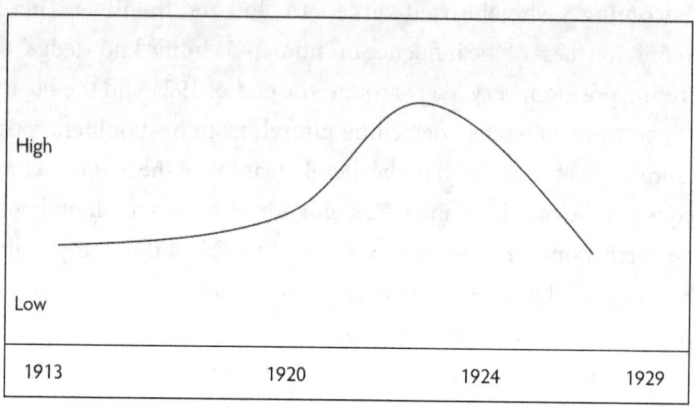

Figure 3: A Chart of the Development of Zhang's Nonliteral and Nonconcordist Position

5.4.2 Prioritizing between Zhang's Two Interpreting Approaches

From the discussion above, we have understood that Zhang saw a positive relationship between the literal interpretation line and his Christian identity. We also have delineated the waxing and waning of his nonliteral and non-concordist approach, but it is still not clear how Zhang prioritized the two interpreting approaches at different stages. This section will be devoted to it so that we can gain a general idea about his subjective feeling of his relationship with Christ.

5.4.2.1 Around 1913

Except for the early chapters of Genesis, Zhang's literal and concordist approach to the Bible was very consistent. In 1910, in his *Jesus and Confucius*, he insisted on the miracles of Christianity, including the virgin birth. In 1928, when he edited *A Quarter of a Century of True Light, Selected*, he included this article and said that, although the views in *Jesus and Confucius* were not accepted by new theologians, he loved and kept this text because they were in accordance with the Bible.[251] It is worth remembering that science had won the Debate on Science and Metaphysics in 1923 and become a part of Chinese culture. It must have taken courage for Zhang to say things counter to fashion and culture.

Concerning Jesus's miracles in the Bible, Zhang believed that these things really happened and that those miracles were necessary to prove that Jesus was God. One had to talk about miracles in preaching the gospel.[252]

In 1914, several Congressmen proposed that the practice of awarding posthumous titles be resumed because it was believed to be no different from the Western idea of going to heaven. Zhang felt obliged to respond to it because this proposal hinted that the spirits and souls of the dead could still move around freely and enjoy the honour, as in making sacrifice to the ancestors. Using Chinese materials in history to expose the errors with this proposal, Zhang stated the reason for his objection.[253] Punishment and reward were decided by God. It was not for us to decide whether or not a person would go to heaven. Awarding posthumous titles would give the impression that the dead had risen into heaven. Zhang urged the advocates and President Yuan Shikai at the time to believe in Jesus for the assurance of entering heaven instead of hell.[254] Zhang often wrote about hell as a warning, not minding if this would make him appear superstitious and naïve, which reveals the strength of his belief in hell.

One reader, Chen Xiaohan, said that Jesus had only divine nature, and not human nature, because human nature was sinful. Zhang corrected him and then praised him, saying that the majority of Christ's worshippers among the Chinese intellectuals would rather call Jesus "the best model among human beings" than confess he was God.[255] They would acknowledge Jesus's human nature but deny his divine nature. If Mr. Chen was also an admirer of science, even though he recognized only one nature of Jesus, his insight had been very much deeper than theirs.

---

251. Zhang, "Jesus and Confucius," 26.
252. Zhang, "Correcting Errors in Dr. Chen," 113–14.
253. Zhang, "Denouncing Fallacies of Awarding," 98–99.
254. Zhang, 101.
255. Zhang, "Answering Chen Xiaohan's," 6.

In calling the other Chinese intellectuals "admirers of science," Zhang had pinpointed the reason for intellectual Christians' rejection of Jesus as God, namely their admiration for science. To Zhang, recognizing Jesus as God was much more important than seeing Jesus as the best model among human beings. However, admiration for science caused people to deny Jesus as God. By contrast, Zhang's own effort in being scientific did not lead him to deny Jesus's divine nature and worship Jesus only as the perfect man. His articles demonstrate this.

Around 1913, Zhang's literal and concordist approach to Jesus, God, and the accounts in the Bible was more significant than his allegorical and nonconcordist position in his dealings with a few incidents in Genesis.

5.4.2.2 Around 1920

In 1920, Zhang's response to the challenge of scientism on the accuracy of the biblical account of Creation shifted from his literal understanding approach to a nonliteral and nonconcordist interpretation held by James Jackson and Bishop Rev. Francis Lushington Norris. Zhang wrote in 1920 to prove the reality of God, Jesus, the Holy Spirit, Satan, heaven, and hell in response to Mo He.[256] Zhang's swing to the nonliteral and nonconcordist approach occurred mainly with regard to the first two chapters of Genesis. Once the battle moved to other supernatural events like Jesus's miracles and the virgin birth, Zhang became again insistent on their literal accuracy.

Another question from Mo He was whether God could send Jesus directly into the world and give him a fleshly body without human parentage. Zhang replied:

> Ten years ago, I have answered a similar question. Now I want to quote my former writing to answer this question. Yes, He can. He can not only do this, but also ask a stone to give birth to all descendants of Abraham.[257]

Zhang had written this answer in 1910, and he had quoted it in 1920. Once again, he chose this piece of writing for reprinting in 1929. He persisted in his literal understanding of God's omnipotence.

---

256. Zhang, "Refuting a Plagiarism," 225.
257. Zhang, 252–53.

He also insisted on the literal reality of Jesus's omniscience and salvation. Mo He questioned how Jesus could know if a person had enough faith and good deeds to be healed. Seeing that Mo He was also confused over faith in healing and faith in salvation, Zhang said that the two faiths were different.[258] Jesus could see into a person's heart and know whether the person had faith in his healing. Healing was not brought about by good deeds. Salvation through faith in Jesus meant that after listening to Jesus's gospel and realizing that they would be eternally damned if they did not quickly repent of their sins, people humbled themselves to receive Jesus's teaching and asked Jesus to be their Saviour. Salvation meant believing in Jesus as the Saviour, walking in the light and upward, having no part in wickedness, and going to the Father after death.

Zhang always held to the literal reality of devils and God in the Bible. Mo He thought the Bible was no more than a fairy tale because it contained stories of devils and gods. Since the Chinese of his time still had high esteem for the traditional classics and took them as a truthful record of the past, Zhang reminded Mo He that the classics in China also spoke of devils and gods.[259]

In the same text, Zhang revealed his shift between the two approaches. His nonliteral and nonconcordist approach was shown in his acceptance of the idea that the sun, moon, and stars were created before the fourth day, while his literal and concordist line was shown by his faith in most of the other supernatural records. Therefore, his literal and concordist approach is more significant than his allegorical and nonconcordist approach.

5.4.2.3 Around 1924

In the 1920s, many Chinese Christians under the influence of liberal theology endeavoured to reform the world and build heaven on earth, of which Zhang was not sure. He said that the world after reformation might be called heaven, but it would still not be the ultimate home for our souls; that the soul could only enter heaven on the strength of good deeds done through faith in Jesus; that no evildoer could enter heaven; and that the body after resurrection would not have the capability to choose evil.[260] Zhang's conservative

---

258. Zhang, 257.
259. Zhang, 262.
260. Zhang, "Questions from Huang Rongzeng," 72–73.

attitude towards the attempt to build heaven on earth resulted from his literal conviction of the reality of the soul, of resurrection, and of heaven, all of which scientism defined as unreal.

It was in 1924 that Zhang experienced his greatest confusion over the accuracy of the accounts in Genesis, especially the part before the creation of Adam. Even so, he was more inclined to believe that all the records were literally true because they were inspired by God. In the second issue of *True Light* in 1924, he said:

> Often the teaching in the Church was that the Bible was inspired by God. Some people might not be convinced, but there was no other better answer. Someone said that Genesis was not totally from the revelation of God because the materials had existed before Moses, which was not completely dependable. Since Moses with God's inspiration had chosen them, more probably they were truthful. Though the records of creation sounded too strange, shallow, and naive to the educated people, it was more trustworthy than other theories because: (1) we know there is a God who is the creator and Genesis also says that God did the creation; (2) according to *The Book of Changes*, the sky and earth first came into being, and then all things and finally man and woman, which was verified by the modern geologists. The creation in Genesis followed the same sequence, which was in accordance with the academic discoveries. So it was the most reasonable and convincing.[261]

Zhang doubted the accuracy of creation accounts because they were unable to satisfy his reason and that of other people. On the other hand, since he wanted to believe, he sought reason and evidence for his confidence in his literal and concordist understanding.

There are three issues in the quotation above. The first was Moses. Since Moses was inspired by God, Moses's choices must be right. This reasoning was based on Zhang's faith – God must be right. The second was the inborn sense of the existence of the creator god: "We know there is a God who is the creator." This observation was based on a kind of feeling which could

---

261. Zhang, "Three Questions about the Bible," 86.

still be viewed as a kind of faith, although this belief in the existence of one true God is observed in hundreds of cultures throughout the world.[262] The third point was that the order of creation both in *The Book of Changes* and in Genesis was verified by modern geology. This reasoning seemed rational on the surface, but was partly also based on faith. First, *The Book of Changes* gives no proof for the sequential order in the formation of the universe as Genesis does, so the parallel between them could only offer a support based on faith. Second, modern geology could only detect what had happened on earth while skies, light, and time were beyond its limit. Thus, modern geology could not verify the sequential creation order, at least not completely. However, Zhang borrowed faith in *The Book of Changes* and in science (modern geology) to authenticate faith in Genesis. Just as Rau notes, each theological interpretation of Scripture must take on faith.[263]

Strictly speaking, faith in *The Book of Changes* and science could not be counted as Christian faith, a biblical faith; however, Zhang transplanted them to validate his literal and concordist interpretation, which he was determined to justify. Furthermore, Zhang's approach to other parts of the Bible was still literal and concordist as firmly as ever. Again, Zhang's insistence on a literal and concordist line takes priority over his adoption of a non-literal and nonconcordist position.

5.4.2.4 Around 1929

By 1929, Zhang still insisted on his opinion of the great flood, but in the same text, he held on firmly to the literal accuracy of the Bible that it is divine work in its entirety, with human ideas playing no part. He warned about the unpredictability of the time for Jesus's second coming and believed in the necessity of always being prepared.

Zhang regarded the miracles of Jesus as science at the highest level.[264] The reason why people denied that Jesus's miracles had happened was that they were themselves unable to reach that level. He was expressing the idea that Jesus's miracles were as real and undeniable as science.

---

262. Don Richardson, *Eternity in Their Hearts*, rev. ed. (Ventura, CA: Regal Books, 1984).
263. Rau, *Mapping the Origins Debate*, 189.
264. Yijing Zhang, "Miracles of Healing the Deaf and Mute by Science (科学的聰聋启瘖神迹)," *True Light* 真光 28, no. 1 (1929): 45.

So, compared with his adoption of an allegorical and nonconcordist line, Zhang's primary biblical interpretation approach was still literal and concordist.

In the following section, for comparison and contrast, an analysis is made of two Chinese liberation theologians in light of the influence of science (as defined by scientism) on them.

5.5 Two Christian Leaders' Response to "Scientistism"

As seen in chapter 4, Xu Qian became a Christian in 1916 after the death of President Yuan. One of the reasons for his former refusal of conversion was his belief in science and reason. He believed that Christianity was unscientific and violated reason.[265] When he told his brother and friends that he would believe in Jesus if President Yuan died, such an event must have seemed impossible in his view: like many people, he was asking for a miracle in the confident hope that it would not occur. However, President Yuan did die shortly after Xu proposed his condition. He received baptism to keep his promise. However, he must have also felt somewhat mystified about the connection between his mindset and Yuan's death, which challenged his commitment to science and reason. Thus, during the first couple of years after his conversion, he accepted the supernatural aspects of Christianity. For example, in his reply to a friend who challenged his Christian faith with science, he affirmed that God really existed and was the Creator of all things. People could sense his existence. The Bible was inspired by God. God was almighty and omniscient. Scientific discoveries would help people to understand more about God, but they would never undermine the fact that the universe was created by God.[266] People sinned because they fell into the temptation of the devil.[267] He who believed firmly in God and did good would be given eternal life and would enter heaven, but he who did not believe in God and did evil would be destroyed and would go to hell. This would be decided at the last judgment.[268]

---

265. Ying, "Christian Doctrine and National Salvation," 27.

266. Qian Xu, "Answering Three Questions from a Friend Based on Science (答友人基于科学观念对基督教之三大疑问)," *The St. John's Echo* 约翰声 27, no. 6 (1916): 28.

267. Xu, "Answering Three Questions," 29.

268. Xu, 30.

In short, although Xu did not believe that the seven days of creation in Genesis literally meant seven days of twenty-four hours duration each, he completely believed in God as the Creator. He also accepted the reality of the devil, the Bible as God's word, heaven, hell, and the last judgment.

However, while he was studying Christianity, he was also absorbing the ideas of scientism, at least through a close contact with a few journals: *La Jeunesse* (新青年), *The Pacific Ocean* (太平洋), *Science* (科学), *The Renaissance* (新潮), and *Weekly Review* (每周评论) which often published articles to publicize science and debase religion.[269] Most of the writers and editors of such journals were returned students or people from abroad and many names have been mentioned above. Among them, Chen Duxiu, Hu Shi, Ding Wenjiang, and Ren Hongjun are taken as representatives of scientism by Kwok.[270] Other significant figures included Wu Zhihui, Wang Jingwei, Li Dazhao, Fu Sinian, Ma Junwu, and Cai Yuanpei.

La Jeunesse was initiated by Chen Duxiu and was most famous for its promulgation of Western science and democracy. *Science* was started by a group of Chinese students in New York. In its Foreword, it charged religion (Christianity) with being superstitious, a shackle on people's minds, and an obstacle to progress and knowledge. It promised to defeat religion, improve morality, and bring peace in the world. People's future and well-being could only depend on science.[271] The professional writers of *The Pacific Ocean* were often Chinese stationed in Japan and the West and its focus was on the textual criticism of the scientific principle.[272] *The Renaissance* originated in Peking University and its goal was to direct Chinese into the modern trend of thought, which was scientific, and into critical thinking. It praised the Renaissance and Reformation scholars for fighting against the devil of the world, which might be a veiled reference to the church.[273]

Gradually, Xu's commitment to scientism gained on his Christian identity. Two years after his conversion, Xu proposed his "Saving Nations through Christianity" (which, in essence, was "Saving China through Christianity")

---

269. Qian Xu 徐谦 and Shijie Bao 包世杰, "A Letter to the China National Education Conference (致全国教育会议书)," *Chinese Christian Advocate* 兴华 16, no. 8 (1919): 14.
270. Kwok, *Scientism in Chinese Thought*, 8–18.
271. "The Foreword (发刊词)," *Science* 科学 1, no. 1 (1915): 5–7.
272. "The Declaration (本志宣告)," *The Pacific Ocean* 太平洋 1, no. 1 (1917): 1.
273. "Foreword (发刊词)," *The Renaissance* 新潮 1, no. 1 (1919): 4.

in the summer of 1918. In this proposal, he interpreted sin as social oppression, Jesus as a Liberator of the nations, and Christians' mission as liberating their nations.[274] Three years later, Xu regarded it superstitious and ridiculous to believe in the Trinity and in the existence of soul, spirit, and heaven after death.[275] There was no heaven other than this visible world.[276] This time he interpreted sin as the fear of death, and repentance as a willingness to die to encourage people to die for the China cause. When people became willing to die, they had their second birth which was their resurrection. Therefore, everyone could repeat Jesus's resurrection.[277]

What did he mean by the resurrection of the Chinese? According to Xu, soul and spirit would die, so people should not seek the eternity of their soul and spirit. However, the nation, as a form of communal life, could last forever, so people should seek the long durability of their nations. A forever lasting China which already had a history of five thousand years was the eternal life for the Chinese Christians.[278] God was not the other being, God was in people, God and people were one, and everyone could become God provided that they did not seek their own interest.[279] He no longer mentioned the authority of the Bible. Later on, he held that Christianity was a superstition and its only function was to save nations.[280]

As seen above, the process of the development of Xu's "Saving Nations through Christ" was a process of reducing the supernatural element of Christianity and increasing the use of scientific terms. God the Creator whose existence as another being was undeniable was reduced to anyone when he or she was unselfish. The devil and the Bible disappeared from the discussion. Reinterpretation removed all the divine aspects of Jesus, heaven, hell, eternal life, victory over death, and resurrection. At the same time, the label of superstition was frequently used for belief in the traditional aspects of

---

274. Xu, "Are Chinese Willing?"; "Practicing Saving Nations"; "Gospel of National Salvation."

275. Qian Xu, "The Speech at Guangzhou Bible Study – Part Two (广州研经会讲演)," *New Autonomy* 新自治 1, no. 2 (1921): 5.

276. Xu, "Bible Study – Part Three," 5.

277. Xu, "Bible Study – Part Two," 3–4.

278. Xu, 5–6.

279. Xu, "Bible Study – Part Three," 1, 9.

280. Xu, "Course of My Involvement," 1850; Lu, "About Xu Qian," 102.

Christianity, such as the Trinity. In the end, the whole of Christianity was dubbed a superstition.

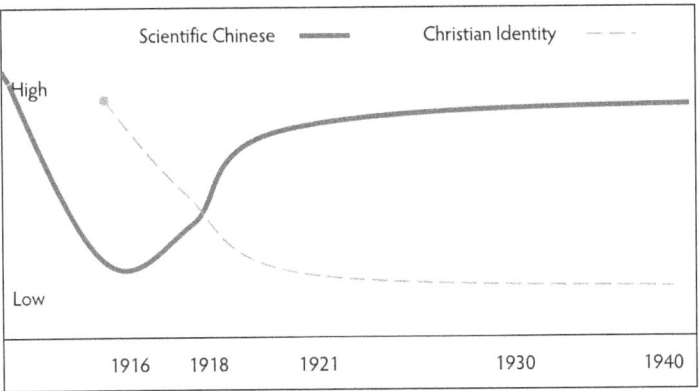

Figure 4: The Changes of Xu's Identity as a Scientific Chinese and Christian Identities

In one sense, Xu's Christian identity experienced a transformation in its contents and its direction was to meet the scientistic standard of being scientific. All aspects that could not be tested and proved by scientific methods were discarded or declared false and superstitious, a typical feature of scientism. Thus, this process demonstrated the rise and fall in Xu's commitment to scientism. Scientism had formerly led to his refusal of Christianity, but later, the strength of his commitment to it was weakened by a supernatural happening, and finally, it regained its strength and he condemned Christianity once more as a superstition. Obviously, his wish to be a scientific Chinese took priority over his Christian identity, so that the contents of his Christian identity were transformed according to the needs of his scientific Chinese identity. It is reasonable to say that Xu's concept of saving nations through Christ was motivated mainly by his identity as a scientific Chinese. If his Christian identity was also involved in his China-saving project, its function was nominal and subsidiary. Christianity was, in Xu's view, the root of the democratic system.[281] Therefore, the interaction of the two identities of Xu led to his way of relating Christ or gospel to culture.

---

281. Xu, "Independence of Chinese Christianity," 50–53.

In light of Xu's various identities, the change in his attitude towards Communism becomes easier to comprehend. The fact that CCP presented itself as the representative of national interests and science appealed to his identity as a scientific Chinese, so he included Communism in his concept.[282] However, after a few years of cooperation, he did not become a Communist. There are two possible reasons: either because he found it different from the image it projected, or because it did not seem to him to contain any possibility of democracy. The second possible reason was noticed in Ying's research.[283]

The second leader was Jian Youwen whose version of loving China was discussed in chapter 4. Jian was born in Guangdong in 1896 and educated at Lingnan School, where he was baptized as a Christian. From 1914 he attended Oberlin College in the US and gained his undergraduate degree in 1917. In 1919 he obtained his Master's degree in Religious Education from the University of Chicago. He returned to China in 1921. He accepted a position as general editor at the Hong Kong YMCA's publications division in 1922, and in 1924 he was appointed associate professor of religion at Yenching University, a post he held until 1927.

The University of Chicago was very important in the development of liberal theology.[284] Around 1900, all the scholars at its Divinity School were modernists influenced by the developing philosophy of American pragmatism. They attempted to adapt the scientific method in order to advance the critical study of the Bible and religious history.[285] This endeavour was part of the intellectual revolution propelled by the findings of Charles Darwin and the broader development of the scientific method.[286] In the 1920s, Jian introduced many of the works on the liberal wing to China[287] such as George Burman

---

282. Xu, "I Bear Witness," 6.
283. Ying, "Christian Doctrine and National Salvation," 88–94.
284. Dorrien, *American Liberal Theology*.
285. Peden, *American Liberal Religious Thought*, 101–2.
286. Peden, 243.
287. Youwen Jian 简又文, "The Function of Death in the Experience of Humankind (人类经验中死之功用)," *Youth Progress* 青年进步, no. 26 (1919): 34–39.

Foster,[288] Gerald Birney Smith,[289] and Harry Frederick Ward[290] who gave a series of speeches on Christianity and revolution, and industrialism in China.[291]

As a student majoring in religious education at the University of Chicago, Jian himself could not be free from the influence of liberal theology. He must have been deeply influenced by the early Chicago School because almost all the key figures of the School except for Edward Scribner Ames were quoted by him to explain Christianity.[292]

To Jian, life was the adaptability of organisms to the environment. The better one adapted to one's surroundings, the more life one had. The best tool of adaptation was religion which helped people to recognize a superior force in the universe, overcome their anxieties, and fulfil their responsibilities.[293] He thought he shared Bertrand Russell's view of religion; namely, that religion must change according to people's needs.[294]

Christianity was also a way of adaptation in the progress of history. Jesus reformed the Israelite religious tradition into a new religious experience with his genius and insight. He expressed this religious experience in his words

---

288. George Burman Foster (1858–1918) was part of the faculty in the Divinity School (Baptist) at the University of Chicago. His views were often thought by his contemporaries to support scientific naturalistic and humanistic views that contradict a Baptist view.

289. Gerald Birney Smith, "Translation: Social Idealism and the Changing Theology (译述:伦理的基督教观)," trans. Youwen Jian 简又文, *Life (Beijing)* 生命(北京) 5, no. 1 (1924): 26–42.

290. Harry Frederick Ward Jr. (1873–1966) was a British-born American Methodist minister and political activist who emerged as a leading fellow traveller of the Communist Party in the US. Ward is best remembered as the first national chairman of the American Civil Liberties Union (ACLU), leading the group from its creation in 1920 until his resignation in protest of the organization's decision to bar Communists in 1940. Ward received a Bachelor's degree in 1897 and a Master's degree in Philosophy from Harvard University in 1898. Following graduation, Ward took a position as head resident of Northwestern University Settlement, a settlement house located in Chicago which sought to educate and improve the lives of impoverished immigrant workers in the city's meatpacking district. Ward evangelized the social gospel, sermonizing on matters of economics and poverty and the potential role of the church in the rectification of the structural failings of society.

291. Harry F. Ward and Youwen Jian 简又文, "The Function of Religion in Social Reform (社会改造中之宗教地位)," *The Supplement to Morning News* 晨报副刊, 19 April 1925: 1–5; Harry F. Ward and Youwen Jian 简又文, "The Revolutionary Christianity – Part One (革命的基督教 一)," *The Supplement to Morning News* 晨报副刊, 1 July 1925: 2–4.

292. Jian, "What Is Christianity?"; Youwen Jian, "What Is Christianity – Part Two (什么是基督教 续第二卷第一期)," *Life (Beijing)* 生命(北京) 2, no. 2 (1922): 1–7; Peden, *American Liberal Religious Thought*, 102.

293. Jian, "What Is Christianity? (什么是基督教)," 1.

294. Jian, 2.

and deeds and passed this experience down to his apostles. As it was passed down, a mass movement was formed. By a strained and far-fetched interpretation, Jesus became the Messiah. In order to adapt to the environment, Paul produced the theory of Jesus having both human and divine nature. Later on, the notion of the Trinity was evolved. So the contents of Christianity kept changing.[295] Jian called his way of understanding Christianity "the historical method," the best tool for the new modern theology.[296]

In Jian's view, the Bible was the servant of life, and as the records in it were outdated, it was arbitrary to take it as the sole authority in life.[297] It was a stick for the blind, had only an aesthetic value, and had nothing to do with science.[298] Therefore, people should go directly to Jesus to ask for life and he only passed it down to living persons.[299] After receiving the traditional teachings of Christianity, Christians should examine, test, and reform them, because the Christian doctrines were the same as the hypotheses of a scientific experiment in nature and function.[300] It was ridiculous for people to believe that a few doctrines of Christianity were unchangeable, as Kant's critical philosophy proved that everything was evolving and time-related.[301] Therefore, theology and doctrines of Christianity should keep changing according to the best scientific discoveries and philosophical theories. The church must be ready to accept all facts and truths found by science and make partial or complete reform according to them.[302] In the case of China, Christianity should get rid of the supernatural aspects, the prospect of the next world, individual salvation, and the old theologies in order to cater to democracy, natural science, patriotism, and socialism.[303]

The old theologies focused on the existence and nature of God, Christ, and humankind, such as the Creator, the Trinity, the virgin birth, miracles, sin, atonement, and resurrection. Such theologies were based on metaphysics and

---

295. Jian, 3.
296. Jian, 4.
297. Jian, 6.
298. Jian, 7.
299. Jian, 6–7.
300. Jian, 7.
301. Jian, 8.
302. Jian, "Ethnic Church," 38; Jian, "Christianity – Part Two," 1.
303. Jian, "Christianity – Part Two," 6.

were unsuitable for China and the new culture, because the Chinese valued moral principles and pragmatic considerations while the new culture featured science, social progress and salvation, and democracy. Thus, it was not fitting for a revolution.[304] The core of the gospel should be pragmatic and ethical, focusing on the reform of Chinese ethics.[305] The touchstone was its capability of saving China.[306] This new Christianity was different from both the Catholic and the Protestant church, but it was the true Restoration church.[307] The new Christianity would be welcomed by all churches.[308] Finally, Jian used the language of a scientist by saying: "This is only a scientific hypothesis and its authenticity needs to be tested by experiment."[309]

Jian supported Xu Qian's "Saving Nations through Christ,"[310] and his own version of loving China could be understood as inherited from Xu. The analysis has centred on the relationship between the prominence of Jian's national identity and the contents of his Christian identity. An analysis of the reason for the contents of Jian's Christian identity still needs to be done.

Jian understood life as adaptability and Christianity as a tool for survival, which was based on two implications: (1) the theory of evolution was unchangeably correct and applicable in all contexts, which seems to be contradictory to the changing nature of evolution in his mind; and (2) the fittest would survive.

Jian's "historical method" by nature was an application of his conviction of both the theory of evolution and the standards of natural science to Christianity in history; that is, everything must continually change and no truth could be undetectable by scientific methods and experiments. Consequently, all the elements in Christianity to which science has no access become useless, outdated, and ridiculous whereas all the elements within the limits set by science must be invariably explained according to the theory of evolution and the philosophy of Kant as he understood them. In other words, evolutionary theory and science had the right to determine

---

304. Jian, "Ethnic Church," 37–39.
305. Jian, 39.
306. Jian, "Christianity – Part Two," 7.
307. Jian, "Ethnic Church," 42–43.
308. Jian, 44.
309. Jian, 44.
310. Jian, 43; Jian, "Christianity – Part Two," 6.

the legitimacy of the contents of Christianity. His faith that evolution never failed and that science set the limits of knowledge and reality was typical of scientism. Moreover, when he called his idea a scientific hypothesis waiting to be tested, he was extending the methodology of natural science into the discipline of Christianity or religion. This is also typical of scientism.

In brief, Jian's commitment to scientism led to his reduction of all the supernatural aspects of Christianity to a version he called a "True Restoration Church" in order to have the richest life or the best adaptability in China. Just like Xu's, Jian's version was mainly motivated by his identity as a scientific Chinese. His Christian identity held a lower position because Christianity was just a tool and the Bible a servant. In other words, the two identities of Jian facilitate a deeper understanding of his type of relating Christ or gospel to culture.

Regarding Zhang Yijing, for a quick comparison, here is the quotation of Zhang's expression of his faith written in 1923 when liberal theology was popularized in China:

> I do not know what is old or what is new. I believe God is the Creator in the Trinity; Jesus is the son of God and he is the only Saviour for all people; the Holy Spirit is the comforter whose help could be obtained by all true believers in Jesus; after death, people have two destinations: heaven or hell; when the truth of Jesus is universally accepted, this world truly could be turned into the heavenly kingdom, but it would be arbitrary to say that there would be no final judgment; I know from my thirty years' experience that there is God's will in everything.[311]

The words "old" and "new" refer to "the old theology" and "the new theology." In fact, Zhang was expressing his attitude towards the "Fundamentalist-Modernist Controversy" in China. It is not difficult to see the difference between Zhang Yijing, Xu Qian, and Jian Youwen. Almost all the supernatural aspects of Christianity discarded by Xu and Jian were the points stressed by Zhang as literally real. The influence of scientism on Xu and Jian was not traceable in Zhang; however, as analyzed above, he was not free from its hegemony.

---

311. Zhang, "How I Became a Christian," 8.

The question has been raised above: Where was the boundary between being scientific and being scientistic? It is hard to draw a dividing line. The question may be better reframed as: Whose definition of science counts?[312] If science is defined by scientism, Xu and Jian could be viewed as more "scientific" than Zhang because he was even determined to become "superstitious."[313]

5.6 Conclusion

In this chapter, the Western root of scientism in China has been briefly reviewed. Moreover, the Chinese root of scientism was also pointed out. More importantly, it was found that Chinese scientism resulted in an attitude similar to scientism from the West, at least in the area of the Christian message. Then the chapter showed Zhang's positive attitude to science and negative response to scientism and his defence of Christianity against the attacks of scientism.

Although Zhang did not espouse scientism, in a context which was dominated by the scientistic version of science, sometimes he was unconsciously brought to terms with it. The hegemony of scientism was especially obvious in his articles written in 1913, 1920, and 1924, when he dealt with Genesis (especially the first two chapters). During the same period, the power of scientism kept increasing in China, claimed victory in the Debate on Science and Metaphysics in 1923, and finally became a part of Chinese culture.

The year 1924 was the most confusing year for Zhang, as seen in the swinging and alternating between a literal and concordist approach and an allegorical and nonconcordist one. By the end of 1924, his adoption of the second approach gradually began to decline.

All through Zhang's life as a Christian, he consistently tended to believe in the supernatural accounts in the Bible according to their literal meaning, except for the part of creation. Even in 1913, 1920, and 1924, Zhang's insistence on literal understanding was in the mainstream. Therefore, his literal and concordist approach is shown to have taken priority over his allegorical and nonconcordist position all through his life after his conversion.

---

312. Rau, *Mapping the Origins Debate*, 176, 189.
313. For the sake of saving space, the influence of scientism on other Christian leaders like David Z. T. Yui and Xu Baoqian will be analysed on a future occasion.

Zhang's efforts to interpret the Bible in a way satisfactory to the requirements of scientism could be viewed as his pursuit of being a "scientific" Chinese. Since there was a positive link between the literal and concordist approach and a strong Christian identity in his mind, the examination of his shift between his two approaches of biblical interpretation could reveal to us how he evaluated his Christian identity and his identity as a scientific Chinese. As analyzed above, his Christian identity was his superordinate one and he reconciled his two identities by integrating the conflicting dimensions: reason being at a stage lower than faith and resuming his belief in the literal meaning, and by compartmentalizing the great flood. Only once in 1924, he subjectively felt his pursuit of being scientific had gone so far that his relationship with God and Christ was hindered. However, he quickly repented and vowed to put things right by studying only the knowledge the Holy Spirit would direct him to. Therefore, for the rest of his life, he subjectively felt a union between his Christian identity and his identity as a scientific Chinese, with his Christian identity as the most important one.

This chapter has also shown that being scientific would not be esteemed as being "scientific" by scientism unless its terms were met. Thus, being scientific would not necessarily prevent a Christian from being labelled as superstitious. In an era or a country which has scientism as the dominant ideology, the popular or official conceptualization of the nation would usually exclude Christians as useless. As a result, Christians upholding their faith would find it very hard to gain popular and official recognition of their belonging to the nation. Examples can be found in Xu Qian, Jian Youwen, and Zhang Yijing. However, Zhang's subjective perception of his self-sameness and continuity in seeking to be scientific has been sufficient to convince him that he was a genuine Chinese in terms of being scientific, in spite of his perception of the fact that, externally, other non-Christians still denied it.

CHAPTER 6

Conclusion

This research has accomplished the goal set out in chapter 1: To what extent did Zhang demonstrate that being a Christian Chinese at his time was possible, or how did Zhang reconcile his personal identity as a Christian and his social identity as a Chinese?

Chapter 1 suggests an additional perspective for the study of Christianity in China – the perspective of identities. It presents the literature reviews of the sociological theory of identities and of the research on Zhang.

Chapter 2 consists of a review of the history and the context in China before and during the 1920s. Then there is a description of Zhang Yijing's life and contributions. Three appendices are added to clarify the description of Zhang's life.

Chapter 3 analyses the formation of Zhang's Christian identity, its early development, and its relationship to his Confucian identity. The hierarchical structure of his two identities distinguished him from many other Confucian Christians concerning the method of contextualizing the Christian message. Though he was a genuine Confucian, he was externally viewed as a traitor of Confucianism by many other Confucians because of the priority of his Christian identity over his Confucian identity. In his own perception, his Christian identity and Confucian identity were in union after the latter was transformed by the former.

Chapter 4 analyses the later development of Zhang's Christian identity, his national identity, and the interaction between these two identities. From 1906, his Christian identity generally took priority over his national identity, which distinguished his contextualization in a milieu of nationalism from many other Chinese Christians. This chapter finds that in an environment dominated by radical nationalism, being a patriotic Christian like Zhang was would not necessarily lead to a public or an official recognition of being Chinese. However, he himself knew he was a true Chinese with a genuine love for China. After being transformed, his national identity was also in concord with his Christian identity.

Chapter 5 finds that Zhang welcomed science but resisted the standards of being scientific as laid by scientism. His biblical interpretation methods reflected how he understood his Christian identity and he perceived the requirements of being a scientific Chinese. It shows that, with the Chinese science market being monopolized by the scientistic version, one's efforts in being scientific would not win the recognition of scientism. Though Zhang consistently resisted the terms of scientism, his interpretation of the Bible could not be completely free from the impact of scientism, as he himself realized. However, this impact was only observable in his dealing with the first two chapters of Genesis (for a short period) and the great flood. By the means of integration and compartmentalization, he felt his Christian identity and his identity as a scientific Chinese were in harmony. And he was confident in his efforts in being a scientific Chinese, though he was continually labelled as "superstitious" by the people instilled with scientism.

The preceding chapters show that the content of Chinese identity, what was required to be considered Chinese, did not remain intact; rather, it had a shifting, malleable, and processual nature. In addition to race and language, being Chinese used to mean identification with Chinese culture, specifically Confucianism. Then the discourses and practices of modern nationalism at the beginning of the twentieth century created a community of individuals who emphasized the past humiliation and their rights, especially the sovereign rights, as the central facet of their identities. In the 1920s, a radical nationalism defined the true Chinese as people whose love for China was their highest priority. Since the 1910s, some intellectuals successfully envisioned and utilized the Western category of science to illustrate what constituted authentic and legitimate Chinese practice: a Chinese must believe in science as the only truth. Whatever discourses and practices were considered authentic and legitimately Chinese, these shaped and reflected Chinese Christians' notion of belonging, including that of Zhang Yijing.

Chapters 3, 4, and 5 have delineated Zhang's search for a Chinese Christian or a Christian Chinese identity. This was, in fact, a search for a reconciliation between his Christian identity and his identities as a Confucian and as a modern Chinese which also included a dimension of being "scientific."

When Chinese identity was defined in terms of culture, especially Confucianism, Zhang was a model Chinese because he sincerely strove to live up to its values. His Confucian identity was extraordinarily strong and there was no obstacle to his feeling of being a Confucian (with just one exception when he was engaged in a polemic with the Confucian Association in 1913). However, he believed that people were first and foremost God's people. In his life, he revealed that his Christian identity took priority over, though in union with, his Chinese identity in its cultural sense, which explains why the officials and intellectuals of the Qing dynasty viewed Chinese Christians as "*jiaomin*" and "traitor," a denial of their Chinese identities.

When Chinese identity was appropriated by modern nationalism, Zhang should have been highly praised and taken as a model by most nationalists for his strong national identity. According to the terms of modern nationalism, Zhang felt confident that he was even more Chinese than those Chinese who worked on Shamian Island, took trams in Shanghai, or bought Japanese products. He should have received public recognition of his "being Chinese." Nonetheless, he believed that Christians' patriotism should be guided by Jesus's teaching and that love for one's country should be like parents' love for their children. With this transformed comprehension, in practical living, he insisted on positioning his national identity under his Christian identity to reach a concord. This inevitably incurred the disapproval of radical nationalists who required a reversed order of the two identities.

When the whole country of China was led into believing that the Chinese should apply the principle of "being scientific," as defined by scientism, to every aspect of their lives, Zhang proved to be a scientific and modern Chinese who was very useful to the development of his country. His commitment to reason and empirical evidence went so far that he even denied the extent of the great flood. Thus, he felt that he and many other Chinese Christians were more useful to China because their scientific knowledge was richer and their scientific spirit was not less than that of anyone else. They should have been recognized as scientific Chinese. Nevertheless, he insisted on believing in things science has no access to and continually opposed the notion that people could judge the existence of God by empirical evidence and reason. For the most part, he was scientific rather than scientistic. According to his own understanding, generally his Christian identity took priority over his identity as a scientific Chinese and the two were in a harmonious relationship. However, according to the standards of scientism, he was still viewed as a superstitious and outdated person who was of no use for the development of China and, consequently, should be got rid of.

As can be seen, Zhang and many Chinese Christians had an unavoidable concern with the seemingly endless crisis of Chinese identity. In the main, this crisis was caused by the denial of their "being Chinese" by officials and intellectuals, as perceived by Zhang and others. Their perception of this public denial affected their personal sense of belonging to the group of Chinese. The public opinion of what "being Chinese" meant was influenced by its shifting, malleable, and processual nature, but their denial of Christians being Chinese was caused by their frustration with Zhang and many Christians who refused their demand of positioning "being Chinese" above "being Christian." However, Zhang demonstrated that his perception of public denial could not essentially undermine his sense of his own genuine Chinese identity after his comprehension of being Chinese had been transformed by his Christian identity, which had risen to be his primary identity or even functioned as his ego identity.

In order to contextualize the Christian message in a way that Chinese listeners would perceive as Chinese, relevant, and meaningful, Zhang selected different strategies to deal with the changing constituent elements of Chinese identity. These included adopting and adapting to Chinese culture, admitting the love of the Chinese for China, redefining nationalism, and pursuing being scientific but resisting scientism. As seen in the chapters above, his selections resulted from his way of being a Christian and a Chinese.

From another perspective, Zhang's contextualization was also a reflection of the process of moulding Chinese Christian or Christian Chinese identity because his contextualization expressed how he understood the balance between Christian identity and "being Chinese." Nonetheless, his version of Chinese Christian or Christian Chinese identity did not meet the conceptualizations of identity and the priority of identities by the Chinese intelligentsia.

If Zhang had submitted to the conceptualizations of those ideologies whenever they were in conflict with the teachings of the Bible, he would have had fewer problems and fewer criticisms. However, on the other side, he would not have had the motivation to argue so strongly against the advocates of Confucianism as China's state religion, the promoters of reason and science as the only standard for the truth, and the radical nationalists targeting Christianity and its religious education. He would not have felt as hurt as he was in the 1920s when Chinese Christians were rejected as authentic and legitimate Chinese. If the whole community of Chinese Christians had adapted like this to the discourses and practices of those ideologies, Christianity in China might have presented a totally different image. It may have been seen as an anthropological, moral, philosophical, and cultural system which is a beneficial complement to Chinese culture and a bridge between China and the West, ready to collaborate with any cultural, political, or ideological agenda. In terms of religiosity, such an image might have been inferior to Buddhism and Taoism, but might have won a wider recognition as being "authentic and legitimate."

However, Zhang was first and foremost a Christian and this identity endowed his life and work with excitement and meaning, among other things. Accordingly, his way of being a Chinese Christian or Christian Chinese guaranteed the tension between his identity as a Christian and the public recognition of his Chinese identity. Such tension was not caused by his lack of will and energy to meet the expectations of those discourses and practices, but rather by the irreconcilable conflict between the different ideological conceptualizations of the state, identity, and the truth.

A similar case of conflict between different conceptualizations is found in an Old Testament story in 1 Kings 18. After three years of famine, Elijah presented himself to King Ahab. When Ahab saw him, Ahab accused him of making trouble for Israel, but Elijah reacted by accusing Ahab of causing the trouble by abandoning the worship of the Lord to follow Baal's commands. Both Ahab and Elijah attributed the famine to each other and called the other one a traitor. From the perspective of Ahab, the truth was in Baal. A loyal citizen should never criticize the state or its king, the representative of Israel. Anyone who denied one's identity in Baal and censured the king or Israel would be viewed as the cause of the sufferings of the nation. Getting rid of such people could solve this problem. While from the perspective of Elijah, the truth was in the Lord. The state was led by Ahab, but under the final authority of the Lord. The ruling class and the masses that denied their identity in the Lord and assumed an identity in Baal were the cause of national suffering. Their criticism was the first step leading to a correction.

If no change occurred on either side, it seems predictable that tension would always exist.

Therefore, some people naturally view the key to contextualization as the unification of conceptualizations. However, opinions on the way of unifying are frequently different. Ahab wanted the submission of Elijah, Elijah wanted a change in Ahab, and Obadiah, as the assistant of Ahab and the sympathizer of Elijah, might suggest a compromising plan, and so on. A similar case was seen in China at the beginning of the twentieth century. If one person wanted unification by Sinicizing Christianity, another wanted a Christianization of China, and there would have been others who wanted a mix of both, and so on.

Very probably, the search for a Chinese Christian identity will never end. Perhaps such tension is not meant to disappear, but to remain as a touchstone or a reflection of identities and their prioritization. For people like Zhang who insisted on Christian identity as the top priority of a Christian's multiple identities, they might want to take Elijah as a reference, since the officials and intellectuals' lack of recognition did not influence Elijah's personal feeling of being an Israelite.

Doyle's research shows how Zhang Lisheng insisted on safeguarding Chinese theology against uncritical indigenization and located the issue of indigenization within a biblical and historical-theological framework, and how his work provides critical resources to reflect on the contemporary quest to indigenize theology in China.[1]

In the same way, Zhang Yijing's insistence on the priority of his Christian identity over his other identities in his search for a Chinese Christian or Christian Chinese identity has offered a significant precedent and reference for the current Christians in China, whose similar efforts are partly reflected in their own endeavours of contextualization under the political pressure and demands of Sinicization.

Such a tug-of-war between different ideologies for top priority faced by the contemporary Chinese Christians is also observed in Li Liang's research. He says that Chinese Christians are marginalized. They are still Chinese, but they no longer belong to the mainstream culture. The core of this problem is

---

1. Doyle, "Lit-Sen Chang."

faithfulness to the culture.² In fact, the "faithfulness to the culture" is "commitment to the culture" or "a commitment to 'being Chinese'" defined by the current culture. And the theme of the current culture has been regulated as "patriotism."³ In other words, Li Liang also sensed that the problem with the public recognition of Christians "being Chinese" is a problem of the prioritization of identities.

As seen in recent years, some scholars and officials have been advocating or hailing that Christianity in China must become or has become Chinese Christianity. In one sense, this can be celebrated as a diversification of the ways of relating Christ to culture. At the same time, a question must be asked: What model of relating does "Chinese Christianity" denote? As this study has shown, the deeper reason for the way of relating Christ to culture is identity and the priority among the identities. Therefore, it is predictable that Christians in China who insist on placing their Christian identity in a supreme position will continually be viewed as unwanted and peripheral to the imagined community of China and to mainstream Chinese cultural and political spheres. Maybe the feeling of being peripheral (or unrecognized by the public) is something which they should get used to. Instead, they should view this as a necessity in their pilgrimage and turn their efforts to articulate their own conceptualization of the state, identity, and the truth.

Next, I turn to the perspective of "identities." A part of the literature review on identity has revealed that some people may wonder how applicable the concept of identity as developed by Erickson and other theorists, a theory developed in the West, is to a non-Western context like China. Scholars realize how little identity development in non-Western contexts is known. However, it is remarkable to discover that Chinese Christians had touched upon the same idea of identity, without using that specific term, in the 1920s, almost forty years earlier than the debut of Erickson's theory of identity. Lu Boai and Zhang Yijing debated over which should take priority, one's national identity or one's Christian identity. Zhang called on Western missionaries to position their Christian identity over their national identity and encouraged Chinese Christians to make their national identity more salient so that their Christian

---

2. Liang Li 李亮, "中国基督教现状的考察 A Survey of the Current Situation of Chinese Christianity," Orient 东方, no. 2 (1995): 53–58.
3. "How Are We Patriotic?"

identity might be accepted as a part of being Chinese. Zhang analyzed why Zhang Chunyi, a former Christian, had become an advocate of Buddhism by listing his three identities: Buddhist, Confucian, and Christian. Such instances offer evidence from non-Western contexts for the argument of Stryker that:

> across cultural contexts, identity achievement is perceived as making and identifying with commitments. It does not matter if commitments are developed using individualistic and internal standards or based on group norms, they likely serve the same function which is to anchor the person within a set of social roles and responsibilities. So in both the Eastern society and Western countries, the commitments one makes will lay a set of expectations upon one's future choices and behaviour.[4]

This may also offer verification for my assumption that the perspective of identity has at least two advantages: personalization and decentralization. When Zhang separated some missionaries' identity into their Christian identity and national identity, he was trying to balance Lu Danlin's totally negative view of Westerners. When he listed Zhang Chunyi's three identities and showed his consistently strong commitment to Buddhism, it became easier to view Zhang Chunyi as a sincere religious inquirer once, and to understand his departure with sympathy rather than treat him as a defector or apostate.

Furthermore, through the analysis in this study, Zhang's search for a Chinese Christian or Christian Chinese identity as exemplified in his contextualization can be viewed as a reflection of the results of the interaction of his multiple identities under the influence of the external and internal elements in his milieu. The examination of his internal identities has facilitated the understanding of the reason why his personal and communal experiences were critical elements in distinguishing his external way of relating Christ or gospel to culture. Thus, the perspective of identities can shed light on the question: Why do people, in similar contexts, relate Christ or gospel to culture differently in the first place, which results in the different types and models as summarized by Niebuhr, Carter, and Bevans?

While this brief and tentative analysis does not do justice to the complexities of identities of Chinese Christians at the beginning of the twentieth

---

4. Sheldon Stryker (2003), cited in Schwartz et al., "Identity Development, Personality," 355.

century, it made clear that identity can be regarded not only as a tool for the study of Christianity in China, but also as an object of analysis. This includes not only a theory for psychological analysis, but also for political ideology or doctrine. As Erikson says, only psychoanalysis and social science together can eventually chart the life cycle interwoven throughout with the history of the community.[5] This research has examined how Zhang negotiated and reconciled his personal identity as a Christian and his social identity as a Chinese. I have also briefly touched upon the hierarchical relationship of his other identities. A more detailed comparison of Zhang's other identities is not impossible, provided that they are clearly manifested in a particular event. If carried out, this perspective proves to be a very useful framework. Since this study aims at examining Zhang's search for a Chinese Christian or Christian Chinese identity at the beginning of the twentieth century in the space of a few chapters, the events chosen are naturally inclined to be the three most heated topics in discussion. However, on other topics like Chinese Christians' attitudes towards Western missions, more than two identities may have been involved simultaneously. This will be left for future research.

This survey also suggests a further agenda for comparative research, namely the study of how identities have developed over time among Chinese Christians in different periods and how those identities have shaped their contextualization, particularly in their search for what it means to be Christian and what it means to be Chinese. In other words, a comparative research of identities between different Chinese Christians of the same period is needed.

Experimenting with the perspective of identities is just one of the goals for this research. This study also aims at discovering Zhang's heritage and reappraising his life and contributions.

Just as the importance of Dietrich Bonhoeffer's life and work were not fully recognized until several decades after his death, so the heritage of Zhang Yijing, as significant a figure as any other Chinese Christians in the twentieth century, also requires more research.

Recently a scholar asked: "Zhang Yijing, so well-known [sic] Christian writer at that time, in fact now has almost been forgotten by ordinary Chinese Christians of today in China. Not only Zhang himself, also other Christian leaders at that time. Why?" One possible reason is that Zhang was the product

---

5. Erik H. Erikson, *Identity and Life Cycle* (New York: W. W. Norton, 1979), 17.

of Sino-western Protestant establishment, while the Christians in mainland China from the 1980s are grown up from Chinese folk, not so much with Zhang's generation. Another possible reason is that they were deliberately marginalized, ignored, and dismissed by the governing body. Maybe there are more reasons, but just as this scholar points out insightfully, this is a good point to analyze the discontinuity of Chinese Christianity in the first half of the twentieth century and after that.

In this study, the terms "Chinese Christian identity," "Christianity in China," and "Chinese Christianity" have been used. If Zhang Yijing could have read this work, he might have corrected this by saying: "Maybe you can consider changing 'Chinese Christian identity' to 'Christian Chinese identity,' and 'Chinese Christianity' to 'Christianity in China' because, in the Chinese language, word order demonstrates priority of value."

APPENDIX 1

The Chronology of Zhang Yijing – My Deceased Father (先严亦镜年表), by Zhang Qiutao (张秋涛)[1]

The original name of my deceased father was Zhang Wen Kai (张文开) and his courtesy name was Jianru (鉴如). As he often used Yijing (亦镜) as his pen-name, people were not familiar with the two names of Zhang Wen Kai (张文开) and Jianru (鉴如).

In 1871, when the Tongzhi Emperor (同治) of the Qing dynasty was in power for the tenth year, on 26 March, my father was born in Huangbao village (黄宝) of Zhongshan County (钟山) in Guangxi Province (广西). After his birth, he did not cry till a month later when he was shown a book. That was why he was named as Wen Kai (文开) which meant "book opens." While he was a baby, he was no different from other children. When he grew older, he became very refined. He was intelligent and studious. He was not an associate of the urchins in the village. The elder generation was very fond of him. Although his family was poor, they still kept him in school.

In 1887, when the Guangxu Emperor (光绪) was in power for the thirteenth year, he was seventeen years old. In spring, he was sent to study at a school at Shatianxu (沙田圩) of Hexian County (贺县) by his father. By accident, he obtained a New Testament from a store named Tian Cheng (or

---

1. This chronology was written by Zhang Qiutao, Zhang Yijing's son, "The Chronology of Zhang Yijing, My Deceased Father (先严亦镜年表)." He worked as a medical doctor in a Christian hospital. Parts of this chronology can be seen in Zhang Yijing's self-description in Zhang, "How I Became a Christian."

365

Heaven Achieves It, 天成). He gladly borrowed and read it. Since he could not understand it very well, he put it away in his book box. In winter, he went to Tong An area (同安) and married the daughter of Chen's family.

During 1888–1889, when he was eighteen to nineteen years old, he taught in his hometown. At his father's command, he began to study geomancy. Within one year, he mastered it, but he did not believe it.

In 1890, he was twenty years old. He followed other teachers to study poetry and classical Chinese in the Tong An area (同安). He made great progress.

In 1891, he was twenty-one years old. He moved his home from Huangbao village (黄宝) to a new house in Tuntangkou (屯塘口) in the Tong An area (同安). There he taught a dozen students at home. By then, the wall of the living room in the new house needed repairs. Out of his curiosity, he deliberately chose a day of evil spirits according to geomancy to do the repairs in order to see if the curse would come true. Out of his expectation, nothing happened. Then he had a great awakening. Afterwards, he did not talk about geomancy anymore.

In 1892, he was twenty-two years old. A village teacher came to borrow books including the New Testament. My father joked that the New Testament was his treasure and it should not be lost. The village teacher agreed. In a few days, he brought the New Testament back and said that it was indeed a special book in the world. The description of Jesus was so extraordinary. My father answered that it was why he treasured it so much. Afterwards, my father began to read it diligently, but he did not understand the purpose of this book.

One new neighbour was Chen Shousheng (陈受生) whose hometown was in Jieyang (揭阳) of Guangdong Province (广东). My mother and his wife were friends and treated each other as relatives. They visited each other often. My grandfather's hometown was in Chaozhou (潮州), a place next to Jieyang (揭阳). For this reason, my grandfather kept a close relationship with Chen Shousheng. At that time, my family did not know that Chen Shousheng was a Christian. In winter, the church in Guangzhou (广州) sent three men including Tan Baode (谭保德) to visit Chen Shousheng. My father had a good talk with them. When my father found they also opposed geomancy, he took them as people with the same inclination. Then he made progress in learning the truth.

In 1893, he was twenty-three years old. In March, my father was baptized. Since then, my grandfather was very displeased with him because it was impossible for him to achieve my grandfather's original dream that my father was educated to pass the provincial civil service examination. Facing my grandfather's anger, my father had to pray silently that God would change the hearts of my grandparents.

In summer, with the help of Tan Baode (谭保德), my father went to study the Bible in the church of Guangzhou without saying farewell to his family. However, he left a letter to tell them where he went. At that time, the church in Guangzhou did not have a seminary. They only had a seasonal Bible-reading class for church members in the gospel church on Wu Xian Men (五仙门). Qiutao noted: now the place is used by YMCA and the church has moved to Dong Shan District 东山. In summer, he was sent to sell Christian publications in the areas of Guangning (广宁) and Sihui (四会) where he suffered a lot of insults from anti-Christians. At that time, he was given 4 yuan for his meals.

In autumn, he returned to his home on his business trip. Then he became aware that my grandparents were very anxious and worried after his departure because the inconvenient traffic and the lack of the post office made them unable to know any news about him.

In 1894, he was twenty-four years old. After his return, my grandparents calmed down, but they kept a close watch over him. It was difficult for him to leave again. My father accepted this situation. He learned a lot by carefully studying the books brought back from Guangzhou including *Ge Wu Zhi Yuan* (*To Study the Phenomena of Nature to Acquire the Original Knowledge*, 格物致原). Sometimes Mr. Zhang Yunwen (张允文) and Mr. Liao Zhuoan (廖卓庵) would bring him *The Review of the Times* (万国公报, founded by Young John Allen 林乐知) and the newspapers published in Guangdong Province and Hong Kong. He read them to increase his knowledge and to drive away loneliness.

In 1895, he was twenty-five years old. In spring, Qiutao (the author, 秋涛), his eldest son, was born. My father spent this year in tutoring and farming. In winter, my grandfather died. My father mourned deeply because he was unable to convert my grandfather into a Christian.

From 1896 to 1898, when he was twenty-six to twenty-eight years old, he abided by the rite of spending three years to mourn the death of his father (a rite of Confucianism). During this period, he read books, tutored students, and farmed.

In 1899, he was twenty-nine years old. He was invited to be a journalist for the *Chinese Huan Newspaper* (中国郇报) in Hong Kong. This weekly newspaper was founded by Chinese Christians and Mr. Liao Zhuoan (廖卓庵) oversaw it. As the rite of three years mourning was over and my grandmother did not stop him, my father could accept this job which was located far from home. This was a preparation for him to be a preacher through writing.

Hong Kong was governed by the UK and Chinese people were bullied there, which left a deep impression on my father. He then doubted that Westerners in the church should be associated with because they were not Chinese. Therefore, he quit his job, left for his hometown, and severed his relationship with the church.

In 1900, he was thirty years old. In addition to his studying, teaching, and farming, he did a surprising thing when he scolded a government official for saving innocent prisoners. Pingle County (平乐) was under the power of a county magistrate named Xu (徐). He mistakenly imprisoned a father and his son with a family name Zhuo (卓) for a robbery and he sentenced them to death. The father and the son were going to be executed. My father had sympathy for them and he wrote and aired a complaint for them. The magistrate saw Zhang's signature at the bottom of the complaint and took it as insulting. As soon as he saw my father, he had my father beaten with a stick for more than one hundred times. A military officer recognized my father as one of his friends and he went to plead with the son of the magistrate. So the magistrate was stopped. At the same time, my father kept scolding the official loudly and angrily for the way the official mistreated the ordinary people. The father and the son who were falsely accused were also released. Someone said to my father that "If you had indicated your identity as a *jiaomin* or a churchman (a term meant a church member in the late Qing dynasty with a derogatory sense, 教民), you certainly would not have suffered this beating." My father answered, "I have become a believer without any connection with any church. Furthermore, at present many people have joined the Church so that they could play like overlords. If I had called myself a *jiaomin*, the magistrate would have been more likely to believe that I had been trying to protect the bad people by the power of the Church. Maybe he would not have beaten me, but the two people would have been more likely taken as bad people." My father truly did not want to shame the church. Afterwards, his fame of "scolding the official and saving the innocent from death" was spread among the neighbouring counties. (Qiutao noted: An elegiac couplet from Mr. Zhuo (卓) of Rongjin Li Jiechong (榕津里结冲) was published in *True Light* vol. 31, no. 9. This Mr. Zhuo was the one saved from this lawsuit by my father.[2])

In 1901, he was thirty-one years old. He tutored students at home as before. In this year, my father enjoyed writing couplets. In my memory, long couplets hang in the living room. One read: "It is good to have peace with people with humility and to protect family with thorough thinking; otherwise, it is dreadful." The other one read: "It is content to have a good sense by reading and to make a living by farming; besides, there is no want." My father could be known through this couplet.

In 1902, he was thirty-two years old. My father lived his life as before. Since his fame of "scolding the official to save innocent life" was spread, a group of seven gentries from Gongcheng County (恭城) used my father's name to scare their magistrate to save their servant who was going to be executed for a false charge. Though it was funny, it showed how the officials at the end of the Qing dynasty preyed on people and had a guilty conscience.

In this year, the China Baptist Publication Society (美华浸会印书局) was founded and *True Light* began to be issued.

In 1903, he was thirty-three years old. He helped militia with recording the statements of those robbers under examination and then they would be sent to the government for execution. After thirteen cases,[3] my father was unhappy with it and he quit this job to focus on teaching.

In 1904, he was thirty-four years old. He taught in Tong An area (同安) and enjoyed a co-operation with his co-worker Zhang Zhilin (张智林). Many students came to follow them.

In winter, a local merchant bought a lottery in my father's name and he won a lot of money. My father refused his offer of sharing the money. He said that he did not want to be viewed as a "gambler."

During the past few years, my father lived like a ship without a rudder. When Yu Jianpan (余建磐), the preacher in the area of Tong An (同安),

---

2. The elegiac couplet said "Recalling the past, I realize that you gave me the second life; Being unforgettable now, I mourn deeply that we are separated into different worlds" (回忆当年, 恩同再造; 难忘今日, 哀吊遥天), from Zhuo Lianyou (卓廉佑) of Rongjin Li Jiechong (榕浸里结冲). "Elegiac Couplets for Pastor Robert E. Chambers and Mr. Zhang Yijing, 76."

3. In Zhang Yijing's memory written in 1923, there were seventeen cases.

heard how my father refused the money won through the lottery, he visited my father and expressed his comfort and admiration. Because of this, my father was determined to devote his life to Christ, which was the beginning of his life mission. How important is the role of the preacher!

1905, he was thirty-five years old. All my father's brothers have become Christians and the family was filled with joy. My father was happy with this. He set a class at home to lead people to believe in Jesus. Every evening, people read the Bible, sang praising songs, and gave glory to God. My father took this year as his spiritual restoration.

In winter, he accompanied one of his students to Guangzhou for the student's further study. Accidentally, he met Mr. Liao Zhuoan (廖卓庵) on the street who was responsible for writing comments on articles published in *True Light*. He strongly recommended my father to help with this job. Then my father went back to his hometown to bring his family to Guangzhou. This was the second time my father joined the circle of the press to do preaching through writing.

In November, he wrote *On Moses* (摩西论) under the name of Jianru (鑑如).

In 1906, he was thirty-six years old. In spring, my father reached Guangzhou by ship with my mother and me and we lived temporarily at the home of Pastor Robert E. Chambers (湛罗弼) in Fang Cui (芳村).

In summer, we had a summer retreat at Culing (牯牛岭) of Lu Shan Mountain (庐山) in Jiangxi Province (江西) with the family of Robert E. Chambers (湛罗弼) who was the leader of *True Light*. In August, we went back to Guangzhou.

In 1907, he was thirty-seven years old. We moved to Hao Xian Street (豪贤街) in Guangzhou. My father worked as before. Now he did not have to go to work in Shamian Island (沙面) by boat. He could walk there.

In that year, the believers in Guangzhou began to be enthusiastic about the church becoming self-supporting and Christian schools being established. My father gave full support.

In May, my father wrote *On Jesus Will Not Desert His Followers* (耶稣不离其徒论) with a name of Qiuchan (秋蟾). In this year, Zhang Wenren (张文仁), one of my father's younger brothers, and Xiaobai (小白), his younger sister, came to live with us for their further study. The income did not increase, but there were more mouths to feed. Our life of poverty could be imagined.

In 1908, he was thirty-eight years old. In January, he wrote *Against Song Shixiang's Christianity Allows Offering Sacrifices to Ancestors* (驳宋史香耶稣教不禁人祭先说) under the name of Jianyu (检余).

In spring, we moved to Zha Fen Street (炸粉街) for a cheaper place. My father walked to work at Shamian Island (沙面) with Mr. Liao Zhuoan (廖卓庵) every day. According to the former regulations at Shamian Island (沙面), Chinese could only enter through a small door instead of the main gate. My father felt painful about it.

In March, my father wrote *The Importance of Preaching through Writing* (以书传道之关系) under the name of Zhishui (止水). In these two years, he loved making poems praising the Lord for *True Light* under the name of Heyin (荷寅). Such poems could be seen in *A Quarter of a Century of True Light, Selected* (真光丛刊).

In 1909, when the Xuantong Emperor (the last Emperor of the Qing dynasty, 宣统) took his throne for the first year, my father was thirty-nine years old. We moved to Pi Shan Academy (劈山书院) at Fu Rong Li (福榕里).

In spring, he wrote *Against the Speech of Atheism* (驳无神论之演说). In August, he wrote *The Relationship between the Advancement of Civilisation and the Church* (文明进步与教会之关系) under the name of Mujun (亩均). In September, he wrote *On Death* (说死) under the name of Jianyu (检余). In November, he wrote *On the Greatest Person in God's Sight* (论上帝所视为至大之人) under the name of Liusheng (流升).

In 1910, he was forty years old. He worked as before.

In 1911, he was forty-one years old. We moved to Si Bei Di Village (寺背底村), Qian Jian Street (前鑑街), and Dong Shan District (东山).

On 7 March according to the lunar calendar, Yangfen (扬芬), his second son, was born.

In April, he finished *Jesus and Confucius* (耶儒辩). Moreover, he also wrote *Jesus and Mo Zi* (Mo-tse) (耶墨辩) and *Cleansing the False Accusations against Christianity* (诬教雪). These were all long apologetical writings. From this year onwards, my father began to write long articles.

In December, he wrote *Against the Accusation of Changing Huaxia or China by Yi or Foreignness* (用夷变夏辩, 1909).

In this year, the offices of the Baptist church and the living places of Westerners moved to Dong Shan District (东山). Since my father had been provoked by discrimination during the last year, he swore he would never enter Shamian Island (沙面) again. Every day, my father gave his articles to Pastor Robert E. Chambers (湛罗弼) who would bring them to Shamian Island for publication. Though my father did not enter Shamian any longer, the business of *True Light* was not interfered with.

From this year onwards, my father loved to use the name of Yijing (亦镜) in his writings. He loved to buy paintings and books for entertainment.

In 1912 when the Republic of China was founded, he was forty-two years old. He left his job at *True Light* and carried boxes of books to his hometown with the expectation that he could enjoy the pleasure of reading books. Afterwards, out of his expectation, just after nearly half a year, Pastor Robert E. Chambers (湛罗弼) made every effort to urge him to carry on with his work. His resignation was not approved. He took his family back to Guangzhou once again. However, during that half a year, he read a lot of books. Therefore, in his future written polemics against anti-Christians, he was invincible.

In 1913, he was forty-three years old. He worked harder at writing apologetical articles. *A Hoe for Brambles* (去荆锄) and *Dissecting the Theory for a State Religion* (国教说解剖) were completed in this year, which should be owed to his half-year reading in his hometown. Mr. Wei Bian (韦编) praised him by composing a poem: "His words are wind and thunder and his pen gives a cold and sharp feeling like frost; the beauty in his words was from his reading of ten thousand of books; from the dynasties of Xia, Shang, and Zhou he searched for origins; In China, his articles ablaze gorgeous."

Between June and August, he wrote *Correcting Errors with Wang Jingwei's Words for Destroying Christianity in the First Issue of Min De Newspaper* (纠正汪精卫巴黎民德报发刊词毁教语之谬).

In October, he completed *Refuting Chen Huanzhang's Petition for Establishing Confucianism as the State Religion* (驳陈焕章等请定孔教为国教呈文).

In 1914, he was forty-four years. During these years, we lived at Xin He Pu (新河浦) in Dong Shan District (东山), because the China Baptist Publication Society (美华浸会印书局) and *True Light* had moved here and built dormitory houses for staff.

In March, he wrote *On the Great Harmony* (说大同). He also wrote *The Explanation of Becoming Republic* (共和之的解) which was published as a separate edition.

In August and September, he wrote *Correcting Errors with Dr. Chen Huanzhang's Speech on Confucianism* (读陈焕章博士孔教讲义辩谬).

In 1915, he was forty-five years old. He quit his job and moved to Hong Kong to teach Chinese to Miss Chen Shuzhen (陈淑贞), the daughter of Dr. Yin Wenkai (尹文楷), with St. Stephen. During the time, he wrote *A Detailed Annotation of Correspondences of Qiu Shui Xuan* (详注秋水轩尺牍) which could serve as a book on Chinese etymology. Regretfully, it has not been published. He also wrote an incomplete work *Essence of Zhuang Zi* (a representative of Taoism, 庄子, 369–286 BC).

Before he quit, when he wrote comments on current issues for *True Light*, he criticized President Yuan Shikai (袁世凯), and Long Jiguang (龙济光), the governor of Guangdong Province. After reaching Hong Kong, he received secret reports from friends in Hong Kong and Macao that Governor Long offered a heavy reward for his head. His friends asked him not to return to Guangzhou anymore. It was God that had directed him to Hong Kong.

In this year, he and Dr. Yin Wenkai (尹文楷) started *Tan Tian Weekly* (谈天周刊) which was for preaching.

In 1916, he was forty-six years old. On the tomb-sweeping day, he wrote *Study of Tomb-Sweeping at the Qingming Festival* (清明扫墓考) which was published in *Da Guang Newspaper* (大光报). He published *Study of the Source and History of Ancestor-Worshipping* (祭先源流考) on *Tan Tian Weekly* (谈天周刊). These two have been published as separate editions. They were very popular and they have been reprinted many times.

In summer, Pastor J. Speicher (师雅各), the acting director of *True Light*, firmly demanded him to take over the editing of a series of books for preaching in Hong Kong. Out of his strong sense of duty, my father accepted. So he laid aside *Tan Tian Weekly* (谈天周刊) to focus on editing.

In August, he wrote *Thoughts over A Western Pastor's Plan on Mastering Chinese with His Colleagues* (闻某西牧欲联同志精习汉文感言) with the name of Zhang Wen Kai (张文开).

In 1917, he was forty-seven years old. He quit his work in *True Light*. Then he started *Da Guang Weekly* (大光周刊) as a continuation of *Tan Tian Weekly* (谈天周刊).

In February, he was engaged in written polemics against the anti-Christian writers of *Guo Shi Newspaper* (国是报). He had all his articles published in *Da Guang Newspaper* (大光报). *Guo Shi Newspaper* (国是报) changed its writers three times and all the writers were silenced. *True Light* (author notes: it should be a mistake for *Da Guang*) won the final victory. The denominations in Hong Kong rejoiced greatly and put the arguments from both sides into a collection with a printed name *Da Guang Po An Ji* or *The Collection of the Great Light Breaking Darkness* (大光破暗集) which was published by *Da Guang Newspaper*.

After this written polemics, he resumed his responsibility for *Da Guang Weekly* (大光周刊). Shortly after this, Pastor J. Speicher (师雅各) arrived in Hong Kong and asked him to resume his responsibilities in *True Light*. So *Da Guang Weekly* (大光周刊) was stopped.

After *Study of Tomb-Sweeping at the Qingming Festival* (清明扫墓考), *Study of the Source and History of Ancestor-Worshipping* (祭先源流考), and *Against Atheism* (驳无神论) have been published as separate editions, his *Study of Burning Incense in the Two Testaments* (二约焚香典礼考), *Wang Yun Questioned Kong Zheng or Confucius* (王允问孔正), and *The Relationship between Taoism and Buddhism* (道释关系) were also published as separate books.

In 1918, he was forty-eight years old. He still lived in Hong Kong.

In March, he wrote *On Writing for Preaching* (论传道文字) under the name of Zhenmei (珍枚). Then he wrote *Lao Zi* or *Tai Shang Lao Jun* (太上老君) and *Bodhisattva* (观世音). They were all published by *True Light*.

In July, the editing department of the China Baptist Publication Society (美华浸会印书局) and *True Light* moved to Shantou (汕头). My father also moved to live at Zhi Nan Li (指南里) of Shantou (汕头).

In August, he wrote *Talk with an Old Pedant* (与老学究语).

In September, he wrote *Against Atheist Zhang Taiyan's Anti-Religion Article* (驳抄太炎无神论之非宗教文).

In 1919, he was forty-nine years old. He still lived in Shantou (汕头) and worked as before. At the birthday of Confucius, Shantou Presbyterian Huaying School (华英学校) had a Confucius-worshipping storm. Zhang organized *A Special Issue of Confucius Worshipping Storm* (拜孔风潮专号) to defend the school and church. This *Special Issue* was published as a book *The Record of Confucius Worshipping Storm at Huaying* (华英拜孔风潮记).

Most of his articles written in Shantou were under the name of Pingji (萍寄).

In March, he wrote *The Qualifications for a Preacher* (传道人当具何资格) under the name of Donghong (冬烘).

In 1920, he was fifty years old. As the editing department was five hundred kilometres away from the printing house in Guangzhou, many errors happened from the poor co-operation between proofreading and printing. On 13 November, the works in Shantou (汕头) were moved back to Guangzhou. All the responsibilities of *True Light* were entrusted to my father by Pastor Robert E. Chambers (湛罗弼) and Pastor J. Speicher (师雅各). Since then, my father used the name of Zhang Yijing (亦镜) for his articles and business card and he seldom used other names anymore.

In autumn, he wrote *A Study of Christianity and Confucianism* (耶儒之研究).

From August to February 1921, he continued with writing *Against Atheist Zhang Taiyan's Anti-Religion Article* (驳抄太炎无神论之非宗教文). In November, he wrote *Investigating the Rite of Fu of Nestorians in Tang Dynasty* (大秦穆护祓考) under the name of Pingji (萍寄).[4]

In 1921, he was fifty-one years old. He lived in the new house at Xin He Pu (新河浦) in Dong Shan District (东山).

In this year and the next year, because of the defamation of Christianity by *Wuzhou Saving China Daily* (梧州救国日报), Zhang published a thick book *New Collection of Correcting Absurdity* (纠谬新编). In response to the Anti-Christian Student Federation (非基督教学生同盟) and the Anti-Religion Alliance (非宗教大同盟), he published another two thick books of *A Special Issue of Criticising the Theories of Anti-Christian Movement* and *A Sequel to Criticising the Theories of Anti-Christian Movement* (正续 批评非基督教言论汇刊) which sold over fifty thousand volumes. *A Special Issue of Criticising the Theories of Anti-Christian Movement* sold more than twenty thousand copies within the first month of its publication and it had to be reprinted within the same month, which had never been seen before among the publications by the churches in China. These two special issues were compiled into a book named *Answering Attacks upon Christianity* (批评非基督教言论汇刊全编).

In 1922, he was fifty-two years old. He worked in the Dong Shan District (东山) as before.

---

4. Tang dynasty AD 635 – 845.

In 1923, he was fifty-three years old. His second son Yangfen (扬芬) died of diphtheria at the age of thirteen. When Yangfen was ill, my father paid no attention to him because he was too busy with writing. Later on, Yangfen's illness became too serious to be cured. After Yangfen's death, my father often described his feeling by reciting the poem, "Where to look for? Only the moon is sure." He became so sad that he became ill. After his recovery, he was not as lively as before.

In 1924, he was fifty-four years old. He worked in the Dong Shan District (东山) as before.

In 1925, he was fifty-five years old. He moved to Hong Kong to do the same job.

In 1926, he was fifty-six years old. There were many workers' demonstrations. The China Baptist Publication Society (美华浸会印书局) had to stop its work. Then *True Light* was moved to Shanghai.

In summer, at the time of moving from Hong Kong to Shanghai, Pastor Zhang Zhuling (张祝龄) introduced Mr. Li Qianli (李千里) to my father. Mr. Li was a poet. Since then, his poems were often published in *True Light*. (After my father died, Li composed more than one hundred poems to commemorate him. Those poems were published in a tract as a gift for friends. Those poems were excellent.

While he was in Shanghai, he made friends with Dan Tu (丹徒) and poet Yan Jiqing (严霁青). They often composed poems to respond to each other. My father preferred Fragrance Hill style (the style of famous poet Bai Juyi 白居易, 772–846) in his poem writing. In spite of this, few were published.

In this year, my father and Mr. Lu Danlin (陆丹林) joined Shanghai Jing She Club (Qiutao noted: This club was for literati. Its purpose was to learn from each other and they discussed topics concerning the ancient and modern times. It was a respectable place for the entertainment of the literati. Shanghai 上海景社).

In 1927, he was fifty-seven years old. In May, my mother caught a cold which finally led to an illness, brain fever. She felt very painful. On 26 June, she was admitted to Bethel Hospital founded by Dr. Shi Meiyu (石美玉). At a quarter past three on 2 July, she died at the age of fifty-five. On that morning I arrived from Nanchang (南昌) of Jiangxi Province (江西). In the afternoon, she was buried at the cemetery of the Baptist church in the Zha Bei district (闸北).

Around that time, my father was busy with compiling *The Special Issue for the 25th Anniversary of True Light* (真光二十五周年纪念特刊). *Answering Attacks upon Christianity* (批评非基督教言论汇刊全编) which was finished in 1926 was also to be printed. *A Quarter of a Century of True Light, Selected* (真光丛刊) was also close to its publication date. My father worked over sixteen hours each day (Qiutao noted: the working hours of my father were over ten hours each day on average). He forgot meals and sleep and felt sorrowful over the loss of his wife.

In 1928, he was fifty-eight years old. On 17 January, *A Quarter of a Century of True Light, Selected* (真光丛刊), a great work, was published. This book was a collection of important articles published by *True Light*. It had more than 900 pages and more than one million words. Hou Shuxian (侯述先), Lu Danlin (陆丹林), and Yan Jiqing (严霁青) wrote forewords for it. From that time, my father's health became even weaker.

In 1929, he was fifty-nine years old. My father had a summer retreat in Qingdao (青岛) while my aunt Xiaobai (小白) and I went back to Guangxi Province (广西). He enjoyed sole fish and mailed some to my grandmother.

In November, he decided to donate 1000 yuan (taken from his salary) for the new building of *True Light* in Shanghai, starting from the spring of the next year.

In this winter, my father started to live a life of poverty. In addition to three meals, he had no other spending. He practised saving the country by living a simple life. He decided to sell his calligraphy to help with the family life.

In 1930, he was sixty years old. In June, his left leg suffered a sprain. The medicine did not work. So he had a soft foot syndrome. A swelling developed on his shin and finally, he was not able to walk anymore. He had to do all things in bed. Mr. Lu Danlin (陆丹林) used to say he was accompanied by a pen, two bottles of ink, a pair of scissors, a bottle of paste, a bag of China tobacco, and a bottle of water. In addition to these things, he had two more new companions: a bed and a mat. His suffering was in the extreme. He had an emaciated and dried-up appearance and a pale face. He was kept indoors for months, which weakened his health further.

My father's illness developed this way. It started on his left hip and it spread to his left shin. Then his right shoulder became infected. The boundaries of the swellings were not clear. At first, the colour remained the same. He felt pain when people pressed such parts with their fingers. When his position was not right, he also felt painful. The painful parts had a pulse.

In 1931, he was sixty-one years old. This year, my father's works sold very well. More than one hundred thousand copies of *Five Answers to the Basic Truth* (要道五答) were sold.

Chinese Christian Advocate in Shanghai (兴华报, a publication by the Methodist Publishing House) carried out a survey on who were the ten most famous Chinese Christians. My father got twenty votes and became the tenth one on the list.

When *China Monthly Review* (密勒评论报) with J. B. Powell as the editor looked for twelve thousand famous Chinese from all walks of the society and their curriculum vitae, my father was one among the chosen from the press. A book with the information of these people was published.

On 6 March, my father set out for Guangdong Province (广东) for treatment after the medical help in Shanghai had achieved no effect for a long time. Three Western pastors whose names were W. H. Tipton (贴威林), Jas. T. Williams (威林士), and Mr. C. J. Lowe (卢信恩) showed to my father the love Jesus demonstrated in washing his disciples' feet. They carried him down from the third floor, took him to the dock by car, and carried him to the cabin of the ship. Many Christians came to say farewell and gave gifts of food. My father was moved to tears to such a degree that he lost his voice. At ten o'clock on the evening of 11 March, we safely reached the house on Pei Zheng South Road (培正南路) in Dong Shan District (东山) of Guangzhou (广州). The smooth trip resulted from the preparations made by Mr. Huang Shigong (黄石公).

On 22 March, he was admitted to the Baptist Hospital in Dong Shan District (东山). The X-ray showed that the tumours had extensively spread to good tissue. His left shin bone had been decayed by a tumour. His shin bone looked like it has been broken. Many doctors came but this could not be cured by surgery.

On 2 April, his right shoulder could not move. A new tumour was found there.

On 4 October, my father was determined to return to his hometown and we set out. On 2 December, we reached his hometown. He felt happy and he could eat more. However, very soon the former condition resumed and he lost his appetite even more than before. He sometimes coughed and spat yellow phlegm. Occasionally he coughed up stagnant blood. Then his urine had blood in it. Later on, there was a big decrease in the amount of his urine.

On 9 December, his speech was blurred. The next morning, he asked his family to sing a song. My aunt Xiaobai (小白) chose *The Place of the Lord's Rest*, the fifty-fourth song in the song book, *Praising the Lord* (颂主诗歌). After singing, my father said, "It is enough." Then he was soaked in sweat. Seeing this, my family knelt down and prayed for him. After prayer, my father also said "Amen." After one o'clock in the afternoon, his breathing quickened and then he died at the age of sixty-one.

APPENDIX 2

The Works of Mr. Zhang Yijing[1] (张亦镜先生的著作)

Zhang's Apologetical Writings

1. *The Collection of the Great Light Breaking Darkness* (大光破暗集, 1916). This was a collection of the war of words between Zhang who took *Da Guang Newspaper* or *The Great Light Newspaper* (大光报) as his battlefield and the Confucian Association (孔教会) which advocated the establishment of Confucianism as China's state religion through *Guo Shi Newspaper* or *National Affairs* (国是报).
2. *Cleansing the False Accusations against Christianity* (诬教雪, 1910). In 1910, a newspaper in Guangdong Province made accusations against the missionaries and claimed: "They intend to destroy Confucianism in order to demolish China (灭国先灭教)." Following this, Zhang wrote this book to refute this article.
3. *Jesus and Confucius* (耶儒辩, 1910). In this book, Zhang first listed the advantages and disadvantages of Christianity and then he listed the similarities and differences between Christianity and Confucianism.
4. *Jesus and Mo Zi* (耶墨辩, 1911).
5. *Brothers Chen Xiang and Chen Xin* (陈相兄弟辩). Some people viewed Confucian scholars who became Christians as traitors, just as brothers of Chen Xiang (陈相) and Chen Xin (陈辛) who deserted Confucianism to

---

[1] This list is based on Yijing Zhang, "How I Became a Christian"; Cheng, "Works of Mr. Zhang Yijing"; Jiang, "Works of Mr. Zhang Yijing (张亦镜先生的著作)"; and Zhang, "Chronology of Zhang Yijing." The author is the son of Zhang Yijing. These works were printed in separate editions.

follow Xu Xing (许行) to learn the theories of Shennong (神农氏, 3245–3080 BC) in the book of *Mencius* (孟子, 372–289). Zhang refuted this view.

6. *Against the Accusation of Changing Huaxia or China by Yi or Foreignness* (用夷变夏辩, 1909).
7. *Against the Atheism of Irreligious Socialism* (驳无宗教社会主义之无神论, before 1918).
8. *Talk with an Old Pedant* (与老学究语, 1918). This was an argument against an old pedant instead of a friend. In this book, Zhang based his assumptions on the old learning in China by the old pedant.
9. *Talking with Wang Jingwei about the Truth* (与汪精卫论道).
10. *Argue against Chen Duxiu and Shen Xuanlu over Christianity* (与陈独秀沈玄庐论道). This was to refute Chen Duxiu's *Christianity and the Chinese* (基督教和中国人) and Shen Xuanlu's *Doubts about Christianity and the Chinese* (对于基督教和中国人的怀疑).
11. *Refuting a Plagiarism of Zhang Taiyan's Atheistic Attack on Religion* (驳抄太炎无神论之非宗教文, 1920).
12. *New Collection of Correcting Absurdity* (纠谬新编). During 1921 and 1922, because of the defamations of Christianity by *Wuzhou Saving China Daily* (梧州救国日报), Zhang published this thick book *New Collection of Correcting Absurdity* (纠谬新编) to refute it.
13. *On Socialists' "No Reckless Action"* (谈社会主义的"莫要乱来").
14. *Against the Speech of Atheism* (驳无神论之演说, 1909).
15. *Comments on Zhu Zhixin's "What the Heck Is Jesus"* (关于朱执信'耶稣是什么东西'的杂评).
16. *Answering Attacks upon Christianity* (批评非基督教言论汇刊全编, 1927).
17. *The Records and Comments on the Ferocious Anti-Christian Movement in 1924* (民十三之剧烈反基督教运动记评).
18. *Review of the Anti-Christian Agitation* (最近反基督教纪评, 1925).
19. *Criticism of Wu Zhihui's "The Views on Universe and Life of a New Faith"* (批评吴稚晖先生的一个新信仰的宇宙观及人生观). (A special issue with Zhang Yijing as the editor.)
20. *The Record of Confucius Worshipping Storm at Hua Ying* (华英拜孔风潮记, 1919).
21. *A Hoe for Brambles* (去荆锄, 1913).
22. *Dissecting the Theory for a State Religion* (国教说解剖, 1913).
23. *Xu Guangqi's Refutations of Fallacies* (徐光启辟谬).
24. *Wang Yun Questioned Kong Zheng or Confucius* (王允问孔正, 1916).
25. *Answering Dr. Chen Huanzhang's Error concerning Religion* (驳陈焕章博士说教之谬, 1919). This book had two parts. The first is *Refuting Chen Huanzhang and Other Four People's Petition for Establishing Confucianism as the State Religion* (驳陈焕章等请定孔教为国教呈文, 1913). The second part is

Correcting Errors with Dr. Chen Huanzhang's Speech on Confucianism (读陈焕章博士孔教讲义辩谬, 1914).

Zhang's Writings for Preaching

1. *Five Answers to the Basic Truth* (要道五答). This book had been reprinted six to seven times before Zhang's death in 1931.
2. *Challenging Equivocation from the Unbelievers* (诘推诿不信者, 1911).
3. *The Exploration of the Origin of the Word* (道源一勺, 即神学管窥, 1916).
4. *The Current Needs of China* (中国今日之需要).
5. *An Experienced Man* (过来人).
6. *Jia Kunshan* (贾坤山, before 1918).
7. *The Shadow of the Lamb* (绵羊影, before 1918).
8. *The Truest Sayings of Lu Lun* (鲁论至言, before 1918).
9. *The Strategies for Supporting the Church* (养会策).
10. *A Giant Fish among the Sea of People* (人海巨鱼).
11. *War and Religion* (战争与宗教).
12. *Folk Proverbs for Alerting the Secular* (警俗俚言, before 1918).
13. *A Song of the Cross* (十字歌).
14. *On Cultivating Integrity* (养正论).
15. *Translation of Excerpts of Prophecies* (预言摘译).
16. *The Only Teacher of All People* (普世人类唯一之尊师).
17. *The Heavenly King* (上帝).
18. *The Genuineness of Christian* (基督徒之真).
19. *On Races* (人种辩, before 1918).

Zhang's Works of Textual Criticism

1. *Study of the Source and History of Ancestor-Worshipping* (祭先源流考, 1916).
2. *Break the Obstinacy in Ancestor-Worshipping* (破祭先执, 1925).
3. *Study of Tomb-Sweeping at the Qingming Festival* (清明扫墓考, 1916).
4. *The Relationship between Taoism and Buddhism* (道释关系, 1916).
5. *Two Cases of the Hatred of Taoism towards Buddhism* (道仇释两大案).
6. *The Explanation of Becoming Republic* (共和之的解, 1914).

Zhang's Works of Biography

1. *Clear Evidence from the Autobiography of Sun Yat-sen* (孙中山自历明证). This was written after Sun Yat-sen was rescued from dangers he met in London.
2. *Huang Naishang, A Great Man among Christians* (基督徒中之伟大人物黄乃裳).
3. *The Biography of Adoniram Judson* (耶德逊传).

4. *Lao Zi or Tai Shang Lao Jun* (太上老君, 1918).
5. *Bodhisattva* (观世音, 1918).
6. *Investigating the Rite of Fu of Nestorians in Tang Dynasty* (大秦穆护祓考, 1920). Tang dynasty AD 635 – 845.
7. *The Biography of Śākyamuni* (释迦摩尼传, 1924).
8. *Study of Burning Incense in the Two Testaments* (二约焚香典礼考, 1916).

Other Works

1. *A Detailed Annotation of Correspondences of Qiu Shui Xuan* (详注秋水轩尺牍, 1915) which could serve as a book on Chinese etymology. It was published probably before 1941.
2. He also had an incomplete work, *Essence of Zhuang Zi* (a representative of Taoism, 庄子, 369–286 BC).
3. On his sickbed in 1931, Zhang edited all his works into *The Collection of Zhang Yijing's Works* (张亦镜先生论道集). This collection was sent back to the China Baptist Publication Society for publication;[2] however, there is no trace of it.

---

2. Cheng Hao 郝城. "The Works of Mr. Zhang Yijing (张亦镜先生的著作)," 33–38.

APPENDIX 3

A Brief History of *True Light* (1902–1927)[1] (真光小史)

In 1902 when *True Light* was founded, its name was *True Light Monthly* (真光月报). It contained 32–38 pages. The yearly fee was 3.5 cents for the Chinese and 5 cents for the foreigners.

In 1903, the number of pages reached 40. The yearly fee was 5 cents for the Chinese and 6.5 cents for the foreigners.

In 1905, the yearly fee was 6 cents for the Chinese and 6.5 cents for the foreigners.

In 1906, *True Light Monthly* was changed to *True Light Newspaper* (真光报). It was still a monthly publication. The number of pages reached 57–60.

In 1910, the yearly fee was 1 yuan for the Chinese and 1.2 yuan for the foreigners.

In 1912, a new weekly paper *True Light Newspaper Attachment* (真光报附张) was issued. This was specifically for news of the church and the current news. *True Light Newspaper* (真光报) stopped including any news. The yearly fee was 1.2 yuan for the Chinese and 1.3 yuan for the foreigners.

In 1916, *True Light Newspaper Attachment* (真光报附张) was stopped. The news was incorporated into *True Light Newspaper* (真光报). The name *True Light Newspaper* (真光报) was changed to *True Light* (真光). Since then, the monthly publication became a semi-monthly. Each issue had 40 pages.

---

1. This is based on Zhang Yijing's description. Zhang, "Last Twenty-five Years," 1–7.

Habitually, Chinese just call this publication "*True Light* 真光." For the sake of clarity, in this study, "*True Light* 真光" is used to stand for all the names used by this publication except *True Light Newspaper Attachment* (真光报附张).

In 1917, *True Light* (真光) was changed to *True Light Magazine* (真光杂志) which was still a semi-monthly. Each issue had 48–50 pages. The yearly fee was 1.2 yuan for the Chinese and 1.5 yuan for the foreigners.

From the date of the first issue until April 1916, there were 170 issues in total. All of the 170 issues were numbered by their corresponding ordinal numbers. For example, the issue of April 1916 was no. 170 (第170册).

From May 1916 to December 1916, there were 16 issues in total. They were still numbered by their corresponding ordinal numbers. For example, the last issue of December 1916 was no. 186 (第186册).

From 1917, the year number was added to the number of issues. The first issue of 1917 should have been marked no. 1 of 16th year (第一六年第一册) while the last issue of 1917 should have been no. 24 of 16th year (第一六年第二十四册). Nevertheless, a counting mistake happened, so all the issues in 1917 were marked with 15th year (第一五年).

In 1918, all the issues were marked with 17th year (第一七年). So the first issue was no. 1 of 17th year while the last issue was no. 24 of 17th year. This practice lasted until the end of June 1920.

From July 1920, "year (年)" was changed into "volume (卷)." The first issue in July 1920 was called "volume 19, no. 13 (第十九卷第十三号)." The numbers of lines and words on each page increased. The titles of the articles were printed on the cover page so that the contents became clearer to the readers.

From the beginning of January 1923, it became a monthly again. Each issue had 96 pages. The former issues were published on the first day of each month, but the current monthly was published on the 15th of each month.

Since 1924, the second half of the monthly used a smaller font so that more materials could be included.

In 1927, the fee was 1.5 yuan for the Chinese and 2 yuan for the foreigners.

Bibliography

Archives

Southern Baptist Historical Library and Archives, Nashville (SBHLA)
Chambers, Robert Edwards. 1926. "Rev. T. B. Ray D. D., USA," 25 August 1926. FMB AR 551-2, BOX 81, Chambers Robert Edwards, Ex Secretary, 1925-26.
Lide, R. W. 1934. "Dr. Rosewell H. Graves." FMB AR 551-1, MISS. MINUTES, BOX - 229, Mission South China, Articles, 1925-39, 229-34.
Tipton, W. H. 1936. "Annual Report of China Baptist Publication Society." FMB AR 551-1, MISS. MINUTES, BOX - 229, Mission South China, Articles, 1930-40, 229-35.

Other Sources

Aikman, David. *Jesus in Beijing: How Christianity Is Transforming China and Changing the Global Balance of Power.* Oxford: Monarch Books, 2006.
Alisat, Susan, and Michael W. Pratt. "Characteristics of Young Adults' Personal Religious Narratives and Their Relation with the Identity Status Model: A Longitudinal, Mixed Methods Study." *Identity: An International Journal of Theory and Research* 12, no. 1 (2012): 29-52.
Amiot, Catherine E., Roxane de la Sablonnière, Deborah J. Terry, and Joanne R. Smith. "Integration of Social Identities in the Self: Toward a Cognitive-Developmental Model." *Personality and Social Psychology Review* 11, no. 4 (2007): 364-88.
Anderson, Benedict. *Imagined Communities: Reflections on the Origin and Spread of Nationalism.* London: Verso, 1991.
Annual of the Northern Baptist Convention. American Baptist Publication Society, 1921.

Barrett, Matthew, and Ardel B. Caneday, eds. *Four Views on the Historical Adam*. Grand Rapids: Zondervan, 2013.

Bays, Daniel H. *A New History of Christianity in China*. Malden, MA: Wiley-Blackwell, 2012.

———. "Protestantism in Modern China as 'Foreign Religion' and 'Chinese Religion': Autonomy, Independence, and the Constraints of Foreign Hegemony." In *Confucianism and Spiritual Traditions in Modern China and Beyond*, edited by Fenggang Yang and Joseph B. Tamney, 229–46. Leiden: Brill, 2012.

Bevans, Stephen B. *Models of Contextual Theology*. Rev. and exp. ed. Maryknoll: Orbis Books, 2004.

Billioud, Sébastien, and Joël Thoraval. "Anshen Liming or the Religious Dimension of Confucianism." *China Perspectives* 3, no. 75 (2008): 88–106. https://www.jstor.org/stable/24054196.

Bodde, Derk. "Henry A. Wallace and the Ever-Normal Granary (1946)." In *Essays on Chinese Civilization*, edited by Charles Le Blanc and Dorothy Borei, 218–34. Princeton: Princeton University Press, 1981. http://www.jstor.org/stable/j.ctt7zvh5f.16.

Bonhoeffer, Dietrich. 做门徒的代价 *(The Cost of Discipleship)*. 北京 Beijing: 新星出版社 New Star Press, 2013.

Bosch, David J. *Transforming Mission: Paradigm Shifts in Theology of Mission*. Maryknoll: Orbis Books, 1991.

Brockman, F. S. 巴乐满. "Seeking Not for One's Own Greatness." *China's Young Men* 16, no. 1–2 (1913): 41–42.

Brown, Hubert O. "Tao Xingzhi: Progressive Educator in Republican China." *Biography* 13, no. 1 (1990): 21–42.

Buoye, Thomas. "Capital Punishment and Confucian Justice: The Limits of Leniency under Traditional Chinese Law." *Studies in Qing History*, no. 4 (2006): 51–58.

Burke, P. J. "Identity Change." *Social Psychology Quarterly* 69 (2006): 81–96.

Cai, Yuanpei 蔡元培. "On Substituting Aesthetic Education for Religion (以美育代宗教说)." *La Jeunesse* 新青年 3, no. 6 (1917): 1–5.

Campbell, William S. *Paul and the Creation of Christian Identity*. London: T&T Clark, 2006.

Cao, Xinming 曹新铭. "In Commemoration of Mr. Zhang Yijing the Former Chief Editor (纪念本志前主编张亦镜先生)." *True Light* 真光 40, no. 12 (1941): 1.

Carter, Craig A. *Rethinking Christ and Culture: A Post-Christendom Perspective*. Grand Rapids: Brazos Press, 2006.

Chambers, Robert Edwards. "Rev. T. B. Ray D. D., U.S.A.," 25 August 1926. FMB AR 551–52, Box 81, Chambers Robert Edwards, Ex Secretary, 1925–26.

Chan, Wai Keung 陈伟强. "Christianity Meets the Chinese Religions: A Case Study of Xu Dishan 基督教與中國宗教相遇—許地山研究." PhD diss., The Chinese University of Hong Kong, 2002.

Chan, Wing-Tsit. "Neo-Confucianism: New Ideas in Old Terminology." *Philosophy East and West* 17, no. 1/4 (1967): 15–35.

———. "Neo-Confucianism and Chinese Scientific Thought." *Philosophy East and West* 6, no. 4 (1957): 309–32.

Chao, T. C. 赵紫宸. "Discussion over the Indigenization of the Church (本色教会的商榷)." *Youth Progress* 青年进步 76 (1924): 8–15.

———. "My Opinions on Creating Chinese Christian Churches (我对于创造中国基督教会的几个意见)." *True Light* 真光 26, no. 6 (1927): 1–13.

Chen, Chunsheng 陈春生. "Ruan Xiaoxian Who Called Others Sordid Jerks (骂人肮脏东西的阮啸仙)." In *Answering Attacks upon Christianity* 批评非基督教言论汇刊全编, edited by Yijing Zhang, 351–52. Shanghai 上海: China Baptist Publication Society 中华浸会书局, 1927.

Chen, Duxiu 陈独秀. "Christianity and Chinese (基督教和中國人)." *La Jeunesse (新青年)* 7, no. 3 (1920): 15–22.

———. "My Patriotism (我之爱国主义)." *La Jeunesse* 新青年 2, no. 2 (1916): 1–6.

———. "On Destroying Idols (偶像破坏论)." *La Jeunesse* 新青年 5, no. 2 (1918): 89–91.

Chen, Jing 陈静. "Question about Yang Guangxian's Hui Nationality or Muslim Identity 杨光先回族或回教徒问题质疑." *Study of Hui Nationality* 回族研究, no. 2 (1993): 78–82.

Chen, Yong. *Confucianism as Religion: Controversies and Consequences*. Leiden: Brill, 2013.

Chiu, King Pong. *Thomé H. Fang Tang Junyi and Huayan Thought*. Leiden: Brill, 2016. https://doi.org/10.1163/9789004313880.

Chow, Tse-tung. *The May Fourth Movement: Intellectual Revolution in Modern China*. Cambridge: Harvard University Press, 1960.

Chu, Samuel C. 朱昌峻. "Early 20th Century Chinese Christian Writers and the Church Indigenization Movement (二十世纪初期中国基督教作家的教会本土化运动)." In *Bulletin of the Institute of Modern History, Academia Sinica* 中央研究院近代史研究所集刊 12, 195–217. Taipei 台北: Institute of Modern History, Academia Sinica 中央研究院近代史研究所, 1983.

Cohen, Paul A. *China and Christianity: The Missionary Movement and the Growth of Chinese Antiforeignism, 1860–1870*. Cambridge: Harvard University Press, 1963.

———. "Cultural China: Some Definitional Issues." *Philosophy East and West* 43, no. 3 (1993): 557–63. https://doi.org/10.2307/1399582.

———. *Discovering History in China: American Historical Writing on the Recent Chinese Past*. New York: Columbia University Press, 1984.

Conant, Judson Eber. *The Church, the Schools and Evolution*. Chicago: Bible Institute Colportage Ass'n, 1922.

Côté, James E. "Editor's Note: The Hope and Promise of Identity Theory and Research." *Identity: An International Journal of Theory and Research* 1, no. 1 (2001): 1–5.

Crocetti, E., M. Rubini, and W. Meeus. "Capturing the Dynamics of Identity Formation in Various Ethnic Groups: Development and Validation of a Three-Dimensional Model." *Journal of Adolescence* 31, 2 (2008): 207–22.

Crocetti, Elisabetta, and Wim Meeus. "The Identity Statuses: Strengths of a Person-Centered Approach." In *The Oxford Handbook of Identity Development*, edited by K. C. McLean and M. Syed, 97–114. New York: Oxford University Press, 2015.

Cui, Aiguang 崔爱光. "On Sinicization of the Church (论中国化教会)." *True Light* 真光 23, no. 11 (1924): 16.

Culp, Robert. "Teaching Baihua: Textbook Publishing and the Production of Vernacular Language and a New Literary Canon in Early Twentieth-Century China." *Twentieth-Century China* 34, no. 1 (2008): 4–41.

Deng, Zigang 邓子刚. "The Contemporary Significance of Confucius' Idea of Cultivation and Reading 儒家耕读传家思想的现代意义." *Journal of Hunan First Normal College* 湖南第一师范学报 7, no. 1 (2007): 63–66.

Dorrien, Gary. *The Making of American Liberal Theology: Crisis, Irony, and Postmodernity, 1950–2005*. Louisville: Westminster John Knox Press, 2006.

Doyle, Wright. "Lit-Sen Chang (1904–1996) and the Critique of Indigenous Theology." *International Journal for the Study of the Christian Church* 15, no. 4 (2015): 345–61.

Duan, Zhiwen 段治文. "Influence from Modern Scientism on Marxism's Spread and Localization in China." *Journal of Jiaxing University* 嘉兴学院学报 30, no. 4 (2018): 68–73.

Duara, Prasenjit. "Transnationalism and the Predicament of Sovereignty: China, 1900–1945." *The American Historical Review* 102, no. 4 (1997): 1030–51.

Dunch, Ryan. "Beyond Cultural Imperialism: Cultural Theory, Christian Missions, and Global Modernity." *History and Theory* 41, no. 3 (2002): 301–25. http://www.jstor.org/stable/3590688.

———. *Fuzhou Protestants and the Making of a Modern China, 1857–1927*. New Haven: Yale University Press, 2001.

Dunlop, William L., and Lawrence J. Walker. "The Life Story: Its Development and Relation to Narration and Personal Identity." *International Journal of Behavioral Development* 37, no. 3 (2013): 235–47.

"Elegiac Couplets for Pastor Robert E. Chambers and Mr. Zhang Yijing (文艺:湛罗弼牧师、张亦镜先生挽联)." *True Light* 真光 31, no. 9 (1932): 71–80.

Erikson, Erik H. *Identity: Youth and Crisis*. New York: W. W. Norton, 1968.

———. *Identity and Life Cycle*. New York: W. W. Norton, 1979.
Fairbank, J. K. *The Chinese World Order: Traditional China's Foreign Relations*. Cambridge, MA: Harvard University Press, 1968.
Fan, Bihui 范皕诲. "The Missions of YMCA in China (中华基督教青年会的使命)." *Association Progress* 青年进步, no. 55 (1922): 90–93.
———. "A Preface to the Bound Edition of True Light Volume Twenty-Seven 真光杂志合订本序." *Youth Progress* 青年进步, no. 120 (1929): 93–94.
Fan, Daming 范大明. "A Dialogue between God and Confucius: Are the Sun and the Moon? Setting Zhang Yijing as the Center 上帝与孔子的对话：日与月乎？" *Journal of Hunan City University* 湖南城市学院院报 34, no. 2 (2013): 32–38.
———. "Exploring Zhang Yijing's Indigenization 审判与选择: 寻索基督教与中国文化的关系——张亦镜本色神学之探." 世界宗教研究 *Studies in World Religions* 3 (2014): 130–42.
———. "New Culture Developed from the Church–Focusing on the Ideas of Zhang Yijing (新文化源于教会论—以张亦镜为中心)." 史林 *Journal of History* 3 (2014): 81–91.
Fan, Daming 范大明, Ling Li, 李灵, and Jianming Chen 陈建明. "True Light: Search for the Relationship between Christianity and Chinese Culture – Taking Zhang Yijing as a Case (真光杂志: 寻索基督教与中国文化的关系 – 以张亦镜为中心的考察)." In *Christian Text Media and Modern China* 基督教文字传媒与中国近代社会, 446–49. Shanghai 上海: Shanghai People's Press 上海人民出版社, 2013.
Fang, Dongmei 方东美. *Philosophies of the Original Confucianism and Taoism* (原始儒家道家哲学). Taibei 台北: Taibei Dawn Culture Company (台北黎明文化公司), 1983.
Fitzgerald, John. "The Misconceived Revolution: State and Society in China's Nationalist Revolution, 1923–26." *The Journal of Asian Studies* 49, no. 2 (1990): 323–43.
"Foreword (发刊词)." *The Renaissance* 新潮 1, no. 1 (1919): 1–4.
Fung, Edmund S. K. "Nationalism and Modernity: The Politics of Cultural Conservatism in Republican China." *Modern Asian Studies* 43, no. 3 (2009): 777–813.
Fung, Yu-Lan, and Derk Bodde. "The Rise of Neo-Confucianism and Its Borrowings from Buddhism and Taoism." *Harvard Journal of Asiatic Studies* 7, no. 2 (1942): 89–125.
Galliher, R. V., K. C. McLean, and M. Syed. "An Integrated Developmental Model for Studying Identity Content in Context." *Developmental Psychology* 53, no. 11 (2017): 2011–22.
Gao, Like 高力克. "'Replacing Religion with Science': Chen Duxiu's Scientism View of Religion." *Journal of Historical Science* 史学月刊, no. 1 (2017): 89–97.

Gardner, Ruth Carver, and Christine Coffee Chambers. *Builder of Dreams: The Life of Robert Edward Chambers*. Nashville: Broadman, 1939.

Gellner, Ernest. *Nations and Nationalism*. Oxford: Basil Blackwell, 1983.

Graham, Carolyn W., Gwendolyn T. Sorell, and Marilyn J. Montgomery. "Role-Related Identity Structure in Adult Women." *Identity: An International Journal of Theory and Research* 4, no. 3 (2004): 251–71.

Gries, Peter Hays. *China's New Nationalism: Pride, Politics, and Diplomacy*. Berkeley: University of California Press, 2004.

Guo, Jichuan 郭济川. "Are the Records in the First Chapter of Genesis Really Not in Accordance with Science? (创世记第一章的记载果与科学不合吗?)." *True Light* 真光 24, no. 2 (1925): 13–21.

Guo, Yingcai 郭英材. "Another Discussion with Mr. Yijing over Three Bowing before the Image of the Deceased Parents at Their Funerals (再与亦镜先生讨论关于追悼会时向先亲像行三鞠躬礼的问题)." *True Light* 真光 23, no. 8 (1924): 27–32.

Hao, Cheng 郝城. "The Works of Mr. Zhang Yijing (张亦镜先生的著作)." *True Light* 真光 31, no. 9 (1932): 33–38.

Harrison, Henrietta. "Newspapers and Nationalism in Rural China 1890–1929." *Past and Present* 166, no. 1 (2000): 181–204.

Harvey, Thomas Alan. "Sermon, Story, and Song in the Inculturation of Christianity in China." In *Sinicizing Christianity*, edited by Yangwen Zheng, 138–66. Studies in Christian Mission Series 49. Leiden: Brill, 2017.

Haslam, Alexander, and Naomi Ellemers. "Identity Processes in Organizations." In *Handbook of Identity Theory and Research*, edited by Seth J. Schwartz, Koen Luyckx, and Vivian L. Vignoles, 715–44. Vol. 2. New York: Springer Science + Business Media, 2011.

He, Zhonghua 何中华. "The Debate on Science and Metaphysics and the Direction of Philosophy in China in the 20th Century ('科玄论战'与20世纪中国哲学走向)." *Journal of Literature, History and Philosophy* 文史哲, no. 2 (1998): 5–15.

He, Zhongxiao 何仲萧. "Jinde Women's School in Wu Xing and Chinese Women (吴兴进德妇女学校与中华妇女界)." *True Light* 真光 23, no. 2 (1924): 65–67.

Henderson, Ailsa, and Nicola McEwen. "Do Shared Values Underpin National Identity? Examining the Role of Values in National Identity in Canada and the United Kingdom." *National Identities* 7, no. 2 (2005): 173–91.

Hendry, Leo B., Peter Mayer, and Marion Kloep. "Belonging or Opposing? A Grounded Theory Approach to Young People's Cultural Identity in a Majority/Minority Societal Context." *Identity: An International Journal of Theory and Research* 7, no. 3 (2007): 181–204.

Hoare, Carol. "Identity and Spiritual Development in the Papers of Erik Erikson." *Identity: An International Journal of Theory and Research* 9, no. 3 (2009): 183–200.

Hobsbawm, Eric. J. *Nations and Nationalism since 1780: Programme, Myth, Reality*. 2nd ed. Cambridge: Cambridge University Press, 1992.

Hong, Xiaonan 洪晓楠. "Effects of the Polemics between Science and Metaphysics on the Development of Chinese Cultural Philosophy ('科玄论战'对中国文化哲学的影响)." *Journal of Nanchang University* 南昌大学学报 (人社版) 33, no. 3 (July 2002): 12–18.

Hou, Shuxian 候述先. "Reflections on Zhang Yijing's Return to Guang Dong Province (对于张亦镜先生返粤的感想)." *True Light* 真光 30, no. 5 (1931): 67–68.

Hu, Hongtu 胡鸿图. "Can Christianity Save China? (基督教可以救国吗?)." *Chinese Christian Advocate* 兴华 17, no. 17 (1920): 30.

Hu, Shi 胡适. "The Thoughts of Wu Zhihui 吴稚晖先生的思想." In 民国吴稚晖先生敬恒年谱 *The Chronicle of My Teacher Mr. Wu Zhihui*, edited by Kailing Yang 杨恺龄, 147–86. Taipei 台北: Commercial Press 商务印书馆, 1928.

Huang, Paulos. *Confronting Confucian Understandings of the Christian Doctrine of Salvation: A Systematic Theological Analysis of the Basic Problems in the Confucian-Christian Dialogue*. 3rd ed. Leiden: Brill, 2009.

Hunsberger, Bruce, Michael Pratt, and S. Mark Pancer. "Adolescent Identity Formation: Religious Exploration and Commitment." *Identity: An International Journal of Theory and Research* 4, no. 1 (2001): 365–86.

Innis, H. A. "Nationalism." *The American Economic Review* 25, no. 1, Supplement, Papers and Proceedings of the Forty-Seventh Annual Meeting of the American Economic Association (1935): 136–39.

Jensen, Lionel. *Manufacturing Confucianism: Chinese Traditions and Universal Civilization*. Durham: Duke University Press, 1997.

Jian, Youwen 简又文. "An Ethnic Church – Part One (民族的教会 上篇)." *Youth Progress* 青年进步, no. 52 (1922): 33–44.

———. "The Function of Death in the Experience of Humankind (人类经验中死之功用)." *Youth Progress* 青年进步, no. 26 (1919): 34–39.

———. "A National Salvation Seeking Christianity (救国的基督教)." *True Light* 真光 24, no. 11–12 (1925): 24–32.

———. "What Is Christianity (什么是基督教)?" *Life (Beijing)* 生命(北京) 2, no. 1 (1921): 1–8.

———. "What Is Christianity – Part Two (什么是基督教 续第二卷第一期)." *Life (Beijing)* 生命(北京) 2, no. 2 (1922): 1–7.

Jiang, Jianbang 姜建邦. "Visiting the Family Members of Zhang Yijing (访问张亦镜先生的家属)." *The Voice of Evangelization* 宣道声 8, no. 4 (1948): 31–33.

———. "The Works of Mr. Zhang Yijing (张亦镜先生的著作)." *True Light* 真光 40, no. 12 (1941): 12–15.

Jiang, Zhongzheng 蒋中正. "Saving China by Character (人格救国)." *Zhejiang Youth (Hangzhou)* 浙江青年(杭州) 3, no. 3 (1937): 1–4.

Jianru 鉴如. "Woe to Those Who Do Not Preach the Gospel (不传福音有祸)." *True Light* 真光 5, no. 2 (1906): 1–4.

Jianyu 检余. "Church's Prosperity and China's Hope (教会兴与中国之希望)." In *(1928), A Quarter of a Century of True Light, Selected* 真光丛刊, *Part 1: Concerning the Scriptures* 说经文, edited by Yijing Zhang, 18–22. Shanghai 上海: China Baptist Publication Society 中华浸会书局, 1906.

———. "The Descent of the Holy Spirit Came on the Day of Pentecost (五旬节圣神降临)." In *(1928), A Quarter of a Century of True Light, Selected* 真光丛刊, *Part 1: Concerning the Scriptures* 说经文, edited by Yijing Zhang, 12–18. Shanghai 上海: China Baptist Publication Society 中华浸会书局, 1906.

Jin, Guantao 金观涛, and Qingfeng Liu 刘青峰. *A Study of Conceptual History: The Formation of the Key Political Terms in Modern China* 观念史研究：中国现代重要政治术语的形成. 1st ed. Beijing: Law Press 法律出版社, 2010.

Kanamori. "The Testimony of Kanamori (刊南慕利保罗的见证)." *True Light* 真光 26, no. 6 (1927): 8–17.

Kane, Anne. "Narratives of Nationalism: Constructing Irish National Identity during the Land War, 1879–82." *National Identities* 2, no. 3 (2000): 245–64.

Karl, Rebecca E. "Journalism, Social Value, and a Philosophy of the Everyday in 1920s China." *East Asia Cultures Critique* 16, no. 3 (2008): 539–66.

Kiesling, Chris, and Gwen Sorell. "Joining Erikson and Identity Specialists in the Quest to Characterize Adult Spiritual Identity." *Identity: An International Journal of Theory and Research* 9, no. 3 (2009): 252–71.

Kiesling, Chris, Gwendolyn T. Sorell, Marilyn J. Montgomery, and Ronald K. Colwell. "Identity and Spirituality: A Psychosocial Exploration of the Sense of Spiritual Self." *Developmental Psychology* 42, no. 6 (2006): 1269–77.

Korostelina, Karina. "History Education and Social Identity." *Identity: An International Journal of Theory and Research* 8, no. 1 (2008): 25–45.

Kui, Ge 奎阁. "Christianity Can Save China – Mandarin (基督教救国论-官话)." *The Women's Messenger* 女铎 7, no. 4 (1918): 28–31.

Kulyk, Volodymyr. "The Media, History and Identity: Competing Narratives of the Past in the Ukrainian Popular Press." *National Identities* 13, no. 3 (2011): 287–303.

Kunnen, E. Saskia. "Are Conflicts the Motor in Identity Change?" *Identity: An International Journal of Theory and Research* 6, no. 2 (2006): 169–86.

Kunnen, E. Saskia, and Harke A. Bosma. "Fischer's Skill Theory Applied to Identity Development: A Response to Kroger." *Identity: An International Journal of Theory and Research* 3, no. 3 (2003): 247–70.

Kuo, Huei-Ying. "Chinese Bourgeois Nationalism in Hong Kong and Singapore in the 1930s." *Journal of Contemporary Asia* 36, no. 3 (2006): 385–405.

Kupfer, Kristin B. "Christian-Inspired Groups in the People's Republic of China after 1978: Reaction of State and Party Authorities (English)." *Social Compass* 51, no. 2 (2004): 273–86.

Kwok, D. W. Y. "Review of Charlotte Furth 'Ting Wenchiang: Science and China's New Culture.'" *China Quarterly* 45 (1971): 186–87.

———. *Scientism in Chinese Thought 1900–1950*. New Haven: Yale University Press, 1965.

Kwok, Wai Luen. "Jia Yuming's Doctrine of Sanctification and the Confucian Nurturing Doctrine of Xin (Heart-Mind)." *Sino-Christian Studies*, no. 17 (2014): 75–109.

Lam, Wing-Hung 林荣洪. *Fifty Years of Chinese Theology: 1900–1949 (中华神学五十年: 1900–1949)*. Hong Kong: China Graduate School of Theology 中国神学研究院, 1998.

———. *Rising Chinese Church in the Storms (风潮中奋起的中国教会)*. Hong Kong: Tien Dao Publisher 天道书楼, 1980.

Lan, Weibin 蓝渭滨. "Saving China by Character (人格救国)." *Jiangsu Party Affairs Weekly (江苏党务周刊)*, no. 5 (1930): 12–13.

Lannegrand-Willems, Lyda, and Harke A. Bosma. "Identity Development-in-Context: The School as an Important Context for Identity Development." *Identity: An International Journal of Theory and Research* 6, no. 1 (2006): 85–113.

Leak, Gary K. "An Assessment of the Relationship between Identity Development, Faith Development, and Religious Commitment." *Identity: An International Journal of Theory and Research* 9, no. 3 (2009): 201–18.

Lee, David. *Contextualization of Sufi Spirituality in Seventeenth- and Eighteenth-Century China: The Role of Liu Zhi (c. 1662–c. 1730)*. Eugene: Pickwick, 2015.

Legge, James. *The Chinese Classics: With a Translation, Critical and Exegetical Notes, Prolegomena, and Copious Indexes*. 3rd ed. Vol. 1. Hong Kong: Hong Kong University Press, 1982.

———. *The I Ching*. 2nd ed. New York: Dover Publications, 1963.

———. *The Sacred Books of China: The Texts of Confucianism*. Part 1. Oxford: Clarendon Press, 1879.

———. *The Works of Mencius*. 3rd ed., with A Concordance Table, and Notes by Dr Arthur Waley. Vol. 2. The Chinese Classics: With a Translation, Critical and Exegetical Notes, Prolegomena, and Copious Indexes. Taipei: SMC Publishing, 1991.

Lei, Guang. "Realpolitik Nationalism: International Sources of Chinese Nationalism." *Modern China* 31 (2005): 487–514.

Levenson, Joseph R. *Confucian China and Its Modern Fate*. Berkeley: University of California Press, 1965.

———. "The Day Confucius Died." *The Journal of Asian Studies* 20, no. 2 (1961): 221–26. https://doi.org/10.2307/2050487.

Levine, C. "Questions Concerning Ego Identity and Its Health: A Commentary on Schwartz's 'The Evolution of Eriksonian and Neo-Eriksonian Identity Theory and Research.'" *Identity: An International Journal of Theory and Research* 1 (2001): 77–80.

Li, Chunfan 李春蕃. "Anti-Christian Week (非基督教周)." *Awakening* 觉悟. 9 December 1924.

———. "The Cicada in Winter Started to Chirp Unexpectedly (寒蝉居然也鸣起来了)." *Awakening* 觉悟. 26 August 1924.

———. "Comments on Christians' Slogan 'Saving the Country by Character' (人格救國！這是基督教教徒所拚命嚷的)." *Awakening* 觉悟. 28 October 1924.

———. "The Mission and Imperialism (传教与帝国主义)." *Awakening* 觉悟. 19 August 1924.

Li, Dazhao 李大钊. "Youth (青春)." *La Jeunesse* 新青年 2, no. 1 (1916): 1–12.

Li, Lanfen 李兰芬, and Qingjiang Zhang 张清江. "Guangzhou's Christian Intellectual Community in the Era of ROC and Their Efforts in Indigenizing Christianity: With Zhong Rongguang and Zhang Yijing as Examples (民国广州基督徒知识分子与基督教中国化的努力 - 以钟荣光、张亦镜为例)." *Open Times* 开放时代, no. 3 (2017): 61–71.

Li, Li 李丽. *Scientism in China* 科学主义在中国. Beijing 北京: People's Publishing House 人民出版社, 2012.

Li, Liang 李亮. "中国基督教现状的考察 A Survey of the Current Situation of Chinese Christianity." *Orient* 东方, no. 2 (1995): 53–58.

Li, Shen 李申. "The Author's Preface to History of the Religion of Confucianism in China 中国儒教史自序." *History of Chinese Philosophy* 中国哲学史 4 (1997): 6–7.

———. *History of the Confucian Religion* 中国儒教史. Shanghai: Shanghai People's Press 上海人民出版社, 1999.

Liang, Jialin 梁家麟. *Blessings on China - Ten Lessons on the Modern Church History of China* 福临中华—中国近代教会史十讲. 香港 Hong Kong: 天道书楼 Tian Dao Press, 1988.

Liang, Junqing 梁俊青. "Questioning Mr. Zhang Yijing's Answers to Mr. Huang and Mr. Liao (读亦镜先生答黄廖二君的疑问的质疑)." *True Light* 真光 23, no. 2 (1924): 27–29.

Lide, R. W. "Dr. Rosewell H. Graves," 1934. FMB AR 551-61, MISS. MINUTES, BOX - 229, Mission South China, Articles, 1925-39, 229-34.

Lie, Ying 列英. "Worthy to Be Answered (值得答复)." *Lingdong Republican Daily News* (岭东民国日报), 1 December 1926.

Liezi. *Liezi*. Translated by Xiaopeng Liang 梁晓鹏. Beijing 北京: Zhonghua Book Company 中华书局, 2005.

Lin, Changmin 林长民. "Christianity the Essential Factor in the Welfare of Society and the Nation." *China's Young Men* 16, no. 1–2 (1913): 32–34.

Liu, Weihan 刘维汉. "About the Editing Office (关于编辑室_编辑者言_终日埋头案前)." *True Light* 真光 27, no. 7 (1928): 94–97.

Liu, Zhongping 刘中平. "On the Sacrifice System of Qing Dynasty 论清代祭典制度." *Journal of Liaoning University (Philosophy and Social Sciences Edition)* 辽宁大学学报(哲学社会科学版) 36, no. 6 (2008): 85–89.

Lü, Banjiao 吕半教. "With the Trend or Against the Trend (随潮流与不随潮流说)." *True Light* 真光 29, no. 1 (1930): 69–71.

Lu, Boai 陆博爱. "The Ideal Church (理想的教会)." *True Light* 真光 24, no. 3 (1925): 65–67.

———. "Talking over Patriotism with Mr. Zhang Yijing (与亦镜先生谈谈爱国)." *True Light* 真光 25, no. 9–10 (1926): 31–34.

Lu, Danlin 陆丹林. "About Xu Qian (关于徐谦)." *Chat at Tea* 茶话, no. 2 (1946): 100–104.

———. "Biography and Comments of Mr. Zhang Yijing (评传:张亦镜先生)." *Beacon* 明灯, no. 275 (1940): 18–21.

———. "Commemorating Mr. Zhang Yijing Who Widely Spread the Way (纪念道满人间的张亦镜先生)." *True Light* 真光 31, no. 9 (1932): 27–33.

———. "Mr. Yijing: We Are Looking Forward to the Combined Issues of No. 4 to 6 in Volume 25 . . . (通讯:亦镜先生:盼望许久的真光杂志廿五卷四至六号合刊 . . .)." *True Light* 真光 25, no. 9–10 (1926): 125–26.

———. "Preface." In *(1928), A Quarter of A Century of True Light, Selected* 真光丛刊, edited by Yijing Zhang, 1–7. Shanghai 上海: China Baptist Publication Society 中华浸会书局, 1927.

———. "Recollection of Zhang Yijing (追怀张亦镜)." *Spring and Autumn (春秋)* 5, no. 3 (1948): 33–35.

Lu, Fang-Shang. "The Intellectual Origins of Guomindang Radicalization in the Early 1920s." *Chinese Studies in History* Fall (1992): 3–39.

Lu, Zhouxiang, and Hong Fan. "From Celestial Empire to Nation State: Sport and the Origins of Chinese Nationalism (1840–1927)." *The International Journal of the History of Sport* 27, no. 3 (2010): 479–504.

Luo, Yijun 罗义俊, ed. *Comments on New-Confucianism (评新儒家)*. Shanghai: Shanghai People's Publisher (上海人民出版社), 1989.

Lutz, Jessie G. "Chinese Nationalism and the Anti-Christian Campaigns of the 1920s." *Modern Asian Studies* 10, no. 3 (1977): 395–416.

Luyckx, Koen, Seth J. Schwartz, Luc Goossens, and Sophie Pollock. "Employment, Sense of Coherence, and Identity Formation: Contextual and Psychological

Processes on the Pathway to Sense of Adulthood." *Journal of Adolescent Research* 23, no. 5 (2008): 566–91.

Marcia, J. E. "Development and Validation of Ego Identity Status." *Journal of Personality and Social Psychology*, no. 5 (1966): 551–58.

Markstrom-Adams, C., G. Hofstra, and K. Dougher. "The Ego Virtue of Fidelity: A Case for the Study of Religion and Identity Formation in Adolescence." *Journal of Youth and Adolescence* 23 (1994): 453–69.

McAdams, Dan P. "Narrative Identity." In *Handbook of Identity Theory and Research*, edited by Seth J. Schwartz, Koen Luyckx, and Vivian L. Vignoles, 99–115. Vol. 1. New York: Springer Science + Business Media, 2011.

———. "What Do We Know When We Know a Person?" *Journal of Personality* 63 (1995): 365–96.

McLean, Kate C., and Monisha Pasupathi. "Processes of Identity Development: Where I Am and How I Got There." *Identity: An International Journal of Theory and Research* 12, no. 1 (2012): 8–28.

McNeal, Robin. "Constructing Myth in Modern China." *Journal of Asian Studies* 71, no. 3 (2012): 679–704.

Meissner, Werner. "China's Search for Cultural and National Identity from the Nineteenth Century to the Present." *China Perspectives*, no. 68 (2006): 41–54. http://chinaperspectives.revues.org/3103.

Metzger, Thomas A. *Escape from Predicament: Neo-Confucianism and China's Evolving Political Culture*. New York: Columbia University Press, 1977.

Metzger, Thomas A., and Ramon H. Myers. "Chinese Nationalism and American Policy." *Orbis* (1998): 21–36.

Miscevic, Nenad. "Nationalism." In *The Stanford Encyclopedia of Philosophy*, edited by Edward N. Zalta. Metaphysics Research Lab, Stanford University, 2018. https://plato.stanford.edu/archives/sum2018/entries/nationalism/.

Mitter, Rana. "Complicity, Repression, and Regionalism: Yan Baohang and Centripetal Nationalism, 1931–1949." *Modern China* 25, no. 1 (1999): 44–68.

———. "Modernity, Internationalization, and War in the History of Modern China." *The Historical Journal* 48, no. 2 (2005): 523–43.

Mostert, Christiaan. "Christian Identity as Baptismal Identity." In *Studies in Reformed Theology, Vol. 16 : Christian Identity*, edited by E. van der Borght, 51–65. Leiden: Brill, 2008.

Mote, Frederick W. 牟复礼. "The Preface of The Way, Learning and Politics – On Confucian Intellectuals (道、学、政 – 论儒家知识分子)." In *A Collection of Tu Weiming's Works (杜维明文集第三册)*, edited by Qi Yong Guo 郭齐勇 and Wen Long Zheng 郑文龙, vol. 3. Wuhan 武汉: Wuhan Publisher 武汉出版社, 1988.

"Mr. Zhang Yijing – A Good Housekeeper (一个好管家张亦镜先生)." *The Voice of Evangelization* 宣道声 9, no. 1 (1949): 37–39.

"Mr. Zhang Yijing – Top-Notch Player in the Ministry of Preaching through Writing from the Baptist Church (浸会文字布道的健将:张亦镜先生)." *The Voice of Evangelization (宣道声)* 3, no. 1 (1940): 19–22.

Mu, Fu-Sheng. "Review of D. W. Y. Kwok 'Scientism in Chinese Thought, 1900–1950.'" *The China Quarterly* 28 (1966): 136–38.

Mu, Zongsan 牟宗三. "The Reason for Reviving Goose Lake Academy and the Rules (重振鹅湖书院缘起暨章则)," in *The Complete Works of Mr. Mou Zongsan 牟宗三先生全集*, 1st ed., vol. 26 (Taibei 台北: Linking Publishing 联经出版社, 2003), 13–20.

Murata, Y. "Nationalism, Historical Aspects of: East Asia." *International Encyclopedia of the Social & Behavioral Sciences*, 2001, 10348–51.

Narváez, Rafael F., Ilan H. Meyer, Robert M. Kertzner, Suzanne C. Ouellette, and Allegra R. Gordon. "A Qualitative Approach to the Intersection of Sexual, Ethnic, and Gender Identities." *Identity: An International Journal of Theory and Research* 9, no. 1 (2009): 63–86.

Needham, Joseph, and Ling Wang. *Science & Civilisation in China, Volume II (2): History of Scientific Thought*. 1st ed. New York: Cambridge University Press, 1956.

Niebuhr, H. Richard. *Christ and Culture*. Exp. 50th Anniversary ed. New York: HarperOne, 2001.

Nuliang 女良. "What Is the Achievement of 'Saving China by Character'? ('人格救国' 的成绩如何?)." *Awakening* 觉悟 9, no. 30 (1924): 5.

Ogden, Suzanne P. "The Sage in the Inkpot: Bertrand Russell and China's Social Reconstruction in the 1920s." *Modern Asian Studies* 16, no. 4 (1982): 529–600.

Okolie, Andrew C. "Introduction to the Special Issue – Identity: Now You Don't See It; Now You Do." *Identity: An International Journal of Theory and Research* 3, no. 1 (2003): 1–7.

Pantsov, Alexander. *The Bolsheviks and the Chinese Revolution 1919–1927*. Honolulu: University of Hawai'i Press, 2000.

Peden, Creighton. *Empirical Tradition in American Liberal Religious Thought, 1860–1960*. New York: Peter Lang, 2010.

Peng, Ping-yi. "The Influence of Early New Culture Movement on the May Fourth Patriotic Movement." *Journal of Hunan University of Technology Social Science Edition* 14, no. 6 (2009): 28–33.

People's Daily Online 人民网. "Today, How Are We Patriotic? Hearing What General Secretary Xi Jinping Said (今天，我们如何爱国？听习近平总书记这样说)." 8 October 2020. https://baijiahao.baidu.com/s?id=1679940990720387510&wfr=spider&for=pc.

Phillips, Andrew, and Paul James. "National Identity between Tradition and Reflexive Modernisation: The Contradictions of Central Asia." *National Identities* 3, no. 1 (2011): 23–35.

Phoenix, Ann, and Ali Rattansi. "Proliferating Theories: Self and Identity in Post-Eriksonian Context: A Rejoinder to Berzonsky, Kroger, Levine, Phinney, Schachter, and Weigert and Gecas." *Identity* 5, no. 2 (1 April, 2005): 205–25. https://doi.org/10.1207/s1532706xid0502_9.

Pingji 萍寄. "On the Guangzhou Crusade's Achievements and Responses (论广州大布道的成绩与反响)." *True Light* 真光 20, no. 2 (1921): 1–8.

Poll, Justin B., and Timothy B. Smith. "The Spiritual Self: Toward a Conceptualization of Spiritual Identity Development." *Journal of Psychology and Theology* 31, no. 2 (2003): 129–42.

Pollard, D. E. "Review of D. W. Y. Kwok 'Scientism in Chinese Thought, 1900–1950.'" *Bulletin of the School of Oriental and African Studies* 30, no. 2 (1967): 437.

Qiao, Fei 乔飞. "From Secretly Prevention to Seriously Protection, Enumeration and Analysis on the Christian Regulations in Late Qing Dynasty 从 '密为防闲' 到 '明为保护' — 晚清基督教法律政策之演变及其法史疏释," 17 October 2016. http://www.chinaaid.net/2016/10/blog-post_78.html.

Qin, Zhen 覃振. "Saving China by Character (人格救国)." *Central Committee Weekly (1928)* 中央周刊 *(1928)*, no. 191 (1932): 1–2.

Rattansi, Ali, and Ann Phoenix. "Rethinking Youth Identities: Modernist and Postmodernist Frameworks." *Identity* 5, no. 2 (1 April 2005): 97–123. https://doi.org/10.1207/s1532706xid0502_2.

Rau, Gerald. *Mapping the Origins Debate: Six Models of the Beginning of Everything*. Downers Grove: InterVarsity Press, 2012.

Richardson, Don. *Eternity in Their Hearts*. Rev. ed. Ventura: Regal Books, 1984.

Rieffer, Barbara-Ann J. "Religion and Nationalism: Understanding the Consequences of a Complex Relationship." *Ethnicities* 3, no. 2 (2003): 215–42.

Robertson, Roy. *The Road to Discipleship*. Singapore: Navigators, 1992.

Rule, Paul A. *K'ung-Tzu or Confucius? The Jesuit Interpretation of Confucianism*. London: Allen & Unwin, 1986.

Saroglou, Vassilis, and Benoît Hanique. "Jewish Identity, Values, and Religion in a Globalized World: A Study of Late Adolescents." *Identity: An International Journal of Theory and Research* 6, no. 3 (2006): 231–49.

Schwartz, S. J., M. B. Donnellan, R. D. Ravert, K. Luyckx, and B. L. Zamboanga. "Identity Development, Personality, and Well-Being in Adolescence and Emerging Adulthood: Theory, Research, and Recent Advances." In *Handbook of Psychology, Vol. 6: Developmental Psychology*, edited by I. B. Weiner, R. M. Lerner, A. Easterbrooks, and J. Mistry, 339–64. New York: John Wiley & Sons, 2013.

Schwartz, Seth J. "The Evolution of Eriksonian and Neo-Eriksonian Identity Theory and Research: A Review and Integration." *Identity: An International Journal of Theory and Research* 1, no. 1 (2001): 7–58.

———. "Self and Identity in Early Adolescence: Some Reflections and an Introduction to the Special Issue." *Journal of Early Adolescence* 28, no. 1 (2008): 5–15.

Schwartz, Vera. *The Chinese Enlightenment*. Berkeley: University of California Press, 1986.

Shen, Grace Yen 沈德容. "Scientism in the Twentieth Century." In *Modern Chinese Religion II: 1850–2015*, 91–137. Leiden: Interactive Factory, 2016. https://brill.com/view/book/edcoll/9789004304642/B9789004304642_004.xml.

Shenzhi. "The Example of Magi from the East (可师法的东方博士)." *True Light* 真光 23, no. 2 (1924): 23–26.

Smart, Ninian. *In Search of Christianity: Discovering the Diverse Vitality of the Christian Life*. San Francisco: Harper & Row, 1979.

Smith, Anthony D. "Nationalism." *Current Sociology* 21, no. 7 (1977): 7–122.

Smith, Gerald Birney. "Theological Thinking in America." In *Religious Thought in the Last Quarter Century*, edited by Gerald Birney Smith, 95–115. Chicago: University of Chicago Press, 1927.

———. "The Theological Thoughts in the U.S.A. during the Last Twenty-Five Years (二十五年来美国神学思想之趋势)." *True Light* 真光 26, no. 6 (1927): 1–13.

———. "Translation: Social Idealism and the Changing Theology (译述:伦理的基督教观)." Translated by Youwen Jian 简又文. *Life (Beijing)* 生命(北京) 5, no. 1 (1924): 26–42.

Standaert, Nicolas. "New Trends in the Historiography of Christianity in China." *The Catholic Historical Review* 83, no. 4 (1997): 573–613. http://www.jstor.org/stable/25025062.

Starr, Chloë. *Chinese Theology: Text and Context*. New Haven: Yale University Press, 2016.

Stauffer, Milton T., Tsinforn C. Wong, and M. Gardner Tewksbury, eds. *The Christian Occupation of China: A General Survey of the Numerical Strength and Geographical Distribution of the Christian Forces in China, Made by the Special Committee on Survey and Occupation, China Continuation Committee, 1918–1921*. Shanghai: China Continuation Committee, 1922.

Stenmark, Mikael. *Scientism: Science, Ethics and Religion*. Ashgate Science and Religion Series. Aldershot: Ashgate, 2001.

Stott, John. *The Radical Disciple*. Nottingham: Inter-Varsity Press, 2010.

Suman, Michael D. *The Church in China: One Lord Two Systems*, Expanded Edition. India: SAIACS Press, 2007.

Sun, Yinwu 孙荫五. "Mourn Mr. Zhang Yijing (悼张亦镜先生)." *The Chinese Christian Intelligencer* 通问报, no. 1496 (1932): 4.

Szucs, Ferenc. "Christian Identity and National Identity." In *Studies in Reformed Theology, Vol. 16 : Christian Identity*, edited by E. van der Borght, 83–90. Leiden: Brill, 2008.

Tajfel, H. "Intergroup Behaviour: I. Individualistic Perspectives." In *Introducing Social Psychology: An Analysis of Individual Reaction and Response*, edited by C. Fraser and H. Tajfel, 423–46. New York: Penguin, 1987.

Tang, Wenfang, and Benjamin Darr. "Chinese Nationalism and Its Political and Social Origins." *Journal of Contemporary China* 21, no. 77 (2012): 811–26.

Tang, Xiaofeng 唐晓峰. "T. C. Chao's Ethical Theology 赵紫宸伦理的神学." In *Christianity in China: The Wisdom of Contextualization (Vol. 1 and 2) 基督教在中国-处境化的智慧-(上.下册)*, edited by Shilin Zhao 赵士林 and Qi Duan 段琦. Beijing 北京: Religion and Culture Press 宗教文化出版社, 2009.

Tang, Yijie 汤一介. "Confucianism's Features and Basic Spirit 儒学的特质和基本精神." In *China Confucianism Culture Overview (中国儒学文化大观)*, edited by Yaonan Zhang, Ming Fang, and Yijie Tang. Beijing: Peking University Press, 2001.

Ten Elshof, Gregg A. *Confucius for Christians: What an Ancient Chinese Worldview Can Teach Us about Life in Christ*. Grand Rapids: Eerdmans, 2015.

The Committee of Reference and Counsel Foreign Missions Conference of North America. *Present Situation in China and Its Significance for Christian Missions*. New York: Board of Foreign Missions of the Methodist Episcopal Church, 1925.

"The Declaration (本志宣告)." *The Pacific Ocean 太平洋* 1, no. 1 (1917): 1.

"The Declaration of The Young China Association at Its Suzhou Conference (少年中国学会苏州大会宣言)." *The Young China* 4, no. 8 (1923): 1–4.

The First Selection of the Speeches on Nationalism 国家主义讲演集第一集. Shanghai: Shanghai Awakening Lion Weekly 上海醒狮周报社, 1926, 1–70.

"The Foreword (发刊词)." *Science 科学* 1, no. 1 (1915): 3–7.

The Maritime Custom: Treaties, Conventions, Etc., between China and Foreign States. 2nd ed. Vol. 1. Shanghai: Statistical Department of the Inspectorate General of Customs, 1917.

Tiedemann, R. G. "Anti-Christian Conflict in Local Perspective. The Life and Times of Pang Sanjie: Patriot, Protector, Bandit or Revolutionary?" In *Contextualization of Christianity in China: An Evaluation in Modern Perspective*, edited by Peter Chen-Main Wang, 243–75. Sankt Augustin: Monumenta Serica, 2007.

Tiedemann, R. G., ed. *Handbook of Christianity in China: Volume Two: 1800 – Present*. Leiden: Brill, 2010.

———. *Reference Guide to Christian Missionary Societies in China: From the Sixteenth to the Twentieth Century*. Armonk: M. E. Sharpe, 2009.

Tipton, W. H. "Annual Report of China Baptist Publication Society," 1936. FMB AR 551–61, MISS. MINUTES, BOX - 229, Mission South China, Articles, 1930–40, 229–35.

Tu, Weiming 杜维明. "The Prospect for the Development of Confucianism at Its Third Stage (儒学第三期发展的前景问题)." In *Comments on New-Confucianism* (评新儒家), edited by Yijun Luo 罗义俊. Shanghai: Shanghai People's Publisher (上海人民出版社), 1989.

Tuck, L. G. 伍连德. "Medical Progress in China Since the Republic." *The Lancet*, 29 May 1920: 1203–4.

Tucker, J. Brian. "Diverse Identities in Christ according to Paul: The Enduring Influence of the Work of William S. Campbell." *Journal of Beliefs & Values* 38, no. 2 (2017): 139–52. https://doi.org/10.1080/13617672.2017.1291255.

———. *Remain in Your Calling: Paul and the Continuation of Social Identities in 1 Corinthians*. Eugene: Pickwick, 2011.

———. *You Belong to Christ: Paul and the Formation of Social Identity in 1 Corinthians 1–4*. Eugene: Pickwick, 2010.

Uberoi, Patricia. "Chinese Conversion to Scientism: Scientism in Chinese Thought by D. W. Y. Kwok. Published by the Yale University Press, New Haven, 1965." *China Report* 4, no. 2 (1968): 33–35. https://doi.org/10.1177/000944556800400209.

Veer, Peter van der. "Religion, Secularism and National Development in India and China." *Third World Quarterly* 33, no. 4 (2012): 721–34.

Vignoles, Vivian L., Seth J. Schwartz, and Koen Luyckx. "Introduction: Toward an Integrative View of Identity." In *Handbook of Identity Theory and Research*, edited by Seth J. Schwartz, Koen Luyckx, and Vivian L. Vignoles, 1–27. Vol. 1. New York: Springer Science + Business Media, 2011.

Virdi, Jaipreet. "Shaping Science and Scientism." *Science as Culture* 20, no. 4 (2011): 541–45.

Wang, Chih-Ming. "Geopolitics of Literature." *Cultural Studies* 26, no. 5 (2012): 740–64.

Wang, Er Min 王尔敏. *On the History of Modern Thoughts in China* 中国近代思想史论. Beijing 北京: Social Sciences Literature Press 社会科学文献出版社, 2003.

Wang, Fengyan 汪凤炎, and Hong Zheng 郑红. "Confucius' Thirteen Standards for the Noble and the Petty 孔子界定 '君子人格' 与 '小人人格' 的十三条标准." *Morality and Civilization* 道德与文明, no. 4 (2008): 46–51.

Wang, Ji 王玑. "The Anecdote of Mr. Zhang Yijing (张亦镜先生轶事)." *True Light* 真光 40, no. 12 (1941): 15–16.

Wang, Jue. "Neither Xi (洗) Nor Jin (浸), But Fu (被): Zhang Yijing's (张亦镜) Translation of Baptism, Viewed from the Perspective of Identity."

Transformation: An International Journal of Holistic Mission Studies 34, no. 3 (2016): 214–22. https://doi.org/10.1177/0265378816667276.

———. "Opium Supporters, Missionaries, and Opium (1874–1906) 鸦片贸易支持者、在华新教传教士、与鸦片 (1874–1906)." Master's thesis, Peking University, 2007.

Wang, Miaoyang 王淼洋. "An Exploration into the Responsiveness between Chinese and the Western Scientific Thoughts (中西科学思想的相应性初探)." *Quarterly Journal of the Shanghai Academy of Social Sciences* 上海社会科学院学术季刊, no. 2 (1992): 71–79.

Wang, Xiuyu. "Review on The People's Peking Man: Popular Science and Human Identity in Twentieth-Century China by Sigrid Schmalzer." *Journal of World History* 21, no. 2 (2010): 356–59.

Wang, Y. C. *Chinese Intellectuals and the West, 1872–1949*. Chapel Hill: University of North Carolina Press, 1966.

Wang, Zhixin 王治心. "Writing and Christianity (文字事业与基督教)." In *(1928), A Quarter of A Century of True Light, Selected* 真光丛刊, Part 3: General Articles 通论, edited by Yijing Zhang, 39–47. Shanghai 上海: China Baptist Publication Society 中华浸会书局, 1924.

Wang, Zuoan. "Building a Harmonious Society and New Ideas of Religious Work (构建和谐社会与宗教工作新理念)." In *Marxism and Religion*, edited by Zhen Chi, Xuezeng Gong, and Dji Lü, 387–96. Vol. 4. Religious Studies in Contemporary China Collection. Leiden: Brill, 2014.

Wang, Zuoyue. "Saving China through Science: The Science Society of China, Scientific Nationalism, and Civil Society in Republican China." *Osiris* 17 (2002): 291–322. https://www.jstor.org/stable/3655275.

Ward, Harry F., and Youwen Jian 简又文. "The Function of Religion in Social Reform (社会改造中之宗教地位)." *The Supplement to Morning News* 晨报副刊, 19 April 1925: 1–5.

———. "The Revolutionary Christianity – Part One (革命的基督教 一)." *The Supplement to Morning News* 晨报副刊, 1 July 1925: 2–4.

Weishuang 味爽. "'Saving China by Character' in the National Day Celebration at Ningbo (宁波国庆大会中的'人格救国')." *Awakening* 觉悟 11, no. 4 (1924): 5–6.

Wilhelm, Helmut. "The Reappraisal of Neo-Confucianism." *China Quarterly* 23 (1965): 122–39.

Wong, Yuet-Sheung Candes 黄月嫦. "The Role of Zhang Wenkai (1871–1931) in the Anti-Christian Movement in the 1920s." Master's thesis, University of Hong Kong, Hong Kong, 1997. http://hdl.handle.net/10722/50446.

Woo, T. B. 拱平. "The Source of Transforming the World into a Paradise." *China's Young Men* 16, no. 6 (1913): 138–40.

Wu, Jianghai 吴江海. "Scientism Thoughts during New Culture Movement: Path, Character and Influence." *Studies in Dialectics of Nature* 自然辩证法研究 24, no. 5 (2008): 88–93.

Wu, Jingheng 吴敬恒. "A Critique of the Thought of Foreign Eight-Leggedism 箴洋八股化之理学." *Advance Together* 共进, no. 44 (1923): 3–4.

Wu, Junsheng 吴俊升. "The Progress of the Nationalistic Education and My Comments 国家主义的教育之进展及其评论." In *The Collection of Papers on Nationalism* 国家主义论文集, edited by Huang Li 李璜, 123–37. Shanghai: Shanghai China Publishing House 上海中华书局, 1925.

Wu, Zhihui 吴稚晖. "A New Belief's Conception of the Universe and the Philosophy of Life 一个新信仰的宇宙观及人生观 (Continuation to Vol. 1, no. 4 续四卷一号)." *Pacific* 太平洋 (Shanghai 上海) 4, no. 3 (1923): 1–36.

Xiao, Chunu 肖楚女. "A Letter on Nationalistic Education 讨论国家主义教育的一封信." In 中国现代哲学史资料选辑1919–1949 (上), edited by Zhenxia Li 李振霞 and Peiyue Guan 管培月, 250–55. Beijing: Philosophy Department of the Party School of the CPC Central Committee 中共中央党校哲学教研室编, 1924.

Xiao, Xiaosui. "The 1923 Scientific Campaign and Dao-Discourse: A Cross-Cultural Study of the Rhetoric of Science." *Quarterly Journal of Speech* 90, no. 4 (2004): 469–92.

Xu, Baoqian 徐宝谦. "An Advanced View of the Bible (进步的圣经观)." *Truth and Life* 真理与生命 2, no. 5 (1927): 117–20.

———. "Another Letter to the Nationalists: About Military Power and Mr. Jingzhi (再质国家主义者:论'武力'兼答竞之君)." *Life (Beijing)* 生命(北京) 5, no. 10 (1925): 1–2.

———. "For Special Issue of Commemorating Zhang Yijing (为张亦镜先生纪念号写)." *True Light* 真光 40, no. 12 (1941): 5–6.

———. "How I Became a Supporter of Internationalism (我讲国际主义的经过)." *Truth and Life* 真理与生命 2, no. 16 (1927): 11–15.

———. "Is It Necessary to Promote Internationalism in Today's China? (今日中国有无提倡国际主义的必要?)." *Truth and Life* 真理与生命 2, no. 16 (1927): 1–3.

———. "The National Obligations of Christians (基督徒对于国家应尽的本分)." *China for Christ* 中华归主, no. 79 (1927): 8–9.

———. "Reminding the Nationalists (敬告今之提倡国家主义者)." *Life (Beijing)* 生命(北京) 5, no. 4 (1925): 1–3.

———. "Write in Memory of Mr. Zhang Yijing (为张亦镜先生纪念号写)." *True Light* 真光 40, no. 12 (1941): 5–6.

Xu, Fuguan 徐复观. "Author's Preface 自序." In *The Continuation on the History of Chinese Thoughts* 中国思想史论集续篇, 417. Shanghai 上海: Shanghai Bookstore Publishing House 上海书店出版社, 2004.

———. "The Similarities and Differences between Cheng Brothers and Zhu Xi (程朱异同)." *The Continuation on the History of Chinese Thoughts* 中国思想史论集续篇. Shanghai 上海: Shanghai Bookstore Publishing House 上海书店出版社, 2004.

Xu, Qian 徐谦. "Answering Three Questions from a Friend Based on Science (答友人基于科学观念对基督教之三大疑问)." *The St. John's Echo* 约翰声 27, no. 6 (1916): 27–31.

———. "Are Chinese Willing to Be Sold (国人岂甘被卖为猪仔乎)?" *Chinese Christian Advocate* 兴华 15, no. 35 (1918): 9–10.

———. "The Course of My Involvement in the Movement of 'Saving Nations through Christ': Or 'Christianity and A New China' (从事 '基督救国' 运动的经过: 一名 '基督教与新中国')." *Typhoon (Hong Kong)* 大风 (香港) 61 (1940): 1850–54.

———. "The Facts about Saving Nations through Christianity (基督教救国事实)." *Chinese Christian Advocate* 兴华 21, no. 1 (1924): 23–28.

———. "The Gospel of National Salvation (救国福音)." *Canton Hospital* 博济, no. 2 (1918): 25–26.

———. "I Bear Witness to Jesus' Truth by Sun Yat-Sen's Faith (我对于孙中山先生的信仰为耶稣所传之真道做证)." *Chinese Christian Advocate* 兴华 22, no. 18 (1925): 5–7.

———. "Love Nation and Save Nation (爱国与救国)." *Typhoon (Hong Kong)* 大风 (香港), no. 44 (1939): 1398.

———. "Practicing Saving Nations through Christianity (基督教救国主义之实行的概念)." *Chinese Christian Advocate* 兴华 15, no. 47 (1918): 3–8.

———. "Preface to the Journal of Freedom of Faith (信教自由丛刊序)." *Chinese Christian Advocate* 兴华 15, no. 33 (1918): 11–12.

———. "The Relationship between the Independence of Chinese Christianity and Saving Nations (中华基督教自立与救国之关联)." *Fellow Christians* 教友, no. 7 (1923): 48–54.

———. "Save Nations through Christ (基督救国主义)." *The International Journal and Institute Record* 国际公报 2, no. 1 (1923): 17–20.

———. "The Speech at Guangzhou Bible Study – Part One (广州研经会讲演)." *New Autonomy* 新自治 1, no. 1 (1921): 1–8.

———. "The Speech at Guangzhou Bible Study – Part Two (广州研经会讲演)." *New Autonomy* 新自治 1, no. 2 (1921): 1–6.

———. "The Speech at Guangzhou Bible Study – Part Three (广州研经会讲演)." *New Autonomy* 新自治 1, no. 4 (1921): 1–9.

Xu, Qian 徐谦, and Shijie Bao 包世杰. "A Letter to the China National Education Conference (致全国教育会议书)." *Chinese Christian Advocate* 兴华 16, no. 8 (1919): 12–16.

Xu, Qian 徐谦, and Xingzhi Su 苏醒之. "A Discussion of Christian Education (基督教育之商榷)." *Christian Educator* 中华基督教育 4, no. 3 (1923): 4–6.

Xu, Songshi 徐松石. "Break into the City of Literature (攻入文学之城)." *True Light* 真光 31, no. 7 (1932): 1–13.

———. "In Memory of Mr. Zhang Yijing (忆张亦镜先生)." *True Light* 真光 40, no. 12 (1941): 2–4.

Xue, Bingyang 薛秉阳. "The Letter of My Repentance (我忏悔经过的一封信)." *True Light* 真光 25, no. 9–10 (1926): 95–98.

Yampolsky, Maya A., Catherine E. Amiot, and Roxane de la Sablonnière. "The Multicultural Identity Integration Scale (MULTIIS): Developing a Comprehensive Measure for Configuring One's Multiple Cultural Identities within the Self." *Cultural Diversity and Ethnic Minority Psychology* 22, no. 2 (2016): 166–84. https://pubmed.ncbi.nlm.nih.gov/26009944/.

Yan, Jiqing 严霁青. "After Reading Mr. Zhang Yijing's Refuting Chen Huanzhang and Other Four People's Petition for Establishing Confucianism as the State Religion (读亦镜先生驳陈焕章请定孔教为国教论题后)." *True Light* 真光 26, no. 10 (1927): 80.

———. "A Poem about a True Confucian (真儒辨)." *True Light* 真光 27, no. 1 (1928): 72.

Yang, Cheng 杨程. "A Criticism of Wu Zhuhui's *The Views on Universe and Life of a New Faith* (批评吴稚晖先生的一个新信仰的宇宙观及人生观,附图表)." *True Light* 真光 24, no. 1 (1925): 2.

Yang, C. K. "Chinese Intellectuals and the West by Y. C. Wang." *Journal of Asian Studies* 26, no. 1 (1966): 115–17.

Yang, Tianhong 杨天宏. 基督教与民国知识分子 *Christianity and Intellectuals of Republic of China*. Beijing 北京: People's Publishing House 人民出版社人民出版社, 2005.

Ye, Xiaowen. "A Brief Discussion on Theories of Religion and Legal Reconstruction over the Past Twelve Years (略谈十二年来我国的宗教理论和法制建设)." In *Marxism and Religion*, edited by Zhen Chi, Xuezeng Gong, and Daji Lü, 376–86. Vol. 4. Religious Studies in Contemporary China Collection. Leiden: Brill, 2014.

Yeung, Maureen W. "Boundaries in 'In-Christ Identity' Paul's View on Table Fellowship and Its Implications for Ethnic Identities." In *After Imperialism: Christian Identity in China and the Global Evangelical Movement*, edited by Richard R. Cook and David W. Pao, 154–74. Cambridge: Lutterworth Press, 2012.

Yin, Yeyong 殷耶傭. "Believing the Christ Is the Key to Saving People and Saving China (信主是救人救国之最要点)." *Christian Advocate* 华美教保 2, no. 3 (1905): 31–33.

Ying, Fuk-Tsang 邢福增. "Christian Doctrine and National Salvation: The Cases of Xu Qian, Feng Yuxiang and Zhang Zhijiang (基督教救國 [electronic resource] : 徐謙, 馮玉祥, 張之江)." PhD thesis, Chinese University of Hong Kong, Graduate School, Division of History 香港中文大学研究院历史学部, 1995.

———. 文化适应与中国基督徒: 一八六零至一九一一年 (Cultural Accommodation and Chinese Christians: 1860-1911). 香港 Hong Kong: 建道神学院 Alliance Bible Seminary, 1995.

———. "知识分子与中国教会 Intellectuals and the Chinese Church," 2002. http://www.godoor.net/text/history/zhjh16.htm.

———. "New Wine in Old Wineskins: An Appraisal of Religious Legislation in China and the Regulations on Religious Affairs of 2005." *Religion, State and Society* 34, no. 4 (1 December 2006): 347–73. https://doi.org/10.1080/09637490600974427.

Yip, Ka-Che. "Health and Society in China: Public Health Education for the Community, 1912–1937." *Social Science and Medicine* 16 (1982): 1197–1205.

Yu, Boxia 俞伯霞. "The Contribution of Mr. Zhang Yijing to Christian Literature (张亦镜先生对于基督教文学的贡献)." *True Light* 真光 31, no. 9 (1932): 43–47.

Yu, Jiaju 余家菊. "The Independence and Unification of Education in China (中国教育的统一与独立)." *Chung Hua Educational Review* 中华教育界 13, no. 8 (1923): 1–8.

———. "The Problems with Christian Education (教会教育问题)." *Young China* 少年中国 4, no. 7 (1923): 1–19.

Yu, Zhaoping 俞兆平. "The Centenary Fate of Scientism in China (科学主义在中国的百年命运)." *Cultural Vision* 文化视野, no. 11 (2014): 70–77.

Yui, David Z. T. 余日章. "Education and Democracy in China (教育与民国之关系)." *The Chinese Students* 中华学生界 1, no. 3 (1915): 1–15.

———. "Saving China by Character: YMCA – an Organization of Saving China and Molding Character (人格救国论:青年会为救国机关,亦造就人格的机关)." *True Light* 真光 20, no. 2 (1921): 17–21.

———. "Why Do I Believe in Jesus (我为什么信仰耶稣)?" *The Shanghai Youth (Shanghai 1902)* 上海青年 (上海 1902) 30, no. 46 (1930): 1–6.

Yun, Daiying 恽代英. "Christianity and Saving China by Character Formation (基督教与人格救国)." *China Youth (Shanghai 1923)* 中国青年(上海1923) 1, no. 3 (1923): 3–5.

Zarrow, Peter Gue. *Anarchism and Chinese Political Culture*. Studies of the East Asian Institute. New York: Columbia University Press, 1990.

Zeng, Qi 曾琦. "The Four Pieces of Evidence for Nationalism Advocates 国家主义者的四大论据." In *The Collection of the Materials of the Modern Philosophy History in China* 中国现代哲学史资料选辑 1919–1949 (上), edited by

Zhenxia Li 李振霞 and Peiyue Guan 管培月, 282–86. Beijing: Philosophy Department of the Party School of the CPC Central Committee 中共中央党校哲学教研室编, 1924.

———. "The Meaning of 'Eradicating Internal National Traitors and Resisting External Powers' 内除国贼外抗强权释义." In *The Collection of Papers on Nationalism 国家主义论文集*, edited by Huang Li 黄璃, 97–100. Shanghai: Shanghai China Publishing House 上海中华书局, 1925.

Zeng, Yugen 曾郁根. "The Baptist Church in Guang Dong and Guang Xi Provinces during the Past Twenty-Five Years (二十五年来两广浸信会概观)." *True Light 真光* 26, no. 6 (1927): 1–13.

Zetzsche, Jost Oliver. "Protestant Missionaries in Late Nineteenth-Century China." In *Handbook of Christianity in China: Volume Two: 1800 – Present*, edited by R. G. Tiedemann, 175–92. Leiden: Brill, 2010.

Zhang, Qiutao 张秋涛. "The Chronology of Zhang Yijing My Deceased Father (先严亦镜年表)." *True Light 真光* 40, no. 12 (1941): 16–22.

Zhang, Wen Kai 张文开. "Author's Preface: A Special Issue for Ten Denominations to Commemorate Robert Morrison (自序:本期报之专载羊城十大公会纪念马礼逊事也)." *True Light 真光* 6, no. 8 (1907): 2.

———. "On 'Our Father in Heaven' (吾侪在天之父论)." *True Light 真光* 5, no. 2 (1906): 2–5.

Zhang, Yijing 张亦镜. "Abolishing the Lunar Calendar (废除阴历)." *True Light 真光* 28, no. 2 (1929): 95–96.

———. "After a Trip to Suzhou City (去苏州一趟回来)." *True Light 真光* 28, no. 5 (1929): 59–66.

———. "After President Yuan Commands to Worship Confucius (书袁总统尊孔命令后)." In *(1928), A Quarter of a Century of True Light, Selected 真光丛刊, Part 3: General Articles 通论*, edited by Yijing Zhang, 76–88. Shanghai 上海: China Baptist Publication Society 中华浸会书局, 1913.

———. "After Reading Mr. Gu Youchen's Reminder to the Elders Who Donated to Jiaying University (读古有成君 '敬告捐款资助嘉应大学诸父老' 书后)." *True Light 真光* 23, no. 6 (1924): 59–63.

———. "After Reading Mr. Lu Banjiao's Criticism of Modern Chinese (读了吕牛教先生白话文的评判以后)." *True Light 真光* 29, no. 6 (1930): 72–79.

———. "After Yan Fu's Speech (书严复民可使由之不可使知之演说词后)." In *(1928), A Quarter of a Century of True Light, Selected 真光丛刊, Part 3: General Articles 通论*, edited by Yijing Zhang, 88–93. Shanghai 上海: China Baptist Publication Society 中华浸会书局, 1913.

———. "Against a Speech for Atheism (驳无神之演说)." In *(1928), A Quarter of a Century of True Light, Selected 真光丛刊, Part 2: The Gospel Discussed and Explained 辩道文*, edited by Yijing Zhang, 17–25. Shanghai 上海: China Baptist Publication Society 中华浸会书局, 1910a.

———. "Against Song Shixiang's Saying That Christianity Allows Offering Sacrifices to Ancestors 驳宋史香耶稣教不禁人祭先说." In *(1928), A Quarter of a Century of True Light, Selected* 真光丛刊, *Part 2: The Gospel Discussed and Explained* 辩道文, edited by Yijing Zhang, 1-17. Shanghai 上海: China Baptist Publication Society 中华浸会书局, 1908.

———. "The Age of Moral Education: Evangelizers and Their Motherland (德育春秋: 传福音之人与其国)." *Shanghai Youth* 上海青年 27, no. 4 (1928): 14-16.

———. "The Anger of the People Who Love Christ (爱基督者之怒)." *True Light* 真光 25, no. 4-5-6 (1926): 233.

———. "Another Three Questions about the Bible (又三条圣经疑问)." *True Light* 真光 23, no. 2 (1924): 87-89.

———. "Answer to the Question about Christianity with Buddhism and with Confucianism (答: 讨论耶与佛及耶与孔)." *True Light* 真光 24, no. 3 (1925): 80-81.

———. "Answering an Old Scholar Instead of a Friend (代友人答复一老学究)." In *(1928), A Quarter of a Century of True Light, Selected* 真光丛刊, *Part 2: The Gospel Discussed and Explained* 辩道文, edited by Yijing Zhang, 175-223. Shanghai 上海: China Baptist Publication Society 中华浸会书局, 1918.

———. "Answering Another Four Questions from Mr. Lu Zhensheng (答吕振声先生之另函四问)." *True Light* 真光 28, no. 12 (1929): 64-68.

———. *Answering Attacks upon Christianity* 批评非基督教言论汇刊全编. Shanghai 上海: China Baptist Publication Society 中华浸会书局, 1927.

———. "Answering Chen Xiaohan's Three Questions (答陈箫寒三大疑问)." In *(1928), A Quarter of a Century of True Light, Selected* 真光丛刊, *Part 5: Answers to Inquiries* 答问, edited by Yijing Zhang, 1-8. Shanghai 上海: China Baptist Publication Society 中华浸会书局, 1913.

———. "Answering Eleven Questions from Shi Jingcheng's Friends Concerning Christianity. (答石精诚函示友人对于基督教的十一条疑问)." In *(1928), A Quarter of a Century of True Light, Selected* 真光丛刊, *Part 5: Answers to Inquiries* 答问, edited by Yijing Zhang, 21: 20-35. Shanghai 上海: China Baptist Publication Society 中华浸会书局, 1922.

———. "Answering Five Questions from Mr. Huang Zhenyan (答黄振雁先生五疑问)." *True Light* 真光 28, no. 11 (1929): 75-78.

———. "Answering Four Questions from Mr. Lu Zhensheng (答吕振声先生四疑问)." *True Light* 真光 28, no. 12 (1929): 59-64.

———. "Answering Lu Danlin's Letter – Mr. Yijing: We Are Looking Forward to the Combined Issues of No. 4 to 6 in Volume 25 . . . (答复陆丹林通讯: 亦镜先生: 盼望许久的真光杂志廿五卷四至六号合刊 . . .)." *True Light* 真光 25, no. 9-10 (1926): 126-29.

———. "Answering Mr. Hou Shuxian (答候述先先生)." *True Light* 真光 28, no. 6 (1929): 60–67.

———. "Answering the Questions from Huang Rongzeng and Liao Yizhi Concerning Why God Did Not Create People Who Would Not Sin (答黃容增廖以智上帝造人何以不使之不会犯罪)." In *(1928), A Quarter of a Century of True Light, Selected* 真光丛刊, *Part 5: Answers to Inquiries* 答问, edited by Yijing Zhang, 68–75. Shanghai 上海: China Baptist Publication Society 中华浸会书局, 1923.

———. "Answering the Questions from Mr. Zeng Guren (答曾骨人先生来函所设问)." *True Light* 真光 29, no. 1 (1930): 58–67.

———. "Answering Three Questions from Zhi Xiang Concerning Genesis (答秩亨创世记三疑问)." In *(1928), A Quarter of a Century of True Light, Selected* 真光丛刊, *Part 5: Answers to Inquiries* 答问, edited by Yijing Zhang, 64–67. Shanghai 上海: China Baptist Publication Society 中华浸会书局, 1923.

———. "Answers to Five Questions (疑问五则)." *True Light* 真光 23, no. 11 (1924): 75–78.

———. "Answers to the Eight Questions from Miss Lin Huizhen (答林惠贞女士八疑问)." *True Light* 真光 28, no. 6 (1929): 67–73.

———. "Answers to Three Questions Concerning the Bible (疑义三则问答)." *True Light* 真光 24, no. 4 (1925): 80–82.

———. "The Anti-Christian Activities during the 'Anti-Christian Week' As I Heard (如是我闻之'非基督教周'的反基督教运动)." *True Light* 真光 24, no. 1 (1925): 89–94.

———. "The Anti-Christian Movement in the Last Christmas in Guang Dong Province (广州本届圣诞节之非教运动 广东)." *True Light* 真光 29, no. 1 (1930): 87.

———. "The Anti-Imperialist Articles by Both KMT Party and Christianity and My Opinions (党教相呼应的反帝文章及我的意见)." *True Light* 真光 26, no. 1 (1927): 68–72.

———. "At the Twenty-First Anniversary of Tong An Church (书同安教会成立廿一周纪念)." *True Light* 真光 17, no. 12 (1928): 51–53.

———. "Atonement (代赎)." In *(1928), A Quarter of a Century of True Light, Selected* 真光丛刊, *Part 6: Brief Selections Translated* 谈薮, edited by Yijing Zhang, 68–70. Shanghai 上海: China Baptist Publication Society 中华浸会书局, 1913.

———. "Attached Comments on a Few Answers to Mr. Yijing (附识: 答亦镜先生几句话)." *True Light* 真光 23, no. 7 (1924): 64.

———. "Attached Comments on the Conflict between Chinese and Westerners in the Church of Guang Xi Province (闻粤西教会中西冲突感言之附识)." *True Light* 真光 25, no. 4–5–6 (1926): 66–68.

———. "Attached Comments on the Telegram of March 17th from the Members of the Anti-Religion Alliance in Peking and Its Manifesto (附评北京各学校非宗教同人霰电及宣言)." *True Light* 真光 21, no. 8–9 (1922): 23–36.

———. "The Attachment to 'Are the Records in the First Chapter of Genesis Really Not in Accordance with Science?' (附: 创世记第一章的记载果与科学不合吗?)." *True Light* 真光 24, no. 2 (1925): 21–22.

———. "Avoid Perishing but Having Eternal Life (免沉沦得永生)." *True Light* 真光 28, no. 7 (1929): 16–23.

———. "Awakening (觉悟)." *True Light* 真光 23, no. 11 (1924): 80–81.

———. "Bible Reading and Praying (读经祈祷)." *True Light* 真光 28, no. 4 (1929): 98.

———. "The Birth of Jesus and the Births of the Founders of Confucianism, Buddhism and Daoism (耶稣之生与儒释道三教教主之生)." *True Light* 真光 29, no. 12 (1930): 42–54.

———. "A Brief History of People in Old and New Testaments (旧新约人物传略)." In *(1928), A Quarter of a Century of True Light, Selected* 真光丛刊, *Part 1: Concerning the Scriptures* 说经文, edited by Yijing Zhang, 145–84. Shanghai 上海: China Baptist Publication Society 中华浸会书局, 1913.

———. "Bullying? (欲欺谁哉)." *True Light* 真光 21, no. 10–11 (1922): 109.

———. "Challenging Equivocation from the Unbelievers (诘推诿不信者)." *True Light* 真光 10, no. 6 (1911): 29–32.

———. "Christian and Freedom (基督徒与自由)." In *(1928), A Quarter of a Century of True Light, Selected* 真光丛刊, *Part 1: Concerning the Scriptures* 说经文, edited by Yijing Zhang, 26–28. Shanghai 上海: China Baptist Publication Society 中华浸会书局, 1907.

———. "The Christian School Interfered with by the Government (在政府干涉下之教会学校)." *True Light* 真光 28, no. 5 (1929): 10–18.

———. "Christian Schools in Belgium (比利时的教会学校)." *True Light* 真光 27, no. 4 (1928): 69.

———. "Christianity and Imperialism (基督教与帝国主义)." *True Light* 真光 26, no. 4 (1927): 22–28.

———. "Christianity under the Government of KMT Party (在既定信教自由于约法既许信仰有完全自由权于党纲的中国国民政府底下的基督教 有按)." *True Light* 真光 29, no. 3 (1930): 48–53.

———. "The Church and the New Thoughts Tide (教会与新思潮)." In *China Christian Yearbook* (中华基督教年鉴), 6: 134–40. Shanghai 上海: China Continuation Committee (中华续行委办会), 1921.

———. "Cleansing the False Accusations against Christianity (诬教雪)." In *(1928), A Quarter of a Century of True Light, Selected* 真光丛刊, *Part 2: The Gospel Discussed and Explained* 辩道文, edited by Yijing Zhang, 46–68. Shanghai 上海: China Baptist Publication Society 中华浸会书局, 1910b.

———. "Clothes Made of Homespun Cloth (布衣)." *True Light* 真光 27, no. 4 (1928): 93–94.

———. "Commenting on Chen Qiulin's On the Anti-Christian Movement (按: 论反基督教运动)." *True Light* 真光 24, no. 1 (1925): 71–83.

———. "Commenting on the Second Letter to Refute a Foreign Female Believer (按: 驳一位外国女信徒的又一封信)." *True Light* 真光 24, no. 3 (1925): 48–53.

———. "Comments: The Lutheran Church in Shekou Seeking Advice on Religious Education (滠口信义会关于宗教教育之广征意见函附识)." *True Light* 真光 28, no. 2 (1929): 83.

———. "Comments on 'My View on Reclaiming the Right to Education' (按: 收回教育权的我见)." *True Light* 真光 23, no. 12 (1924): 1–8.

———. "Comments on Questioning Mr. Zhang Yijing's Answers to Mr. Huang and Mr. Liao (读亦镜先生答黄廖二君的疑问的质疑有批答)." *True Light* 真光 23, no. 2 (1924): 29–34.

———. "Comments on 'Talking over Patriotism with Mr. Zhang Yijing' (与亦镜先生谈谈爱国 -有答)." *True Light* 真光 25, no. 9–10 (1926): 35–42.

———. "Comments on the Christian's Patriotism (按: 基督徒爱国问题)." *True Light* 真光 26, no. 1 (1927): 8–16.

———. "Comments on the Most Inferior Anti-Christian Work (按: 最下乘的反基督教文字)." *True Light* 真光 25, no. 7–8 (1926): 8–9.

———. "Comments on the Theological Thoughts in the U.S.A. during the Last Twenty-Five Years (按: 二十五年来美国神学思想之趋势)." *True Light* 真光 26, no. 6 (1927): 13–14.

———. "Concerning Holding Stick at the Funeral of Parents (亲丧执杖问题)." *True Light* 真光 25, no. 9–10 (1926): 67–81.

———. "Continuation of Tasting the Way (道源一勺续)." *True Light* 真光 29, no. 9 (1930): 1–10.

———. "Correcting Errors in Dr. Chen Huanzhang's Speech on Confucianism (读陈焕章博士孔教讲义辩谬)." In *(1928), A Quarter of a Century of True Light, Selected* 真光丛刊, *Part 2: The Gospel Discussed and Explained* 辩道文, edited by Yijing Zhang, 106–65. Shanghai 上海: China Baptist Publication Society 中华浸会书局, 1914.

———. "Correcting Fallacies in the Sayings of the Anti-Christian Student Federation – General Remarks (纠正非基督教学生同盟的言论之谬误 - 总论)." *True Light* 真光 21, no. 8–9 (1922): 5–12.

———. "Correcting Wang Jingwei's Slander on Christianity in His Foreword to the First Issue of Min De Newspaper (纠正汪精卫巴黎民德报发刊词毁教语之谬)." In *(1928), A Quarter of a Century of True Light, Selected* 真光丛刊, *Part 2: The Gospel Discussed and Explained* 辩道文, edited by Yijing

Zhang, 165–75. Shanghai 上海: China Baptist Publication Society 中华浸会书局, 1914.

———. "Criticizing the Anti-Christian Student Federation's Declaration (批评非基督教学生同盟宣言)." *True Light* 真光 21, no. 8-9 (1922): 12–19.

———. "A Critique of the Anti-Christian Movement (非宗教运动的批评)." *Chinese Christian Advocate* 兴华 21, no. 1 (1924): 23–37.

———. "The Current Trends of Thought in the Church (今日教会思潮之趋势)." *True Light* 真光 26, no. 7-8-9 (1927): 91–100.

———. "Denouncing Fallacies of Awarding Posthumous Title (斥溢法之谬)." In *(1928), A Quarter of a Century of True Light, Selected* 真光丛刊, *Part 3: General Articles* 通论, edited by Yijing Zhang, 95–101. Shanghai 上海: China Baptist Publication Society 中华浸会书局, 1914.

———. "Denouncing Wang Rongbao (斥汪荣宝)." In *(1928), A Quarter of a Century of True Light, Selected* 真光丛刊, *Part 3: General Articles* 通论, edited by Yijing Zhang, 93–95. Shanghai 上海: China Baptist Publication Society 中华浸会书局, 1914.

———. "Discussing over Zhang's Self-Support by Selling Calligraphy (讨论卖字自给问题)." *True Light* 真光 27, no. 2-3 (1928): 114–16.

———. "Discussion about the Presence of Westerners in China's Delegation for Jerusalem Conference (1928) 讨论有外国人加入出席耶路撒冷大会中国代表团问题." *True Light* 真光 27, no. 2-3 (1928): 105–14.

———. "A Discussion of Romans 9:14–18 (讨论罗马人书九之十四至十八)." *True Light* 真光 24, no. 3 (1925): 79–80.

———. "A Discussion over Mr. Zhang Zhongru's Reforming Christianity with Buddhism (讨论张仲如先生之佛化基督教)." *True Light* 真光 23, no. 12 (1924): 77–80.

———. "Discussion with Mr. Wei Qing over the Indigenization of the Church (与唯情先生论本色教会)." *True Light* 真光 25, no. 7-8 (1926): 53–58.

———. "The Enemy Who Could Not Be Loved by Christ Lovers and the Way of Removing the Hatred (爱基督者所不能爱之仇敌与消弭其恨恶此敌仇之方法)." *True Light* 真光 25, no. 4-5-6 (1926): 233–34.

———. "A Fair Judgment on the Liu Hongru's Threat of Slapping Dr. Hu Shi (对刘鸿儒要打胡适之博士嘴巴的话的一个公正评判)." *True Light* 真光 28, no. 12 (1929): 13–24.

———. "The First Part in My Answer to Mr. Jiang Shuai Concerning Tough Questions from Anti-Christians and Passive People (答姜树蔼君来函所列反教及消极两种人的辩难)." *True Light* 真光 29, no. 2 (1930): 74–79.

———. "The Foreword (卷头语)." *True Light* 真光 29, no. 6 (1930): 1.

———. "Foreword: Couplet (卷头语)." *True Light* 真光 29, no. 4 (1930): 1.

———. "Foreword: The Standing Position of the Staff of True Light (卷头语: 我们办真光的人所站的地位)." *True Light* 真光 28, no. 5 (1929): 1.

———. "The Fourth Comments on Mr. Daiying's 'Christianity and Saving China by Character Formation' and 'Why Are We against Christianity' (读代英君的 '基督教与人格救国' 和 '我们为甚么反对基督教' 慨言 - 四)." *True Light* 真光 23, no. 8 (1924): 47–62.

———. "The Fourth Continuation of Recording and Commenting on the Pen War between Two Official Newspapers of Guomindang Party (录评海外两个国民党机关报关于基督教的笔墨官司 - 续四)." *True Light* 真光 23, no. 2 (1924): 35–40.

———. "The Fourth Part in My Answer to Jiang Shuai Concerning Tough Questions from Anti-Christians and Passive People (答姜树蔼君来函所列反教及消极两种人的辩难(四))." *True Light* 真光 29, no. 5 (1930): 65–68.

———. "The Function of Baihua or Modern Chinese (通俗白话之功用)." In *(1928) A Quarter of A Century of True Light, Selected* 真光丛刊, Part 3: *General Articles* 通论, edited by Yijing Zhang, 9–13. Shanghai 上海: China Baptist Publication Society 中华浸会书局, 1911.

———. "Go and Preach the Good News to All People (尔曹往普天下传福音与万民)." In *(1928), A Quarter of a Century of True Light, Selected* 真光丛刊, Part 1: *Concerning the Scriptures* 说经文, edited by Yijing Zhang, 90–94. Shanghai 上海: China Baptist Publication Society 中华浸会书局, 1911.

———. "Going to Cinema and Attending to Sermon (看影戏与赴礼拜堂听讲)." *True Light* 真光 28, no. 5 (1929): 52–55.

———. "Having a Fellowship with Christ (心交基督)." In *(1928), A Quarter of a Century of True Light, Selected* 真光丛刊, Part 1: *Concerning the Scriptures* 说经文, edited by Yijing Zhang, 42–46. Shanghai 上海: China Baptist Publication Society 中华浸会书局, 1907.

———. "How I Became a Christian and My Experiences during the Past Thirty Years after Conversion (我信基督教的缘起和信教后迄今三十年的经过)." In *(1928), A Quarter of a Century of True Light, Selected* 真光丛刊, Part 10: *Conclusion* 备数文, edited by Yijing Zhang, 1–12. Shanghai 上海: China Baptist Publication Society 中华浸会书局, 1923.

———. "How I Became a Christian and My Experiences during the Past Thirty Years after Conversion (我信基督教的缘起和信教后迄今三十年的经过)." *Life* 生命 3, no. 7-8 (1923): 1–10.

———. "Indigenized Church (萍庐笔记: 本色教会)." *True Light* 真光 24, no. 3 (1925): 78.

———. "The Intellectuals in Japan Respect Christianity (日本知识阶级器重基督教)." *True Light* 真光 27, no. 4 (1928): 94–95.

———. "Introducing Mr. Wu Zirui's Blood-Written Petition for Saving China (介绍吴梓瑞先生的救国血书)." *True Light* 真光 23, no. 12 (1924): 21–45.

———. "Introducing to a Sharp Criticism of the Church (介绍一篇针针见血的鍼砭教会文字)." *True Light* 真光 28, no. 5 (1929): 27–32.

———. "Jesus and Confucius (耶儒辩)." In *(1928), A Quarter of a Century of True Light, Selected* 真光丛刊*, Part 2: The Gospel Discussed and Explained* 辩道文, edited by Yijing Zhang, 25–35. Shanghai 上海: China Baptist Publication Society 中华浸会书局, 1910c.

———. "Jesus Asked Peter If He Loved Him for Three Times (主三以爱我语彼得)." In *(1928), A Quarter of a Century of True Light, Selected* 真光丛刊*, Part 1: Concerning the Scriptures* 说经文, edited by Yijing Zhang, 97–100. Shanghai 上海: China Baptist Publication Society 中华浸会书局, 1911.

———. "Lao Zi (太上老君)." In *(1928), A Quarter of a Century of True Light, Selected* 真光丛刊*, Part 4: Religious Evidence and Origins* 关于宗教之考据文字, edited by Yijing Zhang, 57–87. Shanghai 上海: China Baptist Publication Society 中华浸会书局, 1918.

———. "The Last Twenty-Five Years after the Birth of True Light and the Twenty-Two Years of My Humble Involvement (真光杂志出世迄今二十五年及余滥竽其中廿二年之经过)." *True Light* 真光 26, no. 6 (1927): 1–7.

———. "A Letter from Mr. Chen Chonggui (陈崇桂先生来函)." *True Light* 真光 28, no. 11 (1929): 88–89.

———. "The Massacre at Lienchow in the Record of the Sunset of Xixia Mountain (巾峰夕霞记之连州教案)." *True Light* 真光 29, no. 4 (1930): 59–67.

———. "Mining Knowledge of Quintessence: On Funeral by Sima Guang (国粹采适: 司马光葬论)." *True Light* 真光 10, no. 3 (1911): 41–43.

———. "Miracles of Healing the Deaf and Mute by Science (科学的聪聋启瘖神迹)." *True Light* 真光 28, no. 1 (1929): 44–47.

———. "The Most Satisfying Protest Reply from the Governor of Guang Dong Province to the British Consul (粤省长为沙面炸弹案一封最快人意之对英领抗议覆函)." *True Light* 真光 23, no. 7 (1924): 91–93.

———. "Mr. T. C. Chao's 'Discussion over the Indigenization of the Church' and My Thoughts (赵紫宸先生的 '本色教会的商榷' 和我的感想)." *True Light* 真光 23, no. 11 (1924): 12–32.

———. "Mr. Wang Mingdao Preached in Two Cantonese Churches in Shanghai (记王明道先生在上海两个广东教会演讲)." *True Light* 真光 29, no. 4 (1930): 79–83.

———. "My Current View of Jesus (我今日对于耶稣之认识)." *True Light* 真光 27, no. 7 (1928): 45–46.

———. "My Sayings Plagiarized and Twisted in 'The Collection of Researches on Unequal Treaties' (不平等条约研究集引用我的文字的地方)." *True Light* 真光 28, no. 3 (1929): 1–12.

———. "My Two Months in Qingdao (在青岛两个月之经过)." *True Light* 真光 27, no. 10 (1928): 44–51.

———. "My View of Jesus' Resurrection (我也来说说耶稣之复活)." *True Light* 真光 24, no. 5 (1925): 34–38.

———. "My View on Association (我之于社交)." *True Light* 真光 27, no. 7 (1928): 92–93.

———. "My View on Jesus' Atonement (附耶稣赎罪问题之我见)." In *(1928), A Quarter of a Century of True Light, Selected* 真光丛刊*, Part 2: The Gospel Discussed and Explained* 辩道文, edited by Yijing Zhang, 267–71. Shanghai 上海: China Baptist Publication Society 中华浸会书局, 1920.

———. "My View on Preaching through Writing (我之文字布道观)." *True Light* 真光 27, no. 2–3 (1928): 77–79.

———. "My View on the Independence of the Church (我之自立教会观)." *True Light* 真光 27, no. 4 (1928): 18–24.

———. "No Self-Examination Will Lead to the Potential for Disaster (人之患在不知自反)." *True Light* 真光 23, no. 2 (1924): 90.

———. "On Death (说死)." In *(1928), A Quarter of a Century of True Light, Selected* 真光丛刊*, Part 3: General Articles* 通论, edited by Yijing Zhang, 61–65. Shanghai 上海: China Baptist Publication Society 中华浸会书局, 1909.

———. "On Falsehood (说伪)." In *(1928), A Quarter of a Century of True Light, Selected* 真光丛刊*, Part 3: General Articles* 通论, edited by Yijing Zhang, 54–56. Shanghai 上海: China Baptist Publication Society 中华浸会书局, 1914.

———. "On Liang Bichen's Proposal of a Reform Following the Banning of Confucianism (书梁弼臣改革孔教乃可以言维新论后)." *True Light* 真光 10, no. 10 (1911): 1–5.

———. "On Moses (摩西论)." In *(1928), A Quarter of a Century of True Light, Selected* 真光丛刊*, Part 1: Concerning the Scriptures* 说经文, edited by Yijing Zhang, 1–6. Shanghai 上海: China Baptist Publication Society 中华浸会书局, 1906.

———. "On the Anti-Christian Movement on the Christmas Day of 1928 in Shanghai (书民十七耶稣诞日上海的非基运动)." *True Light* 真光 28, no. 2 (1929): 1–8.

———. "On Writing for Preaching (论传道文字)." In *(1928), A Quarter of a Century of True Light, Selected* 真光丛刊*, Part 3: General Articles* 通论, edited by Yijing Zhang, 4–9. Shanghai 上海: China Baptist Publication Society 中华浸会书局, 1918.

———. "The Origin of Making Sacrifice to the Ancestors (祭先源流考)." In *(1928), A Quarter of a Century of True Light, Selected* 真光丛刊*, Part 4: Religious Evidence and Origins* 关于宗教之考据文字, edited by Yijing Zhang, 8–29. Shanghai 上海: China Baptist Publication Society 中华浸会书局, 1916.

———. "Pastor Liang Xigao's Visit (记梁细羔牧师来访)." *True Light* 真光 28, no. 10 (1929): 93.

———. "Personal Comment: Chance for Practising Obedience (随感录: 行道的机会)." *True Light* 真光 26, no. 4 (1927): 101–2.

———. "Poem with the Rhythm Same with Mr. Lu Banjiao (诗歌: 我所学作之诗: 用吕半教先生原韵有序)." *True Light* 真光 30, no. 1 (1931): 78–79.

———. "Preface." In *China Academic History* 中国学术源流, edited by Zhixin Wang 王治心, 1–5. Nanjing 南京: Nanking Theological Seminary 金陵神学院, 1925.

———. "Preface (卷头语)." *True Light* 真光 29, no. 5 (1930): 1.

———. "Preface: Being Sick (卷头语: 记者自去年六月至今,一病八月)." *True Light* 真光 30, no. 2 (1931): 1.

———. "Preface – A Country with Freedom of Faith (序: 以已有信教自由约法之国家)." *True Light* 真光 21, no. 8–9 (1922): 1–2.

———. "Preface: Merry Christmas and Happy New Year (卷头语: 恭祝圣诞,并贺新禧)." *True Light* 真光 29, no. 12 (1930): 1.

———. "The Qualifications for a Preacher (传道人当具何资格)." In *(1928), A Quarter of a Century of True Light, Selected* 真光丛刊, *Part 3: General Articles* 通论, edited by Yijing Zhang, 17–22. Shanghai 上海: China Baptist Publication Society 中华浸会书局, 1919.

———. "The Question of Old and New (旧新问题)." *True Light* 真光 28, no. 4 (1929): 97.

———. "Readers' Responses." *True Light* 真光 28, no. 4 (1929): 79–80.

———. "References about Paul's Teaching of Obeying the Authority (保罗训众宜服秉权者语索隐)." *True Light* 真光 24, no. 3 (1925): 77.

———. "Refuting a Plagiarism of Zhang Taiyan's Atheistic Attack on Religion (驳抄太炎无神论之非宗教文)." In *(1928), A Quarter of a Century of True Light, Selected* 真光丛刊, *Part 2: The Gospel Discussed and Explained* 辩道文, edited by Yijing Zhang, 223–66. Shanghai 上海: China Baptist Publication Society 中华浸会书局, 1920.

———. "Refuting Cai Yuanpei's Speech at the Conference of the Anti-Religion Alliance." *True Light* 真光 21, no. 10–11 (1922): 1–17.

———. "Refuting Chen Huanzhang and Other Four People's Petition for Establishing Confucianism as the State Religion (驳陈焕章等请定孔教为国教呈文)." In *(1928), A Quarter of a Century of True Light, Selected* 真光丛刊, *Part 2: The Gospel Discussed and Explained* 辩道文, edited by Yijing Zhang, 68–106. Shanghai 上海: China Baptist Publication Society 中华浸会书局, 1913.

———. "Refuting Xuanlu Shen's Challenging Non-Religionists' Defending against the Anti-Christian Movement." *True Light* 真光 21, no. 10–11 (1922): 68–85.

———. "The Relationship between the Advancement of Civilization and the Church (文明进步与教会之关系)." In *(1928), A Quarter of a Century of True Light, Selected* 真光丛刊, *Part 3: General Articles* 通论, edited by Yijing Zhang, 37–39. Shanghai 上海: China Baptist Publication Society 中华浸会书局, 1909.

———. "Response to a Letter from Guo Hua (国华) of the Anti-Christian Federation (非基督教同盟)." *True Light* 真光 21, no. 10–11 (1922): 104–8.

———. "Resurrection (复生)." In *(1928), A Quarter of a Century of True Light, Selected* 真光丛刊, Part 1: Concerning the Scriptures 说经文, edited by Yijing Zhang, 126–32. Shanghai 上海: China Baptist Publication Society 中华浸会书局, 1914.

———. "Salvation through Faith in Christ Jesus (尔自幼识圣经因而有智信基督耶稣得救." In *(1928), A Quarter of a Century of True Light, Selected* 真光丛刊, Part 1: Concerning the Scriptures 说经文, edited by Yijing Zhang, 25–26. Shanghai 上海: China Baptist Publication Society 中华浸会书局, 1907.

———. "The Second Telegram from the Anti-Religion Alliance and My Criticism (非宗教同盟第二次通电 – 也有批)." *True Light* 真光 21, no. 8–9 (1922): 36–41.

———. "Seeking to Blame the Chinese (寻求中国人之罪)." *True Light* 真光 25, no. 4–5–6 (1926): 234–36.

———. "Sending Gospel Leaflets Once a Month (逐家每月派书一次之传道新法)." *True Light* 真光 29, no. 4 (1930): 92–93.

———. "Shanghai Park – No Entrance for Chinese and Dogs (华人与犬不许入之上海公园)." *True Light* 真光 27, no. 6 (1928): 96.

———. "The Significance of Religious Education (宗教教育的意义)." *True Light* 真光 28, no. 6 (1929): 90–92.

———. "The Solution of Jesus and Paul to the Economic Problem of Preachers (耶苏与保罗之传道的经济问题解决法)." *True Light* 真光 28, no. 8 (1929): 1–9.

———. "A Spiritual Feast (灵鼎一脔)." *True Light* 真光 28, no. 12 (1929): 44–51.

———. "The Story of Aunty Zhang Si (记张四婶事)." *True Light* 真光 24, no. 2 (1925): 63–68.

———. "Students from Chinese Academy Harrassed Hua Xi University (中文院学生纠众滋扰华大校)." *True Light* 真光 29, no. 1 (1930): 88–91.

———. "A Study of Christianity and Confucianism (耶儒之研究)." In *(1928), A Quarter of a Century of True Light, Selected* 真光丛刊, Part 4: Religious Evidence and Origins 关于宗教之考据文字, edited by Yijing Zhang, 40–57. Shanghai 上海: China Baptist Publication Society 中华浸会书局, 1920.

———. "Tasting the Way (道源一勺)." *True Light* 真光 29, no. 8 (1930): 1–18.

———. "A Ten-Foot High Lampstand (丈八灯台)." *True Light* 真光 21, no. 10–11 (1922): 110–11.

———. "The Third Comments on Mr. Daiying's 'Christianity and Saving China by Character Formation' and 'Why Are We against Christianity' (读代英君的 '基督教与人格救国' 和 '我们为甚么反对基督教' 慨言 – 三)." *True Light* 真光 23, no. 6 (1924): 53–57.

———. "The Third Part in My Answer to Mr. Jiang Shuai Concerning Tough Questions from Anti-Christian and Passive People (答姜树蔼君来函所列反教及消极两种人的辩难--三)." *True Light* 真光 29, no. 4 (1930): 67-69.

———. "The Third Part of My Two Months in Qingdao (在青岛两个月之经过三)." *True Light* 真光 27, no. 12 (1928): 63-66.

———. "Those Bible Stories in Line with the Classics (汉故征经)." In *(1928), A Quarter of a Century of True Light, Selected* 真光丛刊, *Part 6: Brief Selections Translated* 谈薮, edited by Yijing Zhang, 66-90. Shanghai 上海: China Baptist Publication Society 中华浸会书局, 1913.

———. "Thoughts after Reading Mr. Langou's 'Argument against Mr. Xu Dingbang's Criticism of Mr. Wu Zhihui' (读浪鸥君'驳真光杂志徐定邦君批评吴稚晖先生的一个新信仰的宇宙观及人生观'感言)." *True Light* 真光 24, no. 5 (1925): 19-27.

———. "Thoughts over a Western Pastor's Plan on Mastering Chinese with His Colleagues (闻某西牧欲联同志精习汉文感言)." In *(1928), A Quarter of a Century of True Light, Selected* 真光丛刊, *Part 3: General Articles* 通论, edited by Yijing Zhang, 30-37. Shanghai 上海: China Baptist Publication Society 中华浸会书局, 1916.

———. "Three Questions about Genesis (创世纪三个疑问)." *True Light* 真光 23, no. 12 (1924): 76-77.

———. "Three Questions about the Bible from Wang Tuoan (圣经疑问三种)." *True Light* 真光 23, no. 2 (1924): 85-87.

———. "Three Stages (三个时期)." *True Light* 真光 17, no. 12 (1928): 93-94.

———. "True Light Was One of the Best Companies for Mr. Tang Yuanfang (唐元放先生称真光为他最好的伴侣之一函 附)." *True Light* 真光 28, no. 6 (1928): 66-67.

———. "Two Papers of Correcting Errors with Dr. Chen Huan-Chang's Speech on Confucianism (驳陈焕章博士说教之谬两种)." *True Light* 真光 30, no. 7 (1931): 1.

———. "What a Ms. Mei Jianfeng (好一个梅剑凤女士)." *True Light* 真光 21, no. 10-11 (1922): 109-10.

———. "With More Daughters Come Longer Age and More Blessings (多福多寿多女子)." *True Light* 真光 28, no. 10 (1929): 90-91.

———. "A Wonderful Argument against the Saying That Neo-Confucians Were Useless (宋儒不适于用妙辩)." *True Light* 真光 23, no. 10 (1924): 67.

———. "Wong Nai-Siong, A Great Christian (重印绂丞先生七十自叙序)." *True Light* 真光 28, no. 7 (1929): 57-59.

———. "Words from a Female Worship Leader Who Made an Exception (女子破例领礼拜者之言)." *True Light* 真光 28, no. 6 (1929): 85.

———. "Zhang Yijing's Explanation about Why He Did Not Write during the Last Six Months (张亦镜启事:(一)说明半年来不暇作文与不暇作覆书之由)." *True Light* 真光 27, no. 1 (1928): 1.

———. "Zhang Yijing's Notice (亦镜启事:余自三月十一日返至广州后,廿一日进两广浸会医院疗治)." *True Light* 真光 30, no. 5 (1931): 1.

———. "Zhang's First Letter after Returning from Guilin (张亦镜改赴桂林休养报告书第一函)." *True Light* 真光 30, no. 12 (1931): 1.

———. "Zhang's Letter about Recent Situation of Illness (张亦镜覆古尚勤告知最近病状函)." *True Light* 真光 30, no. 8 (1931): 1.

Zhang, Yijing 张亦镜, and Jun Mo Liang 梁君默. "Criticizing Qi Yuan's 'Christianity and Communism' (批评绮园的基督教与共产主义)." *True Light* 真光 21, no. 8–9 (1922): 64–76.

Zhao, Suisheng. "Chinese Nationalism and Its International Orientations." *Political Science Quarterly* 115, no. 1 (2000): 1–33.

———. "A State-Led Nationalism: The Patriotic Education Campaign in Post-Tiananmen China." *Communist and Post-Communist Studies* 31, no. 3 (1998): 287–302.

Zhu, Xiaoming. "On the Socialist View of Religion with Chinese Characteristics (论中国特色社会主义宗教观)." In *Marxism and Religion*, edited by Zhen Chi, Xuezeng Gong, and Daji Lü, 4: 348–75. Religious Studies in Contemporary China Collection. Leiden: Brill, 2014.

Zhu, Xiulian 朱秀莲. "Chinese Apologist's Response in His Era: A Study of Zhang Yijing (中国护教者对时代的回应 – 张亦镜研究)." Master of Divinity thesis, Alliance Bible Seminary, Hong Kong, 2001.

Langham Literature, with its publishing work, is a ministry of Langham Partnership.

Langham Partnership is a global fellowship working in pursuit of the vision God entrusted to its founder John Stott –

to facilitate the growth of the church in maturity and Christ-likeness through raising the standards of biblical preaching and teaching.

Our vision is to see churches in the Majority World equipped for mission and growing to maturity in Christ through the ministry of pastors and leaders who believe, teach and live by the word of God.

Our mission is to strengthen the ministry of the word of God through:
- nurturing national movements for biblical preaching
- fostering the creation and distribution of evangelical literature
- enhancing evangelical theological education

especially in countries where churches are under-resourced.

Our ministry

Langham Preaching partners with national leaders to nurture indigenous biblical preaching movements for pastors and lay preachers all around the world. With the support of a team of trainers from many countries, a multi-level programme of seminars provides practical training, and is followed by a programme for training local facilitators. Local preachers' groups and national and regional networks ensure continuity and ongoing development, seeking to build vigorous movements committed to Bible exposition.

Langham Literature provides Majority World preachers, scholars and seminary libraries with evangelical books and electronic resources through publishing and distribution, grants and discounts. The programme also fosters the creation of indigenous evangelical books in many languages, through writer's grants, strengthening local evangelical publishing houses, and investment in major regional literature projects, such as one volume Bible commentaries like the *Africa Bible Commentary* and the *South Asia Bible Commentary*.

Langham Scholars provides financial support for evangelical doctoral students from the Majority World so that, when they return home, they may train pastors and other Christian leaders with sound, biblical and theological teaching. This programme equips those who equip others. Langham Scholars also works in partnership with Majority World seminaries in strengthening evangelical theological education. A growing number of Langham Scholars study in high quality doctoral programmes in the Majority World itself. As well as teaching the next generation of pastors, graduated Langham Scholars exercise significant influence through their writing and leadership.

To learn more about Langham Partnership and the work we do visit **langham.org**

www.ingramcontent.com/pod-product-compliance
Lightning Source LLC
Chambersburg PA
CBHW061703300426
44115CB00014B/2540